MW01147283

TO THE MEMORY

OF

MY MOTHER

MIASMA

Pollution and Purification in early Greek Religion

ROBERT PARKER

CLARENDON PRESS · OXFORD

Oxford University Press, Walton Street, Oxford OX2 6DP
Oxford New York Toronto
Delhi Bombay Calcutta Madras Karachi
Petaling Jaya Singapore Hong Kong Tokyo
Nairobi Dar es Salaam Cape Town
Melbourne Auckland

and associated companies in
Berlin Ibadan

Oxford is a trade mark of Oxford University Press

Published in the United States
by Oxford University Press, New York

© Robert Parker 1983

First published 1983
Reprinted 1985
First issued in Clarendon Paperbacks 1990

All rights reserved. No part of this publication may be reproduced,
stored in a retrieval system, or transmitted, in any form or by any means,
electronic, mechanical, photocopying, recording, or otherwise, without
the prior permission of Oxford University Press

This book is sold subject to the condition that it shall not, by way
of trade or otherwise, be lent, re-sold, hired out or otherwise circulated
without the publisher's prior consent in any form of binding or cover
other than that in which it is published and without a similar condition
including this condition being imposed on the subsequent purchaser

British Library Cataloguing in Publication Data
Parker, Robert
Miasma.
1. Rites and ceremonies – Greece
I. Title
306'.6 DF121
ISBN 0–19–814742 2 (pbk)

Library of Congress Cataloguing in Publication Data
Parker, Robert.
Miasma: pollution and purification in early Greek religion.
Bibliography: p.
Includes index
1. Purity, Ritual – Greece. 2. Greece – Religion.
I. Title
BL788.P37 1983 292'.2 82–17835
ISBN 0–19–814742 2 (pbk.)

Printed in Great Britain by
Biddles Ltd, Guildford & King's Lynn

PREFACE

This book has developed from an Oxford dissertation. I hope that those I thanked for their help with the thesis, and also its examiners, will accept now a collective expression of gratitude. For subsequent advice on whole chapters I am very grateful to Dr. J. N. Bremmer, Dr. G. E. R. Lloyd, and Dr. C. Sourvinou-Inwood, and on individual points or sections to Professor A. M. Davies, Dr. N. S. R. Hornblower, Dr. D. M. Lewis, and Dr. M. E. Tucker. Mrs. A. M. Cripps kindly typed much of the manuscript, and I am particularly grateful to Mr. R. W. B. Burton for his careful scrutiny of the proofs. For financial aid I thank the Craven committee, the Provost and Fellows of Oriel College, and the Faculty Board of Literae Humaniores in Oxford. My greatest debts are to Hugh Lloyd-Jones, for inspiration and encouragement, and, for reasons too various to mention, to my wife Joanna.

Oriel College, Oxford   *R. C. T. P.*
November 1982.

CONTENTS

ABBREVIATIONS AND EDITIONS ix

Introduction 1

1. Purification: a Science of Division 18

2. Birth and Death 32

3. The Works of Aphrodite 74

4. The Shedding of Blood 104

5. Sacrilege 144

6. Curses, Family Curses, and the Structure of Rights 191

7. Disease, Bewitchment, and Purifiers 207

8. Divine Vengeance and Disease 235

9. Purifying the City 257

10. Purity and Salvation 281

11. Some scenes from Tragedy 308

Epilogue 322

APPENDICES

1. The Greek for Taboo 328

2. The Cyrene Cathartic Law 332

3. Problems concerning 'Enter pure from . . .'
requirements in sacred laws 352

4. Animals and Food 357

5. The Ritual Status of the Justified Killer at Athens 366

6. The Ritual of Purification from Homicide 370

viii

Contents

7. Exile and Purification of the Killer in Greek Myth 375
8. Gods particularly concerned with Purity 393

INDEXES 395

ABBREVIATIONS AND EDITIONS

For ancient authors the abbreviations in *The Oxford Classical Dictionary*,[2] ed. N. G. L. Hammond and H. H. Scullard, 1970, ix–xxii, have been followed where available (with a few trivial exceptions listed below). For other cases those in Liddell–Scott–Jones, *A Greek English Lexicon*,[9] Oxford, 1940 (LSJ), have been used, and where this too offers nothing an easily recognizable form has been chosen. Fragments are cited according to the numeration of the following collections: Hesiod, R. Merkelbach and M. L. West, Oxford, 1967; lyric poets, *PMG* or *SLG* or *PLF* (see below); iambic and elegiac poets, M. L. West, *Iambi et Elegi Graeci ante Alexandrum cantati*, Oxford, 1971–2; pre-Socratics, H. Diels, *Die Fragmente der Vorsokratiker*,[6] revised by W. Kranz, Berlin, 1951–2; historians, F. Jacoby, *Fragmente der griechischen Historiker*, Berlin, 1923– ; Pindar, B. Snell/H. Maehler, Leipzig, 1975; Aeschylus, Nauck *TGF* (see below); Sophocles, A. C. Pearson, Cambridge, 1917 (same numbers in S. Radt, Göttingen, 1977); Euripides, Nauck, *TGF*, except where H. v. Arnim, *Supplementum Euripideum*, Bonn, 1913, or C. Austin, *Nova Fragmenta Euripidea in Papyris Reperta*, Berlin, 1968, are available (in these cases the editor's name is added); Attic comic poets except Menander, T. Kock, *Comicorum Atticorum Fragmenta*, Leipzig, 1880–8; Dorian comedy, Kaibel, *CGF* (see below); comic fragments known from papyri, Page, *GLP* (see below) and/or C. Austin, *Comicorum Graecorum Fragmenta in Papyris Reperta*, Berlin, 1973 (in these cases the editor's name is added); Menander, A. Koerte/A. Thierfelder, Leipzig, 1959; Hellenistic poets, *Coll. Al.* (see below). Specific editors are named when other fragments are cited. Hippocratic texts are cited by the chapters of E. Littré, *Œuvres complètes d'Hippocrate*, Paris, 1839–61, with references to his volume and page numbers in brackets (L. or Littré). But (Hipp.) *Morb. Sacr.* is cited by page and line in the edition of W. H. S. Jones, Harvard, 1923 (J.), and by section in the edition of H. Grensemann (Ars Medica 2.1), Berlin, 1968 (G.).

Abbreviations of the epigraphical collections that are more commonly cited are listed below. For other items the abbreviations of LSJ xli–xliii have been used.

For periodicals the abbreviations of *The Oxford Classical Dictionary*[2] have been used, with some exceptions and additions that are listed below.

1. Abbreviations of ancient authors, periodicals, collections of texts, series, and general reference works

ABSA   *Annual of the British School at Athens*

AJA   *American Journal of Archaeology*

AJP   *American Journal of Philology*

Ant.   Antiphon

Ant. u. Chr.   F. J. Dölger, editor and sole contributor, *Antike und Christentum*

Ath. Mitt.   *Mitteilungen des deutschen archaeologischen Instituts, Athenische Abteilung*

Bacch.   Bacchylides

BEFAR   *Bibliotheque des écoles françaises d'Athènes et de Rome*

Buck   C. D. Buck, *The Greek Dialects*, Chicago, 1955

Coll. Al.   J. U. Powell (ed.), *Collectanea Alexandrina*, Oxford, 1925

CP   *Classical Philology*

Dar.-Sag.   C. Daremberg and E. Saglio, *Dictionnaire des antiquités grecques et romaines*, Paris, 1877–1919

HSCP   *Harvard Studies in Classical Philology*

HTR   *Harvard Theological Review*

IG   *Inscriptiones Graecae*. For details see LSJ, xlii. *IG* I² is being replaced by *IG* I³, ed. D. M. Lewis, Berlin, 1981 –

Kaibel, *CGF*   G. Kaibel, *Comicorum Graecorum Fragmenta*, Berlin, 1899

LSA   F. Sokolowski (ed.), *Lois sacrées de l'Asie Mineure*, Paris, 1955

LSCG   F. Sokolowski (ed.), *Lois sacrées des Cités grecques*, Paris, 1969

LSS   F. Sokolowski (ed.), *Lois sacrées des Cités grecques, supplément*, Paris, 1962

M/L   R. Meiggs and D. M. Lewis, *A Selection of Greek Historical Inscriptions*, Oxford, 1969

Michel   C. Michel, *Recueil d'inscriptions grecques*, Brussels, 1900

Nauck, *TGF*   A. Nauck, *Tragicorum Graecorum Fragmenta*,² Leipzig, 1889

OF   O. Kern, *Orphicorum Fragmenta*, Berlin, 1922

Page, *GLP*   D. L. Page (ed.), *Greek Literary Papyri* I (Poetry), Harvard, 1942

PLF   E. Lobel and D. L. Page (eds.), *Poetarum Lesbiorum Fragmenta*, Oxford, 1955

PMG   D. L. Page (ed.), *Poetae Melici Graeci*, Oxford, 1962

RAC   *Reallexikon für Antike und Christentum*, ed. T. Klauser, Stuttgart, 1950 –

RE   A. Pauly, G. Wissowa, and others, *Real-Encyclopädie der klassischen Altertumswissenschaft*

REA   *Revue des études anciennes*

REG   *Revue des études grecques*

REL   *Revue des études latines*

RGVV   *Religionsgeschichtliche Versuche und Vorarbeiten*

RHR   *Revue de l'histoire des religions*

RML   W. H. Roscher, *Ausführliches Lexikon der griechischen und römischen Mythologie*, Leipzig, 1884–1937

Schwyzer   E. Schwyzer, *Dialectorum Graecarum exempla epigraphica potiora*, Leipzig, 1923

SEG   *Supplementum Epigraphicum Graecum*

SGDI   H. Collitz and others, *Sammlung der griechischen Dialektinschriften*, Göttingen, 1884–1915

SIG   *Sylloge Inscriptionum Graecarum*, ed. W. Dittenberger, ed. 2, Leipzig, 1898–1901, ed. 3, 1915–24

SLG   D. L. Page (ed.), *Supplementum Lyricis Graecis*, Oxford, 1974

Solmsen/Fraenkel   F. Solmsen, *Inscriptiones Graecae ad inlustrandas Dialectos selectae*, ed. 4, revised by E. Fraenkel, Leipzig, 1930

SSR   *Studi Storico-Religiosi*

SVF   H. v. Arnim (ed.), *Stoicorum Veterum Fragmenta*, Leipzig, 1903–24

Thesleff   H. Thesleff (ed.), *The Pythagorean Texts of the Hellenistic Period*, Abo, 1965

Wünsch   R. Wünsch, *Tabellae Defixionum* = *IG* III. 3 appendix, 1897

ZPE   *Zeitschrift für Papyrologie und Epigraphik*

2. *Other works cited in abbreviated form*

Abt   A. Abt, *Die Apologie des Apuleius von Madaura und die antike Zauberei*, *RGVV* 4.2, Giessen, 1908

Adkins   A. W. H. Adkins, *Merit and Responsibility. A Study in Greek Values*, Oxford, 1960

Alexiou   M. Alexiou, *The Ritual Lament in Greek Tradition*, Cambridge, 1974

Amandry   P. Amandry, *La Mantique apollinienne à Delphes* (*BEFAR* 170), Paris, 1950

Andronikos   M. Andronikos, *Totenkult* (Archaeologia Homerica III
W), Göttingen, 1968

Arbesmann   P. R. Arbesmann, *Das Fasten bei den Griechen und Römern,*
RGVV 21.1, Giessen, 1929

Barth   F. Barth, *Ritual and Knowledge among the Baktaman of New*
Guinea, Oslo and New Haven, 1975

Benveniste   E. Benveniste, *Le Vocabulaire des institutions indo-*
européennes, 2 vols., Paris, 1969

Black-Michaud   J. Black-Michaud, *Cohesive Force. Feud in the*
Mediterranean and the Middle East, Oxford, 1975

Blum   R. and E. Blum, *The Dangerous Hour. The Lore of Crisis and*
Mystery in Rural Greece, London, 1970

Bonner/Smith   R. J. Bonner and G. E. Smith, *The Administration of*
Justice from Homer to Aristotle, 2 vols., Chicago, 1930, 1938.

Borgeaud   P. Borgeaud, *Recherches sur le dieu Pan* (Bibliotheca
Helvetica Romana 17), Rome/Geneva, 1979

Boyancé   P. Boyancé, *Le Culte des Muses chez les philosophes grecs,* Paris,
1937

Boyce   M. Boyce, *A Persian Stronghold of Zoroastrianism,* Oxford, 1977

Bremmer   J. N. Bremmer, *The Early Greek Concept of the Soul,*
Princeton, 1983.

Bruneau   P. Bruneau, *Recherches sur les cultes de Délos à l'époque helléni-*
stique et à l'époque impériale (*BEFAR* 217), Paris, 1970

Burkert, *GR*   W. Burkert, *Griechische Religion der archaischen und klassi-*
schen Epoche, Stuttgart, 1977

Burkert, *HN* ——, *Homo Necans. Interpretationen altgriechischer*
Opferriten und Mythen, RGVV 32, Berlin, 1972

Burkert, *LS*   ——, *Lore and Science in Ancient Pythagoreanism,* Cambridge
Mass., 1972, a revised English edition, translated by E. L.
Minar, of *Weisheit und Wissenschaft: Studien zu Pythagoras, Philolaos*
und Platon, Nürnberg, 1962

Burkert, *SH*   ——, *Structure and History in Greek Mythology and Ritual,*
Berkeley, 1979

Busolt/Swoboda   G. Busolt, *Griechische Staatskunde*³, 2 vols. (the
second revised by H. Swoboda), Munich, 1920, 1926

Buxton   J. Buxton, *Religion and Healing in Mandari,* Oxford, 1973

Calhoun   G. M. Calhoun, *The Growth of Criminal Law in Ancient*
Greece, Berkeley, 1927

Campbell   J. K. Campbell, *Honour, Family and Patronage. A Study of*
Institutions and Moral Values in a Greek Mountain Community, Oxford,
1964

Clinton   K. Clinton, *The Sacred Officials of the Eleusinian Mysteries* (Transactions of the American Philosophical Society, new series, 64), Philadelphia, 1974

Cook   A. B. Cook, *Zeus. A Study in Ancient Religion*, 3 vols., Cambridge, 1914–40

Croissant   J. Croissant, *Aristote et les mystères*, Liège, 1932

Davies   J. K. Davies, *Athenian Propertied Families*, Oxford, 1971

Defradas   J. Defradas, *Les Thèmes de la propagande delphique* (Études et commentaires 21), Paris, 1954 (ed. 2, 1972)

Detienne, *Eugénies*   M. Detienne, 'Violentes "eugénies" ', in M. Detienne and J. P. Vernant, *La Cuisine du sacrifice en pays grec*, Paris, 1979

Detienne, *Jardins*   M. Detienne, *Les Jardins d'Adonis*, Paris, 1972

Deubner   L. Deubner, *Attische Feste*, Berlin, 1932

Diels   H. Diels, *Sibyllinische Blätter*, Berlin, 1890

Dodds   E. R. Dodds, *The Greeks and the Irrational*, California, 1951

Dodds, *Progress*   E. R. Dodds, *The Ancient Concept of Progress, and other Essays*, Oxford, 1973

Douglas   M. Douglas, *Purity and Danger. An Analysis of Concepts of Pollution and Taboo*, London, 1966 (cited from the Pelican edition, 1970)

Dover   K. J. Dover, *Greek Popular Morality in the Time of Plato and Aristotle*, Oxford, 1974

Dumont   L. Dumont, *Homo Hierarchichus*, Eng. trans., London, 1970

Durkheim   E. Durkheim, *The Elementary Forms of the Religious Life*, trans. J. W. Swain, London, 1915

Edelstein   E. J. and L. Edelstein, *Asclepius, a collection and interpretation of the testimonies*, 2 vols., Baltimore, 1945

Edelstein, *AM   Ancient Medicine, Selected papers of L. Edelstein*, ed. O. and C. Temkin, Baltimore, 1967

Eitrem, *Beiträge*   S. Eitrem, *Beiträge zur griechischen Religionsgeschichte.* 2, 3, Kristiania, 1917, 1920

Eitrem, *Opferritus*   S. Eitrem, *Opferritus und Voropfer der Griechen und Römer*, Kristiania, 1915

Evans-Pritchard   E. E. Evans-Pritchard, *Nuer Religion*, Oxford, 1956

Farnell   L. R. Farnell, *The Cults of the Greek States*, 5 vols., Oxford, 1896–1909

Fehling   D. Fehling, *Ethologische Überlegungen auf dem Gebiet der Altertumskunde* (Zetemata 61), Munich, 1974

Fehrle   E. Fehrle, *Die kultische Keuschheit im Altertum*, RGVV 6, Giessen, 1910

Fontenrose   J. Fontenrose, *The Delphic Oracle*, Berkeley, 1978

Foucart   P. Foucart, *Les Mystères d'Eleusis*, Paris, 1914

Fugier   H. Fugier, *Recherches sur l'expression du sacré dans la langue latine*, Paris, 1963

Gagarin, *Drakon*   M. Gagarin, *Drakon and Early Athenian Homicide Law*, Yale, 1981

Gebhard   V. Gebhard, *Die Pharmakoi in Ionien und die Sybakchoi in Athen*, diss. Munich, 1926

Gernet   L. Gernet, *Recherches sur le développement de la pensée juridique et morale en Grèce*, Paris, 1917

Gernet, *Anthropologie*   L. Gernet, *Anthropologie de la Grèce antique*, Paris, 1968

Gernet, *Antiphon*   L. Gernet, Budé edition of Antiphon, Paris, 1923

Ginouvès, R. Ginouvès, *Balaneutiké, recherches sur le bain dans l'antiquité grecque* (*BEFAR* 200), Paris, 1962

Glotz   G. Glotz, *La Solidarité de la famille dans le droit criminel en Grèce*, Paris, 1904

Gnoli/Vernant   G. Gnoli and J. P. Vernant (eds.), *La Mort, les morts dans les sociétés anciennes*, Cambridge/Paris, 1982

Goltz   D. Goltz, *Studien zur altorientalischen und griechischen Heilkunde, Therapie, Arzneibereitung, Rezeptstruktur* (Sudhoffs Archiv Beiheft 16), Wiesbaden, 1974

Graf   F. Graf, *Eleusis und die orphische Dichtung Athens in vorhellenistischer Zeit*, RGVV 33, Berlin, 1974

Griffin   J. Griffin, *Homer on Life and Death*, Oxford, 1980

Gruppe   O. Gruppe, *Griechische Mythologie und Religionsgeschichte*, 2 vols., Munich, 1897–1906

Guthrie, *OGR*   W. K. C. Guthrie, *Orpheus and Greek Religion*, London, 1935

Guthrie, *HGP*   W. K. C. Guthrie, *A History of Greek Philosophy*, vols. 1–3, Cambridge, 1962–9

Harrison   A. R. W. Harrison, *The Law of Athens*, 2 vols., Oxford, 1968, 1971

Hasluck   M. Hasluck, *The Unwritten Law in Albania* (ed. J. H. Hutton), Cambridge, 1954

Heldensage   C. Robert, *Die griechische Heldensage*, Berlin, 1920–6 (= part 2 of Preller/Robert, below)

Herter, *Dämonen* H. Herter, 'Böse Dämonen im frühgriechischen Volksglauben', *Rheinisches Jahrbuch f. Volkskunde* 1 (1950), 112–43, reprinted in his *Kleine Schriften*, Munich, 1975, 43–75 (from which I cite)

Hertz R. Hertz, *Death and the Right Hand*, trans. R. and C. Needham, London, 1960

Jacoby F. Jacoby, *Atthis, the Local Chronicles of Ancient Athens*, Oxford, 1949

Jordan B. Jordan, *Servants of the Gods* (Hypomnemata 55), Göttingen, 1979

Kudlien F. Kudlien, *Der Beginn des medizinischen Denkens bei den Griechen*, Zürich/Stuttgart, 1967

Kurtz/Boardman D. C. Kurtz and J. Boardman, *Greek Burial Customs*, London, 1971

Lanata G. Lanata, *Medicina magica e religione popolare in Grecia fino all' età di Ippocrate*, Rome, 1967

Latte, *HR* K. Latte, *Heiliges Recht*, Tübingen, 1920

Latte, *Kl. Schr.* K. Latte, *Kleine Schriften zu Religion, Recht, Literatur und Sprache der Griechen und Römer*, ed. O. Gigon, W. Buchwald, W. Kunkel, Munich, 1968

Latte, *Mord* K. Latte, art. *Mord* in *RE*, reprinted in *Kl. Schr.*

Latte, *RR* K. Latte, *Römische Religionsgeschichte*, Munich, 1960

Lévi-Strauss C. Lévi-Strauss, *La Pensée sauvage*, Paris, 1962, cited from the translation *The Savage Mind*, London, 1966

Lévy-Bruhl L. Lévy-Bruhl, *Primitives and the Supernatural*, trans. L. A. Clare, London, 1936

Lienhardt G. Lienhardt, *Divinity and Experience. The Religion of the Dinka*, Oxford, 1961

Linders T. Linders, *Studies in the Treasury Records of Artemis Brauronia Found in Athens*, Stockholm, 1972

Linforth I. M. Linforth, *The Arts of Orpheus*, Berkeley, 1941

Lipsius J. H. Lipsius, *Das attische Recht und Rechtsverfahren*, 3 vols., Leipzig, 1905–15

Lloyd G. E. R. Lloyd, *Magic, Reason and Experience*, Cambridge, 1979

Lloyd-Jones H. J. Lloyd-Jones, *The Justice of Zeus*, Berkeley, 1971

Lobeck C. A. Lobeck, *Aglaophamus, sive de theologiae mysticae Graecorum libri tres*, Regimontii Prussorum, 1829

Macdowell, *Law* D. M. MacDowell, *The Law in Classical Athens*, London, 1978

Macdowell, *Homicide*   D. M. MacDowell, *Athenian Homicide Law in the Age of the Orators*, Manchester, 1963

Meuli, *Ges. Schr.*   K. Meuli, *Gesammelte Schriften*, ed. T. Gelzer, Basle/ Stuttgart, 1975, 2 vols.

Mikalson   J. D. Mikalson, *The Sacred and Civil Calendar of the Athenian Year*, Princeton, 1975

Moulinier   L. Moulinier, *Le Pur et l'impur dans la pensée des Grecs d'Homère à Aristote* (Études et commentaires 12), Paris, 1952

Murr   J. Murr, *Die Pflanzenwelt in der griechischen Mythologie*, Innsbruck, 1890

Mylonas   G. E. Mylonas, *Eleusis and the Eleusinian Mysteries*, Princeton, 1961

Nilsson, *GF*   M. P. Nilsson, *Griechische Feste von religiöser Bedeutung mit Ausschluss der attischen*, Leipzig, 1906

Nilsson, *GGR*   M. P. Nilsson, *Geschichte der griechischen Religion*, vol. i, ed. 3, Munich, 1969, vol. ii, ed. 2, 1951, (the reference is to vol. i unless otherwise stated)

Nilsson, *Op. Sel.*   *Martini P. Nilsson Opuscula Selecta*, 3 vols., Lund, 1951–60

Nock   A. D. Nock, *Essays on Religion and the Ancient World*, ed. Z. Stewart, 2 vols., Oxford, 1972

Orfismo   *Orfismo in Magna Grecia* (Atti del quattordicesimo convegno di studi sulla Magna Grecia), Naples, 1975

Parke/Wormell   H. W. Parke and D. E. Wormell, *The Delphic Oracle*[2], vols., Oxford, 1956. P/W 50 = response n. 50 in vol. ii

Pollock/Maitland   Sir F. Pollock and F. W. Maitland, *The History of English Law before the Time of Edward I*, ed. 2, 2 vols., Cambridge, 1923

Preller/Robert   L. Preller, *Griechische Mythologie*, ed. 4 by C. Robert, vol. i, *Theogonie und Götter*, Berlin, 1887–94

Pritchett   W. K. Pritchett, *The Greek State at War*, 3 vols., Berkeley, 1974–9

P/W   cf. Parke/Wormell above

Read   M. H. Read, *Culture, Health and Disease*, London, 1966

Reverdin   O. Reverdin, *La Religion de la cité platonicienne*, Paris, 1945

Richardson   N. J. Richardson, *The Homeric Hymn to Demeter*, Oxford, 1974

Robert, *Oidipus*   C. Robert, *Oidipus*, 2 vols., Berlin 1915

Robertson Smith W. Robertson Smith, *Lectures on the Religion of the Semites,* new edition 1894 (cited from the edition London, 1901)

Rohde E. Rohde, *Psyche,* ed. 2 Heidelberg, 1897, cited from the translation by W. B. Hillis, London, 1925

Rudhardt J. Rudhardt, *Notions fondamentales de la pensée religieuse et actes constitutifs du culte dans la Grèce classique,* Geneva, 1958

Schwenn Fr. Schwenn, *Die Menschenopfer bei den Griechen und Römern,* *RGVV* 15.3, Giessen, 1915

Simon B. Simon, *Mind and Madness in Ancient Greece,* Cornell, 1978

Snodgrass A. M. Snodgrass, *The Dark Age of Greece,* Edinburgh, 1971

Srinivas M. N. Srinivas, *Religion and Society among the Coorgs of South India,* Oxford, 1952

Steiner F. Steiner, *Taboo,* London, 1956 (cited from the Pelican edition, 1967)

Stengel P. Stengel, *Die griechischen Kultusaltertümer*³, Munich, 1920

Stiglitz R. Stiglitz, *Die grossen Göttinnen Arkadiens,* Vienna, 1967

Stroud R. S. Stroud, *Drakon's Law on Homicide* (Univ. Cal. publ. in class. stud. 3), Berkeley, 1968

Thomas K. Thomas, *Religion and the Decline of Magic,* London, 1971 (cited from the Penguin University Book edition, 1973)

Töpffer J. Töpffer, *Attische Genealogie,* Berlin, 1889

Turner V. W. Turner, *The Ritual Process,* London, 1969 (cited from the Pelican edition, 1974)

van Gennep A. van Gennep, *The Rites of Passage,* trans. M. B. Vizedom and G. L. Caffee, London, 1960

Vernant, *Pensée* J. P. Vernant, *Mythe et pensée chez les Grecs,* 2 vols., Paris, 1965

Vernant, *Société* J. P. Vernant, *Mythe et société en grèce ancienne,* Paris, 1974

Vernant, *Tragédie* J. P. Vernant and P. Vidal-Naquet, *Mythe et tragédie en grèce ancienne,* Paris, 1973

Vickers B. W. Vickers, *Towards Greek Tragedy,* London, 1973

Wachsmuth D. Wachsmuth, Πόμπιμος ὁ δαίμων, *Untersuchungen zu den antiken Sakralhandlungen bei Seereisen,* diss. Berlin, 1967

Wächter T. Wächter, *Reinheitsvorschriften im griechischen Kult, RGVV* 9.1, Giessen, 1910

Whitehead   D. Whitehead, *The Ideology of the Athenian Metic* (Cambridge Philological Society Supplementary Volume iv), Cambridge, 1977

Wilamowitz, *Glaube*   U. von Wilamowitz-Moellendorff, *Der Glaube der Hellenen,* Berlin, 1931–2 (cited from ed. 3, Darmstadt, 1959, with altered pagination)

Williger   E. Williger, *Hagios, RGVV* 19.1, Giessen, 1922

Ziehen   L. Ziehen, *Leges Graecorum sacrae e titulis collectae,* 2.1, Leipzig, 1906

Zuntz   G. Zuntz, *Persephone,* Oxford, 1971

INTRODUCTION

Anyone who has sampled a few of the most commonly read Greek texts will have encountered pollution. In tragedy, the plague at the opening of the *Oedipus Tyrannus* is caused by it, it precipitates Creon's repentance in the *Antigone*, while Orestes in the *Oresteia*, although he is driven to the matricide by the fear of one pollution, is seized by another after performing it. In history, it plays, perhaps, a larger part than any other religious motif in the austere Thucydides. A Greek state in the fifth century, we learn from him, might attribute a natural disaster to a pollution it had incurred, and he shows us the Athenians expelling the Delians from their island to ensure the purity of this religious centre.[1] In the fourth century, Aeschines could envisage Demosthenes as the 'demon who pollutes all Greece', and brings it to misfortune.[2] A glance at evidence of a different kind, inscriptions regulating cult, shows how the concern for purity affected the individual in his everyday religious practice. The threat of pollution is, it seems, the dominating concern of the Superstitious Man of Theophrastus.[3]

Many questions are worth asking about a phenomenon of this kind. The reader of tragedy will wish to know whether he is confronted, in pollution, with a literary mechanism or a living preoccupation. States intervened in the internal affairs of others to 'drive out the pollution', or made war on account of it;[4] pollution was usually a pretext, but the historian may be interested in the unchallengeable validity assigned to such a justification for aggression. The student of Greek values will consider how the fear of pollution functions as an inhibiting factor in a society whose dominating values are of a different kind. Some have seen here a historical development; thus the postulated growth of pollution fears is central to the famous

---

[1] Thuc. 1.128.1, 5.1. Cf. 1.126–135, 4.97.2–99, 3.104.1–2, 5.32.1 for pollution in this author.
[2] 3.157 f., and often.
[3] Theophr. *Char.* 16
[4] Hdt. 5.72.1. Wars: see pp. 165 ff. below.

hypothesis that describes the spiritual history of early Greece as a transition 'from shame culture to guilt culture'.[5] Still in the sphere of values, a question arises about the relation of pollution to morality; the irrationality of the former, perhaps, makes it hard for a rational system of the latter to develop. The religious historian may wonder how pollution relates to 'sin', prime source of religious danger in a different tradition; this question becomes of central importance in the case of those alternative religions of the Greek world whose goal was salvation and principal route towards it 'purification'. The subject is not irrelevant even to the historian of science, since the Hippocratic doctor, in seeing 'impurity' as a cause and symptom of disease, is an heir to the prophet or oracle. The origin of disease raises the more general question of how the early Greeks, individually and collectively, responded to the afflictions that befell them.

These problems, and more, present themselves to the Hellenist from the Greek material alone. Further questions are raised by anthropology, which shows that pollution belief is closer to being a human universal than an idiosyncrasy of the Greeks. What is it there for? It is not a product of the ill-focused terror that permanently invests the savage mind, because that terror is an invention of nineteenth-century anthropology.[6] Does it perhaps shore up those areas of the social structure and value system that lack any other sanction? That would help to explain the central problem of the divergence in these beliefs between one society and another. For pollutions that derive from involuntary acts, however, an explanation in terms of some other form of order which men seek to impose on their experience will obviously be required. There are rules, too, that govern the minutiae of everyday life. 'Don't cut your hair or your nails at a festival', urged Pythagoras. Can such trivial injunctions be related to a broader system of Pythagorean order, and how could such a system be explained?

Pollution, then, is a pervasive phenomenon which raises diverse questions. The first problem is that of establishing a working definition of the thing itself. The title of this book seems to announce a precise area of inquiry – a single Greek word denoting, one might hope, an easily isolable theme whose clar-

[5] Dodds, Ch. 2.
[6] See Douglas, 11 f.

ity would be in happy contrast to the ambiguity[7] which surrounds the concept of pollution in anthropological literature. The hope proves delusive; the *mia-* word group is applied to a diverse range of things, and if one isolates within it a category that seems to have real unity, the same criteria that have been applied in order to constitute it demand that phenomena described by different words should also be included. An English example will illustrate this simple point: 'innocent' thoughts associate better with a 'pure' mind than does 'pure' alcohol. Not merely words are involved, of course, but forms of behaviour – avoidance, expulsion, ablution, and the like. As a simple appeal to vocabulary will not serve, some further attempt to define what is here understood by pollution becomes indispensable. The approach may seem disconcertingly scholastic, but it is clear in practice (witness the debate about pollution in Homer) that discussion in this area is likely to be conducted at cross purposes without an explicit definition of terms.

The basic sense of the *mia-* words is that of defilement, the impairment of a thing's form or integrity. Things that in English we term 'dirty' are a common source of such defilement, but there are defilements deriving from things that are not dirty in themselves, or not deriving from matter at all. *Miainō* can be used for the pollution of a reputation through unworthy deeds, or of truth through dishonesty;[8] justice, law, and piety are in danger of defilement.[9] This book treats, among all the possible defilements to which *mia-* words could be applied, a sub-category that is to a considerable extent marked out by linguistic usage. The verb *miainō* is more freely applied, but where the noun *miasma* or the adjective *miaros* (except in the sense of 'revolting') occur, they almost always[10] refer to a condi-

[7] See e.g. Buxton, 190 n. 2, A. S. Meigs, 'A Papuan Perspective on Pollution', *Man*, n.s. 13 (1978), 304–18.

[8] Solon, fr. 32.3, Pind. *Pyth.* 4.100, Eur. *Hel.* 1000, cf. Pind. *Nem.* 3. 16 (a citizen's disgrace 'defiles' his *agora*). αἰσχύνω similarly used, Hom, *Il.* 23.571, 6.209; ἀπορρυπαίνω, Soph. fr. 314.159 Radt; κηλίδα προσβαλεῖν, Eur. *Stheneboea*, prologue 37 f.v. Arnim.   [9] Aesch. *Ag.* 1669, *Sept.* 344, Eur. *Supp.* 378.

[10] In Hipp. *Flat.* 5, 6 (6. 96, 98 Littré) *miasmata* in the air cause disease. The reading *miasma* in *SEG* xxv 447.6 (Arcadia, 3rd c. BC) is uncertain, as the editor Dr. G. J. te Riele kindly informs me after re-inspection of the stone (cf. *Bull. Épig.* 1969 n. 267); if correct, it has a secular sense, 'offence'. *Miaros* of ritual status, *LSCG* 56, *LSS* 115 A 10, 18; of ritual/legal status, *SEG* xxvi 1306.25 f.,? *Die Inschriften von Ilion* 25.86 (Michel 524 C 1). It is not used of e.g. dirty clothes.

4 *Miasma*

tion that has some, and usually all, of the following characteristics: it makes the person affected ritually impure, and thus unfit to enter a temple: it is contagious: it is dangerous, and this danger is not of familiar secular origin. Two typical sources of such a condition are contact with a corpse, or a murderer; a polluted reputation, on the other hand, does not qualify on any of the three counts. A specialization rather like that of *miasma* can be seen in its opposite, *katharmos*, which tends to be restricted to a limited category of cleansings. While *kathairō* would be the normal verb to use for washing a wound, it would be odd (though possible)[11] to speak of the process as a *katharmos*; the sacrifice, on the other hand, that remedies the desecration of a sacred grove is so described.[12] This is not, therefore, a book about Greek ideas of dirt and defilement in general – a good comprehensive treatment of that theme already exists[13] – but about certain dangerous conditions to which the metaphor of defilement is often applied.

This means that a large amount of evidence on what is merely 'disgusting' is excluded. Disgusting things in English start with the physically repugnant but include what is morally outrageous; indeed it is not clear that a thing can be strongly disapproved of without becoming 'disgusting'. This is even more true in Greek, in which *miaros* and its near synonym *bdeluros* are among the commonest and strongest terms of abuse. They can be applied to dirty habits – belching at someone, for instance[14]– but only in a minority of their uses do they concern what is felt to be repugnant physically. Often it is impossible to give them a preciser sense than 'villain' or, more playfully, 'rogue'. The essence of disgustingness, however, seems to be deficiency in

[11] Pl. *Soph.* 226d – scarcely, in context, evidence for colloquial use.
[12] Soph. *OC* 466.
[13] Moulinier, *passim*. His book contains an enormous amount of helpful lexicographical material. It is less strong on the subjects I shall attempt to tackle, cf. Vernant, *Société*, 121–40, H. Jeanmaire, *RHR* 145 (1954), 99–104. It will be clear that my usage has nothing in common with that of J. M. Redfield, *Nature and Culture in the Iliad*, Chicago, 1975, 161 f. and Ch. 5, *passim*. Redfield here offers a brilliant analysis of the Homeric sense of order, but his use of the language of purification and pollution to describe it has little justification in either Greek or English usage.
[14] e.g. Ar. *Vesp.* 914, 1151.

shame; 'disgusting and shameless/brazen/bold' are constant conjunctions.[15] This bad boldness can be directed against oneself or against others; thus Timarchus, who prostituted himself,[16] and Meidias, who wantonly attacked Demosthenes, are both alike revealing the *miaria* of their natures.[17] Traitors and law-breakers are *miaroi*, because it is shamelessness that causes them to disregard normal constraints.[18] The *miaros* is an animal,[19] lacking the self-control that is the first requisite of life in society. The criteria just outlined, however, exclude beastliness of this kind from the category of pollution. Normal people try to avoid such *miaroi*, but to prevent them playing some foul trick, not from fear of contamination. If one did try to include all 'disgusting' behaviour, pollution would become a category of alarming and perhaps vacuous comprehensiveness, since it does not seem that in Greek terms disgustingness clings merely to a restricted set of deviations; any outrageous act makes its perpetrator, viewed in a certain light, *miaros*.

It is natural to associate with *miasma* a few other words whose primary reference is to dirt but which are also used in connection with contagious religious danger.[20] Much more important is the noun *agos*, with its adjective *enagēs*, 'in *agos*'. *Agos*, too, it is natural to associate with *miasma*, and no one who has discusssed the subject of Greek pollution seems ever to have thought of doing otherwise; the condition of *agos* has all the three characteristics of *miasma* mentioned above, and can actually be referred to as *miasma*[21] (although the relation is not fully reciprocal). It should be emphasized, however, that the partial

---

[15] e.g. Ar. *Eq.* 304, *Pax* 182–4, *Ran.* 465 f., Xen. *Hell.* 7.3.6, Dem. 8.68, 19.17, (cf. μιαρῶς, 'shamelessly', 21.69); at least 15 further instances occur. Theophr. *Char.* 11.1. defines βδελυρία, if the MSS are right (Diels changed παιδιά to ἀναίδεια), as 'blatant and reprehensible jesting'; this is the thing in its mildest form.

[16] See Aeschin. 1, *passim*. The link with πορνεία e.g. 54, 88, 192, Dem. 19.287. Sexual perversion, Aeschin. 1.70; sexual violence, Dem.19.309. Having an erection, Ar. *Lys.* 989; making advances, Ar. *Plut.* 1069. βδελύττομαι as proper response to the sexually impure, Ar. *Eq.* 1288.

[17] Connection with ἀσέλγεια and ὕβρις: e.g. Dem. 21.98,123,143; 47.81; Isae. 5.11.

[18] Treachery: e.g. Ar. *Ach.* 182, *Eq.* 239; Dinarch. 3.18. Lawlessness: Andoc. 1.122, Isae. 8.42, Dem. 25.27, 35.26.

[19] Dem. 25.58, 43.83, 45.70 (ἄγριος), 58.49, Dinarch. 1.50.

[20] Principally μύσος, κηλίς, λύμα, χραίνω.

[21] Cf. Aesch. *Supp.* 375 with 366, 619. For the respective consequences of *agos* and *miasma* cf. Aeschin. 3.111 and Soph. *OT* 25–30.

overlap between the two concepts is perhaps due to a convergence rather than to a real similarity in origin. On this view they would be two distinct forms of contagious religious danger, created by different acts and to some extent conceived in different ways, which were assimilated because for the outsider their practical consequences were the same. In semantic origin, certainly, there seems to be no resemblance between the two terms. The etymology of *agos* is controversial, but it now seems most probable that ancient scholars were right to connect it with the *hag**– root (*hagnos, hagios*) whose sense is 'to be revered, sacred'.[22] Even if the etymological connection is fallacious, it is plausible that Greeks of the classical period imagined it to exist, and certain that they did not regard 'pollution' as the basic sense of *agos*. The decisive text is the passage in the *Oedipus Tyrannus* where the chorus refer to Creon, who has invoked upon himself a terrible curse should he prove guilty, as *enagēs*.[23] There is nothing polluted about Creon, but he is 'sacred' in the sense that he has surrendered himself conditionally to the gods who will punish him if his oath proves false. (In Latin too an oath is a form of self-consecration.[24]) If it does, he will become *enagēs* not conditionally but absolutely, and for outsiders, who will avoid him for fear of sharing his punishment, his 'sacredness' will amount to pollution. In different language we find the same conception of perilous consecration in an expression like 'I have freed myself from Zeus of *xenoi*' to mean 'I have satisfied my obligations as a *xenos*',[25] or in the Eumenides' claim in Aeschylus that Orestes, who has offended against them, is 'consecrated' to them.[26] It may even be that in Elis in the sixth

[22] See P. Chantraine and O. Masson in *Sprachgeschichte und Wortbedeutung, Festschrift A. Debrunner*, Bern, 1954, 85–107, for a valuable full discussion; cf. Vernant, *Société*, 134–40. Burkert, *GR* 405 denies the connection but admits semantic interference between the two stems. For the rival derivation from Sanskrit 'āgas', sacrilege, see e.g. Williger, 19 ff.; its proponents are required, *inter alia*, to separate ἐναγής from εὐαγής, and ἐναγίζω from its synonyms ἁγίζω and καθαγίζω, and can make nothing of ἄγος = *piaculum* in Soph. *Ant.* 775 and fr. 689 (puzzling admittedly on any view). For a difficulty cf. p. 7 n. 31, below.

[23] 656, cf. 647,653. καθιερόω in a similar context, Dem. 49.66.

[24] *Caput votis obligare*, Hor. *Carm.* 2.8.6; *exsecrari*, cf. Fugier, 235.

[25] Pl. *Ep.* 7, 329b, cf. Eur. *Hec.* 345 πέφευγας τὸν ἐμὸν Ἱκέσιον Δία.

[26] *Eum.* 304 καθιερωμένος; Orestes in 451 protests that he is now deconsecrated.

century a decree of outlawry could be expressed in the form 'Let him go away to Zeus.'[27]

In several other passages *agos* appears as the sanction in a curse. The 'Plataea oath' specifies 'Let there be *agos* for those who have sworn should they transgress their oath.'[28] When Herodotus says that anyone who obstructs a particular right of the Spartan kings is 'held in the *agos*', he is probably referring to a public curse regularly pronounced against offenders of this kind; 'held in the *agos*' is closely parallel to the common expression 'held in a/the curse'.[29] The offender, it seems, is subjected to a perilous consecration. The archaic Roman institution of the *leges sacratae* has often been compared, by which criminals were declared 'sacred' to the god they had offended.[30] They were consecrated only in the sense that they were made over for punishment; from the point of view of human society they became outcasts, to be killed with impunity. *Agos* and *enagēs* are often constructed with a god's name in the genitive,[31] which seems to correspond to the dative of the *leges sacratae* indicating the god to whom the offender is made over. This genitive is not found with words like *miasma* whose basic sense is defilement. Where *agos* is not the sanction to a curse but occurs as a result of sacrilege, the consecration presumably occurs spontaneously.[32] The parallel is evident between the offender who, becoming *enagēs*, is abstracted from human society and consigned to the

[27] *SGDI* 1153 (= Michel 194, Schwyzer 415, Buck 63), as interpreted by Latte, *HR* 62–4. On the consecration of the *dekatos* in the Cyrene cathartic inscription see Appendix 2.

[28] P. Siewert, *Der Eid von Plataiai*, Munich, 1972, p. 7 lines 50 f. For *enagēs* in a curse see Aeschin. 3.110, 121; *agos?* = curse, Soph. *Ant.* 256.

[29] Hdt. 6.56, cf. Solmsen/Fraenkel[4] 52.9, 54 A 20 f., M/L 30 B 34, Pl. *Leg.* 881d, Polyb. 12.6b.9.

[30] Bibliography in Ogilvie's notes on Livy 3.55.5–7; add Fugier, 236 ff. See too *RAC* s.v. *Anathema*, on a comparable Judaeo-Christian institution.

[31] (Aesch.) *Sept.* 1017, Thuc. 1.126.2, 128.1–2, Aeschin. 3.110. It must be admitted that the construction of the noun *agos* often presents a problem on the Chantraine/Masson theory. While one expects the offender to be 'in the agos' (Hdt. 6.56, and *enagēs*), in fact he himself is often virtually equivalent to the *agos* (Soph. *OT* 1426, Thuc. locc. cit., Hdt. 5.72.1, Arist. *Ath. Pol.* 20.2), or an *agos* 'happens to' him (Aesch. *Supp.* 376, Hdt. 6.91.1, Plataea oath). Aesch. *Eum.* 167 has an ἄγος αἱμάτων. Chantraine/Masson would presumably have to explain these usages as an assimilation in construction to *miasma*.

[32] Cf. Durkheim, 320, 'Every profanation implies a consecration, but one which is dreadful, both for the subject consecrated and for those who approach him.'

gods for punishment, and the animal which, in the form of sacrifice known as *enagizein*, is burnt whole for a god with no share left for the human worshippers.

Diverse though they are in origin, *miasma* and *agos* do, as we have noted, overlap in usage. Every *agos* is probably also a *miasma*, and *agos* is often constructed as though it meant pollution rather than something like 'avenging divine power'.[33] It seems, however, that, at least in the early period, not all *miasmata* are *agē*. While certain unavoidable physical conditions are *miasmata*, *agos* is a product of avoidable even if involuntary transgression. A corpse, for instance, diffuses *miasma*, but *agos* is only created if a survivor denies it the divinely sanctioned right of burial.[34] To create *agos*, the offence must probably be directed against the gods or their rules, as simple murder seems not to do so, while murder at an altar certainly does.[35] It sometimes seems as if what causes *agos* is simply contact between *miasma* and the sacred. The historical instances recorded in Herodotus and Thucydides all take the form of killing in violation of sanctuary. Violation of sanctuary without bloodshed, however, is spoken of as *agos* in Aeschylus,[36] and there is no connection between the *agos* invoked in an oath or curse and polluting objects. To defile a sacred place by introducing *miasma* is one way, but one way only, of incurring that perilous consecration which seems central to the idea of *agos*.

It was suggested earlier that *miasma* and *agos* are perhaps in origin two theoretically distinct forms of communicable religious danger. The most important difference concerns the relation of the two to the gods. To *miasma* gods seem irrelevant; it is a dangerous dirtiness that individuals rub off on one another like a physical taint. *Agos* by contrast has its source in a sacrilegious

[33] See p. 7 n. 31.

[34] Soph. *Ant.* 256 (where, however, the meaning 'curse' also seems possible, cf. the schol.'s reference ad loc. to Bouzygean curses), (Aesch.) *Sept.* 1017.

[35] Hdt. 6.91.1, Thuc. 1.126.2, 128.1–2. If a murderer enters a sacred place, the place incurs *agos*, Aesch. *Eum.* 167. For *agos* used of plain murder, however, see Aesch. *Cho.* 635 (a compelling conjecture), Soph. *OT* 1426: in both cases the extreme horror of the deed perhaps evokes the more charged word. From the 4th c. *agos* and *enagēs* become virtual synonyms of *miasma* and *miaros*: Theophr. *ap.* Porph. *Abst.* 2.29, p.159.12 N., Alexander *ap.* Diod. 18.8.4, Polemon *ap.* Macrob. *Sat.* 5.19.26, Ap. Rhod. 3.203, 4.478, *Anth. Pal.* 14.74.2.

[36] Aesch. *Supp.* 375.

act, and the *enagēs*, as the attached genitive suggests, is in the grip of an avenging power; the reason for avoiding him is not fear of contamination but to escape being engulfed in the divine punishment that awaits him. We encounter here a crucial ambiguity in what is understood by the term pollution. While some scholars think of it as the impersonal taint, analogous to dirt or an infectious disease, others regard shared danger rather than the metaphor of contamination as the essential. This could be rephrased to say that one group confines pollution to *miasma* in the strict sense, while the other also includes *agos*. It would be possible in these terms to offer a compromise solution to the notorious problem of pollution in Homer; while *miasma* cannot be shown to be present in him, *agos* (not the word, but the experience) he undeniably recognizes.[37]

Agos seems, in fact, to provide middle ground between two sources of religious danger that are sometimes supposed quite distinct, and, in some cultures, may actually be so – on the one hand, impersonal pollution, and on the other, the anger of a personal deity. One reason for drawing this distinction may be the feeling that belief in divine anger is primitive but comprehensible, while belief in pollution is wholly irrational. But, even though pollution may operate 'with the same ruthless indifference to motive as a typhoid germ',[38] divine anger is not always more discriminating. There is no point in avoiding polluted shipmates before putting to sea, only to fall in with others the gods are angry with; you will finish at the bottom just the same.[39] This is why the *enagēs*, who is consecrated to an avenging god, becomes in practical terms polluted. Divine anger, *agos*, and *miasma* can become inextricably intertwined. In Aeschylus' *Supplices*, we find the consequence of disregarded supplication expressed,[40] sometimes in close juxtaposition, as *miasma*, *agos*, the 'wrath of Zeus of Suppliants', the hostility of the 'all-destructive god' from whom even the dead are not free,

[37] Lloyd-Jones, 74 f.
[38] Dodds, 36.
[39] Shipwreck is caused by, in general terms, injustice (Hom. *Od.* 3.133), impiety (Aesch. *Sept.* 602–4), pollution (Ant. 5. 82, Eur. *El.* 1350). Specific causes are sacrilege (Ajax and Cassandra, Odysseus' companions and cattle of sun), perjury (Eur. *El.* 1355), and blood-guilt (Ant. 5.82). For much further evidence see Wachsmuth, 265–71.
[40] See 366, 375 f., 385, 414–16, 478, and for juxtaposition 616–20.

and the presence of an avenging Zeus perched on the roof-top, perhaps polluting[41] and certainly damaging the house. The same convergence can be seen on the ritual level. In theory sacrifice and purification may seem to be distinct operations, the one intended to appease a deity and the other to efface an impersonal pollution. In practice, what is spoken of as a purification often takes the form of a sacrifice,[42] while the effects of divine anger, at least when it manifests itself as a disease, can sometimes be washed away.[43]

As a result, it becomes extraordinarily hard to draw lines of demarcation between pollution and the consequences of divine anger. Religious danger is almost always potentially communal in Greece; a punishment that is confined to the guilty parties deserves special comment.[44] It may be more natural to envisage the murderer, for instance, as endangering his associates, and the perjurer his descendants, but the other form of contamination is possible in both cases.[45] If the consequences of different offences had once been more distinct, they had been assimilated by the date of most of our sources to an extent that makes them now almost inextricable. There is no question of formal 'purification' from the consequences of perjury,[46] but nor is there from temple-robbing, and the temple-robber is certainly *enagēs*.[47] It is very hard, therefore, to separate from pollution any situation where breach of a religious rule has created danger. As the chapter on sacrilege will show, quite minor violations of sanctity are 'pollutions' both in the sense of causing communicable danger, and in that of requiring 'purification'. To unite all these situations in an undifferentiated category of pollution

---

[41] So the MS in 650, but see Page's critical note.

[42] Hdt. 6.91.1, Soph. *OC* 466–92, Eur. *HF* 922 ff., with Moulinier, 88, Rudhardt, 270, Paus. 1.34.5 ἔστι δὲ καθάρσιον . . . θύειν, below, p. 209 on Epimenides. Such cathartic sacrifice could be denoted by a distinctive use of ἐκθύομαι, Hdt. loc. cit., Eur. fr. 912.12 (with object of the god appeased), Theophr. *Char.* 16.6 (a certain conjecture). Cf. J. Casabona, *Recherches sur le vocabulaire des sacrifices en grec*, Aix-en-Provence, 1966, 96 f.; there were ἱεροποιοὶ ἐπὶ τὰ ἐκθύματα in Athens, Arist. *Ath. Pol.* 54.6, and for ἐκθυσίαι in Delos see Bruneau, 286–8. An ἔκθυμα may well have differed from the characteristic form of Olympian sacrifice, but the point remains that this is a deistic rite.

[43] See Ch. 7.

[44] Diod. 15.49.6, Plut. *Timol.* 30.7–9.

[45] e.g. Eur. *El.* 1355, *Hipp.* 1379.

[46] But for the informal possibility see Ov. *Fast.* 5.681 f., cited *Ant.u. Chr.* 6 (1950), 73.

[47] e.g. Diod. 16.60.1.

would be unacceptable; the language of defilement is more natural in some cases than in others, and will not always have the same implications. It seems better, however, to operate with a concept that is flexible and, at its edges, ill-defined, than to impose a demarcation by force. Care will have to be taken in determining what, in a particular case, the label 'pollution' actually means.

The partial convergence between *miasma* and a word whose etymological connections seem to be with sacredness does not support the often repeated paradox that 'the sacred is at once "sacred" and "defiled" ', because 'in the savage mind the ideas of holiness and pollution are not yet differentiated'.[48] These claims are based on the Polynesian taboo, which does in fact unite sacred things and ritual impurity within the single category of prohibition;[49] no word is available to indicate the special status of the one, it is said, which is not also applicable to the other. It has come to be recognized, however, that taboo is a specialized phenomenon quite unsuitable for the indiscriminate international application that it has often received.[50] Certainly, in Greek as in other religions, there is a similarity between sacred and impure objects in that both are subject to restrictions.[51] In different contexts the one adjective *hosios*, in its sense of 'safely available for profane use', can indicate freedom from either consecration or pollution.[52] There is, however, no difficulty in Greek in distinguishing between the source of restriction in the two cases; a sacred law spells out with welcome clarity the three estates of the world as 'sacred, profane, and polluted'.[53] A Greek would be puzzled by the suggestion that there is anything impure about the sacred, or vice versa. As we have seen, impure things are *miasmata*, not *agē*. The sacred is indeed contagious, in the sense that the offender falls into the power of the offended god; but, although he becomes dangerous, and thus 'polluted', for the outsider, it is not pollution

[48] M. Eliade and J. G. Frazer, cited by Douglas, 18,20.
[49] Steiner, 33–6.
[50] Steiner, *passim*, esp. 35.
[51] Cf. T. O. Beidelman, *W. Robertson Smith and the Sociological Study of Religion*, Chicago, 1974, 62 f.: 'he saw that the concepts of holiness and pollution both depended upon restrictive rules of avoidance, and that formally these prohibitions were alike.'
[52] See Appendix 1.
[53] *LSS* 115 A 9 f.

in the god but avenging power that makes him so. In Latin, even the limited connection between 'sacred' and 'accursed' contained in the use of *sacer* in the *leges sacratae* came to be puzzling;[54] similarly in Greek, if the etymological link of *agos* with *hag-* is correct, differentiation occurred early, through the loss of the aspirate, between beneficial and destructive forms of consecration.[55]

The two words that have been given such prominence so far are not especially common. Whole literary genres can be found from which one or the other is virtually absent. The verb *miainō* is more often found in relation to pollution than the noun *miasma*, and the common way of saying 'polluted' is simply 'not clean' (*katharos*). Often the language used in relevant contexts is that of *hosiā*, what is religiously safe, rather than specifically that of purity. It is as a focusing device that the words *agos* and *miasma* have here been given almost emblematic significance. But alongside them can be set another distinctively religious word which by contrast is very common. *Hagnos* means 'pure', but has no etymological connection with physical cleanliness.[56] Thus, though pollution is elusive, purity stands forth palpably; and the clear reality of its opposite helps to justify the kind of definition of pollution that we have adopted.

The deficiencies in the evidence for our knowledge of Greek pollution belief will repeatedly be apparent. The gravest consequence of the state of the evidence is that it has been impossible to centre this study on a particular time and place. A historical and geographical synthesis becomes inevitable because no one state offers a corpus of contemporary documents, homogeneous or not, sufficiently dense to form a basis for a synchronic local study. Even fifth-century Athens, for which literary evidence is comparatively abundant, offers little forensic oratory, few accounts of relevant behaviour, and almost nothing by way of explicit codes of rules. The perils of such a synthesis are obvious. Place matters; the Greeks were not a homogeneous cultural mass, and did not see themselves so. Several historical instances show that the Spartans, for instance, were ready to respect

---

[54] See Macrob. *Sat.* 3.7.5; cf. W. Warde Fowler, *Roman Essays and Interpretations*, Oxford, 1920, 16 f.

[55] But on the ancient lexicographers' belief in ambiguous words see Appendix 1.

[56] See pp. 147 ff.

religious claims (such as that of the festival calendar) even to their own obvious detriment. Across the boundary in Argos, however, lived men fertile in legalistic devices for evading religious obligations, and quick to exploit to their own ends their neighbours' piety.[57] Time matters even more; the passage from the world that seems to be implied by Homer, where the effects of literacy are scarcely perceived, and the community has few claims as against the individual household, to the society whose administrative complexities are laid out in Aristotle's *Constitution of the Athenians*, did not leave religious values unaffected. It is obvious, for instance, that the implications of a belief like that in collective punishment change drastically when the collectivity threatened is no longer a village community, where everybody could know everyone else, but the city of Athens, conventionally reckoned by the Greeks as containing 30,000 citizens. The actual range of regional and temporal variation in pollution beliefs will certainly not have been captured in this book, but the effort has been made to present as differentiated a picture as the evidence permits.

Another delicate synthesis is that between different classes of evidence.[58] The noun *miasma*, ubiquitous in the tragedians, does not occur at all in Herodotus, Thucydides, or Xenophon. This might be taken to prove that the word's stylistic level is too high for prose, that the concerns of tragedy are unreal, or simply that tragedy and history treat different areas of experience. The status of imaginative literature as evidence is, in fact, a particular problem. Modern social historians view such evidence with suspicion; court records, not extrapolations from Shakespeare, form the backbone of a classic modern study of English popular religion.[59] Literary texts can only be safely exploited, it might be argued, to illustrate the human implications of beliefs and attitudes the existence and significance of which can be independently established. Classical scholars, whose knowledge of subjects like pollution derives largely from their reading of tragedy, have tended to be less cautious, partly because alternative sources of information on these subjects are hard to find.

[57] See pp. 154 f.
[58] Cf. Dover, 8–33; excellent remarks on the relevance of literary purpose in Lloyd-Jones, 76 f.
[59] K. Thomas, *Religion and the Decline of Magic*, London, 1971.

There are most delicate problems here, and some differentiation is required. Works of art may convey incidental factual information that need not be mistrusted. We learn from Shakespeare that the cold maids of England give the name of 'dead men's fingers' to certain flowers, and tragedy contains a good deal of reliable information about matters of cult. Where, on the other hand, a religious motif has an obvious function in the mechanics of the plot, like the ghost in *Hamlet* or the plague in the *Oedipus Tyrannus*, no more can be inferred than that the motif was comprehensible to the audience; neither audience nor playwright need be committed to belief in the phenomenon. Religious themes that are embedded in the outlook of a work are harder to assess. 'Thinking more than mortal thoughts', 'envy of the gods', 'the family curse': these, we believe, are prime religious dangers in the 'archaic world view'. Yet it is chiefly through literature that we hear of them; we scarcely know what their correlates may have been in the everyday experience of the fifth-century Athenian who was so often invited to reflect on them in the tragic theatre.

The spectator of tragedy was also the spectator of comedy, and it is instructive to compare the world-views of the two genres. Divine justice may in tragedy often be an obscure ideal in hopes of which men grope in pain; the gods of Old Comedy are decent sorts, who do their best to keep erring humans on the right track.[60] They punish wrongdoers,[61] but theirs is no savage justice; unlike the Dionysus of Euripides, they can forgive a temporary aberration, and a humble plea for pardon will not find them adamant.[62] This is a world against which no grandiose resentment is possible, and those who display it are explicitly marked by their language as intruders from the tragic stage: 'O savage god, o destiny . . .'.[63] Comedy's nearest equivalent is undignified grumbling: 'Some god's got the house into a proper mess.'[64] Erinyes are known from literature, not life,[65]

[60] Ar. *Nub.* 587–9. This is the standard civic view, cf. Solon, fr. 4 (an influential text), fr. 11.1–2, Dem. 1.10, 2.1, 18.153, 195, 19.254–6, Aeschin. 3.57, 130; with 'luck' instead of gods, Dem. 1.1, 4.12.
[61] Ar. *Nub.* 395–7, 1458–62, *Thesm.* 668–85, *Ran.* 148–50.
[62] Ar. *Nub.* 1478–80, *Pax* 668 f., cf. *Vesp.* 1001 f.; contrast Eur. *Bacch.* 1344–9.
[63] Ar. *Nub.* 1264, cf. *Pax* 1250, *Thesm.* 1047, *Ran.* 310.   [64] Ar. *Vesp.* 1474 f.
[65] Ar. *Plut.* 423, cf. Aeschin. 1.190, Timaeus 566 *FGrH* fr. 55; underworld punishments too are known from art, Dem. 25.52.

and the big words with which tragedy speaks of crime and punishment acquire here more homely meanings.[66] In a fourth-century comedy, the 'curse of the Pelopidae', typical tragic theme, will be a conception to laugh at, and the only *alastores*, polluting demons, who are recognized will be men – philosophers, for instance, who too little appreciate the value of pleasure.[67] While in high literature the seer is always right,[68] in comedy he is always wrong.[69] Not just comedy saw a cleft between tragedy and the familiar world. When, in the fourth century, an orator mounts unaccustomed religious or emotional heights, his opponent will draw him back by an accusation of *tragōdia*, or sham.[70] It is in continuation of this usage that the historian who detects unreal patterns of divine vengeance in the events he records is accused of composing 'tragic' history.[71]

These facts do not, of course, expose the tragic world-view as mere melodrama. If some of its religious preoccupations seemed unreal in the fourth century, they may not have done in the fifth; and the relation of comedy to tragedy is not that of real life to 'lies of poets', but of one polar extreme to another.[72] What does emerge is the crucial influence of a literary work's genre in determining the religious emphasis it contains. Certainly there is also scope for large diversity within a genre (*Iliad* and *Odyssey*, Homer and the epic cycle, the three tragedians), but works of the same genre, because they have a common subject-matter and, in Aristotelian terms, a common aim, are liable to focus on similar areas of experience and belief to the exclusion of others. If one consults works of different genre for information about ideas of fate, or the continuing influence of the dead on human life, one receives answers that, if not contradictory, are at least notably different in emphasis. Thus it is particularly dangerous

---

[66] ἀλιτρία, villainy, Ar. *Ach.* 907; ἀτηρός, impossibly troublesome, *Vesp.* 1299; Ἐρινύων ἀπορρώξ, a real old curmudgeon, *Lys.* 811.

[67] Xenarchus, fr. 1.3 *ap.* Ath. 63 f; cf. Baton, fr. 2.5; Moulinier, 266.

[68] Poulydamas in the *Iliad*, Teiresias in Soph. *OT*, *Ant.*, Eur. *Bacch.*

[69] Ar. *Pax* 1047 ff., *Av.* 521, 959 ff., Cratinus, fr. 57,62, Callias, fr. 14, Eupolis, fr. 211, 212, Epicharmus, fr. 9, 'Aristoxenus' *ap.* Hephaest. 8.3.27 Consbruch (Kaibel, *CGF*, p. 87); cf. Lloyd, 17 n. 41.

[70] LSJ, s.vv. τραγῳδία, τραγῳδέω.

[71] On Plutarch's derogatory use of *tragikos* see P. de Lacy, *AJP* 73 (1952), 159–71, and, summarizing the debate on 'tragic history', F. W. Walbank, *Polybius*, Berkeley, 1972, 34–9, with references.

[72] Arist. *Poet.* 1448b 24 ff.

to base hypotheses of cultural change on works of different centuries that belong to different genres. The belief that pollution fears settled over Greece like a cloud in the post-Homeric period is largely based on a comparison between two separate genres, eighth- or seventh-century epic and fifth-century tragedy; but the prominence of murder pollution in tragedy is a consequence of its preferred subject-matter, and the phenomenon that requires explanation is not an upsurge of pollution fears but the emergence of a genre that so extensively explored the consequences of violence within the family. If we take a fifth-century genre whose aims are closer to the epic, the choral lyric of Pindar, we continue to find pollution fears as inconspicuous as in Homer, while it is possible to read right through the works of Xenophon and scarcely become aware that such a thing exists. The evidence of one genre needs to be controlled by comparison with that of others, literary and non-literary. When this is done, some conceptions best known from high literature – god-sent delusion, for instance – do turn out to occur, in slightly altered guises, at every level.[73]

The spasmodic appearance of pollution in literature raises a final and more general point of method. It is not just in literary texts that pollution fears surprise now by their presence, now their absence. In the late seventh century, the great Athenian family of the Alcmaeonids incurred a celebrated pollution.[74] They were tried and exiled, and the very bones of the dead members expelled. More than half a century later, Peisistratus, later the tyrant, married an Alcmaeonid girl for political reasons, but was unwilling to beget children from the polluted stock; when the girl's father, Megacles, learnt of the insult, a crisis in their alliance resulted. At the end of the sixth century, the Spartans arrived in Athens to expel the Alcmaeonid Cleisthenes and his followers; their motives were political, but the pretext was to 'drive out the *agos*'. The taint still clung to the slightly Alcmaeonid Pericles, and was exploited against him by Sparta in 432. Yet the Alcmaeonids had been able to re-

[73] For comic *atē* see p. 14 n. 62; for history (Hdt. aside), Xen. *Hell.* 6.4.3, Arr. *Anab.* 2.7.3; for oratory, (Lys.) 6.22,27,32, Aeschin. 3.117,133, Dem. 9.54; *atē* as a mechanism of divine punishment, Andoc. 1.113, Lycurg. *Leoc.* 91–3, Dem. 24.121.

[74] See Hdt. 1.61, 5.62–3.1, 5.70–2, 6.126–30, Thuc. 1.126–7, Arist. *Ath. Pol.* 20.2; cf. Davies 368–85.

instate themselves in Athens not long after their trial; the same Megacles whose daughter Peisistratus spurned was himself chosen as son-in-law by Cleisthenes of Sicyon, in preference to the finest men of Greece; at the end of the century, the great temple at Delphi, home of the pure Apollo, was built with funds provided by the tainted family. In this case, it seems that pollution had soon ceased to be an actual source of religious anxiety, and become instead an inherited disgrace, one factor among others in the general reputation of the family, which enemies would denounce and friends ignore. The explanation here is primarily political, but other factors too could cause concern about pollution to appear spasmodic or unpredictable. The individual was most sensitive to the added threat when he was most endangered in other ways; thus we find fear of pollution, like many other religious concerns,[75] at its most intense in connection with seafaring. The consequences might prove that a particular act, merely doubtful in itself, was in fact polluting, or that an *agos* which men hoped had been 'sacrificed out' was still active. The Greeks expressed something like this through the metaphor of a pollution that 'sleeps' and then 'wakes up'.[76] During Sophocles' *Oedipus at Colonus*, the chorus are half persuaded that their initial revulsion was wrong and Oedipus is not a threatening person; but, when a terrifying thunderclap is suddenly heard, they at once suppose that the consequences of associating with the polluted have caught up with them.[77] The Athenians seem to have observed their fortunes during the Peloponnesian war in order to evaluate their policy of religious tinkering with Delos; if battle went ill, the right formula had not yet been found.[78] The implications of all this for method are easily seen. An account of pollution beliefs will be sterile and unreal unless it considers the complicated process by which belief is translated into behaviour.

---

[75] Wachsmuth, *passim*.
[76] Aesch. *Eum.* 280, Hdt. 7.137.1.
[77] 1482–4.
[78] Thuc. 5.32.1.

1

PURIFICATION:
A SCIENCE OF DIVISION

In the longest extant analysis of the activity called *katharmos*,
Plato in the *Sophist* presents it as an aspect of the 'science of
division'. 'Of the kind of division that retains what is better but
expels the worse, I do know the name . . . every division of that
kind is universally known as a purification.'[1] The purifications
envisaged here by Plato are purely physical – washing, carding
of wool, and the like – but such physical acts of division are
readily and unconsciously exploited to create divisions of a
different kind. We see this from Dickens's lawyer Mr Jaggers:

I embrace this opportunity of remarking that he washed his clients
off, as if he were a surgeon or a dentist. He had a closet in his room,
fitted up for the purpose, which smelt of scented soap, like a per-
fumer's shop . . . When I and my friends repaired to him at six o'clock
next day, he seemed to have been engaged on a case of a darker
complexion than usual, for we found him with his head butted into
this closet, not only washing his hands, but laving his face and
gargling his throat . . .

And again, after a dinner party, 'I found him in his dressing
room surrounded by his stock of boots, already hard at it,
washing his hands of us.'[2] Mr Jaggers, therefore, a man whose
imperious control of his environment Dickens emphasizes,
separated the different areas of his experience by elaborate rites
of lustration. Jaggers is an extreme case, but this is a familiar
form of behaviour. Few of the ordinary individual's daily purifications, clustered as they are around points of transition (before and after bed, on return from work, and so on), are without
some symbolic content. What is remarkable about Jaggers is
the ease with which he could remove unpleasant associations by

---

[1] Pl. *Soph.* 226d.
[2] *Great Expectations*, Ch. 26.

the application of soap. His clerk Wemmick required a drawbridge for the same purpose.

Purification is one way in which the metaphysical can be made palpable. Although it can perhaps operate as a divider in a quite neutral sense, it more naturally separates higher from lower and better from worse. Its most obvious use of this kind in Greece is to mark off sacred areas from profane. 'We ourselves fix boundaries to the sanctuaries and precincts of the gods, so that nobody may cross them unless he be pure; and when we enter we sprinkle ourselves, not as defiling ourselves thereby, but to wash away any pollution we may already have contracted.'[3] There is abundant evidence from literature, vase paintings, and excavation for these stoups of lustral water sited at the entrance to sanctuaries, for the purification of those who entered. In inventories, they appear as part of a temple's normal furnishing; Hero, in his *Pneumatica*, tells of a mechanical device that gave forth lustral water at the drop of a coin.[4] It is very revealing for Greek conceptions of the sacred that in Athens the *agora*, civic and political centre of the city, was marked off by similar lustral stoups. Whether the normal Athenian would actually have purified himself before entering is not known, but certainly this was the barrier beyond which those deprived of civil rights might not pass, on threat of prosecution.[5] A kind of ring of purity excluded the disgraced from communal life.

Fixed lustral bowls are first attested around the end of the seventh century, but the custom because of which they were set up is already embedded in Homer. Without purification there is no access to the sacred. 'Respect forbids me to pour a libation to Zeus with unwashed hands', says Hector, and we find Homeric characters not merely washing their hands but bathing and

[3] Hippoc. *Morb. Sacr.* 148.55 ff. J., 1.46 G.
[4] Cf. *SIG*³ index s.v. περιρραντήριον; Hero, *Spir.* 21. Full treatment by Ginouvès, 229–310 (my debt to this learned and comprehensive work is very large). For the earliest *perirrhanteria* see J. Ducat, *BCH* 88 (1964), 577–606. On their function cf. Lucian, *Sacr.* 13, Pollux 1.8.
[5] See G. E. M. de Ste. Croix, *The Origins of the Peloponnesian War*, London, 1972, Appendix 43; and R. Martin, *Recherches sur l'agora grecque*, Paris, 1951, 164–201, on the *agora*'s religious significance.

changing their clothes as a preparation for prayer or sacrifice.[6]
Before any sacrifice, the participants were united by a rite of
symbolic washing. Lustral water was carried round in a special
bowl, and those taking part washed their hands in it, or at least
sprinkled themselves or were sprinkled.[7] Once the ritual space
and the participants had been marked off in this way, the
sacrifice could proceed. Most sanctuaries had a spring near at
hand, a hallowed source of material for 'purifications and lustral water'.[8] Really elaborate rituals of preparatory washing are
not attested, but the more closely involved psychologically the
mortal was in the ceremony to be performed, the greater and
more formal the preliminary requirements became. Thus before incubation, initiation, mysteries, and prophecy the bath
was a regulated and ceremonial event.[9] About civic sacredness
we are less well informed, but Peisetairos is probably following
at least an occasional Athenian practice when he calls for water,
to cleanse his hands, and a crown, before addressing the assembly of the *Birds*.[10]

Greeks observed these customs even though purity was not
an obviously important attribute of their gods. The gods ruled
the universe because they were powerful and immortal, not
because they were pure. It was in practical rather than theological terms that divine purity became an important conception.
Sacredness is elusive, irreducibly metaphysical; purity, though
also metaphysical, can at least be expressed symbolically in
concrete terms. Cleanliness is, in fact, not a special preparation
for worship but a requirement for formal, respectful behaviour
of any kind; there is no generic difference between the lustrations that precede a prayer and those that precede a meal,[11]

---

[6] Hom. *Il.* 6.266–8, cf. e.g. 9.171 f., 16.228–30 (libation cup cleansed with sulphur).
Od. 4.750–2 (bath and clean clothes), Moulinier, 26. Later evidence e.g. Hes. *Op.* 724 f.,
Eur. *El.* 791–4, Moulinier, 71–4.
[7] Hom. *Il.* 1.449, and *passim*. In classical times the sprinkling was often done with a
torch or olive branch dipped into the lustral water, Eur. *HF* 928 f., Ath. 409b. For
details see Eitrem, *Beiträge* iii, 1–19, also Ginouvès, 311–18.
[8] See p. 227 n. 108 below.
[9] Incubation: see p. 213 n. 31. Initiation, mysteries: see Ch. 10 below, also Ginouvès,
380–6 (water installations in sanctuaries of Demeter and other goddesses; cf. *LSCG*
65.37, 107–12). Prophecy: e.g. schol. Eur. *Phoen.* 224, Fontenrose, 224, Ginouvès,
327–44.   [10] Ar. *Av.* 463 f.
[11] e.g. Hom. *Od.* 1.146, Ar. *Av.* 464. No generic difference: cf. J. Gould, *JHS* 93
(1973), 79 n. 34.

which is itself, for the Greek, a ceremonial occasion. In both cases the person affected sheds a little of his everyday self.

These purifications can be looked at from the other side: not only do they prepare the individual for a special event, but they also serve to lift the event itself out of the familiar plane and to imbue it with sanctity. This was often achieved by creating a clear spatial frame for the important occasion. Before every meeting of the council and assembly at Athens, a young pig was killed and its corpse carried round the circumference of the meeting-place by special officials known as *peristiarchoi*.[12] Though quite different in form from any washing process, this was still a 'purification'. Its function in creating a division was so clearly felt that Aristophanes, no doubt echoing popular usage, could speak of taking a seat on the Pnyx as 'coming inside the purification'.[13] Temples too were sometimes cleansed before festivals, and some lexicographical sources tell of the theatre, public buildings, 'the city', and meeting-places in general being treated in the same way.[14] However that may be, the name of the officials concerned, the 'round the hearth leaders', shows that the rite derives originally from household practice.[15] These are clearly symbolic acts, not misguided provisions for public hygiene; it would, one imagines, not have made sense to purify the assembly providently in advance, when no one was there to see. On at least one occasion the custom permitted the Athenians a vivid symbolic action. During a session of the assembly in 370, news arrived from Argos of the civil conflict in which 1,500 men were killed. A fresh purification of the assembly was ordered at once.[16] Much later, we hear of the Mantineans conducting an elaborate purification of their land after a troop of murderous Cynaethans had passed through. Slaughtered animals were carried round the city and entire

---

[12] Most of the sources are printed by Jacoby in his commentary on Istros 334 *FGrH* fr. 16. The γαλῆ of Ar. *Eccl.* 128 is probably a comic mistake. The remains went to the crossroads, Dem. 54.39.

[13] Ar. *Ach.* 44.

[14] Phot., Suda s.v. περιστίαρχος, cf. Harp. s.v. καθάρσιον, schol. Aeschin. 1.23. *Inscr. Cret.* 4.146 (*LSS* 114) has a purification of shipyards, according to the interpretation of Guarducci, ad loc.

[15] Cf. Eitrem, *Opferritus*, 177, *RE* 8.1280 f., 19.859. Hesych. s.v. περίστιον makes this domestic purification post-funerary.

[16] Plut. *Praec.Reip. Ger.* 814b, cf. Diod. 15.57.3–58.

territory.[17] In these cases the traditional rites of division were being re-exploited to express horror and rejection, by separating the citizens from the abhorrent events.

Those within one of these purifying encirclements were marked as having something in common. The purification of the *boulē* and *ekklēsia* defined the participants as the Athenian people in council or assembly, while membership of a religious community was commonly expressed in terms of 'sharing lustral water'.[18] This unifying function is well seen in the practice of purifying an army before the campaigning season.[19] Each spring, when the Macedonian army reassembled, it was marched between the two halves of a sacrificed dog, which created what has been called an 'absorptive zone' for all its impurities. (This, incidentally, is the only form of Greek purification for which a really close near eastern analogue has been demonstrated.[20]) After the purification had, as it were, reconstituted the men as an army, they divided into two halves and proceeded to behave as an army in simulated fight. Plutarch records an identical rite for Boeotia, and though he says nothing of its context it was no doubt similar. If such annual purifications were performed elsewhere in Greece, they have left no trace in the sources, but an incident in the *Anabasis* shows the same ritual being exploited to weld an army back into a unity. Some of the Greeks had made unauthorized raids on villages, and there had been Greek casualties; when ambassadors came to offer restitution of the corpses, they were slain by the dead men's companions. Indiscipline seemed to be increasing, and so Xenophon summoned an assembly and made a stirring

---

[17] Polyb. 4.21.8–9.

[18] e.g. Aesch. *Ag.* 1037, *Eum.* 656, Soph. *OT* 240, Eur. *Or.* 1602, Dem. 20. 158, and esp. Ar. *Lys.* 1129 f. The point is made by Ginouvès, 313.

[19] See most recently Pritchett, iii, 196–202, with references. Macedonia: Livy 40.6.1–5; Polyb. 23.10.17 = Suda s.v. ἐναγίζων; Hesych. s.v. Ξανθικά. Boeotia: Plut. *Quaest. Rom.* 111.290d. For a possible purification of a fleet before embarkation see *Inscr. Cret.* 4.146 (*LSS* 114), with Guarducci's commentary.

[20] To avert an evil omen, the Hittite army was marched through the halves of a slaughtered prisoner of war: see O. Masson, *RHR* 137 (1950), 5–25, H. M. Kümmel, *Ersatzrituale für den hethitischen König*, Wiesbaden, 1967, 150–68. Survival or recollection of the practice in Anatolia, Hdt. 7.39.3. Greco-Roman parallels for this cathartic 'zone d'absorption' (Masson's term) in Masson, loc cit., Eitrem, *Beiträge* ii, 8–16. For a Hittite ritual battle, commemorating a historical victory, see H. Eheloff, *Sitz. Preuss. Ak. Berl.* 1925, 269–72.

speech. 'How are we to pray to the gods with a clear conscience', he asks, 'if we behave so wickedly? What city will receive
us, what honour will we enjoy at home?' His eloquence
triumphed; the troops insisted on the restoration of discipline
and punishment of offenders, and Xenophon with the seers'
support proposed that the whole army be purified.[21] Repentance, change of heart, rejection of anarchy, reassertion of the
army's corporate identity as a disciplined unity: such was the
message of this purification.

Restored to itself after an external incursion, a community
might express its sense of recovered integrity by purifying the
places and elements tainted by the invader's presence. After the
Persian withdrawal in 479, the Greek leaders at Plataea consulted Delphi 'about a sacrifice', but were told 'not to sacrifice
before they had extinguished the fire in the country, since it had
been polluted by the barbarians, and fetched pure fire from the
common hearth at Delphi'.[22] As the bringing of new fire was an
annual ceremony in several places,[23] this was, like the Athenian
re-purification of the assembly, an adaptation of a regular ritual
for a specific expressive purpose. It was the most potent renewal
a Greek community could undergo, since, lodged in the individual hearths of houses and the collective hearth of the city, fire
was the symbolic middle point around which the life of the
group revolved. Although this is not recorded, there was no
doubt also much purification of surviving temples from the
Persian presence. The Messenians, it is said, once expelled all
Epicurean philosophers, and then purified the shrines and the
entire state.[24]

Purification, therefore, marks off sacred places from profane,
creates special occasions, and unites individuals into groups. A
further area of experience which it helps to organize and articulate is the perception of time. Few people, in their informal
thoughts about time, consider a year as a succession of 365

[21] *Anab.* 5.7.13–35. A similar purification of the Macedonian army to end a period of
dissension after the death of Alexander, Curt. Ruf. 10.9.11.

[22] Plut. *Arist.* 20.4.

[23] Nilsson, *GF* 173, cf. W. Burkert, *CQ* 20 (1970), 1–16. On fire symbolism Xen. *Lac.*
13.3 is revealing.

[24] Aelian, fr. 39, p. 201.13–24 Hercher. Rome was purified after the expulsion of the
Tarquins, Dion. Hal. *Ant. Rom.* 5.1.3, and the Gauls, Livy 5.50.2, Plut. *Cam.* 30.3; cf. too
Tac. *Hist.* 4.53, Sil. *Pun.* 12.752.

homologous days, or even twelve cycles of the moon. It is made up of seasons, of festivals, of holidays, changing activities and the intervals between them.[25] Purification, which removes dirt from the past and so makes ready for the future, is ideally suited as a ritual to mark transition. Roman examples are particularly clear. The *tubilustrium* of March and the *armilustrium* of October indicated start and finish of the campaigning season.[26] The pentennial lustration of the people in arms included both thank-offerings for the previous five years and prayers for the following,[27] and the word *lustrum* itself actually came, by way of this ceremony, to denote a period of time. As well as marking change in a neutral sense, purification is also, of course, well suited to satisfy the urge periodically felt by most people to make a new start, and feel a tainted environment grow fresh again.

It will, as often, be most convenient to consider Athens, where the evidence is most abundant. The chief public purification lay in the dispatch of scapegoats,[28] a practice which, though it seems in mood and symbolism to belong to a restricted rustic community, probably still took place in the metropolitan Athens of the late fifth century,[29] and cannot be shown to have been abandoned even in, or after, the time of Aristotle. These wretched individuals were the animate form of the 'offscourings' (*katharmata*) which, in many Greek purifications, were expelled from the area of human habitation, carrying impurity with them. Scapegoats are said to have been sent out in response to specific crises, such as drought or plague, and obviously the ceremony ought primarily to be discussed in the context of communal reaction to danger. Since, however, such rites also had a fixed place in the festival cycle (not just in Athens, but almost wherever in the Greek world they are known to have been performed), they must also count among the

[25] Cf. E. E. Evans-Pritchard, *The Nuer*, Oxford, 1940, 94–108.
[26] Latte, *RR* 117, 120.
[27] Suet. *Aug.* 97.1, T. Mommsen, *Römisches Staatsrecht³*, Leipzig, 1887, 2.1.412 f. On *Lustrum condere* see R. M. Ogilvie, *JRS* 51 (1961), 31–9.
[28] Cf. p. 258 below.
[29] Ar. *Ran.* 733.

purifications that articulate the movement of the year.[30] Indeed
no reliable instances of the dispatch of scapegoats outside the
regular seasonal framework are anywhere recorded.

At Athens, scapegoats were sent out on Thargelion 6, as a
part of the Thargelia, a festival of Apollo; on Thargelion 7,
offerings of the still ripening corn, further first fruits, and the
Greek equivalent of the Maypole (*eiresiōnē*) were carried in
solemn procession, and new-corn cakes were baked.[31] The same
connection with the Thargelia is found at Ephesus,[32] and may
well be ancient. The scapegoat ritual has therefore sometimes
been seen as a magical protection for the new year's ripening
produce at a perilous time.[33] There is, however, no need to see
the relation between the two days of the festival in magical
terms; on Thargelion 6, bad things are driven out, while on
Thargelion 7, good things are carried in, in a pattern whose
appeal on an expressive level is self-evident. The scapegoats
were not, to our knowledge, led among the crops, and they were
said to purify the city[34] and not the fields. Scapegoat-like ceremonies were performed in other states at different times,[35] and
Apollo, honorand of the rites at Athens, was a god more concerned with purification than farming. Concentration on the
harvest obscures the more general sense in which the Thargelia
was for Athens a festival of purification and renewal. These
days were perhaps the two most auspicious in the entire Athenian calendar. On the sixth of Thargelion, Socrates (and
Artemis) were born, Plato on the seventh. Most of the victories
of the Persian wars (Artemisium, Mycale, Plataea) came in time
to be set on Thargelion 6, as well as both the birth and death of
Alexander.[36] New fire, powerful symbol of renewal, arrived

---

[30] On the regular/occasional contrast see Deubner, 184–8. Even for Massilia, where
the source speaks of an occasional ritual only, what is described sounds regular (Serv.
Aen. 3.57 = Petronius, fr. 1). The Delphic rite of the Septerion is interpreted as an
eight-yearly expulsion of a scapegoat by e.g. J. Fontenrose, *Python*, Berkeley, 1959,
453–61.

[31] Deubner, 188–92. Deubner denies use of the *eiresiōnē* at the Thargelia, but cf.
Nilsson, *GGR* 125, Vernant, *Tragédie*, 119 f., and on the *eiresiōnē* Burkert, *SH* 134.

[32] Hipponax, fr. 104.49.

[33] Nilsson, *GF* 113–5, followed by Deubner, 192 f.   [34] Hipponax, fr. 5.

[35] Porph. *Abst.* 2.54 (Rhodes), Deubner, 187 f. (Terracina).

[36] Plut. *Quaest. Conv.* 717b, D.L. 2.44, Ael. *VH* 2.25. But for the birth of Apollo on
Thargelion 7 (Nilsson, *GF* 209) I can find no authority (contrast Plut. *Quaest. Graec.*
9.292e).

from Delphi at some time during the month Thargelion, very probably during the actual festival of the Thargelia.[37]

Cleansing is also the theme of the two remaining festivals of Thargelion, the Kallynteria and the Plynteria,[38] which are regularly associated in the sources and were probably in fact closely related. Most of our knowledge of the Plynteria is due to the coincidence that when Alcibiades returned from exile in 408, he unluckily chose the day of this festival for his landfall in Athens.[39] On this day, we learn, members of the Praxiergidai removed the adornments of Athena Polias' ancient image, veiled it, and performed secret rites. Since the goddess's image was covered, this was among the most inauspicious days of the entire year; the temples were closed,[40] and no Athenian would have thought of choosing it to begin an important undertaking. It seemed that with her covered head the goddess herself was spurning Alcibiades' presence.

Very little more is known of the festival than what can be learnt from this anecdote. Literary sources differ between Thargelion 25 and 29 for its date;[41] a recently discovered deme calendar seems to place it in the following month, but, as other epigraphic texts support a celebration in Thargelion, its precise location is at present obscure.[42] The name Plynteria indicates that the goddess's robes were washed before being replaced. The two noble girls who performed this function could be called either *loutrides* or *plyntrides*,[43] and as *louō* is used of washing a person, whereas *plunō* applies to clothes, we can perhaps infer

---

[37] *SIG³* 711 with n. 8.

[38] See, in addition to the festival handbooks, L. Ziehen in *RE* 21.1.1060–5, D. M. Lewis, *ABSA* 49 (1954), 17–21, W. Burkert, 'Buzyge und Palladion', *Zeitschrift f. Religions– und Geistesgeschichte* 22 (1970), 356–68, and, for possible Plynteria in Tegea, L. Koenen, *ZPE* 4 (1969), 7–18.

[39] Xen. *Hell.* 1.4.12, Plut. *Alc.* 34.1–2.

[40] Pollux 8.141: impossible to tell whether all the temples (Deubner) or only some (Ziehen) were affected. *IG* I³ 7.20–22, as restored and interpreted by Lewis, loc. cit., has a temple locked throughout the month of Thargelion.

[41] Cf. D. M. Lewis, loc. cit., Mikalson, 160–4, Burkert, *GR* 347 n. 5.

[42] Lines 52–4 of the Thorikos calendar, *SEG* xxvi 136; for the text and commentary see G. Dunst, *ZPE* 25 (1977), 243–64, J. Labarbe, *Thorikos, les Testimonia*, Gent, 1977, n. 50. But for Plynteria during Thargelion cf. *IG* I³ 7 (*LSCG* 15), 20–2, *IG* I³ 246 (*LSCG* 2), C 26. As the start is fragmentary, the evidence of the Thorikos calendar is not utterly unassailable (one could substitute Kallynteria, for instance); but the alternatives are unconvincing.

[43] Phot. and Hesych. s.v. *loutrides*.

that the statue itself was bathed. Where and how this was done, if indeed it was done, is unknown. (It has recently been shown that the procession in which the ephebes escorted 'Pallas' to the sea almost certainly formed part of a different festival.[44]) About the Kallynteria almost nothing is recorded,[45] but its name suggests 'sweeping clean', and it is tempting to suppose that at the Kallynteria the temple precinct was cleaned, as the image itself was at the Plynteria.

The cleaning of statues was to some extent a practical necessity. At Eleusis, a special functionary is early attested, and at Olympia, the same task is said to have been bestowed as a privilege on the descendants of Pheidias.[46] It might be performed before sacrifice, or accompany the purification of a shrine with animal blood.[47] Even in these cases, however, it was a way of creating a sense of occasion in preparation for a rite; and when, as at Athens, it gave its name to an important public festival, it had clearly acquired a symbolic religious significance quite distinct from the practical requirements of cleanliness. A month-name Plynterion is attested for Chios, Paros, Ios, and Thasos, which suggests that the Plynteria may have been an ancient Ionian rite.[48]

The bathing of statues, particularly the statues of goddesses, in springs, rivers, or the sea was not rare in Greek cult.[49] In addition to regular annual rituals, the statue might be taken out for washing, or washed on the spot, if a temple was polluted by death or bloodshed.[50] There is no reason to look for a single explanation for all such cases, because an image-bath may imitate any of the various motives that an actual goddess might have for bathing. The bath that Hera's image receives in Plataea is pre-nuptial,[51] but it seems from Callimachus' *Hymn*

[44] By Burkert, op. cit.; doubts already in C. J. Herington, *Athena Parthenos and Athena Polias*, Manchester, 1955, 30 n. 2. Plynteria procession: Phot. s.v. ἡγητηρία.

[45] For its date see Mikalson, 164, and for activities Lewis, loc. cit.

[46] *IG* I³ 1 A 14 (*LSS* 1), Paus. 5.14.5, Clinton, 95, *RE* 19.1559 f.

[47] *LSCG* 58.12 f., 39.26.

[48] See A. E. Samuel, *Greek and Roman Chronology*, Munich, 1972, index 2 (month names).   [49] Cf. Ginouvès, 283–98.

[50] Eur. *IT* 1199, *LSCG* 154 B 24 f., ? *LSA* 79.14 f., 532 *FGrH* D (2). Merely an extension of the common practice of purifying the precinct after a pollution, p. 145 n. 6.

[51] Paus. 9.3.5–9, Plut. *ap.* Euseb. *Praep. Evang.* 3.1. 1–3 = fr. 157 Sandbach; the nuptial interpretation of the rite is secondary (cf. Nilsson, *GF* 50–56, *RE* 20.2. 2319–25, Burkert, *SH* 132–4), but the bath clearly belongs to it.

that 'Pallas' bath' in Argos is simply taken for bathing's sake,[52] and in the case of the Plynteria, there is no hint of any specific motivation for whatever cleansing the goddess received.[53] She was, it seems, participating in the general renewal characteristic of the season, and, by her participation, involving her citizens too. If the day of the cleansing itself was, for all the Athenians, an inauspicious time, the succeeding days will, by a familiar process of contrast,[54] have been a period of especial liberation, with life beginning anew in purity. The ancient *aition* represents the Plynteria as the occasion when the women of Athens first washed their clothes after their year-long grief for the daughter of Cecrops Aglaurus;[55] it was a time, therefore, of revival and renewal of hope.

The sixth month after Thargelion was Maimakterion. Thargelion meant the rising of the Pleiades, the beginning of summer and of the harvest; Maimakterion the setting of the Pleiades, the beginning of winter and of the ploughing. These were the two turning-points of the year.[56] Like Thargelion, Maimakterion was characterized by ceremonies of purification. It may have been during this month that the ephebes solemnly escorted the Palladion down to the sea at Phaleron for cleansing.[57] It was certainly then that the Pompaia were celebrated.[58] The evidence for this ceremony is scanty, but we are told that, 'among the purifications', the fleece of a ram

---

[52] *Hymn* 5. The mythical baths that serve as precedent are just baths (vv. 5–12, 70–4).

[53] The once popular pre-nuptial theory (e.g. Fehrle, 176 f.), well criticized by Ginouvès, 292 f., is still upheld by L. Koenen, *ZPE* 4 (1969), 14–18. Such theories ignore or distort the Kallynteria.

[54] Cf. Deubner's Roman parallel, p. 22.

[55] Phot. s.v. *Kallynteria*, Hesych. s.v. *Plynteria*. Close correlation between *aition* and rite is sought by A. Mommsen, *Feste der Stadt Athen*, Leipzig, 1898, 497–502.

[56] Cf. Hes. *Op.* 383 f., 614–17; Hippoc. *Vict.* 3.68 (6.594 L.); Theophr. *Sign.* 1.6 (fr. 6. 1.6, p. 117 Wimmer), διχοτομεῖ τὸν ἐνιαυτὸν Πλειάς τε δυομένη καὶ ἀνατέλλουσα; *BCH* 85 (1961), 39 (Euctemon); Pliny, *HN* 18.280 *namque vergiliae privatim attinent ad fructus, ut quarum exortu aestas incipiat, occasu hiems, semenstri spatio intra se messes vindemiasque et omnium maturitates conplexis.* For ploughing in Maimakterion (denied by Mikalson, 86) cf. Deubner, 250, and the link with the setting of the Pleiades (Hes. loc. cit.): at 38° in 500 BC the Pleiades rose May 20 and set November 3, according to E. J. Bickerman, *Chronology of the Ancient World²*, London, 1980, 112.

[57] See Burkert, cited p. 26 n. 38 above.

[58] Eustath. ad Hom. *Od.* 22. 481, p. 1935. 5 ff. (cited Deubner, 158 n. 2): cf. Hesych. s.v. μαιμάκτης: μειλίχιος, καθάρσιος.

sacrificed to Zeus Meilichios (a *dion*) was carried out of the city. The sense of this rite is clear from the verb derived from it, *apodiopompein*, to purify by expulsion; the fleece was an inanimate scapegoat, an object that absorbed evil and was then expelled. So one of Thargelion's most important rites has a close parallel in Maimakterion; if the bathing of the Palladion were more securely dated to this time, one could almost speak of a mirror image.

Like the Thargelia, the Plynteria and the Pompaia have both been interpreted as mechanisms of agricultural magic.[59] There is a revealingly large element of the *a priori* in such interpretations, since neither ritual is addressed to a farming god or contains the least agricultural element in its aitiology or symbolism. Though it is true, as we have noted, that these festivals of renewal approximately coincide with important moments in farming life, what this proves is perhaps not that purification serves agricultural ends, but that in a farming community the emotional year, as it might be called, is shaped around the agricultural year.[60] The obvious landmarks that give shape to the dull succession of days are events such as harvest, ploughing, or the sprouting of the young corn. But the informal calendar put together in this way acquires emotional functions and can readily be festooned with symbolic meanings. One has only to think of the associations of transience, but also transformation, that attach to the purely arbitrary new year in our own society to see what harvest time could have meant to a Greek in extra-agricultural terms.

On a smaller scale, we find the housefold purifications of private cult articulating the experience of time in the same way. Even within the month, religion could distinguish between superficially similar days.[61] The concept of *dies fasti* and *nefasti* may be associated with Rome more than with Greece, but the hemerology of Hesiod or his continuator was influential enough to provoke the criticism of Heraclitus; Orphic poets were fascinated by it, but the scholarly Philochorus, too, devoted a monograph to the theme, and Plutarch in his commentary on

[59] Deubner, 21, 158.
[60] Cf. Durkheim, 349 f., 'The seasons have only provided the outer framework for the organization [of festivals] and not the principle upon which it rests.'
[61] Cf. Mikalson, 13–24.

Hesiod characteristically discovered scientific justifications for the ancient beliefs.[62] From the meagre remains of this literature, we learn, for instance, that the Athenians favoured the eighteenth and nineteenth days of the month 'for rites of purification and aversion'.[63] The turning-points of the month in particular were marked by regular rites of expulsion. At the new moon, those householders who could afford it sent out 'meals for Hecate' to the crossroads.[64] These meals for Hecate are constantly associated with the purificatory offscourings thrown out in the same place, and, although their exact relation to such relics[65] is not quite clear, it is certain that like them they were a way of carrying evil away from the place of habitation, or at least of pinning the dangerous goddess at the crossroads by prophylactic offerings. Apollo's Delian temple too was purified by pig's blood once a month.[66] That model of restrained piety, Clearchus of Methydrion, cleansed and crowned his statues every new moon.[67] But at Athens, offerings were also sent out to

---

[62] Hes. *Op.* 765–828; Heraclitus B 106 *ap*. Plut. *Cam.* 19.3; *OF* pp. 274–9; Philochorus 328 *FGrH* fr. 85–8, 189 f.; Plut. fr. 100–112, 142 Sandbach.

[63] 328 *FGrH* fr. 190 – but perhaps this referred originally to one month only, Mikalson, 21.

[64] Ar. *Plut.* 594–7 with schol., Apollodorus 244 *FGrH* fr. 109.

[65] Dem. 54.39 distinguishes Hecate's meals from the remains of pigs used to purify assemblies, Lucian, *Dial. Mort.* 1.1, *Catapl.* 7 from cathartic eggs. Not all *katharmata* therefore become *Hekataia*. It is possible, however, that *Hekataia* are the *katharmata* left by a specific form of purification, that of the house (cf. Theophr. *Char.* 16.7). On the other hand, Plut. *Quaest. Rom.* 68.280c, 'dogs are carried out to Hecate with the other *katharsia*', perhaps indicates merely that the purpose of Hecate's meals was broadly cathartic, not that they themselves were exploited in a specific ritual of purification before being taken out: the offering itself would have been the purification. In the confusing ancient controversy on ὀξυθύμια (see Harpoc. and *Et. Mag.* s.v. ὀξυθύμια; other lexica add nothing), *Hekataia* seem sometimes to be identified with *katharmata*, but not with the specific *katharmata* from house purifications (which are, according to Didymus, ὀξυθύμια). Plut. *Quaest. Conv.* 708 f seems to indicate that Hecate's meals were cooked. Attested constituents were *magides* (Soph. fr. 734, cf. p. 231 n. 141), puppies (Ar. fr. 204, Plut. *Quaest. Rom.* 68.280c, Hesych. s.v. Ἑκάτης ἄγαλμα), and perhaps certain fish (Antiphanes *ap*. Ath. 358 f). They were sometimes eaten, from poverty (Ar. *Plut.* 594–7, ? Theophr. *Char.* 16.4, Lucian, loc. cit.), or bravado (Dem. 54.39).

[66] Moulinier, 106; Bruneau, 93, cf. ibid., 270–4, 286–7 for purification of the Thesmophoreion. Purification of the sacred area, usually by pig's blood, before an important festival or on a regular calendar basis was no doubt a general practice: see *IG* II² 1672.126–7 (= *SIG²* 587, temple at Eleusis and priestess's house), *LSCG* 39.23 f. (Aphrodite Pandemus at Athens, using a dove, because Aphrodite abhorred pigs; similarly *LSA* 36.36, Sarapis/Isis), *LSCG* 65.50, 66, 67 f. (mysteries of Andania), Aelius Aristides 48.31 (Asclepieion of Pergamum).

[67] Porph. *Abst.* 2.16.

the crossroads for Hecate on the sixteenth, exactly half a month after the new moon.[68] These two purifications of private cult divide the month as the public ceremonies of Thargelion and Maimakterion divide the year. Time is articulated on both levels by the same rhythms of cleansing and renewal.

The account of this science of division has been provisional, and in some respects one-sided. It seemed useful, however, to begin with a way of looking that relates purification to the desire for order, and that treats it as a form of behaviour rather than as a product of an explicitly formulated set of ideas. The purifications of this chapter have mostly not been intended to remedy pollutions – lapses below the level of purity required for everyday life – but to impart a touch of sanctity, a state of purity above the average. Purifications such as these create or restore value rather than averting danger. The distinction, however, is not absolute, as 'sacred: not-sacred: polluted' are points upon a continuous line. (This trinity may sound like an analyst's abstraction, but it appears in just this form in a Greek text.[69]) To specific pollutions, and to danger, we must now turn.

[68] Philochorus 328 *FGrH* fr. 86, cf. Jacoby, ad loc., and on the form of offering Borgeaud, 230 f.
[69] *LSS* 115 A 9 f.

2

BIRTH AND DEATH

Eclipses, earthquakes, and monstrous births are commonly seen by primitive peoples as fearful portents. The fact is well known, and easy enough to understand; these are phenomena that disrupt nature's normal, observable course. It is at first sight more paradoxical that the most intimately natural of all experiences – begetting, birth and death – should also be seen by people living close to nature as potent sourses of impurity and danger. Religious teachers and philosophers have rejected the world of coming-to-be and passing-away with scorn. One might suppose their stance the late product of speculation, a kind of estrangement from nature, but the restrictions that hedge around the natural processes throughout the world suggest that it has deeper roots. Almost any book of exotic travels, any ethnographic study will tell of the perils of sexuality and fertility, and the monstrous impurity of the corpse. This vast diffusion does not mean that the phenomenon is readily understood; on the contrary, it is one of those universals or near universals that are often taken to be comprehensible merely because they are common, and that prove under investigation too deep-seated, diverse, or complex for any simple or single explanation. The same impurities take on in different cultures very different significance. In Hinduism, the uncleanness to which the body is liable provides a theoretical basis for the caste structure, since the lower castes are rendered impure by washing the laundry, cutting the hair, and tending the corpses of the higher. In Zoroastrianism, by contrast, the implicatio s of impurity are not social but cosmic; it is a weapon of the evil principle Ahriman in his unceasing struggle with the creator, Ohrmazd.[1] Belief in the body's impurity may be a phenomenon, like animal sacrifice, about which little can usefully be said in general terms.

[1] See Dumont, 84–93; Boyce, 94.

The two natural pollutions most often referred to in Greek
sources are those of birth and death.[2] To avoid the pollution of
death, Artemis in the *Hippolytus* abandons her dying favourite:
'Farewell. Sacred law forbids me to look upon the dead, or stain
my eye with the exhalation of death.' Hippolytus necessarily
undergoes the pollution of death and Artemis necessarily shuns
it; that is the inescapable difference between mortal and immortal. Human sympathy is all with Hippolytus when he complains
'You find it easy to leave our long friendship'; but it is a truism
of Greek theology that Euripides has exploited to achieve the
pathetic effect.[3] In the *Antigone*, too, the pollution of death is
dramatically used. The dispute about Polyneices' burial has
been conducted in terms of rights, deserts, and duties. With the
entry of Teiresias and his report we receive decisive proof that
Antigone is in the right. Birds of prey have carried scraps of the
unburied corpse to the very altars, and all commerce between
man and god is impossible. When an unrepentant Creon insists
that mortals by their acts cannot pollute the gods, we can only
understand this rejection of plain fact as lunatic defiance.
Through pollution, the universe has given an unambiguous
verdict on the moral question.[4]

As these examples have shown, the natural pollutions are
especially repugnant to the gods. Birth or death within a temple
is sacrilege;[5] the sacred island of Delos must be free from all
taint of the processes of mortality.[6] Even a human who has

[2] Birth and death together: Eur. *Cret.* fr. 79.17–18 Austin, D.L. 8.33, Chrysippus, *ap.*
Plut. *de Stoic. Rep.* 1044f–1045a, Schol. Theoc. 2.11/12 b, Men. *Asp.* 216 ff., Porph. *Abst.*
4.16, p. 255.7 Nauck.
[3] Eur. *Hipp.* 1437 ff., cf. Griffin, 189; for the same motif see Eur. *Alc.* 22 f., Ael. fr. 11,
Men. *Asp.* 97 f., Heliod. *Aeth.* 1.2.7. Apollo and death inassociable, Aesch. *Sept.* 859 (cf.
Ag. 1075).   [4] Soph. *Ant.* 999–1047.
[5] *IG* II² 1035.10 πάτριον ἔστιν ἐν μηδενὶ τῶν τεμενῶν μήτ' ἐντίκτειν μήτ' ἐναποθνήσκειν,
Paus. 2.27.1, 6 (Epidaurus), *LSA* 83, Ant. Lib. *Met.* 19.3. Leaving temple to die or give
birth: Thuc. 1.134.3, Xen. *Hell.* 5.3.19, Plut. *Dem.* 29.6, Ar. *Lys.* 742 f., *SIG*³ 1168.1.
Death in the temples a symptom of the extreme demoralization caused by the plague,
Thuc. 2.52.3. It is clear from these texts that these purity requirements applied to all
sacred precincts, not just those of specific gods.
[6] Thuc. 3.104.1–2, Callim. *Del.* 276 f., Strabo 9.5.5 (486). As the latter 2 texts say
nothing of the birth taboo, it has been suggested that the Delians relaxed it once free
from Athenian domination: see Bruneau, 48–52. The temple accounts list payments for
the disposal of corpses washed up on Delos; in the first such case the purchase of a 'pig
for purification' is mentioned, but not subsequently (Bruneau, loc. cit.). Plague
(fictional) on Delos as consequence of a burial there, (Aeschines) *Epistle* 1.2. But the
purification spared tombs of 'heroes' (Bruneau, 49).

come into contact with birth or death is excluded for a period
from worshipping the gods. As Euripides' Iphigeneia complains: 'I criticize Artemis' clever logic. If a mortal is involved in
bloodshed, or touches a new mother or a corpse, she shuts him
out from her altar as polluted; but she herself takes pleasure
in human sacrifice.' Auge reproaches Athena directly; if the
goddess is happy to receive the dedication of blood-stained
spoils, how can she be angry that Auge has given birth in her
shrine? And yet she was; Auge's crime brought barrenness on
the entire land. Many people in the fifth century and afterwards
no doubt felt the same unease as these Euripidean heroines
about such amoral rules of impurity; the Stoic Chrysippus
branded them 'irrational'; but the rules survived. It was useless
to apply blustering moral dialectic to them because, though
pollution belief might sometimes, as in the *Antigone*, reinforce a
principle of morality, these rules were essentially as amoral as
the natural processes themselves.[7]

The description of the rules that follows is necessarily eclec-
tic. There is no Greek community to which all the details that
will be mentioned can be shown to have applied. For many
parts of the Greek world there is no actual evidence that such
regulations existed at all. We never hear of Greek communities
that 'did not use purifications', but it is clear from the local
regulations which define how long impurity lasts and whom it
affects that at this level, at least, there was no Panhellenic norm.
For death,[8] with which we begin, a law of the fifth century from
Iulis on Keos provides a framework,[9] while further details can
be added from Athens. The Iulis law is partially modelled, as
several verbal echoes show, on the funerary legislation of Solon,

---

[7] Eur. *IT* 380–4; Auge's crime, Ar. *Ran.* 1080 + schol.; its consequences, Apollod.
3.9.1; her complaint, Eur. fr. 266 *ap.* Clem. Al. *Strom.* 7.23.5, p. 17 St. (the following
point in Clement, 'other animals do it', is no doubt still Euripidean, cf. Hdt. 2.64); on
Euripides' Auge see *ZPE* 4 (1969), 7–18.

[8] On death-pollution see Wächter, 43–63, Moulinier, 76–81, Nilsson, *GGR* 95–8,
Ginouvès, 239–64. The basic account of the funerary rites is Rohde, 162–74; cf.
Kurtz/Boardman, Ch. 7, Alexiou, 4–23, and more generally the papers collected in
Meuli, *Ges. Schr.*, 1.301–435. See now the valuable discussion by C. Sourvinou-Inwood,
'A Trauma in Flux: Death in the 8th century and After', in R. Hägg and N. Marinatos
(eds.), *The Greek Renaissance of the Eighth Century B.C.: Tradition and Innovation*,
Stockholm, 1983(?).

[9] *IG* XII 5.593 = *SIG³* 1218 = *LSCG* 97. The Solonian law, Dem. 43.62; I speak of
'Solon' for convenience without wishing to commit myself on the law's origin.

but differs from Solon in treating questions of purity explicitly. Solon's silence is characteristic of our evidence; although funerary pollution was familiar at Athens, literary texts often fail to speak of it when treating of death or mourning. It is as though being polluted were, like wearing dark clothes, just one aspect of the state of mourning, and required no special mention.

At the moment of death, the house of death became polluted. A special water vessel was set outside, for the purification of those coming out; this and other conventional tokens used to indicate a house of death will have warned those unwilling to incur pollution not to enter at all. We do not know whether a sprinkling from this vessel was in itself full purification for those who attended the wake but not the funeral, or whether they were subject to further restrictions. The water was fetched from a neighbouring house, as the house of death's own supply was polluted. At Argos, we hear of new fire brought from next door, at the conclusion of mourning, for the same reason.[10] The women of the household prepared the corpse for the ceremonial laying-out and viewing; it was washed, anointed, crowned, dressed in clean robes, generally white or red, and laid upon a bier strewn with branches and leaves.[11] Thus the dead man was symbolically made pure, in despite of the contamination all around him; of all those present at the wake, he alone wore the crown, emblem of purity.[12] Certain obscure practices which the Iulis law alludes to perhaps occurred at this stage. 'Do not put a cup under the bier' (presumably during the laying-out), it orders, 'or pour out the water, or take the sweepings to the tomb.' Interpretation here is guesswork, but modern parallels[13]

[10] Water vessel: Ar. *Eccl.* 1033, Eur. *Alc.* 98 ff., and lexicographers (Rohde, 188 n. 38). Water brought from next door: Pollux 8.65, Hesych. s.v. ὄστρακον. Cypress boughs outside house of death: Serv. *Aen.* 3.681, Rohde, 189 n. 39. New fire at Argos: Plut. *Quaest. Graec.* 24. 297a. Houses may even have been sealed off when death was imminent, Men. *Asp.* 466 f.

[11] Rohde, 162–6 with notes 36, 37, 40, 61; add Callim. fr. 194.40–3. On bathing the corpse see Andronikos, 2–4, Ginouvès, 239 f.; this was the preparatory act that carried most symbolic weight. Libations to the corpse after burial could be spoken of as χέρνιψ or λουτρόν, as though the process of purification continued (Soph. *El.* 84, 434 etc.; cf. P. Stengel, *Hermes* 57 (1922), 539 ff., Ginouvès, 244).

[12] Dead crowned: Rohde, 189 n. 40; mourners not crowned: Arist. fr. 101 Rose³ *ap.* Ath. 675a.

[13] B. Schmidt, *ARW* 24 (1926), 317 f., *ARW* 25 (1927), 82; M. Guarducci, *SMSR* 2 (1926), 89–98. Ritual sweeping of death house at Rome: Latte, *RR* 101; in Byzantium: Alexiou, 25.

make it plausible that the point of these rituals was to banish
death pollution from the house, the first two by catching it in a
vessel of water which was then poured away, and the third by
sweeping it out with the household's physical dirt and deposit-
ing it where it belonged, at the tomb. If this is correct, it is
remarkable to find the Ceans legislating against practices that
are, it seems, socially objectionable only in being superstitious,
and superstitious only in the sense that they take too far that
belief in death-pollution on which several of the law's positive
requirements are founded.

Early on the third day occurred the 'carrying out'. Solon
required that this should be performed before dawn; when the
emperor Julian passed a similar measure almost a thousand
years later, his aim was to protect passers-by from pollution,
but Solon was probably more interested in discouraging the
ostentation of the traditional aristocratic funeral by depriving it
of an audience.[14] The place to which the body was carried lay
outside the city, away from the temples, and, of course, no priest
attended it. The disposal of the body was the turning-point
within the sequence of events that followed the death. Purification could now begin, and the activities of everyday life be
gradually resumed. After the funeral, it was traditional for the
mourners to wash or bathe.[15] There followed, in the funerary
banquet, an important reassertion of the values of life and of the
will to live; the mourners resumed the crown, and sat down
together to share the pleasures of the table.[16] Very probably,

---

[14] Julian, *Epistle* 136 Bidez/Cumont. Solon: Dem. 43.62, cf. Pl. *Leg.* 960a, Cic. *Leg.*
2.66, Ziehen, 264.
[15] I repeat this standard view on the authority of schol. RV Ar. *Nub.* 838, but without
absolute confidence. The bath that purifies the mourners in *LSCG* 97 A 30 (the Iulis
law) did not necessarily follow the funeral immediately (cf. e.g. *LSCG* 124.4). Thus the
funerary bath lacks firm early attestation. The ἀπόνιμμα in the obscure exegetic
fragment of Cleidemus *ap.* Ath. 410a (323 *FGrH* fr. 14) is taken by K. Meuli (in
Phyllobolia für P. von der Mühll, Basle, 1945, 205 n. l, = *Ges. Schr.* 2.928 n. 2) as dirty water
in which the mourners have washed, secondarily 'offered' to the dead as token of a duty
performed; this is plausible, but such an act might as well have occurred at e.g. the
ninth-day rite as at the funeral itself. The lexicographical sources on the mysterious
ἐγχυτρίστριαι give them no other function at funerals than pouring libations, although
in other contexts they are said to 'purify the polluted' (schol. (Plat.) *Min.* 315c, and
other sources quoted ad. loc. by W. C. Greene, *Scholia Platonica*, Pennsylvania, 1938).
[16] On the funerary meal see Fr. Pfister, *RE* s.v. *Perideipnon.* Crowning: Cic. *Leg.* 2.63.
Reassertion of life at the funeral: R. Huntington and P. Metcalf, *Celebrations of Death,
The Anthropology of Mortuary Ritual*, Cambridge, 1979, 34–42, 93–118, cf. of course

however, they were not yet permitted to return completely to normal life. Iphigeneia's remark that Artemis 'keeps away from her altar' anyone who has 'touched a corpse' loses its point if the pollution could be immediately effaced by ritual washing. In post-classical sacred laws, contact with death normally causes exclusion from the shrine for a fixed period of days, and this is surely what is implied in Euripides.[17] Although Iphigeneia is speaking only of Artemis, it is most implausible that rules of this kind should have been confined to one cult: all our other evidence suggests that all the Olympian gods were equally concerned to keep the natural pollutions at a distance.[18] At first sight the Iulis law is more liberal. The legible part of the first side ends: 'those who are polluted . . . after washing . . . shall be pure', but there may well have followed a temporal specifica-

---

funerary games. A mourning fast was perhaps seldom observed in classical times (one case, Arr. *Anab.* 7.14.8), but mourning at Sparta ended with a sacrifice to Demeter (Plut. *Lyc.* 27.4).

[17] Eur. *IT* 380–4. Sacred laws: *LSCG* 55.6 (Attica, Men Tyrannos, 2nd c. AD) 10 days; *LSCG* 124.2–4 (Eresus, unknown cult,? 2nd c. BC) 20 days for a relative, 3 for acquaintance; *LSCG* 139.13 (Lindos, unknown cult,? 2nd c. AD) 40 days for a relative; LSS 91. 13–14 (Lindos, Athene,? 3rd c. AD) 41 days for a relative, 7 for washing a corpse, 3 for entering the death house; *LSS* 119. 3–4 (Ptolemais, unknown cult, ? 1st c. BC) 7 days; *LSA* 12. 7–9 (Pergamum, Athene Nikephoros, after 133 BC) one day for a relative, immediate access, after washing, from a 'burial and carrying out', i.e. a non-relative's funeral; *LSA* 18.7–9 (Maeonia, Meter, 147–6 BC) 4 days for a relative, two for an acquaintance; ? *LSA* 29.2; *LSA* 51.5 (Miletus, Artemis, ? 1st c. BC) two days; *LSA* 84.6–9 (Smyrna, Dionysus, 2nd c. AD) 10 days for a relative, 3 for acquaintance; conceivably *BCH* 102 (1978), p. 326, line 15. Scraps of earlier evidence: *LSCG* 56.13 (Cleonae, early 6th c. BC), but this probably refers to murder, not natural death; *LSS* 31.10 ff. (Tegea, ? 4th c. BC), apparently prescribing a short period of impurity after a burial; ? *LSS* 106 (neither the first editor nor Sokolowski offers a date); Eur. *Alc.* 1143–6, Alcestis consecrated to death for 3 days after return from Hades. At Cyrene pollution lasted 3 days after contact with a birth, and it would be strange if death-pollution was effaced more quickly (*LSS* 115 A 17–19). Coan priests were excluded from the house of death for 5 days from the carrying out; it is plausible that mourners should have been excluded from the sacred for the same period (*LSCG* 156 A 11, cf. 154 A 24–6, 39–41). For death in the house preventing attendance at a festival see Ath. 46e–f, D.L. 9.43. If such rules did exist at Athens, the silence of the epigraphical record suggests that they remained, in significant contrast to the practice of other states, at the level of unwritten laws.

[18] Cf. notes to p. 33. Documents like the Cyrene law regulate what conditions pollute, and for how long; there is no question of being pure enough to visit one shrine but not another.

tion ('on the third day') or other qualification ('but not enter the temples').[19]

The place that had harboured the corpse required purification no less than the mourners who had touched it. At Iulis, the house of death was sprinkled with sea water on the morning after the carrying out; it was now pure, and contact with the gods could be resumed through offerings at the hearth.[20] (The bereaved must have ceased by now to be contagious, or the house would, of course, have been immediately contaminated anew.) If death occurred in a public place, the entity requiring cleansing was no longer the house but the whole deme, and responsibility for this task was specified with some elaboration.[21] Even after the 'carrying out', pollution could still be incurred. There is appended to the Iulis law a further regulation apparently of rather later date. Funerals were succeeded by further rites performed at the tomb, at gradually increasing intervals of time, and it is the power of these rites to pollute that is here defined. 'The council and people decided. On the third day (and) the annual festival those who perform the rites shall be pure, but not enter a temple.'[22] There follows an obscure regulation about the purity of the house in the same circumstances. These questions are decided, we note, by plebiscite and not by consultation of an oracle. It is not surprising that even the annual commemoration of the dead causes a mild pollution. Impurity lingers in the physical relics; the timid and the pure shrink from stepping on a tomb, and a Coan law calls for purification if a human bone or uncovered grave is discovered

---

[19] The transcript in *IG* XII 5.593 in fact offers, after κα[θαϱ]οὺς ἐναι, εωι (from Attic-Ionic ἕως, dawn?).

[20] *LSCG* 97 A 14–17: for the reading in 16 see G. Klaffenbach, *Philol.* 97 (1948), 372 f. Home purification at Athens: Ant. *Chor.* 37, ? Dem. 47.70; for the house as recipient of death-pollution cf. Eur. *Hel.* 1430. A purificatory encircling of the hearth may have been performed at this stage: see Hesych. s.v. πεϱίστιον

[21] Dem. 43.57 f., cf. *Inscr. Cret.* 4.76, *LSCG* 154 B 17–32.

[22] *LSCG* 97 B 1–11. For the restoration καί, not ἐπί, in B 5 see Ziehen, 267 f., E. Freistedt, *Altchristliche Totengedächtnistage* (Liturgiegeschichtliche Quellen und Forschungen 24), Münster, 1928, 112–14. It seems almost inevitable that here 'the third day' is counted from the funeral, not the death; otherwise it would coincide with the *ekphora*, and a special rule about the purity of the celebrants would be unnecessary (Freistedt's answer, op. cit., 96 n. 1, is inadequate: the only alternative is to suppose that the rule on side B replaces that on side A.)

in a public place.[23] This impurity probably diminished with time; a community could, in an emergency, re-use its own old grave monuments for building – but a besieging force that tampered with the tombs of the besieged was justly punished when disease supervened.[24] As the cult of heroes was celebrated at their tombs, the participants were sometimes required to purify themselves afterwards, and people like priests who lived in conditions of special purity might be excluded from them altogether.[25] Elaborate apotropaic precautions were taken in Athens at the Anthesteria, when the dead returned to earth.[26]

Iphigeneia defined the source of pollution as 'touching a corpse'. That is to put the thing in its most concrete form. Birth- and murder-pollution were contracted by entering the same area of social space (typically the same house) as the con- taminated person, and it would be surprising if death-pollution worked differently. 'Touching the corpse' might, of course, have formed a part of the mourning ritual, but this would be merely a translation of social contact into physical, and would not prove the real primacy of the physical.[27] There may have been another determinant, more important than 'touching' or even 'entering the same roof'. In many societies, death-pollution is spread by relationship as well as contact:[28] the dead man's kin are contaminated from the moment of death, even if they are a hundred miles away when it occurs. Thus, in early Rome, the

---

[23] Tombs: Theophr. *Char.* 16.9, Eur. *Cret.* fr. 79.18 Austin. Coan law: *LSCG* 154 B 17–32 (if the μ of δά]μωι in 17 is secure; ἱεϱ]ῶι would much improve the sense).

[24] Diod. 11.40.1, Lyc. *Leoc.* 44, P. M. Fraser, *Rhodian Funerary Monuments*, Oxford, 1977, 7; disease, Diod 13.86.1–3. No harm, however, in overthrowing a tyrant's tomb, Plut. *Tim.* 22.2

[25] Paus. 5.13.3; *LSCG* 154 A 22, 37; 156 A 8–10; *LSS* 115 A 21–5; Nock, ii, 577 f.

[26] Deubner, 112.

[27] The women who prepared the corpse of course touched it. Two Homeric mourning gestures, touching the dead man's chest and cradling his head, involved physical contact; the latter at least survived as a woman's gesture in classical times, but in Homer they are performed only by the dead man's closest associates, and the typical male gesture at the classical *prothesis* seems to have been a greeting from a distance with outstretched arm (*Il.* 18.317; 23.18. 136 f.: 24.712, 724; G. Neumann, *Gesten und Gebärden in der Griechischen Kunst*, Berlin, 1965, 86; ibid., 89, for cradling). I know of no Greek evidence for the farewell kiss (Roman texts in C. Sittl, *Die Gebärden der Griechen und Römer*, Leipzig, 1890, 72). Cf. however, Plut. *Pel.* 33.8, Thessalians eager to touch Pelopidas' corpse, and Xen. *Cyr.* 7.3.8.

[28] e.g. India: Dumont, 88, H. Orenstein, *Ethnology* 4 (1965), 3; Borneo: Hertz, 39. Hundreds of miles: Lévy-Bruhl, 254 (Thonga).

important unit of pollution was the '*familia funesta*'. It is very
likely that this was also the case in early Greece. The Cyrene
cathartic law states that birth, in contrast to death, pollutes 'the
house [*or*, household] itself'. Nothing is said about how death-
pollution operated, but the necessary contrast would be provided if it affected the broader kin group rather than the
restricted family resident under the same roof. In later sacred
laws, relatives are certainly polluted by a death for longer than
outsiders, and it is hard to see why this distinction should be an
innovation. There is, unfortunately, no clear evidence either to
prove or disprove that relatives could be automatically polluted
without coming into contact with the corpse.[29]

In the Iulis law the pollution group is actually defined, but
the stone becomes illegible at a crucial point. It begins 'No
woman shall go to the house where a man dies when he is
carried out, except those who are polluted [*or*, pollute
themselves]. There shall be polluted [*or*, pollute themselves]
mother, wife, sisters and daughters, and in addition to these not
more than five women.' At this point the reading becomes
uncertain,[30] but a probable reference to 'children of cousins'
suggests that the Iulis pollution group resembled the Attic
kinship group of *anchisteia*, which extended to cousins' children
and under Solon's law determined the right of participation in
mourning.[31] The 'not more than five women' might well be
relations by marriage.[32] The regulation is intriguing in its suggestion that pollution, rather than being an incidental but
inevitable by-product, is a temporary status to which not
everyone associated with the funeral is admitted. It would be
possible, although in this case illegal, for a woman to enter the

[29] *Familia funesta*: Latte, *RR* 49. Therefore the dictator Sulla divorced his dying wife,
Plut. *Sull.* 35.2. Cyrene: *LSS* 115 B 24–7. Later sacred laws: p. 37 n. 17 above. No clear
evidence: the anecdotes in (Plut.) *Cons. ad Apoll.* 118c–119d (cf. parallels in the Teubner
ad loc.) are ambiguous and unreliable: cf. the conflicting reports in the Roman
tradition over the ritual status of Horatius Pulvillus after his son's death (*RE* 8.2402).

[30] Hoffmann's restoration of 28 f., commonly accepted, is impossible; see Bechtel on
SGDI 5398. If the gender of ἄλλον δὲ μεδένα in 29 is taken literally, no men are polluted
except any there may be among the 'children' of the preceding clause. More probably
the masculine is generalizing, and only the female pollution group is here regulated.

[31] M. Broadbent, *Studies in Greek Genealogy*, Leiden, 1968, 119–50.

[32] Note, however, that R. F. Willetts's theory of a special funerary role for affines,
adopted by Alexiou, 10 ff., is refuted by H. Meyer-Laurin, *Gnomon* 41 (1969), 162 f.,
H. J. Wolff, *Zeitschrift der Savigny-Stiftung für Rechtsgeschichte, Römische Abteilung*, 85
(1968), 422–6.

house of death without becoming 'one of those polluted.' As this inner group of the polluted is not determined simply by relationship, there was presumably some specific act or duty by which it was defined. One possibility is that they handled the corpse, but this scarcely suits Herodotus' report of what is apparently the same phenomenon in Sparta: 'At the death of a king two free individuals from each household, a man and a woman, must be polluted [*or, pollute themselves*]; there are severe penalties if they do not.'[33] More probably the reference is to self-defilement of some kind; female mourners in classical times might still rend their clothes, pluck out their hair, and tear their cheeks.[34] Whatever the precise interpretation, it is clear that in both cases 'being polluted' is more like going into mourning than catching a disease.

A man's status is seldom so clearly revealed as at his passing. The death of a stranger is met with indifference in societies that are thrown into turmoil by the death of a chief.[35] It is hard to believe that in Greece a female slave would have been honoured by the same elaboration of funerary ritual as the master of the house, and it is tempting to wonder whether her power to pollute the household may have been less too. The many Greek communities that tolerated the burial of children but not adults within the settlement area presumably felt that no great contagion could proceed from such insignificant bones. Further than this we cannot go; the written sources tell us no more about this than any other aspect of the death of the poor.[36] There is evidence, however, that pollution might vary in intensity according to the manner of the death. No special taint attached to the bed on which a man died naturally, but, in a case of suicide

[33] Hdt. 6.58.1. Plut. *Apoth. Lac.* 238d, Lycurgus περιεῖλε τοὺς μιασμούς, seems to have the same sense; cf. *Papyri from Tebtunis part II*, ed. E. M. Husselman and others, Michigan and London, 1944 (*Michigan papyri* 5), n. 243.11, 244.17, members of guilds in Egypt in 1st century AD fined if they refuse μιαίνεσθαι for death of guild members.

[34] Neumann, op. cit., 86–9, cf. Aesch. *Cho.* 22–31; wearing of soiled mourning clothes banned, *LSA* 16.6. For self-defilement with dust or mud (common in Homer) cf. Eur. *Suppl.* 826 f., *Anth. Pal.* 7.10. 3–4 (evidence from later antiquity in E. Reiner, *Die rituelle Totenklage der Griechen*, Tübingen, 1938, 43 n. 5); not washing, Eur. *Or.* 42.

[35] Hertz, 76; more evidence in L. R. Binford, *An Archaeological Perspective*, New York and London, 1972, 220, 228 f., and on children 234. On child and slave burial in Greece see Bremmer, and on differential burial G. Buchner and L. Cerchiai in Gnoli/Vernant, 275–98.

[36] But note Dem. 47.70.

by hanging, the rope and the branch were destroyed or thrown outside the boundaries of the city. The extra pollution here obviously derives from that same moral revulsion against suicide that caused punitive measures to be take against the corpse.[37] The body of a soldier who died in battle, by contrast, scarcely polluted the comrades who burned or buried him. Nothing is ever said on the subject in the many relevant passages in Greek historians, and Xenophon describes himself sacrificing to the gods on the day after burying corpses too putrescent to be lifted from where they lay.[38] At the most, the survivors may have purified themselves by washing. The dead man's relatives, of course, might well have 'polluted themselves' on receiving the news.

The absence of pollution is here a matter of convenience, but it might be made into a point of ideology. In the classical period, extramural burial was in most cities a strictly observed norm, but many communities set the tombs of their 'founders' and 'saviours' in the *agora* itself.[39] The connection between *agora* and tomb probably persisted from the period when political assemblies occurred at the grave monument of a heroic ancestor, outside the settlement area, but by the historical period, when the *agora* was within the city, special values must have been invoked in defence of this breach of the rules. Plutarch's account of the death of Aratus, liberator of Sicyon, is revealing. The Sicyonians, though eager to bury him with the highest honours, were disconcerted by 'an old law forbidding burial within the walls' to which 'great superstition attached'. They therefore consulted Delphi, but on receiving a satisfactory answer 'switched from grief to festivities, and clad in garlands and white clothes brought his body up to the city to the accompaniment of paeans and choruses, and choosing a con-

---

[37] *LSCG* 154 B 33–6, Plut. *Them.* 22.2, Harpocr. s.v. ὀξυθύμια. Only a Diogenes would eat the fruit of a fig tree where a man had hanged himself, D.L. 6.61. Punitive measures: Aesch. 3.244, Rohde, 187 n. 33.

[38] Xen. *Anab.* 6.4. 9–13.

[39] R. Martin, *Recherches sur l'agora grecque*, Paris, 1951, 194–201; cf. O. Broneer, *Hesperia* 11 (1942), 128–61; G. V. Lalande, *Hesperia* 49 (1980), 97–105. Hero tombs left during the purification of Delos: p. 33 n. 6 above. Non-polluting hero tombs in Cyrene: *LSS* 115 A 21–4. Political assemblies at grave monuments: Martin, op. cit., 47–56. See too N. S. R. Hornblower, *Mausolus*, Oxford, 1982, 255 f.; C. Berard in Gnoli/Vernant, 275–98.

spicuous spot buried him like a founder and saviour of the city'. We may compare Plato's account in the *Laws* of the magnificent state funerals with which his scrutineers are to be honoured. Dirges are forbidden; all participants are to be dressed in white, and choruses of boys and girls will sing hymns of praise to the dead man. At the rear of the funeral procession, if Delphi agrees, the priests and priestesses are to walk, even though they are excluded from all other burials; this one will not pollute them.[40] Plato is here adopting and perhaps expanding the ideology originally developed for those who 'showed themselves good men' by death in their country's service. 'Their tomb is an altar; in place of lament they have remembrance, grief becomes praise', said Simonides, and the theme was taken up in many a funeral oration; displays of mourning in such cases might even be controlled by law. 'Here Saon sleeps a sacred sleep. Do not say that good men die.'[41] By the quality of their lives, such outstanding individuals have overcome death itself. Their passing, triumph rather than defeat, cannot be mourned and (Plato draws the consequence) cannot be thought to pollute. For them the tired platitudes of epitaphs – let no one lament my passing – are acted out in ritual, and so the community as a whole participates in their victory.[42] But where an unworthy individual insists on being treated as non-polluting in death, plague ensues.[43]

The individual's right to receive burial was, of course, supported by powerful social and supernatural sanctions. The 'common law of the Greeks' agreed with the 'unwritten, un-

[40] Plut. *Arat.* 53.2–4; Pl. *Leg.* 947b–d. Cf. Plut. *Tim.* 39.3 on Timoleon's funeral: ὄψις μὲν ἦν ἑορτῇ πρέπουσα, πάντων ἐστεφανωμένων καὶ καθαρὰς ἐσθῆτας φορούντων, idem, *Pel.* 33.5, priests at receipt of Pelopidas' body.
[41] Simonides, *PMG* 531.3–4, cf. Eur. *IA* 1437–48, 1466. Legal control: *LSS* 64. 1–4 (Thasos, 5th – 4th c. BC, cf. J. Pouilloux, *Recherches sur l'histoire et les cultes de Thasos* 1, Paris, 1954, 371–6). Saon: Call. *Epigr.* 9 Pf., 41 G/P: cf. Gow/Page's note.
[42] Lienhardt, Ch. 8 describes the rite whereby aged Dinka priests, carriers of the 'life' of their people, voluntarily submitted to burial alive as a means of publicly repudiating normal physical death. Mourning was forbidden. 'For the rest of the master's people . . . the human symbolic action involved in the 'artificial' burial must be seen to transform the experience of a leader's death into a concentrated public experience of vitality' (317). Lienhardt's account is suggestive as a parallel for the passing of Greek heroes like Oedipus (mourning forbidden Soph. *OC* 1751–3) and Amphiaraus. The ideology of 'not mourning brave men' perhaps developed in Sparta: cf. Plut. *Ages.* 29.7, mothers of Leuctra dead thronging shrines in thanksgiving.
[43] (Aeschin.) *Epist.* 1.2.

shakeable laws of the gods' in insisting that even the body of an
enemy should be given up after battle for burial. There was a
generally recognized obligation for anyone who encountered an
untended corpse – a drowned man on the seashore, for instance
– to perform at least a token act of burial; at Athens those who
neglected this minimum human obligation were threatened by
one of the 'Bouzygean curses'.[44] An unburied corpse was an
outrage, and one possible consequence was pollution. Sophocles, in the *Antigone*, as we have seen, offered a remarkable vision
of the form that this pollution took:[45] scraps of the corpse,
dropped by birds of prey on the altars, doused the sacrificial
fires, and doomed the city to godlessness. No doubt Greeks did
not normally consider the nature of *miasma* so precisely, but it is
interesting that when his dramatic purpose forced Sophocles to
be explicit he should have given it so concrete a form. It is clear
that this, in context, is less a 'natural pollution' than a cosmic
sanction operating against the violation of a fundamental social
principle, the individual's right to burial. A drowned man's
corpse lying unnoticed beneath the banks of the Ismenus might
in theory pollute the city no less severely; but it is scarcely an
accident that the one case of pollution by a corpse which we find
vividly described derives from human crime.

Sophocles' picture of the consequences of denying burial is
dramatic and alarming. These consequences, however, often
fail to appear in the contexts where they might have been most
expected. In the extended debates about burial in the *Ajax* and
Euripides' *Supplices*, for instance, the law of the gods is brought
freely under appeal but the threat of pollution is never mentioned; when the Thebans in 424 refused to return the Athenian
dead, they were accused, according to Thucydides, of illegality
and impiety, but not specifically of 'polluting the gods', and in
declaring themselves only conditionally willing to return these
corpses the Thebans were obviously defying pollution.[46] It is

[44] Law of the gods: e.g. Soph. *Aj.* 1130 f., 1335, 1343, *Ant.* 77, 745, 749, Eur. *Suppl.* 19,
311, 526, 563, Thuc. 4.98.8. Requirement to bury: Soph. *Ant.* 255 + schol. (Bouzyges),
Ael. *V.H.* 5.14, idem, fr. 242, Nisbet/Hubbard on Hor. *Carm.* 1.28.23.
[45] 999–1015.
[46] Thuc. 4. 97.2–99; similar Theban conditions, Xen. *Hell.* 3.5.24. For denial of
anairesis, actual or threatened, cf. Diod. 17.25.6, Dem. 7.38. In Greek/barbarian
relations the convention might not apply, Hdt. 9.83, Plut. *Tim.* 25.5; cf. F. Jacoby, *JHS*
64 (1944), 42 f. The general's obligation to protect his own dead: Diod. 13.61.6 with
75.4, Xen. *Hell.* 1.7 (Arginusae generals), Diod. 17.68.4.

not that, while 'pollution' is absent, 'divine anger' against the violators of the divine law impends. Such debates can be conducted in the name of custom, justice, and humanity, without any serious appeal to the threat of supernatural retribution. The divine origin of the law of burial is a guarantee of its justice rather than of swift divine intervention in support of it. While it may to some extent be true that threats of heaven's vengeance are simply squeezed out by a superabundance of human indignation, it looks as if in the late fifth century fear of supernatural punishment was a rather weak and remote deterrent against maltreatment of the corpse.

One reason for this may have been that the obligation to grant burial was never absolute. It was not merely in the upsurge of popular fury or similar ungovernable passions that exceptions occurred; it was the 'common law of the Greeks', not excluding the Athenians, that temple-robbers and their like should be 'thrown out unburied', and many of the *Antigone's* audience will have voted for the decree that declared 'it shall not be permitted to bury Antiphon in Athens or in the territory the Athenians control.' Not even Plato in the *Laws* was prepared to grant all his citizens an inalienable right to burial in their native land.[47] It is often suggested that the Greeks, in contrast to modern Europeans, were abnormally sensitive to the fate of their corpses. The presumed modern indifference is exaggerated; the thought of a relative's body devoured by scavengers is as hateful as it ever was, and the reason why this is no longer a haunting fear is perhaps merely that it is most

[47] Popular fury: Nic. Dam. 90 *FGrH* fr. 60, Diod. 16.16.4. (cf. Plut. *Dion* 35.5–7). Dynast's hatred: Diod. 17.118.2 (the possibility, Quint. Curt. 7.2.32, 8.2.12). Oligarchic brutality: Theopomp. 115 *FGrH* fr. 96 (Hyperbolus thrown in sea), Lys. 12.21,?96. Tyrant throws offenders in sea as means of terror, Theopomp. 115 *FGrH* fr. 227 (cf. *RE* Suppl. 7.1605 f.). Enemy's revenge: Plut. *Nic.* 28.5, cf. *Dem.* 29.5. 'Common law about temple robbers': Diod. 16.25.2, cf. 16.35.6 (throwing in sea), Aeschin. 2.142 (pushing over cliff, cf. Dem. 19.327, Paus. 10.2.4). Traitors and temple-robbers at Athens: Xen. *Hell.* 1.7.22, cf. Thuc. 1.138.6; subverters of the second Athenian league, *SIG*³ 147.62. The punishment exercised at Athens: Thuc. 1.138.6 (Themistocles), (Plut.) *X Orat.* 833–4 (Antiphon), Lyc. *Leocr.* 112–15 (Phrynichus), Plut. *Phoc.* 37.3–5, Lys. 19.7, cf. Hyp. 1.20, 4.18 Kenyon. Those long dead dug up and expelled: Nic. Dam. loc. cit., Thuc. 1.126.12, Lyc. *Leocr.* 112–15, Plut. *Dion* 53.2, *Alex.* 77.2. Plato: *Leg.* 854e–855a, 873b, 909c. More in Bremmer. Cynics (e.g. *SVF* 1.253) and Epicurus (D. L. 10.118) denied the importance of burial, but this was of course not wholly new, cf. Heraclit. B 96, Eur. fr. 176. On the futility of punishing corpses see Aesch. fr. 266, Moschion, frr. 3, 7 Snell (cf. *CQ* 31 (1981), 417) and already? Hom. *Il.* 24.54.

unlikely to occur. The corpse is now sacrosanct, beyond the reach of reward and punishment; even the bodies of suicides are often admitted to consecrated ground, and it is long since the corpse of a debtor was last subjected to distraint.[48] The real difference is that in the ancient world the corpse enjoyed no such exemption. Treatment of corpses remained one of the means by which men could hurt, humiliate, or honour one another, express contempt or respect.[49] This is why the theme could be of central importance in great works of literature. It was the potential for humiliation that was particularly strongly felt. In tragedy, the victim's relatives lament, not his exclusion from the underworld, but his dishonour; 'not to be buried in Attica' is only the familiar punishment of 'deprivation of honour' in its most extreme form. Plato is eager for his citizens to realize that the corpse is a valueless, unperceiving thing,[50] but continues despite himself to treat it as a vehicle of honour in the humiliations he inflicts on it.

It looks as if, in the case of the traitor and temple-robber, the law of the gods ensuring the right of burial ceased to apply. One might even conclude that, with their honour, they lost the power to pollute. This would lead to the paradox that, while no funeral or tomb is pure except that of the outstanding servant of the community, the only corpse that will not cause pollution if left unburied is that of the public enemy.[51] There are many Greeks whom one could imagine maintaining that this was indeed the case – Athens' ferocious Lycurgus would be one – but the conclusion would go beyond the evidence. The Athenians 'threw out' their criminals 'unburied beyond the bounds of Attica'; this allowed the relatives to arrange for burial, and

---

[48] Cf. Mrs Henry Wood, *East Lynne*, London, 1861, Part 1, Ch. 10, for an instance of distraint. For Athens see Diod. 10.30. Jan Bremmer reminds me that modern corpses are used for medical research – but they have to be donated for the purpose. Requisitioning would be unthinkable.

[49] For Homer and the ancient near east see Griffin, 44–7; on Homer, J. P. Vernant in Gnoli/Vernant, 45–76.

[50] *Leg.* 959c.

[51] Logically there is a potential tension betwen *corruptio optimi pessima* and *corruptio optimum non attingit*. Zoroastrians and Hindus thus arrive at opposite conclusions as to whether the death of a person of high or low status pollutes more (Zoroastrians: *The Zend Avesta*, part 1, *The Vendidad*, trans. J. Darmesteter, Oxford, 1880, Fargard 5, §6, 27–38; Hindus: S. J. Tambiah in J. Goody (ed.), *The Character of Kinship*, Cambridge, 1973, 209–12).

even if they did not, the pollution would at least fall outside
Attic territory. Other states' modes of maltreating the corpse –
throwing it over a cliff, or into the sea – were probably intended
to exclude all possibility of burial, but they did serve to dispose
of the remains away from human habitation.[52] The intention of
these methods will scarcely have been to evade pollution – they
were rather a symbolic rejection of the malefactor – but they
probably had the effect that the question of pollution did not
need to be raised. Prolonged public exposure of the corpse, as
prescribed by Creon in *Antigone*, was not the practice of any
Greek state, and when mentioned is treated as shocking.[53] The
law of the gods gave way before society's abomination of certain
of its enemies; pollution might have done so too, but the evidence does not take us so far.[54]

   The *Antigone* at first sight presents an exception. Polyneices is
a traitor; Creon exposes Polyneices; the gods are angry, and
pollution results. The law of the gods has refused to give way. As
we noted, Creon's treatment of Polyneices' corpse differs from
the Athenian practice, but this observation scarcely provides a
solution: few will be convinced that Creon's tragic error lay in
leaving the body on the plain, and that all would have been well
had he carried him off to be eaten by the birds beyond the
boundaries. Though the particular mode of humiliation chosen
by Creon is an aggravating factor, it is the justice of giving
Polyneices anything other than a proper burial that is in dispute.[55] It need not follow, however, that the rights vindicated
for the hero Polyneices belonged also to a shameless pilferer of

[52] See p. 45 n. 47. Burial occurs outside Attica (although no Athenian may participate) Plut. *Phoc.* 37. 3–4, cf. Pl. *Leg.* 909c. At Athens, 'throwing into the pit' was
primarily a mode of execution (see e.g. Gernet, *Anthropologie*, 308–11; Latte in *RE*
Suppl. 7. 1608 f. is hyper-sceptical). There is no evidence that recovery of the body by
relatives was legally forbidden, although it may not have been practically feasible. The
MSS reading in Xen. *Hell.* 1.7.20 indicates a distinct use of the pit for *post mortem*
exposure, but should probably be emended (cf. J. Diggle, *CR* 31 (1981), 107 f.). Even if
corpses were left in the pit, they were at least out of the way. Corpses were thrown out at
Ἁλμυρίδες (Hesych. s.v., cf. Ar. fr. 132); we do not know whose. Cf. too Plut. *Them.*
22.2.
[53] Plut. *Nic.* 28.5 (= Timaeus 566 *FGrH* fr. 101), Phylarchus 81 *FGrH* fr. 45 *ap.* Ath.
521d.
[54] Chariton 1.5.5 offers a novel twist, unfortunately not attested elsewhere: μὴ θάψητέ
με, μὴ μιάνητε τὴν γῆν, ἀλλὰ τὸ ἀσεβὲς καταποντώσατε σῶμα.
[55] Rightly (against Bowra and Ehrenberg) G. Cerri in Gnoli/Vernant, 121–31.

sacred plate. Sophocles may of course have believed, in advance
of his age, that punitive action against the corpse is in all
circumstances an outrage, but the moral premiss of the play
does not seem to be that 'even traitors are human, and deserve a
minimum of respect'. Nothing encourages us to view Polyneices
in this light.[56] Polyneices is a hero who has led an army to
defeat, and Creon's offence is the familiar one of denying an
enemy the right to burial: this is why the corpse remains on the
battlefield where it fell. It is the treatment of enemies and not of
villains that is in question.

We turn now from death to birth.[57] According to Censorinus,
probably echoing Varro, 'in Greece they treat fortieth days as
important. For the pregnant woman does not go out to a shrine
before the fortieth day . . .' (from the moment that she becomes
aware that she is pregnant?).[58] A ritual exclusion of forty days
sounds more Semitic than Greek, but in Greek medical texts the
forty-day period is of particular importance precisely in relation
to pregnancy and birth; during the first forty days after conception, for instance, menstruation continues, and miscarriage is a
constant danger, while by the end of this period the embryo is
formed and the male child begins to move.[59] The dangerous
transitional period therefore lasts forty days, and during this
period, if Censorinus is right, the mother is excluded from
communal life.[60] Seclusion at the onset of pregnancy is a widely

[56] See esp. v. 731. Not even Creon is ever allowed to use the word 'traitor' of
Polyneices. For a different view see Cerri, op. cit., and S. Fuscagni in M. Sordi (ed.),
Religione e politica nel mondo antico, Milan, 1981, 64–72. In Moschion's *Pheraioi*, by
contrast, the right of burial was perhaps vindicated even for a tyrant: see *CQ* 31 (1981),
417.

[57] On birth-pollution see Moulinier, 66–70, Ginouvès, 235–8, Wächter, 25–36.

[58] *De die natali* 11.7.

[59] W. H. Roscher, 'Die Tesserakontaden und Tesserakontadenlehre der Griechen
und anderer Völker', *Ber. Sächs. Ges. Wiss.* 61.2 (1909), 28–34, 40, 85–101: see esp.
Censorinus, loc. cit., Arist. *Hist. An.* 7.3. 583a27–583b15. On wide diffusion of
gynaecological forties cf. G. Eichinger Ferro-Luzzi, *Anthropos* 69 (1974), 148–52.
Views on the timing of these matters were however very various in Greece, cf. E. Nardi,
Procurato Aborto nel mondo greco romano, Milan, 1971, 93–115, 123–32.

[60] The 2 periods would not of course coincide, as most of the 40 days after conception
would pass before the mother perceived her pregnancy. Perhaps in order to bring them
into coincidence, Roscher, op. cit., 28, 30, dated the mother's seclusion from 'the
wedding and conception'. But we would surely have heard of a 40-day seclusion
immediately following the wedding: and what of subsequent pregnancies?

attested rite of passage,[61] and, at the first pregnancy, the Greek woman might have been exposed to the anger of Artemis.[62] There is, however, no trace of Censorinus' rule in any other source, and he, or even Varro, wrote at a time when Greek purity rules were not necessarily restricted to ancient norms.

Later in pregnancy, the woman was not excluded from temples but positively expected to visit them.[63] We do hear, however, of a few sacred rites and places forbidden to her, and there may well have been many more. Pregnant women, and suckling mothers, were excluded from the mysteries of Despoina at Lycosura, while 'no animal or woman in need of Eileithyia' would venture upon the hill in Arcadia where Rheia gave birth to Zeus.[64] These are clearly instances of that same logic of opposition which sometimes required chastity for the service of Aphrodite; it is from rites of fertility, and a mythical birthplace, that those about to give birth are debarred. Except in these special contexts, the pregnant woman was not herself polluting, but it is interesting that she was particularly exposed to pollution by others. When Euripides' Iphigeneia is about to lead the polluted Orestes through the streets, she issues a special warning to three categories of person – to priests, pregnant women, and those about to marry.[65] The pregnant woman is, as we would say, delicate, but it is to ritual dangers that this delicacy relates, and, as the parallel with those about to marry shows, it is from the change she is about to undergo, and not her present physiological condition, that her delicacy derives. These two classes of people are exposed to pollution because they are on the brink.

On the consequences of birth, the earliest explicit evidence comes from the Cyrene cathartic law.[66] The text is fragmentary, but it probably specified that the mother only polluted those who entered the same roof under which she lay; it certainly

---

[61] van Gennep, Ch. 4.
[62] Cf. schol. Theocr. 2.66b, L. Deubner, *JDAI* 40 (1925), 211 f. The evidence of *LSS* 115 B 1–23 is relevant to this whole section, but so obscure that it must be left to Appendix 2.
[63] Arist. *Pol.* 1335b 12–16.
[64] *LSCG* 68.12–13, Callim. *Jov.* 11–13. Callim. *Dem.* 130–2, at least as presented by the poet, is different: a concession and not a rule.
[65] *IT* 1226–9.
[66] *LSS* 115 A 16–20, B 26–7, cf. Appendix 2.

ruled that anyone who did so was impure for three days, but did
not pass that impurity on further. Contact with a new mother is
a normal source of pollution in sacred laws, and three days is
about the average period of exclusion,[67] but the Cyrene law is
isolated and valuable in the specification that pollution is incurred by 'entering the same roof' and not 'touching'. Another
passage of the same law makes birth-pollution pollute 'the *oikia*
itself'. *Oikia* could be interpreted either physically, which
would make it synonymous with 'the roof' of the previous
regulations, or socially, the household; the second interpretation introduces a theoretical inconsistency with the other
rule, as a member of the household could if he wished stay away
from the physical house during the period of impurity, but in
practice both rules would no doubt leave the same individuals
polluted. (Let us not suspect the Greek husband of exploiting
his wife's pollution as an excuse to shun the house during a
trying time.) Birth seems to have polluted a more restricted
circle than death; the further kin were certainly not affected
automatically, and there is no evidence that they were expected
to incur pollution by visiting the house during the time of
impurity. This reflects the fact that deaths (and marriages) pull
together the social group more insistently than births.[68]

The first bath of mother and child was an important occasion. The story of a god's birth was scarcely complete without
mention of it, and even for mortals the water might be fetched

---

[67] Those who come into contact with the mother recover their purity on the 2nd day
(*LSA* 12.7), on the 3rd day (*LSA* 51. 6–10), after 3 days (*LSS* 91.15; ? *LSCG* 124.7; cf.
LSCG 154 A 24, 39; 156 A 13), on the 7th day (*LSS* 54.5, an oriental cult); in *LSS* 119.6
the period is lost. *BCH* 102 (1978), p. 325, line 6 (Isis) seems to attest the 9th day, but
the reference might be to the mother herself; for this and the similar problem concerning *LSCG* 171.16 (10 days) see Appendix 3. For the mother polluted longer than others
see *LSCG* 124.5–8, *LSS* 91.15. In *LSA* 51.6–10 a dog that gives birth pollutes like a
woman, no doubt because dogs share a roof with men (similarly cats in modern Greece,
Blum 47 f.; in *LSS* 91.11 miscarriages of woman, dog, and donkey all pollute alike). In
LSS 115 B 24–7 miscarriage pollutes like death if the foetus is 'distinguishable', i.e. has
recognizable limbs, and, if not, like birth. (Views varied as to when this articulation
should occur, cf. p. 48 n. 59. Aristotle advocated early abortion before the advent of ζωή
and αἴσθησις, *Pol.* 1335b 24–6). In *LSCG* 154 A 24, ? 39 miscarriage pollutes like birth;
the restoration which makes it pollute like death in the closely comparable *LSCG* 156 A
13 is therefore questionable. For the pollution of miscarriage in later sacred laws
see Appendix 3.
[68] Arist. *Eth. Nic.* 1165a 18–21. Husband: cf. S. Beckett, *Company,* 16.

from a special spring.[69] As is often the case, however, the act of physical washing was not sufficient to re-establish purity. The details of the further rites that followed the birth are an unhappy tangle of conflicting and deficient lexicographical evidence, but it is probably right to distinguish two main ceremonies, the *amphidromia* on the fifth day and the name-giving on the tenth.[70] At the *amphidromia*, the child was carried at a run around the hearth. Details are uncertain, but the main point of the ceremony was probably to bring the new member into contact with the household's sacred centre, at which brides and newly-bought slaves were also presented. Ideas of purifying the child by fire may also have been present, although the sources do not say so.[71] On the same day, probably as a part of the same ceremony, the women who assisted at the birth are said to have been purified, but nothing reliable is recorded about the method.[72] The mother had presumably ceased by this time to be an active source of pollution, or all those who attended the fifth-day ceremonies would have gone away infected; certainly on Cos even priests were allowed to venture in four days after the birth.[73] Nothing is recorded of any special ritual for the purification of the house. The mother perhaps entered the state of 'impure, but not polluting others', and only returned fully to purity and normal life with the name-giving and sacrifice on the tenth day. Even after this the cycle of readjustment probably had some way to run. Just as death was followed not just by

---

[69] Gods: *Hymn. Hom. Ap.* 120–1, Callim. *Jov.* 14–16, Paus. 8.28.2, 8.41.2–3, Ginouvès, 235, 238. Special spring: e.g. Callim. fr. 65. This bath occurred immediately; Donatus on Ter. *Andr.* 483.3 (= Men. fr. 36) attests a postponed bath *post puerperium*, but apparently for Rome rather than Greece.

[70] See most recently L. Deubner, *Rh. Mus.* 95 (1952), 374–7.

[71] Presentation: Fustel de Coulanges, *La Cité antique*[25], Paris, 1919, 54 (with the lustral explanation); Nilsson, *GF* 115 f. Purification by fire: Rohde, 318 n. 72; J. G. Frazer, Appendix 1 to Loeb Apollodorus. An ordeal: O. Gruppe, *Bursian Jahresb.* 137 (1908), 342 f., *B. phil. Woch.* 26 (1906), 1137–9, stressing Pl. *Tht.* 160e. Decision by *genos* whether to rear child: Glotz, 41. Cf. further L. Deubner in J. Hastings (ed.), *Encyclopaedia of Religion and Ethics*, Edinburgh, 1909, s.v. *Birth (Greek and Roman)*; Eitrem, *Opferritus*, 173–7; Vernant, *Pensée*, i. 158–64; G. S. Kirk in *Entretiens Hardt* 27, 56–61.

[72] Purification of women: schol. Pl. *Tht.* 160e, Suda s.v. *amphidromia*, Apostolius 2.56. Schol. Pl. *Tht.*, loc. cit. makes the women do the running, and be purified thereby, but in Apost., Suda, and Harp. s.v. *amphidromia*, and by implication Pl. *Tht.* 160e, the runners are male.

[73] *LSCG* 154 A 24, 39, ? 156 A 12–13. Note however, the Superstitious Man's refusal to go ἐπὶ λεχώ, for fear of pollution, Theophr. *Char.* 16.9.

third- and ninth- but also by thirtieth-day rites, so we hear of a joyful 'fortieth-day festival' after birth. Pollution in both cases coincides with the intense early period of the gradual process of assimilating change.[74]

As several instances have already shown, sacred persons were required to hold themselves at the same distance from the natural pollutions as the gods themselves. Any contact with death might impair the wholeness necessary for divine service. In Messene, it is said, if a priest or priestess lost a child, he or she was forced to renounce the office; *amphithaleis*, children both of whose parents were still alive, had an important ritual role.[75] Two Coan inscriptions that prescribe rules of purity for certain local priests and priestesses are largely concerned with keeping them free from the taint of birth and death.[76] It is most plausible, although not strictly demonstrable, that all Coan priests of important cults were subject to similar restrictions. A priest or priestess may not enter a house of death until five days after the carrying out, mount a hero shrine, or eat of the offerings made in heroic or chthonic cult; if he discovers the corpse of a suicide, he can neither ignore it nor touch it, and must summon a passer-by.[77] A house where a birth or miscarriage has occurred he must avoid for three days. Details of dress and diet are influenced too. The priestesses of Demeter seem to be forbidden to wear clothing made from dead animals, or to eat meat slaughtered in a particular way (perhaps strangled).[78] One of the same Coan

[74] 10 days for the mother seem to emerge from Eur. *El.* 654 with 1124–1133. Probably 10 days for mother, 3 for others in *LSCG* 124.7–8 (Eresus, ? 2nd c. BC, cf. p. 355), 21 days for mother in the late *LSS* 91.15. 40th – day festival, Censorinus *D.N.* 11.7 (no earlier attestation). Sacrifice by a λεχώ, *LSCG* 77 D 13, by women 'walking out the *lochia*', *LSA* 52 B 10.

[75] Paus. 4.12.6, Nilsson, *GGR* 118 with bibliography.

[76] *LSCG* 154 A 21–45, 156 A 7–16: interpreted by R. Herzog, *ARW* 10 (1907), 400–15, idem., 'Heilige Gesetze von Kos', *Berl. Abh.* 1928.6, 17, 20–5. They concern priestesses of Demeter and the priest of Zeus Polieus, but the inscriptions to be set up in various other sacred places (*LSCG* 154 A 16–18) presumably contained rules for the priests or priestesses of the relevant cults. For such rules cf. Phrynichus comicus, fr. 70 ἃ δ' ἀνάγκα 'σθ' ἱερεῦσιν καθαρεύειν, φράσομεν.

[77] Corpse of a suicide: *LSCG* 154 B 33–6, well interpreted by Herzog with reference to Serv. *Aen.* 6. 176: *cum pontificibus nefas esset cadaver videre, magis tamen nefas fuerat si visum insepultum relinquerent.*

[78] Clothing made from dead animals: θνησείδια, cf. passages in *LSJ* s.v., Pl. *Leg.* 956a ἐλέφας δὲ ἀπολελοιπότος ψυχὴν σώματος οὐκ εὐαγὲς ἀνάθημα, *LSCG* 124.14, 17 θνασίδια and skins banned, *LSCG* 65.23 leather sandals permitted only if made from sacrificial animals (death by sacrifice no longer counts as death, Xen. *Anab.* 4.5.35); tanner

inscriptions gives an example of the purification that might be required if the taint of death did touch sacred ground: the god's statue is, it seems, carried out of the precinct to be washed, a sacrifice of propitiation is offered, and the whole shrine is purified.[79] Christianity takes control of the natural processes, and particularly of death; the funeral rites are conducted by a priest, and it is beside the church that the body is laid to rest. Greek religion rejects it wholly.[80]

Before considering the interpretation of these pollutions, we must ask what they entailed in practice. The only attested consequence of being polluted is that of exclusion from the temples. It must have involved more than this, or the intermediate condition known from Iulis of 'pure, but excluded from the temples' would not differ from it, but the additional element could have been no more than the property of passing pollution on to others, and thus rendering them in turn unfit for access to shrines. Of the more rigorous restrictions attested in many societies nothing emerges in our sources. We cannot know, for instance, whether a man subject to funerary pollution would engage in agriculture, or a woman who had assisted at a lying-in could go home and cook for her household. 'Hesiod' discouraged intercourse after a funeral, and some may have heeded him, as there is later evidence that contact with death was felt to endanger the reproductive processes; special restrictions might be placed on attendance at funerals by women of childbearing age. They seem to have shared, in attenuated form, the 'delicacy' of the pregnant woman. A plausible guess might be that those who took pollution seriously would stay at

impure, Artemid. 1.51, p. 59.4 Pack; for Rome cf. Ov. *Fast.* 1.629 f., *TLL* s.v. *morticinus*. Bare feet are often required for ritual, but not necessarily for this reason (J. Heckenbach, *De nuditate sacra sacrisque vinculis*, Giessen, 1911, (*RGVV* IX. 3), 23–31). Restoration of the forbidden food]κτων in *LSCG* 154 A 27 is problematic: πνικτων in the New Testament sense of 'strangled' is implausible, as it has a different sense in Greek cuisine (*LSJ* s.v.); for other suggestions see Herzog, op cit., 23.

[79] *LSCG* 154 B 24–32: cf. Eur. *IT* 1040 f., 1176–7, 1199–1201; in the Lindian temple record, 532 *FGrH* D (2), the temple roof is removed for 3 days to admit purifying rain; for Delos see p. 33 n. 6 above.
[80] No priests at funerals, Pl. *Leg.* 947d, ? Erinna v. 19 in Page, *GLP* 488 (cf. C. M. Bowra in *Greek Poetry and Life, Essays presented to Gilbert Murray*, Oxford, 1936, 334). Porph. *Abst.* 2.50. The laurel, sacred plant *par excellence*, not used at funerals, Callim. fr. 194. 39–43.

home, 'engage in no serious undertaking', and avoid exposing themselves to persons in delicate ritual conditions, while the more casual would simply keep away from the temples.[81] It is also not clear how far the chain of pollution might extend away from the original contaminating object. The only evidence on the point is the section of the Cyrene law which, in the case of birth, declares the chain broken after the first link: 'the person in the house shall be polluted himself, but shall not pollute anyone else, wherever he goes'.[82] We never hear of pollution contracted at several removes, but it is impossible to prove that the Cyrene regulation is typical or ancient.

It is inevitable that, given the character of our sources, we know even less about the emotional than the practical implications of these pollutions. It does not seem to be the case that the objects a society declares impure necessarily evoke a response of particular fear or revulsion in its members, or that disgusting things are automatically impure.[83] A pollution attaching to a truly disgusting object may be extended by logical elaboration to something quite innocent; the mark of the corpse is set upon leather shoes. There is, as we have seen, something impure about the tomb; but in vase paintings mourners seem to approach it in a mood rather of sentimental pilgrimage than terrified propitiation.[84] It is unlikely that the woman who had just ensured the survival of a house by bearing an heir felt much degraded by her pollution. Some Greek texts do indeed speak of corpses as repulsive, and tending them as dirty work,[85] but we do not know that the women who helped at a birth had to steel themselves for the task.

The first preliminary to an interpretation should be to ask what the Greeks themselves felt the pollutions of birth and death to be. They clearly saw the two pollutions as similar, since

[81] Pure but excluded from temples: *LSCG* 97 B 7–11. Death and reproduction: p. 70 n. 123 below. Plausible guess: conflated from Arist. *Ath. Pol.* 56.4, Plut. *Ages.* 29.6 (staying at home), Xen. *Hell.* 1.4.12, Eur. *IT* 1227–9.

[82] *LSS* 115 A 17–20.

[83] Boyce, Ch. 5, *passim*, much the best account I know of what pollution feels like. Note too P. M. Kaberry, *Aboriginal Woman, Sacred and Profane*, London, 1939. 238–40 (menstruation dangerous rather than disgusting).

[84] See D. C. Kurtz, *Athenian White Lekythoi*, Oxford, 1975, Plates 18–22 and many others, C. Sittl, *Die Gebärden der Griechen und Römer*, Leipzig, 1890, 74 (kisses blown at grave).

[85] Eur. *Supp.* 767, Pl. *Resp.* 439e, Arist. *Poet.* 1448b 12.

they constantly spoke of them together, and this conjunction
condemns any explanation based merely on emotional response; even Herodotus' Thracians, who wept at births and
celebrated deaths, recognized that in terms of appropriate emotional response the two events have nothing in common. At one
period, impressed by the first revelations of comparative anthropology, scholars did not doubt that pollution was synonymous with the presence of an evil demon;[86] unfortunately, the
swarming nameless demons to which they made constant appeal scarcely appear in the Greek sources before Neoplatonism.
Even if the animist interpretation had been better founded in
the evidence, it would have remained to ask why certain occurrences, and not others, should have let loose a swarm of these
demons into the world. The early texts trace these pollutions to
more concrete origins: again and again, they refer to 'the corpse'
and 'the woman who is lying in', and in Sophocles, as we have
seen, death-pollution is nothing other than scraps of the corpse.
The corpse rotted and the woman bled; once the corpse was in
the ground, the first purifications could be performed, while the
Greek woman probably remained impure for ten days after
birth, about the time for which post-parturient bleeding would
normally continue. (Like menstruation, lochial bleeding was, in
scientific language, a 'purification').[87] Thus the metaphysical
miasma radiated out from a physical centre. In the same way,
the impurity of sexuality was caused by semen, while the pollution of the murderer was expressed in the imaginary stain of
blood on his hands. These facts were noted by Tylor, who was
interested in primitive lustrations because of their survival, in
forms such as sprinkling with holy water, into the formal religious practice of his own day. He saw this as a process whereby

[86] e.g. Arbesmann, Fehrle, Wächter, Eitrem (*Opferritus*, 97), and, influentially,
Rohde. Not just primitives explain the inexplicable in terms of demons, in despite of
evidence. Contrast Herter, *Dämonen*.

[87] *LSJ* s.v. κάθαρσις IIa. The scientific texts make this purification last much longer,
42 days for a girl, 30 for a boy, Hippoc. *Nat. Puer.* 18 = *Mul.* 72 (7.500, 8.152 L.); 30 for a
girl, 40 for a boy, Arist. *Hist. An.* 7.3 583a 30–32; 40 days, Censorinus *D.N.* 11.7. These
figures obviously relate to the total period of lochial discharge (in fact, normally 3–4
weeks); modern doctors distinguish within this an initial period of abundant bleeding
(the subsequent discharge scarcely contains blood), for which, medical colleagues tell
me, 10 days would be a reasonable outside estimate. I am suggesting that the ritual
impurity is based on this initial period, but admit that the scientific texts do not
recognize the distinction.

originally practical measures of hygiene were ritualized, rendered symbolic, and so fossilized and preserved.

It is the plainest proof of the original practicality of proceedings now passed into formalism, to point out how far the ceremonial lustrations still keep their connexion with times of life when real purification is necessary, how far they still consist in formal cleansing of the new-born child and the mother, of the manslayer who has shed blood, or the mourner who has touched a corpse.[88]

It is, however, precisely the 'passage into formalism' that requires explanation. While mundane dirt yields to washing, it is only after a fixed period of time that pollution can be washed away. Dirt does not discriminate, but pollution is liable to afflict a dead man's relatives more than outsiders, and the status of the deceased may influence the intensity of the pollution. Tylor himself quoted examples of peoples who practised elaborate ceremonial lustrations, although conspicuously indifferent, in their daily lives, to what he regarded as the simplest principles of cleanliness and hygiene. 'The Dardanians of Illyria', Greek ethnography noted with interest, 'only take three baths in their lives: when they're born, when they marry, and when they die.' Cleanliness is often an important part of purity, but a dirty robe may be ritually far purer than a clean one.[89] In drawing attention to the dirtiness of the impure, Tylor was perhaps indicating not, as he supposed, the real basis of such impurity, but the concrete vehicle through which more abstract realities were conveyed. Mary Douglas has suggested that a society may use a supposed physical impurity as an unconscious symbol upon which it focuses fears or concerns of a much broader social character.[90] It is obvious, for instance, that in Greece the blood on the murderer's hands clings there because of the act he has committed: crime, not dirt, is at issue. That is perhaps an extreme case, and we need not suppose that physical pollution always bears so heavy a metaphorical burden; but it would be curious if the pollution of corpse and mother did indeed derive

[88] E. B. Tylor, *Primitive Culture*[4], London, 1903, vol. ii, 429.
[89] Dardanians: Nic. Dam. 90 *FGrH* fr. 107. Robes: Srinivas, 105, cf. ibid., 82 f. for the Hindu woman's numerous baths after birth, only certain of which improve her purity. G. Bachelard, *L'Eau et les rêves*, Paris, 1942, 192, observes 'Le Cafre ne se lave le corps que lorsqu'il a l'âme sale'.
[90] Douglas, Ch. 7.

solely from beliefs about dangerous forms and conditions of matter, and owed nothing to feelings about the great human events at the centre of which they lie.

Tylor stressed that pollution focuses around real dirt; medical materialism stresses that it focuses around real danger. Medical materialism is William James's term for the attempt to show that, within apparently arbitrary and superstitious religious laws, sound hygienic principles are enshrined. Maimonides, who in the twelfth century interpreted the abominations of Leviticus in terms of practical dietetics, still has many followers today. This method of exegesis, offering as it does a ready compromise between religious and scientific truth, is particularly welcome to educated, rationalist adherents of faiths that require the observance of such rules. Thus J. J. Modi, a Parsee himself and author of the standard work on Parsee ritual, explains the *Bareshnum*, the elaborate Avestan purification ceremony for mourners, as a technique for isolating the corpse itself and all who come into contact with it, and so preventing the spread of infection. The *Drug Nasu*, the fly demon of death that settles on the corpse, is simply animate contagion; the mourner's seclusion, a proto-quarantine. One chapter actually bears the title 'Old Iranian Purification and Modern Plague Operations'. A special number of the *Health Education Journal* was quite recently devoted to articles by, among others, Hindus, Muslims, and Buddhists, illustrating the hygienic principles embodied in their ritual rules. In the Greek world, it comes as no surprise to find Plutarch applying medical rationalism to explain puzzling religious traditions.[91]

Certainly, rules of purity may resemble rules of hygiene, and might even on occasion have beneficial hygienic effects. It is sometimes claimed that medieval Jews escaped the worst ravages of the plague through observance of the code of Leviticus. Fumigation by sulphur, much practised by the Greeks, does disinfect; but one may doubt whether they applied it with sufficient rigour to receive much empirical confirmation of the

[91] On medical materialism see the exposition and critique of Douglas, 41–4, which I follow closely. J. J. Modi, *The Religious Ceremonies and Customs of the Parsees*[2], Bombay, 1937, esp. 98–101, 149 ff.; *The Health Education Journal* 17.1, March 1959; Plut. *de Is. et Os.* 383a–c, *Quaest. Conv.* 670f–671a. For hygienic rationalizations of beliefs concerning feminine pollutions cf. G. Eichinger Ferro-Luzzi, *Anthropos* 69 (1974), 154.

efficacy of their religious rule, and sulphur was as valuable in the treatment of bewitched livestock as in the purification of a house. We are probably dealing here with a case of coincidence between a substance's symbolic and scientific appropriateness for a particular task.[92] Scientific rationalism would be hard pressed to explain why the sprinkling of the house of death at Iulis had to be done by a free man, or why the house's fire and water but not its tables and blankets suffered especial pollution. Clearly the sprinkling was a ceremonial act, not to be entrusted to the slaves who would perform the more mundane tasks of house cleaning; as for fire and water, it is because they are particularly capable of purity that they are particularly liable to pollution. Empirical observation of the facts of contagion could scarcely have led to the belief that pollution affected a dead man's relatives more severely than outsiders, and it would be easy to amass further examples to show how few sound medical principles Greek religious rules in fact contain. The point is not merely that these laws were not in practice medically effective, but rather that they were not conceived in this light at all. A breach of them might in theory lead to disease, but that is equally true of the obligation to sacrifice or any other religious rule. Some Greeks were aware, at least in time of plague, that disease could be transmitted from person to person,[93] but there is no evidence that they normally saw corpses as a source of infection. One historical text that does, unusually, speak of unburied bodies as a danger to health explains this danger in terms of corruption of the air rather than direct contamination of the survivors by the corpse.[94] And, though gods are ageless and diseaseless, they are particularly exposed to pollution.

It is tempting to seek an analogy between these natural pollutions and the veil of silence drawn over many aspects of man's physical nature in modern western society. Excretion, decreasingly but still in large measure sexuality, increasingly, it is claimed, death, are dirty things that are to be hidden away and never spoken of. We have got into the habit of referring to these as 'taboo' subjects. There is, however, an important difference between these modern taboos and those recorded by

[92] Cf. Lévi-Strauss, 12.
[93] See p. 219 below.
[94] Diod. 17.64.3, cf. Quint. Curt. 5.1.11

anthropology: in the one case the taboo is a veil, while in the other it seems rather to act as a marker. The ultimate objective may perhaps be similar in the two cases, but the intermediate tactics are quite different. There were certainly things that Greek society genuinely sought to hide from view, but in assigning the women who had assisted at a birth, for instance, to a special category of the polluted they were drawing attention to the event rather than obscuring it. We are said today to practise 'death avoidance'; we take no last farewells, shield children from all knowledge of the disruptive event, and refuse to acknowledge explicitly that death is near; when it is imminent, we abandon the dying man to the care of professional nursing staff.[95] This is more like the behaviour of Greek gods than Greek men; mortals are not entitled to hold themselves aloof from pollution. Functionalism went so far as to explain primitive taboo as a mechanism for ensuring the appropriate social involvement in occasions like birth and death: the husband is forced by a taboo to remember that his wife is lying in.[96] The functionalist has not proved his contention that the ritual surrounding these crises creates concern rather than expressing it, but he is no doubt right to assume that this, like all ritual, is a means of display and not disguise.

The most important contribution to an understanding of these phenomena remains that of van Gennep, who in a celebrated work demonstrated the very general human tendency to ritualize important transitions of every type – in space, in time, in social status – and illustrated the typical structure of such rituals, whereby the person undergoing the transition is withdrawn from his previous surroundings, maintained for a time in an intermediate state, and finally reintegrated into society under new conditions or at a new level: rites of separation lead to a period of transition concluded by rites of incorporation.[97] This extension over time is, it seems, the

[95] Ph. Aries, *The Hour of our Death*, London, 1981 (= *L'Homme devant la mort*, Paris, 1977), 559–601, 611–14.

[96] A. R. Radcliffe Brown, 'Taboo', in his *Structure and Function in Primitive Society*, London, 1952, 133–52. Criticisms in Steiner, Ch. 10; cf. however the sympathetic comments of Barth, 166 f.

[97] van Gennep, *passim*; the tripartite schema, 11. The transitional stage is studied, but in relation to initiation only, by V. W. Turner, *The Forest of Symbols*, Cornell, 1967, 93–111 and idem., *The Ritual Process*, London, 1969, Ch. 3.

way in which societies emphasize the changes that are most
important to them. For the individual, the ritual stages provide,
where necessary, a programme for emotional adjustment to the
crises of his experience: in bereavement, for instance, he must
indulge his grief for a fixed period, and then set it aside.[98] The
many rituals that accompany birth and death in Greece fit
neatly enough into van Gennep's scheme. For the central
character, of course, nature has done the work, and rites of
separation are not needed; but after the physical event a cul-
turally prescribed intermediate period must elapse before the
baby is admitted, at name-giving, to the society of the living,
and before the last rites consign the corpse to the ground, and
the soul, still flitting hitherto among the living, to the world of
the dead. As the transitions undergone by those who die or are
born transform the world of their associates, they too become
subject to rites of passage. At birth, it is primarily the mother
who is withdrawn from normal society and requires rein-
corporation, but the other relatives, by attending name-giving
rites and the like, acknowledge and assimilate the change that
has come over the family. After a death, all the relatives and
associates enter an abnormal state, known as mourning, in
which familiar pursuits, interests, dress, and deportment are in
varying degrees forbidden. Obsessed, actually or conventionally, by memories of the dead, they are during this transitional
period half-dead themselves. (To accept death and reject the
period of limbo can be, as the hero of Camus's *L'Étranger* found
out, a serious social crime.) During the period of mourning, a
two-way transition occurs: the dead man moves from the land of
the living to that of the spirits, while the survivors return from
death to life. The last rites finally incorporate or reincorporate
dead and living respectively in their proper communities. As
Achilles says to Agamemnon: 'At dawn, urge your men to fetch
wood, and provide all that the corpse should have when it goes
to the darkness below; so that all the quicker untiring fire may
burn him away from our sight, and the people may turn to their

---

[98] Cf. G. Gorer, *Death, Grief and Mourning in Contemporary Britain*, London, 1965, 72–8,
and esp. the comment quoted on p. 75, 'the week of grief gives you time to get over all
the worry and what not . . . Even though it seems outlandish at the time, it really is a
help . . . you're away for a week and get over all your grief. You get it all concentrated in
one week' (apropos orthodox Jewish mourning rites).

tasks.'[99] In early Greece, as in other societies, this ritual of
separation was so effective that the recipient was now 'dead'
even if it had been performed for him in error, in his absence.
Plutarch tells us that: 'Anyone for whom carrying out and
burial had been performed, as though he were dead, was considered impure by the Greeks, and they wouldn't let such a one
associate with themselves, or enter a temple.' It was only after
Delphi had devised a ritual of reintegration, in the form of an
elaborate pantomime of rebirth, that such unfortunates could
be readmitted to society at all.[100]

It is obviously in the context of the ritualization of transitions
that the pollutions of birth and death belong, and specifically in
the intermediate stage. In a brilliant book, Mary Douglas has
suggested that pollution is in general a property of the betwixt
and between; that which falls between or violates the categories
into which a given society divides external reality is accounted
by that society impure.[101] In Leviticus, for instance, edible land

[99] Hom. *Il.* 23. 49–53. Cf. the Nuer address to the dead man: 'Friend, this beast is
yours. Now turn yourself to the ghosts. Turn yourself away from us' (Evans-Pritchard,
146); their mortuary ceremony is called the 'cutting off' of the dead. For a now classic
study of mortuary rites see Hertz.

[100] *Quaest. Rom.* 264f – 265a: a striking modern case, Evans-Pritchard, 152 f. To be
falsely reported dead was a κακὸς ὄρνις (Eur. *Hel.* 1051) in the 5th century, but not
intolerable in a good cause (Soph. *El.* 58–64); we do not know whether, if the funerary
rites had not been performed, Plutarch's ritual would still have been necessary.

[101] Douglas, *passim*; for her earlier and later thoughts on the topic cf. her collected
papers, *Implicit Meanings, Essays in Anthropology*, London, 1975, and the reader, *Rules and
Meanings*, ed. M. Douglas, London, 1973. E. R. Leach develops similar ideas in 'Animal
Categories and Verbal Abuse', in E. H. Lenneberg (ed.), *New Directions in the Study of
Language*, Massachusetts, 1964, 23–63 (reprinted in P. Maranda (ed.), *Mythology,
Selected Readings*, London, 1972, 39–67): he is effectively criticized by J. Halveson, *Man*
n.s. 11 (1976), 505–16, cf. n.s. 12 (1977), 527 f. S. J. Tambiah offers a theoretical
modification in J. Goody (ed.), *The Character of Kinship*, Cambridge, 1973, 191 f.,
(pollution located in the overlap between two categories, not the gap between them)
and a practical application in 'Animals are Good to Think and Good to Prohibit',
Ethnology, vol. viii, n. 4 (October 1969), 424–59, mostly reproduced in *Rules and
Meanings*, 127–66. Two elements in the original theory should now, it seems, be
jettisoned: (1) the analogy between how perceptual skills are learnt by the child, and
how cultural categories are either learnt by the child or created by societies: cf.
P. Hershman, *Man* n.s. 9 (1974), 292–4, C. R. Hallpike, *The Foundations of Primitive
Thought*, Oxford, 1979, 69–71; (2) the notion that bodily emissions are impure because
they create ambiguity about bodily boundaries: for a more plausible view cf. A. S.
Meigs, 'A Papuan Perspective on Pollution', *Man* n.s. 13 (1978), 304–18. The definition of dirt as 'matter out of place' requires, at least, qualification, cf. Meigs, loc. cit.,
Hallpike, op. cit., 160 n. 4. Hallpike plausibly suggests that the primary form of 'dirt' is
faeces; and on treatment of faeces ethology might well offer guidance.

animals are defined as 'whatsoever parteth the hoof . . . and cheweth the cud'. The pig is therefore an abomination, because 'though he divide the hoof, yet he cheweth not the cud'. Lacking one of the necessary characteristics of the acceptable domestic animal, he is a monster. As a general theory of pollution, this is not wholly convincing; not all pollutions can be seen as products of category violations, and it is not clear that primitive societies are necessarily more disconcerted by classificatory anomalies than we are by, say, the ambiguous status of the tomato.[102] But in the case of the rites of passage, the theory has an obvious plausibility. Persons in the transitional condition are by definition between statuses, and it is not hard to see the corpse and the new baby as situated at the interstices between two worlds. The corpse, in particular, is anomalous both socially (no longer in human society, not yet among the dead) and physically (all the outward marks of a living person, but lifeless). These transitional beings do not, however, fall between categories because the existing categories cannot hold them. There is no intrinsic classificatory problem about the new-born baby; he is alive enough when he enters the world, and it is only because of the characteristic structuring of transitions that he must be suspended for a period in limbo – more a plant than a human being, says Plutarch[103] – before being admitted by baptism, naming, or similar ceremonies to the company of the living. Here, it is not the case that the logic of classifications has generated a misfit who therefore evokes a reaction of alarm; on the contrary, a disconcerting being has been declared a misfit by special manipulation of the classificatory processes. The being is disconcerting not on logical, cognitive, or classificatory but on the simple emotional grounds that it is hard to adjust to decisive change. It is interesting that, in debate about the burial of corpses, we do find arguments that appeal to the breach of category boundaries. By refusing burial, Creon is 'keeping here what belongs to the gods below'; in such a case, 'The gods above are being polluted, and the gods below are not getting what is theirs.' We have seen, however, that it is outrage at unmerited

[102] Cf. Douglas herself, *Implicit Meanings*, 288; J. Goody, *The Domestication of the Savage Mind*, Cambridge, 1977, 45; G. S. Kirk in *Entretiens Hardt* 27, 44–7.
[103] *Quaest. Rom.* 102. 288c.

dishonour that causes this particular demarcation to become so important. It looks as if declaring an object or a person a misfit may be a rationalization for unease, distaste, or anger that is felt on other grounds.[104]

We return to van Gennep. The pollutions of birth and death relate to the disorientation actually or conventionally produced by the great crises in human existence. Not all crucial transitions pollute, however. It is not enough to say that marriage is too joyful an occasion to be polluting, because birth is joyful too. The real difference seems to be that, while marriage is a controlled event, birth and death intrude on human life at their own pleasure. They are an irresistible 'irruption of the biological into social life'.[105] Although they are natural events, they are also violations of order; the dead or dying man and the parturient woman have lost control of their own bodies, and the social group must stand back powerless while crucial changes are worked upon it. The accompanying rites of passage can be seen as reassertions of control; the baby, thrust rudely into the world by nature, still requires social acceptance, and the shade will not be able to reach the world of the dead unless the due rites are performed. This commandeering of the natural processes by society through ritual is so effective that when ritual and physical facts conflict, physical status yields to ritual; living men for whom funerary ceremonies have been performed have been declared 'dead', and, as we saw, dead the unfortunates must remain. Marriage, by contrast, is not an intrusion that requires sealing off, but is itself a harness set upon the rebellious body. Vico defined it as a 'chaste carnal union consummated under fear of some divinity'; it purifies the physical. In viewing the pollutions of birth and death in this way, we are, though doubting Douglas's specific location of impurity in the betwixt

---

[104] Cf. now M. Beard, *JRS* 70 (1980), 20, with references. Creon: Soph. *Ant.* 1070 f., cf. Lys. 2.7. By the 4th c., category ambiguity was a subject for children's riddles, Pl. *Resp.* 479b–c. See too LSJ s.v. ἐπαμφοτερίζειν.

[105] Dumont, 99, cf. 88–9, 'It can be seen that impurity corresponds to the organic aspect of man. Religion generally speaks in the name of universal order; but in this case, though unaware in this form of what it is doing, by proscribing impurity it in fact sets up an opposition between religious and social man on the one hand, and nature on the other.' P. Hershman, *Man.* n.s. 9 (1974), 290 claims 'Pollution is essentially that which cannot be controlled.'

and between, accepting her broader insight that fear of pollution is a product of the urge for order and control.

Natural pollutions are, it appears, complex. Through symbolism of dirtiness that derives from the events themselves (the stench of the corpse, the mess of the birthroom),[106] there is conveyed the disruption wrought in the social group's steady existence by physical events that are of crucial importance to it but beyond its control. This relation to the experience of the social group is particularly clear in the case of funerary pollution. Aristotle observes that mourning is a form of 'homoeopathy' of the mourners with the departed. Death-pollution, too, is a kind of temporary participation in the condition of the dead man, who is through the decay of the corpse 'foul' (*miaros*). In Homer certainly, and possibly in historical times too, the mourners 'befouled' themselves with dust in sympathy; pollution is a transposition of this sympathetic befoulment to the metaphysical plane. 'Being polluted' is a kind of metaphysical suit of mourning. This, and not an erroneous theory of contagion, is why the dead man's relatives are more polluted than outsiders, and why when mourning is forbidden pollution may be excluded too.[107]

Indeed, it can be very hard to distinguish between the socially prescribed consequences of 'pollution' and of 'grief'. Those who have attended a funeral are excluded from sacred places because they are polluted, but sacrifice is a joyous occasion for Greeks and thus they would have been excluded anyway by the conventions of mourning. (Similarly, it would, we sometimes hear, be sacrilegious to mention Dionysus in connection with death;[108] it would also, of course, be bad form to think of the festive god in such a context.) A father who goes about his normal business despite the death of a child is blamed for his unfeeling violation of mourning rather than for 'polluting the temples'.[109] It is as though the gods by their concern for purity

---

[106] On such focusing symbols cf. Hertz, 82–3, V. W. Turner, *The Forest of Symbols*, Cornell, 1967, 98.

[107] Arist. fr. 101 Rose³ *ap*. Ath. 675a. Corpse *miaros*, Hom. *Il*. 24.420.

[108] Hdt. 2.86.2, Dem. 60.30, Pl. *Menex*. 238b. Cf. p. 70 n. 123 on the incompatibility of death and sexuality.

[109] Aeschin. 3.77; a similar attack, Isocr. 19.40, and cf. Lys. 1.14, (Plut.) *Cons. ad Apoll*. 118c–119d.

merely enforce the behaviour that is appropriate in purely human terms.[110]

These observations do not claim to be exhaustive. The belief that 'corpses are dirty' is clearly a possible vehicle for numerous emotions. In the case of birth, it is surely likely that the Greeks will have associated the impurity of mother and child during the first few days of life with their very real physical peril during that period. Pollution would thus have helped to define and so limit a period of danger and anxiety; the ceremony ending it would be a ritual expression of the hope that the child, having surmounted the initial dangers, now belonged to this world and would live on.[111] The polluted mourner too surely felt in contact with an abominable power. Funerary pollution is not explained by man's fear and hatred of death, or birth-pollution would be inexplicable; it must none the less surely have become a focus for these feelings. In such an area Ockham's razor is too blunt an instrument.

In Greek belief these pollutions had a further special application, their role in separating gods and men. ('Special' here does not mean either unique or recent; the same application occurs, in varying degrees, in Roman religion, Hinduism, and Zoroastrianism.[112]) While in most tribal societies it is the protection of fellow humans against these natural pollutions that is the main concern, in Greece real danger seems only to occur if the gods are exposed to them. Thus it is on the altars, not among

[110] The relation of 'pollution' to 'mourning' is in general uncertain. Is the period of abnormality following a Spartan king's death (Hdt. 6.58.3, Xen. *Hell.* 3.3.1, Arist. fr. 611.10) 'mourning' (Hdt.) or 'pollution' (Xen.; for a funerary period as not *hosios* cf. Eur. *Antiope* 80, Page *GLP* p. 68)? Mourning periods could be protracted: e.g. Lys. 1.14 (some restrictions till 30th day), *LSA* 16 (3 months!). Presumably 'pollution' lasted less long; but the matter is obscure.

[111] 'The ritual dangers which are believed to threaten the process of conception and birth are, to some extent, a reflection of pragmatic anxieties about real dangers . . . where pregnancy and childbirth not infrequently lead to the death of both mother and child,' Buxton, 214. Frequent deaths in 1st week, Arist. *Hist. An.* 588a 8–10. Interconnection of physical and ritual dangers in modern Greece, Blum, 12 f., 19 f., 111 (64) (in these accounts mother and child are clearly more imperilled by their own pollution than are outsiders).

[112] Hinduism: C. J. Fuller, *Man* n.s. 14 (1979), 473; L. Dumont, *Une sous caste de l'Inde du sud*, Paris/The Hague, 1957, 345, cf. 210; G. Eichinger Ferro-Luzzi, *Anthropos* 69 (1974), 131–3. We find here a sliding scale: impurity of any kind debars from the temples, while severe pollution also impedes domestic and social activities, cf. Ferro-Luzzi, loc. cit., Srinivas, 106. Zoroastrians: e.g. Boyce, 100.

the houses, that Sophocles' birds of prey drop the scraps of Polyneices' corpse, and, as we have seen, it is hard to identify any certain consequence of contact with natural pollutions apart from exclusion from the temples. This exclusion from the sacred is no doubt in origin, as we have seen, simply an exclusion from social life in its festive forms; there is no celebration, no feeling of community, without sacrifice. It certainly comes to seem, however, as if the real barrier that pollution sets up is not between man and man but between man and gods. By banning birth, death, and also sexuality from sacred places, the Greeks emphasize the gulf that separates the nature of god and man. On one level, of course, the gods have much in common with man in these respects: they underwent birth, and engage in sexual activity. But whereas for men birth and sex are part of a cycle that ends in the grave, the gods enjoy the benefits of the flesh but not its ills. (Philosophers were to seek to free the gods from the taint of the physical altogether.) Excluded from a temple because of the birth of a son, a Greek is reminded, perhaps, that his son has been born to replace himself, and die in his turn, while the gods persist in splendid immortality.[113]

This account may be taken roughly to represent the situation in Athens in the fifth century. In the Homeric world, it has often been argued, attitudes were very different. Despite the countless deaths described in Homer, there is no hint of *miasma* affecting the living. The heroes may return to their normal pursuits after a funeral without apparently even washing. In particular, the absolute revulsion of the gods from scenes of death seems to be missing. They mingle in battle with the dead and dying, and do not disdain to touch a corpse. The river god Scamander, though complaining that Achilles is obstructing his streams with dead bodies, does not speak of this as a desecration. The only pollution known to Homer, on this view, is simple dirt; for his world the metaphysical contagion of death would be a conceptual impossibility.[114]

The postulated growth in pollution fears conflicts, for what it is worth, with Plutarch's picture of the great archaic legislators grappling with powerful superstitious fears attached to death.[115] It is more important that the arguments themselves will scarcely bear investigation. Pollution belief in some form undoubtedly existed in the classical period, and yet it is easy to find passages where classical authors seem oblivious to it. Deaths in Homer occur in battle, but there is no evidence that soldiers were ever polluted by the deaths of their comrades. If Apollo, purest of gods, handles Sarpedon's corpse in the *Iliad* while his sister shuns that of Hippolytus in Euripides, that difference derives from a permanent ambiguity in the relation of god to man rather than a transformation in belief. The gods do care for their human favourites, but fate and the mortality of the favourites impose upon that care limits which men may resent. In the particular contexts, Homer is emphasizing the care, Euripides the limits; both poets are portraying an aspect of the divine nature, not transcribing ritual rules. On a broader level, the gulf between mortal and immortal that Euripides expresses through Artemis' flight before pollution is the unshakeable first premiss of Homer's religion.[116] Even in a fifth-century poet, the same Apollo subjects himself to worse pollution than in Homer; the third *Pythian* shows the pure one snatching a new-born baby from a corpse. The poet who wrote this lived, none the less, in a city that kept temples and tombs well separated.

There is in fact a connection between death and dirt in Homer, although it may not be justified to speak of pollution in the classical sense. Physical cleanliness is an important expression in the poems of wholeness and propriety. The heroes wash before meals, and would be ashamed to pray to the gods when dirty; before pouring an important libation, Achilles first

[114] Cf. Stengel, 156 f.; idem, *Hermes* 41 (1906), 241 (= *Opferbraüche der Griechen*, Leipzig, 1910, 28 f.); M. M. Gillies, *CQ* 19 (1925), 71–4; Moulinier, 25–33. Funerals: Gillies cites *Il.* 23.257 f., 24.801 f., *Od.* 12.10 ff. Corpses: *Il.* 16.666–83, 24.612. Scamander: *Il.* 21. 218–21. Zenodotus athetized *Il.* 16.666–83, as imposing inappropriate work on the 'griefless one'.
[115] *Sol.* 12.8, *Lyc.* 27.1.
[116] *Il.* 5.440–2, Griffin, Ch. 6, *passim*. In *Il.* 22. 213 Apollo in fact abandons the doomed Hector, but this is in a sense cause as well as consequence of the coming death.

purifies the cup with sulphur, then washes it in water, and
finally washes his own hands; it is a rite of ceremonial sprinkling
that unites the participants at every sacrifice in a sacred circle.
Clean clothes are essential to a display of respect or a sense of
wellbeing.[117] Reactions to disaster, by contrast, commonly
focus upon a physical defilement, incidental though it may
seem to the real import of what has occurred. 'His head, beautiful before, lay in the dust': so Homer sums up the humiliation of
the dead Hector. The fall of Patroclus is prefigured in the fall of
the helmet: 'the crest was befouled with blood and dust: yet
before it had not been permitted for the horse-hair helmet to be
befouled with dust, but it protected the head and fair brow of a
godlike man, Achilles.'[118] We are dealing, certainly, with a
great poet's power to express the abstract through the concrete,
but, unless Homer invented the whole system of ritual washing
that he describes, cleanliness must also have been an unconscious symbol of good order in the society that he knew.[119] This
symbolic significance of physical integrity is one reason why it
mattered that the corpse should not be mutilated. Achilles'
immediate reaction to the news of Patroclus' death is therefore
most interesting: 'Taking grimy dust in both his hands he
poured it over his head, and befouled his fair face.' Achilles
pollutes himself in his grief; later, urged to wash off the battle
mire that clings to him from his conflict with Hector, he declares with an oath: 'No water may come near my head, before I
have set Patroclus on the flames, heaped him a monument, and
cut my hair for him.' He speaks of this refusal to wash as a
religious obligation (*themis*); that may be the language of passion, but self-pollution and not washing were probably, if not
fixed rules of mourning, at least traditional modes for the
expression of grief.[120]

[117] Cf. p. 20. Clean clothes: cf. O. P. Taplin, *Greece and Rome* 27 (1980), 9–11.
[118] *Il.* 22.402 f., 16.795–9.
[119] Homeric symbolism is finely described, with reference to the concrete symbolism
of early social, political, and religious life, by Griffin, Ch. 1. On such symbolism
L. Gernet, 'Droit et prédroit en Grèce ancienne', *L'Année Sociologique*, 3ᵉ serie (1948–9),
Paris, 1951, 21–119 (= Gernet, *Anthropologie*, 175 ff.) was most important.
[120] *Il.* 18.23–5, 23.44–6. For self-pollution cf. *Il.* 22.414, 24.163–5, 640, *Od.* 24.316 f.;
for not washing, *Hym. Hom. Cer.* 50. Andronikos observes, p. 2, that not washing cannot
have been a rule, as Achilles is urged to wash, *Il.* 23.39–41; but it may have been a
common practice.

This condition of Achilles may seem to differ from the pollution of the mourner in classical times. The dirt on Achilles is self-inflicted and physical, not automatic and metaphysical; consequently his condition is not contagious, he will become clean again as soon as he washes after the funeral, and there is no suggestion of danger. Under examination, these differences lose their comfortable clarity. The distinction between physical and metaphysical pollution becomes uncertain if one considers that the one may be a symbol for the other. At Iulis, as we have seen, the mourners probably polluted themselves physically, and after the funeral it will have been the marks of this self-defilement that they washed off; but the physical pollution was also metaphysical, or the law would not have needed to specify that, by washing, the mourners recovered their purity. Metaphysical pollution certainly was present at Iulis, because the house of death required purification from it. Conditions in fifth-century Ceos prove nothing about Achilles; but it should be noted that, as long as he remained dirty, he was by Homeric etiquette excluded from social life and divine cult no less than the classical mourner. Thus he was subject to the only practical consequence of pollution that is actually attested at any date. An obvious difference is that, in the Homeric ideology, normal life resumes immediately after the funeral,[121] while pollution may cling to the classical mourner for a further span of days; but Homer tends so to prolong the lamentation at the laying-out that the period of abnormal funerary time is actually longer than in classical practice.[122]

The argument ends, inevitably, in uncertainty; the evidence is not of the right kind. It shows at least that the symbolism of pollution was already linked to death in Homer, even if it lacked the metaphysical extension it was later to receive. Nothing, however, conclusively proves the extension to be a later development. A sharp contrast between Homer and the fifth century will almost certainly be founded on over-emphasis of the importance of death-pollution for the latter, and will give it an undeserved prominence among the symbolic expressions of

---

[121] *Il.* 23.52–3.
[122] *Il.* 24. 784–7, *Od.* 24. 63–5; Patroclus however remains laid out for one day only, Andronikos, 9.

mourning of which it formed a part. If we do not find explicitly attested in Homer the idea of death as an inauspicious event whose dangerous influence persists for those who come into contact with it, it is certainly present in Hesiod or his continuator: 'Do not beget a child on your return from an ill-omened burial, but from a feast of the gods.' No contact is to be permitted between procreation and death, and 'burials' are opposed to 'feasts of the gods'.[123] In a later author we would acknowledge that as pollution belief. All that is lacking is the symbolic connection between 'ill-omened' and 'dirty', and that connection, given the place of physical pollution in the symbolism of mourning, lay close at hand.

There is at all events no doubt that, if a corpse is denied funerary rites in Homer, the consequences may be more than merely physical. Hector warns Achilles that, if mutilated, he may 'become a wrath of the gods' against him; Elpenor issues a similar warning to Odysseus, and in the last book of the *Iliad* Achilles' conduct does stir the gods to indignation and intervention. The language used is that of divine anger and not pollution, but the significance of this distinction is easily over-emphasized: in both cases a human rule is receiving supernatural support. We find here, on an important issue, a clear continuity of value between Homer and the fifth century.[124]

Archaeological evidence on the disposition of graves might also provide guidance on early attitudes to pollution. As we have noted, extramural burial was the norm in almost all classical Greek cities. It would be shocking to mingle the dwellings of the dead with those of the living, still more with those of the gods. Christian burial *ad sanctos* was a sharp break with

---

[123] Hes. *Op*. 735–6. Cf. Buxton, 149: 'The action of procreation belongs to life and must not be introduced into situations associated with death. To mix the two is death-dealing.' The same incompatibility means that death-pollution can be effaced elsewhere by ritual copulation, R. G. Willis, *Man* n.s. 7 (1972), 376. Solon banned women under 60 from attendance at funerals, except for close relatives, Dem. 43.62. This will have served his general aim of reducing the scale of funerals, but in excluding fertile women in particular he may have been influenced by religious motives; even to the magnificent funerals of scrutineers, Plato only admits virgins and women past childbearing (*Leg*. 947d). For Rome cf. Censorinus *D.N.* 2.2 (no blood sacrifice on birthdays), *CIL* I² p. 231 (Fasti Praenestini), Carmentis, goddess of birth, and *morticina* opposed.

[124] *Il*. 22. 358, *Od*. 11.73, *Il*. 24. 33–76.

pagan practice.[125] But this sensitivity to the place of burial was neither universal in the Greek world nor immemorially ancient. Greek tradition knew that, in the old days, burials might be made actually in the houses of the living, and it also knew of historical Greek cities that disposed of their dead within the habitational area. Both these traditions have been confirmed archaeologically,[126] and excavation seems also to have shown that the rule on extrahabitational burial was less strictly applied in early centuries than in the classical period. It is tempting to correlate this increasing desire to separate the dead from the living with increasing fears of pollution. Something of the kind is suggested by Plutarch in the explanation he offers of Lycurgus' funerary legislation:

Another area that he organized admirably was that of burial . . . he destroyed superstitious fears absolutely by allowing the burial of corpses in the city, and the siting of tombs near to temples; thus he made the young men thoroughly familiar with sights of this kind, so that they felt no disturbance or alarm at the thought of death, as though it polluted anybody who touched a corpse or walked between tombs.[127]

This moral stiffening through intrahabitational burial, so well exemplified in warlike Sparta, does not seem to have extended to the other internal-burying city, *inbelle Tarentum.*

There are two difficulties of principle in such an argument. A society may fear pollution from death and the fresh corpse without extending that fear to the site of the grave.[128] Secondly, even if the grave is felt to pollute, it need not be placed right

[125] W. Vollgraff, 'Inhumation en terre sacrée dans l'antiquité grecque', *Mémoires présentés par divers savants a l'Académie des Inscriptions*, xiv. 2 (1951), 315–98, sought to establish hellenistic analogies for burial on sacred ground, mistakenly: see L. Robert, *Opera Minora Selecta* 4, Amsterdam, 1974, 124 f. Shocking to call an altar a tomb, Ar. *Thesm.* 888. (Plut. *Arist.* 20. 6, on burial of Euchidas in shrine of Artemis Eukleia, is a puzzle). On the origins of *depositio ad sanctos* see Ph. Aries, *The Hour of our Death*, London, 1981, 30–40; P. Brown, *The Cult of the Saints*, Chicago and London, 1981, Ch. 1.
[126] (Pl.) *Min.* 315d, = Middle Helladic house burials. Internal burial at Tarentum, Polyb. 8.28.6, cf. Walbank, ad. loc. and Kurtz/Boardman, 308 f.; at Sparta, Plut. *Lyc.* 27.1, *Inst. Lac.* 238d, Paus. 3.14.1–3, cf. 'Αρχ. Δελτ. 19 (1964), A 123 ff., 283–5, *ABSA* 12 (1905–6), 281, 13 (1906–7), 155 ff. Paus. 1. 43.3 shows internal burial to have been exceptional at Megara, not, as is sometimes supposed, normal.
[127] *Lyc.* 27.1.
[128] Nuer are indifferent to graves (Evans-Pritchard, 145), Mandari bury within the homestead (Buxton, 114); both have death-pollution beliefs.

outside the habitational area.[129] Every settlement has its nooks
and interstices which nobody feels to be part of their own
living-space, and this was probably particularly true in the
straggling villages and townlets of early Greece. The disposal of
the corpse is a 'carrying out', but the necessary psychological
separation can be achieved without the corpse in fact being
taken very far. Thus, even if, in a given city, a complete change
from intramural to extramural burial could be demonstrated
over a certain period, that change would not necessarily be
evidence for new beliefs about death or the corpse. (We have
learnt that the theology of inhumation and cremation need not
be very different.) In fact, on the archaeological evidence at
present available, such a complete change cannot be found. If
we ignore the two internal-burying cities, Sparta and
Tarentum, it seems to be true that from the Mycenaean period
onwards extrahabitational burial was everywhere the norm,
though by no means an inflexible one. In the Mycenaean period
internal burial was rare;[130] in the Submycenaean period and
Dark Age, it is attested at Athens, Lefkandi, and perhaps
Iolkos,[131] but in each case the evidence mainly concerns
children, and there is no hint that for adults external burial was
not the rule. At Athens, for instance, a complementary pattern
of intramural child burial and extramural adult cremation has
been suggested.[132] Intrahabitational burial has recently been
claimed for Corinth, and the Argolid; but in the case of the
Argolid it has been pointed out that it is extremely difficult,
both chronologically and topographically, to be sure that when
a particular grave was dug it was felt to fall within the living-
space of a particular village.[133] For later centuries, a cemetery in
Athens, on the lower slopes of the acropolis beside the agora,

---

[129] In Madagascar, tribes that buried within and without the settlement were equally
afraid to approach a tomb (A. van Gennep, *Tabou et totémisme à Madagascar*, Paris, 1904,
66 f.).

[130] V. R. d'A Desborough, *The Greek Dark Ages*, London, 1972, 276.

[131] Snodgrass, 144 f., 361; Desborough, op. cit., 276 f., cf. 369.

[132] Snodgrass, 144 f.

[133] Corinth: C. K. Williams II and J. E. Fisher, *Hesperia* 42 (1973), 4. Argolid:
R. Hägg, *Die Gräber der Argolis in submykenischer, protogeometrischer und geometrischer Zeit*,
i, Uppsala, 1974, 87–91, a good discussion which emphasizes that the perception of a
sharp distinction between internal and external burial is a product of urbanization;
even Hägg's cautious claims are doubted by P. Courbin, *Rev. Arch.* 1977, 328.

has been thought to provide important evidence: it contains adult burials from the late geometric period to the end of the sixth century, but is then abandoned. (A few sixth-century burials have also been found in other parts of the city.)[134] But this proves a hardening of attitudes at the end of the sixth century only if the cemetery, while in use, was within the old city-walls; and this is uncertain.[135]

In a history of attitudes to these pollutions, therefore, the first solid event is the act of Peisistratus, who, according to Herodotus, 'rooted his tyranny firmly . . . taking hostages from the Athenians . . . and purifying Delos in accordance with the oracles'.[136] (He removed all graves from the area within sight of the temple.) It would be easier to understand his motives if we knew what 'the oracles' were that ordained it, and if we could be sure in what sense the purification helped to 'root' Peisistratus' tyranny. A point of obvious significance is that, whatever the origin of the oracles, the effective impulse to purify Delos came not from the Delians themselves but from Peisistratus. By this display of concern for the sanctity of the great Ionian religious centre, Athens' ruler strengthened his city's claim to general spiritual patronage of the Ionians, and to a position of influence among the islands at the centre of which Delos lay.[137]

---

[134] R. S. Young, *Hesperia* 20 (1951), 67–134, esp. 131–3. The ban on intramural burial at Athens is known from Cic. *Fam.* 4.12.3.

[135] F. E. Winter, *Hesperia, Supplement* 19, 1982, 199–204.

[136] Hdt. 1.64.2.

[137] Cf. H. W. Parke, 'Polycrates and Delos', *CQ* 40 (1946), 105–8. For a different but not irreconcilable view see Burkert, *GR* 310: part of a process of theological elaboration of the implications of the traditional mortal/immortal opposition.

3

THE WORKS OF APHRODITE

'Apart from Egyptians and Greeks', says Herodotus, 'almost
the whole of the rest of mankind copulate in sacred places and
go into shrines without washing after sleeping with a woman.'[1]
In Greek ideology, therefore, sexual activity is in some sense
incompatible with the sacred. Such activity is, of course, indisputably natural; for man and woman intercourse is *themis*, that
which is natural and right.[2] It thus joins birth and death to form
a trio of inescapable human processes from which the gods
require insulation. As Herodotus indicates, this takes two
forms, physical separation (no intercourse in sacred precincts)
and lustration (washing after intercourse before entering a
shrine). Both are well attested independently. Cautionary tales
describe the dramatic retribution that strikes those who copulate in shrines,[3] while a long series of sacred laws regulates
access to temples 'from a woman' or the like. The earliest of
these permits immediate entry after intercourse during the
night (passage of time here replaces washing as a mode of
separation), but requires washing after intercourse by day.[4]

---

[1] Hdt. 2.64. The standard collection of material is Fehrle; there is a sane survey by
H. Jeanmaire in *Mystique et continence*, Travaux Scientifiques du viiᵉ Congrès International d'Avon, Les Études Carmélitaines, 1952, 51–60.

[2] Hom. *Il.* 9.276.

[3] e.g. Hdt. 9.116–20 (Aryactes, in Protesilaus' shrine); cf. Burkert, *HN* 72, Fehrle,
242, and, for the rule, Xen. *Ages.* 5.7, Alciphron, *Epistles*, 4.1, Ach. Tat. 5.21.4. But note
p. 76 n. 8 below. Though the crime is commonly located in the temple of a virgin
goddess, the case of Aryactes shows this not to be essential. Ritual origins for such
stories are often suspected (e.g. F. Graf, *SSR* 2 (1978), 75); such rituals would
themselves, however, be based on abnormality. In Ziehen, n.61 = Buck, n. 64,
Schwyzer, 412 (Olympia, 6th c.) fornication in a shrine apparently requires penal
sacrifice and purification only.

[4] *LSS* 115.A 11 ff. (misinterpreted by Sokolowski). But apparently even after washing
there was a certain shrine from which the worshipper was debarred, line 13. Immediate
entry after washing is allowed by *LSCG* 124.9 ('from a woman'), 55.4.('a woman').
LSA 18. 9–13 ('a woman'), ?51. 10–13, *BCH* 102 (1978), p. 326 .14 ('from *aphrodisia*').
Immediate entry, after washing, from licit intercourse, *LSCG* 139. 14–17 ('from lawful
intercourse'), *LSS* 91.17 ('intercourse'). *LSA* 12. 1–3 ('one's own wife or husband')

Such a rule protects the ideological barrier between sex and the sacred without imposing any restraints on sexual activity. We see this in the famous scene in *Lysistrata* where Myrrhine is making excuses to her lustful husband. '[If I yield to you] I won't be pure enough to go back up to the acropolis.' No trouble about that', answers Kinesias, 'you can wash in the Clepsydra fountain.' This passage also shows that, though most of our evidence concerns the purification of man 'from a woman', there is no difference in the purification that woman requires 'from a man'.[5]

Such rules obviously have nothing directly to do with morality. Later sacred laws do try to assimilate them to moral sanctions by distinguishing in point of purity between licit and illicit intercourse (with a prostitute or somebody else's spouse), and excluding the worshipper from the shrine for a period of days after illicit contacts; but the early texts speak merely of purity 'from a woman'.[6] They are not products of asceticism, as they require no abstinence; even the later laws that contain sanctions against sexual irregularities normally allow the effects of licit intercourse to be simply washed away. Nor is it easy to see them as expressions of a strong internalized feeling that the sexual act is degrading or disgusting. Hippolytus, who does see

perhaps omits even washing. Longer periods of purity are required by *LSA* 29. 4–6 (cult of *Meter Gallesia*, 'one's own wife', 2 days), *LSS* 54.4 (a Syrian god, 'woman', 2 days), 119. 7–9 (unknown cult in Egypt, 'men from women, and vice versa', 2 days), *LSCG* 171.17 (a private Coan foundation, 'woman', 3 days), and the new regulations (? 2nd c. AD) for those undergoing incubation in the Asklepieion of Pergamum (*Altertümer von Pergamon*, viii. 3, ed. C. Habicht, Berlin, 1969, p. 168, 11–14, '*aphrodisia*', two days. Rules for those merely entering the shrine were perhaps less strict, as H. Wörrle, the editor of the new law, notes, p. 181). Sexual purity is required without specification of a period by *LSCG* 95.5 ('woman'), *LSS* 59. 15–16 ('woman'), 108.1 ('*aphrodisia*'). Additional impurity derives from intercourse with a courtesan in *LSA* 29.7 (an extra day), *LSS* 91.18 (30 extra days), with someone else's spouse *LSA* 12. 5–6 (an extra day); for the stress on licitness cf. *LSCG* 139.14. In *LSA* 18. 13–15 the prostitute must remain pure for 2 days before entering. Permanent exclusion after 'lawless' contacts in *LSS* 91.19, and the exceptional *LSA* 20. 25–50. Extra period of purity required 'from defloration' *LSCG* 139.18, *LSS* 91. 12. Apart from *LSS* 115 (and, on Sokolowski's dating, *LSA* 29) none of these texts is earlier than the 2nd century BC; several are very late. The earliest evidence is ? Hom. *Od.* 8. 364 f.; impurity of sex, Porph. *Abst.* 2.50, 4.20.

[5] Ar. *Lys.* 912 f. A few of the texts in the preceding note also make intercourse pollute both partners equally.

[6] Later sacred laws: n. 4 above. 'From a woman': *LSS* 115 A 11, *LSCG* 151 A 42.

sex in this way, is not presented by Euripides as a typical Greek. An aura of shame does indeed surround sexuality, but its source seems to be embarrassment about bodily functions rather than guilt. It is within the general structure of respectful behaviour and decorum that these rules find their place. Sex is a private affair; those who are willing to 'couple openly' are characterized by this as extreme barbarians.[7] Keeping private things private is a mark of social distance or respect; to perform a private act deliberately in the presence of another indicates either intimacy or contempt. Old Comedy, a rumbustious and shameless genre, speaks openly of sexual and bodily functions that politer forms of discourse are at pains to conceal. The insulation of sex from the sacred is merely a specialized case of the general principle that sexual activity, like other bodily functions, requires disguise in formal contexts. The symbolic veil that, by washing, the worshipper sets up between his sexual activity and the gods is an expression of respect, rather like putting on clean clothes before approaching a shrine. If lovers sometimes yielded to the tempting seclusion of rustic precincts, they may have reassured themselves with the thought that the easy-going country deities would not stand upon formalities.[8]

'Hesiod' reveals similar ideas in their original context. 'Do not expose your shameful parts, when you are bespattered with seed, before the hearth', he warns. We find here clearly indicated the physical fact that, in Greece as elsewhere, decisively shaped the symbolism through which attitudes to sexuality are expressed. Sex is dirty; it involves a bodily emission. The dirtiness is the same whatever the moral status of the act (and may indeed afflict the male against his will).[9] It is obvious, however, that the belief or assertion that 'sex is dirty' is seldom unin-

---

[7] Xen. *An.* 5.4. 33–4, cited by Dover, 206; cf. G. Henderson, *The Maculate Muse*, Yale 1975, 3–5. The chronological development noted by Dover, 207 does not concern us here.

[8] *Sed faciles Nymphae risere*, Virg. *Ecl.* 3.9. Festivals, and grottoes, of Pan particularly invite such transgression: Ar. *Lys.* 911; Eur. *Ion.* 936–9; R. Herbig, *Pan, der griechische Bocksgott*, Frankfurt, 1949, 48 on his Plate xxxv n. 4, 'Liebesopfer eines ländlichen Paares im Heiligtum und in Beisein Pans'; Ael. *Ep.* 15, cf. Alciphron, *Epistle* 4.13.16. Borgeaud comments, 229, 'La transgression, dans ce cas, est rituelle.'

[9] Hes. *Op.* 733 f. For ἐκμιαίνομαι = ejaculate, voluntarily or involuntarily, see Ar. *Ran.* 753 with schol. For possible pollution by wet dreams in the Cyrene law see p. 342 below.

fluenced by the emotional and social significance of the act to
which it relates: the dirt becomes symbolic. Hesiod's warning is
against 'exposing one's shameful parts when stained with seed',
or making an open display of a fact that should be hidden; and it
is the hearth that he seeks to protect. This is partly due to
respect for fire, a pure element which is liable, it seems, to
metaphysical contamination by this particular form of dirt; for
the same reason, a character in Hipponax apparently 'hides the
fire' before making love.[10] But there is also perhaps a symbolic
opposition between the hearth, public centre of the household,
place of light, and the sexual act, privately performed in darkness in the inner recesses. A further contrast arises from the fact
that the hearth is a goddess, a virgin, who sits all day at home
like an unmarried daughter. Keeping sexuality away from the
hearth is thus also a way of maintaining, on the symbolic level,
the distinction between the married and unmarried estates.[11]

In respect of sexual purity, as of many other areas of concern
about purity, 'Hesiod' offers almost the only evidence as to how
it affected daily life. We are left to wonder, and to doubt,
whether respect of this kind for the hearthfire persisted long.
For Herodotus, it is a peculiarity of Babylonian spouses that
they purify themselves after intercourse before touching any
household utensil.[12] There may, however, have been everyday
contexts in which, in rustic communities, sexual purity was
required. The planting and harvesting of the olive, bee-keeping,
and the preparation of food are tasks to be performed, according
to Roman agricultural writers, by children, or the abstinent, or
only after purification.[13] Unfortunately, we cannot be sure of
the provenance of these rules. The hellenistic agricultural
treatises that to some extent lie behind the Roman writers had
undergone non-Greek influences, and cannot be assumed to
reflect primeval lore.[14] Bees' antipathy to sexuality, however, is

---

[10] Hippon. fr. 104.20 W., interpreted by M. L. West, *Studies in Greek Elegy and Iambus*, Berlin, 1974, 143. But for lamps left alight see Ar. *Eccl.* 7–9 with Ussher's note.
[11] Cf. Vernant, *Pensée*, i. 129–48.
[12] Hdt. 1. 198.
[13] Olive: Palladius 1.6.14 (*Graeci iubent*), cf. *Geoponica* 9.2.5–6; bees: e.g. Columella 9.14.3; food: Columella 12.4.3.
[14] Columella 12.4.2 asserts Carthaginian influence. On the lost Greek literature see E. Oder, Ch. 25 of F. Susemihl, *Geschichte der griechischen Literatur in der Alexandrinerzeit*, vol. i, Leipzig, 1891.

a well-attested Greek belief; there is some reason to think that unmarried girls may have been entrusted with the preparation of food, and Plutarch perhaps records (the text is in doubt) that purity was required in order to begin the harvest.[15] We should therefore consider the Roman rules as at least possible witnesses to Greek practice. They appear to work partly on a level of sympathy (pure trees and animals demand purity of the farmer), partly through metaphysical extension of a requirement of physical purity (food must be clean), and partly on the premiss that important and delicate operations (the harvest) should be approached with the same respect as is paid to the gods. It is hard to go further, when the context of these rules is so insecure. And this is, unfortunately, the sum of our knowledge of domestic requirements of sexual purity.

The separation between religion and sexuality which we discussed earlier is, of course, very restricted. This is true even on the theoretical level, to say nothing of the frequent practical exploitation of festival licence for purposes of sexual adventure.[16] The gods observed the decencies,[17] but many of them were sexually active; on earth, although at some festivals a sexual allusion would have been as untimely as in church today, to the effect of very many others it was central. Sacred activities in Greece are as a class distinguished from the profane by their greater dignity, but they differ greatly in themselves in solemnity and propriety. A festival like the Panathenaea may reflect the dignified decorum of public and social order, but the messy mysteries of fertility also have their place in religious life. Even within the class of festivals that exploit sexuality explicitly, there is great divergence; a solemn mystery like the sacred marriage of Dionysus at the Athenian Anthesteria clearly differs as much in mood from the deliberately outrageous obscenity of the Haloa as do both from the straightforward indulgence of Aphrodisia and the like. It is possible that, for the more frankly hedonistic rites, purity will not have been required;[18] but the contrast between the intrinsic dignity of

---

[15] Bees: p. 83 n. 37 below. Unmarried girls: p. 80 n. 25 below. Harvest: Plut. *Quaest. Conv.* 655d, with Hubert's note in the Teubner.

[16] e.g. Lys. 1.20, Men. *Epit.* 451–4, *Phasm.* 95 ff., *Sam.* 38–49.

[17] Hom. *Il.* 14.330–6, Pind. *Pyth.* 9.40 f.

[18] Cf. *Carmen Priapeum* 14, and p. 76 n. 8 above.

religious activity, and the possibly disreputable character of actual rites, presumably meant that Greeks sometimes purified themselves in respectful preparation for acts they would have been ashamed to perform in everyday life.

We have so far considered only the requirement to wash after intercourse before entering a shrine. Religious rules of sexual purity went beyond this, but from this point onwards, for lack of detailed evidence, it becomes hard to speak with real precision. Though Pausanias offers a good deal of information about virgin priestesses and the like, a congeries of facts about the practice of different parts of Greece in the second century AD is an unreliable basis on which to reconstruct early views on cultic chastity. It is foolhardy to assume that the terms on which priesthoods in a particular cult were held could never change.[19] The safest procedure is obviously to concentrate on the comparatively well-documented case of Athens. Even here, however, large gaps in our knowledge make a certain vagueness inevitable.

At Athens, as elsewhere in the Greek world, many ritual functions fell to those who because of their age were necessarily pure – the 'intact' boys and girls of Catullus' hymn.[20] In postclassical medical and agricultural writers, the virgin and the 'uncorrupted boy' are credited with magical powers that are obviously conceived as deriving from purity.[21] It is not clear, however, that it was because of their purity that such ministrants were chosen for the classical rites, still less that purity was considered magically effective. Often it would be a reversal of the truth to say that the children embody the purity that the ceremony demands; on the contrary, the rite's sole function is as a stage in the induction of the children to adult life. In a famous passage of the *Lysistrata*, the chorus boast of the four ritual roles that they performed when little girls, as 'bearers of secret things', 'corn-grinders for Athene the leader', 'bears at

---

[19] For Delos see Bruneau, 63, 504–6.

[20] Poem 34, sung by *puellae et pueri integri*. Evidence in Fehrle, 112–25.

[21] Fehrle, 54–8; for the much favoured 'urine of an intact boy' cf. texts in *T.L.L.* s.v. *impubes*, col. 706 bottom, M. Wellmann's edition of Dioscorides, vol. ii, p. 381, index s.v. οὖρον παιδὸς ἀφθόρου. Cf. in general H. Herter, 'Das unschuldige Kind', *Jahrb. f. Antike u. Christentum* 4 (1961), 28–36.

Miasma

Brauron', and 'basket-bearers'.[22] Of these, it is certain that
being 'a bear at Brauron' is a case of the kind just mentioned;
the bears were not chaste representatives of the Athenian
people, but little girls seeking ritual protection and preparation
before the onset of womanhood. Although this is more controversial, being a 'bearer of secret things' was probably also
originally one stage in a young girl's initiation.[23] There is no
reason to see the post of 'basket-bearer', attested in many cults,
as an initiatory survival, but the choice of a maiden for it seems
to reflect the division of labour in household cult, where subordinate roles are assigned to the children.[24] Only in the case of
Athene's 'corn-grinder' is it plausible to see chastity as integral
to the role, since abundant comparative evidence is available
for sexual purity being required in the preparation of food.[25] Of
course, purity may have come to seem requisite for all these
posts, since it is the distinctive characteristic of the unmarried
girl. Thus the courtesan Habrotonon in Menander can jokingly
claim, after three days abstinence, that she is now pure enough
'to carry the basket of the goddess'.[26] But it would not have
seemed appropriate to use some other category of ritually
pure person (an old woman, for instance) to serve as basket-
bearer. Ritual functions are divided out between the different
age and sex groups of society, and basket-bearing has fallen to
the unmarried girl; this is her contribution to religious life. It is
a question of status differentiation rather than purity. The
frequency of maiden choirs throughout the Greek world has
been put in a new light by the demonstration that the chorus
was the institution through which young girls were educated for
womanhood.[27] We have only to read the song composed for one
such chorus, Alcman's first *partheneion*, to see that the fresh

[22] Ar. *Lys.* 641–7, cf. A. Brelich, *Paides e Parthenoi*, Rome, 1969, with C. Sourvinou-
Inwood, *JHS* 91 (1971), 172–7.
[23] Burkert, *HN* 171, with references; but note the reservation of P. Vidal-Naquet in
Faire de l'histoire, iii, ed. J. Le Goff & P. Nora, Paris, 1974, 154. A magical interpretation
of their virginity in Deubner, 12.
[24] Cf. Ar. *Ach.* 253 f. For their diffusion see Deubner, index s.v. *Kanephoren*.
[25] Plut. *Quaest. Rom.* 85, with H. J. Rose, ad loc. and in *Mnemos.* n.s. 56 (1928), 79 f.
For the danger of sexual contamination of food cf. p. 99 below on Posidippus, fr. 1.
[26] Men. *Epit.* 440.
[27] C. Calame, *Les Choeurs de jeunes filles en Grèce archaique*, Rome, 1977, vol. i, *passim*,
esp. Ch. 4.

charm of young creatures helped to make them ministrants especially pleasing to the gods.[28]

In the myths told by Attic poets, young people are sacrificed to the gods as well as serving them. One text states explicitly that only the unmarried can be used for this purpose.[29] The explanation may be that the primary myths of this type, which established the story pattern, were reflections of the mock-deaths of initiates, persons by definition not married.[30] It is hard to see why, in terms of simple pathos, the sacrifice of a young bride or groom would not have been equally effective. On the other hand, since unmarried children are property of the father in a way that married are not, the existing pattern is necessary to create Agamemnon's (like Abraham's) dilemma. At all events, here too status seems a more plausible explanation than mere purity.

Some festivals, though celebrated by the sexually active, were characterized by an emphatic anti-sexual ethos. The most important example at Athens is the Thesmophoria.[31] Men were excluded; cautionary tales described the repulse, in one case even the castration, of male intruders.[32] There is evidence, perhaps not wholly reliable, that in some Greek states all the participants were required to abstain from sex for a preparatory period before the festival, and it is certainly true that in Athens three days abstinence was demanded from the women who were most involved in the ritual. The branches or mats on which the celebrants sat came from a plant believed to have an

[28] Other Athenian ritual roles reserved for *parthenoi*: washing Athena's image, at the Plynteria (Deubner, 18 n. 8); celebrating a *pannychis*, at the Panathenaea (ibid., 25); marching in supplication to the Delphinion (ibid., 201 n. 8). Roles reserved for *paides* (the ubiquitous ephebic processions aside): choirs at Thargelia and Dionysia (ibid., 198 n. 2, 140 n. 1); the Oschophoria (ibid., 143 f.); carrying the *eiresiōnē* (ibid., 199 n. 9); being 'boy from the hearth' (ibid., 75). Of these, purity is most likely to be relevant to washing Athena's image, and being boy from the hearth.

[29] Eur. *Phoen.* 944 f. On such sacrifices cf. Schwenn, 121–39.

[30] The obvious case is Iphigeneia.

[31] Burkert, *GR* 365–70; useful collection of testimonia in K. Dahl, *Thesmophoria, En graesk Kvindefest*, Opuscula Graecolatina 6, Copenhagen, 1976; on the anti-sexual ethos see especially Detienne, *Jardins*, 151–5; on feminine self-assertion, idem, *Eugénies*, *passim*, and on the dissolution of social order W. Burkert, *CQ* n.s. 20 (1970), 1–16.

[32] Hdt. 6. 134.2, Aelian, fr. 44, W. Burkert, op cit., 12. Exclusion of men from temples/festivals of Demeter and Kore is common throughout Greece, Wächter, 130 f., *LSCG* 63.10, *LSA* 61.8–9.

antaphrodisiac effect.[33] These regulations seem to have several
levels of significance. Repelling the male is a kind of symbolic
precondition for that assertion of independence which, by their
nature, 'women's festivals' in a male-dominated society represent. In some cases, such as the Lemnian fire festival, this
temporary rejection of normal patterns of existence seems to be
the rite's main point.[34] At the Thesmophoria, however, the
women do not merely secede for secession's sake, but because
they have specific work to do. In the ritual context, the ideological division of labour between the sexes becomes absolute; as
war belongs to men, so fertility belongs to women, and their
ritual labours would be ruined by any contact with the male.
Superimposed on this simple antithesis, at least in the case of
the Thesmophoria, is the idea that, in order to ensure the
healthy continuance of society, woman must subordinate herself to its strictest norms. The Thesmophoria is a festival of
pious and godly matrons, from which all disorderliness is excluded;[35] woman is here tamed, stripped of the apparatus of

[33] All participants: the Pythagorean lady philosopher Theano, asked after how many
days without intercourse a woman was 'pure enough to go down to the Thesmophoreion', answered that after intercourse with her spouse she was pure at once, and after
intercourse with anyone else, never (Clem. Al. *Strom.* 4.19.302. 1–3 St, Theo, *Progymn.*
5, p. 98.3–7 Spengel, Theodoret, *Graec. Aff. Cur.* 12.73; the same *mot* without reference
to a specific shrine in D.L. 8.43 and Stob. 4.23.53 H.) By implication, therefore, 'going
down to the Thesmophoreion' did normally require preliminary abstinence. But the
anecdote, unlikely anyway to be pre-hellenistic, refers to no specific community or
festival (on 'Theano' cf. v. Fritz in *RE* s.v. *Theano*, col. 1380). Ovid's Ceres festival with
9 days of abstinence (*Met.* 10. 434–5), often quoted in this context, in fact reflects the
Roman *Sacrum Anniversarium Cereris* (H. Le Bonniec, *Le Culte de Cérès à Rome*, Paris, 1958.
408–10); this ceremony is Greek in origin (Le Bonniec, 386 f.), but probably derives
from one of the extended Demeter festivals of Magna Graecia (ibid., 420–3) rather than
directly from the Thesmophoria. Ar. fr. 317, cf. 329, indicates abstinence at the
Thesmophoria, possibly preparatory. 3 days abstinence: schol. Lucian 276.5 Rabe
(Deubner, 40 n. 5). Antaphrodisiac plants: Fehrle, 139–54.

[34] Cf. Burkert, loc. cit. Burkert suggests the same for the Skira (*HN* 164), at which
women chewed garlic to keep their men away (Philochorus 328 *FGrH* fr. 89), but they
may have had positive work to do. The exclusion of men from Dionysiac rites (Wächter,
132) is, of course, rebellious. It is almost always from rites of Demeter and Dionysus
that men are shut out (Wächter, 130–3). For the concept of 'women's festival' cf. *LSCG*
36. 8–12, Ar. *Thesm.* 834 f. On the religious role of women cf. Eur. *Melanippe Desmotis*, fr.
6. 12–22 v. Arnim.

[35] Ar. *Thesm.* 330, cf. Detienne, *Jardins*, 152, *Eugénies*, 196 f., quoting Callim. fr. 63.
9–12 against Burkert to prove exclusion of *parthenoi*. Exclusion of non-slave concubines
is not certain, however: cf. Men. *Epit.* 749 f. (more important than Lucian, *Dial. Meret.*
2.1), on which Deubner, 54 is special pleading. Athenian exclusiveness was probably a

sexual attraction,[36] forced to sit, fasting, on the hard ground.
The celebrants of the Thesmophoria are termed 'bees', the pure
type of ideal womanhood.[37] (The respectable bees are, of
course, likely to have relished the conspicuous distinction made
at the Thesmophoria between themselves and rowdy dog-
women of dubious stock.) A final layer of significance derives,
perhaps, from contrast. Sexual abstinence is required before
and during the Thesmophoria precisely because, without sexuality, there can be no fertility. The ritual focuses attention on
the idea of productive sexual union by a paradoxical temporary
insistence upon its opposite. Everything marks the period of
abstinence as abnormal; virgins, who are permanently pure,
have no part in the rites.[38]

A similar argument allows us to see another Athenian
women's festival, the Haloa, as affirming the same moral norms
as the Thesmophoria, although by opposite means. The tone
here was licentious; priestesses whispered to the married women,
urging them to adultery.[39] The festival thus challenged the
rules, but not with intent to overthrow them; once the festival
was over, the rules reasserted their claims with renewed
insistence.

For the logical counterpoise to such women's rites, we must
look outside Athens. At several places in Greece, women were

special development: contrast for Eretria L. Doria, *Cahiers du centre Jean Berard* 5,
Naples, 1979, 62 f.

[36] Sacred laws from Peloponnesian cults of Demeter Thesmophoros or similar goddesses ban embroidered robes, purple robes, make-up, gold ornaments: *LSS* 32, 33, ?
28, *LSCG* 68, 65. 16–23. Such garb denotes the prostitute: Phylarchus 81 *FGrH* fr. 45,
Diod. 12.21.1, Clem. Al. *Paed.* 2.10. p. 220. 6–9 St. Schol. Soph. *OC* 680 records: φασὶ
τὰς θεὰς ἀνθίνοις μὴ κεχρῆσθαι ἀλλὰ καὶ ταῖς Θεσμοφοριαζούσαις τὴν τῶν ἀνθίνων στεφάνων
ἀπειρῆσθαι χρῆσιν ; it is tempting to suppose that the ban extended to 'flowered robes',
typical dress of the prostitute (Sud. & Phot. s.v. ἑταιρῶν ἀνθινῶν). The long list of
female garments in Aristophanes' second *Thesmophoriazousai* (fr. 320, cf. 321) perhaps
relates to such rules.
[37] Apollodorus 244 *FGrH* fr. 89, cf. L. Bodson, 'Ἱερὰ Ζῶια, Brussels, 1978, 25 ff., for
bees and Demeter. Bees and sexual virtue: M. Detienne, 'Orphée au miel', in *Faire de
l'histoire*, ed. J. Le Goff and P. Nora, iii, Paris, 1974, 56–75, H. F. North, *Illinois Classical
Studies* 2 (1977), 35–48. Cf. the oath of marital fidelity in *LSCG* 65.8. Such ideals are not
confined to Demeter cults, however: cf. the skolion *PMG* 901.
[38] Cf. A. D. Nock, 'Eunuchs in Ancient Religion', *ARW* 23 (1925), 25–33, reprinted
in Nock, i, 7–15.
[39] Schol. Lucian 280. 16–17 Rabe (Deubner, 61 n. 5).

excluded from the cult of Heracles, while, in Phocis, the hero
bore the title 'woman-hater'.[40] We have no evidence about
sexual restrictions imposed on ordinary participants in these
cults, but at Phocis the priest was bound, exceptionally, to a
year's celibacy. At first sight there is a contradiction between
the lusts of the mythological Heracles and the misogynism of his
cult. It can perhaps be resolved by seeing Heracles as the hero
who performs male activities, including seduction and procreation, supremely well, but requires protection from certain kinds
of feminine influence to preserve his excellence. Even
mythologically, Heracles is under threat from women; a goddess dogs him, a queen enslaves him, his wife 'man-slaughterer'
eventually destroys him. Through Heracles, we discern a more
general sense of masculine force endangered by the arts of
women; the idea is comprehensible on the level of the seductress
who unmans men, or the wife who poisons them, but also in the
terms of Book 6 of the *Iliad*.[41] Isolated from such dangers, the
worshippers of Heracles the woman-hater prepare themselves
for the work of men. Actual sexual abstinence in preparation for
hunting and warfare is not demonstrable in the historical
period; where abstinence is attested, as for athletes, it can
perhaps be explained pragmatically.[42] It is, however, probably
significant that the separation of the sexes was particularly
emphasized in connection with certain characteristically
masculine activities: women might not set foot in the council
house of at least one Greek state, or in the stadium at

[40] *LSS* 63, *LSA* 42 A, Ael. *NA* 17.46, Plut. *De Pyth. Or.* 20, 403f (Phocis). Cf. L. R. Farnell, *Greek Hero Cults and Ideas of Immortality*, Oxford, 1921, 162 f.; Ch. Picard, *BCH* 47 (1923), 246–9; B. Bergquist, *Herakles on Thasos*, Uppsala, 1973, 85.

[41] Seductress: Hom. *Od.* 10.340 f. Poisons: Eur. fr. 464, Men. fr. 718.9. Antiphon 1, Dem. 25.79. *Iliad* 6: J. Kakridis, *Homer Revisited*, Lund, 1971, Ch. 3, Griffin, 6, W. Schadewalt, *Von Homers Welt und Werk*⁴, Stuttgart, 1965, 207–33.

[42] War: *pace* G. Murray, *The Rise of the Greek Epic*⁴, Oxford, 1934, 133. Hes. *Scut.* 14–22 is a rather different case. Hunting: Burkert, *SH* 118, cf. *HN* 72 n. 12, sees a reflection in e.g. Hippolytus; but the well-attested link of hunting and virginity in Greek mythology seems rather to reflect the values and activities of an age set, cf. M. Detienne, *Dionysos mis à mort*, Paris, 1977, Ch. 2. Athletics: Aeschylus *Theori/Isthmiastae*, 29–31, with Lloyd-Jones's comment, Loeb Aeschylus vol. ii, p. 544; Pl. *Leg.* 839e–840a; Burkert, *HN* 117 n. 43.

Olympia.[43] It was probably for similar reasons that women were sometimes excluded from the cults of Poseidon, Zeus, and Ares, all emphatically masculine gods. A brief entry in a sacrificial calendar from Mykonos is revealing: 'To Poseidon Phykios, a white lamb with testicles. Women not admitted'.[44]

While these cults that emphasized sexual division were quite common, it was only seldom, to judge from the surviving evidence, that the layman was required to keep himself pure in preparation for a festival. Apart from the Thesmophoria, only two instances are attested early, and even these, like the Thesmophoria on the more sceptical interpretation, concern not the whole body of participants, but restricted groups who were to play an important part in the ritual. At the Athenian Anthesteria, the women who prepared the *archon basileus*' wife for her sacred marriage to Dionysus swore that they were 'pure from unclean things in general, and especially from intercourse with a man'.[45] There seems to be a parody of oaths of this kind in the *Lysistrata*, and they may well have been much more frequent than we know.[46] In the attested case, the symbolic point was surely to keep the mystic union with the god free from all taint of merely human sexuality. For the same reason, in myth, gods always chose virgin brides.[47] During the festival of Zeus Polieus

---

[43] Council house: Ath. 150 a (Naucratis); S. G. Miller, *The Prytaneion*, California, 1978, 11, states that the rule applies more widely, but without citing evidence. If magistrates celebrate Aphrodisia at the end of their term (Xen. *Hell.* 5.4.4), that is partly because Aphrodite is patroness of magistrates, but also an expression of responsibility laid aside (Plut. *Comp. Cim. et Lucull.* 1.3, cf. F. Croissant and F. Salviat, *BCH* 90 (1966), 460–71). Stadium at Olympia: Wächter, 126 (maidens were admitted but not married women, Paus. 6.20.9).

[44] *LSCG* 96.9. Women excluded from cults of Zeus: *LSCG* 109, *LSS* 88b, 89 (the exceptional exclusion of women from the cult of Athene Apotropaios in *LSS* 88a, b seems to derive from her close relationship to Zeus). From cult of Ares: Paus. 2.22.6 f., with Nilsson, *GF* 408. From the shrine of the Anakes at Elateia: *LSCG* 82. The character of the violently misogynist hero Eunostos (Plut. *Quaest. Graec.* 40) is uncertain. Uncertain cult: *LSCG* 124. 18–20. A few further exclusions, Wächter, 126–9; cf. Halliday on Plut. *Quaest. Graec.* 40.

[45] (Dem.) 59.78; on the marriage, Burkert, *HN* 255–63. On abstinence by laymen cf. Fehrle, 126–154, and p. 82 n. 33 above.

[46] Ar. *Lys.* 181–237, note esp. the hieratic word ἀταύρωτος in 217. And in Men. *Epit.* 440 ἁγνὴ γάμων γάρ, φασίν, ἡμέραν τρίτην|ἤδη κάθημαι, note esp. φασίν.

[47] Cf. P. Maas, *Kleine Schriften*, Munich, 1973, 66. The mothers of Plato and Alexander were, in popular story, avoided by their husbands after the divine visitation that sowed the famous sons, D.L.3.2, Plut. *Alex.* 2.6, Fehrle, 3.

on Cos, the citizen appointed to sacrifice the bull was required 'to keep pure for a night from woman and [? man]'.[48] In this case, it is hard to find an explanation in the character of the ritual, beyond the fact that this was a sacrifice of high dignity and importance. If more evidence were available, we might find that preliminary abstinence could be imposed on any layman who was to participate significantly in a ritual of especial solemnity, whatever the source of that solemnity might be. It is very plausible, for instance, that there were rules of this kind for the Eleusinian initiate; no trace, however, remains.

Abstinence was probably sometimes observed in response to oracles or other divine signs. When he consulted Delphi about his childlessness, Aigeus was told not to indulge sexually for a fixed period, and it is not implausible that the mythological response reflects actual oracular practice.[49] By the logic of contrast, there is an obvious suitability in refraining from sexual contact as a preparation for procreation. Religious fear might lead to abstinence, if we accept the implications of the story that King Agis shunned his wife for ten months after an earthquake in the night.[50] But in such cases it is not purification from the taint of sexuality that is desired.

If abstinence is sometimes required of laymen performing priestly functions, it might *a fortiori* be expected of priests. The idea of religious abstinence was certainly a familiar one. When Euripides' Electra reveals that her husband has never approached her, her brother asks at once 'Is he under some sacred requirement of purity?'[51] It should be stressed at once, however, that 'sacred requirements of purity' that imposed long periods of abstinence were exceptional. In the classical period, most priests and priestesses throughout the Greek world were either married people conducting normal family lives, who may at the

---

[48] *LSCG* 151 A 42–4 (only the 'slaughterer' is so bound, not all participants, *pace* Fehrle, 155 n. 1). According to Nilsson, *GF* 21, chastity is required because this is a guilty sacrifice, like the Athenian Buphonia. Is the link with Hestia (lines 19, 25, 28) relevant?

[49] Eur. *Med.* 665–81, Plut. *Thes.* 3.5.

[50] Plut. *Alc.* 23.9, *Ages.* 3.9; the story is based on a misunderstanding of Xen. *Hell.* 3.3.2, but might none the less reflect a real possibility.

[51] Eur. *El.* 256, cf. *Tro.* 501; cf. Fehrle, 75–111 (interpretations very dubious). On Greek priests see Stengel 31–48, Ziehen in *RE* s.v. *Hiereis*, Burkert, *GR* 157–63: a monograph is required.

most have been bound to temporary periods of chastity, or married people past the age of frequent sexual activity. It is because they are not the rule that we hear specifically from Pausanias of 'virgin priestesses' and the like. Any more rigorous requirements would be surprising in a society where sacred functions were often attached to political office, and tenure of a priesthood seldom formed the centre of the holder's existence.

About the marital status required for the many priesthoods in Athens,[52] explicit evidence is almost entirely lacking. Of the careers of individual incumbents we sometimes know something, but in the case, for instance, of a statue of a priestess dedicated by her son, it is impossible to be sure whether she already held the office during her child-bearing period. Plato and Aristotle agree that in the ideal state priesthoods should be assigned to the elderly. Plato's specification is particularly interesting: 'The man who is going to be sufficiently pure for divine service, as sacred laws require, should be over 60 years old.'[53] A priesthood, therefore, might impose requirements of abstinence which a younger man would find hard to observe and, as Plato does not seek to justify or explain such requirements, they must have been familiar in Athenian practice. His remark does not indicate in itself whether abstinence would be expected throughout tenure of the office (a year, by Plato's rule) or merely for a few days in preparation for particular ceremonies. A year's abstinence for a male is once attested, but that, as we have seen, is outside Attica, and in the fiercely anti-sexual cult of Heracles 'woman-hater'.[54] Since many priesthoods were held 'for life', it is more attractive to suppose that they entailed, at most, short periods of purity. Eleusis is the only cult for which restrictions of this kind are mentioned in the sources, and there, though the view that the hierophant was bound to permanent chastity from the moment of taking up office cannot be formally refuted, it is more plausible to suppose, since he could retain his wife while in office, that he was simply required to remain

---

[52] The antiquated book of J. Martha, *Les Sacerdoces Athéniens*, Paris, 1882, has not been replaced, except for Eleusis, on which see Clinton. For priestesses cf. H. McClees, *A study of women in Attic Inscriptions*, diss. Columbia, 1920, 5–16, 45; Jordan, 28–36.

[53] Pl. *Leg.* 759d, Arist. *Pol.* 1329a 27–34. Plato specifies the same age for priestesses.

[54] Plut. *De Pyth. Or.* 20, 403f.

chaste for a period before the mysteries.[55] Details, unfortunately, are not available either for this or for any other cult in Attica or Greece as a whole.[56]

As the typical image of the priest in Attic literature is of an old man, it is likely that Plato and Aristotle, in their preference for the old, are reflecting a tendency of Athenian practice.[57] But we hear explicitly of aged ministrants only in the case of Athena's sacred lamp, tended by women who had 'finished with sex',[58] and there is no doubt that Athenians could be appointed to priesthoods while still in their sexual prime. Lysimache, priestess of Athena Polias for sixty-four years, obviously took up office while still young; she almost certainly had offspring, and it is scarcely plausible to assume that the sixty-four years of office began only after her child-bearing days were over.[59] The first priestess of Athena Nike perhaps held office for almost half

[55] cf. Foucart, 171–3; Töpffer, 54; Burkert, *HN* 313; Clinton, 44. The relevant facts are: (1) various texts, of which Arrian, *diss. Epict.* 3.21.16 is the earliest, refer to the hierophant's abstinence, often referring it to the use of antaphrodisiac drugs; (2) Paus. 2.14.1, in a list of differences between the hierophants of Phlius and Eleusis, mentions that the former may 'take a wife, if he wishes'; it is hard to see why Paus. includes this point unless it constitutes one of the differences. Note, however, that Paus. speaks of 'taking' and not 'having' a wife; (3) numerous children of hierophants are attested; they may, of course, have been begotten before their father was hierophant; (4) *IG* II² 3512 shows that a hierophant could have a wife while in office. (2) and (4) are readily reconciled on the view that a hierophant could retain a wife while in office but not acquire one. It is conceivable, though scarcely credible, that the hierophant could have avoided all sexual contact with the wife he retained; but Arrian, loc. cit. uses the term ἁγνεύω, normally applied to temporary abstinence. For the idea of προειρημένον ἡμερῶν ἀριθμὸν ἁγνεύειν see Dem. 22.78, quoted p. 97 below.

[56] Non-Attic evidence for *ad hoc* priestly *hagneia* is almost non-existent. Nothing in *LSCG* 154 A, 156 A 1–16; *LSCG* 156 B 29–35 may have treated the subject, but is beyond reconstruction; *LSCG* 83.40 is vague (as is *LSA* 79.6).

[57] Soph. *OT* 18, and in general Hom. *Il.* 1. 26, 6. 298–300 (Antenor, the priestess's husband, is a δημογέρων, 3. 149), Hes. fr. 321. Cf. Clinton, 44.

[58] Plut. *Num.* 9.11; on this lamp cf. R. Pfeiffer, *Ausgewählte Schriften*, Munich, 1960, 4–7. Burkert, without argument, seems to identify these aged attendants of the lamp with the actual priestess of Athena Polias (in whose temple the lamp was), *HN* 168 n. 59, *GR* 337; but the case of e.g. Lysimache, discussed in the text, refutes this. One might rather see the lamp's attendant in the kind of aged διάκονος to the Polias priestess mentioned Paus. 1.27.4 (cf. *IG* II² 3464). For priestly office held by those who have 'done with sex' cf. Fehrle, 95 n. 1, Paus. 2.10.4, 7.25.13, *GRBS* 14 (1973), 65–73.

[59] 64 years: Pliny, *NH* 34.76. Offspring: *IG* II² 3453, with D. M. Lewis, *ABSA* 50 (1955), 4–6, who ibid., 7–12 collects the evidence for priestesses of Athena Polias (cf. Davies, 170–3). The daughter of Polyeuktos (Lewis, n. 4) had a husband while priestess (*IG* II² 776. 22–30); the husband at some date had a son, presumably by her (*IG* II² 5610, Davies, 72). Chrysis (Lewis, n. 10) had 'descendants', *IG* II² 1136.15. In favour of seeing the Polias priestess as post-sexual, there is only (Plut.) *X. orat.* 843b on

a century, and the regulation that established her post contained no specification about marital status.[60] It has even been argued that Aristophanes' Lysistrata and Myrrhine, the latter at least wedded to a demanding husband, are none other than the priestesses of these two cults of Athena.[61]

The two most important male officials of the Eleusinian cult, the hierophant and the daduch, could both be married, although the hierophant was probably not permitted to take a new wife while in office. Priests in other cults, it may be assumed, will not have been more restricted than the hierophant.[62] The chief female officials at Eleusis, the priestess of Demeter and Kore and the hierophantids, had normally been married, and, though it is not demonstrable that their marriages continued while they held office, there is no positive evidence to the contrary; the fact that they might live in special 'houses of the priestess(es)' does not seem necessarily to exclude the presence of a husband.[63] The priestess of Nemesis at Rhamnus could be a mother, but here too it is possible that she had 'finished with sex' before assuming office.[64] For the cult of Demeter Thesmophoros, however, an honorific decree fortunately pays tribute to a lady indisputably equipped with a husband while serving as priestess.[65]

Philippe (Lewis, n. 11) who 'afterwards became priestess of Athene, but before that Diokles married her and begot . . .'. In view of the other evidence cited, that must represent an isolated case, or at most a later development. Other married women involved in Athene cult: *SEG* xxiv 116, *IG* II² 2342.31.

[60] First priestess *SEG* xii 80; regulations *IG* I³ 35 = M/L 44. For the chronological problems see M/L. Or was this post annual?

[61] D. M. Lewis, *ABSA* 50(1955), 1–7; note however K. J. Dover, *Aristophanic Comedy*, London, 1972, 152 n. 3. Jordan believes (35) that Athena Parthenos must have had a distinct priestess, a virgin.

[62] Hierophant: p. 88 n. 55 above. Daduch: Clinton, 67. There remains, as a possible Eleusinian celibate, the mysterious ἱερεὺς παναγής (Clinton, 95 f.), but we can only guess what restrictions governed him, and his very existence before the late 1st century BC relies on a restoration in *IG* I³ 6 C 48. For other Athenian priests who had wives while in office cf. e.g. *IG* II² 3629, 4076 (exegete), 4851.

[63] Priestesses of Demeter and Kore with children: nn. 3, 6, 10, and 16 in Clinton's catalogue (68–76). Hierophantides with children: nn. 3, 4, 5, 7, 10, 11 (86–9). Houses: Clinton, 20, 71 (the celibate Pythia had a special house at Delphi, Parke/Wormell 44 n. 84). Cf. n. 65 below.

[64] *IG* II² 3462. For a priestess of Helios dedicated by her son cf. ibid., 3578.

[65] *Hesperia* 11 (1942), p. 265 n. 51, whose evidence remains important even if the cult is of a deme and not, as its editor thinks (270–2), of the state. If Clinton, 71, were right that this priestess of the Thesmophoroi was none other than the priestess of Demeter

In contrast to the considerable evidence for those who were or had been married, it is very hard to identify virgin priests or priestesses at Athens. The priestess of Artemis at Brauron was perhaps one, but might, if so, have renounced her office at marriage.[66] Virgin priestesses of Artemis reflect the nature of the goddess and, more particularly, of her young adherents; rather than reflecting a general ideal of virginity, they embody the values of a particular age set.[67] The priestess of Demeter Thesmophoros has now been released, as we saw, by inscriptional evidence from the perpetual virginity to which a scholion on Lucian condemned her; and scholars have been too hasty in establishing a community of celibate priestesses at Eleusis.[68] A

and Kore (but why then the different title?), the problem about the marital status of the latter would be resolved. At all events, the new text refutes the wild fantasies (surprisingly accepted by Burkert, *GR* 368) of schol. Lucian *Dial. Meret.* 7.4, p. 279. 21 Rabe, and *Timon* 17, p. 112.5 R. Lucian himself in *Tim.* 17 (the other passage is vaguer) refers to a man who does not approach his young bride, but neglects her, καθάπερ ἱέρειαν τῇ Θεσμοφόρῳ τρέφων διὰ παντὸς τοῦ βίου. I am not sure that this implies more than temporary abstinence ('for life' can be referred to the boorish man, not the priestess), but even if it does, it will not make the priestess of Thesmophoros a virgin. Anyway, Lucian surely alludes not to Attica but to the kind of rite that lay behind the *Sacrum Anniversarium Cereris* (p. 82 n. 33), in which similar regulations for the priestess are found (unless indeed we are dealing with a late development that affected the cults both of 'Ceres' and 'Thesmophoros'). Further evidence for priestesses married while in office: *IG* II² 1316 (cf. *SEG* xvii 36), 3607, 3725, Posidippus, fr. 26.21 *ap.* Ath. 377b.

[66] There is no direct evidence (for the allusions to her cf. Jordan, 34; the identification of a married incumbent in *CJ* 74 (1979), 361 is unfounded.) Indirect evidence, not conclusive, comes from Eur. *IT* 1462– 3 (the virgin Iphigeneia to be first priestess, cf. 130–1). Her responsibilities (Linders, 52 f.) seem too great for a young girl. *IG* II² 2874 gives a lifelong priestess of Artemis, probably in the cult at Oinoe (cf. S. Solders, *Die ausserstädtischen Kulte und die Einigung Attikas*, Lund, 1931, 30).

[67] On virgin priestesses of Artemis cf. Fehrle, 98–102 – whose argument, however, that the presence of virgin ministrants proves the goddess to have been originally a fertility mother is quite misguided. This relation of contrast between god and servant does occur (Paus. 2.10.4 is the paradigm case, cf. Burkert, *GR* 162), but perhaps not for contrast's sake; Fehrle's own material shows virgin priestesses to be much commoner in the cult of virgin goddesses, married women observing abstinence, or women 'finished with sex', in the cult of Demeter and the like. U. Pestalozza, *Religione mediterranea*, Milan, 1951, 235–59 (= *SMSR* 9 (1933), 173–202) has wild speculation on 'Sacerdoti e Sacerdotesse impuberi nei culti di Athena e di Artemide'.

[68] Pollux 1.35 reads in Bethe's text: ἱεροφάνται, δᾳδοῦχοι, κήρυκες, σπονδοφόροι, ἱέρειαι, παναγεῖς. The comma before παναγεῖς should probably go, as there is nothing distinctively Eleusinian about ἱέρειαι, but 2 MSS of Poll. give not ἱέρειαι but ἱερεῖς, and this should surely be accepted, as the ἱερεὺς παναγής is inscriptionally attested (Clinton, 96), and παναγής for Pollux (1.14) is a male title. Entries like Hesych. παναγεῖς· Ἀθήνησι ἱέρειαι, ibid., παναγία· ἱέρεια ἥτις οὐ μίσγεται ἀνδρί (cf. Foucart, 214 n. 5), seem to be

fine imaginative portrait of a virginal temple servant we do have, however, in Euripides' Ion.[69] This fresh, innocent, devoted youth warns us against interpreting the ideal of purity, in the case of the young, too narrowly. In Ion, an intact body houses a mind uncontaminated by joyless and cynical thoughts. Ion's chaste temple service, however, is no more than a stage in his life.

After this survey of the evidence, some tentative conclusions about cultic chastity can now be drawn. A possible line of interpretation would be structural.[70] The Greeks, like other societies, divided the affairs of the world into sacred and profane, and this basic dichotomy was naturally extended into the sexual sphere. Profane life is, necessarily, sexual; to approach the sacred men must therefore become asexual. A minimum division from the profane is achieved by the worshipper who washes before access to the temples, a maximum by the lifelong virgin priestess. Such an account is probably an accurate description of some part of a Greek's sentiments: the closer a mortal comes to sacred objects, the more acute becomes his need for sexual purity.[71] If an explanation is needed as to why sexuality is drawn into the contrast between sacred and profane at all, it must lie in that embarrassment about bodily functions discussed earlier, which naturally aligned sexuality with the less honourable pole in the antithesis. We must emphasize, however, that the opposition between gods and mortals is not the only one in play; there is also that between statuses (unmarried and married) and between sexes. The significance of chastity or abstinence varies accordingly: the hierophant before the mysteries seeks to free himself from the taint of the physical: the Phocian Heracles priest shuns women to protect his god

based on corrupt texts or misunderstanding and are perhaps influenced by Christianity. References to 'priestesses' in an Eleusinian context (Foucart, 215) can be applied to the hierophantids and the priestess of Demeter and Kore (so too the probably Eleusinian ἱρείας . . . σαόφρονα Κύπριν ἐχούσας of *IG* II² 3606.15, which anyway does not imply absolute celibacy). For probably chaste Demeter priestesses in Hermione, but only attested late, cf. Th. Reinach, *BCH* 32 (1908), 505.

[69] His virginity, 150. Other virginal temple servants in Eur. *IT* 130.
[70] E. R. Leach, *Culture and Nature or La Femme Sauvage*, Stevenson Lecture for 1968, 11.
[71] Whence, in the practice of later antiquity, most magical acts demand preliminary abstinence: Fehrle, 50 n. 6.

from contamination by the feminine: the virgin priestess of
Artemis provides a model of virtue appropriate to young girls
not yet in flower. The language of 'purity' is used in all three
cases, but it can indicate resistance to several distinct forms of
contamination.

It is also important to note that these ritual rules give rise to
no positive ideal of chastity. Abstinence, though equipping the
worshipper to approach the temples and sacred objects of the
gods, does not render him godlike himself. Even Hippolytus by
his purity wins the favour of but one goddess. It is less in order
to be a certain kind of person that chastity is required than in
order to enter certain places, touch certain objects, view certain
sights.[72] It may have been more common to appoint humble
sacristans than actual priests from among those who, by
reason of their age, were necessarily pure, because their
mundane duties brought them into more frequent contact with
the temple.[73] Connected with this is the failure to assign positive
value to the self-denial that continence demands. Control over
sexual desire was indeed, in Greek values, an important part of
both male and female excellence, but this was rather because
indulgence might divert both sexes from their essential virtues
than because self-mortification was esteemed in itself. The
answer of the Cynics to the problem of lust was submission
without emotional commitment, not resistance.[74] In ritual
practice, it is hard to find even a limited attempt to present
continence positively as an aspect of self-mastery. Young
children and the aged are chosen for the posts that would
impose real restraints on the sexually mature, while sacred fires
are guarded, not by perpetual virgins, but by women who 'have
done with sex'.[75] Purity and innocence may be associated with
the 'intact boys and girls' of cult, but they are treated as the
virtues of a particular stage of life rather than as a general ideal,
or a necessary consequence of celibacy. It is for marriage that
Artemis' 'bears' are preparing themselves.

To these generalizations, the 'virgin priestess for life', where

---

[72] Dem. 22.78 (entering, touching); (Dem.) 59.73, 85 (sacrificing, seeing, entering,
doing), 78 (touching).
[73] e.g. Plut. *Num.* 9.11, Eur. *Ion* 150, Paus. 2.10.4.
[74] Dover, 208, 212 f.
[75] Eur. *Ion* 150, Plut. *De Pyth. Or.* 20, 403f, Pl. *Leg.* 759d, Plut. *Num.* 9. 11.

she existed, was an exception. There is a significant distinction, seldom drawn sufficiently sharply, between the virgin priestess who laid down her office at marriage, and the 'virgin priestess for life'; for the one, her office was a mere preliminary to the natural goal of women's life, while in the other case it was a substitute for it. It may thus be no coincidence that firm evidence for the 'virgin priestess for life' is very hard to find.[76] The prophetess at Delphi was in theory a maiden (the god could not possess a body given over to the pleasure of a mortal) and was certainly bound to strict chastity during her tenure of office, but in practice the post was normally filled by an old woman, who will, since spinsterhood was not a recognized estate, certainly once have been married.[77] As we have seen, no such priesthoods are securely attested at Athens. The most interesting evidence comes once again from Euripides. His Theonoe is and will remain a virgin; she is wrapped in a mysterious sanctity, peculiarly righteous, and has abnormal understanding of the inner counsels of the gods. There is no doubt that positive religious capacities are here being treated as dependent on virginity.[78] It might be wrong, however, to relate Theonoe's powers merely to purity from a physical taint. Withdrawal from the sexual structure of society brings with it withdrawal from the social structure, and it seems that Theonoe can submit herself to the gods so completely because like submission is not required of her by a husband. There is a kind of analogy between such a woman and sacrificial animals, or sacred land, 'let go' by mortals for the use of the gods.[79] This conception may often have

[76] The only case I can find is Paus. 9.27.6, Heracles' priestess at Thespiae. In the more reliable tradition the 'Locrian maidens' served for a year only, cf. F. Graf, *SSR* 2 (1978), 61–79 (with persuasive initiatory interpretation).

[77] Parke/Wormell, 1.35; cf. 36 for a Pythia with progeny. Apollo's prophetess at Argos, γυνὴ ἀνδρὸς εὐνῆς εἰργομένη (Paus. 2.24.1), was perhaps also post-sexual. The conception of the prophetess as the god's bride (Fehrle, 7 ff., 79; K. Latte, *HTR* 33 (1940), 9–18, *RE* 18. 840; Burkert, *HN* 143) is hinted at mythologically, esp. in the figure of Cassandra (Aesch. *Ag.* 1202–12), but was certainly not enacted ritually in Greece; the sacred marriage in Patara is for Hdt. (1.182) a foreign custom, tinged with charlatanism. It is in a less precise sense that the prophetess is reserved for the god (on this reservation cf. Eur. *Tro.* 251–8). Old women at Dodona too, Strabo 7.7.12, cf. L. Bodson, Ἱερὰ Ζῶια, Brussels, 1978, 101 ff.

[78] Eur. *Hel.* 10–15, 865–72, 876–91, 894, 939, 1006–8. R. Kannicht (*Euripides Helena*, Heidelberg, 1969, i, 75) points out that Theonoe's vocation appears as a substitute for marriage in 12 f.

[79] See Eur. *Tro.* 41–2.

been important where virgin priestesses existed; and the independence that virginity offered was certainly significant in
forming the image of virgin goddesses.[80] But it is hard to know
how far familiar Greek attitudes are expressed through the
exotic Theonoe.

The regulations we have considered so far have been concerned, almost exclusively, with sexuality, not sexual morality.
Only in the hellenistic period, as we have noted, does intercourse with another man's wife become more polluting than
intercourse with one's own. A Coan law cited earlier shows, if
correctly restored, that on the ritual level no distinction is
drawn between heterosexual and homosexual contact.[81] Not all
the forms of union, however, which create impurity in the later
laws were subject to moral stigma in the classical period. In
sleeping with a courtesan, or a boy, there was no necessary
disgrace. At Athens, it is really only the adulterous male who
was subject to legal penalties and moral disapproval, but free,
so far as the evidence goes, from ritual disabilities. And it is
worth stating with some emphasis that the two classes of sexual
offender whom society most savagely condemned were permanently excluded from the shrines. There was no question of the
convicted adulteress, or the male prostitute, acquiring the right
to worship with respectable citizens through a simple period of
abstinence.[82]

These exclusions are, of course, aspects of *atimia*, deprivation
of citizen rights, and similar restrictions were placed on other
classes of discredited persons, such as state debtors and
deserters.[83] Deserters are excluded from the shrines not because
they are polluted and dangerous, but because they have sacrificed their right to a place in the community of citizens. It is

---

[80] See Wilamowitz on Eur. *HF* 834, Burkert, *GR* 284 f.

[81] *LSCG* 151 A 42 (addressed to a man), ἀγνεύεσθαι γυναικὸς καὶ ἀ [   ]ς where either
ἀνδρός or ἄρσενος is hard to avoid (ἀμίδος Paton-Hicks, cf. Ath. 150a, too demand-
ingly). This text apart, the possibility of homosexual contact seems not even to be
envisaged in early ritual rules.

[82] Adulterous woman: (Dem.) 59. 85–7; Aeschin. 1.183; prostituted male: Aeschin.
1. 19, 21, 160, 164, 188; Dem. 22.30, 73, 77; 24.126.

[83] Harrison, ii, 168–76; G. E. M. de Ste. Croix, *The Origins of the Peloponnesian War*,
London, 1972, 397 f.

natural to interpret the case of the sexual offenders in the same way; although their deeds are described in the language of pollution,[84] it is because they are disgraced, not because they are dangerous, that they are banned from religious life. The point is an important one, as it distinguishes the position in Greece from that of the many societies where sexual irregularities are indeed seen as sources of religious danger, causing disease or crop failure.[85] The Greeks very probably saw incest as a pollution of this kind, although this is surprisingly hard to demonstrate; but in expressing the wish that sodomy and adultery could become unthinkable acts like incest, Plato acknowledges their actual status to be different.[86] It is hard to show that the adulteress or male prostitute is endangered or dangerous on any supernatural level. If the people of Cyme avoided as 'impure' the stones on which they exposed adulteresses to humiliation, the ascription of impurity was itself part of the process of humiliation. One can imagine that a wronged Athenian husband might have purified the marriage bed, or might have feared the consequences if he disobeyed the legal requirement to put his 'polluted' wife away, but such unease would be a consequence of society's moral condemnation of the adulteress rather than its cause. The worst automatic punishment for sexual crimes is no more than attack by bees; hostile to sexuality in any form, they especially abhor adulterers, and sting them savagely, disgusted by their smell.[87]

A question arises about the application of the term 'pollution'. If we mean by it behaviour that is felt to subvert the moral foundation of society, so that the guilty persons must be ex-

---

[84] Adultery 'pollutes' the bed: Eur. *Hipp.* 1266, *Or.* 575, *Hel.* 48 (cf. *Hec.* 366), *Anth. Pal.* 3.5.2; it pollutes those threatened by it: Eur. *Hipp.* 601–6, 653–4, 946, ? Soph. *Inachus*, fr. 269 a 24 Radt. Αἰσχύνω similarly used: Hes. fr. 176.7, Eur. *Hipp.* 408, 420, 944, 1165, 1172, Men. *Sam.* 507, and regularly to denote rape. Adulteress excluded from shrines 'to prevent pollutions', (Dem.) 59.86. Male prostitute 'impure in body': Aeschin. 1.19, 188; 2.88; on the 'unclean mouth' he acquires see below.

[85] Douglas, Ch. 8.

[86] Pl. *Leg.* 838a–9a.

[87] Cyme: Plut. *Quaest. Graec.* 2, 291e–f; for archaic institutions preserved at Cyme see Arist. *Pol.* 1269a 1–3, Latte, *HR* 32, and for public humiliations of adulterers (and others) Halliday on Plut. loc. cit.; Latte, *Hermes* 66 (1931), 155–8 = *Kl. Schr.* 290–3; Lloyd-Jones in *Dionysiaca, Studies presented to Sir Denys Page*, Cambridge, 1978, 58 f.; p. 195 below. Purifying the bed: cf. Prop. 4.8.83–6. Legal requirement: (Dem.) 59.87. Bees: Plut. *Quaest. Nat.* 36.

pelled if that society's essential values are to be preserved,[88] male prostitution and female adultery are clearly pollutions; they undermine respectively the essential qualities of the man – his masculinity[89] – and of the woman – her stewardship of the purity of the stock.[90] Within pollution so defined, however, we will also have to include desertion, debt to the state, and most of the capital crimes. If we require of pollution that it be contagious, and dangerous on a supernatural level, all these offences, including the sexual ones, will be excluded. What matters, of course, is not dispute about the presumed essence behind a word, but a clear distinction between separate phenomena. For the sake of such clarity it might be helpful to put the sexual offences in a category of 'metaphorical moral pollutions': pollutions because they are so described, metaphorical because they are not contagious or dangerous in the same sense as, for instance, murder, and moral to emphasize that the impurity of the adulteress has quite distinct origins from that of the corpse. We are dealing with breaches of social rules – just like desertion in battle – which are spoken of as pollutions because they derive from 'dirty' acts.

The response to these offences is interesting. That there should be unchaste women and boys in the world is no matter for concern; they provide, indeed, a useful outlet for the not unreasonable desires of honest men. It is only among the possessors of 'honour' (full citizen rights) that they are out of place. Offenders are not exiled or put to death but deprived of 'honour' and forced to find a place amid the flotsam of foreignness and vice that laps around the citizen body.[91] The *atimoi* are in an almost literal sense the 'out-casts' of Athenian society.

In respect of the relation between ritual purity and morality, the conclusion must be that, even if 'purity' is in itself amoral, strong factors of a different kind kept the morally discredited from the altar. It is quite misleading to view Greek religion, at

---

[88] Aeschin. 1.183, adulteress excluded ἵνα μὴ τὰς ἀναμαρτήτους τῶν γυναικῶν ἀναμιγνυμένη διαφθείρῃ.

[89] Political enemies revealed by their sexual practices as 'women': Aeschin. 2. 129, 179, Hyp. fr. 215, (Dem.) Ep. 4.11.

[90] Woman as steward in general: T. E. V. Pearce, *Eranos* 72 (1974), 16–33.

[91] Cf. Whitehead, 67 n. 109. But citizens must go out to enjoy the floating world: to introduce *meretrices* to the marital home is appalling, Andoc. 4.14, Ter. *Ad.* 747.

least in its public aspects, as standing beyond or beneath the moral demands of society. This religion was rigorously status-conscious, and status, as we have seen, could be affected by moral conduct. Like its magistrates, those who prayed on the city's behalf had to be truly representative of it; they were required to be of especially pure stock,[92] and they could not have lived licentiously, since those who did were unfit to be citizens at all, let alone to represent the citizen body. Aeschines tells the Athenians not to be surprised at the failures that beset them, when they have a man like Timarchus to draft prayers on their behalf. Thus forms of behaviour that are, in themselves, shameful but not dangerous, become actual sources of religious danger when perpetrated by those holding an office that demands an honourable incumbent. Demosthenes' denunciation of Androtion concludes: 'you have Androtion as repairer of sacred vessels. Androtion! what could be a worse offence against the gods? The man whose job it is to enter temples, touch lustral water and sacred baskets, and take charge of the cult we pay to the gods, ought to have kept pure not just for a fixed number of days, but throughout his life, from the things Androtion has done.' Demochares, having prostituted 'even the upper parts of his body', was 'unfit to blow the sacred fire'. The speech against Neaera is extended testimony to the shock felt at tenure of an important priesthood by a woman of shameful life.[93] One may add that it is very doubtful whether a convicted adulterer, ritually pure though he may have been, would have been considered a suitable candidate for a priesthood.[94]

As was noted earlier, it is difficult to prove that incest is a 'pollution'. Here, too, problems arise about the definition of the term. Incest is nowhere spoken of as a *miasma*, and it does not seem that it was even formally illegal at Athens, much less that the offender was publicly expelled to purify the state.[95] In one passage in Euripides, however, Oedipus is said, immediately after a reference to his marriage, to be 'polluting the city', and

[92] (Dem.) 59.92, Pl. *Leg.* 759c, Ar. *Pol.* 1329a 29 f., *LSA* 73.4–8.
[93] Aeschin. 1.188, Dem. 22.78, Archedikos, fr. 4 = Polyb. 12.13.7 (same point against Demosthenes 76 *FGrH* fr. 8, and cf. Aeschin 2.23, 88), (Dem.) 59.72–117.
[94] cf. Andoc. 1. 124–9, on Callias.
[95] See Harrison, i, 22 n. 3, M. Broadbent, *Studies in Greek Genealogy*, Leiden, 1968, 155. Adkins, 110 n. 17 excludes incest from the pollutions on these grounds.

the idea of religious danger is present in the common claim that such a match is *anosios*, offensive to the gods.[96] The incestuous could be socially isolated without exile, by exclusion from sacrificial communities and marriage exchanges.[97] It was believed in later antiquity that Cimon incurred actual ostracism because of his relations with Elpinice, and the recently discovered ostracon that urges him to 'get out and take his sister with him' suggests that this may indeed have been a factor. The Aeolus of Euripides, sterner than Homer's, put his incestuous daughter to death.[98] On an imaginative level, an analogy is clearly felt between incest (and other gross sexual offences) and the worst pollutions. In the myth of Oedipus, it is associated with parricide. A connection between sex and eating, and thus between forbidden sexual contact and forbidden food, is said to be found throughout the world, and becomes almost explicit in the myths of Thyestes, Tereus, and Clymenus. Thyestes seduced his brother's wife, Tereus his wife's sister, Clymenus his daughter; all were subsequently forced to eat their children's flesh. Plato, too, associates cannibalism and incest, while Aeschylus' Danaids ask, in reference to a forced and perhaps incestuous marriage, 'How could a bird that eats another bird be pure?'[99] Incest, particularly that between generations, is, therefore, one of the supreme horrors of the imagination that define by contrast the norms of ordered existence. It lies in a sense beyond pollution, because it is beyond purification.

   In most societies, sexual behaviour is regulated, in addition to the restraints of decency and morality, by a canon of the 'natural'. This canon may declare illicit any form of sexual relation between certain classes of people, such as members of the same sex, or it may forbid certain acts even when performed by those between whom sexual contact is in itself permissible. It

---

[96] Eur. *Phoen.* 1050; Soph. *OC* 946, Ar. *Ran.* 850, Pl. *Leg.* 838b; pollution language in Ael. *NA* 6.39. cf. too (Plut.) *Par. Min.* 19a, 310b.

[97] Glotz in Dar.-Sagl. s.v. *Incestum*, 450.

[98] Cimon: first in (Andoc.) 4.33, Plut. *Cim.* 4.5–7. The ostracon: see p. 270 below. Other imputations of incest in orators: Lys. 14.28, Lys. fr. 30 Gernet, and cf. Andoc. 1.124–9, (Andoc.) 4.22, ? Isae. 5.39. Aeolus: see Nauck, *TGF*, 365 f.

[99] Pl. *Resp.* 571c–d; Aesch. *Supp.* 226, cf. μιαίνειν γένος in 225. On the relevance of incest to *Supp.* see A. F. Garvie, *Aeschylus' Supplices: Play and Trilogy*, Cambridge, 1969, 216–20; J. K. MacKinnon, *CQ* 28 (1978), 74–82. Note that ἅπτομαι is used both of sexual and dietary crime.

is hard to know quite what belongs in such a category in Greece. The 'unnatural vice' most familiar from our own culture was, it seems, not seen as such, whether performed homosexually or heterosexually, before Plato.[100] Oral sexual acts done by a man conform to the definition in that they are considered revolting even when not morally shameful. 'Anyone who doesn't abominate such a man', says an Aristophanic chorus about Ariphrades, whom it revealingly describes as the 'inventor' of such practices, 'will never drink from the same cup as us.' As we have seen, another comic poet declared that Demochares had in the same way made himself 'unfit to blow the sacred flame'. A cook might, it seems, claim that a rival indulged in these pleasures, and so would taint the food, while the kiss of such a man was to be avoided.[101] These texts agree in expressing revulsion against the practice through a strikingly physical view of the 'pollution' that it causes. The state is not endangered by the fact that people do such things, but those who do them become very dirty, and their misused mouths contaminate all they touch or breathe on. The source of the revulsion seems to be the offence against the body's hierarchy. The most honourable part of the body, and the purest, is the head, and of the head the purest part should be the mouth, which receives food, utters prayer, and implants chaste kisses;[102] it is thus in particular danger of contamination by contact with dirty and shameful

---

[100] K. J. Dover, *Greek Homosexuality*, London 1978, 60, 165–170; heterosexual anal intercourse, ibid. 100–1, and note Hdt. 1. 61. 1 ('irregular', not 'unnatural'). This is not surprising in a culture where homosexuality was probably once a required phase in a youth's education: J. N. Bremmer, 'An Enigmatic Indo-European Rite: Paederasty', *Arethusa* 13.2. (1980), 279–98; cf. P. Cartledge, *PCPS* n.s. 27 (1981), 17–36.

[101] Ariphrades: Ar. *Eq.* 1280–9; he 'pollutes' his tongue, and 'soils' his chin, licking the 'disgusting dew'. Demochares (and Demosthenes): p. 97 n. 93. A cook: Posidippus, fr. 1.5–6 *ap.* Ath. 662a (some textual uncertainty). A kiss: Ar. *Eccl.* 647. Oral sexual acts by the male are not portrayed on vases, G. Henderson, *The Maculate Muse*, Yale, 1975, 51, Dover, op. cit., 99–102. Henderson's belief (51–2) that no disgust is felt about such practices is based on a failure to distinguish between oral sex performed by men and women; the latter is not disgusting, at least when performed by *hetairai*, but might perhaps become so if performed by citizen wives (H. D. Jocelyn, *PCPS* n.s. 26 (1980), 12–66, proves the abusive term *laikazein* to refer to fellation by the woman; in later texts, for which see Courtney on Juvenal 6.51, and Artemid. 4.59, p. 283. 8–16 Pack, oral sex pollutes man and woman alike).

[102] On the head cf. *LSJ* s.v. κεφαλή; the fact that it can become μιαρά proves its normal purity. Religious importance of 'pure mouth': Aesch. *Eum.* 287, *Supp.* 696. Kisses: Kroll on Cat. 79.3.

organs. Considerations of social hierarchy, however, become confused with this simple hierarchy of the body. When performed by a woman, such acts are not revolting, because woman is naturally degraded in relation to man; even when done by a man, it is only when combined with the absolute self-degradation of homosexual prostitution that they are sufficiently outrageous to become a focus for political abuse.[103] Incest, finally, though it was pronounced 'natural' by nature's aggressive supporters, was surely in conventional belief just the opposite, as it violated an unwritten law.[104]

Throughout this discussion of sexual matters, one idea that has played no part is that of the inherent impurity of women, manifested through menstruation. This absence is surprising, both because menstruation is viewed as a pollution by innumerable societies, and particularly because it commonly acts as a symbol on which men's attitudes of suspicion and hostility towards women can focus.[105] For its status as an unconscious symbol of this kind, evidence from New Guinea in particular is quoted, where, it is said, fear of menstrual pollution is much stronger among tribes who 'marry [the daughters of] the people we fight' than among those who marry from friendly tribes;[106] that may be an extreme case, but a connection of some kind between menstruation and woman's status as an inferior, threatening, or mistrusted being is widespread.[107] There un-

[103] Woman: see n. 101. Political abuse: no orator, to my knowledge, accuses opponents of doing such things to women.

[104] Xen. *Mem.* 4.4.19–23, Pl. *Leg.* 838a–b; nature's supporters: *SVF* 1.256, 3. 743–6, cf. Eur. fr. 19.

[105] Douglas, 173 ff., cf. her *Implicit Meanings, Essays in Anthropology*, London, 1975, Ch. 4.

[106] M. J. Meggitt, 'Male–Female Relationships in the Highlands of Australian New Guinea', *American Anthropologist*, 1964, vol. 66, special publication on *New Guinea, the Central Highlands*, ed. J. B. Watson, 204–24; cf. e.g. M. Strathern, *Women in Between*, London and New York, 1972, Ch. 7, and, for further references on sexual pollution in this area, A. S. Meigs, *Man* n.s. 13 (1978), 304–18. M. R. Allen, however, *Male Cults and Secret Initiations in Melanesia*, Melbourne, 1967, 54, draws attention to societies that marry friends but have strong sexual pollution beliefs, and E. Faithorn (in *Towards an Anthropology of Women*, ed R. R. Reiter, New York and London, 1975, 127–40), points out that menstrual blood is only one of a number of dangerous bodily wastes, produced by both sexes.

[107] See, to cite only modern Mediterranean parallels, J. Pitt-Rivers, *People of the Sierra*[2], Chicago, 1971, 197; J. Cutileiro, *A Portuguese Rural Society*, Oxford, 1971, 99, 276; Blum, 46 (12), cf. 99(16); J. du Boulay, *Portrait of a Modern Greek Village*, Oxford, 1974,

doubtedly existed in Greece considerable unease and suspicion
about women that could have found expression in this way. The
first woman came to man as 'a beautiful evil in place of good',
bringing with her disease and old age.[108] As we have seen,
woman threatened man's virility, his valour, and his life. Apart
from the direct damage she could do him, there was also, more
threatening still, the power she possessed to bring dishonour on
his name. Lustful and uncontrollable, she was the weak link in
the family chain of honour.[109] And when she abandoned the
modest, submissive role through which society wisely sought to
restrain her volatile nature, the whole structure of ordered
existence was thrown into jeopardy. Prudent states had instituted a special magistracy of 'women-controllers'.[110]

It does not matter that this a tendentious selection from the
many ways in which Greeks could view women. Such attitudes
existed, and could readily have been expressed in terms of
impurity. We do occasionally find women spoken of as 'dirty' or
'revolting'; and the fact that the ideal woman was compared to
the pure bee perhaps indicates what might be thought of the
rest.[111] What cannot be demonstrated is a connection between
this idea and menstruation, or any strong fear of menstrual
blood as a polluting force. Purity from menstrual contamination only appears as a condition for entering a temple in late

102–3; J. Okely in S. Ardener (ed.), *Perceiving Women*, London, 1975, 55–86. Admittedly
here too, as in the Roman agricultural writers discussed in the text, though menstrual
blood symbolizes the dangers inherent in female sexuality, what is directly imperilled
by it is the life of farm and field.

[108] Hes. *Op.* 57–105, *Theog.* 570–602, cf. Dover, 99–102 (woman shameless, deceitful,
'prompt to devise evil', vindictively jealous, ungrateful, spreader of malicious gossip),
and particularly J. Gould, 'Law, Custom and Myth: Aspects of the Social Position of
Women in Classical Athens', *JHS* 100 (1980), 38–59.
[109] Eur. fr. 662; 'pollution' inflicted on marriage bed, p. 95 n. 84 above; 'doglike
mind', Hes. *Op.* 67 with West's note, P. Friedrich, *The Meaning of Aphrodite*, Chicago,
1978, 135.
[110] Jeopardy: e.g. Aesch. *Cho.* 585–638. Magistracy: Ar. *Pol.* 1322b 37–1323a 6 ,
Busolt/Swoboda, i, 494 n. 1.
[111] Alc. fr. 346.4, with particular reference to lust (D. L . Page, *Sappho and Alcaeus*,
Oxford, 1955, 305; W. Rösler, *Dichter und Gruppe*, Munich, 1980, 258 n. 344, unconvinc-
ingly suggests a specific reference to lubrication); Ar. *Lys.* 253, 340; Men. fr. 718.6; but
in all these the sense 'revolting' – a sense in which *miaros* is often applied to individual
men – is more prominent than that of dirty. For dirty types of women see Semonides 7.
Female sexual secretions dirty, Ar. *Eq.* 1285 (whence, in part, revulsion at cunnilingus).

sacred laws of non-Greek cults.[112] Menstruation is, in fact,
something about which, outside medical texts, we hardly hear.
It seems almost certain that there will have been rituals relating
to it, but nothing of the kind is recorded.[113] Possibly it was a fact
so secret and shaming that it could not be alluded to at all, even
to the extent of requiring purity from it in a sacred law. It is,
certainly, almost the only bodily function which Old Comedy
never mentions.[114] Chance allusions in scientific texts, however,
suggest that the widespread taboo against intercourse during
menstruation was not observed.[115] This is particularly surprising in that, although the process of menstruation was
commonly spoken of as a 'purification', one might, by analogy
with other purifications, expect the waste matter discharged
thereby to be particularly impure.

What seems to be the only early evidence for magical properties of menstrual blood comes, curiously, from Aristotle, who
asserts that the menstruating woman dims the mirror in front of
which she stands. This detail reappears in Roman agricultural
writers in company with further powers; menstrual blood sours
wine, blights trees and crops, blunts knives, kills bees, rusts

---

[112] *LSS* 54. 7–8. ? 91.16, 119.13, *LSCG* 55.5, *BCH* 102 (1978), 325 line 9. Cf. Porph.
Abst. 2.50, and probably Heliodorus *Aeth.* 10.4.5.

[113] A connection between menstruation and the Thesmophoria is suggested by
K. Kerenyi, *Zeus and Hera*, London, 1975/6, 157, cf. Burkert, *GR* 369 f., and Detienne,
Eugénies, 213. A. Mommsen, *Philol.* 58 (1899), 343–7, argues that, in the temple
inventories of Artemis Brauronia, ῥάκος sometimes indicates a valuable garment. He
suggests that it acquired this meaning, via that of offering, from a custom of young girls
dedicating their first menstrual rags to Artemis (ῥάκος in this sense *Geopon.* 1. 14.1,
10.67.3, Plut. *Quaest. Conv.* 700e,, cf. Goltz, 229 f.) But there is no evidence for such a
custom, and Aeolian βράκος means 'robe' in Sappho, fr. 57, Theoc. 28.11. Linders
argues (58 f.) that ῥάκος does mean 'rag' in the records. I suspect there was originally a
connection between the three 'polluted days' at the end of the month (p. 158) and
menstruation. Menstruation naturally fell, according to Aristotle, at the month's end
(*Hist. An.* 582a 35–6, *Gen. An.* 738a 16–22, 767a 1–13); on the moon and menstruation
cf. C. Preaux, *La Lune dans la pensée grecque*, Brussels, 1973, 88 f.

[114] K. J. Dover, *Greek Homosexuality*, London, 1978, 173, mentioning the possibility that the 'things a man may not name' dedicated by a retired *hetaira* in Philetas
1.5 Gow/Page (*Anth. Pal.* 6.210) are menstrual towels. If so, that is relevant to
A. Mommsen's theory mentioned above; but one rather expects the reference to be to
something salacious.

[115] Arist. *Gen. An.* 727b 12–23, Hippoc. *Nat. Mul.* 8 (7.324 Littré). The excuse in Ach.
Tat. 4.7.7. (ἀνδρὶ συνελθεῖν οὐ θέμις during period) comes therefore from some other
tradition. Of course, willingness to have intercourse during menstruation does not
necessarily mean that menstruation is positively evaluated (cf. Blum, 46 (12)), although it may (Buxton, 212).

metals and maddens dogs. (It can be put to beneficial use too, but even here its utility, like that of a poison, lies in its destructiveness. Locusts fall dead to the ground at sight of a girl at her first menstruation.[116]) It is unfortunately impossible to tell whether this whole complex of beliefs already existed in Aristotle's time.[117] Whatever their date, it is not to male health and potency that the menstruating woman poses a threat.

One might of course argue, not implausibly, that it is indeed male fear of women that endows menstrual blood with such fearful powers, and only by a Freudian process of displacement is its destructive force diverted to operate against plants and field. The only text, however, that makes woman, by her mere physical nature, a source of danger to man is 'Hesiod', who warns 'Let a man not clean his skin in water a woman has washed in. For a hard penalty follows on that too for a time.'[118] There is no reason to see in that a reference to menstruation. It is none the less interesting, as containing the idea of contamination; but it finds no echo in later texts. In the classical period, to judge from the surviving evidence, the threat which woman poses to ordered society proceeds not from the dark recesses of her body but of her mind.[119]

[116] Arist. *de somniis* 459b 23–460a 23; Pliny, *HN* 7.64, 28. 78–80, Columella 11.3.50, *Geoponica* 12.20.5, 25.2; locusts: Colum. 10.357 ff., 11.3.64, Ael. *NA* 6.36, Pliny, *HN* 17.266, 28.78, *Geop.* 12.8.5 f.; menstrual blood, or indecent exposure by a woman, averts hail and whirlwinds from vineyard: Plut. *Quaest. Conv.* 700e, Pliny, *HN* 28.77, *Geop.* 1.14.1; medicinal powers: Pliny, *HN* 28.82–6. Cf. H. Wagenvoort, *Roman Dynamism*, Oxford, 1947, 173–5.

[117] For the locust charm, Colum. at 10.358 cites 'Dardanus', at 11.3.64 'Democritus' on antipathies (for the link of the two cf. Pliny, *HN* 30.9); Pliny, *HN* 28.78 cites Metrodorus of Scepsis, who claims the discovery to have been made in Cappadocia. On medicinal powers Pliny, *HN* 28. 82–6 quotes various unrevealing authorities.

[118] Hes. *Op.* 753–5 . To the same kind of context belongs the idea of woman 'burning up' and 'withering' man, *Op.* 704–5, cf. Detienne, *Jardins*, 224 f.

[119] But note Simon, 242, 260–6, on the Hippocratic doctor's 'need to be ignorant' of the inside of the female body.

4

THE SHEDDING OF BLOOD

That the blood of his victim clings to the hand of a murderer, and, until cleansed, demands his seclusion from society, is a belief attested in a bewildering variety of literary, oratorical, historical, mythographical, and pictorial sources – although other sources preserve a stolid and no less perplexing silence on the same subject. Two texts illustrate the matter in some detail, Book 9 of Plato's *Laws*, and the *Tetralogies* ascribed to Antiphon. The *Tetralogies* are an obvious starting-point for a discussion, although not an ideal one. Their sophistical author, whether Antiphon or another, is perhaps not himself committed to the doctrines he manipulates, and may not know where to draw the line in his imitation of belief; and the relation of these hypothetical cases to actual legal process is a long-standing difficulty. On the other hand, it is now generally agreed that the audience to which they are addressed is Athenian,[1] which means that they can be confronted with the one body of homicide law that is well known to us; and the very form of the tetralogy, designed to show how the same topic of argument can be exploited and re-exploited by both parties, means that the full potential of the argument from pollution is here displayed as in no other text.

It may be useful to give a summary of such arguments in the order in which they appear. The 'you' of the speakers refers to the jurors. The first tetralogy concerns a case of premeditated homicide; the defendant denies his involvement.

First speech for the prosecution: It would be against our interest to prosecute an innocent man and let the guilty escape. The whole city is polluted by the guilty man until he is prosecuted, and if we connive at this by charging the innocent, the guilt for this pollution of the city becomes ours, and the punishment for the

---

[1] See Gernet, *Antiphon*, 8–13; K. J. Dover, *CQ* 44 (1950), 58; M. Gagarin, *GRBS* 19 (1978), 291–306.

mistake you would make falls upon us. Thus the whole pollution falls upon us if we act unjustly (3). It is against your interest to allow this polluted man to enter divine precincts and pollute their sanctity, or pass on his contamination to the innocent by eating at the same table with them. This is the kind of thing that causes crops to fail, and affairs in general to go wrong. The vote you are about to cast concerns your own interest: make this man bear his sins on his own head, and purify the city (10–11).

First speech for the defence: As I am innocent, I will not pollute the shrines. It is my opponents who, by prosecuting the innocent and letting go the guilty, cause crop failure (11).

Second speech for the prosecution: As his guilt is manifest, in seeking acquittal he is merely asking you to transfer his own pollution upon yourselves (9). If you acquit him unjustly, the dead man will not be a visitant against us, but you will have him upon your minds. So avenge the victim, punish the killer, and cleanse the city. Thus will you be free of the pollution you would otherwise incur on the guilty man's behalf (10–11).

Second speech for the defence: Remember the victim's right to vengeance. If you condemn me, the real culprit will never be found (11).

The second tetralogy concerns a boy killed by another at a javelin practice. Both parties agree that the death was accidental.

Prosecution 1: My son's death, if unavenged, will be a source of religious anxiety to us. Exclude the killer from the places the law requires, and do not allow the whole city to be polluted by him (2).

Prosecution 2: Even if the killing was a simple accident, the killer should pay the penalty; it may, however, be a taint sent against him by the gods for some act of impiety (8). As the whole pollution is liable to be transferred to you, take great care. Don't involve yourselves in the killer's pollution (11–12).

Defence 2: The victim killed himself, in effect; thus he cannot be said to be unavenged (8). The dead boy, punished by his own fault, can leave no form of visitant against anybody. But if an innocent boy is destroyed, this will be a source of religious anxiety to those who condemn him (9).

The third tetralogy relates to a death in a brawl. The fact of the killing is agreed, but the degree of provocation disputed.

Prosecution 1: The victim of murder leaves behind him the anger of the avenging spirits, which acts as an agent of god's vengeance on behalf of one robbed of the divine gift of life. Those who judge unjustly bring this anger, a pollution that does not belong to them, into their own houses (3). If we, the dead man's natural avengers, prosecute the innocent, we will have the visitants of the victim acting as avenging spirits against us; and we will ourselves be guilty of murder (4). We have therefore prosecuted the guilty party; do you punish him and cleanse the city (5).

Defence 1: Consider your own interest. Should you acquit me unjustly, because the prosecution has failed to convince you, the dead man's visitant will turn against the prosecution and not against you. But if you condemn me unjustly, it is against you and not the prosecutor that I shall turn (?) the anger of the avenging spirits (8). Acquit me: thus shall we all avoid defilement as best we can (9).

Prosecution 2: We adjure you, on behalf of the victim, to appease the wrath of the avenging spirits by this man's death, and so cleanse the whole city (7).

Defence 2: Don't kill an innocent man. If you do, the dead man's avenging spirit will still be a visitant against the guilty (*perhaps – the text is corrupt*), and the innocent man by his death will double the pollution of the avenging spirits against his killers (10).

The first question raised by these texts about the pollution of bloodshed is the apparently simple one of what it is. This question has, of course, an obvious answer, which is fundamental to the way in which the murderer is normally described, imagined, and portrayed: his pollution is the blood of his victim clinging to his hands.[2] In these speeches, however, this obvious answer is entirely disregarded. Most openly, perhaps, in the third tetralogy, but by implication throughout the work, pollution appears not as a mess of blood, but as the anger of the victim, or of avenging spirits acting on his behalf, against the man who has robbed him of the life that is his right. 'Appease the wrath of the avenging spirits by this man's death, and so cleanse the whole city', 'the pollution of the avenging spirits',

---

[2] e.g. Aesch. *Eum.* 41 f., and the common expression οὐ καθαρὸς τὰς χεῖρας.

'bring upon themselves the anger of the avenging spirits, a pollution that does not belong to them' – such expressions illustrate unambiguously, in the case of murder, that 'demonic' interpretation of pollution which we noted to be unattested for birth and death.[3] The literal image of murder-pollution as a stain on the hands, where it does appear, is manifestly a symbol of something beyond itself, since the stain is invisible; the *Tetralogies* unabashedly substitute the thing symbolized for the symbol.

The idea that it is his victim's anger that makes the murderer dangerous or endangered is not confined to the *Tetralogies*. Plato refers to an 'ancient myth' which explains the killer's exile in just these terms, while Xenophon's Cyrus can even appeal to the murdered man's power to send out 'avenging demons' as an acknowledged fact which will support the more doubtful general proposition of the soul's survival.[4] Legend told how the regent Pausanias was haunted by the ghost of a Byzantine girl he had summoned 'for her shame' and accidentally killed.[5] The identification between pollution and the victim's anger is obvious in an expression like 'the pollution coming from the dead man'.[6] The Erinyes, above all, are animate agents of pollution who embody the anger of one slain by a kinsman. Although they are not formally identical with pollution (rather they 'arrive where a man hides bloody hands'),[7] there is no difference between its effects and theirs, and the operations of the two are normally co-extensive; even where, in the exceptional poetical conception of Aeschylus' *Eumenides*, they continue their assaults after the murderer's hands are clean, the evils with which they threaten Athens for harbouring the murderer are familiar effects of pollution.[8] This co-extensiveness of pollution and the victim's anger is implicit in the formal rites of purification, in which 'washing off the blood' is followed by appeasement; the

---

[3] *Tetr.* 3·γ 7, δ 10 (cf. K. J. Maidment's note, ad loc. in the Loeb), α 3; cf. Rohde, 215 n. 176.

[4] Pl. *Leg.* 865d–e, cf. 872e–873a; Xen. *Cyr.* 8.7.18.

[5] Plut. *Cim.* 6.4–7, *De sera* 555c, Paus. 3.17.8–9. On haunted houses in antiquity see Dodds, *Progress*, 157 n. 2.

[6] Soph. *OT* 313 – unless the genitive is objective, as it seems to be in Eur. fr. 82. Cf. Soph. *OT* 1012.

[7] Aesch. *Eum.* 316–20.

[8] 778–92.

same is true of the savage self-protective devices of murderers,
who 'wipe off' or 'spit out' the victim's blood, and seek to
incapacitate him for revenge by mutilation.[9] In exempting
from all legal sanctions, therefore, the killer who had been
pardoned by his dying victim, the Athenians were not bidding
defiance to pollution,[10] but acknowledging its source.

Against the identification of pollution and angry spirits, it has
been objected that such spirits are virtually confined to tragedy
and the *Tetralogies*. In forensic oratory, history, and comedy,
alastores and *alitērioi* are not supernatural beings but polluted,
sacrilegious, dangerous humans.[11] The contrast, however, between Aeschylus and the *Tetralogies* on the one side, and the
orators and comedians on the other, perhaps reflects the difference between different ages as much as that between literature
and life. The atmosphere of Aeschylus and the *Tetralogies* is too
thick with spirits for everyday habitation; but they perhaps, by
their imaginative exaggeration, set before us the fundamental
structure of popular belief. The evidence of language is revealing.[12] The same word (*prostropaios*) can be used of the polluted killer himself, of the victim's polluting blood, and of the
victim himself in his anger, or his avenging spirits;[13] *palamnaios*
is applied to the killer, the demons that attack him, and the
(demonic) pollution that radiates from him;[14] words like *miastōr*,

---

[9] Cf. Ap. Rhod. *Argon*. 4. 699–717, 477–9; Rohde, 180 f., 582–6.

[10] Dem. 37.59, Eur. *Hipp*. 1447–51 (explicitly said to purify Theseus), Pl. *Leg*. 869a
(where a requirement of purification remains). Similarly, Iolaus would be polluted by
the sacrifice of his daughter but not by her voluntary self-oblation, Eur. *Heracl*. 558 f.

[11] Moulinier, 259–70. But there are exceptions: for supernatural *alitērioi* cf. Andoc.
1.130, Pl. *Ep*. 7. 336b; supernatural *palamnaioi*, Xen. *Cyr*. 8.7.18. Moulinier's position is
criticized by Vernant, *Société*, 127, 132 f.

[12] On most of these words see W. H. P. Hatch, *HSCP* 19 (1908), 157–86.

[13] Killer:.Aesch. *Eum*. 176, 237, 445; Eur. *HF* 1259, ? cf. *Heracl*. 1015. The word is also
used of suppliants, Aesch. *Ag*. 1587, Soph. *Aj*. 1173, *Phil*. 930, *OC* 1309, esp. killers,
Aesch. *Eum*. 41, 234. There has clearly been semantic interference between the 'turning' of the suppliant to an altar, and the 'turning' of pollution against those it infects.
Victim's blood: Eur. *HF* 1161, *Ion* 1260. Victim, or his spirits, as visitant: ? Aesch. *Cho*.
287, Ant. *Tetr*. 1 γ 10, 2 δ 9 (a 'pre-animistic' neuter), 3 α 4, β 8, δ 10; polluting visitant,
without specific reference to murder, Aeschin. 2. 158, Eupolis, fr. 120. προστρέπομαι of
the victim turning his anger against the killer: Ant. *Tetr*. 3 β 8 (by conjecture), Pl. *Leg*.
866b.

[14] Killer: Aesch. *Eum*. 448, Soph. *El*. 587, *Tr*. 1207, Phryn. Com. fr. 58. Demons:
Xen. *Cyr*. 8.7.18. Demonic pollution: Eur. *IT* 1218 (doubted by J. Diggle, *Studies on the
Text of Euripides*, Oxford, 1981, 88 f.; but for demons shooting out from a polluted person
see e.g. Eur. *Med*. 1333).

alastōr, and *alitērios* work in very similar ways.[15] These are remarkable sets of meanings. The killer is *prostropaios*, but so is the victim; the killer, a *palamnaios* himself, is also attacked by, and emanates, supernatural *palamnaioi*. The unifying factor is the polluting act, which sets up a chain of abnormal relations between humans – victim, killer, associates of killer – the connecting links in which are supernatural powers. It is hard to believe that semantic configurations of this kind correspond to no felt reality.

There are, certainly, many passages where the pollution of murder is referred to and yet there is no suggestion that the avenging spirits of the victim are at work. Often, no doubt, the claim that a particular individual 'has impure hands' is a reproach or a simple description of what, in customary terms, his ritual status now is, rather than an expression of a real belief that supernatural dangers threaten. Even where the idea of danger is certainly present, however, it is not necessarily derived from the dead man's anger. Nothing is said about the victim in the famous passage of the forensic Antiphon that explains how the ships that a murderer sails in run into danger, and the sacrifices he attends go awry.[16] Even though the Erinyes take account, remarkably, of the fact that Oedipus slew his father unwittingly, and do not in the extant texts pursue him, Oedipus remains one of the great polluted figures of Greek literature; in the *Hercules Furens*, it does not seem to be the wrath of his tiny children that makes the mighty Heracles so polluted. In the latter two cases, both of them instances of kin-killing, it seems that pollution derives not from the wrong to the victim, but from the violation of the order of the family; there is expressed through it universal shock, not the particular anger of the victim and his kin. Of the Antiphon passage, and others like it, we can perhaps say that although murder-pollution derives its dynamic charge from the victim's wrath, it can to some extent retain that dynamism even when separated

[15] On *alitērios* see Hatch, op. cit., 157–62; on *alastōr*, Fraenkel on Aesch. *Ag.* 1501, and on Zeus Alastoros, C. Rolley, *BCH* 89 (1965), 454–6. Killers are *miastores*, Aesch. *Cho.* 944, Soph. *El.* 275, *OT* 353, Eur. *El.* 683, *Andr.* 615; they are threatened by *miastores*, Aesch. *Eum.* 176 f., Soph. *El.* 603, Eur. *Med.* 1371. *Erinys* can work similarly, cf. Soph. *El.* 112 with 1080.
[16] Ant. 5. 82–4.

from it. If it seems arbitrary to represent the 'avenging' pollution of the *Tetralogies* as primary, and other forms as derived, the
justification must be that it is as an avenger that murder-
pollution appears in the texts where its threats are most vividly
presented.

The significance of this identification with the victim's anger
is that it affects the way in which pollution is diffused. According to the logic of the metaphor of 'defilement', it ought to
operate, in Dodds' phrase, 'with the same ruthless indifference
to motive as a typhoid germ',[17] and there are certainly texts in
which it is regarded as liable to do just this. In Euripides, for
instance, the barbarian king covers his head when Orestes
passes 'so as not to get a polluting spirit upon me'.[18] (The
protective device is as mechanically conceived as the threat.) In
the *Tetralogies*, by contrast, pollution appears as a stern and
discriminating upholder of the moral order. Although diffusion
by physical contact is not excluded, the pollution that is emphasized attaches to those who, by omission or commission,
obstruct the victim's right to revenge. It threatens in the first
instance the dead man's kin, should they fail to find and prosecute the true killer, and secondly the jury, should they fail to
condemn him. In this case the prosecution would have done
their duty, and be safe, but the jurors, and through them the
city which they represent, deeply endangered. For Plato too,
pollution 'comes round to' kinsmen of the victim who fail to
bring a prosecution. Because they make pollution operate in
this discriminating way, both authors can identify it with the
'vengeance' or 'enmity' of the gods.[19] Before courts existed, it
was the threat of the same fierce but purposeful pollution that
imposed on Orestes his terrible revenge.[20] Even when pollution
is spread by simple contact, it remains purposive, though in a
different sense; the purpose is to impose social isolation upon
the killer, and those who suffer through involuntary association

---

[17] Dodds, 36.

[18] Eur. *IT* 1218.

[19] Ant. *Tetr.* 1 α 3, γ 9,11; *Tetr.* 2 γ 11–12; *Tetr.* 3 α 3,4, β 8; Pl. *Leg.* 866b, 871b.
Identification: Ant. *Tetr.* 3 α 3, Pl. *Leg.* 871b (in Eur. fr. 82 the gods 'avenge' pollutions).

[20] Aesch. *Cho.* 269–96 (cf. Eur. *Or.* 580–4); 'attacks of the Erinyes' are spoken of, but
the symptoms are precisely those of pollution. It was the same with Alcmaeon: Eur. fr.
69 with the testimonia.

with him are unlucky victims of a rule chiefly aimed at others.[21]

In turning to consider how murder-pollution is incurred, we enter a quicksand. The prosecutor in the second tetralogy states intention to be irrelevant to pollution; Sophocles' Oedipus can declare, 'pure before the law, unknowing did I come to this.'[22] All murderers are excluded from sacred places; yet the chorus in the *Agamemnon* in one place imply that it was only the complicity of his wife in the murder of Agamemnon that caused 'pollution of the land and the country's gods'.[23] Creon in Sophocles at first supposes that, by leaving a few scraps of food in the tomb to which he consigns Antigone, he is 'pure in respect of this girl'; later in the play, humbled, he acknowledges himself her killer.[24] It is possible to attach pollution either to the physical agent, or to the person ultimately responsible for the act. A dialogue in Euripides presents this tension in extreme terms:

Menelaus: Do you mean to say you deserve to live?
Orestes: Yes, and be a king . . .
Menelaus: Yes, you'd be just the man to handle holy water.
Orestes: What prevents me?
Menelaus: And perform sacrifice before battle.
Orestes: Have you the right to do so?
Menelaus: Of course. My hands are clean.
Orestes: But not your heart.[25]

Such contentions were no doubt often heard. When Euripides' Achilles, outraged to learn of the proposal to sacrifice Iphigeneia, says that he himself is polluted by the abuse of his name in the plot to lure her to Aulis, he is obviously expressing moral revulsion in ritual terms.[26] Since the stain on the murderer's hand is in fact invisible, it is just as possible to dispute whether a particular person is touched by pollution as by guilt, and, since its social consequences are serious, just as necessary.

[21] In Pl. *Euthphr.* 4c Euthyphro, not obviously by way of paradox, in fact confines pollution to conscious association.

[22] *Tetr.* 2 α 2; Soph. *OC* 548.

[23] Aesch. *Ag.* 1644 f.

[24] Soph. *Ant.* 775f., 889, 1339–46.

[25] Eur. *Or.* 1600–4. For the ascription of pollution to a person only distantly responsible for a death cf. Eur. *Andr.* 614 f. Persons morally responsible for a death (even one that doesn't occur) spoken of as 'killers': Soph. *Aj.* 1126, *OT* 534, Eur. *Hel.* 280, *Med.* 1364, Andoc. 1. 58.

[26] Eur. *IA* 938–47.

Amid all this ambiguity, it would be reassuring to turn to the precision of a code of rules. At Athens, both sets of the exegetes could be consulted on religious questions arising from violent death; of their traditions, unfortunately, virtually nothing is known. A law of the early sixth century from Cleonai probably treated murder-pollution, but no certain or even probable information can be extracted from it. The Cyrene cathartic law contains regulations for the purification of the *autophonos*; it is frustrating that we cannot be sure whether this means 'kin-killer', 'killer with one's own hand', or merely 'killer'. A hellenistic sacred law from Lato in Crete seems to declare pure the perpetrator of certain forms of involuntary homicide (pushing a person in a fire, or pouring boiling water over him).[27] From such desultory scraps of information there is little to be learnt. For an extended code we must turn to Plato's in Book 9 of the *Laws*. Its most striking feature is the acute sensitivity to circumstances with which he credits pollution. He lists a series of conditions under which 'the killer would rightly be pure': killing of a night thief, or of a footpad in self-defence: killing of a person sexually violating a relative of the killer: killing in defence of a relation.[28] (Elsewhere he declares pure the man who kills in self-defence or during civil strife, even, remarkably, if the victim is a brother; retribution against a homicidal slave is also non-polluting.[29]) Plato has limited the Athenian category of justified killing to acts which positively serve social or family solidarity. Those accidental killings, in athletics, military training, or war, which at Athens fell into the same justified category, have been transferred to the lowest level of his class of 'involuntary acts of violence'; they carry no penalty, but require purification.[30] Thus Platonic pollution can distinguish between deliberate, justifiable homicide, wholly pure, and non-culpable, accidental homicide, which by robbing the state of a useful life[31] causes a mild pollution. Plato continues to legislate for the manifold forms of homicide with similar casuistry. The killer of a slave, by

---

[27] Exegetes: Jacoby, 41–51. Cleonai: *LSCG* 56, with bibliography. Cyrene: *LSS* 115 B 50, cf. p. 351 below. Lato: *LSS* 112.
[28] 874 b–c.
[29] 869 c–d; 868 b–c.
[30] 865 a–b.
[31] Cf. 831a.

accident or in anger, must undergo 'more and greater' purifications than the perpetrator of accidental non-culpable homicide, but apart from compensating the owner is subject to no further sanction.[32] Anyone who 'involuntarily' kills a free man, except in the particular mitigating circumstances already mentioned, must suffer exile, which is for Plato a form of purification, for periods varying according to the character of the deed.[33] The whole graduated scale of purification and punishment reaches its culmination in the deliberate parricide, for whom death itself is too little; the magistrates carry his naked corpse to a crossroads outside the city, take each a stone and cast it at his head, to 'cleanse the whole city', and then hurl the body unburied over the boundaries of the land.[34]

It would be misleading to say that Plato has moralized pollution, although he is moving in that direction. Traces of a material, objective conception remain.[35] Purely accidental killings may require purification, and even exile. The man who murders through a hired assassin is, Plato insists, 'polluted in soul' and must be punished exactly like the physical killer; but Plato allows him that burial in his native land that the deliberate murderer is normally denied.[36] Pollution distinguishes in terms of social order as well as moral intention, and reacts differently to the killing of slave by free man and free man by slave. It is clear, however, that though Plato surely regards pollution as a real thing and no legislator's fiction, he is not moved by an indiscriminate horror of shed blood.

Many of the Platonic differentiations undoubtedly derived from Attic practice. For Athenians, as, apparently, for all Greeks at all times, blood shed in battle could simply be washed off.[37] The perpetrator of 'justified homicide', or at least certain

---

[32] 865c, 868a.

[33] See the table in W. Knoch, *Die Strafbestimmungen in Platons Nomoi*, Wiesbaden, 1960, 162 f.

[34] 873b.

[35] Cf. Reverdin, 177 ff.

[36] 872a.

[37] The only text suggesting that Greek soldiers purified themselves formally after battle is Aesch. *Sept.* 679–82. It cannot be allowed to weigh against the total silence of the historians, whose implication is echoed by Eur. *Ion* 1334 καθαρὸς ἅπας τοι πολεμίους ὃς ἂν κτάνῃ, Pl. *Leg.* 869 d καθάπερ πολέμιον ἀποκτείνας ἔστω καθαρός; cf. Andoc. 1. 97, and the declaration of war on the Spartan helots by the ephors. A regular purification after hunting is claimed only by Arr. *Cyn.* 33.

categories of it, was formally considered pure; private scruples might have caused him to seek purification, but no one could prosecute him for entering the temples without it.[38] Certain killings in literature that fall into no precise legal category are probably thought of in roughly these terms. Thus in Euripides, though Heracles does speak of 'cleaning his hands' from the killing of Lycus, it is clear that this absolution will be automatic and final; the simplest ritual can efface the blood of a villain.[39] The 'involuntary' killer, by contrast, incurred exile, and could not return before he had 'sacrificed and been purified'.[40] Plato's partial extension of pollution to the author of a murder as well as its agent is also Attic. By law, 'the deviser was subject to the same penalties as the man who did it with his hand' and, since 'the deviser' could thus be prosecuted for murder, he will have been excluded from the shrines for the period before the trial. We hear of an informer, whose murders were performed by legal process, being shunned 'like a polluting demon', 'as a murderer', and eventually being brought to trial for entering the sacred places although 'manifestly' a killer.[41]

The real problem that the subject presents has begun to emerge in this discussion. In assessing the intensity of pollution, we have been appealing not merely to ritual criteria but also to legal penalties. This has been in accord with the practice of Attic authors, who commonly treat exile itself as a form of purification.[42] To consider merely the number and intensity of ritual lustrations that a particular act required would be quite to miss their conception of what the implications of pollution are. Ritual and legal status are assimilated to the extent that in contexts of homicide 'pure' and 'not subject to legal sanctions' are often synonymous.[43] A few acts, such as the killing of a

[38] See Appendix 5.

[39] Eur. *HF* 940. The ritual envisaged is unclear; 923 speaks of 'rites to purify the house', 940 and 1145 of 'cleansing the hands', but what Heracles seems to be preparing is a normal sacrifice (Rudhardt, 270, Moulinier, 88). Odysseus purifies his house, but not himself, after the murder of the suitors (*Od.* 22. 481–94).

[40] Dem. 23.72.

[41] Deviser: Andoc. 1. 94, cf. Aeschin. 1.172 with 2.148. Informer: Lys. 13.79,81,85–7 (cf. MacDowell, *Homicide*, 131–3).

[42] e.g. Aesch. *Ag.* 1419 f., *Cho.* 1038, Eur. *Hipp.* 35, Ant. *Tetr. passim*, Pl. *Leg.* 865 d–e; see too Nic. Dam. 90 *FGrH* fr. 45.

[43] See Appendix 5.

dependent, may have required purification, and even some seclusion of the killer, without being subject to legal penalty, but an Athenian would probably have said that they were 'polluting, but not sufficiently polluting to require exile', rather than acknowledging them as a real exception to the principle. (Another special case, which will be mentioned later, is that of kin-killing.) This correlation between legal and ritual requirements, however, imposes the question of the causal relation between the two. Do they coincide because the threat of pollution is one factor among others, or even the dominating factor, that the legislator took into account? Or has pollution, a religious idea and not, in itself, a powerful determinant of action, wrapped itself round the law like ivy round the oak and proudly claimed the shade the latter casts to be its own?[44]

The difficulty with the first approach is that it is hard to give meaning to the idea of a fear of pollution that is somehow quite distinct from all the other motives that determine responses to homicide. If it is fear of pollution alone that causes the killer to be exiled, the unattractive conclusion seems to follow that, without it, his victim's kin would let him live on unmolested. It is also impossible on this hypothesis to explain why, in Greek society, some forms of killing are entirely pure, while even in societies that require purification after war and the hunt these socially approved forms of killing are much less polluting than is murder. Some have supposed that, though Greek responses to homicide derive in origin from such familiar motives as the desire for revenge, pollution intruded at a particular historical moment to push the institution in a new direction. Thus it has often been argued that the first codification of murder laws by Draco in the seventh century was a response to the growth of hitherto unknown fears of pollution.[45] If this were true, the novel fears would themselves await an explanation. But the postulated transformation, sudden and otherwise inexplicable,

---

[44] A view close to this is well put by MacDowell, *Homicide*, 1–5, 141–50; but note T. J. Saunders, *JHS* 85 (1965), 225. Gagarin, *Drakon*, 164–7 sees doctrines of pollution as post-Draconian.

[45] e.g. by E. Meyer, *Geschichte des Altertums*, III², Stuttgart, 1937, 528–34; Wilamowitz, *Das Opfer am Grabe³*, Berlin, 1907, 8 f.; Bonner/Smith, i.53. Vigorous and effective criticism in Calhoun, 25–41; a subtle discussion by L. Gernet, *Annales* 10 (1955), 530–3. Glotz, 225–37 has a more ingenious variant, well criticized by P. Fauconnet, *L'Année sociologique* 10 (1905–6), 475–8.

in the treatment of killers simply does not occur. Draco passed a homicide law, but in a society in which authority was gradually being centralized, murder was unlikely to be left uncontrolled by law, since public cognizance of homicide seems to be a distinctive mark of a centralized political system.[46] He or a successor probably forbade the acceptance of blood-money (the details are quite obscure)[47] but such a restriction on the power of individual citizens to barter with life and death could also have been predicted as part of the process of centralization of authority. Even if these reforms were justified as a defence against pollution (as is the ban on accepting compensation in the Old Testament),[48] a self-moving fear of pollution was clearly not their true inspiration. But it has often been noted that there is no mention of pollution in the surviving portions of Draco's law, and other authors of the period who have much to say about justice and the welfare of the community (Hesiod, Archilochus, Alcaeus, Solon) do not seem to be haunted by the spectre of the unpunished murderer lurking in its midst.

The alternative conception, which makes pollution a kind of shadowy spiritual *Doppelgänger* of the law, is therefore more attractive. Not just Draco's but all surviving homicide laws ignore it almost entirely.[49] Sometimes the appeal to pollution in classical authors appears as almost a rationalization of an institution whose historical origins we can actually see to be different. The 'involuntary' killer under Athenian law was required to go into exile until pardoned by the victim's kin, for a period that could in theory be indefinite although it seems normally to have been fixed at a year. This withdrawal can be explained as a response to pollution. Plato quotes an 'old myth': the free man, freshly dead and angry at his premature and

[46] J. Beattie, *Other Cultures*, London, 1964, 156. On the introduction of legal process for homicide see E. Ruschenbusch, Φόνος, *Historia* 9 (1960), 129–54; Latte, *Mord*; Gagarin, *Drakon*; above all H. J. Wolff, 'The Origin of Judicial Legislation among the Greeks', *Traditio* 4 (1946), 31–87. The 6th-century Sicilian homicide law *SEG* iv 64 is unfortunately too mutilated to be revealing.

[47] See for different views Rohde, 211 n. 154; Glotz, 314 f., 439 f.; Bonner/Smith, ii. 196–8; Latte, *Mord*, 284 = *Kl. Schr.* 387 (a different nuance *Kl. Schr.* 274); M. Gagarin, *GRBS* 20 (1979), 303. Survival or revival of blood-money outside Attica: *Inscr. Prien.* 84; Michel 524 C 20 f. (Ilion).

[48] Numbers 35:31–3.

[49] The only Attic exception (MacDowell, *Homicide*, 148) is Dem. 23.72.

violent end, cannot bear to see his killer at large in the places he himself frequented, and may seek revenge.[50] In mythology and Homer, however, we find the involuntary and even the 'justified' killer (of later classification) subject to permanent exile, and the force that drives him out is not just pollution but pursuit by the victim's kin.[51] The classical institution is a mitigated survival of the pre-legal procedure. There is, of course, an element in such a case that in modern terms appears irrational, and that some might wish to explain through fear of pollution. The victim's kinsmen, faced by the monstrous fact of his extinction, decline to take account of motive. 'He did it involuntarily', says the prosecutor in the second tetralogy, 'but the affliction he brought upon me is not less than it would have been had he done it with intent.' (He adds that even apparent accidents may be instruments of divine vengeance; the suggestion is most revealing, but not essential to his point.[52]) An innocent man has suffered violent death, and his death must be taken out on its 'cause', regardless of whether an intention to kill was present or even possible.[53] In Athens, animals or inanimate objects that had caused death were tried at the Prytaneum and, if found guilty, expelled beyond the boundaries of Attica.[54] The accidental killer had therefore to try to demonstrate, not that he was morally innocent, but that he was not causally responsible for what occurred at all.[55] But the basis of the institution seems not to be fear of pollution but the urge to exact retribution, and be seen to exact it, for an injury that has been received. Similar practices are found in societies which lack the metaphor of blood pollution, and the reason why the irrational or inanimate killer is 'cast outside the land' is by assimilation to the fate

[50] *Leg.* 865d–e.
[51] *Il.* 23.85–8, *Od.* 22.27–32. Exile for accidental killing in the myths e.g. of Aetolus, Cephalus, Oxylus, Perseus (Appendix 7), and the story of Adrastus (Hdt. 1. 35), for justifiable homicide in the myth of Hyettus (Hes. fr. 257). Cf. Glotz, 49 f. Life-exile for accidental homicide in classical Sparta, Xen. *An.* 4.8.25.
[52] *Tetr.* 2 a 2, γ 7–8.
[53] See Gernet, 305–88 on the 'objective crime', also Dover, 152 f., 159; on 'the cause of death' Gernet, 368–71, Adkins, 103–7.
[54] MacDowell, *Homicide*, 85–9, cf. Pl. *Leg.* 873e–874a. Similar practices elsewhere in Greece, Paus. 5.27.10, 6.11.6.
[55] Adkins, 103–7. Such evasions are, however, primitive, not sophisticated, cf. e.g. the punishment of the axe at the Bouphonia (Paus. 1.24.4), and for the form of argument already Aesch. *Cho.* 923.

of the rational killer. (By a similar assimilation, homicidal pigs in the Middle Ages were hung.[56]) The idea that the homicidal axe is polluted, or that the victim would be angry if his accidental killer were not expelled, is a secondary elaboration upon the primary desire for retribution.

Another clear instance of the way in which the concept of pollution fits round the legal or pre-legal institution is the status of the killer in exile. His taint, ineffaceable at home, disappears, or at least becomes open to purification, as soon as he reaches foreign soil. The victim is only angry, it is said, at seeing the killer roaming at large in the places he himself once frequented (he shares, therefore, the probable feelings of his surviving kin).[57] A few crimes were, it is sometimes claimed, so horrendous that no city would provide refuge for their perpetrators[58] (there is a hint in Sophocles that at Athens the Areopagus may have intervened in such cases), but in general the principle of 'but that was in another country' must have applied. 'Those who are in exile for killing, once they move to another city, are not treated as enemies by those who receive them', says Lycurgus.[59] But while the permanent exile was pure in respect of his new surroundings, but still polluted should he seek to return home, for the involuntary killer temporary exile was itself a kind of cleansing, during which his pollution 'was rubbed off' or 'fell asleep' (since 'time purifies all things'),[60] ready to be finally removed by purification when he came back to his native soil.

A further instance where pollution offers an extra explanation of an institution that can also be explained in other terms is

[56] E. P. Evans, *The Criminal Prosecution and Capital Punishment of Animals*, London, 1906; on deodand (penal surrender of homicidal objects) see Kenny's *Outlines of Criminal Law*, 19th edn. by J. W. C. Turner, Cambridge, 1966, 7 f. In old English law '*Legis enim est qui inscienter peccat, scienter emendet' vel. sim.* (*Leges Henrici Primi*, ed. L. J. Downer, Oxford, 1972, 88.6a, 90.11a, 70.12b: followed however in each case by a recommendation to mercy, see Downer's references on 70.12a), 'the thought of man shall not be tried, for the devil himself knoweth not the thought of man' (a late medieval lawyer cited Pollock/Maitland, 2.474).

[57] Pl. *Leg.* 865e; for the kin's sentiment cf. the quotation in Campbell, 198: 'I suddenly saw him there, drinking and putting on airs. I remembered that his brother Vasili drew blood from my brother. I could not stand it.'

[58] Soph. *OC* 944–50 (Areopagus), Eur. *El.* 1194–1200, *HF* 1286–90, *Hipp.* 1066 f., *Med.* 847–50, Lys. 12.35, (Lys.) 6.16,30, Lyc. *Leoc.* 133.

[59] *Leoc.* 133, cf. Dem. 23.39.

[60] Aesch. *Eum.* 238, 280, 286.

that of the minor Athenian court 'at Phreatto', which heard the case of anyone accused of deliberate murder while already in exile for homicide. It met on the shore, and the accused man approached it from the sea; he was not allowed to set foot on land, but pleaded his case from the boat.[61] Obviously these regulations can be interpreted as a device to protect the land from pollution, and this is no doubt how many Athenians understood them. Equally, however, they protected the exile himself who, if he set foot in the forbidden territory, became an outlaw to be killed with impunity. The site of the court emphasizes with formal archaic symbolism that the exile is not breaking bounds.

Pollution's lack of real coercive force of its own is clear from the case of the victim without a patron, mentioned by Antiphon.[62] He is probably thinking of the slave killed by his own master, although it is not impossible that the child killed by his father is also envisaged. 'Even when a man kills somebody he controls himself, so that there is no one to avenge him, he still, in respect for custom and the gods, purifies himself and keeps away from the places laid down by law, thinking that this will be best for him.' Unless Antiphon is being disingenuous, we must assume that the killer here avoids the forbidden places not for fear of a prosecution by seizure, but from private scruples. Having shed blood, he fears the consequences (disease, madness?), and hopes to escape them by voluntary submission (Antiphon does not say for how long) to the restrictions that were normally imposed on the killer perforce. This is indeed most striking, and warns against too external a view of what pollution means. The danger, however, seems to be confined to the killer himself, since his pollution does not require him to be driven into exile or subjected to any legal restraint. The son who actually prosecutes his father for causing an unprotected dependent's death, claiming to fear pollution, is branded thereby as a fanatic.[63]

[61] MacDowell, *Homicide*, 82–4, cf. Paus. 2.29.10, Pl. *Leg.* 866c–d, 867e (scrutiny at the frontier).

[62] 6.4, cf. 5.87. Plato requires no more than purification in such cases, *Leg.* 865d, 868a.

[63] Pl. *Euthphr.* 3e–4d. The killing of one dependent by another, the same passage shows, required purification, and punitive measures against the homicide, but not of course legal process.

Pollution by itself makes nothing happen. But to speak of it as a rationalization is unjustified, because there is no reason to see it as chronologically secondary, while to treat it as merely the religious shadow of a legal institution would separate the two areas in a way that seems untrue to archaic Greek attitudes. It may be helpful at this point to seek guidance from ethnography.[64] The belief that killing pollutes is very widespread and, in its detailed application, very diverse. This diversity is itself important. Some pollutions threaten the killer only, others the killer and his victim's kin, others again the whole society. Some can be cleansed immediately or after a short period, while others demand the expulsion of the offender from the group. These divergences are found both between societies and in the treatment by the same society of different forms of killing. Often socially approved killing causes a mild pollution and shameful killing a very severe one. Another and even more important point that emerges from any careful ethnographic account is that pollution is a kind of institution, the metaphysical justification for a set of conventional responses to the disruption of normal life through violent death. Killing causes pollution just as, among us, death causes mourning; because of pollution various avoidances are practised, just as because of mourning black suits are donned. Classical scholars, by contrast, have tended to interpret the phenomenon in terms of emotions, crediting the Greeks with that horror of spilt blood that they imagine they themselves might in the circumstances have felt. But though such horror is no doubt the source of the imagery of pollution, it cannot explain the way in which 'the polluted' continue to perform a set of standardized acts, and continue to be avoided by outsiders, however little horror may be felt in the particular case. A clear example of pollution as a kind of institution comes from the Nuer.[65] When a killing occurred, the

---

[64] See e.g. J. G. Frazer on Pausanias 2.7.7, idem., *The Golden Bough*[3], iii, London, 1911, 165–90; P. Bohannan (ed.), *African Homicide and Suicide*, Princeton, 1960; references in I. Schapera, 'The Sin of Cain', *Journal of the Royal Anthropological Institute*, 85 (1955), 33–43; references in following notes. For differential pollution note e.g. G. M. Wilson, in P. Bohannan, op. cit., 182 (manslaughter pollutes the killer, murder the whole community); Douglas, 106 f. (only the killing of fellow-tribesmen causes hunting failure).

[65] See Evans-Pritchard, 293–7, idem, *The Nuer*, Oxford, 1940, 152–5; similarly among Mandari, Buxton, 227 f.

murderer himself required immediate purification. He received
it from a chief, in whose house he then lived until the feud was
settled. There remained a kind of relation of pollution between
the kin of the victim and of the killer. If a member of either camp
ate or drank from a vessel belonging to the other, he would
surely die. The pollution would also come into effect if a third
party inadvertently used the vessels of both sides. This state
continued until cattle were paid in compensation, to buy the
dead man a levirate bride, and the feud was wiped out by
sacrifice. These sanctions obviously gave symbolic expression
to the social gulf created between the two sets of kin by the act of
killing. When the order dislocated by the murder was restored,
the pollution ended. They also operated as a discreet pressure
towards settlement, since the need to guard against a third
party setting the pollution off imposed tiresome restrictions on
all concerned.

Pollution, therefore, is not so much a rationalization as a
vehicle through which social disruption is expressed. Naturally
it is closely associated with the dead man's anger, but even this
is just another way of expressing the same sense of disruption.
Since the disorder is the pollution, any action that restores the
normal equilibrium of things becomes a purification. A word
that is often found in this context is the verb *hosiō* or *aphosiō*,
which conveys the idea of restoring religious normality and
thereby putting oneself in the clear. The ways of doing this are
various. The verb is used in relation to exiling a killer, to
bringing him to court, and to hurling stones at a parricide's
naked corpse. A householder who cannot prosecute the killers
of an elderly female dependent, because she is unrelated to him,
can only purify his house, but, since this is all he can do, even
this puts him in the clear.[66] The crucial point is that whatever
can be done should be done. As we have seen, pollution nudges
the victim's relatives into bringing a prosecution to avenge their
kinsman, and then turns its attentions to the jurors and,
through them, the entire community.

The order whose restoration pollution demands is not simply
a matter of peace and quiet. The solution for which it works is
not the easiest, but the one which reflects the society's sense of

[66] Eur. *Or.* 515, Pl. *Euthphr.* 4c, *Leg.* 873b, 874a, Dem. 23.73, 47.70. Cf. Appendix 1.

Miasma

what is proper. Thus, though the Nuer pollution encourages an honourable settlement between the two sets of kin, it renders shameful connivance without payment of cattle impossible. Strong religious sanctions of the same kind are also found in Greece. Antiphon explains that murder trials are held in the open air not merely to protect the jurors from pollution, but also 'so that the prosecutor should not share a roof with his kinsman's slayer',[67] and numerous texts speak of voluntary association with a kinsman's killer as the worst of crimes, compulsory association as the bitterest of degradations. In Euripides' *Andromache*, Menelaus can profess to be shocked that Peleus is prepared to enter the same roof as Andromache, ex-wife of the brother of the killer of Peleus' son that she is.[68] This sense of a special corrupted relation created between families by the act of killing is reflected semantically in the word *authentēs*, which in early usage is constructed with a dative of disadvantage: X is *authentēs* to Y if he has killed one of Y's kin.[69] Murder within the family creates the same kind of relationship of pollution between the killer and the surviving relatives. For expiable forms of kin-killing (fratricide in anger, killing of child by parent, but not the reverse, in anger) Plato in the *Laws* imposes restrictions on the killer even after his return from exile. He may not resume any form of association with his family, because he has destroyed one of their relatives, and if he does, both he and they are liable to prosecution for impiety. Plato is certainly reflecting Athenian sentiment here, although we know nothing of the formal legal position.[70] 'The law' forbids Heracles to bury the

---

[67] 5.11, cf. Arist. *Ath. Pol.* 57.4. O. Weinreich, Hermes 56 (1921), 326–31 (= *Kl. Schr.* i, Amsterdam, 1969, 552–7) refers this custom to the purifying power of sun and rain (cf. 532 *FGrH*, p. 513 para. 2); Antiphon's explanation in terms of the symbolic meaning of the shared roof (cf. *Il.* 9.640, *LSS* 115 A 16–20, and many texts about to be cited on the '*authentēs* relation') is far superior.

[68] Eur. *Andr.* 654–9. On the '*authentēs* relation' between families and social groups cf. Soph. *El.* 262–76, 358, 587, 1190, *OT* 821 f., Eur. *Andr.* 170–4, Thuc. 3.58 (!), Isae. 9.20, (Andoc.) 4.22, Arist. *Ath. Pol.* 18.6, Dem. 18.257: all this abhorrence lies behind Hom. *Il.* 24.505 f. The relation disregarded, Hes. *Scut.* 11.

[69] L. Gernet, *Droit et société dans la Grèce ancienne*, Paris, 1955, 29–38 (= *REG* 22 (1909), 13–32); see esp. Hdt. 1.117.3, Soph. *El.* 272, Eur. *Andr.* 172, *IA* 1190, *Tro.* 660, *Rhes.* 873, Ant. 5.11. The special usage with dative of disadvantage (expressed or implied) that Gernet establishes remains a fact even if Chantraine ('Ἀφιέρωμα Τριανταφυλλίδῃ, Thessaloniki, 1961, 89–93) is right to make the basic meaning 'responsible'. F. Zucker, 'Authentes und Ableitungen', *Sitz. Leipz.* 107.1962.4, does not yet know Chantraine.

[70] Pl. *Leg.* 868c–869a. But cf. n. 79 below.

children he has slain, and it would be sinful (not *themis*) for
Agamemnon, having sacrificed one of his children, to embrace
the others;[71] in a historical case, continued association by the
victim's brother with a presumed father-killer leads to a prosecution for impiety.[72] Society's practical power to insist upon
what it believes to be right is here very weak. Kin-killing is
utterly abominable,[73] but since revenge (and subsequently prosecution[74]) belongs exclusively to the victim's relatives, who are
also relatives of the killer, the pressure towards connivance is in
practice very strong.[75] The father with two sons, one of whom
kills the other, is left helpless in his old age if he expels the
offender as he should. Pollution does its best to reassert the
claims of the victim against those of convenience (or even, as in
the *Oresteia*, against those of broader social order). Family
members who disregard it invite divine punishment. Too much
trust is placed in the gods' clemency, we hear, by the 'father
who shares his house with sons who have shed kindred blood'.[76]
Its practical success, of course, in forcing kin-killers into exile is
hard to assess. Expulsion of homicidal relatives by the rest of the
clan, and voluntary withdrawal 'in obedience to the law', are
both found in mythology,[77] but about the fate of actual kin-
killers in Athens there seems to be no scrap of evidence.

[71] Eur. *HF* 1361, *IA* 1191 f.; cf. Aesch. *Cho.* 909, Hdt. 3.50.3.
[72] Dem. 22.2. That 'Athènes appliqua systematiquement ce principe' (Reverdin,
188, cf. Glotz, 436–8) the evidence of one malicious prosecution does not demonstrate.
MacDowell, *Homicide*, 9 f. goes too far in inferring that failure to prosecute in any
homicide case could lead to an impiety charge; the case in question in Dem. 22.2 is one
of parricide, and the offence is 'association' with the killer, not failure to prosecute;
where the killing had occurred between families, 'association' would not normally
arise. The analogy with Plato (*Leg.* 866b, 871b, etc.) is misleading here, as Plato is very
free with impiety charges.
[73] On the horror of kin-killing, which is in fact 'self-killing' (cf. p. 351 below on *auto-*
compounds), see e.g. Aesch. *Sept.* 681 f., Eur. *HF* 1074–6, *Med.* 1268–70, fr. 82, Pl. *Leg.*
872c – 873b. Its taint may persist abroad, cf. most of the passages cited p. 118 n. 58.
Parricide forbidden burial in native land?: Soph. *OC* 407. For discussion see Glotz, 44
f., 232–6, 321–3, 434–8.
[74] See most recently M. Gagarin, *GRBS* 20 (1979), 302–13.
[75] See I. Schapera, op. cit.; Black-Michaud, 228–34.
[76] Eur. fr. 645.4.
[77] Expulsion: Hom. *Il.* 2.665 f., 16.573 f., Hdt. 1.35.3, Apollod. 3.12.6; Glotz, 44 f.
Voluntary withdrawal by tyrants in historical romance: Nic. Dam. 90 *FGrH* fr. 45, 61,
Parth. *Amat. Narr.* 14.5. Other voluntary responses to pollution, Apollod. 2.4.12, 2.7.6.
Note too the moral pressure supposedly exerted on the tyrant Periander, who had killed
his wife, by his son, Hdt. 3.50–53.

Because pollution expresses a sense of disorder, little or none of it results from killings that are felt to be quite appropriate. This is why its demands and those of the law normally coincide so closely. Where public sentiment swings in favour of a particular form of killing (of the adulterer, or the tyrant) there pollution gives way without a fight. Even in civil strife, pollution was held either not to be incurred at all, or to be willing to yield to a simple collective purification.[78] In the occasional cases where there is a clash of interest between pollution and moral feeling or the law, pollution is still standing out in favour of a principle of order whose validity in normal circumstances is universally accepted. Parricide is the most appalling of acts. A slanderous imputation of it is one of the 'unsayable things' and liable to legal action, and the possibility that it might occur inadvertently is an objection of self-evident validity to the sexual communism of the *Republic*.[79] (The particular horror is that such cases would not even be recognized, and thus the 'customary solutions' could not be applied; this danger impressed Aristotle himself.) In contrast to the normal pattern, such a violation of the order of the family can, it seems, be polluting though legally pure.[80] It would be hard to prosecute Oedipus, who killed his father unknowingly in self-defence, and yet he is a dangerous man to encounter. But it is, of course, the crucial importance of the father's inviolability that causes the pollution to spill over even on to involuntary cases; the horror is even increased by the fact that the violation of fundamental order has occurred at random. In the same way, it is because the mother's right not to be killed by her son is in general unquestioned that pollution attaches to Orestes and Alcmaeon, even though in the particular case their act may be justified.

It is obvious that murder-pollution differs in important respects from those caused by birth and death. All these pollutions are produced by breaches of order, but the source of disturbance is quite distinct in the different cases. Murder-pollution is caused by an unnatural act, and for this reason is virtually identified, as we saw, with the anger of the man

[78] Pl. *Leg.* 869c, Xen. *An.* 5.7.35, Paus. 2.20.2. In most cases of *stasis* we hear nothing at all of ritual consequences.
[79] Lys. 10, *passim*; Ar. *Eccl.* 638–40; Arist. *Pol.* 1262a 31 f. 'Solutions': exile followed by dissolution of the family, as in Plato, Glotz suggests, p. 234.
[80] Soph. *OC* 548.

unnaturally killed. This anger then directs itself in ways that in theory enforce the expulsion of the killer from the community. Birth- and death-pollution, by contrast, merely cause those most affected to lie low for a while.

The appropriate context for beliefs of this kind about murder-pollution is surely a society that lacks more formal legal institutions. They express and focus concerns that cannot be discharged through fixed channels of procedure: if Orestes had been taken in charge by a policeman, there would have been no need for the Erinyes. (In this modified sense, there is truth in the often expressed view that murder-pollution is too 'primitive' a belief to be an innovation of the seventh century.) As a result, many aspects of the institution's original workings must remain obscure. But one detail that we can point to with some plausibility, because it survived with various ramifications into the age of the orators, is the proclamation against the killer.[81] As Draco's law takes familiarity with it for granted, it is evidently very ancient. In the historical period, the proclamation by the victim's kinsmen was supplemented by one by the *archon basileus*, which formally excluded the killer, in the period before trial, from 'lustral water, libations, mixing bowls, shrines, agora'.[82] It is scarcely rash to infer that the original relatives' proclamation was to the same effect. Oedipus' proclamation against Laius' killer in Sophocles probably gives a fair impression: 'I forbid anyone in the land . . . to receive or address the man, or admit him to prayers to the gods or sacrifices, or give him lustral water; but let all thrust him from the house.'[83] It seems that proclamations of this kind were often respected in the early period, because there is no real trace in legend of the kind of blood feud familiar from many non-centralized societies.[84] Instead of remaining with his kinsmen to fight it out, or seeking refuge with a powerful lord in his own land, the killer persuades the victim's relatives to accept blood-money, or flees

---

[81] *IG* I³ 104 (M/L 86) 20, MacDowell, *Homicide*, 23–6; on the origins see Latte, *Mord*, 283 f. = *Kl. Schr.* 386; Gernet, *Anthropologie*, 227–9.

[82] Dem. 20.158.

[83] Soph. *OT* 236–41; cf. Hdt. 3.50–53.

[84] This point, crucially important (and constantly neglected) in relation to the supposed Homeric indifference to pollution, is emphasized by Nilsson, *GF* 99 n.1, Wilamowitz, *Kleine Schriften*, 5.1, Berlin, 1937, 120. Contrast the protection that for other offences could be sought within the same community, Hom. *Od.* 16.424–30.

to another country where he is purified and starts life anew. The advantages of such a convention, which saved the Greeks from the ravages of feud, are obvious, but its imaginative vehicle must have been the 'pollution' of the killer, which debarred his countrymen, however sympathetically disposed, from sheltering the shedder of a 'fellow tribesman's' blood.[85]

If the proper place for a belief in murder-pollution is in a society without courts, we would expect it to wither away or change in meaning once courts are established. This would not necessarily happen immediately, because time would be needed for the courts to entrench themselves and win recognition as a satisfactory form of procedure. Pollution temporarily acquires a new function, as a threat directed by the original avengers against the surrogate avengers, the jurors, and through them against the city that they represented. We see this most clearly in the *Eumenides*, where the Erinyes, defeated in the first of all murder trials, at once propose to turn their malice against the whole city by which Orestes has been acquitted. (Normal prosecutors, like those of the *Tetralogies*, can merely warn of the dangers of pollution, but because of their dual nature as prosecutors and animate pollution the Erinyes can also inflict it.) The numerous and distinctive oaths sworn at homicide trials seem to have been intended to transfer responsibility for a false decision from the jurors to the perjured participants.[86] After Aeschylus and Antiphon, however, the dangers of pollution seem to recede. Even within 'Antiphon', there is a noticeable contrast between the *Tetralogies*, where the argument from pollution recurs with obsessive regularity, and its merely intermittent presence in the forensic speeches. The speech *Against the Stepmother* (admittedly a weak case probably undertaken only in obedience to the dead man's order) contains no reference to the temples she pollutes, no attempt to trace the working of the divine curse in her life after the murder, no threats of divine vengeance against the prosecutor's conniving half-brothers; although the crime itself is repeatedly spoken of

[85] For the concept of killing an *emphylos* (admittedly designating, in some cases, kinsman rather than tribesman) see Hom. *Od.* 15. 273, Hes. fr. 190.2, Pind. *Pyth.* 2.32, Pl. *Resp.* 565e, *Leg.* 871a, Ephorus 70 *FGrH* fr. 100, *P. Oxy.* 1241, col. 3, 28 ff., Theophr. *ap.* Porph. *Abst.* 2.27, Paus. 2.20.2.

[86] MacDowell, *Homicide*, 90–100. On the motivation see Aeschin. 2.87 f.

as an impiety, the only suggestion that its consequences may be supernatural is the final sentence, 'I think the gods below too care for those who have been wronged.' The defendant in the Herodes case does indeed advance the celebrated argument from safe contact as a proof of his innocence (81–4), but, though he reminds the jurors that they have often in the past come to regret capital sentences (69–71, 91), and speaks of such a false verdict as 'not just a mistake but also an impiety' (88, 91, 92), he does not claim that they have suffered as a consequence, or will necessarily do so if they go wrong in the present case. On the contrary, when a man is unjustly executed, 'along with his body his hope of revenge dies too.' His friends will not care to avenge him; even if they do, 'what good will that do him once he's dead?' (95). The defendant in the speech *On the Choreutēs* points out to the jurors the solemnity of their charge (3–6), but does not advance further towards a threat than the remark that a correct verdict is desirable 'principally for the sake of the gods and piety, but also for your own sakes' (3). Arguments familiar from the *Tetralogies* recur, but in the most muted tones. An unjust acquittal is 'less religiously offensive' (*hosiōteron*) than an unjust condemnation; in the *Tetralogies*, it is a question of which way the avenging spirits will turn.[87] The jury cannot 'transfer the responsibility' for an unjust decision upon anybody else; here too, in the *Tetralogies*, it would be pollution or spirits that the jurors could not evade.[88]

In other orators, supernatural threats have receded even from the position they occupy in the forensic Antiphon. Gorgias' *Palamedes* contains only the faintest hint that an unjust condemnation might be a source of danger to the assembled Greeks; the consequences on which the orator really insists are those of remorse and everlasting disgrace.[89] The idea that the gods are watching the jurors as they vote is not extinguished in fourth-century oratory – it occurs particularly in cases of impiety – but it has settled down as no more than one argument

[87] 5.91; *Tetr.* 3 β 8. Xen. *Hell.* 1.7.19 makes an unjust capital condemnation 'a great offence against the gods' without explicit mention of pollution.
[88] 6.6, cf. 5.89; *Tetr.* 3 β 8.
[89] Gorgias B 11.34–6. The 'impious deed' they will have on their consciences perhaps hints at danger.

among many.[90] Even in religious cases, the injustice of the deed
is often emphasized more than the impiety.[91] The first speech of
Lysias, a defence in a case of justified killing, is quite free from
the language of pollution, and it appears only fleetingly even in
the prosecution of Eratosthenes.[92] A comparison is difficult
because of the accident[93] that has preserved for us three murder
speeches of Antiphon but none of later date except for Lysias I,
which is a defence. But it is reasonable to suppose that, in a
fourth-century prosecution, murder would have been presented
as a threat to society on a secular far more than on a religious
level. This secularization probably has complex causes, but it is
tempting to suggest as one of them that murder-pollution had
outlived its utility. The prominence of pollution in the *Laws* is
characteristic of that work's profound religious conservatism.

The approach adopted here puts no emphasis on fear and
horror. The polluted murderer is by definition dangerous, but
this does not mean that fear was the origin of the belief, nor even
that, provided the proper procedures were followed, the danger
presented by the killer was any more a source of anxiety than
the high-voltage cables that run through our cities. The idiom
was, of course, well suited to express any fear or horror that
might actually be felt, as in the case of Oedipus, but that does
not tell us anything about the origin of the belief.

On the other hand, since the doctrine of pollution does
postulate intense dangers, it would always be possible for an
individual or a community to worry whether the customary
procedures were adequate in order to cope with them. The
polluted murderer lurking undetected could become a source of
imaginative terror. There is obviously a question here about
intimate feelings that we are scarcely equipped to answer, but
such evidence as is available suggests that intense anxiety was
not the norm. If we consider the different sets of people involved, it is the killer himself whose peril is most frequently

---

[90] (Lys.) 6.13 μὴ βούλεσθε εἰς ὑμᾶς τὴν αἰτίαν ταύτην περιτρέψαι, Dem. 19. 220 (cf. 239)
μὴ ... ὑμεῖς τὴν ἀρὰν καὶ τὴν ἐπιορκίαν οἴκαδ᾿ εἰσενέγκησθε, Dem. 29.4, ? 43.84, 59.109 (cf.
126), Lycurg. *Leocr.* 146 (these last two texts both claim that public responsibility
before the gods for an individual's misdeeds only begins once they are brought to trial),
Aeschin. 2.87 f.
[91] e.g. Lysias 30.
[92] 12.99.
[93] K. J. Dover, *Lysias and the Corpus Lysiacum*, Berkeley and Los Angeles, 1968, 6.

mentioned. The murderer goes mad, and not in the elaborate mythological histories of Orestes and Alcmaeon alone; in the *Hippolytus*, the nurse reacts to Phaedra's derangement by asking 'Are your hands clean of blood, child?' and Amphitryon in the *Heracles* supposes for a moment, remarkably, that the hero has been driven mad even by his justified revenge against Lycus. The same belief is still attested in fourth-century texts.[94] The killer of a parent, according to a 'doctrine of priests of old' recorded by Plato, is surely destined himself to perish at the hands of a child, in this incarnation or another.[95] For the threat to the victim's kin, should they fail to seek revenge, the most eloquent testimony is Apollo's oracle to Orestes in the *Choephori*, which mentions cancerous diseases, leprosy, and madness.[96] We do not hear, however, of any defaulting avenger, mythological or historical, who was actually believed to have been afflicted in this way. As to the dangers undergone by those who associate with the killer, Antiphon states that they are demonstrated by numerous instances, while Orestes too, in Aeschylus, can point to his 'harmless association' with many households as proof of his purity.[97] But it is interesting that the only specific risk which Antiphon refers to is that of shipwreck. There is no suggestion that disease or madness is contracted by contact with a murderer and, though the possibility is envisaged in tragedy,[98] no exemplary mythological tale is based upon it. When in myth a purification proves ineffective, this is revealed through the killer's renewed madness and not the affliction of his associates. Xenophon offers a purely secular version of the belief: 'So far have men gone in their precautions against murder that many have made a law that not even the man who associates with the murderer should be pure.'[99] There is, finally, the danger to the community at large. This appears to be excellently attested; the prosecutor in the first tetralogy

[94] Murder madness: see Appendix 7 on the myths of Alcmaeon, Heracles and Iphitus, Ixion, and Orestes; Aesch. *Cho.* 1055 f., Eur. *Hipp.* 316, *HF* 966 f., *Or.* 339, Xen. *Cyr.* 8.7.18, Pl. *Leg.* 865d–e, Plut. *Cim.* 6.4. But murder-madness is a common belief in societies that do not talk of murder-pollution.
[95] Pl. *Leg.* 872e.
[96] 278–96.
[97] Ant. 5. 82, Aesch. *Eum.* 285. In Ael. *VH* 8.5 blood-guilt causes contrary winds.
[98] Eur. *Or.* 793.
[99] *Hiero* 4.4.

warns the jurors that unavenged murders lead to crop-failure, while the *Oedipus Tyrannus* opens with all nature out of joint as a consequence of the death of Laius. Specific instances, however, prove surprisingly hard to discover. In myth, when plague follows upon the murder of an individual, the victim is normally someone especially dear to the gods (priest, prophet, or poet), the guilty party not a private citizen but the whole community, and the purport of the story aitiological. Historically, we do not find afflicted states instituting hunts for the murderers in their midst; the commonest religious explanation for public disaster is sacrilege, and the only kind of killing that seems to be identified as a cause is the collective massacre, with numerous victims and communal responsibility, which was already a source of scandal before the affliction occurred.[100] Even in Sophocles, plague would not perhaps have bitten so deep had not both victim and killer been kings, and one the father of the other. It seems that the author of the *Tetralogies* has taken the doctrine of pollution to a theoretical extreme some way beyond the level of unease that in practice it created.

We turn in conclusion to the factor that has long bedevilled discussion of this issue, the 'silence of Homer'. It has deliberately been postponed to the end, so that readers with little taste for speculation about the unknowable can pass straight on to the following chapter.

Homer's silence was first noted in antiquity. 'We don't find the killer being purified in Homer, but either going into exile or being killed in turn (*or, paying compensation*)', says one scholiast, and another, detecting at one point an allusion to purification, comments 'perhaps an anachronism, like "the trumpet sounded." '[101] It should be emphasized that these two texts, although often taken to indicate that Homeric man's attitude to homicide was relaxed, admit the opposite interpretation just as readily. The Homeric killer cannot merely be purified, but must flee instead. It is interesting to contrast the first securely attested purification, that of Achilles in the

---

[100] See pp. 273 ff. below.
[101] Schol. T. *Il.* 11.690 (the ambiguous word is ἀντιτίνοντα); schol. T. *Il.* 24.480.

Aethiopis (a poem perhaps of the mid-seventh century).[102] Having, under provocation, slain Thersites, Achilles sailed to Lesbos (a temporary symbolic exile), sacrificed, was purified, and rejoined the Greek army. We see here, some say, the first imprint of the novel doctrine of pollution: Achilles would not hitherto have been incommoded for putting down such a low fellow. The alternative to purification for Achilles, however, might well have been permanent exile, hounded out by Thersites' cousin, Diomede. It has similarly been suggested that the Athenians first established their *exēgētai pythochrēstoi* to make possible the return of the tainted Alcmaeonids. 'You were all too lax', exclaims Ovid of the ancients, 'in thinking that the grim crimes of bloodshed can be washed away in river water.'[103]

Purification is not mentioned in Homer; the customary responses to homicide that appear in the poems, however, are quite reconcilable with the institution we have postulated, and may even be taken to presuppose it.[104] There is no possibility for the Homeric killer, any more than for the 'polluted' killer of classical times, of finding refuge within his own country. He may, it is true, be able to persuade the victim's kin to accept compensation (this was probably particularly common in cases of accidental killing)[105] but, as the African evidence shows, the payment of blood-money is not irreconcilable with a doctrine of pollution. No absolute moral revulsion is felt against deliberate killing, which may even be a subject for boasting,[106] but this

[102] OCT Homer v, p. 105. 28 ff. The arguments advanced for dating Arctinus (W. Schmid/O. Stählin, *Geschichte der Griechischen Literatur*, i.i, Munich, 1929, 211 f., G. L. Huxley, *Greek Epic Poetry*, London, 1969, 144) are fragile. Other purifications ascribed by late sources to early poets (adduced by Lloyd-Jones, 73) must be treated with caution (Calhoun, 26–9). Whereas in Hes. *Scut.* 13 Amphitryon merely 'supplicates' the Thebans, in Apollod. 2.4.6. and hyp. D, E to Hes. *Scut.* (pp. 269–71, Rzach, *ed. maior*) he is purified there. We cannot therefore be confident that Procris was really 'purified' at Thebes in the *Epigoni* (OCT Homer v, p. 115, fr. ii). On the supposedly Hesiodic story in Schol. D. *Il.* 2.336 see p. 382 below. But the purification ascribed by Proclus to the *Aethiopis* is unlikely to be a late accretion, as subsequent accounts of Thersites' death ignore it (*RE* s.v. *Thersites*, 2461–3). Stengel, 157 claims that the purification is of early and untypical form because sacrifice precedes purification; but cf. Dem. 23.72, ? *LSS* 115 B 58.

[103] Exegetes: Jacoby, 40 f., 272 n. 225. Ov. *Fast.* 2.45 f.

[104] For the evidence see Bonner/Smith, i. 15–22.

[105] Cf. Hasluck, 239 f. But the definition of the 'accidental' can depend as much on the mutual disposition of the two kin groups as the facts of the case, Black-Michaud, 19 f.

[106] e.g. *Od.* 13. 258 ff.; cf. Hasluck, 228, and for public indifference Campbell, 201.

could scarcely be looked for in a society without centralized authority, where the threat of violence is the individual's only final protection against encroachment by his neighbour. In the classical period, by contrast, killing is much closer to being the same absolutely horrific act that it is today. It is 'impious', a 'public offence', 'among the worst of crimes'.[107] 'Man-slayer' is, like 'temple-robber', a term of everyday abuse, and orators concoct murderous plots in which they claim their opponents to have been involved.[108] This change in attitude is obviously due to the development of alternative institutions through which the individual can vindicate his rights. Arms are no longer worn, and the only motives for killing that can remain are shameful. But it is again clear from the ethnographic evidence that pollution may antedate moral revulsion against killing. The disorder that it expresses is not moral but social, a disturbance of the equilibrium between two family groups. It may become a vehicle for moral revulsion once this is felt, but this is a kind of reapplication.[109] Even in Homer, however, as in most non-centralized societies that condone honest killing,[110] there exists a special category of shameful killings that are fiercely condemned. (Most of the murders of modern society would fall into this category.) Killing 'by stealth', later condemned in all circumstances, is still admissible in defence of honour, but it is clear from the case of Aegisthus that killing for material and sexual gain invites divine punishment; we see the gods

---

[107] See e.g. Ant. *Tetr.* 3 a 2, Ant. 5.10, Dem. 21.45. Among the West Locrians, by the early 5th century, the killer and his *genea* were exiled in perpetuity, and his house destroyed (M/L 13. 12–14); at Athens the property of the deliberate killer was confiscated, in apparent contrast to the Homeric practice (*Od.* 13. 258 f.) – a penalty reserved for serious crimes against the community.

[108] Man-killer: Men. *Dysc.* 481 with Sandbach's note, and note Pl. *Euthphr.* 4d. Imputations of murder: Lys. 10.1, 26.8–13, Isae. 8.41, 9.17, Isoc. 18.52, Dem 21. 104, 22.2, 59.9, Aeschin. 1.172, 2.148.

[109] It is tempting to suppose that in Greece a pollution originally confined to killer and victim's kin became extended for this reason to the whole community (so Durkheim in his review of Glotz, *L'Année sociologique* 8 (1903–4), 469), particularly through the institution of courts; but the killer's exile suggests that he was always generally polluted. For the same reason it is unsatisfactory to suppose that pollution originally attached only to shameful killers (*miaiphonoi*).

[110] See e.g. Hasluck, 244–5; P. P. Howell, *A Manual of Nuer Law*, Oxford, 1954, 40, 42, 55; Pollock/Maitland, i.52, ii.458 n. 1, 486 on non-emendable offences; Black-Michaud, 117 f.

themselves discussing it.[111] Kin-killing, strongly condemned by
public opinion, will surely not have escaped the notice of the
Erinyes, and the threat of divine anger is a powerful deterrent
from guest-killing.[112] It is very revealing that legalistic
stratagems, rather like that of Creon in the *Antigone*, are employed to avoid the literal taint of these kinds of murder. The
offensive person is marooned, or dispatched abroad to be killed
by a stranger, or sent out to face impossible dangers in the
hunt.[113] The supernatural dangers that are apparent in these
cases are not mentioned in connection with ordinary killings,
because the chief responsibility for achieving revenge lies not
with the gods but with the victim's kinsmen. Fear of disgrace is
the chief pressure that drives the Homeric kin to seek revenge,
and in some modern Mediterranean feuding societies it is the
only one.[114] (There is therefore no reason to see the Homeric
picture as an idealized aristocratic rendering of an institution
whose real basis is the peasant's fear of ghosts.[115] There is less
evidence for fear of the dead in Hesiod than in Homer.) But in
Homer the dead can intervene to nudge the living and remind
them of their duties; maltreatment of a corpse provokes divine
revenge, and the Erinyes ensure that each member of a family

[111] Stealth: *Od.* 13. 258 ff., *Il.* 7. 142–6, contrast Soph. *Tr.* 274–9, Pind. *Pyth.* 2.32. It
was particularly after δολοκτασίαι that the killer sought to protect himself by 'spitting
out' the blood, *Etym. Magn.*, p. 118. 31–6 citing Aesch. fr. 354 and Ap. Rhod. 4.479.
Aegisthus: *Od.* 1. 35–47; for possibly violent public response to a shameful killing cf. *Od.*
16. 376–82.

[112] Especial inhibitions against kin-killing: *Il.* 9. 461, *Od.* 10.441. The Erinyes uphold
rights, whether of parents, elder brothers, or beggars (Lloyd-Jones, 75), living or dead
(*Od.* 11. 280). Guest-killing: *Od.* 14. 406, 21. 28, *Il.* 24. 583–6 (cf. Eur. *Hec.* 25–7, 714 ff.,
789 ff.)

[113] Soph. *Ant.* 775 f., *Od.* 3. 267–72, *Il.* 6. 155 ff., with Tzetzes on Lycophron 17. An
errant sent away to be killed: Apollod. 1. 8. 4 (= Hesiod, fr. 12, Periboea); given away
for killing: Apollod. 3. 9. 1 (Auge); exposed to mortal dangers: Apollod. 3. 13. 3 (Peleus).
For marooning cf. the Philoctetes myth, Eur. *Hec.* 1284–6, *Paroem. Gr. Coislin.*, p. 123
Gaisford s.v. Ἀνάγυρος (testimonium to Aristophanes Ἀνάγυρος).

[114] *Od.* 24. 433–6. Cf. e.g. Hasluck, 219–260, Campbell, 193–203, Black-Michaud,
passim.

[115] So e.g. Stengel, 156: 'und wo ritterliche Adelsgeschlechter herrschen, trotzig ihrer
Kraft vertrauend, wie die homerischen basileis, findet der ängstliche Glaube der
niedrigen Bürger schwer Eingang'. For emphasis on the 'peasant' basis of Homeric
society cf. H. Strasburger, *Gymnasium* 60 (1953), 97–114; P. A. L. Greenhalgh, *Historia*
21 (1972), 532 f.; P. Walcot, *Greek Peasants Ancient and Modern*, Manchester, 1970, 16–19.

pays to the others their due.[116] It seems inevitable that the victim's kin would have been exposed to supernatural danger as well as public scorn if they failed to seek revenge.

Thus, of the bundle of phenomena that constitute, or are explained by, pollution in the classical texts we find in Homer the killer's exile, divine anger provoked by particular forms of killing, and the potential at least for ghostly sanctions against inactive kin. The actual metaphor of pollution is absent, but there exists an epithet *miaiphonos* (it is applied to Ares) which means, presumably, 'one who kills in a polluting way' and in later texts is applied to the most culpable murderers.[117] The celebrated silence, therefore, reduces itself almost entirely to the matter of the actual rite of purification. Of the exiled killer, Homer says merely that he 'makes supplication to' a powerful prince, without mention of purification.[118] Even in later texts, however, the request for purification appears merely as a sub-division or special aspect of supplication. Zeus is god of the one because he is god of the other, and in ritual rules from both Athens and Cyrene the killer seeking purification is a 'suppliant'.[119] His most pressing requirement is for a home in which to start life anew. By consenting to purify him, the foreign lord accepts the obligation to provide one, and this is the source of the purified man's strong indebtedness towards him.[120] But this, the really important service, is already provided by the Homeric lord who 'receives' a homicidal 'suppliant'. If the actual rites of purification were introduced in post-Homeric times – an importation from Lydia, perhaps[121] – the importance of this innovation was slight. It is hard to accept, however, that such rites were a complete novelty, though modification and extension in their application there may well have been. They are not products of the same kinds of anxiety as the compulsive

---

[116] *Il.* 23.65–107, 22.358; for the Erinyes see Lloyd-Jones, 75. For the dead man's claims see E. Bruck, *Totenteil und Seelgerät im griechischen Recht*, Munich, 1926, 27–34, Rohde, 38, Glotz, 59–76, above all *Il.* 24. 592–5.

[117] LSJ s.v. μιαιφόνος

[118] e.g. *Il.* 16.574.

[119] 356 *FGrH* fr. 1; *LSS* 115 B 50 ff.

[120] For this see Hdt. 1.44, Eur. *Stheneboea*, prologue 22–5, p. 44 v. Arnim, Apollod. 3.13.3, and *e contrario* Ixion's crime against Zeus.

[121] G. Grote, *History of Greece*[2], London, 1883, i.25, citing Hdt. 1.35 – but sceptics might regard Hdt.'s remark as a story-teller's improvisation.

washings of the patients of Freud, but ceremonial expressions, exploiting concrete symbolism, of social realities. Bloodshed has caused the killer's exclusion from society and, to permit his readmission, that blood must be washed away. These rites are performed in the classical period not by vagabond priests but by high-born representatives of the community; a Nestor would doubtless have been happy to preside over such a ceremony.[122] Purification of the suppliant in his new home abroad is deeply embedded in mythology and, in the autonomous prince who acts as purifier, presupposes a figure who was becoming extinct in the archaic period.[123] If Homer had been lost, indeed, and only the mythological evidence survived, no one would have doubted for a moment that these rites were primeval. It is tempting to revive the unfashionable view that, in 'supplicating' a foreign lord, the Homeric killer implicitly requests purification; the actual ritual is omitted by the poet, not by the society the poet describes.[124] The author of the Hesiodic *Shield*, who certainly lived in a period when purifications were performed, was content to describe a killer's arrival in a new country in terms of supplication.[125] The passages that have been quoted to prove that Homer cannot have been familiar with these practices are quite inconclusive.[126]

[122] See Appendix 6. Dodds designates the rituals 'elaborate and messy' (36); were Homeric rituals as a rule anything else?

[123] See Appendix 7. The myth of Ixion is based upon the archaic institution of bride-price (Diod. 4. 49.3; on bride-price cf. A. M. Snodgrass, JHS 94 (1974), 114–25).

[124] K. O. Müller, *Aeschylos Eumeniden mit erläuternden Abhandlungen*, Göttingen, 1833, 137. For the subsequent debate cf. references in Glotz, 228 n. 3, Bonner/Smith, 16 n. 1, Calhoun, 16 n.2. Nilsson, *GGR* 91 f., Lloyd-Jones, 83 revive Müller's position, without citing him. Müller's positive arguments for the presence of murder purification were fallacious. He observed (134 n. 10) that schol. T. *Il.* 24.480 apparently read ἀνδρὸς ἐς ἀγνίτου; it notes τὸν δὲ καθαίροντα καὶ ἀγνίτην ἔλεγον. But the tradition makes excellent sense, as supplication was made ἀνδρὸς ἐς ἀφνειοῦ (see Appendix 7), and murder purification was not performed by a specialized 'purifier'; ἀγνίτης, which first appears in Lycophron 135, is a formation of a kind very common in technical and poetical Hellenistic Greek, rather rare in Homer: cf. G. Redard, *Les Noms grecs en -ΤΗΣ, -ΤΙΣ*, Paris, 1949, 110–15, 260 n. 2. (But Müller's reading is accepted by E. Fraenkel, *Geschichte der griechischen Nomina agentis auf -τήρ, -τωρ, -της*, ii, Strasburg, 1912, 128 n. 2, and defended by Williger, 49–52.) The *thambos* of the spectators in *Il.* 24.482 need imply no more than surprise and curiosity, cf. *Od.* 7. 144–5. Nor does *Od.* 23.118 ff. support Müller, cf. Lipsius, 9 n. 25.

[125] Hes. *Scut.* 13.

[126] *Od.* 15.223 ff., 22.480–94. As to the first, the sea-shore was no place for a formal purification (Theoclymenus does not even perform a formal supplication, contrast *Od.* 7.133 ff.); as to the second, Odysseus considers the killing of the suitors justifiable homicide with no compensation payable (cf. Appendix 5).

We have so far discovered no really surprising discontinuity between Homer and the fifth century. It is, however, sometimes claimed that those heroes whose monstrous pollution fills the Attic stage are viewed by Homer and other early poets with a certain complaisance.[127] In the *Odyssey*, Orestes is an exemplary figure, untroubled by Erinyes. Still in the *Odyssey*, Oedipus lives on as king in Thebes after the discovery of his crimes, while in the *Iliad* he is honoured with funeral games like any other hero; he perhaps even, in one of the old Theban epics, makes a new marriage. Another early poem may have let Alcmaeon, with his mother's blood upon him, march out against Thebes at the head of the Epigoni. Killing a parent is, it seems, just one of the ordinary ups and downs of a hero's career.

Such a conclusion becomes paradoxical, if one considers the character of the myths themselves; is not their point to imagine the unimaginable?[128] We would have to suppose that the tragedians rediscovered in these stories that original significance which the early poets had forgotten. It does not seem, however, that Homer was unconscious of the horror of the events he alludes to, even though it does not suit his immediate purpose to emphasize it. He presents Orestes as a glorious and prosperous figure, as do all the fifth-century poets, in the long term, except Euripides; to do so, however, he finds it necessary to focus attention on the death of Aegisthus, and suppress all allusion to the matricide.[129] (Some have even supposed that it did not yet form a part of the legend.) His Oedipus, though king, is suffering all the pains that the Erinyes of a mother can create;[130] if Homer knew of any further marriage, this detail too he suppressed. As for lost poems, we cannot assess their moral colour, or how they treated these delicate incidents in their heroes' careers. The mere existence of a myth that allowed Oedipus to marry again cannot properly be used as an argument, because

---

[127] Glotz, 233 f., Dodds, 36. For the evidence on these legends see Appendix 7.

[128] On Orestes' dilemma see Hasluck, 217. The correct response would have been for Menelaus to kill Clytaemnestra; was it to prevent this tame solution that he was sent wandering so long in Egypt?

[129] Cf. A. Lesky, *RE* s.v. *Orestes*, 968 f.; M. Delcourt, *Oreste et Alcméon*, Paris, 1959, 21, 89; J. Griffin, *JHS* 97 (1977), 44 n. 32; contrast the clear statement of Hes. fr. 23 a 30.

[130] *Od.* 11. 275–80: all here is mysterious and dire. For the sufferings cf. Hes. fr. 193.4 πολυκηδέος Οἰδιπόδαο (probably in the context of his funeral games), Ibycus, *SLG* S. 222.5.

mythical persons attract to themselves stories of diverse origins and tendencies, and it is left to the poets to extract from them such coherence as they can.[131] Even Oedipus' life as a wandering outcast, sublimely imagined by Sophocles, seems to have as its origin nothing more significant than Athenian pretensions to possess his grave.

Because these stories have nothing to do with what is typical or legally exemplary,[132] the imaginative response to them of poets becomes elusive evidence. For the fifth-century tragedian, Orestes' situation has been further removed from everyday experience by the fact that an Orestes of the day would perhaps have sought redress through the courts.[133] To ask what treatment an actual Oedipus would have received is a rather fantastic question, but it is clear even from the *Oedipus Coloneus* that the issue would have been controversial;[134] the poet, however, has other interests than the precise ritual status of involuntary incestuous parricides. To descend to this level, it is instructive to compare the chorus's horrified response in Aeschylus' *Septem* to the impending fratricide with Plato's regulations on the subject in the *Laws*. 'The death like this of two brothers, one slain by the other – this is a pollution which can never grow old', say the chorus. For Plato, fratricide is 'pure' in civil strife, and requires three years exile, admittedly associated with dissolution of the family, when it occurs through anger; only the murder of a brother in cold blood demands the severest penalties.[135]

---

[131] Cf. M. Delcourt, *Oedipe, ou la légende du conquérant*, Liège, 1944, ix: 'Il n'y a pas d'Oedipe primitif. Ce qui est primitif, ce sont les thèmes qui, en s'articulant les uns aux autres sont devenus d'abord les gestes d'Oedipe, puis sa vie et enfin son caractère.' H. Jeanmaire, *Rev. Phil.* 21³ (1948), 163, speaks of 'une biographie romanesque dont il était réservé à de grandes artistes de dégager l'élément tragique'.

[132] In the case of Orestes, L. Gernet, the legal historian, insists on this, *Annales* 10 (1955), 531.

[133] Eur. *Or.* 500–4. For the possibility of prosecuting a kinsman (denied by Glotz, 437) cf. Ar. fr. 585, Pl. *Euthphr.* 4a, Poll. 8.117.

[134] Soph. *OC* 427–44, 765–71 (cf. *OT* 1438 f., ask the god). The reception of Oedipus at Athens is similarly contentious, contrast 225 ff. (chorus), 551–68 (Theseus), 944–50 (Creon).

[135] Aesch. *Sept.* 681 f., Pl. *Leg.* 868c, 869c–d, 873a–b. Cases of wholly accidental kin-killing Plato unfortunately does not consider. Sentimental tradition was eventually to declare the daughters of Pelias pure from the accidental killing of their father, see *Appendix* 7 s.v. *Peliades*.

There is no need therefore to postulate a sudden transformation in the eighth or seventh centuries. But it is worth considering some of the explanations that have been offered by those who believe in this transformation, because of their relevance to our main theme. The most popular has been the nascent influence of Delphi, and a chronological observation seems to lend support. Delphi rose to prominence in the post-Homeric period, exactly when, it is claimed, the need for purification was first making itself felt. The first attested purification from murder, that of Achilles in the *Aethiopis*, was preceded by sacrifice to 'Apollo, Artemis and Leto'.[136] The character of Delphi's influence has been defined in various ways. Some see the essence of the Delphic doctrine as the absolute debt of vengeance to the dead man's soul, and detect its expression in Draco's ban on compensation.[137] Others stress rather the need for purification and expiation. Did not Apollo himself serve Admetus for a year, and submit to complicated rites after the murder of the dragon Pytho? There has even been talk of 'the new religion of expiation' (*Sühnereligion*), founded by 'the Delphic church' in the eighth century.[138] Some appeal, without specific reference to Delphi, to the character of Apollo as the god *par excellence* of purity and cleansing, whose prophets, the archaic Men of God, carried to all corners of Greece their mission of healing, appeasement, and purification.[139]

The Greeks, of course, spoke of Apollo, the 'ancestral exegete', with immense respect, and would not have scorned the idea that he had exercised a civilizing influence upon their lives. None the less, when the word 'church' appears in the context of Greek religion, it is hard not to discern behind Apollo and his Delphic servants the image of prophets and priests of a very different kind. Apollo, it seems, introduced into Greek religion that spiritual and moral element in which it had been hitherto so lamentably deficient.

---

[136] OCT Homer v, p. 105.28 ff.

[137] Wilamowitz, *Das Opfer am Grabe*³, Berlin, 1907, 14 ff.; *Glaube*, ii. 36. Similarly Rohde, 174 ff.

[138] L. Deubner, *Neue Jahrb.* 43 (1919), 403; more cautiously Nilsson, *GGR* 632–7, 647–52, Burkert, *GR* 232, and cf. Glotz, 237.

[139] L. Gernet, *Annales* 10 (1955), 541. In his commentary on *Laws IX* (Paris, 1917, 122) he had credited 'la religion apollinienne' with the doctrine of graduated pollution according to responsibility. Further doxography in Defradas, 12 f.

A categorical denial of all Delphic influence is out of the question, when so little is known, but it is surprising how meagre the solid evidence in favour of it turns out to be. It is unsafe, for instance, to draw an argument from the nature of the god himself. Apollo, it is true, is in the fifth century the 'purifier of men's houses', he who 'washes away' evil; from his epithet *Phoibos* verbs meaning 'purify' are formed.[140] This cleansing function is obviously an aspect of Apollo's healing function, and is therefore likely to be very ancient.[141] With murder purification, however, Apollo has, on the level of cult, no connection; his priests do not perform it, at Delphi or, very probably, anywhere else.[142] The evidence is extensive that the god at whose altars murderers sought purification was Zeus; he acquired this function, which fell to him naturally as god of suppliants, when he performed for Ixion the first of all such rites, and he never surrendered it to his son.[143] Apollo, by contrast, was a god of oracles who became an authority on murder purification because pollution was an issue on which, like other oracular gods,[144] he was repeatedly consulted. When he cleansed Orestes in Aeschylus, he was performing a task that would normally have fallen to a human purifier. He felt himself responsible because his own oracle had enjoined the matricide,

---

[140] Aesch. *Eum.* 62 f., Pl. *Cra.* 405b, *LSJ* s.v. ἀφοίβαντος, φοιβαίνω, φοιβάω, φοῖβος.

[141] See Burkert, *GR* 232, *Rh. Mus.* 118 (1975), 19:

[142] R. R. Dyer, *JHS* 89 (1969), 38–56, pointed this out, correcting a general misconception. The conclusion is not weakened by the fact that, *pace* Dyer, Orestes in Aeschylus obviously was cleansed by Apollo at Delphi. There is no single cult of Apollo to which cathartic rites were definitely attached. The ancient temple of Apollo Thearios at Troizen (Paus. 2. 31. 6–9) claimed to have been the site of Orestes' purification, but in order to explain a banqueting custom (cf. the *Choes aition* at Athens, Eur. *IT* 947 ff.), not a cathartic ritual. His cure was elsewhere linked with Zeus (Paus. 3. 22. 1) and Artemis (Pherecyd. 3 *FGrH* fr. 135a). Heracles' purification at Amyclae from the blood of Iphitus (Apollod. 2. 6. 2) is not necessarily connected with the cult of Apollo there. Apollo Katharsios, scholars write note with surprise, does not exist (*RE* 10.2519).

[143] Aesch. *Eum.* 717 f. (Ixion). For Zeus Katharsios see Hdt. 1.44.2, Ap. Rhod. 4.708 f., ps.-Arist. *Mund.* 401a 23 f., Pollux 8.142, Cook, ii.ii. 1097 n. 2, 1100 n.l. For cults see ? *LSS* 65.4, *LSA* 56.11, Plut. *Thes.* 12.1 (*aition* for a cathartic cult of Zeus Meilichios at the old boundary of Attica), Paus. 5.14. 8, schol. Eur. *Tro.* 90 = 84 *FGrH* fr. 38. Other titles of Zeus are of course also relevant, Meilichios (Paus. 2.20.2), Phyxios (Paus. 3.17.9), Palamnaios, Hikesios, Alastoros. See Farnell, i.64–9, J. W. Hewitt, *HSCP* 19 (1908), 61–120, Nilsson, *GGR* 411–17, M. H. Jameson, *BCH* 89 (1965), 159–65, C. Rolley, *BCH*, ibid., 454–6. Nilsson's view that Apollo replaces Zeus as god of expiation (*GGR* 417) seems to misconceive the separate relation of the two to the process.

[144] Cf. *SEG* xix 427.

but he was not the god to whom the rites were addressed. His role in the *Aethiopis* is isolated, and puzzling.[145] Thus it seems to be a reversal of history to suppose that, once the oracle of the pure Apollo attained Panhellenic importance, it inevitably spread the doctrine that murder demands purification throughout Greece. In this area, it was the functioning of the oracle itself that made the god into a 'purifier of other people's houses'.

Argument from the god's original nature is mistaken. It might none the less be the case that the Delphic priesthood, constantly confronted by inquiries on just these matters, was responsible for the creation (or at least systematization) and diffusion of a new doctrine. The controversial question of Delphic teaching arises here.[146] Was Delphi a true fountain-head of new wisdom, or a sounding-board that amplified perhaps but did not create its clients' typical religious conceptions and preoccupations? The doctrine of purification is an excellent test case. Plato in the *Laws* submits certain aspects of his legislation on this subject to the Delphic god and his interpreters.[147] What Apollo is required to expound, however, is the ritual, while the more important issues of exile, punishment, and pardon Plato himself determines. Moreover, Plato's artificial state is reliant on Delphi because it lacks ancestral traditions of its own. It is very doubtful to what extent Delphi influenced even the ritual of historical Greek states; a glance at the sacred laws shows that they followed divergent local traditions, not directives from the centre of the earth. Even in the case of the great cathartic law of Cyrene, which is almost unique among sacred laws in presenting itself as an oracular response of Apollo,[148] it is generally agreed that the actual regulations, both in dialect and content, were formulated in Cyrene itself. Either the ascription to Apollo was simply fictitious, or the laws had been sent ready drafted for the god's formal approval, which he, with his deep-seated respect for local tradition,[149] had no cause

---

[145] Is Thersites' scapegoat nature (below, p. 260) relevant? Apollo was god of the Thargelia.

[146] References to earlier discussion in Defradas, 12 f. On Defradas's work see H. Berve, *Gnomon* 28 (1956), 174–81, L. Gernet, *Annales* 10 (1955), 526–42, H. Jeanmaire, *RHR* 149 (1956), 231–5, P. Amandry, *Rev. Phil.* 30³ (1956), 268–82.

[147] Cf. G. R. Morrow, *Plato's Cretan City*, Princeton, 1960, 423–7; Jacoby, 13–15.

[148] See Appendix 1.

[149] Xen. *Mem.* 1. 3. 1, 4. 3. 16, Isoc. *Paneg.* 31.

to refuse. At Athens, the situation was probably very similar. Though the *exēgētai pythochrēstoi* have sometimes been seen as local representatives of the Delphic god, Apollo's role was confined to selecting these interpreters from a list of candidates; once in office, they will have expounded essentially Athenian lore without reference to Delphi.[150] The most important purifications at Athens, those of 'suppliants', are performed by the Eupatrid exegetes, a college of obvious antiquity who had nothing to do with Delphi.[151]

Occasionally, every state was forced to look beyond its own recognized ritual procedures. When plague raged or crops failed, there was no other recourse but Delphi. In the *Oedipus Tyrannus*, Apollo makes a long-forgotten crime the cause of the city's misfortunes, but no single dependable historical parallel can be quoted.[152] Though it concerns a different oracle, the question put by the Dodonaeans to their Zeus is revealing: 'Is it because of some mortal's pollution that we are suffering this storm?'[153] The suggestion came from the citizens themselves.

Apart from a moralizing story of obviously post-classical origin,[154] there remains only the evidence of myth. It has repeatedly been argued that ours is a Delphic Oresteia,[155] which embodies the teaching that killing is sometimes a duty, but always requires purification. The connection lies near at hand (it was made in antiquity[156]) with the court of Apollo Delphinios at Athens, which tried cases of justified homicide,

---

[150] Jacoby, 30–3. Even if their *patria*, unlike those of the Eupatrid exegetes, were sanctioned by Delphi (Jacoby, 33, 38), the Cyrene inscriptions shows how such a sanction is probably to be understood. Even in Plato we can infer a similar procedure. Despite the role of 'prophecies' and 'the god', the detailed draft legislation in sacred matters is the work of exegetes, priests, *nomothetai* (*Leg.* 828a–b, 871c–d).

[151] See Jacoby, loc. cit.; suppliants, 356 *FGrH* fr. 1.

[152] See Ch. 9.

[153] *SEG* xix 427. On the way that most oracles tell their clients what they expect or want to hear see Thomas, 257, with references.

[154] Aelian, *VH* 3.44, Parke/Wormell, nn. 575–6: the young man who killed his friend while seeking to defend him is pure, while he who abandoned him is polluted. For the moral tone of this cf. e.g. the 'oracles' *Anth. Pal.* 14.71, 74 (P/W 591–2), below, p. 324. P/W 339 has a 'Pythian purification of Phoebus', in P/W 74 Apollo banishes polluted inquirers from his temple.

[155] e.g. Defradas, 160–204. Delphic influence on the myth is still asserted by H. Hommel, *Antike und Abendland* 20 (1974), 15.

[156] Dem. 23.74. But his trial, of course, was on the Areopagus.

and also with the various expiations undergone by the god himself.[157] As a vehicle for establishing that a category of justified homicide exists, however, a case of matricide is unnecessarily problematic; justified homicide seems not in fact to have required purification at Athens, and the choice of the Delphinium as a court need have nothing to do with Delphic doctrine (Apollo Delphinios is an older god than Apollo of Delphi).[158] Against any attempt to exploit the evidence of myth, there is an obvious objection of principle: it is not necessary or even plausible to suppose that whenever the Delphic god appears in a myth, he owes his place there to his priests. It is hard to see, for instance, what motive a devotee would have for ascribing to Apollo ultimate responsibility for Orestes' matricide. We seem rather to be dealing with the invention of a story-teller whose chief interest was the psychology of the mortal. How could Orestes bring himself to slay his own mother? The answer was obvious: only at the instance of a god.[159]

A still more hypothetical source of influence, possibly connected with Delphi, is Crete.[160] From Crete came Epimenides to Athens; to Crete went Apollo himself for cleansing from the blood of the dragon, to a town quite obscure in historical times.[161] There are other hints too that Crete was a land of ancient renown in the arts of purification.[162] Perhaps it was from there that these rites were reintroduced into Greece; an available channel would have been the Cretan priests who,

---

[157] See Appendix 7 s.v. *Apollo*.

[158] On the god see now F. Graf, 'Apollon Delphinios', *MH* 36 (1979), 2–22. His temple is suitable as a court because he is a god intimately associated with civic life, Graf, 7–13. I can find no evidence for the assertion (Wachsmuth, *RE* 4. 2513, Herter, *RE* Suppl. 13.1092) that defendants whose plea of justified homicide was admitted at the Delphinion were then purified there. On the ritual status of justified homicide see Appendix 5.

[159] Cf. M. Delcourt, *L'Oracle de Delphes*, Paris, 1955, 179; *Oreste et Alcméon*, Paris, 1959, 103–12. Fontenrose, 109 admits possible Delphic influence – but exerted to publicize the oracle, not instruct the Hellenes.

[160] See e.g. L. Deubner, *Neue Jahrb.* 43 (1919), 394–5.

[161] See Paus. 2.7.7, 2.30.3; 10.6.6–7, 10.7.2, 10.16.5; hypothesis C to Pind. *Pyth.* (p.4 Drachmann); W. Aly, *Der Kretische Apollonkult*, Tübingen, 1908, 49–52.

[162] Cretan purifiers, Aelian, *VH* 12.50; Cretan asceticism, Eur. *Cretans*, fr. 79 Austin. In an Orphic tradition, purificatory materials come from Crete (*OF* 156). Killers often flee there (Apollod. 3.15.8, Porph. *Abst.* 2.29, *Certamen*, 237–8 in OCT Homer v, p. 234), but perhaps merely as a safe refuge.

according to tradition, served Apollo in the early times at Delphi.[163] So speculative a reconstruction can neither be refuted nor confirmed. The new need in Greek society that encouraged the importation of the rites would anyway remain to be identified.

A more interesting possibility concerns Orphism. Orpheus, we learn, taught men 'rites and to abstain from murder', and 'mutual slaughter' was probably presented in Orphic poetry as a characteristic of man's barbaric past.[164] It seems almost certain that some connection exists between the central importance of 'not killing' (animals or men) in Orphism and the new horror of killing that was developing, as we saw, in a society that was shedding its arms. But the eccentric religious movement, though it may have focused and intensified these attitudes, can scarcely have created them from nothing and then foisted them on society at large.

This historical excursus ends negatively. Nothing has emerged to explain the post-Homeric transformation. But, very probably, there was nothing to explain.

---

[163] *Hymn. Hom. Ap.* 388–544, cf. P. Bourboulis, *Apollo Delphinios*, Thessaloniki, 1949, 35–8, M. Guarducci, *SMSR* 19–20 (1943–6), 85–114, G. L. Huxley, *GRBS* 16 (1975), 119–24.

[164] Ar. *Ran.* 1032, *OF* 292, Graf, 34 ff. Cf. Pl. *Leg.* 870d–e, 872d–873a.

5

SACRILEGE

A chapter on sacrilege in a book about pollution perhaps requires justification. In contrast to murder, there is, it might be argued, nothing dirty about temple-robbing; the temple-robber seeking cleansing in a foreign home is not among the standard personnel of mythology, and sacred laws, or exegetic traditions, relating to the purification of the sacrilegious are not attested. Sacrilege has sometimes, therefore, been excluded, implicitly or explicitly, from the possible categories of pollution even in serious and significant discussions.[1]

'Purifications' after acts of sacrilege do occur, however, and in good number. They escape notice because they relate to minor and, as it might seem, technical offences. If purification from spectacular forms of sacrilege is not attested, that is rather because such offences are inexpiable than because no contagious danger attaches to them. In mythology, while the murderer flees and is purified, the man who fights the gods suffers immediate and drastic punishment. But on the day to day level of cultic practice, since sanctity is defined in terms of purity,[2] minor infractions are treated as pollutions that must be met by purification. Purification will obviously be required if something intrinsically polluting is allowed to come into contact with the sacred,[3] but the principle is broader than this.[4] In several Peloponnesian cults of Demeter, for instance, the participants are forbidden the use of elegant and alluring clothing,[5] and in

[1] Cf. Gernet's remark, *Recherches*, 36 'On paraît (Glotz au moins) ne vouloir considérer, en fonction de l'idée de souillure, que l'homicide: mais l'homicide est un délit récent; des anciens délits – essentiellement sacrilèges – on ne dit rien.' Sacrilege is explicitly excluded by Adkins, 110 n. 117.
[2] Above, pp. 19f.
[3] See p. 27 n. 60, p. 33 n. 6, Ziehen, n. 61 = Buck, n. 64, Aesch. *Eum.* 167, 715 f., Ant. *Tetr.* 1α 10, β 11.
[4] Cf. H. J. Stukey, *TAPA* 67 (1936), 295.
[5] *LSS*, p. 71 for a list. Purification: *LSS* 33. Dedication: *LSCG* 68, ? *LSS* 32. Ideology of these festivals: p. 83 n. 36 above.

one case it is specified that a transgression will require purification of the shrine. There is nothing intrinsically impure about a
purple gown (indeed the offending object is sometimes required
to be dedicated to the goddess); but it is polluting in this context
because it offends against the ethos of a festival that requires
women temporarily to renounce the paraphernalia of sexual
attraction. A pollution like this is wholly metaphysical, unlike
those that have been considered in previous chapters, which
at least had their origin in tangible impurities. Several other
sacred laws demand a purification of the shrine in the event of
transgression, and if such documents had more commonly
specified a penalty, the list could no doubt have been extended.[6]

A further difference between these cases and those discussed
in earlier chapters is that the object of purification is the shrine
and not the guilty human. This is because, through such acts,
the pure gods suffer defilement. This conception came to be
criticized as crediting men with an unacceptable power over
immortals,[7] but it undoubtedly existed in popular speech,[8] and
must be counted as an anomaly in traditional belief. In the case
of suppliants, defilement might be said to fall on the emblem of
their sanctified status, the suppliant crown.[9] Though mortals
can pollute the gods, however, the gods do not seem to suffer by
it; the idea, found in some mythologies,[10] of divine power wan-
ing beneath clogging pollution is not attested in Greece. On the
contrary, it is upon the offending mortal that the pollution

---

[6] *LSCG* 136, allowing a pack-animal to enter the shrine of Alectrona at Ialysus, or
entering wearing leather shoes or products of the pig; *LSCG* 152, throwing cakes into
the springs in a shrine of Asclepius and the Nymphs in Cos; *LSCG* 154 B 1–16, various
offences; *LSS* 115 A 26–31, making an illicit sacrifice at Cyrene; *LSS* 28, 31, both
obscure. In *LSCG* 76, 149, 'propitiation' is required. Any alteration, however
necessary, of temple goods or fittings required an ἀϱεστήϱιον (propitiatory cake): see
LSJ s.v., Stengel, 134, Sokolowski on *LSCG* 32.58.

[7] Soph. *Ant.* 1044, Eur. *HF* 1232: perhaps under sophistic influence, W. Schmid,
Philol. 62 (1903), 9. The cautious formulation in Lys. 2.7 might be a response to such
criticisms: ἱεϱῶν μιαινομένων τοὺς ἄνω θεοὺς ἀσεβεῖσθαι. In modern popular Hinduism
opinions seem to differ by region as to whether the gods can be polluted: see C. J. Fuller,
Man n.s. 14 (1979), 469, with references.

[8] Aesch. *Ag.* 1645,? Eur. *HF* 757, Eur. *Heracl.* 264, *Ion* 1118, fr. 368, Pl. *Leg.* 917b,
Alciphron *Ep.* 4.1. Moulinier, 256 f. interprets expressions like τὸ ἄγος τῆς θεοῦ (p. 7 n.
31) as the pollution suffered by the goddess; that is scarcely the expression's origin, but
it may sometimes have been so understood.

[9] Eur. *Heracl.* 71.

[10] Burkert, *SH* 89

rebounds; he falls into the power of the god whose purity he has violated, becoming *enagēs*. When, in *Oedipus at Colonus*, Oedipus unwittingly desecrates the grove of the Eumenides, the chorus insist that he perform a 'purification of these goddesses', who have been polluted by him. But a subsequent remark by the chorus shows that it is mortals, not deities, who are endangered: 'If you do that, I will be happy to associate with you; otherwise, stranger, I would be frightened about you.'[11] Practically, therefore, the difference between sacrilege and other forms of pollution disappears.

It was not merely in the narrow ritual sphere that a violation of religious rules was seen as a pollution. Pollution occurs if the divinely sanctioned rights of suppliants are violated in any way, not merely if they are slain at the altar,[12] and even an offence of thought can be spoken of in the same way: he who denies the efficacy of divine vengeance 'lawlessly defiles the gods'.[13] It may be more common in such cases to use the language of divine anger or revenge rather than that of pollution, but, as we have seen, the word-group round *agos* forms a bridge between what are anyway not two sharply circumscribed concepts.[14] The reality of infectious religious danger is the same in either case, whatever language it is described in.

These ideas of polluted temples, suppliant crowns, and gods are merely a specialization of a very general tendency to envisage devaluation, the failure to pay honour where honour is due, in terms of defilement. The consulate would be polluted, Roman aristocrats felt, should a new man attain it; in Greek, honour, trust, justice, and piety are all liable to taint, and this is also the context in which the polluted marriage bed belongs, although here the threatened ideal has found a concrete symbol for itself.[15] It might be hard to find a language in which degradation and defilement are not connected. In the idea of polluted gods, therefore, a form of conceptualization is at work which is no less natural than that which sees pollution issuing from the stain on the murderer's hands. The different source of the sense

---

[11] Soph. *OC* 466, 490–2.
[12] Aesch. *Supp.* 375, Eur. *Heracl.* 71, 264.
[13] Eur. *HF* 757 – but cf. G. W. Bond ad loc.
[14] pp. 8 ff.
[15] Sall. *Cat.* 23.6; above p. 3 nn. 8, 9 and p. 95 n. 84.

of defilement in the two cases, however, leads to that difference in its diffusion that was mentioned earlier: just as an insult pollutes the honour of the person insulted, but leaves its perpetrator pure, so too sacrilege initially defiles the gods and their sacred places and only rebounds upon the guilty human by way of punishment. Where, of course, the consequences of devaluation cannot be turned back in this way upon the source of disrespect, the value itself disappears.

It is possible that the adjective *hagnos*, the standard term used to express the purity of the worshipper, originally denoted no more than that respect which access to the sacred required. *Hagnos* is unusual in the Greek religious vocabulary in that it can be applied to both gods and men. It used to be assumed that the meaning in both cases was the same, 'pure' and more specifically 'chaste'; but there was always difficulty in seeing what the chastity of Zeus, Apollo, and Demeter consisted in, and, even when used of mortals, *hagnos* is a vague term, which requires qualification from its context to describe purity from a specific taint such as sexuality. It is etymologically related to *hazomai*, 'I feel or display reverence/respect', and when applied to gods, their precincts, or their festivals, seems to mean not 'pure' but 'demanding respect'.[16] Strong support for this interpretation comes from the parallel case of *semnos*, an adjective which unquestionably means 'reverend' and is used in just the same contexts as *hagnos*. Artemis, Graces, Nymphs, Muses, Nereids, Poseidon, Demeter, Kore, Athene, Apollo, Chthonians, Zeus, personified abstractions, divine images, seats of gods, rivers, fires, and *aither* all receive both epithets, and there are no significant areas in which one is applied but not the other.[17] While some deities, almost certainly on the basis of cult, are given them as by right,[18] they are applied to others where the idea of awesomeness is particularly appropriate. Ajax as-

---

[16] Williger, 37–72. In prose, *hagnos* in its sense of venerable was supplanted by *hagios*, applied to temples, rites, mysteries, and subsequently deities, but never to pure mortals: see Williger, 72–84, Moulinier, 281 f., Benveniste, ii, 202–7.

[17] Cf. W. Ferrari, 'Due Note su *hagnos*', *Stud. Ital. di Fil. Class.* 17 (1940), 33–53. Ferrari in this valuable study suggested the parallelism but did not work it out to its limit; I tried to do so in pp. 329–35 of my Oxford doctoral thesis (1977, same title as this book), but have omitted the detailed evidence here, as anyone who cares to do so can recover it from lexica.

[18] See *IG* XIV 204, 431, Stiglitz, 64–5, *RML* 1. 1814 f.

saulted Cassandra in the temple of '*hagna* Pallas, she who of all
the blessed gods is most terrible to sacrilegious mortals'. Whèn
the gods divided up the earth, Helios was absent, and 'they left
him, a reverend god, without a share of land': a god, that is, who
little deserved to be treated in such a way. In 'they show respect
for the suppliants of reverend Zeus' the etymological connection is alluded to explicitly.[19] *Hagnos* and *semnos* or its cognates
are both used, often together, in the same highly charged way to
denote the inviolable sanctity of mysteries,[20] supplication,[21]
sanctuary,[22] oaths,[23] or any overriding claim.[24] While the rendering 'taboo' that is sometimes proposed for *hagnos* is imprecise
– one can display respect for a person or place without actual
avoidance – it brings out the inhibitions upon normal freedom
of action that *hagneia* imposes. 'Now is the time of the god's
festival among the people, a festival that demands respect: who
would draw a bow today?'[25]

   This interpretation of divine *hagneia* leaves its relation to
human *hagneia* problematic. The parallel with *semnos* fails us
here, because the two words, so closely comparable as epithets
for gods and their possessions, diverge completely when used of
mortals. *Semnos* moves outside the specifically religious sphere
but keeps the sense of 'requiring respect'; *hagnos* remains principally religious but now means 'uncontaminated, fit to approach
the gods', with no very obvious undertone of 'reverend'. It does
not appear in this sense in Homer, but this is perhaps coincidence, as we find in Hesiod the instruction to perform sacrifice
'reverently (*hagnōs*) and purely', which might already be the

[19] Alcaeus, *SLG* 262. 16–19, Pind. *Ol.* 7. 59 f., Aesch. *Suppl.* 652 f. The verb is
obviously felt as closely related also in Aesch. *Eum.* 885, ἀλλ᾽ εἰ μὲν ἁγνόν ἐστί ϳοι Πειθοῦς
σέβας.
   [20] Ar. *Ran.* 386 f., cf. *Hymn. Hom. Dem.* 476–9.
   [21] ἱκέται δ᾽ἱεροί τε καὶ ἁγνοί, oracle of Dodona *ap.* Paus. 7. 25. 1, the only case of *hagnos*
being applied to a mortal in the same sense as to a god (for *semnos* used similarly cf.
Aesch. *Eum.* 441).
   [22] Aesch. *Suppl.* 223 f. ἐν ἁγνῷ . . . ἵζεσθε, i.e. at the altar: cf. Eur. *Andr.* 253, 427, *HF*
715, *Suppl.* 33, 359.
   [23] ἀλλ᾽ ἁγνὸν ὅρκον σὸν κάρα κατώμοσα, Eur. *Hel.* 835, cf. Soph. *Phil.* 1289, and for the
ἁγνὸν σέβας of the gods Soph. *OT* 830, Eur. *Cycl.* 580, cf. Aesch. *Eum.* 885.
   [24] σέβας δὲ μηρῶν ἁγνὸν (so Canter for ἅγιον) οὐκ ἐπῃδέσω, Aesch. fr. 135.
   [25] Hom. *Od.* 21. 258 f. Williger, 38 renders *hagnos* 'religiöse Scheu erweckend';
Vernant, 136 says '*hagnos* et *hagios* marquent la distance, la barrière à ne pas franchir, le
mystère à respecter . . . ce qui rend le divin, en tant que tel, intouchable' (the final
phrase perhaps goes too far).

fixed phrase it later became.[26] Used without specification, *hagnos* indicates fitness to worship,[27] freedom from religious contamination of every kind; priests at Cyrene are distinguished from laymen as *hagnoi*, and a Euripidean chorus-leader, after stating in general terms that his life is *hagnos*, goes on to list the specific pollutions that he avoids.[28] Where it means 'chaste', this limitation is indicated by context or by an added genitive; it can also according to context express purity from blood-guilt, birth, and death.[29] Such human *hagneia* is essentially negative, freedom from this or that pollution; it is the necessary minimum if a god is to heed the worshipper's prayers, and its absence will not go unavenged, but it does not bridge the gap between god and man. Consecration is expressed through words from the root *hosi-*, not *hagn-*.[30] To gods *hagnos* is always applied affectively, to express the speaker's attitude to them rather than to convey information, but of mortals it merely states an objective fact about their ritual status. It is difficult, therefore, to reconcile divine and human *hagneia* by saying that the mortal, by his heroic abstinence, comes to share in the divine awesomeness.[31]

The two usages do, certainly, sometimes converge. The worshipper expressed his 'respect' for the 'sanctity' of a sacred place chiefly by protecting it from pollution; thus its *hagneia* was for him defined and felt in terms of purity. The Erinyes in Aeschylus warn Apollo that if he continues to patronize blood-guilty persons, his oracle will no longer be *hagnos*.[32] An oracle

---

[26] *Op.* 336 f., cf. West's note and Ion. fr. 27.5.

[27] See e.g. Aesch. *Suppl.* 364, 696, Xen. *Mem.* 3.8.10, *SGDI* 5112, *LSCG* 130, indices to *LSCG, LSS, LSA*, Fehrle, 48.

[28] *LSS* 115 A 21, 24; Eur. *Cretans*, fr. 79.9–20 Austin.

[29] See e.g. Men. *Epit.* 440, Eur. *Hipp.* 316, *LSA* 12.1–9, indices to *LSCG, LSS, LSA*, s.v. *hagnos, hagneuō*.

[30] Eur. *Cretans*, fr. 79.15 Austin, Ar. *Ran.* 327, 336, Pl. *Resp.* 363c, M. H. Van der Valk, *Mnemos.* 10³ (1942), 125 f., and on the negative character of *hagneia* Williger 53 f. But for a special use of ἁγνίζω in tragedy see Appendix 1.

[31] Fr. Pfister, *Phil. Wochenschr.* 1923, 359 f., *RE* Suppl. 6.153; but see Williger, 53, and on the lack of positive esteem for chastity above, p. 92.

[32] *Eum.* 715f., cf. e.g. Ant. *Tetr.* 1 α 10, β 11, Xen. *Ages.* 11.2, Theophr. *ap.* Porph. *Abst.* 2.19, p. 49.8–10 Nauck. This is Williger's explanation, 55–60, for the 'pure' sense of *hagnos*. Other coincidences/interferences between the two forms of *hagneia: hagnē* applied to a virgin goddess certainly came to be understood as 'chaste', (Arist.) *Probl.* 894b 34 f., and perhaps in e.g. Aesch. *Suppl.* 1030–2, Ar. *Ran.* 875; *hagnos* of a sacrifice means sometimes 'solemn' (Soph. *Tr.* 287, cf. 756, Xen. *Symp.* 8.9), sometimes 'pure' in the sense of bloodless (Thuc. 1. 126.6, Pl. *Leg.* 782c, Theophr. *ap.* Porph. *Abst.* 2.31, p. 162.1 N.).

was normally *hagnon* in the sense of 'demanding respect'; here, however, where it is contrasted with pollution, the word obviously also contains the idea of undefiled, and the divine and human senses become inseparable. But it is not clear that such cases of interference or coincidence between the two senses of the word are sufficient to explain the original bifurcation, and it may be worth considering the possibility that *hagnos* began as a Janus-faced adjective like *aidoios*, indicating both sides of a relation involving respect: 'demanding respect' of gods, 'displaying respect' of men. The other two archaic verbal adjectives in -*nos* (*semnos* and *deinos*)[33] are normally confined to a passive sense, but Gorgias and Isocrates found it possible to apply *semnos* actively,[34] 'respectful'. If this quite speculative hypothesis were correct, it would show that 'purity' is merely the most distinctive aspect of that 'respect', the lack of which 'defiles the gods'. It is at all events clear that the *hagneia* which fits a mortal to approach the gods is not in conceptual origin a matter of physical cleanliness. *Hagnos* never means 'clean' in a secular context, and even in reference to ritual purity is not normally applied to inanimate objects such as the clothes of worshippers. That would, perhaps, be as bizarre as to speak of 'respectful' clothes. Where it is used of an object – a precinct, lustral water, even an axe[35] – it establishes for that object, as something sacred, a claim to reverence.

Where the barrier of respect that hedges round the sacred is violated, pollution occurs. The characteristic form of this respect is, of course, inhibition. Sacred things are commonly surrounded by interdiction; a simple example comes from Thucydides, who mentions a spring in Boeotia which was 'not to be touched' for any except cultic purposes.[36] The 'untouchable' spring suggests other familiar phenomena of Greek religion – things not to be spoken, or moved, places not to be entered. Durkheim supposed that the sacred is typically defined

---

[33] A. Debrunner, *Griechische Wortbildungslehre*, Heidelberg, 1917, 159.

[34] Gorgias B 6, p. 286.12 D/K, Isocr. *Bus.* 25 (which also contains a unique active use of *hagios*, Williger, 83 f.). Sophocles' phrase εὔσεπτος ἁγνεία (*OT* 864) is a nice illustration of *hagneia* as reverence, and this meaning would suit the first attestation of the word in reference to mortals, Hes. *Op.* 336 f., perform sacrifice ἁγνῶς καὶ καθαρῶς.

[35] See Ferrari, op cit., Moulinier, 40, and Pind. fr. 34.

[36] 4.97.3.

by just such a complete abstraction from ordinary human use, as the opposition between the categories of sacred and profane is one that admits of no compromise.[37] But though the gods must obviously make demands of men in order to insist on the reality of their presence at all, there is no logical reason why these demands should take the form of prohibitions rather than commands, nor why sacredness should be determined negatively (this spring is not used for profane purposes) rather than positively (this spring is used for ritual). In practice it may be hard to discover, or even conceive of, a religion in which there is no connection between sacredness and interdiction,[38] but it is certainly the case that the emphasis given to this connection varies both between religions and within them. Both Panathenaea and Eleusinian Mysteries are sacred occasions of the highest importance in the same state; this does not mean that both are subject to the same intensity of interdiction. The normal Greek word for sacred, *hieros*, does not contain in itself the notion of 'forbidden', but merely marks out things that are in some way associated with the gods.[39] This association often but not always takes the form of ownership; sacred diseases, sacred wars, and sacred days are nobody's property, while Delos is the sacred island of Apollo even though most of the territory belongs to individual Delians. When sacred things are contrasted to *hosia*,[40] things over which the gods have no claim and that may be used freely without offence to them, 'sacred' has come to entail 'restricted', but the character of the restriction will vary from case to case, and *hieros* is often used without the opposition to *hosios* being either stated or implied. *Hagnos/ hagios* differs from *hieros* in emphasizing the majesty of the divine – a cooking-pot used in a temple, though certainly *hieros*,[41] is not necessarily *hagnos* – but, as we have noted, the respect that is required of the worshipper need not be synonymous with avoidance.

[37] Durkheim, 299–325 and *passim*; criticized e.g. by S. Lukes, *Émile Durkheim, His Life and Work*, London, 1973, 24–8.
[38] Steiner, 129 f.
[39] Burkert, *GR* 402 f. Note Dem. 21.16. On the expression ἄνθρωπος ἱερός see Burkert, 403 n. 5.
[40] Latte, *HR* 55 n. 16, 75 n. 40, 114; Busolt/Swoboda, 514.
[41] See e.g. Ar. *Nub.* 254.

Whereas Durkheim perhaps saw the relation between profane and sacred as unique, it has been pointed out that it merely
reflects, in intensified form, the patterns of respectful behaviour
that are found in everyday life.[42] Each man is a temple, surrounded by a *temenos* on which no outsider may intrude without
due cause; an incursion is felt as a pollution, and it is this sense
of personal defilement that is perhaps the unconscious model
for the pollution of gods, shrines, and values in general. The
more respected a person is, the less conceivable does it become
to tamper with his clothes, enter his room unasked, or even,
though property rights are not here in question, make free with
his name or occupy his special seat. Human awesomeness,
however, like divine, demands positive as well as negative
tribute; celebratory dinners here take the place of sacrificial
feasts. And even the most revered individual is not condemned
to absolute untouchability; a working relationship can be established which will allow his worshippers some access to him and
some exploitation of his resources, even though the original
respect will not perhaps survive unchanged too great an
intimacy.

The argument that respect for gods differs only in degree
from respect for men can be rephrased to say that there are
many sacred objects outside temple walls. In some societies,
this seems to be true even on a linguistic level, sacredness being
determined not by relation to supernatural powers but by a
particular attitude of reverence associated with it. If I appeal to
you by what you hold most sacred, I probably have a value
rather than a religious relic in mind. Although *hieros* seems not
to be used in this way (the appropriate word would be *hagnos*), a
Greek could certainly make a similar appeal in the name of a
value or valued object in addition to the gods or instead of
them.[43] It was even possible to seek sanctuary at the tomb of
one's oppressor's father rather than at a sacred place.[44] The
herbalist might extend his display of respect for the mysterious
and temperamental plants he culled to the point of bringing

[42] E. Goffman, 'The Nature of Deference and Demeanor', *American Anthropologist* 58
(June 1956), 473–502, also in his *Interaction Ritual*, Harmondsworth, 1972, 47–96.
[43] e.g. Hom. *Il.* 22.338.
[44] Eur. *Hel.* 980–7, Timaeus 566 *FGrH* fr. 50 *ap.* Ath. 520b, cf. Fontenrose, 309. For
supplicating the oppressor's wife see J. N. Bremmer, *Mnemos.* 33 (1980), 366 f.

them offerings,[45] while men who inspired exceptional awe by their deeds revealed themselves as gods thereby and earned cult. A more mundane instance of the practical diffusion of sacredness would be the garland and the values associated with it. Although it is left to the observer to say that the garland is a mark of consecration, anyone who wore one enjoyed, in principle, the benefits and suffered the liabilities of sacredness (respectively inviolability, and the obligation of purity).[46] The garland marked with a certain sanctity many areas of Greek life outside the strictly religious sphere; the participants at dinner parties put one on, but certain public offices too were 'garland-wearing'.[47] This last detail shows, as do the lustral stoups around the *agora* and the preliminary purification of the assembly,[48] that the community itself was in a sense a sacred entity.

The sacred, therefore, appears as the intensely venerable rather than the absolutely other. Though sacredness is commonly surrounded by interdiction, the relation between men and the things they hold in awe is more complex than one of simple avoidance. The gods' claims over things they actually own are naturally large, and to cede ownership to the gods is obviously a notable abnegation by men; on the other hand, divine rights in these cases may be reduced to property rights, so that the mortal is scarcely more restricted in his use of sacred property than of any other property not his own. Like other proprietors, gods let out their land and lend their money at interest. Where sacred things are not owned by the gods, the prohibitions, if any, that derive from sacredness are very varied. Athenian 'sacred triremes', for instance, were not exempt from use in war.[49] To appreciate the flexibility of sacredness in its

[45] Theophr. *Hist. Pl.* 9.8.7.
[46] Ar. *Plut.* 21, Aeschin. 1.19. Removal of the crown in contexts of death or execution, Arist. fr. 101 Rose³, *ap.* Ath. 675a, *Ath. Pol.* 57.4, Lycurg. *Leocr.* 122, (Plut.) *Cons. ad Apoll.* 119a; pollution of suppliant crown, Eur. *Heracl.* 71. Note too Pl. *Phd.* 58a–c. The essential point about crowns was made by Wilamowitz on Eur. *HF* 677; subsequent writings (listed by Burkert, *GR* 101 n. 5 and Wachsmuth, 312) have obscured the issue by treating a symbol as a magical device (Ganszyniec in *RE* s.v. *Kranz* is a partial exception).
[47] Ar. *Av.* 463–5, Aeschin. 1.19. A certain sacredness of public office appears also in the restriction of archonships, like priesthoods (p. 175 n. 177), to the physically intact, Lys. 24.13.
[48] Above, pp. 19 and 21. On the close relation between piety and patriotism see Dover, 250 f., idem, *Talanta* 7 (1975), 26.
[49] Wachsmuth, 285.

practical implications (as well as to confront one of his own
sacra), an Englishman might substitute the notion of 'royal'; the
restrictions placed upon the commoner's use of crown property
are not of one kind (royal parks and crown jewels), while an
occasion can be 'royal' without being owned by the crown or
subject to restriction. In what follows, different categories of
sacred things will be considered to see what are the implications
of their sacredness for human activity, and what the consequences of their desecration.

The institution of 'holy days' is one that few people, perhaps,
associate with Greece; certainly the Jewish sabbath was an
observance that might earn the contempt of a Greek author.[50]
There existed, none the less, a special term, *hieromēnia*,[51] to
denote the sacred time associated with a festival, and it is
commonly in the context of restrictions placed upon profane
activity that we find it used. The original sense of the word must
be 'sacred month', although it is unclear whether any Greek
state retained so long an observance in the historical period.[52] It
was the *hieromēnia* of the Carneia that prevented the Spartans
from marching out in full force to Thermopylae, perhaps also to
Marathon,[53] and on several other occasions Peloponnesian
states were obstructed in their campaigning by the *hieromēniai* of
the most important festivals.[54] Greeks enjoyed festivals, but it
cannot have been mere love of pleasure that caused serious
matters to be neglected in all these cases. There is a religious
obligation here, and one that, remarkably, could not be satisfied by magistrates acting on behalf of the people, but fell upon
the entire citizen body. When the obligation became intolerable, it was countered, like other binding religious rules, by
sophistic evasion rather than simple neglect; to avoid cam-

[50] Agatharchides of Cnidus, 86 *FGrH* fr. 20.
[51] G. Rougemont, 'La Hieromenie des Pythia et les "trêves sacrées" d'Eleusis, de Delphes et d'Olympie', *BCH* 97 (1973), 75–106, at p. 81.
[52] Rougemont, op. cit., 86–9. Note also p. 26 n. 40 above.
[53] Hdt. 7.206.1, 6.106.3 (but against referring the latter to the Carneia see Pritchett, i, 116–21).
[54] Main texts: Hdt. 9.7.1, 9.11.1, Thuc. 4.5.1, 5.54.2–4, 5.75.2, 5.82.3, Xen. *Hell.* 4.5.11: cf. H. Popp, *Die Einwirkung von Vorzeichen, Opfern und Festen auf die Kriegführung der Griechen*, Erlangen, 1957, 75–122, Pritchett, i, 121–6. Only major festivals seem to have constituted *hieromēniai* of this kind, and the demands even of these major festivals seem to have varied: the Gymnopaidia could be postponed (Thuc. 5.82.3), the whole Spartan army was not required for the Hyakinthia (Xen. *Hell.* 4.5.11).

paigning during a *hieromēnia*, the Argives manipulated the calendar so as to stick fast on.the last available profane day.[55] It is hard to be clear whether the suspension of activity, and especially of warfare, was essential to the ideology of the festival, or a mere negative by-product of the positive requirement to celebrate the rites at the due time. If the original *hieromēnia* was indeed a month, abstention from profane activity must surely have been valued in itself, as the positive celebrations could scarcely last so long. A Delphic response preserved by chance in Demosthenes shows that a period of communal inaction might still be of religious advantage in the fourth century.[56]

In certain circumstances, a *hieromēnia* might prevent aggression against a state as well as by it. The term was applied to the truces, between the host state and the participating states, that permitted the celebration of the Attic Eleusinia and the four Panhellenic athletic festivals even in time of war.[57] These truces are normally seen as compacts for mutual benefit, and it is certainly true that all Greek states strongly desired the opportunity to participate in the festivals, and that without the truces this would have been impracticable. But it is not implausible that they grew out of a feeling that respect is due to an enemy's festivals no less than to his shrines. Certainly the sacred truces had a special character, in that, unlike normal truces, decent states were expected to accept them automatically if proffered in good faith.[58] In 387, the Argives, threatened by a Spartan invasion, had recourse to their usual stratagem of declaring a sacred truce (probably that for the Nemean games)[59] 'not when the time came due, but when the Spartans

---

[55] Thuc. 5.54.3 (cf. Plut. *Alex.* 16.2). Sophism in connection with supplication, p. 184 n. 219, with oaths e.g. Hdt. 4.154.4, and cf. Latte in *RE* s.v. *Meineid* 348 = *Kl. Schr.* 369 f.

[56] Dem. 21.53.

[57] G. Rougemont, op cit.; F. J. Fernandez Nieto, *Los Acuerdos Belicos en la Antigua Grecia*, Santiago, 1975, i, 147–84. The Olympic inviolability was in the 4th c. claimed, falsely, to have once extended to the Eleans themselves: see Walbank on Polybius 4.73.6–74.8.

[58] Cf. Aeschin. 2.133–4. As for Xen. *Hell.* 4.5.1–2, the Spartans no doubt denied the Argives' right to proclaim an Isthmian truce.

[59] See references in Popp, op. cit., 144 n. 229. The identification depends on dating the incident to 387, a Nemean year; it is recommended by the fact that a Nemean truce did exist, while truces for local festivals are not attested until much later (Busolt/ Swoboda, 1263). Pritchett, i, 123 plumps, without argument, for the Carneia; an annual festival would, of course, have served the Argives' game better than a biennial.

were about to invade'. When confronted by this stratagem previously, the Spartans, characteristically, had withdrawn; on this occasion, the invasion went ahead, but only because Agesipolis had providently checked with Zeus at Olympia that it was 'safe to reject a truce unjustly offered', and subsequently confirmed with Apollo at Delphi that on this point he 'agreed with his father'.[60] For a Spartan army to disregard a Nemean truce without this explicit sanction would have been impossible, and breaches of the festival truces are in general very rare.[61]

A much broader ideal is suggested by the Plataeans' complaint against Thebes in Thucydides that they were set upon 'during a *hieromēnia*';[62] as there is no question here of a Panhellenic festival, this seems to imply that all sacred occasions should be exempt from attack. But, although the truces for the games and Eleusis are perhaps specializations from some such original ideal, there is no other secure evidence for its persistence in the classical period,[63] and a good deal of evidence that it was not in practice observed; festivals were the ideal moment for a surprise attack.[64] Such methods may have been somewhat improper, but they were not comparable to violation of a publicly heralded, and accepted, festal truce; in the hellenistic period, it was by proclaiming their own festal truces that local festivals sought to protect themselves.[65]

In contrast to the Peloponnese, there is no question at Athens of sacred time interfering with military activity. Presumably her festivals could be performed satisfactorily even with the army away.[66] What we do find at these times is a suspension of important aspects of the life of the community. Festivals were

[60] Xen. *Hell*. 4.7.2–3.

[61] Aeschin. 2.12 (cf. Dem. 19, 2nd hypothesis, para. 3); Athenian decree in *Hesperia* 8 (1939), 5–12; imputed breach, Thuc. 5.49–5.50.4. Sanctions against violation, Thuc. loc. cit., *LSCG* 78.47–9. For observance, note Thuc. 8.9.1–8.10.1; but for possible suspension of the Olympia in 428 and 424 see Pritchett, i, 120 n. 26. Host states could apparently decline to offer the truce to enemies, Thuc. 8.10.1; the Eleusinian truce, possibly for this reason, seems to have been ineffective during the Peloponnesian war, Xen. *Hell*. 1.4.20.

[62] Thuc. 3.56.2, 65.1.

[63] Cf. however p. 155 n. 59.

[64] Hdt. 6.87, Thuc. 3.3.3, Xen. *Hell*. 5.2.25–36, Aeneas Tacticus 4.8 (cf. Burkert, *SH* 174 n.20), Plut. *Pelop*. 5.

[65] Busolt/Swoboda, 1263.

[66] The battle of Naxos was won in 376 during the Eleusinia, Plut. *Phoc*. 6.7 (noted by Pritchett, i, 121 n. 28).

not necessarily general days of rest (stalls were open and building work went on)[67] but courts, council, assembly and other
administrative bodies did not hold sessions during them.[68]
Exceptions, while not actually illegal, were stigmatized as
highly irregular. There is no reason to go beyond the obvious
explanation suggested by a fourth-century decree,[69] that people
wanted time off to celebrate the rites and enjoy themselves; the
festival calendar determined the pattern of holidays, in an
association that seems to us, perhaps, more self-evident than it
is because it persists in our own culture. If it were true that the
assembly tended to avoid the monthly 'sacred days' of Olympian gods even when they were not the occasion of a public
festival, this might indicate a more disinterested respect for the
sacred; but the fact is very uncertain.[70] A more specific ideology
of the festival is suggested by Demosthenes: 'the city gave each
one of us a guarantee against being subjected to any unpleas-
antness or outrage at this time, by making it a *hieromēnia*', and
'when you were all celebrating a *hieromēnia*, and a law existed
that at this time no-one should wrong anyone else either
publicly or privately.'[71] Bans on the seizure of debtors and the
execution of criminals happen to be attested in connection with
particular festivals,[72] and it is very likely that they extended to
all publicly recognized *hieromēniai*. The festival is a time of
peace, when even legally sanctioned violence is inadmissible.
Special legal procedures protect the peace against 'wrong doing

[67] Mikalson, 203.
[68] Ar. *Nub.* 620, (Xen.) *Ath. Pol.* 3.2–8, Lys. 26.6, Ath. 98b (courts); council and assembly, Mikalson, 186–204, with D. M. Lewis, *CR* n.s. 27 (1977), 215 f. For the expression ἀφέσιμοι ἡμέραι see *LSS* 14.47 f.
[69] *Ap.* Ath. 4.171e, cf. P. J. Rhodes, *The Athenian Boule*, Oxford, 1972, 30; cf. Plut. *Nic.* 28. For the same reason there may have been a tendency for business to proceed during women's festivals, from which men were excluded anyway: see Mikalson, 189, and for Thebes Xen. *Hell.* 5.2.29. At Athens, however, there were no meetings on at least the central day of the Thesmophoria (Ar. *Thesm.* 80); conceivably it counted as 'polluted' (Pritchett, iii, 212).
[70] D. M. Lewis, *CR* n.s. 27 (1977), 215 f.
[71] Dem. 24.31, 29.
[72] Dem. 21.11, 175 f., Pl. *Phd.* 58a–c. Xen. *Hell.* 4.4.2 makes the stay of execution at festivals Panhellenic. The law against 'placing a suppliant branch', a mode of initiating legal action, during the Eleusinia, belongs in this context (Andoc. 1.110–6). Chains and sacredness incompatible, Eur. *IT* 468 f. For the taint of punitive legal procedure cf. p. 175 n. 177.

concerning the festival'.[73] Punishment under these procedures seems to have been fiercer than for a comparable offence committed in profane time; an individual who whipped an enemy at a festival was put to death.[74] It was a particular affront to Athenian feeling that the execution of Phocion should have occurred on a sacred day, and that the city 'should not even have been pure of public bloodshed during a festival'.[75]

The same conception is to be found in the hellenistic period in several Greek cities, where festivals were the occasion of a 'truce' involving holidays for children and slaves, perhaps the release of prisoners from chains, and a cessation of legal activity.[76] The earliest of this non-Athenian evidence is a law from Thasos, perhaps of the late fourth century, specifically forbidding 'denunciation and seizure', the most aggressive modes of direct legal action, during a list of named festivals.[77] A passage in Homer that has already been quoted shows that the peace of the festival is an early value: 'Now is the time of the god's festival among the people, a festival that demands respect. Who would draw a bow today?'[78]

There was at Athens another group of days abstracted from normal use, that of 'impure days', on which temples were closed and 'nobody would begin any serious undertaking'.[79] A few festival days counted as impure because of the inauspicious rites performed on them,[80] but no one would have thought of describing the Panathenaea, for instance, or Dionysia as impure, and there were impure days, connected originally, perhaps, with phases of the moon,[81] that were distinct from festivals. In much the same way in Sparta, warfare might, it

---

[73] MacDowell, *Law*, 194–7 (whose interpretation is more pragmatic than that adopted here).

[74] Dem. 21.180.

[75] Plut. *Phoc.* 37.2, cf. ibid., 28.2–3 for feeling about the arrival of a Macedonian garrison during the mysteries.

[76] L. Robert, *Études Anatoliennes*, Paris, 1937, 177–9; F. J. Fernandez Nieto, *Los Acuerdos Belicos en la Antigua Grecia*, Santiago, 1975, i, 151 n.1.

[77] *LSS* 69, cf. F. Salviat, *BCH* 82 (1958), 198.

[78] *Od.* 21.258 f.

[79] Xen. *Hell.* 1.4.12. Cf. J. D. Mikalson, ἡμέρα ἀποφράς, *AJP* 96 (1975), 19–27; a different view, in some respects less convincing, in Pritchett, iii, 209–29.

[80] Plynteria: Xen. *Hell.* 1.4.12, Plut. *Alc.* 34.1, cf. p. 26 above; Choes: Phot. s.v. μιαρὰ ἡμέρα (but cf. Mikalson, loc. cit.); other possibilities in Pritchett, iii, 211 f., 215.

[81] Pritchett, iii, 209–14.

seems, be impeded not just by a ceremony but also by an unpropitious phase of the moon.[82] Thus normal days were contrasted to both 'sacred' and 'impure' days. This is an instance of the kind of phenomenon that has often been explained by the supposed primitive confusion of the sacred and the unclean. [83] On such a view, there would originally have been a single category of forbidden days, only gradually separated out into two classes of holy and impure. Two causes are not necessarily identical, however, merely because they lead to the same effect (the abstraction of a day, or thing, from normal use); and, though both were subject to restriction, sacred and impure days were not of the same character. On the contrary, their relation was one of polarity, and activities especially appropriate to one (like sacrifice or marriage) would be unthinkable on the other.[84] The polarity is particularly marked in the case of legal process; whereas on sacred days even the execution of judgement ceased, the Areopagus, most solemn instrument of public justice, held its sessions on 'impure days'.[85]

The festival peace is a limited and temporary assertion of the value of community against the divisions that characterize normal, profane life.[86] The Greeks themselves saw religion as the cohesive force in every kind of social grouping. But the openness and unguardedness that made the festival a time for the experience of fellowship also made it an open invitation to those who wished to subvert that fellowship. Murder at the sacrifice is a frequent theme,[87] while Aeneas Tacticus, most pragmatic of Greeks, points out that festivals are the commonest occasion for uprisings within the state.[88] It is surprising to note the extent to which in such cases feelings about the justice of the cause prevailed even in third parties over religious scruples. An observer who disapproved politically was likely also to experience revulsion at the impiety,[89] but murder at a

[82] Cf. Pritchett, i, 116–21, on Hdt. 6.106.3.
[83] Cf. p. 11.
[84] Lys. fr. 53 Thalheim (5 Gernet), cf. Pl. *Leg.* 800d–e.
[85] Pollux 8.117, *Etym. Magn., Et. Gud.* s.v. ἀποφράδες, Pritchett, iii, 210. For the impurity of punitive legal procedure cf. Pl. *Ep.* 356d–357a, Arist. *Ath. Pol.* 57.4.
[86] Cf. Turner, Chs. 3–5.
[87] Eur. *El.* 774–858, *Andr.* 1085–1165, Ephorus 70 *FGrH* fr. 216, Nic. Dam. 90 *FGrH* fr. 52, Diod. 14.12.3, Plut. *Timol.* 16.5–6, cf. *Dion* 56.6, Polyaenus, *Strat.* 1.23.2.
[88] 22.17; for instances see ibid., 17.3, Diod. 13.104.5, Xen. *Hell.* 4.4. 2–4.
[89] Xen. *Hell.* 4.4.2–4.

festival is not explicitly identified as *agos* in our sources. After a violation of sanctuary perpetrated in the best of causes, the Athenians found it necessary to purify their city and expel the guilty family; yet at their drinking parties they regularly celebrated Harmodius and Aristogeiton for killing the tyrant 'at the sacrifice of Athene'.[90] If political developments had been different, of course, more might have been heard of how the accursed pair 'polluted the *hieromēnia*'.

From sacred time, we turn to sacred space. Land 'taken out' for the gods is a well-recognized category, commonly mentioned, for instance, in connection with the apportionment of land at the foundation of a colony.[91] A curious incident of the 330s shows the Athenians concerned not to profiteer in land at the expense of the gods. The territory of Oropus had fallen to Athens and was to be divided among the tribes, but the suspicion arose that a portion of it belonged by right to Amphiaraus. Luckily the god in question was proprietor of an oracle and could be consulted directly about his claims. A commission was sent to settle the issue by incubation in the shrine.[92]

Sacred land, like any other, was marked out by boundary stones, which normally made a declaration about ownership. '[Sacred area] of Chiron', an early example announces.[93] The god occupied an area 'cut off' (*temenos*), but did not differ in this from an early king; it was only after Homer that the word *temenos*, apparently secular in origin, became specialized in its familiar religious sense.[94] In the classical period, land belonging to the gods fell in practice into two categories.[95] The first was that which was genuinely abstracted from human use and left uncultivated; the second, also termed sacred,[96] was let out for

[90] Alcmaeonids: p. 16 above. Harmodius: *PMG* 895.

[91] e.g. Thuc. 3.50.2, *IG* I³ 46 A 14–15 (M/L 49), Pl. *Leg.* 738d, (Arist.) *Rh.'Al.* 1425b 22. Sacred land is not a legal category (Harrison, i, 235), but the point does not concern us here.

[92] Hyperides, *Euxen.* 14–17, cf. L. Robert, *Hellenica* 11–12, Paris, 1960, 194 ff.

[93] On *horoi* see M. Guarducci, *Epigrafia Greca* iv, Rome, 1978, 46–73, with bibliography, p. 73; Chiron, ibid., p. 48.

[94] K. Latte, *RE* s.v. *Temenos*, 435. For *temenos* in Linear B, see M. Gérard Rousseau, *Les Mentions religieuses dans les tablettes mycéniennes*, Rome, 1968, 208.

[95] Latte, op. cit.; for leased sacred land see Stengel, 19–21, O. Schultess in *RE* s.v. *Misthosis*, D. Behrend, *Attische Pachturkunden* (Vestigia 12), Munich, 1970, 55 ff., and on the extensive Delian evidence Busolt/Swoboda, 64 n. 4.

[96] P. Guiraud, *La Propriété foncière en Grèce*, Paris, 1893, 368, citing *IG* XIV 645. 98 and *passim*; cf. *IG* I² 377 (M/L 62) 16, 21.

agriculture like any other land. The unworked land would normally be that immediately surrounding the sacred buildings or altar, while the broader periphery, and fields belonging to a shrine but not attached to it, might be cultivated; it seems, however, from leases that agriculture will have lapped right round the bases of certain minor private shrines.[97] The distinction of the two kinds of land is shown clearly by an Athenian decree of 418 to 417 regulating the sanctuary of Codrus, Neleus, and Basile; the *hieron* itself is to be fenced off, but the *temenos* leased out to become an olive orchard of at least 200 trees.[98] It looks as if the orchard is being created out of hitherto uncultivated land, the change of use being sanctioned by a simple decision of the people. When, in the mid-fourth century, the possibility was raised of bringing part of the Eleusinian 'sacred *orgas*' under cultivation, oracular authority was sought by a curious and elaborate procedure; Delphi disapproved, and the land remained untilled.[99] That particular tract of land had so long been controversial that special procedures were necessary, but in the case of a normal sacred field it was presumably felt, rather surprisingly,[100] that a human decision was sufficient, because leasing was a re-definition rather than a negation of the god's claim.

Unworked sacred land was certainly supposed to be pure

---

[97] e.g. *SIG³* 963, *LSCG* 47, *IG* II² 2501. In a Thespian lease of *c.* 230,100 feet are to be left free around the shrine of Meilichios, *BCH* 60 (1936), 182 f.

[98] *IG* I³ 84 (*LSCG* 14), cf. R. E. Wycherley, *ABSA* 55 (1960), 60–6.

[99] *LSCG* 32.23 ff. In 26 I would supplement not ἐν]τὸς (as editors) but ἐκ]τὸς τῶν ὅρων, and suppose the Athenians to be asking leave to cultivate the γῆ ἀόριστος of Thuc. 1.139.2, the area around the edges of the 'sacred *orgas*' in its narrow sense. (On this view, the decree will be using 'sacred *orgas*' in 30 in a broad sense to include the 'unbounded land', while Thucydides contrasts them.) A year or so later, an Athenian campaign against Megara for encroachment on the *orgas* was concluded with the *orgas* marked out anew, and the ἐσχατιαὶ ὅσαι ἦσαν πρὸς τῆι ὀργάδι left uncultivated, ἀνελόντος τοῦ θεοῦ λῶιον καὶ ἄμεινον εἶναι μὴ ἐργαζομένοις, 324 *FGrH* fr. 30, cf. 328 *FGrH* fr. 155. The oracle referred to is likely to be the one solicited in *LSCG* 32 (P. Foucart, *Memoires de l'Academie des Inscriptions et Belles-Lettres* 38 (1909), 179–82), which would confirm that *LSCG* 32 concerns ἐσχατιαί, land outside the boundaries. But even if that connection is false, it is implausible that, within a year or two of a campaign against Megara for encroachment, the Athenians should be thinking of bringing the *orgas* itself under cultivation. On this Megarian war see Jacoby on Philochorus 328 *FGrH* fr. 155, G. L. Cawkwell, *BCH* 82 (1969), 328–32.

[100] Contrast e.g. *LSCG* 72.3–8, ibid., 129, for oracular consultations in comparable situations, and cf. *SIG³* 987. In *SIG³* 965. 15–17 the deme Peiraeus specifies rental terms for such *temenē* as 'it is possible and *themiton* to bring under cultivation'.

from the taints of birth, death, and sexuality discussed in previous chapters, and also no doubt from bodily functions. (The pollution of temples could of course occur in the most literal way.)[101] In 424, the Thebans made it a serious charge against the Athenians that their troops had camped in the sacred precinct at Delion, 'contrary to the Greek custom', and were doing there 'all the things that men do on profane ground'.[102] A temple should be situated away from the common path, so that all who approach it can ensure that they are properly pure.[103] It seems that in Attica requirements of purity also in theory extended to worked sacred land. Private cult organizations that let out their land regularly required the tenant to treat the property 'as a sacred place'.[104] Lease contracts for publicly owned precincts do not contain explicit rules about purity, but they might have formed part of the 'law about *temenē*'[105] upon which such contracts are based; certainly a decree of the Roman period declares that birth and death are traditionally forbidden 'in all *temenē*', an expression which in context ought to include those that are rented out.[106] Worked sacred land thus probably retained a measure of notional sacredness beyond the fact that the rent was paid to the god; there were, of course, degrees of sanctity, and such land was not sacred enough to be used, for instance, as a place of sanctuary. (It would be interesting to know whether a pious invader might have felt obliged to exempt

[101] Ar. *Vesp.* 394, *Ran.* 366, and for defilement as a political weapon Hesych. s.v. *ἐν Πυθίῳ χέσαι* (a reference I owe to Simon Hornblower). Later evidence in Fehling, 34; cf. Courtney on Juvenal 1.131.
[102] Thuc. 4.97.3. For occupation of shrines and hero precincts through pressure of space cf. Thuc. 2.17.1, and *LSA* 55 with Sokolowski. On the rules of war in Greece see J. de Romilly in J. P. Vernant (ed.), *Problèmes de la guerre en Grèce ancienne*, Paris, 1968, 207–20. Actual fighting in the *temenos* at Olympia, Xen. *Hell.* 7.4.28–32.
[103] Xen. *Mem.* 3.8.10.
[104] *LSCG* 47.5–7; *IG* II² 2501. 4, 15; H. W. Pleket, *Epigraphica* i, Leiden, 1964, n.43; cf. Behrend, op. cit., 96 ff.
[105] *IG* I³ 84.25 (*LSCG* 14).
[106] *IG* II² 1035. 10 f., cf. Behrend, op. cit., 68. On the date, which hovers between 1st c. BC and 2nd c. AD, see *SEG* xxvi 121, with bibliography. The decree seeks to remedy the illicit appropriation of *temenē*, clearly cultivated fields and not temple precincts, by private persons. The word *temenos* can be used of sacred land of any kind, K. Latte, *RE* s.v. *Temenos*, 435. The trees in rented *temenē* are sometimes protected in the lease (e.g. *IG* II² 2494. 15 f., *IG* XIV 645. 135 f.), but probably not for specifically religious reasons; the same is true of the ban on constructing tombs in *IG* XIV 645. 137 (although note the insistence in this context that this is 'sacred' land).

leased *temenē* from ravaging.) A requirement of purity might even in special circumstances extend to land that was owned by private individuals, and was sacred to a god only in the sense of being particularly dear to him. The sanctity of Delos, religious centre of the Athenian empire, became so intense that the Athenians found it necessary to expel the existing graves from the sacred island, and protect it in future from all taint of birth and death;[107] it was useless for the individual Delian to complain that he had the right to die on his own property if he chose. The sacredness of other, obscurer 'sacred islands' was probably of this kind.[108] Sacredness could thus exercise effective claims, distinct from those of ownership, even over something in which property rights did exist. Alexander, some maintained, had incurred the wrath of Dionysus by sacking the god's city of Thebes, for all that he spared the sacred places.[109] The patron goddess of Athens would not tolerate the abuse by individuals of olive stumps growing on their own land.[110]

Untilled sacred land could be spoken of as 'let go', which brings out what it has in common with days, animals, and persons 'let go' in favour of the gods.[111] It would be interesting to know whether at any period real religious renunciation had been practised, in the sense that large areas of good land were left unused. Some gods in historical times had substantial areas leased out, but it cannot be assumed that they had owned this land from of old, and that it had originally, like the Neleus sanctuary, lain uncultivated. Although the gods do not seem commonly to have bought land,[112] they could acquire it by gift or confiscation, and, in the case of colonies, may have received in the original allotment fields intended from the first to provide them with a revenue through leasing. The two substantial areas of unworked land that are famous, because violation of them helped to precipitate two major Greek wars, may both be special cases. The Eleusinian 'sacred *orgas*' lay on the boundary

---

[107] Thuc. 3.104.1–2. Sexuality they tolerated.
[108] For the category cf. Xen. *Cyn.* 5.25 (dogs excluded).
[109] Ephippus 126 *FGrH* fr. 3, Plut. *Alex.* 13.4.
[110] Cf. p. 165 n. 120.
[111] *LSCG* 32.30, cf. *LSJ* s.v. ἄνετος, ἄφετος.
[112] On this and the following see P. Guiraud, *La Propriété foncière en Grèce*, Paris, 1893, 362–7.

between Athens and Megara,[113] and its original consecration might have occurred through a mutual renunciation of disputed territory. Otherwise the explanation probably lies in the character of the divinities concerned; the goddesses of agriculture demand the renunciation of one tract of 'swelling, teeming,' land (*orgas*) in exchange for the fructification of the rest. As for the Cirrhaean plain below Delphi, its special status came to be explained through a curse imposed upon the wicked Cirrhaeans after a sacred war;[114] the explanation may be fictitious, but there would not have been scope here for a propagandist's invention if unworked land had been a familiar phenomenon. We do not hear of any state renouncing a large area that fell unambiguously within its own territory. Smaller tracts, however, that were 'better unworked', like the Athenian Pelargikon, may well have been common. Some Athenians attributed some part of the disasters of the Peloponnesian war to the occupation of the Pelargikon that it made necessary.[115]

The sanctity of the unsullied meadow, where 'no shepherd ventures to feed his flock, and iron has never come', is unforgettably evoked by Euripides.[116] The Euripides of popular conception might have been expected to dismiss reverence for such places as rank superstition; the poet himself, however, invests his meadow with peculiar moral value. In mythology and historical moralizing, the consequence of grazing, burning, or felling a sacred grove may be death, madness, or a curious and humiliating disease.[117] Such supernatural dangers were not in themselves sufficient deterrent, as the protection of unworked

---

[113] On its identification see U. Kahrstedt, *Ath. Mitt.* 57 (1932), 9 f., E. Meyer in *RE* s.v. *Megara*, 159. On the etymology of *orgas* see *LSJ* and the etymological dictionaries; E. Norden, *Aus altrömischen Priesterbüchern*, Lund, 1939, 22–4, followed by Nilsson, *GGR* 179 n. 7, was misled by lexicographical evidence in his interpretation of *orgas* as 'wild wooded landscape', cf. Latte, *Philol.* 97 (1948), 155 n. 1 = *Kl. Schr.* 102 n. 13.

[114] Aeschin. 3.107–112. First reference to this sacred land, *LSCG* 78.15 ff. (380–79 BC). Fictitious: N. Robertson, *CQ* n.s. 28 (1978), 38–73, but cf. *Historia* 29 (1980), 242 f.

[115] Thuc. 2.17. 1–2. For concern over the Pelargikon cf. *IG* I³ 78.54–7 (*LSCG* 5), Pollux 8.101, Nilsson, *GGR* 79 n.6. All this anxiety arose, it has been suggested (Ziehen, 22 n. 14), from a misquoted and misunderstood oracular fragment, *Anth. Pal.* 14.73.1, τὸ Πελασγικὸν Ἄργος ἄμεινον.

[116] *Hipp.* 73–81. Cf. *Hymn. Hom. Ven.* 264–8.

[117] Hesiod, fr. 43 (*a*) 5–9, (*b*), (*c*) (Erysichthon), Hdt. 6.75.3 *bis* (Cleomenes), 9.116.3, 120 (Artayctes), Suda s.v. Ἀναγυράσιος δαίμων.

groves and meadows is one of the commonest themes of sacred laws.[118] The need for human legislation does not, of course, discredit the god's powers; divine vengeance operates through the humans who 'come to the god's aid'.[119] At Athens, the death penalty originally threatened anyone who tampered with Athena's sacred olives, but that is quite exceptional;[120] in general, sacred laws treat pasturing a flock or cutting wood in a god's grove as an offence against property rather than a threatening sacrilege. While theft of sacred goods was a capital offence, the punishment here is a fine, and varies according to the damage actually caused. An errant shepherd may be let off with an obol for each animal pastured, but to fell one of Asclepius' stately cypresses in Cos costs 1,000 drachmas.[121] One law even declares that, provided the proper price is paid to the god, sacred wood may be used for 'sacred, profane and unclean' purposes.[122]

Sacred land did, however, have a special status in that offences against it offered a particularly valuable handle for political manipulation. Accusations under this head could be constructed in such a way as to threaten crippling penalties, which made them an ideal device for the pursuit of personal vendetta or class strife behind a veil of legal process.[123] Similar methods proved no less serviceable in inter-state relations. A Greek state would not admit to going to war without just cause,[124] and none could be juster than 'coming to the god's aid'

---

[118] See Sokolowski's lists, *LSS*, p. 143, *LSCG*, pp. 72, 211.

[119] For the expression see Aesch. *Sept.* 14, Soph. *OT* 136, Hdt. 8.144.2, Ar. *Lys.* 303, Xen. *Hell.* 1.2.6, Aeschin. 3.120, Diod. 16.25.1, 28.3, etc., *LSCG* 177.139. Observers have sometimes misunderstood this kind of relation, Steiner, 142 f. In Isocr. 18.3 human punishment is said to avoid the delays of divine. Cf. Dio Cass. 51.8.3.

[120] Arist. *Ath. Pol.* 60. 2, cf. Lysias 7.

[121] *LSCG* 136.32, 150 A 5. Other attested penalties: cutting or carrying off wood, *LSCG* 37.15, 50 drachmas (the fine seems small, but the legislator seems to have had minor offences like carrying off broken branches chiefly in mind); 65.78 ff., discretionary; 91.10, 100 drachmas; *LSS* 81.10, ? 100 drachmas per tree; Thuc. 3.70.4, one stater per vine-pole; Pollux 8.101 (but cf. *IG* I³ 78.54–7), 3 drachmas; pasturing herds, *LSCG* 91.11, ? 67, ? 79.29 ff., *SIG*³ 963.37 f., confiscation of the herd; *LSCG* 116.12, *hēmiekton* per animal; both offences, *LSCG* 84.14, ? 50 drachmas. I have not been able to find out what penalty comparable damage to profane property would carry; but for the offence cf. Pl. *Leg.* 843c–d.

[122] *LSS* 115 A 8–10.

[123] Thuc. 3.70.4–5.

[124] Pl. *Alc.* 109c, cf. H. Bengtson, *Historia* 12 (1963), 100–4.

in defence of sacred land. The path between cynicism and gullibility is here a narrow one, and hard to follow. While it is true that 'a Greek state champions the cause of "its own" deities . . . to avoid the anger of these deities',[125] it is also true that religious offences were often exploited, or condoned, for political ends with blatant opportunism. Both the third and fourth sacred wars began with accusations of cultivating the sacred Cirrhaean plain, and in both cases the political designs of the accusers are palpable and undisputed.[126] When Aeschines launched the second of these accusations, the illicitly cultivated land was, he maintained, clearly visible from the terrace where the Delphic Amphictyons held their sessions;[127] yet, in this as in the earlier case, the encroachment had apparently been tolerated until political hostility provoked action. Political motivation is much less certain in the Athenian interventions against Megara over the sacred *orgas*, but that may partly be because so little is known at all of the detailed background to these events. The famous Megarian decree that, many contemporaries felt, precipitated the Peloponnesian war is hard to call in evidence on either side; it professed itself a response to Megarian abuse of the *orgas*,[128] but the suspicion, rife in ancient times, that Pericles' motives went deeper than that has not yet been wholly allayed.[129] In the mid-fourth century, further trouble over the *orgas* led to actual war against Megara. There is no reason in this case to doubt that the Athenians' concern was religious, as they gained no temporal advantage from the successful campaign that they conducted; but there may have been particular reasons why Athenian sensitivity to Megarian impiety became acute at just this time, and we should not neglect as a factor simple human resentment that the territory which the Athenians piously denied themselves should suffer encroachment by the 'cursed Megarians'.[130]

[125] K. J. Dover, *AJP* 87 (1966), 207.

[126] See e.g. Parke/Wormell, i, 222, 236. H. W. Parke, *Hermathena* 53 (1939), 65–71, argues for a similar accusation in connection with the second sacred war.

[127] Aeschin. 3. 118 f. A supervisory procedure was supposed to have been established in 380/79, *LSCG* 78. 15–21.

[128] Thuc. 1.139.2, Plut. *Per.* 30.

[129] Despite Geoffrey de Ste. Croix's fine book, *The Origins of the Peloponnesian War*, London, 1972.

[130] For the war see Dem. 13.32, 3.20, cf. 23.212, 324 *FGrH* fr. 30, 328 *FGrH* fr. 155, p. 161 n. 99 above. For the offence of encroachment on profane land cf. *SIG*³ 56.25.

Even further abstracted from human use than the 'unsullied meadow' is the area to which entry is absolutely forbidden, the *abaton*. In some religions, it is said, the more sacred a thing is, the less touchable it becomes, so that absolute holiness implies absolute inaccessibility. That conception can be only partially applied to the Greek evidence. The classical temple, it is true, contains in theory an inner room that is not to be entered (*adyton*); but archaeology has shown that a common early form of temple, perhaps indeed the earliest form, was built round a central hearth and used for communal feasting.[131] As for the *abaton*, the inaccessible grove or area like that of the Eumenides at Colonus, there is no reason to think that it was ever the natural form for the precinct of the most powerful gods. Although the rationale of a particular *abaton* is sometimes obscure, the clearer cases suggest that divine force of a particular kind, not divinity in general, was hedged off in this way. In marking out *abata* of persons struck by lightning, and of the Eumenides, the Greeks were protecting themselves against the universe's destructive and avenging powers.[132] It is not a coincidence that powers of just the same kind were propitiated through the sacrificial ritual known as *enagismos*, which involved the total

---

[131] See H. Drerup, *Arch. Anz.* 1964, 199–206, idem, *Griechische Baukunst in geometrischer Zeit* (Archaeologia Homerica II.O), Göttingen, 1969, 123–8. Snodgrass, 408–13 argues for the hearth temple as the earliest form; contrast Burkert, *GR* 150. The reality of the hearth temple is, however, disputed by B. Bergquist, *Herakles on Thasos*, Uppsala, 1973, 61.

[132] *Abata* where lightning has struck e.g. Eur. *Bacch.* 10, Pollux 9.41, *IG* II² 4964,5 (Zeus Kataibatēs), cf. W. Burkert, *Glotta* 39 (1961), 208–13 with references. *Abaton* of the Tritopateres: *IG* I² 870 (cf. *IG* II² 2615, *SEG* xxi 650). Of the Eumenides: Soph. *OC* 126. Of a heroized dead woman: *IG* XII. 3 suppl. 1626 (*SIG*³ 1223). Of the Hyacinthids: Eur. *Erechtheus*, fr. 65.87 Austin. Unspecified: *IG* XII. 3. 453–5 (probably tombs, cf. *SIG*³ 1223 commentary); *IG* XII. 3 suppl. 1381; XII. 5. 255; *LSCG* 121; *LSS* 34, 128 (access to the last 3 might have been occasionally permitted); inscr. in F. Courby, *Le Portique d'Antigone* (Delos 5), Paris, 1912, 97–102 (a further Athenian instance is cited ibid., 101 n. 2); *The Inscriptions of Cos*, ed. W. R. Paton and E. L. Hicks, Oxford, 1891, n. 8, line 11 (cf. S. M. Sherwin-White, *Ancient Cos* (Hypomnemata 51), Göttingen, 1978, 135 n. 283). The phenomenon is commoner in Arcadia, Paus. 8.30.2, 38.6 (Zeus Lykaios), 8.31.5 (a grove, unspecified), 36.3 (cave of Rhea, open to priestess). This is all the evidence for actual *abata* I have found (the idea of an untreadable island is comprehensible, Arr. *Indica* 37.4, but I know no Greek instances). Shrines open once a year only are found, Dem. 59.76, Paus. 6.20.7, cf. Pl. *Criti.* 116c, but the habitual inaccessibility here is perhaps a by-product of the positive idea of performing ritual in a special spot once a year. Extensive material on the theme, uncritically arranged, in J. W. Hewitt, 'The Major Restrictions of Access to Greek Temples', *TAPA* 40 (1909), 83–92.

destruction of the sacrificial offering. Great goddess though she was, it would not have made sense to shun Athena thus, or refuse all share in offerings made to her.

The sanctity of temples and sacred images, and the divine anger striking those who violate them, are almost too familiar to need illustration.[133] Even when Alexander razed Thebes to the ground to intimidate the Greeks, he spared its sacred places.[134] It was mutilation of divine images that, at Athens in 415, led to a spectacular series of impiety trials. It is worth pausing over the events of 415, because they are better documented than any comparable incident in Greek religious history, and are often thought to illustrate the reserves of superstitious fear that were ready to come bubbling through once a crisis had cracked the smooth surface of late fifth-century rationalism. Even scholars who did not grudge the Greeks their belief in gods have spoken of 'enormous hysterical fuss' and 'real religious hysteria', and the proceedings did not escape the censure of Thucydides, who noted that 'good men were convicted on the testimony of bad'.[135] All our sources agree, however, in showing that the hysteria, if hysteria it was, was not exclusively religious.

When all the herms were mutilated by unknown persons in a single night, shortly before the Sicilian expedition set sail, the Athenians reacted with 'anger and fear'. Repeated emergency meetings of council and assembly were held, a board of investigators established, and rewards offered for information, from any quarter, about the mutilation and any other acts of impiety. When these measures provoked the revelation (or fabrication) that Alcibiades and others had parodied the mysteries, alarm only grew, and something like a witch-hunt developed.[136] Genuine anxiety about the religious conse-

---

[133] See e.g. Aesch. *Ag.* 338–42, 527, *Pers.* 809–15; Hdt. 1.19. 1–2 (accidental burning of temple causes disease), 8.33, 53.2, 109.3, 129. 2–3, 143.2; instantaneous self-inflicted punishment for those who tamper with images, Hdt. 5.85. 1–2, Dem. 24.121. The good general respects enemy *hiera*, Xen. *Ages.* 11.1; one's own side burns temples by accident only, Hdt. 5.102.1, Diod. 16.58.6 (contrast Paus. 10.35.3).

[134] Arr. *Anab.* 1. 9.9.

[135] Dodds, 191, M. P. Nilsson, *Greek Folk Religion*, New York, 1961, 122; Thuc. 6.53.2. On these events I have found most useful D. M. MacDowell's edition of Andocides *On the Mysteries* (Oxford, 1962), and K. J. Dover in A. W. Gomme, A. Andrewes, K. J. Dover, *A Historical Commentary on Thucydides*, vol. iv, Oxford, 1970. 264–88.

[136] Plut. *Alc.* 18.8, Andoc. 1.40, 36, Thuc. 6.27.2 with Andoc. 1.27–28, 40.

quences of impiety was certainly felt. It was information about 'other acts of impiety', not other threats to the state, that was solicited by offers of rewards and immunity, and Andocides vividly presents the language of religious danger in which the first such denunciation was made. 'You, Athenians, are about to send out this enormous expedition and expose yourselves to danger. But I will show you that your general Alcibiades has along with others been parodying the mysteries . . .'.[137] This brings out two characteristic religious preoccupations, the especial need for sound relations with the gods when danger threatens, and the particular danger that attends on an impious commander.

The other side to the affair is indicated by Thucydides. The mutilation was believed, he says, to be not just a 'bad omen for the voyage', but also 'part of a revolutionary conspiracy for the overthrow of the democracy'.[138] This is not Thucydidean bias,[139] as it is just as clear from the other accounts that the most extreme manifestations of panic were products of political fear. The atmosphere of a witch-hunt so vividly evoked by Andocides was created by demagogues who insisted that a large conspiracy was at work, and when the Athenians left their homes to spend a night under arms in the Theseum, they were anticipating an invasion from without timed to coincide with an uprising from within.[140] The mutilation was held to be a pledge in crime given to one another by the conspirators;[141] had it been merely a drunken prank, it would have remained an act of impiety, but there would have been no great cause for alarm.[142] Even if the profanation of the mysteries was not originally seen as part of the conspiracy, it certainly came to be associated with it, and the jurors responsible for the condemnation probably thought that they were casting their votes against treacherous as well as impious men.[143]

[137] Thuc. 6.27.2, Andoc. 1.11.
[138] 6.27.3.
[139] So Dodds, 202 n. 78.
[140] Andoc. 1.36,45, Thuc. 6.61.2.
[141] Andoc. 1.67, cf. Dover, op. cit., 286; for such pledges cf. Diod. 13.112. 4, Thuc. 3.82.6.
[142] Plut. *Alc.* 18.8.
[143] Plut. *Alc.* 21.3, Thuc. 6.61.1; on the timing see MacDowell, op. cit., 184 §4.

'All you people ever think about is conspiracies', says a conservative in Aristophanes, mocking the irrationality of democratic fears.[144] But the mutilation of the herms was a systematic undertaking, not a drunken exploit, which demanded investigation even if it did not constitute proof of conspiracy.[145] The Greeks believed that respect for the gods and respect for the laws of men were products of the same inhibitory process,[146] and this being so it is presumably true that the person prepared to defy society in the one respect might also defy it in the other. The real irrationality lay in the conduct of the investigation, as Thucydides points out. It is striking to observe how quickly in this charged atmosphere one accusation of impiety led to another, and all were believed;[147] but it is also necessary to ask what had charged the atmosphere. In a different political context, a surprising number of the impious wretches were able to return to Athens and resume public life.[148]

Sacred equipment belongs on sacred premises, and is not to be put to profane use.[149] Actually to steal sacred property, of course, is an offence the enormity of which is indicated in several ways. At Athens the temple-robber, like the traitor, was denied burial in his native land, and many Greek states chose methods of execution apparently intended to prevent any form of burial.[150] When Alexander issued his famous 'recall of exiles' decree in 324, only temple-robbers and murderers were excluded.[151] The emotional charge attaching to the offence was

[144] Ar. *Vesp.* 488 f., cf. L. Woodbury, *Phoenix* 19 (1965), 180.
[145] On this and the following see Dover, op. cit., 285 f.
[146] Burkert, *GR* 372 f., cf. e.g. Lys. fr. 53 Thalheim, 5 Gernet, καταγελῶντες τῶν θεῶν καὶ τῶν νόμων τῶν ἡμετέρων.
[147] Interesting modern parallels in G. Grote, *A History of Greece*, new edn. in 10 vols., London, 1888, vi, notes on pp. 11, 37, 47, 49.
[148] (Lys.) 6.13 f., Andoc. 1. 35, 53, 55. For particular cases note Alcibiades and 2 figures who apparently returned in his wake, Adeimantus and Axiochus, both politically active in 407 (M/L, p. 246). Most of them, though, presumably had to wait for the recall of exiles in 404. The affair could be joked about, Ar. *Lys.* 1094, Plut. *Alc.* 20. 6–7.
[149] *LSCG* 116.22–5, *LSS* 24, 27, 117, *LSA* 74; disrespect to sacred property, Andoc. 4.29, Dem. 21.16, 22.73.
[150] Athens: Xen. *Hell.* 1.7.22, cf. Diod. 16.25.2. Throwing over a cliff, Aeschin. 2.142, Plut. *Praec. Reip. Ger.* 825b; throwing in the sea, Diod. 16.35.6.
[151] Diod. 17.109.1.

sufficient to make 'temple-robber' a term of everyday abuse; orators exercised ingenuity in devising ways in which their opponents had deprived the gods of their due and so fell into the abominated category.[152] Disrespect for sacred money was a mark of extreme social decay, the behaviour of a tyrant or barbarian.[153]

The temptation to temple-robbery was, of course, enormous, particularly in time of war. Nowhere else was so much movable wealth so readily available.[154] At the start of the Peloponnesian war, the Athenians seem prudently to have removed the temptation by transferring to the acropolis the treasure from most of the outlying sanctuaries. The pious Nicias, we are told, deliberately delayed in order to allow the Syracusans time to guard their rich Olympeion against his eager troops.[155] But although such precautions were necessary, piety surely posed its own restraints. Looting might occur on impulse, but the sacred places of the enemy were never an explicit target; when a dedication sent by the tyrant Dionysius fell into Athenian hands on the way to Delphi, they kept it to pay the mercenaries,[156] but would scarcely have appropriated it if it had reached a temple. If barbarians sacked Greek shrines, that was why barbarian invasions of Greek territory were always unsuccessful.[157] The Panhellenic sanctuaries displayed their wealth, unprotected and unmolested. It was not, it seems, until the hellenistic period that the traditional inviolability of such places came under serious threat, and even then at the hands of pirates living on the fringes of the Greek world.[158]

---

[152] Abuse: *LSJ* s.v. ἱερόσυλος. Orators: Dem. 22.69–71, 24. 111 f., 120 f., 129 f., 137, 49.65, cf. Lys. 30.21, Isae. 5.44. Framing on a charge of *hierosulia* occurred in legend (Aesop), and no doubt also in reality: Arist. *Pol.* 1304 a 3, Plut. *Praec. Reip. Ger.* 825b. Several states extended the category of *hierosulia* to include a variety of related offences, Latte, *HR* 83–6.

[153] Social decay: Solon, fr. 4.12, Soph. *OT* 883–96. Tyrant: Xen. *Hieron* 4.11, Diod. 14.67.4. Barbarian: n. 157 below.

[154] Cf. Diod. 16.56.6 on Delphi.

[155] *IG* I³ 52 (M/L 58) A 18–22, cf. M/L, p. 158; Plut. *Nic.* 16.7, cf. *Demetr.* 30.2. Guards employed against domestic temple-robbing: *LSCG* 60 with Sokolowski.

[156] Diod. 16.57.2–3.

[157] See the passages of Hdt. 8 cited in p. 168 n. 133 (cf. 1.105), Diod. 14.63. 1–2, 70.4, 76. 3–4, 77.4.

[158] E. Schlesinger, *Die griechische Asylie*, diss. Giessen, 1932, 63–8. Dionysius, a tyrant, sacked a rich Etruscan temple, Diod. 15.14.3–4, Alexander's governors were unreliable, Arrian *Anab.* 7.4.2.

The perpetrators of the most striking exception brought upon
themselves a torrent of execration. Under pressure from the
Delphic Amphictyony in 356, the Phocians amazed Greece by
occupying the unprotected Delphi; to finance the war that
followed they were eventually compelled, despite their initial
protestations, to melt down Delphic treasure into coins for
mercenaries.[159] Over the details of their subsequent fates pious
historians gloated with an insistence that recalls early Christian
literature on the deaths of the persecutors. Philomelus hurled
himself from a cliff, Onomarchus was crucified, Philon died
under torture, while Phayllus suffered the prolonged punishment of a lingering disease. If Phalaecus lived on for a while, the
gods were holding him in reserve for further humiliation and
torment.[160] As for the troops, many were killed by the avenging
Amphictyones; some were burnt to death when, miraculously, a
temple where they had sought refuge took fire.[161] The mercenaries who escaped came in the end to no good, although
some were exploited by the divine providence to do Timoleon
good service before perishing themselves.[162] King Archidamus
was punished for his involvement by loss of burial, the Athenians and Spartans by loss of liberty.[163] The Phocian wife who
received Eriphyle's necklace out of the Delphic spoils was killed
by her son, or at least plotted murder against her husband – we
touch here upon tragic history's freest fantasies.[164] Later
sources may have introduced elaborations, but this religious interpretation was already firmly fixed in the earliest accounts.[165] In the concluding treaty, the Phocians involved in the

[159] Main source, Diod. 16.23–39, 56–64: cf. N. G. L. Hammond, *JHS* 57 (1937),
44–78, Parke/Wormell, i, 221–31.
[160] Diod. 16.61.1–3, 56.4.
[161] Diod. 16.35.6, 58.4–6 (in Paus. 10.35.3, however, the Thebans light the match).
[162] Diod. 16.63.5, 78.4, Plut. *Timol.* 30.7–10.
[163] Paus. 3.10.5, in the context of Theopompus 115 *FGrH* fr. 312 (cf. 232), Diod.
16.64.1. 'Diodorus, however, entirely fails to mention the fate which overtook Thebes,
the ardent and persevering champion of Apollo, eleven years later', comments C. T. H.
R. Ehrhardt, The Third Sacred War, unpublished B. Litt. thesis, Oxford, 1961, 73.
[164] Diod. 16.64.2, Damophilus 70 *FGrH* fr. 96, Theopompus 115 *FGrH* fr. 248; more
in Parke/Wormell, i, 231 f., nn. 30–1.
[165] Elaborations: see Parke/Wormell, i, 228. The earliest accounts: cf. preceding
note. Unfortunately Diodorus' source is unknown. He can scarcely be Damophilus,
because of the discrepancy between Diod. 16.64.2. and 70 *FGrH* fr. 96. Hammond's
ascription of Diod. 16.64 to a different source from 16.61–3 (*CQ* 31 (1937), 83) is
unconvincing; 64 is the climax to which 61–3 lead.

'temple-sacking' were declared 'accursed', and, some fifteen years later, Aeschines could interpret the tumultuous events of the intervening years through the operation of divine favour or enmity to the various states, in accordance with their role in the sacred war.[166]

The Phocian action, however, was less monstrous and un-exampled than their eventual failure and disgrace has made it appear. By the end of the fifth century, various exceptions to the theoretical untouchability of sacred money had come to be accepted. A temple might lend out its spare resources in coined money to individuals at interest, just as it leased its *temenē* for cultivation; both practices are found in the accounts of Apollo's temple on Delos.[167] More analogous to the Phocian case was the tradition, first attested at Athens in connection with the Samian campaign of 440,[168] of financing wars by public borrowing from temple funds. The gods could not refuse these loans, for which they received no security and on which the interest might be reduced to an almost nominal rate;[169] such borrowing was not confined to coined money but extended to dedications, which would be melted down, and even, in Pericles' famous phrase, to the very gold on the images of the gods. If the god-fearing felt unease about these measures, their dissent is not recorded, and the fact that the loans made by the gods during the Peloponnesian war were for the most part never repaid cannot be shown to have been a source of serious guilt to the Athenians. As an initial justification, there was the interpretation of such requisition as mere borrowing, with interest payable; Thucydides' Pericles insists on this. It was probably more important psychologically, and in the eyes of the Greek world, that the treasures which were now being used in defence of Athenian interests had been dedicated, for the most part, by Athenians, in honour of Athens' divine patroness. It was their own money, in origin, that they were exploiting, and in a cause of which the goddess herself would approve.

[166] Diod. 16.60.1, Aeschin. 3.132–4.
[167] Cf. *IG* I³ 248, Nemesis of Rhamnus; ibid., 402, Delos, loans, and leases (M/L 53,62).
[168] *IG* I³ 363 (M/L 55). For Pericles see Thuc. 2.13.4–5.
[169] M/L, p. 215; in the early years of the war it seems to have been charged at more or less the going rate (H. T. Wade-Gery, *CR* 44 (1930), 163–5, A. B. West, *TAPA* 61 (1930), 234 f.)

This was the crucial difference between the Athenian and the Phocian case.[170] The Phocians undoubtedly professed to be merely 'borrowing' Delphic funds, but few of the offerings in question will have been made by Phocians, and their claim to administer Delphi at all was fiercely disputed. What rendered the Phocian action so outrageous, therefore, was not the exploitation of sacred property in itself, but the fact that Phocians were turning to their advantage what members of other states had piously renounced. There is an analogy with feelings about the cultivation of sacred land, where too it is human indignation that fires the sense of sacrilege. Acts like that of the Phocians had often been mooted in the past, sometimes with rather more justification, but never carried into practice. During the Ionian revolt, Hecataeus had proposed that Croesus' dedications in Apollo's shrine at Didyma should be put to use; at the start of the Peloponnesian war, there was talk on the Spartan side of exploiting Delphic and Olympic treasure; in the 360s, when the Arcadian league had occupied Olympia, and was in a position exactly analogous to that of the Phocians at Delphi, moderate opinion within it had swung against expropriation of the treasure 'lest we leave the gods a complaint against our children'.[171] By their initial undertaking to leave the dedications intact, the Phocians themselves implicitly condemned their subsequent action.

Despite their sacrilege, however, the Phocians did not lack sympathy and promises of assistance. The Athenians and Spartans, united to Phocis by hostility to Thebes, may initially have hoped that it would be possible to conduct the war without broaching the sacred funds; when that hope failed, they did not withdraw their support, and it was not because of religious scruples that it proved in the main ineffective. It would be interesting to know what at this time the feelings of god-fearing pro-Phocians were. Some hardy spirits may have argued that the gods forgive even crimes committed under duress, and turn their anger against the authors of the constraint (in this case Thebes).[172] More, no doubt, will have seen in the affair a choice

---

[170] Cf. G. L . Cawkwell, *Philip of Macedon*, London, 1978, 64–6.

[171] Hdt. 5.36.3, Thuc. 1.121.3, 143.1 (a hint of sacrilege in the word κινεῖν?), Xen. *Hell.* 7.4.33–5, cf. 6.4.30.

[172] Cf. Thuc. 4.98. 5–7.

of evils. Despite moralizing stories of instantaneous punishment, most Greeks thought of the consequences of sacrilege as 'bad hopes' for the future.[173] On this occasion, the expectation of distant evil must have seemed preferable to the present threat of domination by Thebes.

By the terms of the final settlement the defeated Phocians were required to repay the full amount they had appropriated.[174] A treaty on any other terms would have been hard to conceive of, as debts to gods were a serious matter. Not all states claimed the right, as did Athens,[175] to annul sacred no less than public debts by plebiscite. (The Athenians appear here as more Erastian than most Greeks, and it is possible that their exploitation of sacred resources during the Peloponnesian war, which was treated above as an acceptable model, was in fact viewed in some quarters as sacrilegious.) The Eleans in 420, eager to placate the Spartans in exchange for the return of Lepreon, offered to remit their half of the fine they had imposed on them for breach of the Olympic truce, and pay themselves the half that was due to the god.[176]

A minor beneficiary of sacredness is the priest. The priest is a kind of walking temple; he avoids those categories of polluted persons who are debarred access to shrines,[177] but in return acquires a claim himself to the inviolability of the sacred place. He is defiled if profane hands are laid upon his untouchable robes.[178] When Alexander captured Thebes, he made over all the territory for distribution among his allies 'except the sacred parts', and enslaved all the inhabitants 'except the priests and

[173] For 'good' or 'bad' hopes consequent on conduct see e.g. Pl. *Resp.* 331a, Isoc. 8.33–4, Dem. 19.240, Xen. *Ages.* 1.27, Men. fr. 494.

[174] Diod. 16.60.1–2. Captured Phocian arms were destroyed, ibid., 3. For the smelting and re-dedication by the pious Opuntian Locrians of the coins struck by the Phocians from the temple treasure see Parke/Wormell, i, 229.

[175] Dem. 24.55; for the counter-evidence see Latte, *HR* 51 f.

[176] Thuc. 5.49. 5. Cf. *Bulletin Épigraphique* 92 (1979), n. 185 for a decree specifying that revenue from Heracles' sacred quarries at Eleusis may not be diverted for non-sacral purposes.

[177] For priestly purity see pp. 52 (birth and death), 86 ff. (sexuality); also Pl. *Ep.* 356d–357a (no contact with imprisonment, execution), *Leg.* 759c (priest to be true-born, physically intact, pure both in himself and in descent from pollutions such as blood-guilt): cf. Arist. *Pol.* 1329 a 29–30 (citizen), Anaxandrides, fr. 39.10, *LSCG* 166.9 with Sokolowski's note (physically intact), *LSA* 73. 6–8 (citizen stock for three generations).

[178] Eur. *IT* 798 f.

priestesses'. He may have had his Homer in mind; for Homer
describes how the sage Odysseus spared a captured priest of
Apollo, and how the headstrong Agamemnon brought plague
upon the Greek host through disrespect to another. Alcibiades
even released captured priests without a ransom.[179] In certain
circumstances, the ordinary individual could benefit from the
sacred inviolability by donning the emblem of sacredness, the
crown, or by performing temporary service to a god. The blows
that Meidias dealt Demosthenes when he was Dionysus'
khorēgos smote, the victim tells us, religion itself.[180] For the same
reason it might be dangerous to obstruct the due performance
of rites. When, in the fourth century, Helike and Boura
were engulfed by a tidal wave, traditionalists countered loose
scientific talk of the subterranean compression of air by dis-
covering an offence of this kind by the two villages against
Poseidon.[181] Punishment even awaited those who harmed a
god's humbler dependents, his sacred herds. The companions
of Odysseus learnt this to their cost, while, in the late sixth
century, a citizen of Apollonia is said to have been blinded by
his fellow citizens because he fell asleep on watch and let wolves
devour the sacred cattle of the sun.[182] Xenophon once found
himself in possession of an old and sickly sacred horse. Fearing
it might die naturally (and so be lost to the god?), he fattened it
up for immediate sacrifice.[183]

Ritual is a final area of manifold restriction. Every sacred
precinct and every festival had its own distinctive rules; of
precinct rules we have some knowledge through surviving examples of the inscriptions set up at the entrances, while for

[179] Arrian *Anab.* 1.9.9, Plut. *Alex.* 11.12; Hom. *Od.* 9.197–201, *Il.* 1.9–100 (but note
*Il.*5.76–83, *Od.* 22.310–29); Plut. *Alc.* 29.5 . On Creusa's crime see p. 185 n. 224.
[180] Dem. 21.126. On the crown see p. 153 above.
[181] Diod. 15.48–9, cf. H. B. Gottschalk, *Heraclides of Pontus*, Oxford, 1980, 94 f.
Delians condemned to permanent exile for expelling Amphictyones from temple, *IG* II²
1635.134–140. .
[182] Hom. *Od.* 12.374–419, Hdt. 9.93.1–3. On sacred cattle of the sun cf. *Hym. Hom.
Ap.* 411–13, Burkert, *SH* 94. To eat of the sacred fish in Arethusa's pool at Syracuse
meant instant death, Diod. 5.3.6, from Timaeus. On sacred flocks see *LSCG* 79 with
Sokolowski's commentary, ibid., 67.15, Stengel, 93 f. Unfortunately the penalty for an
offence against them seems not to be specified.
[183] *Anab.* 4.5.35.

festival rules we are dependent on chance allusions in literary sources. Major categories of rule concern:[184]

(1) right of access to the shrine or festival (typical excluded categories are men, women, slaves, foreigners)
(2) conditions of purity required for access
(3) dress
(4) mode of sacrifice
(5) forbidden objects (e.g. knots, swords, metal objects, pack animals, skins).

A full treatment would require an interpretation of most of Greek religion and much of Greek society, and cannot be attempted here. Through the first class of rules, major demarcations of society find intensified expression. We have seen, for instance, how the division of capacities and duties between the sexes is accentuated in the ritual sphere.[185] Rules of class 3 support rules of class 2 (cleanliness) or 1 (avoidance of the clothing of the prostitute).[186] Sacrificial rules also relate to demarcation, but of the divine rather than human sphere. Incense, typical accompaniment of Olympian sacrifice, is not to be used in the cult of the underworld goddess Hecate.[187] (Seldom, unfortunately, is the meaning of such a regulation as perspicuous as this.) Rules of class 5 are diverse;[188] they derive partly from concern for purity, partly from the symbolic classification of animals and animal products, partly from magical dangers, and no doubt from other motives besides. Certain rituals, most notably the Eleusinian mysteries, are further protected by rules of secrecy, and it is probably here that we find at its most marked in Greek religion the connection between sacredness and interdiction. Superficially, secrecy divides profane knowledge from guarded sacred knowledge; it is probably more important, however, that a division is thereby created between those who have access to this knowledge and those denied it. The secrecy of the Thesmophoria emphasized the separation of

---

[184] Cf. H. J. Stukey, *TAPA* 67 (1936), 286–95 , and, on a crucial principle for the interpretation of these documents (the laws only specify mistakes that are likely to be made), H. Seyrig, *BCH* 51 (1927), 197 f.

[185] pp. 82 ff.

[186] See p. 83 n. 36.

[187] *LSS* 133.

[188] See *LSCG* 65, 68, 124, 136, 154b, 170; *LSS* 28, 32, 33, 59, 60, 91; *LSA* 6, 14.

the sexes, that of the Eleusinia the exclusive good fortune, in the after life, of the blessed élite.

Breach of ritual regulations might, as we have seen, require purification of the shrine. Often the sanction is not stated, and we are left to wonder whether it would be an uneasy conscience, a purification, or actual legal action. In cases judged serious, prosecution was certainly a possibility. At Athens in the fourth century, a hierophant who had made an illicit sacrifice to please a lady was convicted; his punishment is unfortunately not recorded.[189] A spectacular violation is said to have been perpetrated by the daughter of Neaera, who, though disqualified on two counts (non-citizen birth, and prostitution), succeeded in becoming wife of the *archōn basileus* and performing the solemn rites required of the *basileus'* wife. The Areopagus called her husband to account for marrying such a creature, but, assured that he had done so in ignorance, and would now put her aside, took no further action.[190] The council seems to have taken an interest in another such case, although here too no actual punitive measures are recorded.[191]

There can be little doubt that Athenian courts would have been prepared to strike hard in defence of the Eleusinian mysteries. In 415, there were aggravating political factors, but persons suspected of profaning the mysteries would surely have been condemned to death anyway.[192] The reasons for this were not exclusively religious. Eleusis had too important a place in the image the Athenians had of themselves as benefactors and civilizers of Greece for any attack on it to be tolerable. There is no historical evidence to show what might have happened if comedy's fantasy had been fulfilled, and a male usurper detected at the Thesmophoria, but we do have in this connection

---

[189] (Dem.) 59.116 f. As it would have suited the orator's argument to emphasize a severe sentence, we can perhaps infer that it was not severe. The hierophant's real offence, of course, concerned status and rights as much as religion: he made a sacrifice that belonged to another official. For an accusation of illicit sacrifice see Lycurgus, fr. 4.1, in the Loeb *Minor Attic Orators*, ii, ed. J. O. Burtt, 1954, p. 142.

[190] (Dem.) 59.72–84.

[191] Isae. 6.49 f.

[192] For Aeschylus' profanation see Nauck, *TGF*, p. 28. One of the few secure facts about Diagoras of Melos is that his offence was against the mysteries: see e.g. schol. RV Ar. *Av.* 1073 – the decree may of course have been passed in the wake of the Hermes affair. On Diagoras see F. Jacoby, *Berl. Abh.* 1959. 3, L. Woodbury, *Phoenix* 19 (1965), 178–211.

two good instances of the popular sub-literary genre of 'impiety instantly punished'.[193] Miltiades, seeking to enter the temple of Demeter Thesmophoros on Paros for nefarious purposes, was seized by panic at the entrance; as he fled he wrenched his hip, and died from an infection that entered the wound. Battos of Cyrene insisted on viewing the goddess's forbidden mysteries; the priestess tricked him by showing him harmless things, but the women celebrants, blood-stained from sacrifice, rushed on him and unmanned him. In both cases the goddess prevented the impiety but punished the intent; the existence of the stories proves the intensity of the taboo.

In discussing some cultures, it would be necessary at this point, having listed the restrictions that bar the passage from profane to sacred, to turn to the further set that bar the path back. Desacralization after contact with the gods is sometimes just as necessary as sacralization in preparation for it. The worshipper in the Old Testament washes after touching a sacred book or garment. What the pagans told Isaiah was not 'stand by thyself, come not near to me, for I am holier than thou' but 'for I would sanctify you'.[194] In catholicism today the communion chalice must be wiped ('purified') after the mass before a profane person like the sacristan can handle it.[195] Sacred rules have thus become 'two-way';[196] the gods must be protected from human profanity, but men too must be protected from divine sanctity. Objects like clothes once used in a religious context become unusable for any other purpose.[197]

---

[193] Hdt. 6.134–6, Aelian, fr. 44 Hercher, cf. Detienne, *Eugénies*. For the genre cf. p. 168 n. 133, Aelian, fr. 10, 35–7, 43. It was obviously cultivated in priestly circles, (Lys.) 6.1, Andoc. 1.29, and the *Strafwunder* in the Epidaurian temple record. Such stories seem to be universal; in modern India, untouchables about to exercise their newly acquired and hotly disputed right of temple entry are driven off by bees, debarred by militant cobras, drowned or eaten by crocodiles during preparatory bathing (E. B. Harper ed., *Religion in South Asia*, Washington, 1964, 180). For 16th-century England see J. Carey, *John Donne, Life and Art*, London, 1981, 21; for 19th-century Oxford, G. Faber, *Oxford Apostles*², London, 1936, 442. The broader genre of 'impiety punished', perhaps after long delay (Plut. *Ser. Num. Vind.*), acquired a certain intellectual respectability in the context of philosophical debates on divine justice, cf. H. B. Gottschalk, *Heraclides of Pontus*, Oxford, 1980, 95. There is a great deal of material of this kind, often with Epicureans as victims, in the fragments of Aelian's *On Providence* and *On Divine Appearances* (pp. 190–283 Hercher, cf. *RE* 1.486).
[194] Leviticus 16:23–4; Isaiah 65:5; Robertson Smith, 450–3.
[195] E. des Places, *La Religion grecque*, Paris, 1969, 376.
[196] Douglas, 18.
[197] Robertson Smith, loc. cit.

(This is yet another source of the doctrine of the 'primitive confusion of the sacred and the unclean'.) In Greece, however, it seems that the sacred becomes contagious only in particular circumstances. A Greek naturally washed before a rite, but it would be strange to find him washing again after it, as a Hebrew did.[198] He might have done so after participating in the cult of heroes, or 'gods of aversion',[199] but these were powers of a special kind, whose precincts were sometimes 'untreadable', and offerings to whom were commonly burnt whole without human participation. The 'exit' or desacralization process is little developed in the ritual of Olympian sacrifice.[200] It was customary for the Eleusinian initiate to dedicate the clothes in which he was initiated,[201] but this is not necessarily because they had become too sacred for normal use; it may be an example of the common practice of marking a transition in status through an appropriate dedication. Normally it was only through transgression that infection occurred; the offender against a religious rule became *enagēs*, while the object introduced illicitly into a shrine had to be left behind.

The aspects of sacredness that have been discussed so far represent, one might say, the self-protection of the gods, the rules by which they mark out their place in the world. Though such rules have social implications, they cannot be seen as specific products of the social process, and would not if removed leave an immediate cleft in social life. The mantle of sacredness is also extended, however, over crucial areas of the relations between men. Occasionally, perhaps, it would be appropriate to speak of a conscious exploitation of the sacred inviolability for pragmatic ends: fines for secular offences, for instance, were hard to evade and impossible to recover if they were declared payable to a god.[202] More commonly the process seems quite

---

[198] *LSCG* 151 B 23 looks like a case: 'the priest sacrifices and is sprinkled with sea-water,' but it is not certain that the washing follows the sacrifice.

[199] Porph. *Abst.* 2.44. On the impurity of hero cult see p. 39 n. 25.

[200] H. Hubert and M. Mauss, *Sacrifice: Its Nature and Functions*, trans. W. D. Halls, London, 1964, 45–9; indeed the utility of the concept in a Greek context is questionable, cf. G. S. Kirk in *Entretiens Hardt* 27, 68–70.

[201] Ar. *Plut.* 845. οὐκ ἀποφορά sacrificial rules are perhaps more relevant.

[202] Latte, *HR* 48–61. For a law declared 'sacred' see M/L 13.14. For dedication of property by individuals to protect it see Latte, *HR* 100, and for dedication in connection with manumission, ibid., 101–11.

unstudied. A prominent example of this unconsciously applied sacredness is the protection afforded by the gods to suppliants.[203] As the institution seems to some extent to have developed in the period covered by our sources, it will be convenient to consider the Homeric and classical evidence separately. Even in Homer, 'supplication' occurs in diverse contexts, and, what is more important, with very differing power to constrain the person supplicated. From the many possibilities, two forms can be singled out, which might be termed 'help me' and 'spare me' supplication. In the first, the suppliant entered territory controlled by the person supplicated, performed a ritual act of self-abasement, and made a request. Such supplication was commonly addressed to a member of a different community, and the 'help me' suppliant (literally 'comer') is clearly assimilated to the stranger.[204] A characteristic request, made by exiled homicides, for instance, was for admission to the foreign community, which is why a social group like the phratry which would be confronted by appeals of this kind might honour Zeus of Suppliants among its patron deities.[205] Such a suppliant had an absolute claim not to be harmed by the person he had supplicated; this claim, guaranteed by Zeus of Suppliants,[206] was an intensification of the stranger's similar claim, guaranteed by Zeus of Strangers. His right to receive the aid he sought was perhaps not absolute, but if the request was reasonable it was certainly very strong. If the supplication was successful, a social bond was created that entailed lasting mutual obligations.

'Spare me' supplication is the appeal for mercy in battle in exchange for ransom. 'Supplication' here is a term of convenience, because, although 'help me' and 'spare me' supplication exploit the same ritual gestures, the second would perhaps not have been described by Homer as *hiketeia*. Lycaon, entreating mercy, grounds his appeal on the claim that he is, because of a

---

[203] See John Gould's fine article '*Hiketeia*', *JHS* 93 (1973), 74–103. On rejection of supplication as pollution see p. 146 above. An ostracon perhaps accused Aristeides of an offence against suppliants, M/L, p. 42. Cf. too p. 152 n. 44.

[204] J. Gould, op. cit., 90–4.

[205] See R. Herzog, 'Heilige Gesetze von Kos', *Berl. Abh.* 1928, 35, and for related phratry gods C. Rolley, *BCH* 89 (1965), 455.

[206] Hom. *Il.* 24.570.

previous encounter, 'like a suppliant' of the 'help me' category to Achilles.[207] If he needs to argue that he is 'like a suppliant', clasping Achilles' knees can scarcely have made him into a real suppliant. This is not a mere linguistic quibble; the consequence is that the 'spare me' suppliant has no Zeus of Suppliants to invoke in his defence, and thus nothing like an absolute title to mercy.[208] The victor often in practice takes pity, because the battle suppliant's self-abasement has a strong emotional appeal, both intrinsically[209] and by association with true supplication; but for a hero to dispatch a malefactor who has clutched his knees does not present a moral problem.[210]

The role of Homer's Zeus of Suppliants is readily understood. Plato explains that offences against strangers and suppliants are particularly offensive to the god because such people are particularly helpless;[211] all that needs to be added is that the god is safeguarding a necessary social institution, because, in a world where innocent people are constantly being driven into exile, the avenue of reintegration that supplication provides is indispensable.

In classical supplication, two changes can be observed. When there is any kind of threat of constraint, the supplication now normally takes place at an altar[212] and, although the appeal for protection in a foreign country still occurs, more commonly the altars serve as a place of refuge either in normal

---

[207] *Il.* 21.75. For the claim to be an actual suppliant contrast *Od.* 5.450, 9.269, 16.67. The only case I find in Homer of a *hik-* word applied to a 'spare me' supplication is *Il.* 22.123, *hikesthai* (less formalized than *hiketeuō* or *hiketēs*). This is a movement towards the classical convergence of *lissomai* and *hiketeuō* (for a weak use of the latter cf. *Od.* 11.530). On the two stems cf. A. Corlu, *Recherches sur les mots relatifs a l'idée de prière* (Études et commentaires, 64) Paris, 1966, 298 f. Benveniste, ii, 253 f. argues that one becomes a *hiketēs* by 'reaching the knees' (*Il.* 18.457, *Od.* 5.449, 9.266 f.) of the person supplicated. But the emphasis on 'reaching' the knees might be a secondary application of the idea of arriving contained in *hiketēs*; Benveniste mistranslates Lycaon's plea ('je saisis tes genoux; je suis ton suppliant') to make it fit. Gould, op. cit., 93 n. 100a suggests on different grounds that 'help me' supplication is primary, 'spare me' 'merely a crisis extension, a metaphorical adaptation'.

[208] For the gods' primary concern with stranger supplication see esp. *Od.* 5. 447–9, 9.269–71. *Od.* 14.278–84 is a partial exception, but this is half-way between the two forms of supplication.

[209] Burkert, *SH* 45–7.

[210] *Od.* 22. 310–29.

[211] *Leg.* 729e–730a.

[212] Already a possibility in Homer, *Od.* 22.334–6: other early instances, the Cylonian conspirators, and, probably, Alcaeus in exile (fr. 129, 130).

warfare or civil strife. These two developments together are responsible for the peculiar dilemmas that constantly surrounded the classical institution. The suppliant now in theory enjoys absolute inviolability, because he shares the sacredness of the altar to which he clings;[213] and this inviolability is available to the malefactor in the middle of the society which he has wronged. For the Spartans, once the traitor Pausanias had reached an altar, no satisfactory line of conduct was available.[214] To leave him to die of starvation in the sacred area meant pollution, but, as they found, to carry him out against his will when on the point of death was no better; the only policy safe in religious terms – free pardon – was socially intolerable. Fierce spirits might claim that religious protection did not extend to villains,[215] but, in the case of Pausanias, Apollo of Delphi had declared that it did. Whereas the Homeric institution was socially functional, classical supplication may appear an abuse; the suppliant's sanctity is no longer a necessary religious shield held by society over an important social relation, but a concession dragged from an unwilling society by desperate individuals exploiting the logical consequences of the sanctity of sacred places.[216]

The real dilemma that this situation created is illustrated by the propaganda war in which Sparta and Athens engaged before the outbreak of the actual Peloponnesian war.[217] All three of the outrages then cited took the form of killing of suppliants, and all three were still remembered although they had occurred far in the past, one of them almost 200 years before. In none of the three cases, with a partial exception,[218] did death actually occur on sacred ground; in two of them the

---

[213] Cf. vividly *Com. Adesp.* 239 Austin (= Page, *GLP* n. 48), fr. 1.12–13, 18–20.

[214] Thuc. 1.134. The later king Pausanias who, threatened by a capital charge, lived out his life as a *hiketēs* in the *temenos* of Athena at Tegea, was at least out of the country, Plut. *Lys.* 30.1.

[215] Lycurg. *Leocr.* 128 f., Eur. fr. 1049 (= *Oedipus*, fr. 98 Austin), cf. Eur. *Heracl.* 259 f.

[216] Tac. *Ann.* 3.60. (For this reason the Athenian acropolis was guarded to prevent runaway slaves achieving sanctuary, *IG* I³ 45.) The contrast is not seriously affected by two riders that caution demands: (1) 'dysfunctional' supplication, though not attested, may well have occurred and caused problems in the early period; what would Odysseus have done if a suitor had reached an altar? (2) it is natural, given the nature of the evidence, that only the problematic cases from the classical period should be recorded.

[217] Thuc. 1.126.2–135.1.

[218] The τινές of Thuc. 1.126.11.

victims were lured out through promises and then killed, while in the third the suppliant, debilitated by starvation, was carried out to die. The pressure to avoid death at the altars was obviously intense, but to have succeeded in doing so was no guarantee against pollution.[219] In two cases, the victims were traitors or subverters of the constitution and, in the third, persons of the lowest rank. In two of the cases, again, the state concerned had attempted public purification, while, in the third, the Spartans believed that their murder of helot suppliants in a shrine of Poseidon had caused the great earthquake of 462.[220] Another example of the long-lasting effects of such a crime comes from Herodotus.[221] During civil strife in Aegina in the 490s or 480s, the rich murdered 700 of the people, one of whom was clutching a temple door. The Aeginetans were 'unable to sacrifice out this pollution (*agos*), but were expelled from their island first' (in 431).

It was hard in normal warfare for men seized by the joy of killing[222] to acknowledge an absolute title to mercy, but it was even harder in the extraordinarily embittered atmosphere of civil strife, when the suppliant spared today might head a counter-coup tomorrow. Violations in civil war became very common.[223] This is probably the context in which belongs a

[219] Casuistic attempts at evasion were none the less popular: see Gould, op. cit., 82 f., and for treachery add schol. Dem. 1.5 (cf. Plut. *Alex.* 42.1), for fire Menander, *Perinthia* 1 ff. with Sandbach's note. Actual killing on sacred ground is rare even among the violations listed below. Faced by fire or force the suppliant will ideally ensure maximum pollution by staying put (Eur. *Andr.* 258–60, *Ion.* 1255–60), but is scarcely to be condemned for not doing so (cf. Plut. *Dem.* 29. 5: *contra*, A. P. Burnett, *Catastrophe Survived*, Oxford, 1971, 160).

[220] Expulsion of Alcmaeonids, 1.126.12; statues for Athene Chalkioikos, 1.134.4; earthquake, 1.128.1. According to later tradition, Pausanias required more elaborate appeasement, Plutarch, fr. 126 Sandbach.   [221] 6.91.

[222] Xen. *Hieron* 2.15 f.

[223] Violation in *stasis* or comparable situtions: Hdt. 5.46.2, Thuc. 3.81.5, Xen. *Hell.* 2.3.52–6 (cf. Lys. 12.96), 4.4.3, 6.5.9, 7.2.6,? Arist. *Pol.* 1303a 29–31, Arr. *Anab.* 1.17.12, Plut. *Dem.* 28.4, cf. 29.5 f., *Praec. Reip. Ger.* 825b, Quint. Curt. 10.9.21. In warfare: Hdt. 6.79 f., Arr. *Anab.* 1.8.8 (Diod. 17.13.6), Paus 10.35.3 (contrast Diod. 16.58.4–6); by barbarians: Hdt. 8.53.2, Diod. 13.90.1. Observance in warfare: Thuc. 3.28.2, Xen. *Hell.* 4.3.20 (cf. *Ages.* 2.13, 11.1), Diod. 11.92, 14.53.2–3, Arr. *Anab.* 2.24.5, cf. Diod. 13.67.7. On Thuc. 3.75, 81 see Gould, op. cit., 83. For later evidence see P. Ducrey, *Le Traitement des prisonniers de guerre dans la Grèce antique*, Paris, 1968, 295– 300. Murder at altars in mythology: e.g. Apollod. 1.9.8, idem, *epit.* 2.13, 3.32, 5.21. For murder at the altars causing disaster in mythologized history see Fontenrose, 76. It is a very common theme of art: see K. Schefold, *MH* 12 (1955), 138 f., cf. G. Roux, *Antike Kunst* 7 (1964), 36f.

famous inscription from Mantinea of the fifth century, which excludes from the shrine of Athene Alea a group of named individuals who have polluted it with bloodshed; the ban extends to their descendants, and is to last for ever.[224] It was hard too for the victors to respect the women who fled to the altars when a city was sacked. The Locrian Ajax failed, and the consequences for himself, his companions, and his descendants were dire.[225]

Even when supplication retained its true Homeric form of a refugee's plea for reception, it might provoke anxiety and guilt. The suppliant had an absolute claim not merely to be done no harm by the individual or city at whose altar he sat, but also to receive from them positive protection against his enemies; the involuntary host was not free to step back and leave the pursuers to risk the consequences of violation, as it was his own altar that would be defiled.[226] Suicide at the altar, a final resource whereby the 'spare me' suppliant could brand an indelible pollution on the enemies he was otherwise powerless to harm,[227] was also available as a threat for use by the 'help me' suppliant. This was the weapon by which the Danaids in Aeschylus forced an unwilling Pelasgus to accept their supplication at the cost of probable war.[228] Faced by a similar choice, a historical state might well have responded differently; but the Cymaeans, under pressure from Persia to surrender a suppliant, went to considerable lengths to ensure his safety, and the Chians, who betrayed him, treated as defiled the land they received as reward.[229]

Despite repeated violations, the sanctity of the suppliant

[224] Schwyzer 661, Solmsen/Fraenkel[4] 5, Buck 17, cf. Latte, *HR* 45–7. Creusa, who attempted to murder a temple servant on sacred ground, was threatened with stoning, Eur. *Ion.* 1112, 1237.
[225] *Iliou Persis*, OCT Homer v, p. 108.2–6, cf. already *Od.* 3.134–5, 4.499–511; Alcaeus, *SLG* 262, with H. Lloyd-Jones, *GRBS* 9 (1968), 137; on the Locrian maidens, F. Graf, *SSR* 2 (1978), 61–79. For rape in a temple duly punished by stoning see Paus. 8.5.12.
[226] Hdt. 3.47.3, Eur. *Heracl.* 255 f.
[227] Thuc. 3.81.3.
[228] *Supp.* 459–79, cf. Hdt. 7.141.2, Eur. *Hel.* 985–7. On morally coercive suicide cf. Gernet, *Anthropologie*, 297 f. Are the corpses hanging in temples that occasionally appear, without explanation, in the sources (532 *FGrH* D (2), p. 513,? *LSCG* 154 B 33–6) actual cases of this? Cf. too Ov. *Met.* 7.603.
[229] Hdt. 1.157–60. A novella about successful war in defence of suppliants, Diod. 12.9.

remained at the end of the fourth century a significant constraint upon action.[230] Some sanctity likewise still clung to
another aspect of social relations brought directly under divine
protection, the oath.[231] Gods witnessed it, sacrificial ritual accompanied it, and it was commonly tendered in a sacred place.
Upon its sanctity depended innumerable relations, both within
states and between them: through his office as guardian of
oaths, Zeus was automatically guardian also of social morality.
'The oath is what holds the democracy together. Our society is
made up of three parts, the magistrates, the jurors, the private
citizens. Each one of these tenders this pledge.'[232] The humblest
citizen was thus constantly forced to choose between 'respect-
ing' and 'defiling' the gods. It is not surprising that perjury
should have been the first offence for which post-mortem
punishment is attested.[233] In serious oaths, the swearer invoked
destruction on himself and his descendants in case of perjury,
and might have present in person the children by whom he
swore.[234] This threat to descendants is constantly mentioned in
connection with broken oaths.[235] When observance of an oath
was intolerable, a casuistic pseudo-fulfilment might be attempted rather than simple violation.[236] Merry rogues exploited the
institution at every period; a direct line runs from Autolycus,
admired in Homer for unsurpassed skill in 'thieving and oaths',

---

[230] A small instance, on an everyday level, Plut. *Alex.* 42.1.

[231] Latte, *HR* 5–47, 96–101, idem, in *RE* s.v. *Meineid* (*Kl. Schr.*, 367–79), Dover,
246–50, Burkert, *GR* 377–82 with bibliography, Glotz in Dar.-Sag s.v. *Jusjurandum*.

[232] Lycurg. *Leocr.* 79. How can one have peace with the Spartans, ask the Acharnians
(Ar. *Ach.* 308), οἷσιν οὔτε βωμὸς οὔτε πίστις οὔθ᾽ ὅρκος μένει?

[233] Hom. *Il.* 3.278 f., 19.259 f., cf. Ar. *Ran.* 150.

[234] Destruction of *genos* invoked in oaths: M/L 5.47–51, *IG* I³ 14.17 (M/L 40), ibid.,
37.55 (M/L 47), *SIG*³ 360.52–5, Ar. *Ran.* 587 f., Andoc. 1.31, 98.1, 126, Ant. 5.11 f.,
Dem. 23.68, 24.151; with presentation of children, Lys. 32. 13, Dem. 29.26, 54, 54.38.
Destruction of *genos* in curses: M/L 13.15; 30, *passim*; Schwyzer 632 A 23, 634 B 46 f.,
Soph. *Aj.* 1178, Ar. *Thesm.* 349 f., Dem. 19.70 f., Aeschin. 3.111. Cf. too Ar. *Plut.* 1102–9.
Much more in Glotz, 572–4, Pease's note on Cic. *Nat. D.* 3.90, R. Lattimore, *Themes in
Greek and Latin Epitaphs*, Urbana, 1962, 112–14, and cf. *SIG*³, index s.v. ἐξώλης.

[235] Hom. *Il.* 3.298–301, 4.160–2, Hes. *Op.* 282–5, Theog. 199–208, Lycurg. *Leocr.* 79.
On the punishment of perjurers see also Hes. *Op.* 219–24, 803–4, *Theog.* 231 f.,
Empedocles B 115.4, Ar. *Nub.* 395–7, Xen. *Anab.* 2.5.7, Antiphanes, fr. 233, epigram in
Polyb. 4.33.3. One person can urge another to perjury by taking the punishment on
himself, Ar. *Lys.* 914 f., Plut. *Arist.* 25.1. There are of course oaths and oaths: no one
expects much from a lover (Hes. fr. 124) or salesman (Hdt. 1.153.1, Pl. *Leg.* 917b).

[236] Above, p. 155 n. 55.

to Lysander, who 'cheated boys with knuckle-bones, men with oaths', while the ordinary word for perjury contains etymologically no further idea than that of 'oath'; but the currency was not devalued.[237] The fate of Glaucus, whose family was obliterated root and branch although he had done no more than consult the Pythia about violating his pledge, might serve as a warning.[238] The very Athenian clubs that existed to provide mutual aid in court cases, where necessary through perjury, were founded upon oaths.[239] 'I'm willing to bring my children wherever you wish', says a lady in Lysias, 'and swear the oath. But I'm not so desperate, or mad for money, as to commit perjury by my children before I die.'[240] The skilled logographer would not have hoped to impose on the jury with an argument that was ludicrously naïve. The arbitrator in a private case might, if required to tender an oath, reach a different verdict than he would have done without it;[241] the shadiest of characters could be shamed out of a deception by the challenge to an oath which would brand him publicly as a perjurer;[242] an enemy's perjury is claimed to be beneficial, since it secures for one's own side the favour of the gods.[243] Perjury influenced the

[237] Autolycus: Hom. *Od.* 19.395 f. Here too deceitful oaths were no doubt involved rather than plain perjury; for the art cf. *Il.* 15.41 with schol. AT *ad. loc.* Lysander: Plut. *Lys.* 8.4–5 (the *mot* was ascribed to others too, Latte, *RE* s.v. *Meineid*, 350 = *Kl. Schr.*, 372). Word for perjury: M. Leumann, *Homerische Wörter*, Basle, 1950, 79–92.
[238] Hdt. 6.86 α 2 – δ.
[239] συνωμοσίαι, cf. E. Leisi, *Der Zeuge im Attischen Recht*, diss. Zürich, 1907, 118 f., G. M. Calhoun, *Athenian Clubs in Politics and Litigation*, Austin, Texas, 1931, 77–82. On the evident mendacity of many witnesses cf. Leisi, op. cit., 114 ff., unfortunately paying more attention to orators' assertions about opponents' witnesses than the direct evidence of the texts. 'Der grösste Fehler in der attischen Rechtsprechung', concludes Leisi, 'ist der Mangel an Ehrlichkeit im Charakter des Atheners.' Not all evidence, except in murder trials, was delivered on oath, Leisi, 57–66, Harrison, ii,150–3.
[240] Lys. 32.13, cf. Dem. 29.26, 47.73, 57.22, 57.53. For the other side see Dem. 54.38, and for both sides (Arist.) *Rh. Al.* 1432a 33–1432b 4.
[241] Dem. 29.58, 52.30 f. (the speaker claims ἐμοῦ δὲ ἄνευ μὲν ὅρκου οὐδὲν αὐτῷ ἔμελεν, μεθ᾽ ὅρκου δὲ ἴσως ἂν οὐκ ἠδίκησεν διὰ τὸ αὑτοῦ ἴδιον). For the juror's concern for his oath cf. Aeschin. 3.233: if he votes unjustly ὁ ὅρκος, ὃν ὀμωμοκὼς δικάζει, συμπαρακολουθῶν αὐτὸν λυπεῖ. Oath as a constraint on the witness, Ant. 5.11 f.
[242] Dem. 33.14, cf. probably 59.60, and for the 'purificatory oath' Hom. *Il.* 23.579 ff., Latte, *HR* 5–28. Contrast Ar. *Nub.* 1232–6. Obviously his loss of social credibility in the event of perjury is as important a constraint on the swearer as the fear of divine anger.
[243] Xen. *Hell.* 3.4.11 (= *Ages.* 1.13; for Agesilaus' own firmness of oath, ibid., 3.2); Hom. *Il.* 4.234–9.

fortunes not just of individuals but of nations. For Xenophon, Sparta's defeats at the hands of Thebes in the fourth century were punishment for her seizure of that city in defiance of an oath.[244] The Spartans themselves thought that they fared ill in the Archidamian war because they had entered upon it in contravention of the thirty years peace, sanctioned, of course, by oaths.[245]

A clear final example of religious protection for an exposed but indispensable social function is that of the herald.[246] His herald's staff in hand, he moves, inviolable, from state to state;[247] included in an embassy in time of war, he extends his protection to the other members.[248] When the murder of a herald occurs, the indignation of the offended state is loud,[249] but the offenders too may in calmer mood recognize the need for expiation, while pious outsiders will watch for signs of divine anger. The wrath of Talthybius which beset the Spartans for the murder of Darius' herald was temporarily allayed by their attempt at appeasement, but 'woke up' again some sixty years after the crime, and found a paradoxical fulfilment which proved to Herodotus the divine character of the affair. How the Athenians were punished for the same crime Herodotus is not certain, but he does not doubt that divine anger should have found some expression.[250]

This survey has covered a very large number of the religious dangers to which Greek life was exposed. Most of the situations where Herodotus detects the operation of divine vengeance, or

---

[244] *Hell.* 5.4.1. That seizure itself, however, punished Thebes for violation of an oath, Isoc. 14.28.

[245] Thuc. 7.18.2.

[246] Cf. L. M. Wery, *Ant. Class.* 35 (1966), 468–86, P. Ducrey, *Le Traitement des prisonniers de guerre dans la Grèce antique*, Paris, 1968, 301–4.

[247] Thuc. 1.53.1 with schol., Dem. 51.13, R. Boetzkes, *Das Kerykeion*, diss. Münster, 1913. The herald's rights might be suspended, however, in an ἀκήρυκτος πόλεμος: see J. L. Myres, *CR* 57 (1943), 66 f.

[248] Hom. *Od.* 10.102, Thuc. 2.12.2, 4.118.6. In time of peace, ambassadors are theoretically inviolable anyway by the state to which they are sent, (Dem.) 12.3–4 (for an infraction Xen. *Hell.* 5.4.22). One explanation for the destruction of Sybaris was divine anger over an offence against heralds, Phylarchus 81 *FGrH* fr. 45. It is not clear whether violence offered to an embassy travelling from an enemy to a 3rd party breaks the rules, Thuc. 2.67, *Hell. Oxy.* 7.1.

[249] Plut. *Per.* 30.3 (Anthemocritus, cf. Paus. 1.36.3), (Dem.) 12.2–4.

[250] Hdt. 7.133–7. Pausanias offers an answer, 3.12.7: Talthybius' wrath smote the family of Miltiades.

where speakers in Thucydides claim that religious rules have
been violated, fall under one of these headings. Despite certain
changes of emphasis (as in the case of supplication), the forms of
religious respect required throughout this long period are in
their broad outlines remarkably constant. Alexander perhaps
learnt from Odysseus the importance of sparing priests, and the
Homeric sacred festival where the bow is not to be drawn
prefigures the legal truce of hellenistic cities. The common view
that fear of pollution is virtually unknown to Homer is obviously based on an implicit exclusion of the pollution of sacrilege,
which is ubiquitous in him.

All the pollution beliefs here discussed might be seen formally as functioning to maintain a category distinction, that
between gods and men. The same category distinction is constantly threatened, and as constantly reaffirmed, in the many
mythological stories of hardy heroes scaling the heavens,
mounting the beds of goddesses, or challenging the gods to tests
of strength or skill.[251] These stories are the mythological correlate of the rules with which we have been concerned. It is
sometimes said explicitly that categories are confused when
these rules are violated. Xerxes, for instance, through disrespect to temples 'put sacred and private dwellings on the same
level'.[252] We need to ask, however, why the maintenance of this
particular category distinction was of such importance. Popular
feeling about the ultimate threat to it, denial of the gods' very
existence, is revealing. The prosecutions of intellectuals for
impiety at Athens in the late fifth century are an obscure
area,[253] but Aristophanes' *Clouds* provides clear evidence that
atheism was felt to lead directly and necessarily to the dissolution of social morality. The institution most obviously
threatened was the oath, but the connection between religion
and an ordered society went much further than this. Order
depends on *aidōs*, self-restraint expressed through respect for
recognized values. *Aidōs* is a quality that you have or you lack; it
is the same *aidōs*, or absence of it, that expresses itself in speech,
dress, deportment, sexual behaviour, relations with men, and

---

[251] e.g. Hom. *Il.* 2.595–600, 5.405–9, 24.602–9; Hes. fr. 30.1–23, 51, 177.11–12.
[252] Hdt. 8.109.3.
[253] See most recently K. J. Dover, *Talanta* 7 (1975), 24–54.

attitude to gods. The inviolable meadow of a god is a fit symbol for the chastity of a virtuous youth, as both are protected by *aidōs*.[254] Respect for the gods entails an ultimate restraint in conduct, a willingness to stick at something. Sparing an enemy's sacred places is, like returning his dead for burial, a recognition of the minimum right to respect enjoyed by any human[255] (or, at least, by any Greek; barbarians cannot absolutely rely on such respect). The man, by contrast, who flouts religion despises, in Athenian eyes, 'both the gods and our laws'.[256] If he will engage in a conspiracy to annihilate sacred images, he is unlikely to feel scruples about subverting the democracy. The superior power of the gods must be vindicated even in morally neutral areas like that of prophecy to keep society sound. Otherwise, religion will decay, and there will be no further motivation for 'reverent purity in word and deed'.[257] When justice does triumph in the world, this is confirmation that the gods are there. The Greek who then eagerly exclaims 'the gods exist' is announcing more than a fact about categories.[258]

---

[254] Eur. *Hipp.* 73–81. Cf. Aesch. *Ag.* 371–2 on the trampling of ἀθίκτων χάρις.

[255] Therefore an alleged violation of sacred places is met by refusal of burial, Thuc. 4.97. 2–99, while temple-robbery normally incurs this punishment.

[256] See p. 170 n. 146.

[257] Soph. *OT* 863–910.

[258] Men. *Dysc.* 639, cf. Aesch. *Ag.* 1578 with Fraenkel.

6

CURSES, FAMILY CURSES, AND
THE STRUCTURE OF RIGHTS

When mortals violated the sacred in the directest of the ways
that were discussed in the previous chapter, the consequence
was that 'an *agos* came upon them.' *Agos* is here a spontaneous
and automatic product of transgression.[1] As was noted in
the introduction, however, it could also be invoked against
offenders in curses: 'let an *agos* come upon those who have
sworn the oath should they transgress it.'[2] Though curses often
demand simply that the offender should 'be destroyed himself
and his family', they sometimes specify familiar consequences
of pollution: crop-failure, sterility of animals, monstrous births
of humans.[3] The Amphictyonic oath contains a provision of this
kind, and continues 'And may they never sacrifice without
offence to Apollo or Artemis or . . .'. It is the impossibility of
sacrificing 'without offence' that, according to Antiphon, often
indicates the presence of a pollution, and that revealed to the
Spartans that 'the wrath of Talthybius had struck upon them'
for the murder of Xerxes' heralds.[4]

Although the *agos* of sacrilege is in principle automatic, while
that of a curse depends upon public proclamation, the distinction is little more than a formal one. In cases of sacrilege, the
divine curse was often supported by a human one; in 415, after
the profanation of the mysteries, 'the priests and priestesses
stood facing west and cursed [the offenders] and shook their
purple robes, according to the ancient custom.' (Only one

---

[1] Hdt. 6.91.1.

[2] 'Plataea oath': see p. 7. Lines 40–6 specify the nature of the ἄγος. There may be an
invocation of *agos* in the *defixio*, Wünsch, n. 90, b 6.

[3] Soph. *OT* 269–72 (where the connection with pollution is explicit); Amphictyonic
oath, *ap.* Aeschin. 3.111; Eupolis, *Demes* 31 f., Page, *GLP*, p. 208 = n.92 Austin fr.
1.33–4. For later epigraphic evidence see L. Robert, *Études épigraphiques et philologiques*,
Paris, 1938, 313 with n. 3, citing *SIG³* 360.55 f., 526.40–7, 527.85–90, Schwyzer
198.23–5.

[4] Ant. 5.82, Hdt. 7.134.2; cf. *LSA* 16.25–7, with Sokolowski's note.

gentle lady refused to take part, saying that she was 'a priestess of prayers and not of curses'.)[5] It was the spoken verdict of a human tribunal or, through oracular consultation, of a god[6] that confirmed the presence of *agos*, and the sacrilegious received their most lasting taint when they were 'written up on the pillar as offenders against the gods'. And if the divine curse against sacrilege often had to await human confirmation in order to become fully effective, in the many archaic Greek communities where the magistrates pronounced curses in advance against certain categories of treacherous behaviour,[7] the offender was in theory 'held in the *agos*' (the expression comes from Herodotus, in this context)[8] from the moment of his crime just as securely as if he had robbed a temple. As a result of this convergence between curses that are automatic and those that are proclaimed, it can be difficult in a particular case to decide which of the two is in question. The passer-by who covers a corpse perfunctorily with soil 'to escape *agos*' may either be avoiding the taint caused by neglecting a fundamental divine law, or more specifically the curse regularly pronounced against such offenders at Athens by a member of the priestly family of Bouzygai.[9]

Between *agos* in its two forms there is, in fact, a deep similarity. Anyone can utter a curse, but the power to curse effectively is normally confined to certain categories – kings, parents, priests, magistrates, and the like – who represent whatever in society most demands reverence.[10] Hippolytus' 'If only mortals could curse the gods' is a bitter acknowledgement that this power is, in fact, dependent upon the hierarchy of authority.[11]

---

[5] (Lys.) 6.51, Plut. *Alc.* 22.5. Purifications, by contrast, were performed facing east, p. 225.

[6] Arist. *Ath. Pol.* 1, Diod. 16.60. 1, Andoc. 1.51, above, p. 185 n. 224. Note too Chryses' prayer, Hom. *Il.* 1.37–42.

[7] E. Ziebarth, *Hermes* 30 (1895), 57–70; idem, in *RE* s.v. *Fluch*; Glotz, 569–76; R. Vallois, *BCH* 38 (1914), 250–71; Latte, *HR* 61–88.   [8] 6.56.

[9] Soph. *Ant.* 256 with schol.; on Bouzygean curses see Töpffer, 139, W. Schulze, *Kleine Schriften*[2], Göttingen, 1966, 191.

[10] R. Vallois, op. cit. – an important article; cf. Douglas, 127.

[11] Eur. *Hipp.* 1415; for the distinctive construction of *araios* with dative of disadvantage cf. Eur. *Med.* 608, Pl. *Leg.* 931c (empowered to curse), Aesch. *Ag.* 237, Soph. fr. 399, Eur. *IT* 778 (working harm through a curse). In Soph. *Tr.* 1201 f. (Heracles to Hyllus); εἰ δὲ μή, μενῶ σ᾽ἐγὼ/καὶ νέρθεν ὢν ἀραῖος εἰσαεὶ βαρύς, the word ἀραῖος seems actually to have become a noun, 'curse-demon'. On the word cf. W. H. P. Hatch, *HSCP* 19 (1908), 157–86.

There is thus a clear similarity between the *agos* that seizes the sacrilegious and the curse pronounced against those who violate whatever is socially 'sacred'. To some extent social sanctity even has supernatural forces working automatically in its defence; the Erinyes of a wronged father will probably seek revenge without formal invocation in a curse. For an idea of the potential awesomeness of a curse invested with the full solemnity of public authority, we can turn to the *Oedipus Tyrannus*, where Oedipus pronounces one against the unknown killers of Laius. It is not the least of his torments, after the revelation, that he has imposed so terrible a sentence upon himself.[12]

Public curses of magistrates were aimed against behaviour that directly threatened public well-being or order. The earliest and most famous example comes from Teos;[13] we learn from an inscription perhaps of the early fifth century that the magistrates were required, three times a year at public festivals, to invoke destruction upon anyone using poisons (or magic spells?) against the Teians, interfering with the import of corn, resisting the authority of the magistrates(?), conducting or condoning piracy against the Teians, betraying their territory, or 'devising any evil concerning the commonwealth of the Teians in respect either of the Greeks or barbarians'; magistrates abusing their authority were probably also included in these curses, which extended in each case to the family of the offender. Both in its inclusions and its omissions (theft, murder, arson, adultery, and the like) the Teian inscription is typical of the institution; at Sparta subversion of regal privilege, at Athens seeking or supporting tyranny, treating with the Mede, betraying the city, taking bribes against the city's interest, deceiving the council and people, adulterating the coinage(?), and exporting vital foodstuffs were subject to curses, while the citizens of the Tauric Chersonese bound themselves by oath (with curse sanctions) not to commit a very similar range of offences.[14] In Athens, at least, these curses were not an assertion

---

[12] 236–75, 744 f., 1381–2.   [13] M/L 30.

[14] Sparta: Hdt. 6.56. Athens: main text Ar. *Thesm.* 332–67, cf. P. J. Rhodes, *The Athenian Boule*, Oxford, 1972, 37; curses against food exports (clearly not a part of the regular curses before assembly and council), Plut. *Sol.* 24.1. Tauric Chersonese: *SIG*³ 360. For the range of offences countered by curses see esp. Latte, *HR* 68–77, with much further evidence.

194 *Miasma*

of the magistrates' authority but an expression of the mood of the people, who 'prayed along' with the heralds who pronounced them.[15] The sacred power whose potential anger they expressed was indeed, in this case, society. (It is interesting that the people of Athens, no less than their gods, had 'unspeakable' mysteries, *aporrhēta*, protected by just these curses.[16])

Part of the point was perhaps that many of these offences were particularly hard to guard against on a human level; but detection was certainly not entirely impossible, and the question arises of what treatment from his fellows the man consigned to divine punishment might receive. Upon the killer of Laius, Oedipus imposes a form of excommunication: 'Let no one receive him, or speak to him, or make him a partner in prayer or sacrifice to the gods, or give him lustral water, but let all thrust him from them.' A story in Herodotus has the tyrant Periander using excommunication of this kind as a punishment, and there are historical instances of public malefactors being subjected to what appears at first sight to be a spontaneous social ostracism, but could be a survival of a more formal earlier institution.[17] It seems unlikely, however, that the seething public indignation would always have been satisfied to express itself in so negative a form. The old Attic law against tyranny made the offender *atimos* in the archaic sense, an outlaw to be killed with impunity,[18] and it is hard to see what objection there could be to killing anybody against whom the curse 'let him perish' had been publicly pronounced. We are dealing, in fact, with just the kind of offence which was liable to provoke particularly violent forms of popular revenge – destruction of the house,[19] stoning,[20]

---

[15] Ar. *Thesm.* 331, 352.

[16] Lys. 31.31, Ar. *Thesm.* 363, cf. *SIG*³ 360.26.

[17] Soph. *OT* 238–41; Hdt. 3.51.2–52.6; Hdt. 7.231, Lys. 13.79, Xen. *Hell.* 1.7.35, Dem. 25.61 (cf. Dinarchus 2.9); cf. W. Schulze, loc. cit. (p. 192 n. 9), also Pl. *Leg.* 881 d–e, Xen. *Lac. Pol.* 9.4–6.

[18] Arist. *Ath. Pol.* 16.10, discussed most recently by M. H. Hansen, *Apagoge, Endeixis and Ephegesis against Kakourgoi, Atimoi and Pheugontes*, Odense, 1976, 75–80.

[19] M/L 13.9–14 (proposal to reassign land; murder); Hdt. 6.72.2, Thuc. 5.63.2 (Spartan kings who failed as generals through suspected corruption); Ar. *Nub.* 1484 (sacrilegious teachings); Krateros 342 *FGrH* fr. 17, (Plut.) *X Orat.* 834 a (Phrynichus and Antiphon, betrayal); Nic. Dam. 90 *FGrH* fr. 60 (Kypselids, tyranny); Diod. 12.78.5 (Argive generals).

[20] e.g. Hdt. 5.38 (tyrant), 9.5.2 (treacherous proposals, cf. Ar. *Ach.* 204–36, Lycurg. *Leoc.* 71), Thuc. 5.60.6 (general who fails to press home advantage), Xen. *Anab.* 5.7.2 (general who 'deceives' troops), 6.6.7 ('traitor'), Diod. 13.87.5, 91.3, Pl. *Ep.* 7.354d

expulsion of the corpse unburied.[21] Already in the *Iliad*, Hector tells Paris that he deserves 'to have a stone tunic put on him' for the affliction he has brought on his homeland.[22] It would be rash to assume that before the institution of special forms of procedure – at Athens, *eisangelia* dealt with such cases[23] – the criminal was simply left to the gods to punish. A recently-published fragment of the Teian curses seems to show that there, at least, the curse could entail outlawry.[23a]

It is clear that, though an offender of this kind may formally be 'accursed' or 'in the *agos*', the important fact about him is not that he is a source of religious danger. The threat he poses is on a secular level – he pollutes not the gods but the constitution[24] – and there is no question, as there can be in cases of murder or even involuntary sacrilege,[25] of his being avoided through unease about supernatural consequences even by those sympathetically disposed to him morally. As a possibility, before detection, he is certainly feared intensely, but once caught, the feeling he provokes is indignant rage. The same distinction, as we have seen, also applies to a milder form of social rejection; though the murderer may be debarred from the *agora* and sacred places to protect them from pollution, in the case of the male prostitute or man who has 'thrown away his shield', exclusion is simply a mark of disgrace, and the only pollution his fellow citizens would suffer through his presence is the social one of mixing with a rogue.[26] (Offenders of this kind were in many archaic communities subjected to humiliating punishments rather like the stocks; these involved a 'taint', but it was

('treacherous' generals), Plut. *Sol.* 12.1 (aspirants to tyranny); see further the scholars cited by Fehling, 63 n. 258, and for stoning of leaders ibid., n. 262.

[21] Above, p. 45 n. 47.   [22] Hom. *Il.* 3.56 f.

[23] Hypereides, *Euxen.* 7–8, 29; cf. most recently MacDowell, *Law*, 183–6; P. J. Rhodes, *JHS* 99 (1979), 103–14.

[23a] *Chiron* 11 (1981), p. 7 face (b), 5–9; cf. *SEG* xxvi 1306. 23–6 (partially vindicating Glotz, 465, against Latte, *HR* 69, n. 21).

[24] Xen. *Hell.* 2.3.23, 26, 51. The verb used is λυμαίνομαι, which is referred by lexica not to λῦμα (pollution) but λύμη (outrageous injury); though this is generally correct (cf. the *figura etymologica* in Eur. *Hel.* 1099), it seems likely that in many contexts Greeks will also have heard λῦμα in the word (note e.g. Eur. *Bacch.* 354, *Hipp.* 1068, of adultery; Xen. *Hell.* 7.5.18, a stained reputation; and above all Ar. *Eq.* 1284, impure sexual pleasures, also the semantic interference between λῦμα and λύμη themselves, *LSJ* s.vv.). For the Greek's sense of being under threat in secular terms this is a crucial word-group.

[25] e.g. Soph. *OC* 490–2, Eur. *IT* 949–57.

[26] Above, pp. 94–6.

upon the victims that it fell.[27]) On the other hand, it is probably
true even in cases of sacrilege that the primary public response
is one of rage rather than of fear. The forms of mob justice that
were mentioned earlier – stoning and the like – were all applied
to sacrilege as well as treachery,[28] but not, in the main, to other
categories of offence,[29] and seem to testify to similar feelings in
the two cases. Stoning the sacrilegious may have been a means
of averting divine wrath,[30] but no one ever cast a stone in a
merely prudential spirit.

The domestic correlate to the cursing power of the king or
magistrate is, of course, that of the father. 'A parent can curse a
child more effectively than anyone can do it to anybody else,
quite rightly', says Plato, and as instances of curses which
everyone agrees to have been fulfilled he cites those of Oedipus
against his sons, Amyntor against Phoenix, and Theseus
against Hippolytus.[31] Such curses are, in the epic, administered
by the Erinyes,[32] who are guardians of the structure of family
authority (younger sons normally have no Erinyes);[33] a mother
can 'curse Erinyes' against her son, and it is as 'curses' that they
describe themselves when formally asked their identity by
Athena in Aeschylus.[34] These are mythological conceptions too
elevated for everyday speech,[35] at least in classical Athens; the
value to which they relate, however, is fundamental, as is clear
in particular from Aristophanes' portrayal of moral anarchy in
the *Clouds*.[36] In its defence, Plato organizes sanctions which take
us right back into the sphere of public curses and outlawry.
Anyone failing to protect a parent from assault by a child is

[27] Above, p. 95 n. 87. 'Taint': Xen. *Hell.* 3.1.9.
[28] Cf. p. 45 n. 47, p. 194 n. 19; stoning of the sacrilegious, Fehling, 63 n. 260. Same law for temple-robbers and traitors, Xen. *Hell.* 1.7.22.
[29] House-destruction for murder among the Locrians (M/L 13.13) is an exception. Tyrants and defective leaders are often stoned; stoning for other categories of offence is sometimes envisaged, but 'so gut wie nie antik und historisch', Fehling, 63.
[30] Alcaeus, *SLG* 262.
[31] *Leg.* 931b–c.
[32] e.g. Hom. *Il.* 9.454, 566–72.
[33] *Il.* 15.204.
[34] Hom. *Od.* 2.135 f. (note the fear it inspires); Aesch. *Eum.* 417. It is as curses relating to rights that they are constantly constructed with a genitive of the wronged party: cf. E. Rohde, *Kleine Schriften*, Tübingen and Leipzig, 1901, ii, 233–5, with the qualification of Dodds, 21 n. 37.
[35] οἳ᾿ ἀγορεύεις/ἀρὰς τε στυγερὰς καὶ Ἐρινύας, Ap. Rhod. 3.710–1.
[36] 1321–450.

'held in a curse of Zeus of kindred', and the man convicted of such assault is to be banished to the countryside and excluded from the shrines for ever; any free man who as much as speaks to him may not enter city, shrines or market-place without being purified.[37] (Secondary though it appears, the contagious impurity of the moral leper here receives from Plato characteristic emphasis.) Plato goes to extremes, but under Attic law conviction for maltreatment of parents entailed *atimia*, a kind of mitigated outlawry.[38] Even Plato's uncomfortable image of aged parents as 'living shrines' is reflected in the claim that they should receive honours 'equal to those of the gods'.[39] Disrespect to them is sacrilege, a pollution,[40] and danger attends upon it. Fear of a parental curse is, in the epic, a real constraint upon action, and the occurrence of one is a dire event which may lead to a drastic reaction.[41] If less is heard of it, outside a mythological context, in the fifth and fourth centuries, that must in large part be because the rights of parents had received such effective protection in secular law.

The curses considered so far have supported the structure of authority, and this is their most characteristic function. It is, however, to rights rather than raw power that they relate, and if they commonly consort with authority that is because the rights of communities and parents are in fact very extensive. Even the strong can perhaps not curse effectively unless wronged, while the weak acquire the power to do so in so far as their recognized rights are infringed. The disguised Odysseus can suggest, tentatively it is true, that 'beggars have Erinyes';[42] the myth of the house of Tantalus shows a charioteer and a younger brother imposing effective curses, and a daughter with Erinyes;[43] 'even dogs have Erinyes', the proverb says (they are, after all, members of the household).[44] Euripides' Medea not merely utters curses against Creousa, but in a more serious sense 'is' a

---

[37] *Leg.* 881b–e.
[38] Aeschin. 1.28.
[39] *Leg.* 869b, 931a, Aeschin. 1.28.
[40] Cf. (Aeschin.) *Epistle* 2.5.
[41] Hom. *Od.* 2.135 f.; *Il.* 9.454 ff., 566 ff.
[42] Hom. *Od.* 17.475.
[43] Aesch. *Ag.* 1433, cf. ibid., 237, Eur. *Med.* 1389; on the rights protected by Erinyes see E. Wüst, *RE* Suppl. 8.116 f.
[44] Macarius 3.54.

curse against Jason, who has wronged her more deeply.[45] This
is, in theory at least, the difference between the curse and the
binding spell; the former has its own intrinsic power, while the
latter, an act of aggression unsupported by right, needs
reinforcement through magical techniques, the impurity of the
grave, and invocation of infernal powers. (In practice, no
doubt, those who believed themselves wronged often had
resource to *defixiones* as well as mere curses.[46]) This power of the
wronged to curse effectively relates to the more general way in
which the world sometimes operates to redress injustice. In
Herodotus, in particular, punishment often comes upon individuals for violent acts that are not affronts to the gods in any
direct sense.[47] But though the possibility exists, it is noticeable
that stories of the 'wronged widow's curse' type are not at all
common in Greece. The Spartan defeat at Leuctra in 371 gave
rise to one famous instance; they lost, it was said, because of a
curse imposed on them centuries before by one Skedasos of
Leuctra, whose daughters died after being raped by passing
Spartan youths and who then himself committed suicide over
their tomb.[48] In this case, however, it was obviously the existence of a tomb of 'the Leuctrian maidens' at the site of the battle
that determined the form of the story. One reason for the
scarcity of stories of this kind may be that they tend to be
subsumed under the 'wronged suppliant' type; but the fact
probably also indicates something about the general ethos of
Greek culture.

It is natural to consider, in connection with curses, the doctrine
of inherited family guilt.[49] Several interrelated ideas need to be

[45] Eur. *Med.* 607 f.

[46] See Wünsch, nn. 98, 102, 158 for the claim by the author of a *defixio* to have been
wronged. Objects, by the same title, can try to curse those who steal or violate them
(Schwyzer 272; *IG* XIV 865). Of the tomb-curse, however, I know no explicit early
instance (Schwyzer 272 need not be one, L. H. Jeffery, *The Local Scripts of Archaic Greece*,
Oxford, 1961, 348).

[47] Cf. J. E. Powell, *A Lexicon to Herodotus*, Cambridge, 1938, s.v. τίσις.

[48] Fullest version (Plut.) *Am. Narr.* 773c–774d, already known to Xen. *Hell.* 6.4.7. Cf.
Fontenrose, 147 f., Burkert, *SH* 74. Suicide here, as often, increases cursing power. For
similar stories see p. 107 above (the regent Pausanias); Plut. *Quaest. Graec.* 12,293d–f
(Charila).

[49] Cf. Glotz, 560–83; J. T. Kakridis, Ἀραί, Athens, 1929, 141–68 (with the comment
of R. Vallois, *REA* 34 (1932), 98 f.), Dodds, Ch. 2.

mentioned, not all of them involving Erinyes and curses, which tend to shade into one another even though they are perhaps theoretically separable. The first and commonest is the famous doctrine of Solon and many later moralists: sooner or later Zeus punishes all wrongdoers, and if they escape themselves, 'their innocent children pay for their deeds, or their descendants afterwards.'[50] Perjury is the offence most commonly punished in this way, but any other might be; the moderates in the Arcadian league, for instance, decided not to touch the sacred treasure at Olympia 'lest we leave the gods a complaint against our children'.[51] A slightly different tone is introduced when it is specified that the ancestral crime is one of bloodshed. The basic conception remains the same, but emphasis shifts from the image of the slow-grinding mills of god to that of a pollution which has tainted the stock.[52] In a much stronger form, this idea of the internal corruption of the family is central to the myths of the houses of Labdacus and Tantalus.[53] In contrast to the preceding cases, it seems essential here that the crimes of the parents are violations of the order of the family, and lead to similar violations on the part of their children.[54] Both myths in their most extended form do indeed begin with acts of violence against outsiders,[55] but both in their central and earliest-attested core portray a family that, through the most manifold perversions, is gnawing out its own heart. The implicit logic is suggested by Pindar's summary of the myth of Oedipus: the Erinys, seeing Oedipus slay his father, proceeded to 'slay his

[50] Solon 13.25–32. In respect of oaths cf. pp. 186 f. above, and more generally Theog. 731–52, Aesch. *Eum.* 934, Eur. fr. 980, Lys. fr. 53 Thalheim (5 Gernet), (Lys.) 6.20, Isocr. *Bus.* 25, Dodds, 33 f., Dover, 260; specific instances will follow.

[51] Xen. *Hell.* 7.4.34.

[52] μιαιφόνον τι σύγγονον/παλαιῶν προγεννητόρων, Eur. Hipp. 1379 f.; cf. Aesch. *Supp.* 265, παλαιῶν αἱμάτων μιάσματα. For pollution language in reference to past kin-killing see e.g. Aesch. *Ag.* 1460, *Cho.* 649 f.

[53] Main texts on inherited guilt or curse: Aesch. *Sept.* 653–5, 699–701, 720–91, *Ag.* 1090–7, 1186–97, 1309, 1338–42, 1460, 1468–88, 1497–1512, 1565–76, 1600–2; Soph. *El.* 504–15, *Ant.* 583–603, *OC* 367–70, 964–5, 1299, Eur. *El.* 699–746, 1306f., *IT* 186–202, 987 f., *Or.* 811–18, 985–1012, 1546–8, *Phoen.* 379–82, 867–88, 1556–9, 1592–4, 1611.

[54] Cf. Pl. *Leg.* 872e–73a, cf. 729c.

[55] Pelops and Myrtilus: attested in Soph. *El.* 504–15, but excluded in Aesch. *Ag.* 1192f. Laius and Chrysippus: not in Aesch. *Sept.* 742 ff. The origin of this motif is quite uncertain: see Lloyd-Jones, 119–21, and against Deubner's analysis of Peisander, 16 *FGrH* fr. 10, M. Delcourt, *Oedipe ou la légende du conquerant*, Liège, 1944, xii ff.

sons by mutual slaughter'.[56] With this conception of the family crime that leads automatically to fresh crime is constantly intertwined the idea of the actual spoken curse which brings descendants to harm. Imprecations against their own kin were uttered by Oedipus, Thyestes, and, in one variant, Pelops,[57] and, in the extended forms of the legends, the Tantalid and Labdacid woes went back to curses by the outsiders, Myrtilus and Pelops.[58] Such a curse seems merely to express in words what pollution would have achieved anyway in its own inarticulate way, and it can be difficult, though scarcely important, to decide whether the *alastores* and Erinyes referred to in a particular passage are spontaneous products of transgression, or due to a spoken curse.

Postponed punishment of the kind envisaged by Solon, seen by some as particularly 'divine', was criticized by others as morally repugnant.[59] Certainly there was nothing quite like it in human justice, by which sons might be punished with their fathers but not normally instead of them. The conception on which the tragedies are based, however, seems to be one of greater moral subtlety. When the smitten Heracles recalls that his father married the daughter of a man he had killed, and comments 'when the foundations of a house are ill laid, the descendants are bound to suffer',[60] his proposition has an obvious plausibility in terms which are not merely those of pollution, or divine anger, waking up late to smite the innocent in the second generation. Agamemnon and Aegisthus are not innocent victims, any more than the Polyneices and Eteocles of Sophocles; even Antigone is a savage daughter of a savage sire,[61] and it is in Clytaemnestra that the curse of the Pelopid line finds embodiment. 'A godless act breeds more such after, true to its own type.' It is through human sin and folly, 'madness in reasoning and an Erinys of the mind', that the house's

---

[56] *Ol.* 2.38–42.

[57] Hellanicus 4 *FGrH* fr. 157, cf. *Heldensage*, 217.

[58] Myrtilus: Apollod. *Epit.* 2.8. Pelops: Byzantine hypothesis to Aesch. *Sept.*, in *Aeschyli Tragoediae Superstites*, ed. W. Dindorf, Oxford, 1851, vol. iii, 297.

[59] Hdt. 7.137.2, Theog. 731–42; cf. Dodds, 33 f.

[60] Eur. *HF* 1258–62.

[61] Soph. *Ant.* 471 f. For the parents' moral deficiencies reappearing in the child cf. Eur. *Hipp.* 337–43. For Greek views on moral inheritance (by no means uniform), see Dover, 83–95.

tragic destiny is worked out, not in a series of external afflictions besetting the innocent.[62] Even when one of the agents is in fact, like Orestes, innocent, it is a compulsion created by past crimes that drives him to his terrible act. We see here the special character of the family crime, for which remedy must be sought 'not from outside, but from themselves, through savage bloody conflict'. In these circumstances it is not surprising to find the doctrine of dual motivation becoming explicit. 'That you are innocent of this murder, who will bear witness? But the demon of the race might be an accomplice.'[63]

It is sometimes suggested that the idea of inherited guilt, in whatever form, is a post-Homeric development, a product of Delphic teaching or of a creeping sense of guilt.[64] Divine revenge against the whole family, however, is certainly attested in Homer, just where one would expect it, in connection with oaths. Zeus punishes perjury in the end, if not at once, and offenders 'pay for it at a high cost, with their own heads, their wives and children'.[65] It is true that what is envisaged here is a delayed reckoning striking both the criminal and his family, not the complete postponement of punishment to the guilty man's children; but it is hard to see how anyone who accepted the former possibility would be offended by the latter. It is, certainly, plausible that the belief in delayed punishment hardened somewhat in the archaic age, the period that saw the development of the Orphic doctrine of inherited guilt. Where a Homeric Greek, faced by unaccountable misfortune, concluded 'I must be hated by Zeus', or 'I must have committed some offence against the gods',[66] one of the fifth century might rather think of some undefined ancestral fault: 'Such was the will of the gods; perhaps they were angry with my family from of old.'[67] It is not clear that such a change of emphasis is of any great importance. Uncomfortable though the doctrine of inherited guilt appears to us, anxiety is not necessarily its origin. It

[62] Aesch. *Ag.* 758–60, Soph. *Ant.* 603.
[63] Aesch. *Cho.* 472–4, *Ag.* 1505–8.
[64] e.g. Kakridis, op. cit., 141, Dodds, 36.
[65] *Il.* 4.160–2, cf. 3.300 f., Hes. *Op.* 282–5 (the latter very close to the Solonian doctrine). For affliction of whole families see *Il.* 6. 200–5, *Od.* 20.66–78; the Homeric Zeus can hate a whole family, *Od.* 11. 436.
[66] Hom. *Il.* 21.83, *Od.* 4.377 f.; cf. still Hdt. 6.12.3, Men. *Asp.* 215.
[67] Soph. *OC* 964 f., cf. Eur. *Hipp.* 831–3, 1379–81.

protects the belief in divine justice against crude empirical
refutation; for the same reason, perjury, typical cause of inherited punishment in later texts, is already liable to post-
mortem punishment in Homer.[68] Though in some contexts it
appeared unjust, in others it could vindicate the gods: Croesus,
deprived of his kingdom despite rich offerings to Delphi, was
merely being asked to hand back, after a generous period of
usufruct, what his ancestor had wrongfully acquired.[69] Poets
and historians might devise ancestral offences as a kind of
explanatory hypothesis to impose pattern on disparate events;
thus Helen and Clytaemnestra both betrayed their husbands
because their father, Tyndareus, had omitted a sacrifice to
Aphrodite.[70] The doctrine was perhaps not even an important
source of anxiety. Innocent suffering was a fact of experience
which might be explained in terms of inherited guilt, but this
need not mean that, when not afflicted, the innocent lived in
fear. When the rich Athenian is persuaded by an 'Orpheus-
initiator' to protect himself from the consequences of ancestral
sin by sacrifice,[71] this is perhaps simply a transposition of
sacrifices he might anyway perform 'for good luck'.

The inherited guilt of towns and communities was perhaps a
more serious preoccupation. Often, of course, it was the actual
occurrence of disaster that provoked the pious to look for an
ancestral crime to explain it; most obviously that is true, as we
saw, of the Spartan defeat at Leuctra. We do not know how
seriously, before the disaster of 431, the Aeginetans had the
sacrilegious deeds of the 490s or 480s on their minds.[72] The
obligation accepted by the Locrians to pay 'maiden-tribute' for
a thousand years in expiation of Ajax's crime long seemed
spectacular evidence for a communal sense of guilt; it has
recently been argued convincingly that the institution
originated in temple service of a familiar kind, and only
acquired its special character by a process of secondary
reinterpretation, and perhaps mere misunderstanding by out-

[68] *Il.* 3.278 f.
[69] Hdt. 1.91.
[70] Stesichorus, fr. 223 Page.
[71] Pl. *Resp.* 364c.
[72] p. 184 above.

siders.[73] On the other hand, ancestral guilt clearly influenced the actual behaviour of the Athenians when they expelled the Delians from their island in the belief that they had been 'consecrated although they were impure because of some ancient offence'.[74] If Thucydides accepted that Athenian motivation in this case was religious, it is not for us to disagree; but it is interesting to note that ancestral like other guilt is easier to see from outside than from within.

A further development in the archaic period, it has been suggested, is the tendency to link together originally distinct myths to form the characteristic tragic vision of a family or race afflicted through three or four generations.[75] In the *Iliad*'s account of how Agamemnon received his sceptre, there is no hint of tainted stock; the *Cypria* first made him a Tantalid.[76] The extension, however, of the Oedipus saga into the third generation through the expedition of the Epigoni is already mentioned in the *Iliad*,[77] while the crimes of the Tantalid house involved monstrous and marvellous elements that Homer might well have preferred to keep out of sight. Even if such a development could be demonstrated, it would be hard to know what conclusion should be drawn about the temper of the age from the fact that poets detected this pattern in the fortunes of two mythical houses. Noble families continued to boast their descent from the Tantalid or Labdacid line.[78]

Few of the ideas discussed so far would be likely to have much influence on behaviour, except to the extent that individuals might be encouraged, or discouraged, in their crimes by the prospect of the reckoning being postponed to their descendants. They do not, that is to say, isolate a recognizable category of

[73] F. Graf, *SSR* 2 (1978), 61–79; differently in details, but not implication, Fontenrose, 131–7. Similarly in Hdt. 7.197 an ancestral sin is invoked to explain a singular religious requirement.

[74] Thuc. 5.1.

[75] F. Wehrli, 'Typologische Richtungen der griechischen Sagendichtung', in his *Theoria und Humanitas*, Zürich, 1972, 71–87; he refers to K. Schefold's argument that scenes of violent crime became popular in art in the early 6th century, *MH* 12 (1955), 138 f.

[76] *Il.* 2.101–8, *Cypria*, fr. 11.4 Allen. Even in the 5th century, the splendour of the Pelopids can prevail over their sufferings, Pind. *Ol.* 1.89.

[77] 4.404–10.

[78] Alcaeus, fr. 70.6, Pind. *Ol.* 2.35–47, *Isthm.* 3.17; on the descent of the Eupatrids at Athens from Orestes see Töpffer, 176 f.

polluted persons, sprung from criminal ancestors. At Athens, one family did notoriously find itself in this position, but it is a little surprising that no specific case besides that of the Alcmaeonids can be quoted. A considerable number of children were, however, deprived of 'honour' (i.e. in rough terms citizen rights) because of their fathers' offences. In addition to various specific crimes for which this penalty is said to have been imposed,[79] one text perhaps implies in general that the children of men put to death by the state became *atimoi*.[80] Such hereditary punishments could still be imposed in the fourth century, as was finally demonstrated by the discovery of Eucrates' law against tyranny.[81] But it is clear that the children's loss of rights is a continuation in mitigated form of the earlier practice, also well attested, by which they shared their father's *atimia* in the sense of outlawry and were liable to be killed with him if caught.[82] The main intention of the institution is the prudential and punitive one of destroying the public offender 'root and branch',[83] and any cathartic motivation is quite secondary. It is in connection with subversive offences that the inherited punishment is specifically attested (aspiration to tyranny, betraying the city, accepting bribes for the harm of the people). Only by inference from the rather doubtful rule mentioned earlier can it be concluded that the children of men executed for murder or temple-robbing became *atimoi*; this granted, it remains possible that the murderer's children retained their rights if he chose to retire into exile before the verdict.[84] In the *Oedipus at Colonus*, Ismene reports that Eteocles and Polyneices initially renounced their claim to the throne of Thebes because of the 'corruption of their race from of old'; but though their subsequent change of heart was impious, the specific point that they were disqualified for kingship by pollution does not receive emphasis.[85]

[79] M. H. Hansen, *Apagoge, Endeixis and Ephegesis against Kakourgoi, Atimoi, and Pheugontes*, Odense, 1976, 71 and 73.

[80] Dem. 25.30.

[81] *SEG* xii 87, cf. Hansen, op. cit., 72.

[82] See Hansen, op. cit., 75–80.

[83] Cf. Fraenkel on Aesch. *Ag.* 535 f.

[84] Cf. Ant. *Tetr.* 1 β 9.

[85] *OC* 367 ff. In 90 *FGrH* fr. 45 a Lydian king goes into exile for 3 years to expiate a murder committed by his father.

Whatever their legal status, there were, certainly, social means by which the children of a polluted father could be made to feel unclean. It was open to any sacrificial community to make its own decision as to who was acceptable as a member. Above all, the marriage prospects of the children and particularly the daughters were jeopardized: 'who will marry me/her/you?' is, in these contexts, a constant refrain.[86] But this too is a difficulty not confined to the polluted but shared by the socially discredited in general. Euripides' Helen mentions that because of her disgrace no one is willing to marry Hermione, and the same problem confronts the daughter of a state debtor.[87] It is interesting that Oedipus, in his portrait of the wretched life that awaits his polluted daughters, seems to draw colours from Andromache's picture in Homer of the hardships that Astyanax will have to undergo as a mere orphan.[88] In the second generation, pollution may indeed be something to be held against a family, but as a 'reproach'[89] not sharply different in kind from any other damage its reputation might incur. A certain residual unease is apparent in Plato's specification that candidates for the priesthood should be investigated to ensure 'that they come from the purest possible families; the candidate himself must be untainted by bloodshed and all such crimes against the gods, and so must both his parents.'[90] Plato is in general opposed to inherited guilt even for the worst crimes. Of the children and family of the man executed for impiety he says: 'If they grow up different from their father, they should be given due credit for their noble achievement in transforming evil into good.'[91] It is therefore significant that the one hereditary disqualification for priesthood that Plato specifies should be the taint of bloodshed. It is also significant, however, that this disqualification should be confined to the narrowly religious sphere.

[86] Soph. *OT* 1492–1502, Eur. Andr. 974–6, *El.* 1198–1200; on the Alcmaeonids see p. 16 above.

[87] Eur. *Hel.* 933, (Dem.) 59.8.

[88] Soph. *OT* 1486 ff., cf. Hom. *Il.* 22.490 ff.

[89] Soph. *OT* 1494. In Eur. *Supp.* 220–8, Adrastus, by contracting a marriage alliance with Polyneices, has 'muddied' his 'bright' house by contact with one that is 'unjust', 'sick', and 'unfortunate' ('sick' in relation to pollution also Eur. *IT* 693) – revealingly vague terms (cf. p. 219 on contagious bad luck).

[90] *Leg.* 759c.

[91] 855a, cf. 909c–d, but note 856c–d.

This argument invites us to consider ancestral pollution of an unfamiliar kind. In Aristophanes, the accusation, 'I say that you are from the family of those who sinned against the goddess', is countered by 'I say that your grandfather was one of the bodyguards of Hippias.'[92] The juxtaposition in Aristophanes suggests that the two forms of taint were not felt to be radically different in kind. The same pillar on the acropolis bore inscribed, for perpetual contumely, the names both of the sacrilegious and of traitors.[93] Of the two taints, one was perhaps easier to efface than the other. When the Spartans brought up against Pericles the Alcmaeonid crime, his popular support, according to Plutarch, only increased,[94] but no Peisistratid could set foot in Athens in the fifth century. If it was through hostility to tyrants that the Alcmaeonids incurred pollution, it was surely their carefully nurtured reputation for the same quality that helped to cleanse it.[95] One has only to read the speeches of Lysias to discover how chronic, contagious, and hereditary, in consequence of the oligarchic revolutions, the taint of 'hatred of the people' had become. And though it may be hard, in the strictly religious sphere, to discover instances of inherited innocence to set alongside inherited guilt, in civic life they exist in abundance. Distinctions bestowed by the Athenian people on foreign benefactors regularly extended to their sons.[96] The appeal to ancestral credit is one of oratory's standard themes; as a consequence of an act of sacrilegious murder performed by their ancestors, for purely personal motives, the descendants of Harmodius and Aristogeiton enjoyed tax relief and free dinners in perpetuity.[97]

[92] Ar. *Eq.* 445-8.
[93] Lycurg. *Leoc.* 117.
[94] *Per.* 33. 1-2.
[95] Hdt. 6.121.1.
[96] e.g. *IG* I³ 23, 27, 92, 95, 181.
[97] e.g. Isae. 5.47. Exploitation by Andocides of his ancestors' hostility to tyranny, 1.106, 2.26.

7

DISEASE, BEWITCHMENT AND
PURIFIERS

A slave in Menander is critical of his master's hypochondria:

What do I suggest you do? If there had really been anything wrong with you, then you'd have had to look for a real cure. But there isn't. Find an imaginary cure for your imaginary disease and persuade yourself that it's doing you some good. Get the women to wipe you round in a circle and fumigate you. Sprinkle yourself with water drawn from three springs, with salt and lentils added.[1]

This passage illustrates both the semi-medical use of religious techniques of purification, and the contempt in which such methods were held by enlightened Athenians of the fourth century. The same contempt emerges from a fragment of Diphilus which describes the most famous purification of mythology, that of the daughters of Proetus by Melampus. 'Cleansing the daughters of Proetus and their father Proetus the son of Abas, and the old woman to make five in all, with one torch and one squill for all those people, and sulphur and pitch and much-resounding sea, drawn from the deep and gentle-flowing ocean.'[2] Diphilus' manner, in metre (hexameter), language (Homeric expressions), and thought is that of burlesque; he ridicules the notion that one torch and one squill could serve to cleanse five people, and seems to have transferred to the legendary Melampus the healing methods of the lowest contemporary charlatans. The great seer emerges as a pedlar of superstitious mummery. It is a hostile observer again, the Hippocratic author of *On the sacred disease*, who gives the most detailed picture of such practitioners at work. These 'magi, purifiers, begging-priests, frauds' who 'purify (epileptics) with blood as though they were polluted' are, he claims, merely

---

[1] *Phasma* 50–6.
[2] Diphilus, fr. 126.

'using the divine as a cloak and a shield for their own helplessness in not having any useful remedy to apply'.[3]

On the sacred disease shows that epilepsy was a typical object of
purification. So too was madness, as we see from the casual
remark that Aristophanes' Bdelycleon had had his lunatic
father 'washed and purified'.[4] But an anecdote telling how King
Cleomenes, in the grip of a long disease, turned to the purifiers
for aid suggests that physical illness could be tackled in the
same way.[5] There is reason to think that certain skin diseases, in
particular, were popularly seen as pollutions that could be
washed away; and a cure for impotence is found in Hipponax
which would almost certainly have been spoken of as a purification.[6] In myth, even a plague afflicting an entire community
could be effaced by a prophet sprinkling lustral water from a
branch of laurel to the accompaniment of magic words.[7]

It is unlikely that the purifier had always been the degraded
figure who appears in most of our texts. Some development is
already apparent in the contrast between the easy contempt of
the fourth-century comedians, and the need felt by the Hippocratic author to attack his magical rivals at length. A fragment
of Sophocles refers with apparent respect to a 'purifier of the
army, skilled in the rites of wiping off (disease)',[8] and it has
often been pointed out that the charlatans of *On the sacred disease*
resemble Empedocles, who claimed like them the power of
controlling the weather, practised as a healer, and wrote a poem
with the title *Katharmoi*.[9] (Although *katharmos* here refers to
escape from the cycle of incarnation, it is plausible that
Empedocles also treated diseases by purification.) We see the
purifier's original prestige above all in the fame of Melampus,
most illustrious member of a famous mantic family.[10] Every-

---

[3] *Morb. Sacr.* 140.II.3–8, 148.36–8 J., 1.10,40 G.   [4] *Vesp.* 118.

[5] Plut. *Apophth. Lac.* 223e(11). Purification from disease at Rome: Tib. 1.5.11–12,
Ov. *Ars. Am.* 2. 329 f.

[6] Skin disease: see below. Hipponax, fr. 92, interpreted by Latte, *Hermes* 64 (1929),
385 f. = *Kl. Schr.* 464 f.

[7] Callim. fr. 194. 28–31, with Clem. Al. *Strom.* 5.8.48, p. 359 St., cited by Pfeiffer,
ad loc.

[8] Fr. 34, cf. Graf, 106.   [9] See e.g. Lloyd, 37 f.

[10] Cf. Hesiod, fr. 203. See on Melampus *Heldensage*, 58–60, 196–202, 246–53;
K. Hanell, *Megarische Studien*, Lund, 1934, 101–5; G. Radke in *RE* s.v. *Proitides*; Nilsson,
GGR 613 n. 2; I. Löffler, *Die Melampodie*, Meisenheim, 1963; A. Henrichs, *ZPE* 15
(1974), 297–301. Dexicreon in Plut. *Quaest. Graec.* 54, 303c is modelled on Melampus.

body knew how he cured the daughters of Proetus, or the women of Argos, from their frenzied wandering through the Peloponnese. There are, too, the great wandering healers of the archaic age.[11] Several are associated with Apollo, as was Melampus himself.[12] At Apollo's behest, the seer Bacis cleansed the Spartan women of an outbreak of madness. Thaletas the Cretan by his music stayed a plague that was raging in Sparta. Abaris taught both Athenians and Spartans sacrifices to avert the onset of plague.[13] These are shadowy or legendary figures, but we approach firm historical reality with Epimenides, and attain it in Empedocles.

There is, however, a difficulty about assimilating the purifiers of the fifth and fourth centuries to the archaic healers. In the earliest reference, it is not as a purifier but as a 'healer-seer' (*iatromantis*) that Melampus appears.[14] The purifier treats symptoms by a magical technique, whereas the healer-seer diagnoses the disease's cause. He can then prescribe the appropriate cure, which need not take the form of a purification. Both for the diagnosis and the prescription his skill as a seer is required. In Calchas in *Iliad* 1 we have a simple example of a healer-seer at work. He identifies Apollo's anger over Chryseis as cause of the plague, and tells the Greeks what restitution to make, and what sacrifices to perform, in order to appease the god.[15] Even Epimenides, who gave his name to the first comprehensive study of ancient purifications,[16] cleansed the Athenians, according to tradition, not by lustration but by an ingenious sacrificial ritual designed to propitiate offended

---

[11] See on them Rohde, 299–303, L. Gernet *Le génie grec dans la religion*[2], Paris, 1970, 118–21, Nilsson, *GGR* 615–20, Dodds, Ch. 5, Burkert, *LS* 147–65, I. P. Culianu, *SSR* 4 (1980), 287–303.

[12] Hom. *Od.* 15.245, Hes. fr. 261, Apollod. 1.9.11. For his Dionysiac connections see Hdt. 2.49, Paus. 1.43.5, Burkert, *HN* 189 f.

[13] Schol. Ar. *Pax* 1071 = 115 *FGrH* fr. 77; (Plut.) *Mus.* 42.1146b = Pratinas, *PMG* 713 (iii); Apollonius, *Mir.* 4, Ar. *Eq.* 729, Sud. s.v. *Abaris*.

[14] Hes. fr. 37.14; cf. Bacch. 11. 95–110 (without Melampus), schol. MV Hom. *Od.* 15.225 (but see *RE* 23.1.120).

[15] Hom. *Il.* 1. 93–100. For other instances see e.g. 3 *FGrH* fr. 33 (with *Heldensage*, 58 f.); Apollod. 3.3 (Polyidus and Glaucus).

[16] J. Lomeierus, *Epimenides, sive de veterum gentilium lustrationibus syntagma*, ed. 1 Ultrajecti, 1681, ed. 2 Zutphaniae, 1700.

gods.[17] On this evidence, Epimenides deserves the title 'purifier' in the sense that he was dealing with a 'pollution', but not on the basis of the actual ritual methods that he employed.

On the other hand, it is probable that 'purification' in the narrow sense had always formed a part of the healer-seer's repertoire. Before the propitiatory sacrifice, the Achaeans in *Iliad* 1 are told by Calchas to 'wash off their pollution and throw the pollution into the sea'.[18] This clearly anticipates the practice of the purifiers of *On the sacred disease*, who 'bury some of (the polluted remains) in the ground, cast some in the sea, and carry others to the mountains'.[19] Conversely, a vestige of diagnostic procedure survives even in the practice of these purifiers, since 'If the patient imitates a goat, or roars . . . they say the mother of the gods is responsible', and similarly with a wide variety of symptoms.[20] The classical purifiers should probably be seen not as figures of a quite different kind from the early healers, but as heirs to a small portion of a divided patrimony. The great empire of the healer-seer was fragmented in the early historical period. Melampus and his descendants are mythical precursors of those great mantic families that played an important role in Peloponnesian history in the archaic age and beyond. Many points of contact can be found between these wandering aristocratic opportunists of hereditary skills – the Iamids, Klytiads, and Telliads – and the Melampodids, from whom some of them in fact claimed descent.[21] Of the historical prophets, however, miraculous cures are not recorded; their sphere of action was above all military. Of Melampus' healing functions, many had obviously been absorbed by secular medicine. In so far as diseases still required diagnosis in religious terms, oracles such as that of Delphi were able to offer it. Much

[17] D.L.1.110. Jacoby, commentary on 457 *FGrH*, p. 310, regards the details as authentic. For Epimenides as 'healer-seer' note Ar. *Rhet.* 1418a 23–6, Epimenides practised divination not about the future but obscure events in the past, and 457 *FGrH* T 4e, 'he professed to purify people by rite from any damaging influence whatever, physical or mental, and to *state its cause.*' Both points are interesting even if they derive from the spurious writings.

[18] *Il.* 1.314. For 'healer-seer' and 'purifier' closely associated see Aesch. *Eum.* 62 f., *Supp.* 262–7.

[19] *Morb. Sacr.* 148.43–6 J., 1.42 G.

[20] 146. 20 ff. J., 1.33 ff. G.

[21] Hdt. 7.221, Paus. 6.17.6. On the characteristics of such seers see I. Löffler, *Die Melampodie*, Meisenheim, 1963, 11–29; and on military prophecy Pritchett, iii, 47–90.

of the custom of the old healer-seers was also, no doubt, diverted by the increasingly important cults of healing gods and heroes. Only the least reputable of functions, the one that most resembled a magical manipulation, remained for the purifier. But this very expressive, manipulative aspect of his technique ensured, perhaps, that he would never entirely lack a clientèle. The drama of purification had a psychological appeal that incubation, prayer, or the observance of a delicately balanced dietetic regime could scarcely rival.

It has often been said that the fame of the healer-seers and purifiers is proof of the obsessive anxiety that was felt about pollution in the archaic period.[22] It is scarcely justifiable, however, to attribute to archaic Greeks *en masse* the mentality of Theophrastus' Superstitious Man, whose days are passed in a perpetual series of precautionary measures against the contamination that threatens him from every side. If the archaic Greek in times of affliction desired 'purification', that is testimony to a cultural idiom but not to an obsession, since a remedy of some kind is sought by all afflicted societies. We have no evidence that healer-seers were summoned in response to mere anxieties. (Unfortunately, the precise circumstances in which Epimenides was fetched from Crete to purify Athens are quite uncertain.[23]) The elimination of evils of very various kinds, and by various means, seems to be seen in this period as a 'purification', without it necessarily being felt that they had been caused by a pollution. Heracles and Theseus, for instance, were seen as having 'purified' the earth from the monsters and brigands that they slaughtered. Though it was open to a pious poet to explain that in such a case earth had brought forth these monsters 'through the pollution of ancient bloodshed', in the popular conception to call Heracles 'purifier' scarcely differed from calling him 'averter of evil'.[24] Purification in this rather broad

[22] See works cited p. 209 n. 11 above, particularly Gernet, 120.

[23] In one of the versions in D.L. 1.110, a mysterious plague afflicts Athens, and Epimenides identifies its cause in the Cylonian pollution. In Plut. *Sol.* 12 (from Aristotle), by contrast, it is to deal with the Cylonian pollution, already a scandal that has led to the trial and expulsion of the guilty Alcmaeonids, that he is summoned. Moderns tend to follow Plutarch, and see the purification as a symbolic anti-Alcmaeonid gesture (e.g. Jacoby, 40 f., W. G. Forrest, *BCH* 80 (1956), 39–42.) On all problems concerning Epimenides see Jacoby, commentary on 457 *FGrH*.

[24] Soph. *Tr.* 1012, Eur. *HF* 225, Apollod. 2.6.3 (Theseus); pious poet: Aesch. *Supp.* 262–7; *alexikakos* and *kathartēs* equivalent, Ar. *Vesp.* 1043.

sense is not necessarily a matter of ritual cleansing (in the case
of Heracles it obviously was not): Epimenides is supposed to
have used sacrifice, Thaletas musical therapy, the priests of
Dionysus ecstatic ritual.[25] And, if the wandering healer-seer's
role is determined not by novel fears of pollution, but by the
age-old need for healing, it becomes implausible to see him as a
newcomer in the archaic period. The scholarly tradition which
insists that he is has no support in the ancient evidence, and has
to ignore Calchas and treat Melampus, distant ancestor of a
character in the *Odyssey*, repeatedly alluded to in Hesiodic
poetry, as a mythological latecomer.[26]

The purification offered by the purifiers of the fifth and fourth
centuries is of a narrower kind. They are called purifiers
because they remove disease by a kind of washing. We have
already seen that a purification in this narrow sense is found in
the *Iliad*, and there is further evidence that the conception of
disease as something to be washed or purged away was deeply
embedded. Healing springs, for instance, sacred to Heracles,
Artemis, or the Nymphs, were widespread.[27] The sick person
bathed in them, and though their symbolic efficacy must have
been based on feelings of relaxation – the springs were normally
hot – as well as purification, the idea that their waters carried
away diseases was certainly also present. It was thought that
skin diseases in particular, by an obvious assimilation to
ordinary dirt on the skin, could be treated in this way. Pausanias
describes how the victim of leprosy, after anointing the diseased
parts of his body, would swim across the Anigrus marsh; the
impurity remained in the water, and he emerged clean.[28]
According to one tradition, Melampus had washed the Proetids

---

[25] On the healing pacan see L. Deubner, *Neue Jahrb.* 43 (1919), 385–406. It has long
been recognized that in one tradition Melampus 'purified' the Proetids by a Dionysiac
pursuit ritual: Apollod. 2.2.2., cf. Paus. 2.7.8., Burkert, *HN* 189–200. On Dionysiac
purification see Ch. 1c.

[26] So Nilsson, *GGR* 616, K. Hanell, *Megarische Studien*, Lund, 1934, 99.

[27] Cf. Ginouvès, 361–73. But J. H. Croon, *Mnemos.* 20[4] (1967), 225–46, argues that
natural hot springs were not exploited for healing before about the 4th century.

[28] Paus. 5.5.11., cf. Strabo 8.3.19.347 *init.* On the washing-off of skin diseases
cf. Ginouvès, 370 n. 2, referring *inter alia* to Hdt. 4.90, Hippoc. *Epid.* 5.9. (5.208 bottom
Littré), Pliny, *HN* 31.11. Nic. *Alex.* 253 speaks of 'pollution' of the skin; ointments used
against scab 'purify' it, Dioscorides *Mat. Med.* 1.1.3 p. 7.10 Wellmann, 2. 163
p. 228.4, cf. 227.17 Wellmann.

with water from the same spring Anigrus,[29] while another
located the cure in the temple of Artemis Hemera at Lousoi
('washings'), in the precinct of which a pool for bathing has
been uncovered.[30] Purification played little part in the temple
medicine of the classical period, but it has been argued that
healing cults first of Apollo, and subsequently of Asclepius,
commonly grew up at the site of a sacred spring.[31]

There is also the evidence of the Hippocratic corpus. It has
come to be recognized that Hippocratic medicine is in many
respects a continuation of traditional practices and beliefs.[32]
This is probably true not merely of the occasional imaginary
ailment that the Hippocratic doctor still knew how to tackle
(wandering womb or excess of black bile), but also of a large
number of the forms of treatment that he had at his disposal.
The central importance in the Hippocratic corpus of *katharsis* is
therefore most interesting.[33] The body is a container whose
purity is naturally maintained by periodic spontaneous 'purifications' (excretion, menstruation, and the like). Health is the
balance of the humours or vital principles present in the body.
When one of them develops in excess, disease occurs, and an
artificially induced purification of the peccant matter becomes
necessary. Although this is achieved through a purgative drug

[29] Strabo 8.3.19.346 end.

[30] Bacch. 11.95–110, cf. Steph. Byz. s.v. *Lousoi*, and p. 230 n. 131 below. On the pool
see Ginouvès, 383, citing *JÖAI* 4 (1901), 15–18, and on this temple Stiglitz, 101–5.

[31] Ginouvès, 327 f., 349 f., R. Martin and H. Metzger, *La Religion grecque*, Paris, 1976,
Ch. 3. Bathing before incubation in Asclepieia, as before other incubation, was
required (Ginouvès, 352–7; see esp. Ar. *Plut.* 656–8, Xen. *Mem.* 3.13.3) but is distinct
from the actual healing process. Preliminary bathing was required in other incubation
cults with healing functions (Paus. 9.39.7, Trophonius; Xen. *Mem.* 3.13.3, Amphiaraus),
but a role for bathing in the healing process is explicitly attested only for the cult of
Podalirios in Apulia, Lycoph. *Alex.* 1050 ff. with schol. (= Timaeus 566 *FGrH* fr. 56):
cf. Ginouvès, 344–9. There is considerable archaeological evidence, however, that from
about the 4th century actual hydrotherapy developed in Asclepieia: see Ginouvès,
357–61, Martin/Metzger, loc. cit. For a cure in which stigmata are wiped off see *SIG*³
1168.47–55, cf. 55–68.

[32] See e.g. O. Temkin, *Isis* 44 (1953), 213–25; Kudlien, *passim*; idem, *Clio Medica* 3
(1968), 305–36; Lloyd, 39–45.

[33] First studied in this regard by O. Temkin, 'Beiträge zur archaischen Medizin',
Kyklos, Jahrbuch f. Geschichte und Philosophie der Medizin, 3 (1930), 90–135 (cited by Artelt
and Goltz: *non vidi*); cf. W. Artelt, *Studien zur Geschichte der Begriffe 'Heilmittel' und 'Gift'*
(*Studien zur Geschichte der Medizin*, ed. K. Sudhoff, 23), Leipzig, 1937, 49–60, 89–91;
Moulinier, 158–68; Goltz, 283–6.

(*pharmakon* – itself a word of important extrà-medical connotations),[34] medical *katharsis* entails more than the simple emptying of the digestive tract. The humours are situated not in the bowels but in the whole body, and *katharsis* affects flesh and veins as well as the digestive organs;[35] localized purifiers can be administered to the nose, head, and other regions, and the effect even of the drugs applied externally to wounds is one of purification.[36] As a result, medical texts contain expressions that strikingly recall the language of pollution. Phrases such as 'such bodies as are impure', or 'it is beneficial for such patients, if they appear unpurified, to cleanse their heads and the rest of their bodies,'[37] with their implication of a general bodily purity that is more than cleanness, sound initially like a simple transference of the religious conception. When the patient, and not just a part of him, is object of the verb *kathairō*,[38] medical and religious purification are distinguished only by the accompanying dative of instrument: Melampus purifies the Proetids with sulphur, while Hippocrates purifies the Coans with diuretic drugs. It is plausible that the negative expression *akatharsia*, unpurified matter, filth, actually entered the language of pollution, where it is common in the fourth century,[39] from the medical side. This conception of disease is certainly not a late development in the Hippocratic tradition, as two texts from the corpus speak of purgative drugs as a primitive technique in contrast to the 'more doctorly' method of dietetics.[40]

Other Hippocratic treatments, too, resemble the methods of the purifier. Processes of 'wiping off', fumigation, and localized drenching have obvious cathartic parallels, and cataplasms based on barley groats recall the bran mashes sometimes used

[34] Artelt, op. cit. For the religious use of ἐλατήριος, which sometimes qualifies φάρμακον, see LSJ.

[35] Artelt, op. cit., 75 f.

[36] Artelt, 58 f., 55.

[37] *Aph.* 2.10 (4.472 L.), *Aff.* 20 (6.230 L.).

[38] e.g. *Epid.* 6.1.5 (5.268 L.) οὐρητικοῖσι καθαίρειν, *Loc. Hom.* 28 (6.322 L.) καὶ λουτροῖσι κάθαιρε.

[39] Dem. 19.199,21.199,25.63; for the Hippocratic use see Goltz, 284 n. 189, LSJ s.v. ἀκαθαρσία.

[40] *De arte* 6 (6.8–10 L.), *Acut.*1 (2.226 L.): cf. I. M. Lonie, *Medical History* 21 (1977), 235–60. Such drugs clearly fall within Temkin's conception of 'leechcraft': see *Isis* 44 (1953), 219 f.

to wipe off pollution.[41] One of the commonest Hippocratic prescriptions is a hot bath, still a form of purification even though the ritual purifier would normally use cold water.[42] The occasional requirement of abstention from baths also has analogues in the religious sphere.[43] For the doctors, of course, an absolute difference of kind separates their methods from those of the religious healer, and the original family likeness is simply not perceived. It is without any sense of incongruity that the author of *On the sacred disease*, having dismissed the purifiers, goes on to explain how the origin of epilepsy is a defective 'purification' of the brain of the still unborn child, and he can even fault his rivals for not submitting their patients to medical treatment by hot baths.[44] But this only shows how far Hippocratic medicine had advanced from its origins; and whatever doctors may have said, patients at an unconscious level no doubt continued to perceive and respond to the similarities.[45]

The relation between these two forms of purification, by rite and by medicine, is a delicate one to define. To see the one as a secular transposition of the other would make it seem secondary, whereas there is, in fact, nothing advanced about the use of purgative drugs. Rather, the two methods both derive from an undifferentiated ideal of purity, physical and metaphysical, necessary both for health and for proper relations with the gods. (Thus in some cultures the purge is a preparation for ritual activity.[46]) The two methods come closest to convergence in the treatment of madness. Though this long remained subject to ritual purification, another popular form of treatment, this too invented by Melampus for the daughters of Proetus,[47] was

---

[41] Wiping off: Goltz, 219 f. Fumigation: ibid., 231–7. For fumigation with sulphur and asphalt, as in ritual purification, see *Morb*. 3.10 (7.130 L.), *Nat. Mul.* 26 (7.342 L.). Drenching: Goltz, 221–4. Cataplasms: ibid., 213 f. (on wiping off with bran mash see p. 231 below). On 'wiping off with mud' in later medicine see Graf, 106 n. 60.

[42] Goltz, 217–20, Ginouvès, 367 f.; see e.g. *Loc. Hom.* 28 (6.322 L.) λουτροῖσι κάθαιρε.

[43] e.g. *Mul.* 1.66 (8.136 L.), *Morb.* 2.67(7.102 L.); the purifiers have the same rule, *Morb. Sacr.* 140. 13 J., 1.12 G., as do Trophonius, Paus. 9.39.5, and Pythagoreans (Burkert, *LS* 199 n. 34).

[44] 154–6 J., 5 G., 142.34 J., 1.21 G.

[45] Cf. Pl. *Crat.* 405a–b on ἡ κάθαρσις καὶ οἱ καθαρμοὶ καὶ κατὰ τὴν ἰατρικὴν καὶ κατὰ τὴν μαντικὴν which, he claims, all serve the same end of making man 'pure in both body and soul'.

[46] Lanata, 53.

[47] Apollod. 2.2.2, Theophr. *Hist. Pl.* 9.10.4: on hellebore see *RE* 8.163–70.

purging by hellebore. Psychologically, the difference between the two methods lay merely in whether the madness was transferred into the purifying materials and carried off with them, or swept away through the body's own channels.[48] A pleasing proof that hellebore was seen not pharmacologically but, in a very general sense, as a 'cure of evil' is the fact mentioned by Theophrastus that 'people use it to purify their houses and their flocks, chanting some kind of charm over it, and for a great number of other jobs.'[49] A house has no digestive system; from its use as a purge, hellebore has become a full purifying agent.

The cathartic medicine of the fifth and fourth centuries perpetuates, it seems, deep-rooted popular conceptions. If we turn, however, to consider how the clients of the purifier interpreted the process to which they were submitting themselves, a paradox at once arises. Purification assimilates disease to dirt that can be washed off: Asclepius stretches out his gentle hand and 'wipes off' diseases,[50] and leprosy becomes an unclean excrescence on the skin that the waters of a special stream will carry away. But although purification thus seems to be a kind of mechanical technique, it is in the treatment of 'divine' diseases that it is applied.

The author of *On the sacred disease* points out the difficulty: if disease comes from the gods, the proper treatment is prayer, sacrifice, and supplication; purification in these circumstances is 'most impious and most godless', one of a series of practices which wickedly imply that mortal techniques can constrain the gods. 'But I do not believe that a man's body is polluted by a god, the corruptest of things by the purest, but that even if it has been polluted by something else, the god would cleanse and purify it, rather than polluting it.'[51] Rites designed to wash away divine anger in the manner criticized are extremely common in the religions of the world,[52] but that is no answer to the Hippocratic author's objection.

[48] See Simon, 317, n. 34.   [49] Theophr. *Hist. Pl.* 9.10.4.

[50] Herodas 4.17 f.: cf. the 'scraping' or 'cleansing' off of old age, Hom. *Il.* 9.446, *Nostoi*, fr. 6 OCT Homer v, p. 141, Aesch. fr. 45. Stigmata are transferred to a bandage in the wonder-cure *SIG³* 1168.47–65.   [51] 144–150 J., 1.28–45 G.

[52] Cf. Lévy-Bruhl, Ch. 8., 'Defilement and Purification'. The same symbolism, not surprisingly, appears in the compulsive acts of neurotics: 'Occasionally patients with a compulsion neurosis can make all their scruples disappear by bathing or changing their clothes, "bad feelings" being conceived of as dirt that can be washed away.' (O. Fenichel, *The Psychoanalytic Theory of Neurosis*, London, 1946, 289).

A distinction might be drawn between the symptoms of the disease and its cause, purification being intended to treat the former only. Thus, after the plague in the *Iliad*, purification is a preliminary to sacrifice, while bathing in the Anigrus marsh to cure leprosy is preceded by prayer to the Nymphs.[53] From the point of view of the patients mentioned in *On the sacred disease*, however, a distinction of this kind would probably be an over-rationalization. It is the sensation of being in the grip of an invasive supernatural force that is, for them, the pollution.[54] What unites dirtiness and divine intervention, and makes the one somehow equivalent to the other, is that both are external intrusions upon the integrity of the body. The body that is itself, free from all outside interference, is clean; an unwelcome incursion of any kind dirties it, but an incursion as mysterious and supernormal as epilepsy is also divine. The epileptic patients do not start from the premiss that the divine pollutes, which would no doubt have shocked them no less than the slightly sanctimonious Hippocratic; it is only in this restricted and temporary context that the gods become unclean. This is one of the anomalies in traditional belief that philosophy was to remedy by the postulate of impure demons acting as agents of the divine vengeance, to whom the rites of purification and expulsion are addressed.[55] Even in the earlier period, however, it was more common to envisage *kēres*, or *daimones*, perched upon the good things in life and polluting them than to identify the polluting power with an actual named god, as happens in *On the sacred disease*.[56]

It would not be surprising to learn that diseases which required treatment by purification were themselves the product of polluting acts or conditions. This appears to be the case in some cultures which practise cathartic medicine; for certain

---

[53] Hom. *Il.* 1.314–317, Paus. 5.5.11.

[54] Dirt and divine anger are close to equation in Soph. *Aj.* 655 f., I shall go to the shore, ὡς ἂν λύμαθ᾿ ἁγνίσας ἐμὰ/μῆνιν βαρεῖαν ἐξαλεύσωμαι θεᾶς (Eitrem, *Opferritus*, 121 n. 2). For the idea of *katharmoi* being addressed to spiritual beings cf. the 'Pythagorean' view in D. L. 8.32, which may reflect early attitudes despite an undeniable Platonic influence (Nock, ii, 601, W. Burkert, *Gnomon* 36 (1964), 564).

[55] Chrysippus *ap.* Plut. *Quaest. Rom.* 51, cf. Herter, *Dämonen*, 68–75. This was the Babylonian conception, Goltz, 1–14.

[56] For *kēres* see e.g. Pl. *Leg.* 937d; Herter, *Dämonen*, 54–6; the δῖος πράκτωρ of Aesch. *Supp.* 646–50 is an intermediate figure.

Bantu peoples, for instance, consumption and leprosy were caused by the pollutions of birth and death.[57] In Greece, madness of course might be due to the blood on a murderer's hands, and there is also evidence that skin diseases could be traced back to pollutions. In a hellenistic story, the people of Delos incurred a leprous disease when they permitted a burial on the sacred island, and the pollution that threatened Orestes should he fail to avenge his father would have taken the same form.[58] Thus the affliction that was a pollution in appearance (uncleanness on the skin) was also interpreted as one aitiologically. Pollution on Delos seems to have been suspected as a cause of the historical great plague at Athens, and we find a rationalization of these beliefs[59] in the Hippocratic doctrine that plagues are caused by *miasmata* in the air. The Roman view that stepping on an impure object causes madness or impotence is also very likely to go back to Greece.[60] But a diagnosis of this kind was not essential in order to attempt a cathartic cure, as the purifiers of *On the sacred disease* do not seem to have offered one. The symptoms themselves, the violation of the body's integrity, were the pollution to be cleansed, without any antecedent pollution being required to explain it.

It is natural to ask what relation there is, if any, between these polluting conditions and the infectious diseases of modern life.[61] We cannot assume, merely because they required purification, that they must have been seen as contagious. The contaminating contact that had to be cleansed was primarily that between the victim and the god and not that between him and his fellow men. In Greek popular belief, there seem to be two kinds of contagious condition, neither closely related to modern infections. On the one hand, there are pollutions such as those of birth, death, and blood-guilt that are communicable

[57] Lévy-Bruhl, 232.
[58] Madness: see p. 129 n. 94. Delians: (Aeschines) *Epistle* 1.2. Orestes: Aesch. *Cho.* 278–82. Skin disease is also inflicted as a punishment for religious offences that are not specifically pollutions: the Proetids, Hes. fr. 133 (cf. Roscher in *RML* 3.458 – thus the connection with ritual masking, Burkert, *HN* 190 f., *GR* 170 f., is unnecessary); (Plut.) *Fluv.* 21.4.
[59] Athenian plague: see p. 276 below. Hipp. *Flat.* 5, 6 (6.96,98 L.).
[60] Hor. *Ars. P.* 471, Petr. *Sat.* 134. See too Xen. Ephes. 5.7.7–9.
[61] Cf. O. Temkin, 'An Historical Analysis of the Concept of Infection', in the collective work *Studies in Intellectual History*, Baltimore, 1953, 123–47, reprinted in his *The Double Face of Janus*, Baltimore, 1977, 456–71.

according to specified principles and demand the formal seclusion of affected persons. On the other, there are a series of undesirable qualities and conditions that can be 'wiped off' on people and with which one may be 'filled' – folly, immorality, bad luck, and the like.[62] The contagiousness of bad luck often appears in comedy. 'Who goes there?' 'An unlucky man.' 'Keep to yourself then.'[63] Ill-omened words and prophecies often provoke a similar reaction.[64] Against contaminations of this kind one can protect oneself by mere words, 'May it turn against your own head', or by the simplest of all purifications, 'spitting out' the pollution.[65] It would be wrong to see the threat of contagion in all these cases as a mere metaphor. We hear, for instance, of unconquered troops who were unwilling to be joined in one division with their defeated comrades, and a Euripidean Theseus warns of the danger of marrying into an unfortunate household.[66] It seems to be in this latter sense that polluting diseases were contagious. People threw stones at madmen and might spit at the sight of a madman or epileptic, but these were protections against something repugnant and frightening rather than against a medical infection or a formally defined pollution. None of the many preserved sacred laws include the diseased among the polluted persons banned from entering a temple.[67] It is not clear that diseases ever truly became infectious in any other sense than this in Greek thought. Greeks were practically aware, in time of plague, that the disease could be contracted by contact,[68] but in popular per-

[62] 'Wiping off': Ar. *Ach.* 843, Eur. *Bacch.* 344. 'Filling': Ar. *Nub.* 1023, Dem. 20.28, Xen. *Lac. Pol.* 14.4 (this word is also used with reference to actual pollutions, Ant. *Tetr.* 1 α 10, Aeschin 2.88).

[63] Ar. *Ach.* 1018 f., *Nub.* 1263.

[64] e.g. Ar. *Pax* 1063, Eur. *Hec.* 1276; cf. Ar. *Ach.* 833, *Pax* 651, *Lys.* 506, Dem. 18.290,19.130,54.16.

[65] See preceding note. For spitting see e.g. Eur. *Hec.* 1276, Gow on Theocr. 6.39, p. 108 n. 9 on the murderer.

[66] Xen. *Hell.*1.2.15; Eur. *Supp.* 220–8 (cf. for contagious luck ibid., 591, and for a 'stain of misfortune' Soph. *OT* 833).

[67] Stones: Ar. *Av.* 524 f. Spitting: Theophr. *Char.* 16.15, cf. Plaut. *Capt.* 550, Pliny, *HN* 10.69,28.35. Sacred laws: Wächter, 43. The view sometimes expressed that madmen were formally excluded from temples seems to be based on misinterpretation of Ar.*Av.* 524 f. Contrast, for formal seclusion in Persia, Hdt.1.138.1.

[68] Thuc. 2.51.4–6 (some awareness of contagiousness was clearly general – note the reference to 'fear' of tending the sick); *SIG*³ 943.7–10;? Soph. *OT* 181. For Rome see *Thes. Ling. Lat.* s.v. *contagium*, a word most commonly (and perhaps originally) applied to infections among sheep (which Greeks too will have observed).

ception this may have been no more than an acute instance of the contagiousness of misfortune. Even Thucydides has no other language with which to describe infection than that of being 'filled with' the disease, an expression commonly applied to contagions of a different kind. It is worth considering the possibility that the Hippocratic doctors ignored the principle of infectiousness[69] because they saw belief in it as mere superstition. It is the Superstitious Man of Theophrastus who spits at sight of an epileptic.

Cathartic medicine aims to restore the sense of personal wholeness that has been disturbed by attack from outside. Seen in this way, illness is not a discrete phenomenon, but one of a set of dangerous intrusions upon the normal tenor of life. The word *nosos* itself is not confined to disease but covers a wide variety of 'bad things',[70] and we have just seen that bad luck, for instance, must be avoided and bad news spat out. The sources do not allow us to establish the full range of 'bad things' against which purification could be employed, but several can be named. A 'divine dream' that portended ill might be washed away, spat out, or purged in other ways; a particularly serious case would require sacrifice to the gods of aversion.[71] Evil omens could also be treated by purification, but the evidence here is surprisingly scanty.[72] It is perhaps characteristic of Greek in contrast to

[69] See J. C. F. Poole and A. J. Holladay, *CQ* n.s. 29 (1979), 295–9.

[70] e.g. Hom. *Od.* 15.407 f., Hes. *Theog.* 527, Pind. *Pyth.* 4. 293; cf. G. Preiser, *Allgemeine Krankheitsbezeichnungen im Corpus Hippocraticum* (Ars Medica II.5), Berlin, 1976, 89–104. On 'badness' see e.g. Hom. *Od.* 5.397,17.384,22.481. But on the limitations of this kind of argument see G. Lewis, *Knowledge of Illness in a Sepik Society*, London, 1975, 142 f., 355 f. (no one ever takes to their bed in response to the disease of poverty, and so on).

[71] Washing: Ar. *Ran.* 1340, Ap. Rhod. 4.670 f. Purification: Plut. *De Superst.* 166a. Sacrifice/libations and prayers, to the *theoi apotropaioi*, or Apollo, or the power (perhaps a dead man) whose anger the dream portended: Aesch. *Cho.* 523–5 (dead man), *Pers.* 201–4, 216–9 (*apotropaioi*), 219 f. (earth and the dead), Soph. *El.* 405–27 (dead man), 634–59 (Apollo), Xen. *Symp.* 4.33 (*apotropaioi*), Men. *Dysc.* 409–17 (Pan). (For offerings after a favourable dream cf. Xen. *Cyr.* 8.7.2–3). Prayer, to sun, Zeus etc. after favourable dreams, to *apotropaioi*, earth, and heroes after unfavourable, Hippoc. *Vict.* 4.89,90 (6.652,656–8 L.). (For prayers cf. Moschus 2.27, 4.123, *CQ* 32 (1982), 233 f.). Consultation of the dream interpreters for advice which god to propitiate: Eur. *Hec.* 87–9, Theophr. *Char.* 16.11, cf. 'Magnes' fr. 4. Declaration of the dream to the open air: Soph. *El.* 424 f., Eur. *IT* 42 f. Spitting out: Aesch. *Ag.* 980. Statement that 'I banish the dream': Eur. *Hec.* 72, 97. On the *apotropaioi* see Nock, ii, 599–602, with references; later evidence on dream procuration in Headlam's note on Herodas 8.11. Similar beliefs appear, thinly rationalized, in Hipp. *Vict.* 4: see esp. §87–8 (6.642 L.).

[72] Plut. *Alex.* 57.3, 75; Theophr. *Char.* 16.14.

Roman religion to view portents not as monstrosities requiring ritual banishment but as signs for which interpretation is necessary.[73] The appropriate response to these signs, once interpreted, will often be an action on a practical level, such as the abandonment of a campaign.[74] The distinction is not absolute, since the impulse simply to eliminate the abnormal is also found in Greece. Monstrous births and other abominations were sometimes burnt on 'wild wood' or the wood of fig-trees (worthless material characteristically being chosen for the disposal of a polluted object).[75] But this, too, is a kind of concern that, in contrast to the conspicuous Roman obsession, scarcely penetrates our sources.

Love, in later antiquity, was a condition the luckless suitor might seek to get clear of by purification, and it would not be ridiculous to postulate classical Greek precedents.[76] Plato urges the man driven by sacrilegious impulses to turn to the rites of expulsion.[77] Particularly interesting for the view of purification as an attempt to restore the personality to its normal state after an alien incursion is a passage of the *Cratylus*[78] in which Socrates playfully speaks of the passion for etymology as a 'wisdom' which has 'fallen upon him' suddenly from an unknown source, probably through contact with Euthyphro, who in his 'inspiration' had filled not just Socrates' ears but also his soul with this 'supernatural wisdom'. He suggests that for the day he and his interlocutors should exploit the alien inspiration, but on the morrow 'expel and purge it' through the offices of whatever priest or sophist was best at performing purifications of this

---

[73] e.g. Plut. *Per.* 6.2.

[74] Cf. the material in Pritchett, iii, Chs. 3–4. On prodigies see R. Bloch, *Les Prodiges dans l'antiquité classique*, Paris, 1963, 9–42, with bibliography.

[75] (Dion. Hal.) *Rhet.* 9.10, p. 309 Usener-Radermacher, on Euripides' *Melanippē* (children born to a cow); Phrynichus *Praeparatio Sophistica*, ed. I. de Borries, Leipzig, 1911, p. 15.12 = *Anecd. Bekk.* 10.26 (τὰ τερατώδη τὴν φύσιν); Diod. Sic. 32.12.2. (hermaphrodites); see too Theocr. 24.89–92 (snakes sent against infant Heracles); Lycoph. *Alex.* 1155–9 + schol. on 1155, citing Timaeus 566 *FGrH* fr. 146 (Locrian maidens); ? Tzetzes *Chil.* 5.735 (but cf. Gebhard, 3 f.) (scapegoats). Burning on fig-wood: comic poet *ap.* Dio Chrys. 33.63 (Kock, *CGF*, iii, p. 398), Lucian, *Alex.* 47. Burning of *katharmata* at crossroads: Eupolis, fr. 120. Throwing of monstrous births over one's shoulder is perhaps implied by Eur. *Andr.* 293 f.

[76] Tib. 1.2.59, Nemes. *Ecl.* 4.62–7; *contra*, Ov. *Rem. Am.* 260.

[77] *Leg.* 854b.

[78] Pl. *Cra.* 396c–e.

kind. This is a clear indication that purification counters such disruptions of the individual's normal personality as are felt to have their origin outside the individual himself.

It is natural in these terms that bewitchment, the 'imported' evil,[79] should have been seen as a pollution. When Euripides' Phaedra makes her famous statement that, though her hands are clean, her mind is polluted, the nurse thinks at once of sorcery, and we know from *On the sacred disease* that the person attacked in this way might be purified by blood.[80] It would be intriguing to know in what circumstances bewitchment of an individual or house was liable to be diagnosed, but on this the sources offer very little guidance.[81] Theophrastus' Superstitious Man was constantly purifying his house, on the grounds that Hecate had been conjured against it.[82] One of the sorcerer's methods, it seems, was to constrain the goddess by magical means to attack his victim's person and home.

We have a fragment of·an invocation of Hecate which, though its context is uncertain, gives a vivid hint of the kind of conception with which the sorcerer must have worked.[83] It is written in a rhythmic-sounding Doric prose that suggests Sophron, and is that part of an invocation which describes the god's location, powers, or condition before the actual request is made. But instead of 'whether you are in x or y' we find 'whether you have come hastening from a hanging, or from grinding to death a woman in childbed, or from ranging among

[79] Witchcraft or spell as ἐπακτός: Eur. *Hipp.* 318, *Inscr. Cret.* 2.xix. 7.20, *SGDI* 3545 (but on the latter two cf. P. Maas, *Hesperia* 13 (1944), 36 f.), and below, p. 348.
[80] Eur. *Hipp.* 317 f., Hipp. *Morb. Sacr.* 148.38 J., 1.40 G. Cf. Suda, Photius, s.v. περικαθαίρων:ἀναλύων τὸν πεφαρμακευμένον ἢ τὸν γεγοητευμένον. For the use of φαρμακεύω = bewitch cf. Pl. *Leg.* 932e–933e; it derives from an original undifferentiated concept of *pharmaka* as forces operating invisibly and mysteriously for good or evil. It is unclear what form the 'destructive drugs' feared by the people of Teos might take (M/L 30 A 1–5, cf. Latte, *HR* 68 n. 18); in Pl. *Leg.* 845e the drugs used to damage wells are presumably poisons rather than spells (cf. Thuc. 2.48.2), but a religious purification prescribed by the exegete remains necessary. Fumigation cures *fascinatum animal* in iate veterinary texts, Vegetius, *Mulomedicina*, 3.12.1; Claudii Hermeri *Mulomedicina Chironis*, ed. E. Oder, Leipzig, 1901, 497, p. 163.
[81] Note, however, Eur. *Andr.* 157 f. (woman's sterility). Other plausible occasions (cf. the *defixiones*) would be disease, unexpected failure in an important enterprise, or a run of bad luck; and of course objects suggesting magical attack might be seen (Pl. *Leg.* 933b).
[82] Theophr. *Char.* 16.7. For what may be a spectacular case see p. 348 below.
[83] Ap. Plut. *de Superst.* 170b; on the text see Wilamowitz, *Griechisches Lesebuch*[13], Berlin, 1936, i.336, ii.210 f.; R. Herzog, *Hess. Blätt. f. Volkskunde* 25 (1926), 219 n. 4. ·

corpses', and there follow references to several other forms of pollution. This remarkable language surely belongs to someone whose aim it was to exploit the goddess's pollution for shameful ends.[84] Love-magic would be one possible context;[85] conjuring against an enemy another. The goddess's power to harm was expressed in her impurity.[86]

It is very likely that an exorcism of Hecate, as performed by Theophrastus' Superstitious Man, was represented at least once in literature. Sophron composed a mime with a title the most obvious translation of which is 'The women who claim that they are driving out the goddess'.[87] (Of the alternative explanations that have been offered, some are linguistically impossible, some simply much less plausible.) Some idea of how the expulsion may have been achieved is given by a papyrus fragment which probably belongs to this mime.[88] An officiant

---

[84] This seems to emerge from the examples of ritual *loidoria* collected by S. Eitrem, *Symb. Osl.* 2 (1924), 43 ff., cf. ibid., 12 (1933), 23 f., 21 (1941), 48 f. If correct. this conclusion excludes the generally accepted ascription of the piece to the mime 'The Women who claim . . .': cf. K. Kerenyi, *Riv.Fil.* 13 (1935), 10. P. Legrand, *REA* 36 (1934), 25–31, argues on other grounds that Sophron wrote several magical mimes.

[85] Cf. the *loidoria* Theocr. 2.12–16. For pollution in magic see Theocr. 5.121 with Gow's note; pollution and magical attack, Orph. *Lith.* 591 (585).

[86] Schol. Theocr. 2.11/12 records, immediately after a Sophron citation, an elegant little folk-tale that explains Hecate's association with death and every form of pollution. Hera bore Zeus a daughter named Ἄγγελος, the Syracusan form of Artemis/Hecate (cf. Hesych s.v. ἄγγελος). Ἄγγελος stole her mother's magic myrrh and gave it to Europa. Hera, furious, pursued her daughter, but Ἄγγελος fled first to the house of a new mother, then into a funeral procession, where the Olympian Hera naturally could not follow her. Zeus instructed the Cabiri to purify Ἄγγελος. They did so at the Acherusian marsh, but this meant that she belonged for ever to the chthonian world. The story almost certainly derives from Sophron or Apollodorus' commentary on him; for different views see Wilamowitz, *Hermes* 34 (1899), 206–9 = *Kl. Schr.* iv, 48–51; G. Kaibel, *CGF* 161 and *Hermes* 34 (1899), 319; O. Crusius, *Neue Jahrb.* 25 (1910), 86–90; K. Latte, *Philol.* 88 (1933), 263 = *Kl. Schr.* 497.

[87] Sophron, fr. 3–9 in Kaibel *CGF*. Doxography in Olivieri, *Frammenti della comedia greca e del mimo*, ii², Naples, 1947, 68 f. Complete scepticism in Page, *GLP* 329; A. S. F. Gow, *Theocritus*, Cambridge, 1950, ii, 33. The most plausible alternative is that of R. Wünsch, *Jahrb f. Klass. Phil. Suppl.* 27 (1902), 111–22, and Latte, *Philol.* 88 (1933), 263 = *Kl. Schr.* 497, 'Women who claim the goddess is riding out.' But ἐλαυνῶ and compounds are repeatedly used of ritual expulsion: see S. Eitrem, *Symb. Osl.* 12 (1933), 11f., and add Aesch. *Cho.* 967 f., *LSCG* 56.1, Lucian, *Philops.* 16, Orph. *Lith.* 596 (590), *Carmen de viribus herbarum*, ed. E. Heitsch (*Die griechischen Dichterfragmente der römischen Kaiserzeit*, ii, Göttingen, 1964), 172,177; cf. *GRBS* 22 (1981), 284 n. 3.

[88] Page, *GLP* 328 with bibliography; vital for the ritual details S. Eitrem, *Symb. Osl.* 12 (1933), 10–29; K. Latte, *Philol.* 88 (1933), 259–64, 467–9 = *Kl. Schr.* 492–8, and Gow, *Theocritus*, ii, 34.

assembles a series of materials – salt, laurel, a puppy, asphalt, a torch – that were commonly used in purifications, in order to 'box against the goddess'. The fragment breaks off at the vital moment but, if it did portray an expulsion, it looks as if the goddess was first propitiated by the offering of a meal;[89] this will then have been carried out, and the goddess with it. The most interesting aspect is the reservation on the part of the mimographer that his title implies: he will not endorse the women's claim to be 'driving out the goddess'. Their haste in assuming bewitchment, their folly in attempting to constrain the gods by magical means, the impiety of supposing that gods pollute men:[90] one of these, perhaps more than one, may have been the target of Sophron's irony. It was, however, to keep Hecate away that pious Athenians carried out meals for her to the crossroads each month.[91]

About further contexts for purification we can only speculate. It would be intriguing to know whether bad luck and poverty, for instance, were diseases for which it would have made sense to try such a cure.[92] Animals as well as men were often purified against harmful influences, but here too precise details escape us.[93]

It remains to consider briefly the techniques that the purifiers used.[94] Some practices will be included which are found in such

---

[89] Lines 17–18. Latte compared the Arval Brothers' offering to the Mater Larum, thrown out down the hill through the temple doors (Dessau, *ILS* 9522 II 23 f. with notes; Latte, *RR* 92). Hecate's meals obviously reflect the same idea, and see p. 347 below.

[90] Haste: cf. Men. fr. 97, Theophr. *Char.* 16.6–7. Folly: Pl. *Leg.* 909b, Men. fr. 210. Impiety: p. 216 above.

[91] p. 30 n. 65 above.

[92] Note the paratragic line Ar. *Pax.* 1250 ὦ δυσκάθαρτε δαῖμον, ὥς μ'ἀπώλεσας. Particularly intriguing is *Morb. Sacr.* 148.38 J., 1.40 G., they purify epileptics ὥσπερ μίασμά τι ἔχοντας ἢ ἀλάστορας ἢ πεφαρμαγμένους ὑπ' ἀνθρώπων. (The run of the sentence makes ἀλάστορας object of καθαίρουσι rather than ἔχοντας, and thus human not demonic.) It indicates that being an *alastōr* is a condition an individual might acknowledge in himself, and not just a taunt hurled by enemies: cf. only Aesch. *Eum.* 236 (itself problematic) and perhaps the cult of Zeus Alastoros (p. 139 n. 143 above). In what circumstances would one admit to being an *alastōr*?

[93] e.g. Theophr. *Hist. Pl.* 9.10.4, Diod. 3.58.2, Orph. *Lith.* 208–218, p. 222 n. 80 above. Animals receive other purifications too, e.g. Theophr. *Hist. Pl.* 9.8.4 (purge), Pl. *Leg.* 735b.

[94] Cf. Rohde, 588–90; Stengel, 155–70; Bouché-Leclerq in Dar-Sagl. s.v. *Lustratio*; Burkert, *GR* 129–32; Eitrem, *Opferritus, passim*. Important sources are the passages of Diphilus and Menander cited above, p. 207, the Sophron mime (p. 223 above), Theocr.

contexts as initiatory cults or the purification of priests and temples, even though they are not attested as actual methods of healing. This is partly an expository convenience, but finds its excuse in the very extensive overlap that does exist between the purifications practised in these different contexts. This overlap is an important factor in the appeal that cathartic medicine exercised. It worked not merely by assimilating disease to dirt, but also indirectly by exploiting all the positive value assigned to purification as a form of action in a wholly religious context. The non-specific character of rites was noted by Durkheim;[95] once their prestige is established, they tend to be employed very widely outside their original context. Communion is taken at weddings and funerals as well as actual communion services, just as no ancient ceremony was complete without sacrifice; mass can be specially celebrated for healing, while a Hindu, weakened by malnutrition and anaemia, may seek to recover his strength by ritual bathing.[96] In a similar way the purifier benefits from the techniques, and the prestige, of the priest.

Though elaborate stage directions seem more characteristic of the ancient near east, there is some evidence for the symbolic exploitation of space in Greek rituals of this kind. It is said that rites of expiation and purification were normally performed facing east.[97] We have already seen the importance of symbolic encirclement. Lustral water was distributed to the ring of participants before sacrifice, and purificatory animals were carried round every Athenian place of meeting; Mantineans were supposed on one occasion to have taken animals around their entire territory.[98] When an individual human was initiated or purified, he was seated submissively in the middle, and the officiants performed whatever ritual was appropriate around him.[99] Verbs like 'purify in a circle' (*perikathairō*) were

24.88–100, Plut. *de Superst.* 166a, 168d, Lucian, *Nec.*7, Clem. Al. *Strom.* 7.4.26.2–3, vol. iii, p. 19 St. (red wool, salt, torches, squills, sulphur), idem, *Protr.* 1.10.2, vol. i, p. 10 St. (laurel leaves and fillets).

[95] *Elementary Forms*, 385 f.
[96] Read, 71.
[97] Schol. Soph. *OC* 477, cf. Orph. *Lith.* 210.
[98] pp. 20 f.; Mantineans, Polyb. 4.21.9; cf. further Lucian, *Philops.* 12, Paus. 9.22.2, the Roman (and Iguvian) *Amburbia*, *Ambarvalia* etc. (Latte, *RR* 41f.); much more in Eitrem, *Beiträge*, ii, 1–19.
[99] Men. *Phasm.* 50–6.

used even when there was no actual encirclement.[100] But the same effect could be achieved by different means. When the Macedonian and Boeotian armies were purified, the dog victim was not carried round them, but divided into two halves through which they marched, the severed animal creating what has been called an 'absorptive zone'.[101] What mattered was to create symbolic contact between the person who was to be purified and the cathartic objects. Another possibility is seen in a ritual described but surely not invented by Valerius Flaccus: two priests carried parts of animals in opposite directions through the middle of the Argonauts, touching the heroes with them as they went.[102] The scapegoat was whipped on the genitals with cathartic plants, while in a wide variety of initiations the virtue of the sacred objects was transmitted to the seated candidate by simply holding them over his head.[103]

Among agents of purification, the most widely used and most basic was water.[104] Natural though this seems, there are differences as well as similarities between secular and religious cleansing. Lustral water had to be pure, and drawn from a flowing source;[105] so too, if possible, water for ordinary washing.[106] But no washerwoman would think of combining the waters of three, five, seven, or fourteen different springs to remove even the deepest stain.[107] This was a distinctively religious source of power. Particular springs were especially favoured for purifications, and the most prized cathartic water was that of the salt-stained sea: 'the sea washes away all evils

---

[100] Cf. *RE* Suppl.6.149–51 (Pfister) for a list of the lustral *peri*-compounds. Similarly Roman *circumferre*.

[101] p. 22 above.

[102] *Argon.* 3.439–443; cf. P. Boyancé, *REL* 13 (1935), 107–36.

[103] Scapegoat: Hipponax, fr. 10. Sacred objects: G. Schneider-Herrmann, *Antike Kunst* 13 (1970), 52–70.

[104] See Eitrem, *Opferritus*, 76–132; Ginouvès, Part 3, *passim*.

[105] Aesch. *Eum.* 452, Eur. *El.* 794, *Hipp.* 653 with Barrett; J. S. Rusten, *ZPE* 45 (1982), 284 n. 3. For Rome see Bömer on Ov. *Fast.* 2.35.

[106] Eur. *Hipp.* 123 f., Hom. *Od.* 6.85–7.

[107] 3 Springs, Theophr. *Char.* 16.2 (if E. K. Borthwick is right, *Eranos* 64 (1966), 106), Men. *Phasm.* 55; 5 springs, Empedocles B 143; 7, Ap. Rhod. 3.860, Philinna papyrus in *JHS* 62 (1942), 36; 14, Suda s.v. ἀπὸ δὶς ἑπτὰ κυμάτων (murderer's clothes); more in Rohde, 589. For repeated washings in the same spring see Borthwick, loc. cit., 108.

from among men'.[108] Religious water could be fortified; when salt was put in this may have been simply a way of creating artificial sea-water (though salt was a purifying agent in its own right), but other additives too are found.[109] Above all, lustration differs from washing in its manner of application. In rite, there is a difference in degree but not in kind between simple sprinkling and total immersion. Religious water is potentially effective in even the tiniest quantity; certain crimes, on the other hand, not all the rivers on earth could wash away.[110]

Greeks sometimes spoke of 'purifying fire'.[111] The element was in itself always bright, never stained, and through the hearth and sacrifice it had powerful sacral associations. Torches were an indispensable part of many ceremonies, and, swung vigorously, they could purify a room or a man.[112] Normally, however, sharp-smelling substances were added to the fire when purification was needed. The smoke and pungent odour of sulphur, lapping round the polluted object and penetrating its every part, rendered vividly perceptible the desired effect.[113] Already in Homer sulphur was a 'cure for bad things', and the purifier held it in honour throughout antiquity.[114] He

[108] Particular springs: e.g. Paus. 2.17.1, cf. Eitrem, *Opferritus*, 84; Moulinier, 71. Sea: Eur. *IT* 1193, cf. 1039, Soph. *Aj.* 655, p. 283 on Eleusinian *mystai*, Diphilus, fr. 126, Theophr. *Char.* 16.13, Ap. Rhod. 4.663, Plut. *Quaest. Graec.* 40, 301a, *LSCG* 97 A 15, 151 B 23, Iambl. *VP* 153, Eitrem, *Opferritus*, 335 f. and exhaustively Wachsmuth, 219–23. Sea's purity, Aesch. *Pers.* 578, D.L.8.35.

[109] Men. *Phasma* 55 (salt and lentils), Theocr. 24.97 (salt), Hesych. s.v. χερνιβεῖον (salt and barley groats): cf. Eitrem, *Beiträge*, iii, 8 f., idem, *Opferritus*, 86. Purifying salt: Sophron and Clement cited p. 224 n. 94, schol. Ar. *Nub.* 1237; Eitrem, *Opferritus*, 323 ff.; *RE* s.v. *Salz*, 2093 f. The point of lentils and barley groats as additives is unclear; but cf. Plut. *Quaest. Graec.* 46, 302b.

[110] Cf. G. Bachelard, *L'Eau et les rêves*, Paris, 1942, 193–4: 'La meilleure preuve de cette puissance intime, c'est qu'elle appartient à chaque goutte du liquide . . . pour l'imagination matérielle, la substance valorisée peut agir, même en quantité infime, sur une très grande masse d'autres substances.' See too Eitrem, *Opferritus*, 126; ineffacable crimes e.g. Soph. *OT* 1227 f.

[111] Eur. *Hel.* 869, *HF* 937, *IA* 1112, 1471. For a pseudo-medical use see Plut. *De Is. et Os.* 383d. For Rome see Börner on Ov. *Fast.* 4. 727. The funeral fire, of course, purged off the impurity of mortality: Rohde, 49 n. 41, 334 n. 127, *Anth. Pal.* 7.49.

[112] Eur. *IT* 1224 f., the Torre Nova sarcophagus (p. 285 below); cf. M. Vassits, *Die Fackel in Kultus und Kunst der Griechen*, diss. Munich, 1899, 6–8.

[113] *Penetrat ad viscerum omnes recessus, ac curat saepius loca, quae potiones non potuerunt curare*, Vegetius, *Mulomedicina*, 3.12.1.

[114] Hom. *Od.* 22.481, cf. *Il.*16.228, Eur. *Hel.* 866, almost all the texts cited above, p. 224 n. 94; *RE* s.v. *Schwefel*, 798–9 (Blümner); Börner on Ov. *Fast.* 4.739. On cathartic fumigation see Eitrem, *Opferritus*, 241–50. Burkert, *Grazer Beiträge* 4 (1975), 77, suggests an original connection between καθαίρω and semitic ktr, 'raüchern'.

esteemed it, of course, not for its actual disinfectant powers, but because its dry acrid smoke was symbolically fit to combat the damp rottenness of impurity;[115] pitch was sometimes burnt for the same purpose.[116] For offerings to the gods, by contrast, sweet-smelling substances were chosen.[117]

'Water is best, and gold shines out like blazing fire', says Pindar; this metallic homologue of the two uncontaminated elements is in fact, like them, a purifier, although the exact mechanism of a 'purification by gold' is nowhere specified (it was perhaps by sprinkling of water from a gold vessel).[118] And it is surely as the purest form of vegetable matter, a title it claims for itself in Callimachus' *Iambus*,[119] that the laurel expels and cleanses evil. The evidence for this function is abundant in Roman sources, and not negligible in Greek; Apollo's priest Branchus cleansed the Milesians from plague by sprinkling them with water from a laurel bough,[120] and the same method seems to be attributed to Apollo himself on two vases showing the purification of Orestes.[121] In other contexts too, laurel has powers for good.[122] It seems to derive its purity not directly from its physical properties, nor from its place within the general

[115] Cf. C. R. Hallpike, *The Foundations of Primitive Thought,* Oxford, 1979, 160 for such patterns of synaesthetic association.

[116] Diphilus, fr. 126, Sophron in Page, *GLP*, p. 330; *RE* s.v. *Asphalt*, 1728 f.

[117] Fr. Pfister in *RE* s.v. *Rauchopfer*, 284.

[118] Pind *Ol.*1.1. Purification by gold: *LSCG* 154 A 29,30,44; B 2,6,15,26;? *LSCG* 156 A 15; Eur. *IT* 1216 (where editors corrupt χρυσῷ to πυρσῷ); Iambl. *VP* 153. Sprinkling from a golden vessel, Eur. *Ion* 434 f. On apotropaic gold see Eitrem, *Opferritus*, 192–7; 'purifying' bronze, Apollodorus 244 *FGrH* fr. 110 (banged against eclipses).

[119] Fr. 194. 37–44; cf. Artemid. 4.57 p. 282.1 Pack, Pliny, *HN* 15.135. Laurel in funerary contexts (Pliny, *HN* 16.239, Tzetzes ad Lyc. *Alex.* 42, *AJA* 11 (1907), 72) is exceptional. On laurel see M. B. Ogle, *AJP* 31 (1910), 287–311; Gow on Theocr. 2. 1; Amandry, 126–34; Bömer on Ov. *Fast.* 1.339; K. Lembach, *Die Pflanzen bei Theokrit,* Heidelberg, 1970, 57–61.

[120] Callim. fr. 194. 28–31 with Pfeiffer.

[121] *JHS* 89 (1969), Plates 3.3,4.5; Apollo and Artemis hold laurel boughs even when the purification is by pig's blood (ibid., Plates 2.1–2,3.4,4.6; cf. Melampus on the cameo *RML* 3.3009). A Lucanian vase in Berlin perhaps shows a purification by laurel (*Archäologische Zeitung* n. f. 1 (1847), Fig. 7, A. D. Trendall, *The red-figured vases of Lucania, Campania and Sicily,* Oxford, 1967, 150 n. 854). Ion swept Apollo's temple with a laurel broom, Eur. *Ion* 80, 103, 113 ff.; those who left a death house sprinkled themselves with water from a laurel branch, schol. Eur. *Alc.* 98, cf. Servius on *Aen* 6.230. Laurel-sprinkling in magical papyri, e.g. *PGM* 5. 200, S. Eitrem, *Gnomon* 4 (1928), 194 f. For laurel used in fumigation, a common practice at Rome (e.g. Pliny, *HN* 15.135, 138), I know for Greece only Plut. *De Pyth. or.* 397a.

[122] Theophr. *Char.* 16.2, D.L.4.57; Ogle, op. cit., 295 f., 307 ff.; Rohde, 198 n. 95; Gow on Theocr. 2.1.

classificatory scheme of plants, but from its ancient status. the origin of which we can scarcely determine, as the sacred tree *par excellence,* dear to all the Olympian gods and especially to Apollo,[123] mark of honour assigned to those who, like prophets or poets, are themselves dear to the gods. Olive branches[124] and wool fillets[125] occasionally appear as purifiers for similar reasons. (Such prior sacral significance is the kind of factor that, as has been pointed out, much complicates a simple structural analysis.[126]) A pure and purifying animal, like the four-eyed dog of Zoroastrianism, seems not to be available to set alongside the pure mineral and vegetable.[127]

While the processes considered so far dissolve pollution through contact with the purest forms of matter, others transfer it into absorptive substances, not especially pure in themselves and perhaps even the opposite, which are then ostentatiously disposed of.[128] The contrast between the two methods, however, is a purely formal one, as both were normally combined in the same ceremony, and even on a formal level not absolute, since at least one of the pure substances, water, is itself contaminated by the dirt it washes away.[129] The passage of *On the sacred disease* that best illustrates the disposal of these offscourings has already been quoted: 'They bury some of them in the ground, they throw some in the sea, and others they carry off to the mountains where nobody can see or tread on them.' (He omits the common expedient of sending them to the crossroads.[130]) Local tradition in the Peloponnese knew the spot

[123] Amandry, 127; Ogle, 305 f.
[124] Theocr. 24.98, Orph. *Lith.* 214 f. Though opposed to the laurel as chthonian to Olympian, and thus associated with funerals (Callim. fr. 194. 40–56), it was united with it against other trees as sacred against profane (Callim. fr. 194. 101 ff., Pliny, *HN* 15.135, cf. Murr, 40–8; Diels, 119–21), and could thus be exploited for purification.
[125] Theocr. 24.98, Nemesianus *Ecl.* 4.63, Clem. Al. *Strom.* 7.4.26.2, vol. 4, p. 19 St. For wool as an *alexipharmakon* cf. J. Pley, *De lanae in antiquorum ritibus usu, RGVV* 11.2,Giessen, 1911, 80–94; Eitrem, *Opferritus,* 380–6; Gow on Theocr. 2.2. For its high social status see Empedocles B 112.6; Pley, 68–79.   [126] Cf. p. 365.
[127] Four-eyed dog: Boyce, Ch. 6. Note, however, the (?sacred) fish held over initiands on vases discussed by G. Schneider-Herrmann, *Antike Kunst* 13 (1970), 52–70.
[128] Rudhardt, 165.
[129] And for the throwing away of lustral torches see Claud. *Cons. Hon.* 329 f.
[130] 148.44 ff. J., 1.42 G.: cf. Hom. *Il.*1.314, Ap. Rhod. 4.710, Paus. 2.31.8, 8.41.2; on the crossroads, p. 30 n. 65; sacred laws restricting where *katharmata* might be thrown out, *LSCG* 108; *IG* I³ 257 = *LSS* 4 (danger of stepping on one, Petron. *Sat.* 134). Only desperate persons or desperadoes would eat such remains, p. 30 n. 35. For their power to 'take up' evil from the purified person see esp. Clem. Al. *Strom.* 7.4.26. 1, vol. 3, p. 19 St.

where Melampus had buried the offscourings of the Proetids, or could point out the spring into which he threw them, thus contaminating it.[131] The verb *ekpempō*, 'send out', normally applied to humans, is sometimes used of the disposal of the polluted remains, as though there were something slightly animate about them.[132] The purifier would emphasize separation from them by 'throwing them over his shoulder', and 'walking away without looking back'.[133]

Most powerful among these rites of absorptive purification was that by blood sacrifice, practised for healing by the purifiers of epilepsy and also, according to a south Italian vase of the fourth century, by Melampus.[134] The symbolism of this ritual is considered elsewhere.[135] It had a variant form, '(purifying) around by puppy', in which the most despised of animals was used to receive the candidate's impurity.[136] The commonest substance into which evil was transferred, by a process that is nowhere made explicit, was the egg.[137] It was perhaps because the egg was a common offering to the dead, and thus 'food for corpses', that it was suitable for this use.[138] In murder purifications, and perhaps in other contexts, the candidate placed his foot on a woollen fleece which absorbed his impurity.[139] Symbolically even more direct was the technique of 'wiping off' the evil through smearing with a clinging substance

[131] *Pharmaka* buried in agora at Sicyon: *Bulletin Épigraphique* 69 (1956), 110, 72 (1959), 157. *Katharmata* thrown into Anigrus marsh: Paus. 5.5.10; thrown into fountain at Lousoi – whence all who drink from it hate wine – Ov. *Met.* 15.322–8; *Heldensage*, 247 n. 4.

[132] Aesch. *Cho.* 98, cf. Aelian, *VH* 14.7 ἐξηλαύνετο τῆς Σπάρτης ὡς τὰ τῶν νοσούντων καθάρσια, and the 'sending away' of evils, by a merely verbal act, to distant regions in *apopompē* (cf. Soph. *OT* 194–7, *Hymn. Orph.* 11.23, 14.14, 36.16, 71.11; the many studies of O. Weinreich on *apopompē* are listed by H. Herter, *Dämonen*, 47 n. 12).

[133] Aesch. *Cho.* 98, Eur. *Andr.* 293 f.; Rohde, 325 n. 104; A. S. Pease on Cic. *Div.* 1.49; Gow on Theocr. 24.96; Bömer on Ov. *Fast.* 5. 439.

[134] The Canicattini crater: see most recently *Antike Kunst* 13 (1970), 67, Fig. 1, with references to other portrayals. The *en passant* interpretation of the Canicattini crater by E. Langlotz, *Die Kunst der Westgriechen*, Munich, 1963, 25, as an initiation scene fails to explain the unmistakable Artemis image.

[135] Appendix 6.

[136] Theophr. *Char.* 16.14, Plut. *Quaest. Rom.* 68, 280b–c; ?cf. Sophron in Page, *GLP*, p. 330.

[137] See p. 30 n. 65; also *Ant. u. Chr.* 6 (1940–50), 57–60. Stengel, 162 speaks of 'wiping off' with egg-yolks, but it is clear from Clem. Al. *Strom.* 7.4.26.3, and Lucian, cited p. 30 n. 65, that after use the cathartic eggs were still edible.

[138] Nilsson, *Op. Sel.* i, 3–20.

[139] See Appendix 6.

which was then washed off, bringing the pollution with it. Mud was an obvious material to choose, since it emphasized the new state of purity by the greatest possible contrast.[140] The use of a bran mash for the same purpose is less easy to explain.[141]

The use of the laurel has already been discussed. Other plants sometimes described as 'purifiers' perhaps owe that title chiefly to their function as *alexipharmaka*, 'averters of drugs/bewitchment', rather than to any specific use in purifications.[142] These *alexipharmaka* seem to be a complex class – the strong smell of the buckthorn is no less effective than the sanctity of the laurel – and to discuss them here would lead too far afield. One plant, however, that is repeatedly mentioned as an actual purifying agent is the squill.[143] It seems safe to infer that the plant used by the purifier was the 'Epimenidean' squill, which, says Theophrastus, 'gets its name from its use'.[144] The squill was used as a whip in scapegoat and other rituals,[145] but its application in purifications, nowhere clearly indicated,[146] was not necessarily the same. In the scapegoat ritual, it is associated with despised wild plants,[147] and is elsewhere sometimes spoken of as contemptible, inedible, even deadly.[148] It is tempt-

---

[140] Dem. 18.259, Graf, 106.

[141] Dem. 18.259, ἀπομάττων τῷ πηλῷ καὶ τοῖς πιτύροις. The *prospermeia* (*hapax*: but cf. *panspermia*) of Cos (*LSCG* 154 A 29, 30, 44; B 2, 6,15,26; *LSCG* 156 A 15 (restored)) was presumably similar. Wiping off with μαγίδες, cheese or bran cakes also offered to Trophonius and Hecate, is attested by Hesych. s.v. μαγίδες; μαγμόν; cf. Soph. fr. 734 with Pearson and Radt, Ath. 149c. This perhaps permits the inference that here too the absorptive substance is 'corpse food': for *panspermia* offered to the dead see Deubner, 112 (Chytroi).

[142] e.g. buckthorn: see Rohde, 198 n. 95; Murr, 104–6; fig: Cook, 2.ii.1103; *RE* 1.55 f.; Murr, 31–5; Gebhard, 69 f.; Rohde, 590; ἱερὰ βοτάνη or περιστερεών: *RE* 1.55; σχῖνος: Cratinus, fr. 232, Ar. fr. 255, Ameipsias, fr. 25 (with asparagus) – I do not understand why in these cases LSJ and others take σχῖνος to be a squill. Trallians used vetch in purifications, Plut. *Quaest. Graec.*46,302b.

[143] In *katharmoi* Theophr. *Char.* 16.14, Diphilus, fr. 126, Lucian, *Nec.* 7, Dio Chrys. 48.17, Artemid. 3.50, p. 225. 13 Pack. Hung at door or buried under sill as an *alexipharmakon*: Theophr. *Hist.Pl.* 7.13.4, Dioscorides, *Mat.Med.* 2.171.4, p. 239.11 W.

[144] Theophr. *Hist.Pl.*7.12.1. Squills are normally identified as *urginea maritima*; W. Thiselton Dyer, however, in the index to the Loeb *Hist.Pl.*, makes the Epimenidean squill *ornithogalum pyrenaicum*.

[145] Hipponax, fr. 6, Theocr. 7.107 f. + schol. A 'squill-battle' in *Inscr. Prien.* 112.91,95.

[146] Possibly for fumigation in Calp. Sic. 5.79. Burkert's Hittite parallel, *GR* 131, wrenches the squill away from its quite complex web of Greek associations, unjustifiably.   [147] Tzetzes, *Chil.* 5.736.

[148] J. N. Bremmer, 'Scapegoat-Rituals in Ancient Greece', *HSCP* 87 (1983), citing *inter alia* Theog. 537, Artemid. 3.50, p. 225.11 Pack, Suda s.v. *skilla*; they grow on tombs, Theocr. 5.121.

ing, therefore, to see it as the vegetable equivalent of the impure puppy, a dishonourable plant appropriately used in a ritual applied to polluted persons. The difficulty, however, in interpreting the symbolism of natural species lies in the complexity of their possible uses. Though the squill might be aesthetically and gastronomically despised, the druggist and the horticulturalist esteemed it. It had a wide variety of medical uses,[149] and was believed (correctly, it is said) to foster the growth of seeds and shoots planted in the surrounding soil.[150] It stayed alive for a remarkable length of time when dug up, and Theophrastus makes this exceptional vitality the reason for its use as an 'averter of spells'. The Epimenidean squill was actually the one edible form,[151] which suggests that it was the positive qualities of the plant that the purifier sought to exploit. But without being able to see and hear him manipulate the magic plant we can only guess at its significance.

These various techniques, which have had to be separated in description, tended to be freely combined in actual use. Diphilus' Melampus employs torch, squill, pitch, sulphur, and sea-water all together, and other texts show a similar profusion. The rites were accompanied by incantations which probably comprised formulas of transference – 'may the evil pass into this egg' – and analogy – 'as I wash off this mud, so may . . .' – as well as more mysterious matters.[152] Expressions sometimes occur which suggest that an incantation could be a 'purification' in itself.[153]

The purifiers of *On the sacred disease* deserve special mention, but as their methods have been well studied in detail it can be quite summary.[154] In addition to the actual purifications, they subjected their patients to various abstentions (from bathing, and from particular forms of food), and rules of life (such as not to wear black, or 'put foot on foot and hand on hand'). These

---

[149] See Gebhard, 69 n. 28; *RE* 1.67 f.; ibid., 3 A 522–6; K. Lembach, *Die Pflanzen bei Theokrit*, Heidelberg, 1970, 63–5; Dioscorides, *Mat.Med.* 2. 171; Pliny, *HN* 20.97–101.

[150] Theophr. *Hist. Pl.* 2.5.5, 7.13.4; *RE* 1.67; ibid., 3 A 523 f.

[151] Theophr. *Hist. Pl.* 7.12.1.

[152] Cf. Hippocr. *Morb. Sacr.* 138.10, 140.13, 148.34 J., 1.4, 12, 39 G.; Arist. fr. 496 Rose; Callim. Fr. 194.30; cf. Boyancé, 37. For surviving incantations see R. Heim, 'Incantamenta magica graeca – latina', *Jahrb. f. klass. Phil. Suppl.* 19 (1893), 463–576 and Fr. Pfister in *RE* Suppl. 4 s.v. *Epode*.

[153] Arist. fr. 496, Diod. 3.58.2–3.   [154] Lanata, *passim*; cf. Lloyd, 37 f.

regulations have close parallels in form, and often in detail, in the abstentions (*hagneiai*) required of participants in particular cults, and in the minute regulations for daily living that are best represented for us by 'Hesiod' and the Pythagorean *symbola*, but certainly derive ultimately from popular belief. The purifiers of epilepsy, therefore, differed from simpler purifiers in digging deeper than them into the resources of traditional religion. Exploiting these resources, they put together for their patients a distinctive way of life to follow. Though their materials and explanations were religious, it is plausible that in doing so they were, consciously or unconsciously, mimicking the special ways of life that non-religious healers of the period were prescribing. That, at least, is the charge brought against them by their Hippocratic critic; their abstinences, according to him, are just dietetic prescriptions in disguise.[155]

A theoretical issue of importance is raised by the use of unclean materials (blood, mud) in some of these rites. One of the true observations out of which the doctrine of the 'ambiguity of the sacred' was built up was that, in some cultures, in some contexts, pollution acquires positive powers; the impure, normally shunned, becomes 'sacred' in the sense that it is marked out as powerful in contrast to the non-polluted objects of familiar use.[156] Obscene or blasphemous language is a commonplace example. Certain currents in the popular medicine of later antiquity made conscious use of the powers of pollution. Although bodily wastes were perhaps used as a *materia medica* simply because they were thought to have specific virtues like any other substance,[157] there were authorities who explicitly recommended the unspeakable. '(In the treatment of fevers) Democritus says pollution is needed, for instance blood guilt (?), menstrual blood, the flesh of sacred birds or forbidden animals given as food, and draughts of blood.'[158] Honourable Roman authors record with revulsion the belief that human

[155] *Morb.Sacr.* 142–4.6 J., 1.12–23 G.
[156] Cf. Steiner, 66, Douglas, Ch. 10.
[157] R. Muth, *Träger der Lebenskraft, Ausscheidungen des Organismus im Volksglauben der Antike*, Vienna, 1954, *passim*.
[158] Theodorus Priscianus, *Physica*, p. 251.2–5 Rose. On the pseudo-Democritean literature see *RE* Suppl. 4.219–23; on Bolus (its most important representative), bibliography in *Oxford Classical Dictionary*², s.v. *Bolus;* index to J. Bidez/F. Cumont, *Les Mages hellénisés*, Paris, 1938.

blood, smeared on the lips or drunk hot from a gladiator's fresh wounds, could cure epilepsy.[159] The abomination, transferred to the blood of martyrs and executed criminals, is said to have continued until recent times.[160] Other cures for epilepsy were water drunk from a murdered man's skull (Artemon), the flesh of a beast slain by the same weapon as had killed a man ('Orpheus and Archelaus'), goat's meat roasted on a funeral pyre ('the magi').[161] But it would probably be wrong to father such attitudes on the purifiers of *On the sacred disease*. Although purification by blood was certainly a confrontation with the horrific, it was a confrontation licensed, in other contexts, by traditional religion, and it was not the defiling power of blood in itself that made the ceremony effective; the blood was a token of the pollution that was to be removed.[162] Similar ceremonies, like the cleansing of the Proetids according to Diphilus, did not use polluting agents at all. In the early period, it is only for harmful magic that we find impurity being sought out and exploited.[163]

As we noted initially, the purifier was an object of contempt to the enlightened by the fourth century. Before intellectuals, his methods could not well be defended. Intellectuals, however, could simply be ignored. These practices continued; the purifier reappears (as an old woman) in Roman love elegy, and in the fourth century of our era still threatened to lure wavering Christians into superstition.[164]

---

[159] e.g. Pliny, *HN* 28.4.

[160] F. J. Dölger, *Vorträge der Bibl. Warburg* 1923/4, 196–214, esp. 204 ff.; Abt, 199 (273), n. 10.

[161] Pliny, *HN* 28.8,34,226. More bloody epilepsy cures in O. Temkin, *The Falling Sickness*², Baltimore, 1971, 22 f., and on the use of blood cf. Eitrem, *Opferritus*, 441–7.

[162] See Appendix 6.

[163] p. 222 and p. 223 n. 85. I am not convinced by the counter-instances of Vernant, *Société*, 137 f. Ritual obscenity, of course, which does occur, is a related phenomenon.

[164] Cf. *Constitutiones Apostolorum* 8.32.11: the μάγος, ἐπαοιδός . . . περιάμματα ποιῶν, περικαθαίρων to be excluded from communion until reformed; *Concilium Ancyranum*, Canon 24, in C. J. Hefele, *Histoire des Conciles*, tr. H. Leclerq, Paris, 1907– , i.324:5 years penance for those who introduce magicians into their houses ἐπὶ ἀνευρέσει φαρμακειῶν ἢ καὶ καθάρσει; the temptation to infidelity cited by Augustine: 'Sed ecce adstat vicinus et amicus et ancilla . . . ceram vel ovum manibus ferens et dixit "Fac hoc et salvus eris. Quid prolongas tuam aegritudinem?" ' (*Revue Bénédictine* 54 (1938), p. 8. 121). For the use of baptism as a rite of exorcism see K. Thraede in *RAC* 7.76 ff.

8

DIVINE VENGEANCE AND DISEASE

A claim such as 'You'll go mad if you enter that precinct' has two levels of significance. It is on the one hand a way of insisting on the sanctity of the gods' property, a threat in support of a value rather than a hypothesis about the causes of disease. The system of taboo is not, as it has seemed to some observers, the product of a cultural neurosis, but a way in which 'attitudes to values are expressed in terms of danger'.[1] On the other hand, it is natural that, if a case of madness occurs in a society where such threats are rife, breach of the rule should be suspected as its cause. In the previous chapters, we have surveyed a large number of religious dangers, but primarily in their role as sanctions. It remains to consider to what extent they were appealed to in explanation of actual afflictions. Where they were not applied, it will obviously be necessary to pay attention to the alternative explanations that supplanted them.

Unfortunately, the programme here outlined is forbiddingly vast. There is no special area of experience to which the operations of destiny, luck, or divine anger are confined, and, although inexplicable happenings are liable to be especially 'divine', there are many instances of the gods' will being worked out through events that Greeks could easily interpret in human terms. A man's standing in relation to the gods or destiny will affect, among other things, his health, wealth, length of days, procreative powers, success in farming, business or politics, marital or parental fortunes. In what follows, the restricted case of responses to disease will, for convenience, alone be considered. As it happens, the evidence is scarcely available through which to consider some of the other situations; our sources do not reveal the inmost feelings of a father whose sons have died on the verge of manhood, of a wife unable to produce heirs for her husband, of any ordinary individual all of whose

[1] Steiner, 21.

projects go inexplicably awry. But the question could certainly be confronted more generally than will be attempted here.

Serious disease is an affliction that wrenches the patient's life out of its customary unreflective course. From an independent agent, master of his own affairs, he has become the prey of external forces he cannot understand. He wakes up one morning ill; but the previous day he had been well, and he has not eaten or drunk anything unusual, or changed his habits in any way. 'By day and by night diseases of themselves (*automatoi*) come upon man, and do him harm, silently; for cunning Zeus took out their voice', says Hesiod.[2] This brings out three crucial facts about diseases, that they are uncontrollable, inexplicable, and hateful. The question of why they occur is not perhaps of great interest in itself (no one ever consulted an oracle to establish the cause of a disease safely overcome); but during the affliction an explanation that will permit control becomes vitally important.

Illness becomes comprehensible when it ceases to be a random event. In Judaism, as famous incidents in the gospels show, it is sin, whether ritual or moral, that causes disease,[3] and this idea seems to have been widespread in the Ancient Near East.[4] The correct procedure for the sick man or his friends is to diagnose the relevant sin, confess it publicly, and make a sacrifice of atonement. If the evil continues, further sins must be established (perhaps with the help of an oracle) and publicly confessed.[5] This link of sin with disease is found throughout the world.[6] Among various Nilotic peoples, for instance, a sin, such as incest, and the disease that it is believed to cause may bear the same name.[7] If such an offence is committed, sacrifice will probably be made immediately to prevent the onset of the

---

[2] *Op.* 102–4.

[3] See Mark 2:1–12 (Matthew 9:1–8, Luke 5:18–26), John 5:1–15, 9.1–2, Epistle of James 5:14–15. In the Old Testament e.g. Psalm 39, 41:4, 103:3, 107:17–20. I have not seen W. v. Siebenthal, *Krankheit als Folge der Sünde*, Hanover, 1950.

[4] See Latte, *Kl. Schr.* 32 n. 42, Goltz, 7–10, and at length R. Pettazzoni, *La Confessione dei peccati*, Bologna, 1929–35, vols. ii and iii.

[5] A good example of this search for the responsible sin is the Hittite 'Prayers of King Mursilis in a time of plague', *Ancient Near Eastern Texts*,[3] ed. J. B. Pritchard, Princeton, 1969, 394–6: cf. R. Pettazzoni in *Occident and Orient, Studies in Honour of M. Gaster*, London, 1936, 467–71.

[6] See R. Pettazzoni, op. cit., vol. i.

[7] Evans–Pritchard, 184, Lienhardt, 284, Buxton, 194.

disease. When illness actually occurs, the diagnostic procedure that follows is likely to identify 'sin' as the cause, though other possibilities exist.[8] In all cases, diseases come for definite reasons. Those sent by spirits can only be cured by religious means, through sacrifice, though this is not to say that medicines should be ignored. On the contrary, everything possible should be done on the practical level; but a final cure will depend on God. Such a set of beliefs serves both to explain the apparently random affliction, and also to indicate a practical course of action: there is a god or spirit to be appeased. The psychological importance of putting the disease in professional hands (whether doctor or diviner) and treating it positively (whether by prescription or sacrifice) is very great, as the effectiveness of the placebo proves.[9]

For Greece, scholars have noted the supposed daemonic or divine origin of various illnesses.[10] But the fact that a god is responsible for disease does not reveal much about it. Has it been sent as a punishment, or in caprice? Or is the idea of the god-sent disease simply a way of expressing human incomprehension? The subject does not seem to have interested historians of divine justice and human responsibility.[11] Yet it allows an interesting confrontation of religious theory and therapeutic practice. Moralists may have seen disease as a punishment; were religious and magical cures based on the same belief?

For such an investigation, the existence of 'scientific' Greek medicine presents a complication. It is not of course that all Greeks at all times accepted a natural account of the causation of disease. Early poets and myths reveal pre-Hippocratic conditions, and behind the imposing edifice of Hippocratic rationalism we can always detect spirits who put less faith than the doctors in the delicate dietetic balancing of the body's

---

[8] For an account of the diagnostic procedure in one case see Lienhardt, 58–62.

[9] On the reassuring function of consultation see Una Maclean, *Magical Medicine*, London, 1971, Ch. 1; on the 'placebo effect' Thomas, 248 f.

[10] Cf. Lanata, esp. 28–39; Edelstein, *AM* 219–24 (rightly restrictive); Herter, *Dämonen*; Lloyd, 29 n. 98.

[11] But cf. Lanata, 28–39 and F. Kudlien, 'Early Greek Primitive Medicine', *Clio Medica* 3 (1968), 305–36. W. R. Halliday, 'Some Notes on the Treatment of Disease in Antiquity,' in *Greek Poetry and Life (Essays presented to Gilbert Murray)*, Oxford, 1936, 277–94, does not discuss the theological problem.

humours.[12] On a simple practical level, it is unlikely that scientifically trained doctors ever penetrated far into the rural areas of Greece.[13] The problem is not so much that rationalism suppressed religious medicine, as that it deprived it of its voice. Apart from documents concerning the cult of Asclepius, such practices are mostly mentioned by those unsympathetic to them, like the polemical author of *On the sacred disease*, or simply passed over in silence. In this sense, Hippocratic medicine is an obstacle to the present inquiry. But it is also in itself a problematic phenomenon that demands explanation.[14] A materialist medicine, in a world where science is powerless to prove its postulates, has no more claim to popular support than the psychologically more satisfying arts of the diviner. Without such proof, its theories can only be a kind of dogma, even for the physician himself. The weakness of natural aitiology can be well seen from the fate of western medicine when introduced into traditional societies. A common reaction seems to be to distinguish 'European' or 'doctor' diseases – acute conditions and others for which western pharmacology is conspicuously successful – from 'native' diseases, 'diseases the doctors don't know', only to be treated by traditional, perhaps magico-religious methods.[15] The doctor may be assimilated to the herbalist, in contrast to the diviner, as one who treats symptoms without seeking out the underlying cause.[16] Western pretensions to treat by natural means clearly supernatural psychological conditions are often viewed with polite scepticism;[17] in general, even when European remedies are used, native methods are applied simultaneously.[18] European medicine is

---

[12] Cf. Lanata, 15 f., 71–6.

[13] The case for a shortage of doctors is put by L. Cohn-Haft, *The Public Physicians of Ancient Greece*, Massachusetts, 1956, 23–31.

[14] Cf. Thomas, Ch. 7, esp. 226, 245. For the English peasant, Galenic prescriptions were no more rational than the methods of the herbalist or conjurer.

[15] See e.g. D. B. Jelliffe and F. J. Bennett, *Journal of Pediatrics* 57 (1960), 252; J. B. Loudon. *The Health Education Journal* 15 (1957), 98; R. H. and E. Blum, *Health and Healing in Rural Greece*, Stanford, 1965, index s.v. *illnesses 'which doctors don't know'*.

[16] See M. Gelfand, *The Central African Journal of Medicine*, 1 (1955), 125.

[17] Not without reason, as 'Primitive psychotherapy, in particular, can compare favourably with its modern rivals' (Thomas, 245 with references); cf. C. Lévi-Strauss, *Structural Anthropology* (trans. C. Jacobson), London, 1968, Ch. 10, 'The effectiveness of symbols'.

[18] See Read, Ch. 4; U. Maclean, *Magical Medicine*, London, 1971 (a detailed study of the phenomenon in Ibadan).

only convincing where it is obviously successful, but Hippocratic medicine can never have enjoyed empirical confirmation of that kind. Its history in later antiquity shows how fragile and ill-protected is a materialist medicine without effective pharmaceutical support.[19] Even in western society today, where most people have formally adopted a scientific view of the causation of disease, research has shown that, under the stress of really serious illness, almost everybody reverts at least in part to different forms of explanation. Children blame their illnesses on petty thefts, or playing too hard, or their parents' unkindness; adults on their own imprudence, their unsatisfactory personal relationships, their moral faults. It is only in terms of what is humanly significant that human suffering becomes truly comprehensible.[20]

The ways in which Hippocratic medicine achieved plausibility have recently been brilliantly analyzed.[21] Its origins in Greek folk-medicine, the continuing resemblance of many of its methods to those of religious healers, and the persuasive skills of its practitioners emerge as important factors. A possible obstacle would have been a strongly held theological doctrine, of the kind already mentioned, that disease is the consequence of sin. There is, of course, no doubt that diseases were on occasion theologically explained by the Greeks, just as death was, and there was certainly nothing repugnant to Greek thought in the idea of divine retribution taking this form. Most of the important myths can be analysed by a schema of crime and punishment,[22] and though the punishment is commonly death, diseases too are found;[23] madness in particular often occurs.[24] Lysias, in his speech against Cinesias, mentioned the impious dining club, the *kakodaimonistai*, to which Cinesias and his friends belonged. The other members, he says, had all died,

---

[19] See Edelstein, *AM* 231–5; O. Temkin, *The Falling Sickness*[2], Baltimore, 1971, 23–7.

[20] See R. H. Blum, *The Management of the Doctor Patient Relationship*, New York, 1960, 63–5. For the remarkable diversity of explanation in a modern Greek peasant community-environment, stress, emotional disturbance, hostile spirits, evil eye, sorcery, ritual and moral failings – see R. H. and E. Blum, *Health and Healing in Rural Greece*, Stanford, 1965, Ch. 9.

[21] Lloyd, Chs. 1 and 2. Cf. p. 213 above.

[22] See Vickers, Ch. 5, esp. 252–5.

[23] See W. Roscher, *Rh. Mus.* 53 (1898), 169–204, and in *RML* s.v. *nosoi*.

[24] See J. Mattes, *Der Wahnsinn im griechischen Mythos und in der Dichtung bis zum Drama des fünften Jahrhunderts*, Heidelberg, 1970, esp. 50–2.

'as one might expect, being the men they were', but the gods had reserved Cinesias himself for a worse fate, as an example to mankind: 'To die or fall ill in the normal way is common to us all; but to live as Cinesias has done for so many years, to be always dying and yet never manage to die – that is kept only for those whose crimes have been like his.'[25] Such is Lysias' diagnosis of the causes of chronic illness. But though it is one possible interpretation, there is no proof that it was the usual one, nor that the victim himself would have looked for an explanation of this kind. Myth, moral principle, and rhetoric need to be tested against the actual responses of the afflicted.

Before the fifth century, evidence is very scanty, and it would be rash to build much on a few passing allusions in Homer and Hesiod. But for what it is worth these suggest a view of disease that is fatalistic rather than moral. The Cyclopes, supposing Polyphemus' cries to be due to an acute internal disease, comment: 'There's no escaping a disease sent by Zeus; so pray to your father Poseidon.'[26] When they speak of the disease as sent by Zeus, they do not seem to be thinking of a punishment; this sounds like an amoral Zeus who distributes 'good and bad to each man, as he wishes'. Of the cause of the disease, no more is said. As to its treatment, there is no hint of a diagnostic process to establish why it has been sent. Polyphemus is recommended to invoke the aid of a god who will on personal grounds be well disposed to him, his father Poseidon. One other Homeric passage is similar in implication. A simile compares Odysseus' delight at sighting dry land to the delight felt by children whose father has long lain tormented by illness, 'and a hateful daimon has attacked him', when the gods finally cure him of his sufferings.[27] 'And a hateful daimon attacked . . .' is an expression that could be used of any misfortune,[28] and one that, even if it does not exclude, certainly does not encourage a theological justification. From this attack by a 'hateful' (not a just) agent, the victim is rescued by the gods. It is the same picture of divine favour opposed to malevolent disease.

[25] Fr. 53 Thalheim = 5 Gernet, *ap.* Ath. 552b. A similar interpretation of chronic disease, Diod. 16.61.3. On the special horror of long disease see Kudlien, 106–24.

[26] *Od.* 9.411 f. But Dodds, 67 and Mattes, op cit., 31, suppose that the Cyclopes take Polyphemus to be mad.

[27] *Od.* 5.394–7. *Stugeros* of disease also *Il.* 13.670.

[28] Cf. *Od.* 10.64.

Hesiod knows the origin of this bane. There was a time, he says, when man lived free from all evil, labour, and disease. Then Pandora's box was opened, and now: 'The land is full of evils, and so is the sea.' There follows the passage about the activities of diseases that has already been quoted. They roam at large, unaccountable and irrational, controlled, it seems, neither by god nor man. They are free agents, and agents of evil.[29] It has been claimed that in this Hesiodic passage we see a moralization of the concept of disease, in that it was a crime, Prometheus' defiance of the will of Zeus, that brought them upon man for the first time.[30] But the myth's ethos is that of the just-so story, not the theodicy; what Greek ever seriously thought of referring his troubles to Prometheus' crime?[31] One has only to contrast the enduring explanatory, justificatory power of the Jewish myth of the Fall to appreciate this.[32] The Prometheus/Pandora myth emphasizes the irreversibility and inescapability of certain ills; but far from moralizing the individual's sufferings it implies much randomness in their distribution.

It is perhaps hard to believe that this is the full story. Divine anger is a ubiquitous theme in Homer,[33] and individuals may, when in trouble, suspect that they have 'sinned against' a god.[34] There was material here for the healer-seer to work with. The same may be said of Hesiod. His general philosophy would favour the attempt to explain disease as a consequence of crime. In particular, it is easy to suppose that the penalty awaiting those who infringed the rules of conduct near the end of the *Works and Days* may have taken this form.[35] Anyone who observed scrupulously rules such as these, or their Pythagorean descendants, will surely have been inclined to seek a religious or

---

[29] *Op.* 90–104.

[30] F. Kudlien, *Clio Medica* 3 (1968), 315 f.

[31] Cf. Lienhardt, 33–7, 53–5 on a similar, essentially non-moral Fall myth; idem, in *International Encyclopaedia of the Social Sciences*, New York, 1968, s.v. *Theology* (*Primitive*), citing Nadel 'The only problem in Nupe theology is the actual power of evil, not its origin.'

[32] For a telling example see J. K. Campbell, 'Honour and the Devil', in *Honour and Shame, the values of mediterranean society*, ed. J. G. Peristiany, London, 1965, esp. 152–9 ('the sins of Adam').

[33] J. Irmscher, *Götterzorn bei Homer*, diss. Berlin, 1949.

[34] p. 201 above.

[35] *Op.* 706–64; early evidence, even if not genuine Hesiod.

at least a magical explanation for his personal misfortune. Unfortunately, it is impossible to advance beyond such general probabilities.

There follows a chronological gulf. Empedocles' *'Purifica-tions'*, Musaeus' *'Cures for disease'*[37] have perished. The next substantial evidence comes from Herodotus, an author with a reputation for pious credulity and insistent moralizing. Despite this, he can speak of serious illnesses and sudden deaths as apparently natural events.[38] A 'wise warner' can number diseases among those amoral trials imposed by a jealous god that render death a sweet refuge for mortals.[39] The interpreta-tion of disease as punishment does, certainly, also occur; thus the horrible fate of Pheretima, who seethed with worms while still alive, shows that the gods resent excessive severity in revenge.[40] Similar beliefs were held, according to Herodotus, by the Greek world at large. In the case of Cleomenes, it was the general opinion that he went mad because he corrupted the Pythia, but the Athenians referred to his devastation of the Eleusinian precinct and the Argives to a similar offence against one of their sacred groves.[41] That division shows the excessive neatness which has brought Herodotus' source indications in general under suspicion,[42] but even on the most sceptical view he ascribed opinions to his informants that he believed they might have held. He mentions the intriguing case of Otanes, who resettled depopulated Samos 'because of a dream-vision and a disease that afflicted him in the genitals'.[43] Physiological and religious explanations of disease are twice presented as alternatives and, interestingly, Herodotus himself judges dif-ferently in the two cases. He cannot accept the Spartans'

---

[37] Ar. *Ran.* 1033.

[38] e.g. 1.161, 7.117.1. On Herodotus' complex attitude to divine and natural causation cf. Lloyd, 30 f.

[39] 7.46.3.

[40] 4.205

[41] 6.75.3, 84.

[42] D. Fehling, *Die Quellenangaben bei Herodot*, Berlin, 1971, *passim*. In 1.105.4 Herodotus ascribes to the Scythians the explanation of their 'female disease' as a consequence of sacking the ancient temple of Aphrodite Ourania at Askalon. W. R. Halliday, *ABSA* 17 (1910–11), 95–102, long ago pointed out how unlikely this was to be a true Scythian doctrine. Other religious explanations of disease attributed to foreigners: 1.138, 2.111.2.

[43] 3.149.

natural account of the madness that destroyed as great a sinner
as king Cleomenes, but thinks it 'not implausible' that
Cambyses' madness was a consequence of congenital epilepsy
rather than of a crime against Apis.[44] It is noticeable that the
choice here is between interpreting disease as a god-sent
punishment and as a natural event. In a fragment of Euripides,
by contrast, where 'divine' diseases are contrasted with those
that are 'self-chosen',[45] the disease's divinity seems to consist
merely in its inescapability, like Homer's 'disease of Zeus'. We
shall see too that there were other ways in which in the fifth
century a disease could come from the gods without being a
punishment.

One problem in judging Herodotus' evidence is to know
whether the diseases of ordinary people had the same causes as
those of the great. The same problem applies to tragedy.
Neither tragedy nor Ionian history can be dismissed, on the
moral level, as mere romance. On the other hand, it is obvious
that the fortunes of a Croesus had a high dignity and significance denied to ordinary people, just as the home life of most
Athenian families was not much like that of the Pelopids. The
lives of kings who exercised a decisive influence on the course of
history were easily absorbed into the schemata of crime and
punishment characteristic of myth. Would Herodotus, smitten
by a chronic disease, have believed his own affliction to be
equally rich in significance?

A recently published comic fragment, probably from Aristophanes' *Heroes,* provides interesting evidence, in a context that
is not elevated or mythological, for the moral interpretation of
disease.[46] The chorus of Heroes here announce that: 'We are the
guardians of good things and ill; we watch out for the unjust, for
robbers and footpads, and send them diseases – spleen, coughs,
dropsy, catarrh, scab, gout, madness, lichens, swellings, ague,
fever. That's what we give to thieves . . .'. Another comic

[44] 6.84, 3.33. Madness from physical causes is an accepted fact in Xen. *Mem.* 3.12.6.
Pl. *Phdr.* 265a distinguishes madness caused by human disease from divine madness.
Physiological madness also *Leg.* 934c–d, *Ti.* 86b; cf. the obscure report of Empedocles
A 98. The 'black bile' theory of madness, common in the late 5th century, may well
have earlier roots: cf. p. 246 n. 61.
[45] Fr. 292; probably, it is true, metaphorical diseases. See too Soph. *Aj.* 1841.
[46] Ar. fr. 58 in C. Austin, *Comicorum Graecorum Fragmenta in Papyris Reperta*, Berlin,
1973.

fragment perhaps testifies to the same belief: 'I committed an offence against a hero.'[47] The new fragment provides welcome support for the idea that the heroes in Greece play the part assigned in other religions to the ancestors. While the dead in general, except for those dispatched violently, seldom seem to intervene in the affairs of the living,[48] the heroes are constantly active. Here, as in a passage of Hesiod, they exercise moral supervision over the conduct of men of the present day like true ancestors.[49] On the other hand, the heroes also had a reputation as trouble-makers, beings liable to attack for slight reason or none;[50] and it seems likely that the Aristophanes fragment attests a belief that also existed in a less moral form.

The diversity of possible explanations is clear from a set of fifth-century texts that treat the causes of mental disturbance. The purifiers of *On the sacred disease* tried to diagnose the deity responsible for each patient's affliction, but their methods were purely external: 'If the patient imitate a goat, if he roar, or suffer convulsions in the right side, they say that the Mother of the Gods is to blame. If he utter a piercing and loud cry, they liken him to a horse and blame Poseidon.'[51] There was apparently no question of seeking a cause for the anger of the god in question, nor of appeasing him by sacrifice. The powers identified by the purifiers as senders of epilepsy – the Mother of the Gods, Poseidon, Enodia, Apollo Nomios, Ares, Hecate, and the Heroes – do not, as a group, seem strongly involved with the moral order. The malicious attacks of Hecate were a terror to the superstitious, and if they had a cause, it was not the guilt of the victim but the conjuring of a sorcerer.[52] Enodia was of the same character.[53] Apollo Nomios probably represented the

[47] Ar. fr. 692a.
[48] Even Plato refers to the specific case of the *biaiothanatoi* to establish the general point, *Leg.* 926e–927a, cf. 865e.
[49] *Op.* 121–6.
[50] Ar. *Av.* 1490–3 with schol., Men. fr. 394, Babrius 63, Ath. 461c, p. 272 n. 73 below; cf. A. Brelich, *Gli eroi greci*, Rome, 1958, 226 ff., and Herter, *Dämonen*, 56.
[51] Hippoc. *Morb. Sacr* 146. 21 ff. J., 1.33 ff. G., trans. Jones. On the gods identified cf. Lanata, 39 n. 94.
[52] Above, p. 222. For later antiquity see Fr. Pfister, *Wochenschrift f. klassische Philologie*, 29 (1912), 753–8.
[53] Enodia exists in Thessaly as an independent chthonic goddess (Wilamowitz, *Glaube*, i, 170–2; T. Kraus, *Hekate*, Heidelberg, 1960, 77–83); in Attica she merges into Hecate (Eur. *Hel.* 569 f., Soph. fr. 535), or Persephone-Hecate (Eur. *Ion.* 1048, Soph. *Ant.* 1199 f.). She is patroness of 'attacks' by night or day (Eur. *Ion.* 1048–50).

same amoral menace of the open air as Pan – the sudden terrors of herds, the midday madness of men. Of the Mother more will be said below. A famous chorus in Sophocles represents Ares as foe to man.[54] The significance of the Heroes is, as we have seen, ambiguous. Almost all the gods specified by the purifiers, therefore, had special associations with mental disorder or other afflictions, which they sent for reasons unconnected with morality.

A similar picture emerges from a passage in the *Hippolytus*, where the chorus speculate on Phaedra's mysterious wasting disease, which they see as a form of madness. 'Are you wandering seized, princess, by Pan or Hecate or the holy Corybantes or the mountain mother?'[55] These gods differ little in character from those of the list in 'Hippocrates'. Living on the fringes of the Olympian world, they lack its involvement with morality. They seize their victims; they do not punish them. An attack may be ascribed to 'Pan's anger',[56] but that anger, if explained at all, has motives that are frivolous.[57] Anyone can fall into the power of gods like the Corybantes, and the only cure is to celebrate their rites. Thus the chorus's first suggestion implies no offence at all on Phaedra's part. They go on to wonder, almost in the same breath, whether Phaedra has omitted an offering to Dictynna. They show no awareness of having passed from one level of explanation to another, and in the next two stanzas speculate on natural causes, both psychological and physical, for the same affliction. Later in the play, the nurse considers whether Phaedra's frenzy might be due to the stain of blood or to witchcraft.[58] This pragmatism, and receptivity to differing and possibly contradictory theories of disease and methods of treatment, is perhaps characteristic of folk-medicine.

There is a similar passage in Sophocles' *Ajax*, where the

[54] *OT* 190–202.

[55] 141 ff., Barrett's translation. For the controversy over *entheos* see Burkert, *GR* 178 n. 1.

[56] A fainting-fit, Eur. *Med.* 1172, delirious terror (Eur.) *Rhes.* 36.

[57] See Gow on Theocritus 1.15. R. Herbig, *Pan*, Frankfurt, 1949, 18 f., stresses that the conception of 'panic' derives from the behaviour of animals; it remains amoral when transferred to men. This aspect is fully treated by W. H. Roscher, 'Ephialtes' (*Abh. Sächs. Ges. Wiss.* 20.2, Leipzig, 1900), 66–84; Pan's amorality is clear from the equation with Ephialtes. See too Borgeaud, 137–75.

[58] 316–19.

chorus consider the hero's madness. It might, they feel, be a
punishment sent by Artemis or Ares for omitted thank-offerings. Of Pan and the Corybantes they say nothing. Later in the
play it turns out that the offended goddess is Athena, and the
offence not a mere failure in cult, but a wanton over-valuation of
human strength against divine, a classic insult to the gods.[59]
This highly moral story is very far from *On the sacred disease*, and
the two texts may be taken as representing extreme possibilities.
There is no reason to doubt that an offence against the gods
could be seen as causing disease, but Sophocles may have been
influenced by the claims of tragic dignity in ignoring all other
possible diagnoses. Aristophanes mentions three religious
treatments for madness – purification, the Corybantic rites, and
incubation.[60] None of them obviously entails the identification
and appeasement of a punishing god. If seers existed who
conducted cures along those lines, they have left no trace in our
sources. The everyday expressions for 'you're off your head'
that are found in comedy treat madness as a product either of
inexplicable daimonic intervention, or of an excess of black
bile.[61]

The opposition which has begun to emerge between madness
as punishment for ritual or moral offences, and madness as
seizure by capricious, amoral spirits, finds parallels among
many peoples. Throughout the world there are cultures that
attribute disease, particularly mental disease, to possession by
spirits. A recurrent pattern can be traced whereby, alongside
the central deities (often ancestors) who send affliction as
punishment, certain peripheral spirits, perhaps of foreign
origin, are also active, and choose their victims regardless of
morality. Such spirits attack people whose position in society is
as peripheral as their own, men without status and, above all,
women. The 'cure', in so far as it is possible at all, characteristically involves lifelong devotion to the cult of the possessing

[59] 172–86, 756–77.
[60] *Vesp.* 118–24.
[61] The contrast in this respect with higher genres is noted by A. O'Brien Moore,
Madness in Ancient Literature, diss. Princeton, 1922, published Weimar, 1924, 10 f.
Daimonic intervention: p. 248 n. 67 below. Black bile: often in Aristophanes (e.g. *Nub.*
833, *Av.* 14, *Pax* 66), and Menander. This is probably in origin a popular, not a
scientific interpretation (see Kudlien, 77–88) and need not be later than the religious
one.

spirit, a cult that will probably take an ecstatic form, and be celebrated by the community of past victims. Though possession is at first seen as an affliction, against which help is needed, these cults undoubtedly have a clandestine significance from which the victims of the spirit gain psychological benefit. The healing cult becomes a personal religion for persons shut out from the central morality cults. It offers women a religious experience, a sphere of interest, and an identity, each of them opposed to the typical female role. But if possession is to be interpreted as an inescapable affliction, the possessing spirit should be guided by caprice. Such a cult cannot be based on the admitted guilt of its members. The tarantism of southern Italy, spirit-possession mediated by an event as amoral as the bite of a spider, is a characteristic example.[62]

We know of one 'foreign' spirit who afflicted Greek women in this way: Dionysus. The social significance of maenadism, a form of behaviour not originally shared by both sexes but performed by one in defiance of the other, has tended to be underestimated.[63] By the fifth century, however, spontaneous possession was no longer attributed to Dionysus but to powers such as the Corybantes.[64] There is no evidence that their rites were especially celebrated either by women or by a particular social class, but in other important respects they conform to the pattern of peripheral healing cults. The Corybantes themselves, senders of madness, also cure it; their healing methods are homoeopathic, by ecstasy; they are explicitly foreign, and they have no interest in morality. Their cult is not attested before the fifth century,[65] but this kind of interpretation of mental disturbance is unlikely to be a novelty. Dionysus was their predecessor, and the indigenous Pan, also a sender of madness, was no guardian of morality. Similar conceptions appear elsewhere in popular thought. In the language of Homer there are hints of the view of madness as due to daimonic

---

[62] On all this see I. M. Lewis, *Ecstatic Religion*, Harmondsworth, 1971, esp. Ch. 3 and 79–85. On tarantism, ibid., 88–92, and E. de Martino, *La Terra del rimorso*, Milan, 1961.

[63] But see Simon, 242–57.

[64] Dodds, 77–80 with bibliography. Pl. *Euthyd.* 277d implies participation of the well-born, as Dodds notes.

[65] E. R. Dodds, *Harvard Theological Review* 33 (1940), 171–4; the 'mother' (Greek or Phrygian?) is already a healer in Pind. *Pyth.* 3. 76–9; cf. Burkert, *GR* 277.

intervention,[66] and that view is preserved in the use of the verb *daimoniō*, though we cannot be sure how literally the idea expressed in it was understood.[67] A striking number of diseases have animal names or nicknames: fox, lion, crab, and many more.[68] Nightmares can be traced to Ephialtes, the 'leaper on', and sudden attacks of fever in the night to similar strangling demons.[69] Such language reveals at the least an immediate perception of disease that is amoral, although the beast or demon with which one struggles could of course also be seen as the agent of an avenging god.

It is obviously relevant to consider the moral stance of Greece's countless healing gods and heroes.[70] Unfortunately, though we can trace the existence of healing cults from early times, we know little of the ideas and expectations that patients brought to them. For one cult, however, of the fourth century we have detailed evidence. The inscription recording the miraculous cures of Asclepius at Epidaurus is obviously a document that requires discreet handling, but the admixture of five-year pregnancies and the like does not entirely disqualify it as evidence. *Pia fraus,* to be effective, must be rooted in the familiar; it glorifies the god by representing the hopes and dreams of every worshipper as achieved fact.[71] Incubation is a particularly revealing technique, because what the patient derives from the experience will correspond to what he himself

[66] Dodds, 67.

[67] e.g. Ar. *Plut.* 372, 501, Men. *Dysc.* 88, fr. 127; cf. A. O'Brien Moore, op. cit., 14–18. Madness as a being 'struck' persists too, e.g. Ar. *Vesp.* 947, Men. *Dysc.* 311, *Perikeiromenē* 496 with Sandbach, Borgeaud, 183 f. Physiological and daimonic are nicely conflated in Men. *Epit.* 880 f., where black bile 'falls on' you.

[68] See W. H. Roscher, *Rh. Mus.* 53 (1878), 173, 180 n. 5; also A. Riess, *Rh. Mus.* 49 (1894), 181. For semi-personified disease see Ar. *Nub.* 243 with Dover's note, Soph. *Phil.* 758 f. with Jebb. The claim that similar ideas still shimmer through in the vocabulary of the Hippocratic corpus is not proven: see G. Preiser, *Allgemeine Krankheitsbezeichnungen im Corpus Hippocraticum* (Ars Medica II.5), Berlin, 1976, 60–3; Goltz, 272–4.

[69] See Sophron, frr. 68, 70; Ar. *Vesp.* 1037 ff. with schol.; W. H. Roscher, 'Ephialtes' (*Abh. Sächs. Ges. Wiss.*, 20.2, Leipzig, 1900), 48–56; for the medical literature denying demonic nature of such seizures ibid., 108–15.

[70] A scholarly account of Greek healing gods in general seems not to exist. For Attica, F. Kutsch, *Attische Heilgötter und Heilheroen, RGVV* 12.3, Giessen, 1913. Some general indications in Nilsson, *GGR* (index s.v. *Heilgötter*), and the chapter 'Disease and Calamity' in W. H. D. Rouse, *Greek Votive Offerings,* Cambridge, 1902.

[71] On the status of the temple inscription as a witness see Dodds, 112 f.; idem, *Progress,* 169–71.

brings to it. The god's diagnosis and cure of his disease depend on his own conception of how a divine healer ought to operate. Given this, it is striking to observe the indifference of the god to the origin of the disease that is to be cured. He appears in a dream and either performs an act of miraculous healing at once, or indicates the course the patient must follow on waking to be cured. What he does not do is to suggest a past offence against another god that might have caused the disease. Apart from a few late anecdotes,[72] the god's concern for human justice did not extend beyond his own perquisites.[73] To questions of morality he had in general the professional indifference of the true doctor.[74]

The parallel with the doctor is important. Many people seem to have made the journey to Epidaurus not as an alternative to medical treatment, but once such treatment had failed.[75] Co-operation between doctors and priests of Asclepius is not demonstrable,[76] but nor is hostility; and, though there are important differences between scientific and temple medicine, there are also important similarities.[77] The divine physician was expected to make prescriptions that were the paradoxical reverse of normal human therapy, and did not disdain the use of magical drugs. But he was not required to suggest a different, essentially religious aitiology of diseases. His was secular medicine, as understood by the layman, with an injection of supernatural power. It is therefore only partially correct to see the triumphant rise of the Asclepius cult as a symptom of growing irrationalism.[78] The genuine achievements and programmatic aspirations of Hippocratic medicine had aroused

[72] Testimonia 394, 395, 397, 517 in Edelstein's collection.

[73] Miraculous punishment of those who mock Asclepius himself: *SIG³* 1168, cures vii and xxxvi; *IG* IV² 123, cure xlvii (cf. *SEG* xi 423 with bibliography). For confession in this context (exceptional for a Greek) see too *IG* IV² 123.67,91. On the 'Strafwunder' cf. O. Weinreich, *Antike Heiligungswunder*, *RGVV* 8.1, Giessen, 1909, 55–62.

[74] Edelstein, ii, 180.

[75] Edelstein, *AM* 245.

[76] See L. Cohn-Haft, *The Public Physicians of Ancient Greece*, Massachusetts, 1956, 26–31, and S. M. Sherwin-White, *Ancient Cos, Hypomnemata* 51, Göttingen, 1978, 275–8, criticizing Herzog; also Lloyd, 48 n. 209. Edelstein, *AM* 244 f. also believed that doctors might implicitly refer cases to temples.

[77] Cf. Dodds, 115 f., Lloyd, 40 f. Paradox, e.g. testimonia 317.8, 408 in Edelstein's collection. Drugs, Dodds, 115.

[78] Dodds, 193.

large expectations as to the possibility of curing all forms of disease, expectations which, naturally, it was in no position to fulfil. To satisfy them, popular imagination created, in the human doctor's image, a divine doctor whose magic powers allowed him to make real the exaggerated claims of rational medicine. Those who underwent incubation dreamed not of angry gods but of skilful surgery and subtly balanced regimen.

Delphi must often have been consulted about disease.[79] One instance recorded in Herodotus is that of the Lydian king Alyattes, who fell ill after accidentally burning down the temple of Athena Assēsiē at Miletus. The disease refused to clear up, and so Alyattes decided to consult the oracle. The Pythia would not give him an answer until he rebuilt Athena's temple. He did so, and recovered at once.[80] This is the classic pattern of a disease caused by a religious offence, diagnosed by a religious specialist, and cured by expiation or restitution. The very neatness of the pattern, indeed, exposes the story to suspicion.[81] More reliable evidence is available for Dodona, because some of the lead tablets on which requests to the oracle were written have survived.[82] Unfortunately their dating is insecure, and none of them seems to be very early. A typical example runs: 'Nikokrateia asks which god she should sacrifice to in order to fare better and be free of her disease.'[83] There are several such requests, some with the exhaustive formula 'which god or hero or daimon should x sacrifice to'.[84] It would be interesting to know what was the usual answer. Perhaps the priests identified a god to whom the inquirer had not sacrificed recently, and the oracle then suggested an offering to him.[85] Perhaps it simply named a healing power.

It is worth mentioning some factors that do not appear or only seldom appear in Greece as causes of disease. Very trivial ritual infractions are not attested. Possibly such subjects were

[79] Cf. *LSCG* 83. 12 f., health and preservation as twin concerns of Apollo's oracle at Corope.

[80] 1.19–22.

[81] Fontenrose, 301. Solid Delphic evidence is quite lacking.

[82] The older ones are in *SGDI* 1557–1598 (Hoffmann); recent discoveries *SEG* xiii 397, xv 385–409, xix 426–432, xxiii 474–6, xxiv 454.

[83] *SGDI* 1561 B = *SIG*³ 1161.

[84] *SGDI* 1564, 1566, 1582, 1587.

[85] Cf. the procedure of the mantis Eukleides in Xen. *An.* 7.8.1–6.

too undignified to penetrate our sources; perhaps the Greeks were unwilling seriously to believe that a god might send disease as punishment for entering a shrine in a dirty robe. It has already been noted that, although pollutions can cause physical disorder,[86] this is not an idea that receives strong emphasis. Nor is there much evidence in this connection for the evil eye or sorcery, though the silence of the sources here may be deceptive. Presumably the bewitchment that the purifier professed to cure[87] could manifest itself in disease. If we think further of the *defixiones*, a few of which specify the disease they are supposed to cause,[88] with Plato's account of the fear such methods inspired,[89] it seems almost inevitable that human malice must often have been diagnosed, or at least suspected, as the cause of a particular misfortune. More than this, unfortunately, it seems impossible to say.

Non-scientific attitudes to disease in Greece are, it seems, too diverse to be covered by a simple formula. A recent study by a medical historian has tried to illustrate the transformation of early Greek society from shame culture to guilt culture by its changing understanding of disease.[90] A shame culture, it is said, sees disease either as random evil, inexplicable fatality, or as a god's revenge for an affront to his own honour, but in neither case as a punishment for moral evil. The moral view is taken as the defining characteristic of a guilt culture, and it is also said to

---

[86] p. 218.

[87] p. 222.

[88] Wünsch, nn. 77–8 (impotence); sherd published by Nilsson, *GGR* 801. Ἀριστίωνι ἐπιτίθημι τεταρταῖον ἐς Ἅιδα; later instances *SEG* iv. 47, E. Ziebarth, 'Neue Verfluchungstafeln aus Attika, Boiotien und Euboia', *Sitz. Preuss. Ak. Berl.* 33 (1934), n. 24.

[89] *Leg.* 933a–b. Charms cause childlessness and aversion, Eur. *Andr.* 155–60; evil eye kills, Ap. Rhod. 4.1669 ff. On early Greek magic see T. Hopfner, *RE* s.v. *Mageia*. 303 (Homer); Abt. 95–100 (tragedy and comedy); Hopfner, loc. cit., 384 (trials of sorceresses).

[90] F. Kudlien, 'Early Greek Primitive Medicine', *Clio Medica* 3 (1968), 305–336, esp. 317. (It is because of this scholar's deserved authority that I take issue with him explicitly.) On the whole question, it is interesting to note that, though psychodynamically shame and guilt can perhaps be distinguished, the differentiation of whole cultures according to these criteria has proved very problematic. Shame is or can be internally felt no less than guilt (G. Piers and M. B. Singer, *Shame and Guilt, a psychoanalytical and cultural study*, Springfield, Illinois, 1953, esp. 48 ff.). A Homeric hero is constrained by *aidōs* to observe certain social rules no less than to assert his own agonistic pre-eminence. Against a sharp distinction see Lloyd-Jones, 24–6, Dover, 220 n. 3; but note the comment of J. Gould, *CR* n.s. 28 (1978), 287.

be the dominating attitude of the fifth-century Greek. But, as we have seen, the view of disease as random affliction still persists in the fifth century, and in the fourth century, in the practice of Asclepieia, seems to triumph. One obstacle to a full moralization of disease was that it might involve an admission of wrong-doing most unwelcome to the patient himself.[91] A Greek would scarcely have cared to proclaim publicly that he was suffering the consequences of his perjury or maltreatment of a guest. His neighbour's affliction, indeed, was no doubt a richly deserved divine punishment, but his own was a random event, the product of malice or sorcery. The one confession that it was readily acceptable to make was that of a ritual omission, a forgotten sacrifice perhaps;[92] the cloud of forgetfulness could envelop the most honourable of men in unpredictable ways.[93] Ajax's Salaminian sailors loyally ascribed his madness to an offence of this kind.[94] In the dark hours when Alexander was consumed with guilt for the murder of Cleitus, tactful seers pointed out that the king had sacrificed to the Dioscuri on a day traditionally reserved for Dionysus: the drunken murder was but the wounded god's savage revenge.[95] Even the idea of inherited punishment can acquire a new significance in this perspective, as a way of evading personal guilt.[96]

It would, of course, be rash to deny that a Greek could, within himself, connect his crimes and his sufferings, whatever he may have maintained before the world. The word group surrounding *enthumios*, 'on one's mind', is of importance here.[97] These words can be applied to any object of anxious thought,[98] but in most surviving instances they have a specialized reference to

---

[91] Cf. esp. Campbell, 325. Also R. H. and E. Blum, *Health and Healing in Rural Greece*, Stanford, 1965, 127: 'In a culture where maintaining *philotimo* requires that a man remain blameless, the peasant does not attribute his sufferings to his own sinfulness.'

[92] Cf. R. H. and E. Blum, loc. cit.: 'although they do attribute illness to their ritual failures, such failures do not imply a personal moral transgression.'

[93] Pind. *Ol.* 7.45.

[94] See above, p. 246; so too the chorus in *Hippolytus*, 141 ff. (cf. p. 245).

[95] Arr. *Anab.* 4.9.5.

[96] Note the context of Soph. *OC* 964 f.; cf. Boyce, 107, and J. K. Campbell, cited p. 241 n. 32.

[97] See Dodds, 55 n. 46, referring to Wilamowitz on Eur. *HF* 722 and W. H. P. Hatch, *HSCP* 19 (1908), 172–5 (Hatch collects the instances of *enthumios* but ignores related uses of *enthumeomai* and *enthumēma*).

[98] e.g. Hom. *Od.* 13.421, Soph. *OT* 739, *Trach.* 109, Eur. *Ion.* 1347.

religious scruples or anxiety. If a murderer is unjustly acquitted, a speaker in the *Tetralogies* points out, the murdered man becomes *enthumios* for the jurors, whose duty it was to avenge him.[99] Xerxes for an unknown reason ordered the Athenian exiles to make sacrifice on the acropolis; perhaps, suggests Herodotus, the fact that he had burnt down the shrine was an *enthumion* for him.[100] An act of potential religious danger might become an *enthumion* at once,[101] or in times of trouble the victims might ponder their afflictions and connect them mentally with past offences.[102] An *enthumion* is not a pang of conscience, although the English concept is often helpful in translating it; whereas conscience is guilt over bad actions, regardless of consequences,[103] an *enthumion* is the anxious anticipation of evil as a result not merely of an act but even of an occurrence, such as a bad omen.[104] But though not confined to the moral sphere, the word could certainly be used in connection with the expectation of evil in consequence of evil deeds.

In its specialized sense, *enthumios* is not attested before the fifth century, but the experience it denotes is certainly much older. Whenever a character in Homer rejects a particular form of behaviour through religious scruples, he implies that, were he to perform it, it would then be 'on his mind'.[105] When the

---

[99] Ant. *Tetr.* 1 γ 10, 2 α 2, δ 9; cf. Democritus' use of ἐγκάρδιον, B 262.

[100] 8.54.

[101] Scruples concerning a future act, Eur. *HF* 722; cf. Soph. *OC* 292.

[102] Thuc. 5.16.1. In 5.32.1 and 7.18.2 *enthumeisthai* is constructed with the present misfortunes as object.

[103] Cf. Dover, 220–3, who is cautious about recognizing allusions to conscience in the moral sense. For the literature on conscience (disappointing) see the bibliography to M. Class, *Gewissensregungen in der griechischen Tragödie, Spudasmata* 3, Hildesheim, 1964.

[104] Hdt. 2. 175, Thuc. 7.50.4.

[105] e.g. Hom. *Il.* 6.266 f., *Od.* 14.406. Attempts to generate religious scruples, *Il.* 22.358, *Od.* 11.73. These obvious remarks are directed against Latte's characterization of Homeric man, *ARW* 20 (1920/1), 258 = *Kl. Schr.* 6: 'Erst das Unheil weckt in ihm das Empfinden, sich vergangen zu haben.' There never was such a man. The *enthumion* is also seen as a later development by Gernet, *Antiphon*, 135 n. 1 and Dodds, 55 n. 46. I cannot accept either Dodds's further claim that: 'The specific usage is confined to this period; it vanished, as Wilamowitz says, with the decline of the old beliefs, whose psychological correlate it was.' Since Wilamowitz's *Heracles* was published, new evidence has been found for the word's survival, and it may be rash to brush it aside as 'archaizing'. See *LSS* 64 (Thasos, late 5th and early 4th c.): if anyone ignores these funeral regulations, ἐνθυμιστὸν αὐτῷ ἔστω; *LSCG* 154 Α 14 (Cos, first half of 3rd c.): if anyone ignores the sacred law, ἐνθύμιον αὐτοῖς ὡς ἀσεβήσασιν; *LSS* 72 Α 5 (Thasos, 1st c.): ἐνθυμιστόν for anyone who fails to pay temple dues. (Later examples *SIG³* 1184.7,

companions of Odysseus do in fact transgress a basic taboo by
slaughtering the cattle of the sun, they are plunged into guilty
anxiety.[106] What may be new in the late fifth century is an
explicit awareness of the mechanism of religious scruple, and
a willingness to speak openly of this private condition.[107]
Antiphon in a remarkable passage describes the mental effects
of guilt and innocence. There is no greater comfort for a defendant, he says, than the knowledge that he has committed no
crime or impiety. That knowledge can sustain him in extreme
bodily weakness. But the guilty man's case is opposite. 'His
spirit fails him while his body is still strong, because it thinks
that this (the illness? the trial?) has come upon him as a punishment for his crimes'.[108] Euripides goes a step further in reducing
the Erinyes that attack Orestes to his consciousness of the dire
act he has performed.[109]

The conceptual framework for a religion of confession therefore existed. In practice, however, it made little headway
against the dominant ethic of 'turning the fair side outwards'.[110]
As a contrast, it is interesting to consider certain Lydo-Phrygian
inscriptions of the second and third centuries AD,[111] written in a

---

Inscr. Cos 319.) Cf. *LSCG* 130 (Astypalaea, 3rd c.): if anyone disobeys, αὐτῷ ἐν νῷ
ἐσσεῖται. There is also the fact that *syneidēsis* seems to have been a concept of popular
morality (Wilamowitz, *Glaube*, ii, 386). Xenophon's threat that 'the goddess will take
care of' violators of his sacred law amounts to the same thing (Xen. *An.* 5.3.13).
Another inscriptional threat, that the violator will have himself to blame, is broader,
since the undesirable consequences are not necessarily supernatural, though they may
be, as in *SIG*[3] 1236 (on this formula cf. A. Wilhelm, *Sitz. Wien.* 224.1 (1946),
21 = *Akademieschriften zur griechischen Inschriftenkunde* iii, Leipzig, 1974, 159; L. Robert,
Études Anatoliennes, Paris, 1937, 415 f.; specifically religious applications of this or
comparable expressions are already found in the 5th c., Ar. *Ran.* 630, Eur. *Med.* 1055).
Note too the characteristic language of 'good hopes', above, p. 175 n. 173. Plut. *de Pyth.
or.* 404a nicely illustrates the *enthumion*.

[106] *Od.* 12.340–51.
[107] In rural Greece today, *filotimo* is 'largely concerned with the protective conceal-
ment of everything internalised in a person or society', M. Herzfeld, *Man* 15 (1980),
346.
[108] 5.93, cf. 6.1.4, and the texts in Stobaeus 3.24 περὶ τοῦ συνειδότος. For an instance
see Plut. *Dion* 56.2.
[109] Eur. *Or.* 396.
[110] Pind. *Pyth.* 3.83. Confession is un-Greek, Latte, *Kl. Schr.* 32 n. 42 (but for a special
case see p. 249 n. 73).
[111] Collected and studied in the valuable dissertation of P. Steinleitner, *Die Beicht im
Zusammenhange mit der sakralen Rechtspflege in der Antike*, Leipzig, 1913. Add *SEG* iv
647–52, xxviii 910, 913 f.; *Monumenta Asiae Minoris Antiqua* iv, ed. W. H. Buckler *et al.*.

form of Greek but revealing a very un-Greek religious climate, in which disease was a direct punishment sent by a specific god for sin, and the principal healing technique was to identify and confess that sin. Once cured, the patient was required to set up a tablet recording his transgression and its punishment. Occasionally a sinner might anticipate the delays of divine revenge by a spontaneous confession.[112] From these tablets we hear of men paying for their offences not only in their own persons, but also in the person of a son, daughter, relative, and even cow.[113] These sins are almost all ritual offences of some kind: the accidental cutting of sacred wood, failure to fulfil a vow, entering a precinct in dirty clothes or a state of ritual impurity.[114] They are, however, also moral offences in the sense that they imply contempt for the sacred. The penitent commonly ends his inscription with solemn advice to all to 'take the stele as a warning and not despise the god.'

How different is the message inculcated by these inscriptions from that of the temple record of Epidaurus! Here that pervasive unease sometimes supposed characteristic of archaic Greece does indeed seem to be present.[115] The Greek by contrast could experience misfortune in the form of disease without necessarily searching his conscience with anxiety for a possible cause. Deity in different Greek authors, sometimes in the same author, seems to operate at different levels: it guards the moral order, rewarding the good and punishing the bad; it upholds the formal rights of gods against men; as fate or the inscrutable divine will it makes occurrences inevitable; and it represents the random malicious element in the universe that causes the good to suffer and the bad to prosper. These levels

Manchester 1933, nn. 279–90. Cf. F. Cumont, *Les Religions orientales dans le paganisme romain*[4], Paris, 1929, 218 n. 40; R. Reitzenstein, *Die hellenistischen Mysterienreligionen*[3], Leipzig, 1927, 137 ff.; R. Pettazzoni, *Essays on the History of Religions* (*Numen* supplement 1), Leiden, 1954, 55–67.

[112] e.g. *MAMA* iv 285.
[113] Steinleitner, nn. 3,7,17,33 (*MAMA* iv 286).
[114] Irrelevance of intention: Steinleitner nn. 11,14,16. Ritual impurity is especially common, ibid., nn. 24,26, *MAMA* iv 283,285,288,289, but moral offences are also possible, e.g. Steinleitner, n. 29 (perjury). Steinleitner, n. 16, referring to an offence committed παιδίον ὤν, suggests that the search for causes could go back very far.
[115] Of course, the Greek who 'turned the fair side outward' may often have accused himself inwardly more bitterly than these ostentatious confessors of footling infractions, but the point about the publicly accepted response to disease in Greece remains.

correspond to as many natural human attitudes: the demand that the natural order should conform to the moral order; the need for automatic sanctions guarding the restrictions that divide god from mortal; fatalistic acceptance of events; and the discouraged perception of cosmic injustice. These four attitudes determine the Greeks' religious explanations of disease. They seem to coexist at all periods, and it would be hard to detect a significant shift in emphasis between them. The choice of interpretation in a given case will be pragmatic. The obviously guilty man's disease is seen as punishment, certainly by his enemies, perhaps by himself too; but the institutionalization of guilt in confession, the dogmatic definition of illness as a consequence of sin, ritual or moral, is lacking. To some extent the idea of disease as a random event was inherent in Greek thought, and this popular attitude had a negative relevance to the success of Hippocratic medicine, in that materialist modes of explanation. were not opposed by theological prejudice.

9

PURIFYING THE CITY

It was noted earlier that there was, in Greek belief, no such thing as non-contagious religious danger.[1] Some dangers were more commonly seen as communicable by contact, while others rather threatened the guilty party's descendants; but the difference was one of degree rather than of kind. Every member of any community, therefore, in principle lived under threat of suffering for his neighbours' offences. The ways in which divine anger against a community could be expressed were diverse. At the beginning of Sophocles' *Oedipus Tyrannus*, Thebes is afflicted in three ways − the crops have failed, women and animals cannot bring forth their young, and plague is raging. This is a typical situation that constantly recurs both in myth and in the Greeks' own perception of historical reality. The name for this whole complex of disasters is *loimos*, which is thus much broader than 'plague' by which it is commonly rendered.[2] It could be called down against the violator of an oath, or its opposite besought in prayer.[3] But though divine anger was typically expressed through disturbances of the natural order such as these (storms too are often mentioned),[4] it might also be the ultimate cause of events readily explicable on the human level. Civil strife and military failure are commonly associated with *loimos*; the Spartan setbacks in the Archidamian war had a religious origin, and the anger of Zeus Xenios against Paris was fulfilled through the Greek expedition against Troy.[5] Moving passages in Hesiod and Aeschylus contrast afflictions of all

[1] p. 10.

[2] See M. Delcourt, *Stérilités mystérieuses et naissances maléfiques*, Liege, 1938, Ch. 1.

[3] Oath: above, p. 191 n. 3. Prayer: Aesch. *Supp.* 659–97, *Eum.* 907–9, 937–48, 956–67. For plague as 'daimonic' or 'god-sent' see e.g. Thuc. 2.64.2; Polyb. 36. 17; sources cited in Erotian, p. 108. 16–19 Nachmanson and Galen, *Comm. in Hippoc. Prog.* 1.4, Corpus Medicorum Graecorum 5.9.2, p. 206. Plague not controllable by medical means: e.g. Thuc. 2.47.4. Crop diseases too are 'from Zeus', (Xen.) *Ath. Pol.* 2.6.

[4] Cf. p. 279, and Wachsmuth, 224 n. 746.

[5] Thuc. 7.18.2, Aesch. *Ag.* 699–705.

these kinds with an ideal picture of the good life that a righteous community may enjoy.[6]

One form of purification that the imperilled community could undergo was that by expulsion of a 'scapegoat' – in Greek he was called either a 'medicine' (*pharmakos*) or 'offscouring' (*katharma*), and the rite's explicit purpose was to 'purify the city'. Scapegoat rituals were mentioned earlier in connection with periodic festivals of renewal, but the sources state that they could also be performed in response to a specific crisis.[7] As their symbolism and significance have been well studied in detail of late, a further analysis would be superfluous here.[8] They seem an archaic feature in the religion of the classical period, to the preoccupations of which it is hard to relate them directly. Indirect reflections and continuations of the same mentality, however, may well appear in classical institutions and forms of behaviour,[9] and to investigate this intriguing possibility it will be necessary to consider, briefly and partially, the conceptions that are associated with the rituals.

The fundamental idea is obviously that of 'one head' (or rather two, in most cases) 'for many', but there is ambiguity as to who the one should be. In practice, it was some miserable creature – physically repulsive, a condemned criminal, a beggar – who could be forced into the role or would even accept it voluntarily in return for the preliminary feeding that it brought with it. (The best evidence now indicates that the scapegoat was not killed.[10]) Aitiologically, however, the *pharmakos* is not merely a wretch but also a villain; the ceremony commemorates the punishment of one Pharmakos, who, detected stealing Apollo's

---

[6] Hes. *Op.* 225–47 (cf. Callim. *Dian.* 122–35), Aesch. *Supp.* 656–709, *Eum.* 902–87.

[7] See p. 24 above.

[8] Burkert, *SH*, Ch. 3; *GR* 139–42; J. N. Bremmer, 'Scapegoat Rituals in Ancient Greece', *HSCP* 87 (1983). It is not clear whether the obscure notice of Hesych. s.v. φαρμακή, ἢ χύτρα, ἣν ἡτοίμαζον τοῖς καθαίρουσι τὰς πόλεις, relates to this or some other ritual. Mannhardt's interpretation of the scapegoat as an embodiment of fertility who must himself be cleansed is criticized, after Deubner, 194–7, by Burkert and Bremmer. But the parallel between the treatment of the scapegoat and contemporary magical cures for impotence (Hipponax, frr. 78, 92, with M. L. West, *Studies in Greek Elegy and Iambus*, Berlin, 1974, 144 f.) suggests that this was a complex ritual in which the idea of 'purifying the scapegoat' coexisted with that of 'purifying the city' by expelling him.

[9] Cf. Vernant, *Tragédie*, 116–31; most important for what follows.

[10] *Diēgēsis* 2.39 f. to Callim. fr. 90.

sacred cups, was stoned to death by the companions of Achilles.[11] By this conception the *pharmakos* ceases to be a mere vehicle on to which, like the original scapegoat of the Old Testament, the ills of the community are loaded by a mechanical process of transference, and becomes instead, through his crime, the actual cause of whatever affliction is being suffered. Accordingly, to exile Andocides will mean, says his opponent, at once 'sending out a *pharmakos*' and 'getting rid of an offender against the gods' (*aliterios*);[12] 'offscouring' is a loaded insult.[13] A quite different element is introduced in the many legends which make military success or the safety of a city dependent on the sacrifice or voluntary self-oblation of a person of especially high value – the fairest virgin in the land, the king's daughter, or even the king himself.[14] This might in origin be a quite distinct conception, since death rather than expulsion is here essential; but, if so, a contamination of the two forms seems early to have occurred. Late sources speak of virgin sacrifice as a 'purification',[15] and a hellenistic romancer introduced the sacrifice of two handsome young men into the account of Epimenides' famous cleansing of Athens.[16] More importantly, Herodotus tells how the Achaeans had once been on the point of 'making Athamas (their king) a purification for the country and sacrificing him'.[17] The language is significant; Athamas is an animate 'purification' just as the scapegoat is an animate 'medicine'. By a final twist the person of high social value may cease to be an innocent oblation and become instead the polluted cause of his nation's affliction. This may have been the case with Athamas in the legend which Herodotus refers to, since he had 'plotted the death of Phrixus', and there is perhaps a reflection of such modes of thought in the *Oedipus Tyrannus*.[18] A

---

[11] Istros, 334 *FGrH* fr. 50; probably *aition* for a festival other than the Attic, cf. Jacoby, ad loc.

[12] (Lys.) 6.53.

[13] LSJ s.vv. κάθαρμα, φαρμακός.

[14] See Schwenn, 121–39.

[15] Seneca, *Ag.* 163, cf. *Tro.* 634 f.; Achilles Tatius 3.12.1, 3.16.3, 3.19.3, 5.18.4.

[16] Neanthes of Cyzicus, 84 *FGrH* fr. 16, *ap.* Ath. 602c–d (cf. D.L.1.110); declared a fiction by Polemon cited in Ath., ibid. (a fact often neglected in modern works).

[17] Hdt. 7.197.3.

[18] See esp. J. P. Vernant, loc. cit., also Burkert, *SH* 65. For Pentheus, Dodds on Eur. *Bacch.* 963.

clear mythical example is Lycurgus, who brought barrenness to the land of the Edonians by his offences against Dionysus. His subjects, instructed by an oracle, put him to death.[19]

One way of relating these conceptions to historical behaviour would be to look at the different categories to which ritual and mythical scapegoats belonged, and consider to what extent it was natural to seek within them non-ritual scapegoats, persons to be blamed for the misfortunes of the community. An approach as general as this may of course obscure important differences, since it is more interesting and more surprising if a general is blamed for crop failure than for failure on the field of battle. It will therefore be necessary to consider not merely what categories of person are identified as threatening or corrupting presences, but also in what circumstances and by what means they are felt to work their harm.

An obvious dichotomy among the scapegoats of myth and ritual is that between the socially elevated and debased. (In the legends of Oedipus and Codrus, it has been noted, the one is transformed into the other.)[20] It is tempting to see here two conflicting diagnoses of the causes of public misfortune, corruption or incompetence on high, and subversion or envy at the bottom. The tension between these diagnoses is perhaps reflected through two familiar characters, the portrayal of whom has been thought to be influenced by the figure of the scapegoat. Aesop was ugly and a slave; in one version he was put to death on a false charge of stealing sacred vessels (like the original Pharmakos).[21] Thersites was base-born and deformed; he died at the hands of Achilles (the companions of Achilles killed Pharmakos), possibly, in one variant, for the same crime of pilfering temple plate.[22] Both figures have relations of a distinctive kind with their social superiors. Thersites' essential activity is to 'quarrel with the kings':[23] he is indeed a kind of

[19] Apollod. 3.5.1.

[20] e.g. Burkert, *SH* 65.

[21] See A. Wiechers, *Aesop in Delphi*, Meisenheim, 1961, 31–42 for Aesop as scapegoat; and now F. R. Adrados, *Quaderni Urbinati di Cultura Classica*, n.s. 1 (1979), 93–112.

[22] The evidence for the last point is a vase apparently illustrating the *Achilles Thersitoktonos* of Chairemon: see J. M. Paton, *AJA* 12 (1908), 406–16 (but for a different interpretation C. Robert, *Archaeologische Hermeneutik*, Berlin, 1919, 278–86: further references in *Lexicon Iconographicum Mythologiae Classicae* i, Zürich, 1981, 171). Usener had already identified Pharmakos and Thersites (*Kl. Schr.* iv, Leipzig, 1913, 239–59).

[23] *Il.* 2.214.

embodiment of 'grudge' or 'envy', a power that was probably associated, in an obscure way, with the ideology of the scapegoat.[24] In Homer, the loud-mouthed cur is silenced and humiliated – but not before he has uttered a number of criticisms of his commander-in-chief that strike home. In the Aesop legend, guilt is even more effectively turned back against the powerful; the accusation against Aesop is false, and his death, caused by the authorities, brings disaster upon the land. Aesop was, of course, inventor of the literary genre through which the weak could tactfully but firmly admonish the mighty.[25] These two figures invite us to consider the dichotomy between noble and debased scapegoats not in merely structural terms – kings and beggars coincide because both are outside the norm – but in terms of debate; is the real villain Thersites, or Agamemnon?

We begin with Thersites. As the Greeks did for ritual purposes, so many cultures have in bitter earnest recruited their scapegoats among despised sections of the community or outsiders. This is the mentality that dictates the witch-hunt, or the pogrom. In Greece, however (or at least in Athens), significant expressions of this attitude are hard to find. Envy threatened the fortunate, both on a pragmatic and magical level, but we do not find the poorer classes being persecuted for performing sorcery against the powerful. Women, a suppressed class, were to some extent threatening,[26] but metics and slaves seem to have evoked contempt rather than fear. Neither group, perhaps, was enough of a unity to be truly formidable either practically or in the imagination. (The Spartans, by contrast, lived in perpetual fear of their helots, and expressed this fear by murdering them individually and, on one horrific occasion, *en masse*; they had, however, good grounds for this disquiet, and there is no evidence that the helots became an imaginative terror on any other level than that on which they were a real threat.[27]) Intense suspicion is found only in connection with one sub-group of metics, who controlled, for their own profit, a

[24] Plut. *De mul. vir.* 252e (*baskanos*) with Parth. *Amat. Narr.* 9.5 (Thargelia): cf. Burkert, *SH* 72 f.

[25] K. Meuli, *Herkunft und Wesen der Fabel*, Basle, 1954 = *Ges. Schr.* ii, 731–56.

[26] p. 101 above.

[27] Fear: e.g. Thuc. 4.80.3, Arist. *Pol.* 1269a 38–9. Murder: Thuc. 4.80.3–4, Isoc. 12.181, Arist. fr. 538. Cf. D. M. Lewis, *Sparta and Persia*, Leiden, 1977, 27–9; P. Cartledge, *Sparta and Lakonia, a Regional History*, London, 1979, 176 f.

delicate and crucial area of Athenian life. More corn-dealers
have been condemned to death, maintains the Lysianic speech
directed against them, than members of any other profession.
In the particular case to which the speech relates, popular fury
had been so strong that they came close to being executed
without trial. 'Their interests', Lysias points out, 'are the opposite of those of other men. For they make their biggest profits
when news of some disaster has reached the city and they can
sell their corn dear.' And so 'they look with joy on your
afflictions.'[28] This argument from lack of common interest is
often used by the orators to cast an opponent as an internal
enemy of the state.[29] The corn-dealer is clearly on the way here
to becoming a Jewish merchant; but he is a special case, and
there is no suggestion that even he threatens the general well-
being by any more arcane methods than hoarding, rumour-
mongering, and price-fixing, or from any more sinister motive
than greed. There was no religious divergence between Athenians and corn-dealers to transform the difference of interest into
a difference of fundamental value. Only once are metics as such
known to have come under systematic attack, and, though
ideology may have lurked in the background, the primary
motive of the thirty tyrants in 404 was to benefit from rich and
easy pickings in a time of financial straits.[30]

The danger that demanded constant vigilance was not so
much that of attack from below as infiltration. Shortly after the
expulsion of the Peisistratids, citizens who were 'impure in
descent' were rejected.[31] (The timing, of course, suggests that
this was a purification from tyranny as well as a cleansing of the
citizen body.) Pericles' law of 451/0, excluding the children of
non-Athenian mothers, rendered the citizen body, in principle,
a sealed and impenetrable unit.[32] Penalties for infiltration were
savage, and it is clear from comedy and oratory that the possibility was one that was constantly present in many people's
minds. The language of 'purity' is sometimes found in this

[28] Lysias 22.20,2,13 f. On the speech cf. R. Seager, *Historia* 15 (1966), 172–84.
[29] Lys. 27.9,29.10, fr. 1. 195–200 Gernet, Andoc. 2.2 f., Dem. 18.198; cf. R. Seager, op. cit., 180–2. This is the trouble with the helots, Arist. *Pol.* 1269a 38–9.
[30] Xen. *Hell.* 2.3.21; cf. Whitehead, 155.
[31] Arist. *Ath. Pol.* 13.5; cf. Whitehead, 143.
[32] Whitehead, 149–51.

context,[33] but there were further grounds for this growing exclusiveness in the real advantages that attached to citizenship in a prosperous state. It was, for instance, a gift of corn from the king of Egypt for distribution among the citizens that in 445/4 provoked a revision of the rolls, and the expulsion of numerous impostors.[34] Provided, however, that the dividing wall of privilege between citizen and outsider was well guarded, Athenians do not seem to have been greatly concerned about what went on outside it. It was left to the philosopher to worry about the contamination of citizen morale by contact with the values of foreigners.[35] At Sparta things seem to have been different, since Xenophon explains the periodic expulsions of outsiders as a device to prevent the city 'catching sloppy ways from foreigners';[36] but, even here, the threat posed by the outsider was practically conceived and, as Spartan history showed, realistically.

For the rich in Athens, a stronger threat from below was embodied in the person of the sycophant. For a reborn Thersites, this would surely have been the natural profession, and many a member of an Athenian propertied family would doubtless have enjoyed the opportunity to drive a sycophant figure beyond the boundary with stones. This is perhaps the level of feeling to which the Thirty Tyrants appealed with their intention of 'purifying the city from the unjust' (a category identified by their supporters with sycophants).[37] The notion of purifying the city by the expulsion of some disruptive element (*ekkathairō*) is one that is quite commonly found: possible targets for this treatment are luxury, bribery, persons with no visible means of support, 'corrupters of youth', and even, under tyranny, 'the best citizens'.[38] The purge, however, is not a form of behaviour confined to societies that practise the ritual expul-

---

[33] Arist. *Ath. Pol.* 13.5, Dem. 57.55.

[34] Philochorus, 328 *FGrH* fr. 119, Plut. *Per.* 37.4. Such distributions among citizens, familiar from Hdt. 7.144.1, were a regular archaic institution: see Latte, 'Kollektivbesitz und Staatsschatz in Griechenland', *Nachr. Gött.* 1945/8 (1948), 64–75 = *Kl. Schr.* 294–312.

[35] Pl. *Leg.* 949e–950a.

[36] Xen. *Lac. Pol.* 14.4.

[37] Lysias 12.5, cf. Xen. *Hell.* 2.3.38. It is tempting to try to connect the sycophant ('fig-shower') directly with the fig-wearing scapegoat: but how?

[38] Pl. *Resp.* 399e, Dinarchus 2.5, Diphilus, fr. 32.17, Pl. *Euthphr.* 2d, *Resp.* 567c; cf. *Com. Nov. Incert. Auct.* fr. 214 (3.449 Kock) τὰ μυσαρὰ ταῦτα θρέμματ' ἐκδιωκτέον.

sion of scapegoats, and, in a detailed discussion of the 'purification of the city', Plato seems to have other models in mind – the
herdsman who purifies his flock by sorting healthy animals
from diseased, the doctor who administers purgative drugs.[39]
Plato does, though, locate the source of danger at the bottom of
the social scale: 'have-nots' who, through starvation, clamour
for the property of the 'haves' are a 'disease' which can be
purged by the dispatch of what is 'euphemistically' termed a
colony.

Of the other ideas that emerged in connection with the ritual
and mythical scapegoats, two can be passed over briefly. The
one which makes the scapegoat an 'offender against the gods'
interprets disaster as the consequence of religious offences by
individual members of the community; this conception's relevance to actual behaviour will be considered later. The sacrifice
of the king's innocent son or daughter lacks, not surprisingly,
close historical equivalents. The nearest approach is perhaps to
be found in Herodotus' story of how the Spartans, suffering
from the wrath of Talthybius for the murder of Darius' heralds,
asked in public assembly 'if any of the Lacedaimonians was
willing to die for Sparta' by being sent up to Xerxes for punishment; two Spartiates, 'well endowed by nature and in the first
rank for wealth', volunteered.[40] If the story were true, it would
provide the most spectacular evidence in all Greek history for
self-punishment as a form of religious expiation, since the affliction was merely the inability to sacrifice successfully, while the
cure was the loss of two Spartiate lives. Unfortunately, even if
the broad outline of the story is considered reliable, the reason
for sending the two men up to Xerxes need not have been the
one recorded by Herodotus. We are therefore left with no secure
evidence that the sacrifice of the innocent was anything more
than a traditional legendary motif. But the motif is not rendered
meaningless by being literally unrealistic, and part of what a
story like that of Iphigeneia's sacrifice seems to convey is that
obligation as well as privilege is concentrated around the person

---

[39] *Leg.* 735a–736c (cf. *Resp.* 501a). In Pl. *Euthphr.* 2d the image is from weeding. On
colonization as scapegoat expulsion see Burkert, *GR* 142.

[40] 7.134.2. The oracle which fortified Leonidas to accept death at Thermopylae
(Hdt. 7.220.3–4) is generally regarded as a forgery.

of the leader. If responsibility is thus placed upon the shoulders of the commander, it is obviously likely that guilt too will be his.

We come finally to the figure of the guilty king. He has often been considered in a retrospective light, as a descendant of Frazer's magical king, but should perhaps also be seen as a forerunner of, for instance, Demosthenes, the 'common polluting demon of all Greece'. From every period of Greek history there is evidence for the concentration of blame upon the figure of the leader. Often, of course, the blame relates to the specific sphere of activity, usually military, with which the leader is most concerned, but we can still find bad weather being caused by an orator's impiety near the end of the fourth century. The special influence that the person in authority exercises over human affairs extends also to the workings of nature.

Some mythological evidence for turning against the king has already been mentioned. A clear example is Plutarch's story that, instructed by an oracle, the Aenianes once stoned their king to end a drought.[41] A hint that this may once have been a common response to misfortune comes from a question put to the king's son Telemachus in the *Odyssey*: 'Is it in obedience to a "voice of god" that the people hate your family?'[42] Though some commentators interpret the 'voice of god' as merely a 'mysteriously inspired movement of feeling', it seems more natural to follow the scholia and take it as an oracle. Rejection of the king in a time of affliction is a logical counterpoise to the belief, attested in a well-known passage of the *Odyssey*, that prosperity too depends upon him:[43] 'A god-fearing king, who, ruling over a large and mighty people, maintains straight justice, and the dark earth bears corn and barley, and the trees are weighed down with fruit, and the flocks give birth unfailingly, and the sea produces fish, because of his good rule, and the people prosper.' A belief of this kind seems to be, in part at least, a kind of moral lever for use by subjects against their ruler. This is certainly how it is deployed in Hesiod's famous diptych

[41] *Quaest. Graec.* 26,297c. Different from cases mentioned already in that there is no indication of the king's guilt.

[42] 3.215.

[43] 19.109–14; cf. W. Speyer, *Jahrbuch f. Antike und Christentum* 22 (1979), 30–9.

of the just and unjust city.[44] Justice brings health, healthy
children, thriving crops and animals, calm seas, and military
success; injustice the opposite. The warning that 'a whole city
often suffers from one bad man' applies in principle to any
citizen; it was indeed true at this date on the most pragmatic
level, since whole communities were liable to reprisal strikes by
their neighbours for the offences of individual members.[45] It is
clear, however, that the injustice which Hesiod wishes really to
present as threatening the general welfare is that of the kings.
Even on the purely practical level that has just been mentioned,
it was only the crimes of the mighty that really threatened
communal well-being: if a Trojan commoner had carried Helen
home from Sparta, he would of course have been handed over to
the avenging Greeks to avoid war. With the powerful, however,
it was different: 'I fear lest the city be overcome along with the
kings'; *quidquid delirant reges, plectuntur Achivi.*[46] This special
potential of the king extends also to the metaphysical level. He
carries and embodies the welfare of his people (and cannot
therefore be deformed in body).[47] His relation to the divine is
unique. He is 'from Zeus'; gods may interfere with the natural
order by sending a thunderclap to honour him; even his dreams
have a meaning not shared by those of the commoner.[48] The
converse, however, is that his crimes too have unique significance on the religious plane, and his eminence is in this respect
perilous. If he makes himself unpopular by injustice, his subjects will know where to lay the blame when disaster occurs.
The plague in *Iliad* 1 is caused by a crime of the commander-in-
chief (once again, anybody else would have been forced to hand

[44] *Op.* 225–47.
[45] Latte, *RE* s.v. *ΣΥΛΑΝ = Kl. Schr.* 416–20. The institution survived in certain forms into the hellenistic period.
[46] Aesch. *Sept.* 764 f., Hor. *Epist.* 1.2.14. Only kings can sin really effectively, Pl. *Gorg.* 525d–e.
[47] Xen. *Hell.* 3.3.3 (Agesilaus), Paus. 7.2.1 (Medon), also Hdt. 4.161.1; cf. J. N. Bremmer, 'Medon, The Case of the Bodily Blemished king', in *Perennitas: Studi in Onore di Angelo Brelich*, Rome, 1980, 67–76. Cf. still 'Ekphantos' the Pythagorean, demanding absolute purity in a king, Stob. 4.7.64 p. 273. 12 ff. Hense (= Thesleff, p. 80. 15 ff).
[48] Hes. *Theog.* 96; Hom. *Il.* 11.45 f.; *Il.* 2. 79–83 (cf. Artemid. 1.2 p. 9.19 ff. Pack, Dodds, *Progress*, 178 n. 1; a priestess's dreams too are significant, Aeschin. 2. 10, and Demosthenes claims his to be, Aeschin. 3.77,219). It is to the king that bad omens portend harm, Arr. *Anab.* 4.4.3–9. Later material on gods and kings in Nisbet/Hubbard's note on Hor. *Carm.* 1.12.50; cf. Soph. *Phil.* 139 f., Xen. *Hiero* 8.5.

back Chryseis immediately). Had he persisted in his refusal to return the girl, the Greek army might have been forced to turn to stoning.

By the historical period, the situation had been in important respects transformed. No 'god-nurtured' kings remained except in Sparta, and the wings even of these were clipped. More direct ways of disposing of unpopular commanders were now available than by accusing them of causing the crops to fail. As a result, though the expulsion of high-ranking scapegoats was endemic in the society of fifth- and fourth-century Greece, the victim was not usually accused of working harm by arcane or impossible means. A general may indeed fritter away an opportunity or lead an army to disaster through folly, cowardice, or corruption. The irrational element in these proceedings was none the less fully evident to many contemporaries. It is already the complaint of one of the first commanders who addresses us in the fifth century, Aeschylus' Eteocles: 'Should we fare well, god is responsible. But if – may it not happen – disaster befalls, Eteocles alone will be blamed throughout the city.'[49] The trials of Athenian generals and Spartan kings are a leitmotif in the history of the period, and the phenomenon seems to have been pan-Hellenic.[50] Disaster was constantly traced back to those maleficent but invisible powers, bribery and treachery. Unlike witchcraft in the seventeenth century, these two powers did work real damage, and there are doubtless good structural reasons why they posed such a threat to Greek states. They are none the less, along with conspiracy, the witches of classical Greek society.[51]

---

[49] Aesch. *Sept.* 4–6.

[50] G. E. M. de Ste Croix, *The Origins of the Peloponnesian War*, London, 1972, 350–3; Pritchett, ii, 4–33. The monthly oath to govern legally which Spartan kings were required to swear (Xen. *Lac. Pol.* 15.7) is also revealing in this connection. For another form of turning against the powerful note the pogroms of Pythagoreans in the 5th century (exact details are unfortunately not available): Burkert, *LS* 115.

[51] Lysias 28 and 29 are instructive in this regard. We here find an initial assumption (our commanders steal our money) being defended against empirical refutation (the money he was supposed to have embezzled was not found among the property of Ergocles after his execution) by an undemonstrated subsidiary hypothesis (it was appropriated in turn by Ergocles' associate Philocrates). This process is familiar to anthropologists from the study of witchcraft beliefs (the spell failed because of a counter-spell). Of course, Philocrates *might* be guilty: K. J. Dover, *Lysias and the Corpus Lysiacum*, Berkeley, 1972, 72.

Though most of the faults with which the powerful were
charged now related to their functions, there also persisted a
conception of the magistrate as a symbolic vehicle of his
people's welfare, which defects of various kinds could
jeopardize. The magistrate, like the priest, was required to be
physically intact; many men in Athens were 'impure in body',
but the community was only endangered if one of them held
office; it was far worse to have a man who had parodied the
mysteries as general than merely serving in the ranks.[52] When a
politician describes his opponent as the 'polluting demon of the
city', he is primarily denouncing his opponent's policies and
their practical consequences, but also seeking to suggest that,
with such an impure rogue in charge, afflictions of every kind
are likely to follow. Aeschines repeatedly uses openly religious
language to represent Demosthenes as a pollution perilous to
general welfare. Demosthenes is the cause of every misfortune;
he brings catastrophe to all he associates with; he is 'the polluting demon of Greece', and should be 'cast beyond the frontiers',
or 'sent away (*apopempō*) as the common disaster of the Greeks'.[53]
The 'luck' of the people depends on the character, or mere luck,
of its leader; it thus becomes worth while for Demosthenes to
argue whether he himself or Aeschines is the luckier man. With
this emphasis on fortune, a characteristic fourth-century note
intrudes, but the framework remains the ancient conception of
the community's magical dependence upon the leader.[54] Outside Athens, some saw Dionysius as the 'polluting demon of
Sicily'. It was noted that battles were won in his absence, but
lost in his presence.[55] Two attacks on Demosthenes neatly bring

[52] Lys. 24.13; pp. 97 and 169 above. Absolute requirement for those holding public
office to be free from other taints, (Lys.) 6.4, Lys. 26.8, Ant. 6.45 f.
[53] 3.57,114 (because of his association with polluted Amphissians), 131, 157 f., 253.
Cf. Dem. 18.159,296, Dinarchus 1.77, and for the idea of 'a country's polluter' already
Eur. *Or.* 1584, Soph. *OC* 788, Eupolis, fr. 120.
[54] Demosthenes unlucky: Aeschin. 3.157 f., Dinarchus 1.31 (bad luck contagious),
41,74,77,91,92. Luckier than Aeschines: Dem. 18.252 ff. Dem. also points out, 18.255,
that his own puny luck could not damage that of the city – a nice parallel to the debate
about mortals polluting gods, above, p. 145. He is said none the less to have feared his
own luck, Plut. *Dem.* 21.3. On 'luck' in the period see e.g. Lys. 30.18, Dem. 1.1,2.22
(linked with 'good will of gods', cf. p. 14 n. 60), 4.12, 20.110, Aeschin. 2.51, Plut. *Tim.*
passim, esp. 16.1, 21.5, 30.7, 36.6–7. Cf. Xen. *Cyr.* 4.1.24, 7.2.24 (charisma of divine
descent). On contagious luck see p. 219 above.
[55] Timaeus, 566 *FGrH* fr. 29, Diod. 14. 69.1–3.

out the dependence of these themes on traditional concepts. Aeschines actually quotes the passage of Hesiod which was discussed earlier: when the poet spoke of one man bringing affliction on many, Aeschines comments, it was creatures like Demosthenes that he had in mind. Dinarchus urges the Athenians to 'put the affairs of the city under better omens, by turning the disasters upon these leaders': he might be the voice of the oracle urging the Aenianes to stone their king.[56] The comic poet Philippides even went back to blaming disturbances in the weather upon a politician's crimes. 'Stratocles, who made the acropolis into a tavern, who lodged whores with the virgin Athena, because of whom the frost scorched the vines, because of whose impiety the goddess' robe was cleft in the middle, he who assigned to men the honours of the gods'.[57] It is perhaps not a coincidence that this reversion to the Homeric and Hesiodic conception in its most magical form relates to a figure who was, like the archaic kings, hard to assail on a direct human level.[58]

It has sometimes been suggested that ostracism is a kind of expulsion of the scapegoat in secularized form.[59] The institution seems, however, to have been functional, if singular; and it is not clear that its symbolic and expressive significance is sufficiently important in contrast to its purely practical effect to make such an explanation appropriate. The original motivation has been much discussed, but the danger that it was designed to meet, whether tyranny or a paralysing clash of rival leaders, was certainly political.[60] It appears as less of a collective ritual if we believe the report that has recently been uncovered in a Vatican gnomologium that the vote was initially intended to be confined to the council.[61] If, however, ostracism is to be mentioned in this connection at all, it should obviously be

[56] Aeschin. 2.158,3.134–6; Dinarchus 1.29.

[57] Fr. 25.2–7, *ap.* Plut. *Dem.* 12.7,26.5.

[58] Stratocles was the tool of Demetrius Poliorcetes. Similarly, a *defixio* against Kassander and his circle has now been found, *Ath. Mitt.* 95 (1980), 230.

[59] Vernant, *Tragédie*, 124–6, developing unpublished ideas of Gernet.

[60] Recent contributions: e.g. G. R. Stanton, *JHS* 90 (1970), 180–3; J. J. Keaney, *Historia* 19 (1970), 1–11; R. Thomsen, *The Origin of Ostracism*, Copenhagen, 1972; A. J. Holladay, *Greece and Rome* 25² (1978), 184–90.

[61] J. J. Keaney and A. E. Raubitschek, *AJP* 93 (1972), 87–91; cf. G. A. Lehmann, *ZPE* 41 (1981), 85–99.

connected with the scapegoat king rather than the scapegoat beggar. On any view, there lies behind the institution some such thought as Solon's: 'It is through big men that the city is destroyed'; in being turned against the low wretch Hyperbolus, ostracism suffered an abuse, and was abandoned.[62]

Some justification for seeing some connection between the ostracized politician and the scapegoat has perhaps been provided by the actual ostraca discovered during this century. The quite unexpected number of candidates that they have revealed has shown how freely individual Athenians exploited the institution to give vent to their own feelings as to which powerful figure the state could best be rid of.[63] From the angry and venomous messages sometimes added, it has become clear that the question, 'Which of our politicians poses the greatest threat to stable government?' was not sharply distinguished from 'Which of our politicians is the greatest rogue?' 'This ostracon says that of all the cursed *prytanes* Xanthippos does most wrong (?).'[64] Against 'traitors' the ostracon becomes the written equivalent of the public curse.[65] Religious factors could certainly play their part in encouraging the feeling that the state would fare better if a particular individual were out of it. Several of the still unpublished ostraca from the Cerameicus are said to allude to the Alcmaeonid pollution, and one to associate Themistocles with a curse hitherto unknown.[66] The Xanthippos ostracon just quoted uses one of the strongest terms denoting a religious offender, *alitēros* (the exact construction is unfortunately unclear). An obscure ostracon naming Aristeides has been interpreted as accusing him of an offence against suppliants.[67] Most interestingly, the tradition found in ancient sources that Cimon was ostracized because of his incestuous relations with Elpinice now finds support in the message urging him to 'clear out, taking his sister with him'.[68] Though a certain sardonic humour

[62] Solon, fr. 9.3. Abuse: Thuc. 8.73.3, Plato Comicus, fr. 187 *ap.* Plut. *Nic.* 11.6–7.
[63] See R. Thomsen, op. cit., 70–80.
[64] M/L, p. 42, with discussion.
[65] Traitors: M/L, p. 42. There is now too 'Kallias the Mede' (but note the reservation of D. M. Lewis, *ZPE* 14 (1974), 3). Cursing of traitors: p. 193 above.
[66] H. Mattingly, *The University of Leeds Review* 14 (1971), 285–7.
[67] M/L, p. 42.
[68] H. Mattingly, op. cit., 284.

is unmistakable, it could disguise real feeling. The sexual scandal will certainly not have caused Cimon's ostracism, but might have helped to focus indignation against the discredited leader. The offences of the many obscurer figures against whom occasional ostraca were inscribed may well have been as much moral and social as political.

This survey of various forms of blame-throwing has taken us far from the original situation of the stricken community seeking a cure for its ills. To this it is time to return, in order to apply to it the kind of analysis attempted for the diseases of the individual in the previous chapter, by considering the diagnoses that were offered and remedies adopted in specific cases of affliction. Some but not all of the material that has been mentioned in relation to the scapegoat is also relevant here. In the preceding discussion, 'scapegoats' were included who were accused of causing harm by familiar human methods. Here, however, it is with specifically religious diagnoses of disaster that we are concerned.

A difficulty arises at once over evidence. Although the pattern of transgression leading to communal affliction is ubiquitous in mythology, aitiology, and legendary history, secure historical evidence for the religious interpretation of public disaster is sparse. Thucydides, for instance, says nothing of what was said or done on this level at Athens during the great plague, although religious diagnoses must certainly have been presented. Of the Delphic oracles, well over fifty, that purport to have been uttered in such circumstances, only one is considered certainly authentic by the latest critic, and that was given in the third century AD.[69] The verdict may be severe, but the number that have much chance of being genuine are certainly very small. This state of the evidence, however, is perhaps not as serious an obstacle as it might appear. Herodotus believed that the Agyllaeans incurred plague by stoning a band of Phocaean survivors to death. Even if incorrect, the belief is good evidence for a possible interpretation of public disaster in the second half of the fifth century. Not all the quasi-historical and legendary instances can claim the same value as evidence as this, particularly when the plague is introduced to explain an

[69] Fontenrose, 442.

272   *Miasma*

existing ritual; but there are enough early stories that are not
narrowly aitiological to suggest the kind of explanation for
public misfortune that might have seemed plausible. The patterns that emerge from the legendary and quasi-historical
material can then be compared with the reliably historical
evidence.

In one pattern, disaster serves merely as a stimulus from the
gods to some form of cultural change. Several stories in
Herodotus are of this type. Crop-failure induces the Epidau-
rians to set up images of Damia and Auxesia, drought the
Therans to colonize Cyrene, military setbacks the Spartans to
bring home the bones of Orestes.[70] Similar stories came in time
to explain the bringing home of the bones of Theseus, Hesiod,
Hector, and Pelops. There is no suggestion that the Epidau-
rians were culpable in having no images of Damia and Auxesia,
but the time had come for them to set some up, as it had for the
Therans to colonize Cyrene. The affliction was an admonition
rather than a punishment.[71]

In another pattern, the explanation lay in a neglect that was
in some degree culpable of proper cult for a particular god or
hero. Plague forced the Locrians to resume the famous tribute;
Spartan girls were born misshapen because their city paid no
sufficient honour to Aphrodite; the Phigaleans were punished
for failing to restore an image of Demeter burnt in a fire, the
Sicyonians for allowing two divine images to remain incomplete.[72] Several striking stories refer to failure to pay proper cult
to a heroized Olympic victor.[73] Mythologically, Oineus

[70] Hdt. 5.82.1, 4.151.1, 1.67.2. Comparable cases are 'Parke/Wormell, nn.
179,223,237, the aitiological n. 569, and the *aitia* for Athenian Demeter festivals,
Parke/Wormell, ii, p. 79 on n. 169, Lycurgus, fr. 82–5 Blass. Other aitiological
plagues/droughts, *Et. Mag.* 252. 11 (Daitis, in Ephesus), P/W 559 (Bouphonia), Paus.
8. 28.5–6, Apollod. 2.5.11 (Busiris) and many of the following. Population movements
explained by plague/crop failure: P/W, nn. 305,402,453;477 *FGrH* fr. 8, and cf. Hdt.
7.171 (population change). Plague prevents a premature population movement, Apollod. 2.8.2.
[71] Parke/Wormell, nn. 113,207,409,563. Cf. Plut. *Cim.* 19.5 for a cult of Cimon
instituted ἐν λοιμῷ καὶ γῆς ἀφορίᾳ.
[72] P/W, nn. 331,554,493,28. Cf. nn. 455,485–7.
[73] P/W, nn. 388–91, cf. 118. For the hero's malice cf. P/W, n. 392, Paus. 9.38.5; for
the sternness of heroes' revenge against insult, A. Brelich, *Gli eroi greci*, Rome, 1958, 226
ff., citing the *Anagyrasios daimōn* (Diogenian 1.25, Suda s.v.), the hero of Temesa
(P/W, n. 392), Protesilaus and Argus (Paus. 3.4.5–6), Minos (Hdt. 7.169). On the
story type cf. J. Fontenrose, 'The Hero as Athlete', *California Studies in Classical Antiquity*
1 (1968), 73–104.

brought the boar against Calydonia by forgetting a sacrifice, and the first assumption of the Greeks in *Iliad* Book 1 is that Apollo has sent the plague in anger for an unoffered hecatomb or a disregarded vow.[74]

Positive affronts to the gods are of course all the more likely to lead to disaster. The story of Laomedon can be taken as representative of a common mythological pattern.[75] Laomedon deprived Apollo and Poseidon of their wages for fortifying Troy. Apollo sent plague, Poseidon a sea-monster; an oracle told Laomedon that release could be secured by exposing his daughter to the monster. In this type the original impious act is performed by the king or a member of his family; disaster strikes the community as a whole, but is abated by an act of renunciation or self-sacrifice on the part again of a member of the royal house. We are back, of course, with the scapegoat king. Occasionally, a particularly impious king involves his people in final destruction.[76] Affronts to gods by commoners normally lead to their direct punishment, but in one or two stories even they can cause communal disaster: Comaetho and Melanippus bring plague by copulating in a sacred precinct, and the rape of Cassandra by Ajax provokes the storms that wreck the Greek fleet.[77] In the case of Auge too, who causes crop-failure by bearing her baby in Athena's precinct, it seems more relevant that she is a priestess of Athena than the king's daughter.[78]

In the quasi-historical rather than legendary material the affront to the gods normally involves a killing on sacred ground. There are several story patterns which make murder a source of disaster. One is that of the killing, usually in civil war, in defiance of sanctuary. Guilt is normally ascribed to a whole people, or a tyrant.[79] In the stories that blame plague on the killing of an individual on profane ground, the victim is almost invariably the son of a god, especially dear to a god, a priest, or

[74] Hom. *Il.* 9. 533 ff., 1.65.
[75] Apollod. 2.5.9; for the pattern cf. ibid., 2.4.3 (Cassiepeia and Andromeda), 3.5.1 (Lycurgus), and Agamemnon in *Iliad* 1. Also perhaps Auge, cf. below.
[76] Hes. fr. 30. 16–19 (Salmoneus).
[77] Paus 7.19.4–6 (P/W, n. 556, but aitiological); Ajax, p. 185 n. 225 above (affects a fleet, not a country).
[78] Apollod. 2.7.4, 3.9.1. The fact of being priestess sufficiently enhances the outrage in itself.
[79] P/W, nn. 27,74,75: on the type see Fontenrose, 76 f. Murder of ambassadors caused the fall of Sybaris, Phylarchus, 81 *FGrH* fr. 45.

fulfilling a mission pleasing to the Olympians; normally too such stories explain the foundation of a cult or temple, and are *ad hoc* creations not involving substantial figures of mythology. A typical example is the murder of Karnos, origin of the Karneian games.[80] Herodotus has two stories set in historical times that conform roughly to this pattern. The people of Apollonia blinded Evenius for allowing wolves to attack the sacred herds of the sun which he was guarding. Animals and land immediately became sterile, and Apollo told the Apolloniates to pay Evenius any compensation he chose; Apollo himself would give him a greater gift. Apollo's gift was prophecy and Evenius became famous as a seer throughout Greece. The Delphians who executed Aesop on a trumped-up charge suffered terribly until at last they found someone willing to receive compensation for his death.[81] Aesop, the poet, was obviously dear to the gods, while Evenius founded a famous mantic family.

Another source of plague is the massacre of particularly defenceless victims by the dominating section of the community. When the Agyllaeans stoned some Phocaean refugees, all living creatures passing the site of the crime became twisted. Excessive savagery against the helpless distorts the natural order in the same way in the legend of the Lemnians who murdered their Attic wives and offspring; and the murder of children often leads to plague in aitiological stories.[82] For disaster due to the simple murder of one individual by another, on the other hand, the evidence is remarkably sparse. Laius' death brings plague in Sophocles, but that, as we saw, is a special case; both parties are kings, and one the father of the other. The murder of Stymphalus by Pelops caused drought throughout Greece, but here too the victim was a king.[83] The plague in

---

[80] P/W, nn. 291–3. Afflictions follow the deaths of Orpheus (P/W 376), Linus (386), the *Poinē* sent by Apollo (387), Scephrus (566), and a μητραγύρτης (572). So too for various introducers of the vine or wine (542,544,551). The death of Charila (570) is an exceptionally bald aition.

[81] Hdt. 9.93–4, 2.134.4. Cf. the plague that struck Athens for the killing of Androgeos, Apollod. 3.15.8. In 90 *FGrH* fr. 45 (from Xanthus?) dearth strikes Lydia because of a murder committed by the reigning king's father.

[82] Hdt. 1.167.1–2, 6.139.1; cf. P/W, nn. 130,199,385.

[83] Apollod. 3.12.6. Killing a king especially portentous, Hom. *Od.* 16.401 f., Soph. *OT* 257.

Psophis due to Alcmaeon's presence is probably Euripides' invention.[84]

A final cause of plague, little attested, is the sacking of a city particularly dear to a god or hero.[85]

The reliably historical explanations for misfortune fall, with certain obvious modifications and limitations, into similar patterns. Although the evidence for religious explanations of plague is slight, we know a certain amount about religious and magical responses. The quasi-legendary plagues that lead to the installation of new cults find their historical correlate in cults or temples founded in response to affliction. The temples of Apollo Helper at Bassae and Pan Releaser at Troezen were said to be thank-offerings for help given during the great plague,[86] and it has been plausibly suggested that the introduction of Asclepius' cult to Athens was a reaction to the same event.[87] Two Delphic responses that might be genuine relate to it. The Athenians were told to set up an image of Apollo, the Cleonaeans to sacrifice a billy goat to the rising sun.[88] The sun probably received the offerings because of plague's symbolic connection with blazing heat,[89] which would make this a semi-magical remedy. The same kind of amoral manipulation appears in the Cyrenaean custom of countering the onset of plague by sacrificing a red goat to Apollo Averter before the gates.[90] Apollo of course was the pre-eminent averter of plague throughout antiquity. He might also be its sender, as in *Iliad* 1, but often enough his reasons for anger, if his anger was suspected at all, must have been obscure, and the appeal to him simply an

[84] Apollod. 3.7.5, cf. Appendix 7 below s.v. Alcmaeon. P/W, n. 398, a hellenistic romance, is an insignificant exception.

[85] P/W, n. 169. Cf. P/W, n. 305.

[86] Paus. 8.41. 7–9, 2.32.6.

[87] See e.g. A. Burford, *The Greek Temple Builders at Epidaurus*, Liverpool, 1969, 20 f. See too D. M. Lewis, *ABSA* 55 (1960), 193 f., on IG I³ 130.

[88] Paus. 1.3.4, 10.11.5 (P/W, nn. 125, 158). Even Fontenrose, 330, seems disposed in their favour.

[89] Soph. *OT* 27, 176, 191.

[90] *LSS* 115 A 4–7, cf. Appendix 2. For further semi-magical techniques see Paus. 2.34.2 (Methana): two halves of a sacrificed cock are carried around a vineyard to create a magic circle against damaging winds; D.L.8.60: Empedocles catches plague-bearing etesians in ass-skin bags; Plut. *Quaest. Conv.* 694 a–b: sacrifice of black bull to Βούβρωστις at Smyrna (the bull perhaps embodying the Βούβρωστις); Paus. 9.22.1: Hermes averts a plague at Tanagra by carrying a ram around the walls (aition for a statue of Hermes Kriophoros); Paus. 2.13.6: the Phliasians set up a bronze goat as protection for their vines against the 'goat' star.

attempt to secure the aid of the relevant divine specialist.[91] Though remedies based on magical manipulation, or supplication of a healing deity, could no doubt coexist with a diagnosis in terms of religious guilt, it is interesting that the attested practical responses should be on the level of sacrificing a billy goat, not 'driving out the pollution'. The Athenian purification of Delos in 426/5 is a partial exception, if we accept Diodorus' very plausible view that this was provoked by the plague;[92] but, even here, the pollution that was identified as a cause was merely a ritual offence against the god specifically associated with the disease.

Most of the actual explanations of other forms of disaster have already been mentioned in other contexts, and can be listed summarily. They fall almost without exception into the category of violation of divine rights. Where mythologically the guilty party is the king or a member of his family, in the historical instances blame lies with the community as a whole, substantial portions of it, or its representatives. If the summoning of Epimenides to Athens was indeed provoked by plague, this was due to a massacre of suppliants by magistrates.[93] The devastation of Athens in 480 was probably caused by Athenian involvement in the burning of the temple of Cybele at Sardis.[94] Impiety against a temple of Poseidon provoked the tidal wave that swept away a Persian battalion.[95] The great Spartan earthquake was punishment for the massacre of helot suppliants, while they suffered setbacks during the Archidamian war because they entered upon it in violation of their oath. That at least was one view at Sparta; others detected pollution on the

[91] Cf. F. G. Welcker, 'Seuchen von Apollon', *Kleine Schriften* iii, Bonn, 1850, 33–45 (but on the coins of Selinus discussed there see A. H. Lloyd, *The Numismatic Chronicle* 15⁵ (1935), 73–93); O. Weinreich, *Ath. Mitt.* 38 (1913), 62–72 = *Ausgewählte Schriften* i, Amsterdam, 1969, 197–206; Nilsson, *GF* 174 (Apollo Hekatombaios); L. Deubner, *Neue Jahrb.* 43 (1919), 385–406; A. Severyns, *Recherches sur la Chrestomathie de Proclos* ii, Paris, 1938, 128 (healing paean); Nilsson, *GGR* 541. Apollo can still send evil in the classical period (cf. the Erythrae paean, J. U. Powell, *Collectanea Alexandrina*, Oxford, 1925, 140), but in general is invoked as averter rather than sender of plague (see e.g. Soph. *OT* 203–15, where the plague is blamed on Ares; and Weinreich, op. cit.)

[92] Diod. 12.58.6–7. Thuc. 3.104.1–2 says nothing of this motive, but his chronology is compatible with it, cf. 3.87.

[93] p. 211 above.

[94] Hdt. 5. 102.1. The connection is an inference from 7.133.2, drawn e.g. by Stein on 7.133.

[95] Hdt. 8.129.

throne, since king Pleistoanax's return, it was said, had been procured by bribing the Pythia.[96] Athenian fortunes by contrast were bound up with the condition of Delos; it was perhaps the plague that first forced them to purify it, but when they extended the purification to the point of expelling the inhabitants, military failure followed, and the Delians were restored.[97] The Aeginetans were expelled from their island because of a murder on sacred ground.[98] Religious diagnoses become rarer in the post-Herodotean period (although several of the most interesting come in fact from Thucydides). The sense of a precise and direct link between crime and punishment, which allowed Herodotus to discuss carefully which of several offences a misfortune was caused by,[99] was probably giving way in the fourth century, even among the religious, to vaguer and thus less potent notions. We hear none the less that Spartan and Theban misfortunes in the first half of the century were due to violation of oaths, while Helice and Boura were obliterated by a tidal wave because they disrupted other communities' devotions to Poseidon.[100] The Spartan defeat at Leuctra was due to an ancient rape, which led to suicide; the culprits were individual Spartans, but stories that represent Spartans as sexual oppressors of dependent peoples are common, and seem to reflect on the Spartans as a community.[101] The distant cause was anyway not sufficient to overcome entirely the Spartan instinct to blame a king; men remembered now the oracle that warned against a lame kingship, in defiance of which Agesilaus had been appointed.[102] A plethora of ancient crimes, finally, was adduced to explain the destruction of Thebes by Alexander.[103] It is intriguing that the same event rebounded against the destroyer; com-

[96] Thuc. 1.128.1, 7.18.2, 5.16.1. For the last cf. 90 *FGrH* fr. 44.7 (from Xanthus?), drought afflicts Lydia under usurping king.
[97] Thuc. 5.1, 32.1. The Athenians also turned against Pericles in response to the plague, and indeed blamed him for it, but not, to our knowledge, on any supernatural level (Thuc. 2.59.1–2, 65.1–3, Plut. *Per.* 34.3–35).
[98] Hdt. 6.91.
[99] Hdt. 6.84.3, 7.133.2.
[100] p. 188 n. 244 and p. 176 n. 181 above.
[101] Leuctra: p. 198 above. Stories: Plut. *Cim.* 6.4–6, *Narr. Am.* 773f–774a.
[102] Plut. *Ages.* 30.1.
[103] Arr. *Anab.* 1.9.7. – medism, destruction of Plataea, proposal to destroy Athens. On delayed punishment of states cf. Isoc. 8.120.

munal responsibility here appropriately gives way once again to that of the king.[104]

From all this evidence there emerges a conclusion that must be surprising to anyone whose picture of communal pollution is based on the opening of *Oedipus Tyrannus*. What is commonly and loosely referred to as collective religious responsibility has two theoretically distinct forms. One makes the crime or impurity of any individual member of a community a danger to the whole, while by the other it is for the offences of its representatives or masters that the citizen body suffers.[105] The former is the doctrine of the *Tetralogies*, which ascribe crop-failure to the presence of a single unpunished murderer in the state;[106] it also appears constantly in connection with sea voyages. The latter, however, has turned out to be the basis not merely for the conception of the scapegoat king, but also for the religious interpretation of communal disaster in general. Virtually no instance has emerged from either legendary or historical material of a collective misfortune blamed upon an ordinary individual's offences. This is a merely empirical observation – in principle, as the *Tetralogies* show, a cat may pollute a king as well as look at him – but not the less interesting for that. For this predominance of pollution from above, two explanations may be suggested. One relates to the size of communities and to synoecism. There is, perhaps, something ridiculous in the idea of a social group as large as classical Athens being punished for the offence of an individual member, unknown to virtually all of its many thousand inhabitants. In relation to a 'city' of the size envisaged by Hesiod, on the other hand, the proposition appears more reasonable; and the smaller the community becomes, the more reasonable it appears. Thus it is upon the other members of restricted and clearly defined social groups (those sharing a ship, or a sacrifice) that pollution is most likely to work its effects. If we had access to the deliberations of an afflicted deme, or phratry, we might find interpretations under consideration of just the kind that we miss for Athens as a

[104] Ephippus, 126 *FGrH* fr. 3, Plut. *Alex.* 13.4.

[105] Cf. D. Daube, *Studies in Biblical Law*, Cambridge, 1947, Ch. 4; also Douglas, 100: 'In general, we can distinguish beliefs which hold that all men are equally involved with the universe from beliefs in the special cosmic powers of selected individuals.'

[106] Above, p. 129; cf. too Pl. *Leg.* 910b.

whole. It is interesting that two towns which do envisage an ordinary individual's conduct affecting the weather (one, it is true, only in Plutarch's day) are both of comparatively small size. The people of Dodona asked their god: 'Is it because of some human's impurity that we are suffering this storm?'[107] Plutarch tells how it was normal practice 'when an earth tremor or drought or other portent had occurred, for the Tanagraeans to investigate and take a lot of trouble about finding out whether a woman had approached the place (shrine of a 'woman-hating' hero) without being detected.'[108] Full collective responsibility, therefore, perhaps properly belongs to life before synoecism. We saw, however, that even Hesiod, man of Ascra, envisages chiefly the injustice of the kings as threatening the natural order, and this leads to the second explanation. The individual is held in check by a tight mesh of human sanctions. The king is not; nor is the community. Supernatural constraints are therefore imposed upon the king (his subjects will remind him of them). In the same way, divine punishment forces the community to adhere to its own general ideals, however free and tempted it might be to violate them in a particular case. There was no one to avenge the rights of the helot suppliants, slain by the Spartans in violation of sanctuary, except Poseidon. The Spartans, however, acknowledged that he had done so.

This ideal of communal moral responsibility is vividly conveyed in two passages in Aeschylus. In the *Supplices*, the daughters of Danaus invoke upon Argos the characteristic blessings – thriving crops, successful births, freedom from disease and civil strife – that mark the just and prosperous city. A similar prayer for Athens is uttered by the Eumenides.[109] Both occur at moments when pollution, whose counterpoise they are, has just been averted, and in both cases the pollution would have been public not merely in effect but also in origin. Pelasgus points out to the Danaids that 'you are not sitting at the hearth of my palace (but at public altars) . . . the (danger of) pollution extends to the whole city . . .'[110] and it is in democratic assembly

[107] *SEG* xix 427.
[108] *Quaest. Graec.* 40, 300f. Note too the story in Ael. *VH* 8.5: a fleet is held in harbour by contrary winds, and seers declare that pollution is the cause.
[109] *Supp.* 659–709, *Eum.* 902–87.
[110] 365 f.

that their admission to the city is agreed. The anger of the Eumenides, which Athena with difficulty allays, extends to the Athenians as a whole, because Orestes has been acquitted by a court representing the entire citizen body. The threat of communal affliction is the price at which, in Aeschylus' impressive vision, the possibility of a truly communal well-being is secured.

A final observation reverts to scapegoats; or rather, the apparent absence of scapegoats in situations of the kind that have been discussed. Eagerly though persons guilty of disaster on the human level were sought out, and possible though it was theoretically to ascribe supernatural afflictions, too, to guilty humans, a certain fatalism is in fact apparent. This is not a fatalism of inaction, since supplications to the gods were of course made, but a cut-off point in the search for a moral and religious explanation of human misfortune, a willingness to accept a certain randomness in 'acts of God'. In a late fiction, Delphi urges a plague-stricken city to seek out 'the impious one';[111] in the *Oedipus Tyrannus*, too, the oracle institutes a hunt. In any Greek community there were no doubt impious individuals enough, lurking undetected or unprosecuted, who could have been sought out in time of crisis and expelled. In historical practice, however, oracles seem to have been more likely to urge communities to set up a statue of Apollo than to drive out the impious one. If the inquiries, just mentioned, of the Dodonaeans and Tanagraeans had revealed pollution as the cause of disturbance, some kind of hunt for the guilty party would perhaps have been started; but it seems equally possible that the recipients would merely have used the information to determine the appropriate form of expiatory sacrifice. Athenians were in many contexts urged vehemently to 'punish the guilty'; but Pericles in time of plague was perhaps merely reiterating an accepted ideal in encouraging them to accept 'what came from the gods' with fortitude.[112]

---

[111] (Plut.) *Parallela Minora* 310b.
[112] Thuc. 2.64.2.

10

PURITY AND SALVATION

Socrates in the *Phaedo* is made to uphold a radical dualism of mind and body. The philosopher cannot but welcome death, because then he will be able to achieve that spiritual contemplation of spiritual reality which he has, indeed, always aspired to, but which the body with its incessant demands and deceptions has barred him from attaining. The separation of body and soul in death does not in itself lead to such a vision. Reality is pure and unadulterated, but during its sojourn in the body the soul may acquire a taint of corporeality that is not dissolved even in death. If he is to enjoy the heavenly vision, the philosopher, while still alive, must seek to escape this taint by resisting the intellectual and emotional demands of life in the body. This purposeful asceticism is repeatedly expressed in the language of purification. The soul that has shunned the body and turned in upon itself escapes 'pure' at death, dragging nothing corporeal with it; but the soul that has been a slave of sensation departs 'polluted', so enmeshed in the physical that it can still be seen as it flits, a spectre, around the place where its body lies buried.[1] Again and again Socrates speaks in the same way of the need to approach death with a soul 'purified' from bodily desire.[2] Such language is by no means unknown elsewhere in Plato,[3] but in its concentration here is a distinctive feature of the *Phaedo*.

Plato is half playfully presenting abnormal doctrine in a familiar guise. The truism 'Religious law forbids the impure to

---

[1] 80d–81d.
[2] 65e–69d, 80d–83e, 108a–c, 113d (*post mortem* punishment as a catharsis), 114c (οἱ φιλοσοφίᾳ ἱκανῶς καθηράμενοι).
[3] *Cra.* 404a, *Resp.* 496d, 611c–d, *Leg.* 716e ἀκάθαρτος γὰρ τὴν ψυχὴν ὅ γε κακός. καθαρὸς δὲ ὁ ἐναντίος, παρὰ δὲ μιαροῦ δῶρα οὔτε ἀνδρ᾽ ἀγαθὸν οὔτε θεὸν ἔστιν ποτὲ τό γε ὀρθὸν δέχεσθαι. μάτην οὖν περὶ θεοὺς ὁ πολύς ἐστι πόνος τοῖς ἀνοσίοις … (mental pollution 777d, 872a, *Soph.* 230e), *Tht.* 177a, κάθαρσις τῆς ψυχῆς *Soph.* 227c: cf. Xen. *Symp.* 1.4. ἀνδράσιν ἐκκεκαθαρμένοις τὰς ψυχάς. The place of purity in Plato's thought cannot be considered here: cf. H. Perls, *Lexicon der Platonischen Begriffe*, Bern, 1973, 284–8; Moulinier, 323–410; H. J. Stukey, *The Conception of Purity in Plato*, diss. California, 1935 (*non vidi*); A. J. Festugière, *Contemplation et vie contemplative selon Platon*[2], Paris, 1950, 123–56.

touch the pure' is applied to the necessary conditions for contemplation of unadulterated reality. Purification becomes the
separation of the soul from the body, and, in place of water,
eggs, and the blood of pigs, its agents are self-restraint, justice,
courage, and intellectual activity itself.[4] The doctrine that Plato
has subjected to this idiosyncratic transposition seems to be
more specific than the normal requirement of every Greek
temple that the worshipper should approach the gods in a state
of purity. Plato is not referring to a temporary preparation for
ritual activity but to a way of life whose aim is purification.[5]
This purity is sought as a way of salvation; what matters is a
pure death, for which a pure life is only a preparation. Through
Plato we detect cults or doctrines that attributed to *katharmos* a
definite eschatological importance.

He himself indicates in one passage the source of his imagery.[6]
He has just argued that the moral virtues, truly understood, are
a form of purification from that anxious weighing of pains and
pleasures which is generally mistaken for virtue; he goes on to
suggest half-ironically that 'those who established our rites'
were hinting at this when they claimed that in Hades the
uninitiated would lie in mud, but those who were 'purified and
initiated' would live there with the gods. It seems clear that
Plato is referring here to doctrines associated with the Eleusinian mysteries,[7] though he may have had other rites in mind
too. It has, however, recently been shown that, by the end of the
fifth century at the latest, the public part of the 'Eleusinian'
promise was expounded in 'Orphic' poems.[8] This means that
any doctrine referred to by Plato in an Eleusinian context may
be Orphic in origin. But where one speaks of Orpheus one
cannot keep silent about Pythagoras. To discover the original
connection between purification and salvation it is necessary in
fact to consider all the cults that made promises about the afterlife to their adherents. It will also be necessary to define the
meaning of 'purification' in this context, and the techniques by
which it was achieved. What was such purification supposed to

[4] 67b, 67c, 69c.
[5] P. Boyancé, *REG* 54 (1941), 164 n. 3, cf. Burkert, *LS* 213, against Festugière, op.
cit., 123–8.
[6] 69c; but not 67c, on which see J. V. Luce, *CR* n.s. 1 (1951), 66–7.
[7] Note ἡμῖν, ἀμύητος. Doxography, Graf, 100 n. 30.
[8] Graf, *passim*, esp. 139–50.

efface? Sins of the present life, sins of a previous incarnation, ancestral sins, or simply an unexplained accumulation of impurity? Did it take the form of a single ritual release, lasting asceticism, or, as in Plato, moral purification? What connection existed between the familiar everyday cleansings of Greek religious life and the saving purification? Wholly clear answers, though, are not to be hoped for. It is perhaps the very imprecision of the concepts involved that makes 'purity' and 'purification' the potent religious metaphors that they are.

We begin with the mysteries of Eleusis. The evidence for purifications, abstinences, and requirements of purity in this context is extensive and varied.[9] A solemn proclamation by the hierophant excluded from the rites all those who were 'impure in hands or incomprehensible in speech'. Three days before the actual procession to Eleusis, all the candidates went down to the sea to bathe. It may well have been during the ensuing period that they were subject to restrictions: avoidance of natural pollutions, of certain foods, and probably also, although this is not explicitly attested, of sexual contact. On one day at least they were required to keep to their houses – a form of preparation for ritual activity that is hard to parallel in Greek religion. At some stage, too, they fasted, although the occasion and duration of this fast are uncertain. The 'mystic pig' which each candidate sacrificed 'on behalf of himself'[10] – an individual relation that is again distinctive – did not serve for purification in any strict sense, as its flesh was eaten,[11] but there were further

---

[9] Cf. Ginouvès, 376 ff. Proclamation: Foucart, 311. Bathing: Burkert, *HN* 285 n. 9. Restrictions: Arbesmann, 76 f., cf. Appendix 4. Natural pollutions: Porph. *Abst.* 4.16 p. 255.6. Eleusinian *hagneiai* perhaps lasted three days, Ar. *Pax* 151, 162 f., cf. Latte, *Kl. Schr.* 26. Keeping to houses: Arist. *Ath. Pol.* 56.4. Fast: Richardson on *Hymn. Hom. Cer.* 47.   [10] Schol. Ar. *Ach.* 747 – not 'instead of himself', as Burkert renders, *HN* 285.

[11] Ar. *Ran.* 338; on the mystic pig cf. Burkert, *HN* 284 with references, on its function Moulinier, 126–9, Ginouvès, 376 n. 7. For the inedibility of purificatory sacrifices see e.g. Ap. Rhod. 4.710, *LSS* 38 A 32,? *LSA* 79.19, p. 30 n. 65. The pig *katharmos* at the Andania mysteries (*LSCG* 65.66–8) cleansed the locale, not the mystai; it is distinguished from the sacrifice offered ὑπὲρ τοὺς πρωτομύστας (ibid.). The Eleusinian pig at most could have been a *katharmos* in the loose sense of p. 10 n. 42. Pl. *Resp.* 378a speaks of it as a sacrifice, stressing its cheapness. It is sometimes inferred from the reference to οἱ σπλαγχνεύοντες in the fragment of Eupatrid laws for the purification of suppliants that the cathartic animal could be eaten (356 *FGrH* fr.1). While that is not impossible, nothing shows that οἱ σπλαγχνεύοντες ate the same animal as was used for purification. Possibly, after the formal purification, representatives of the state admitted the suppliant by sharing a fresh sacrifice with him, just as children were admitted to the phratry through sacrifice.

ritual washings to be performed on the road to Eleusis and on arrival there;[12] we hear of a 'water-man: the purifier at Eleusis'.[13] These final cleansings were merely the culmination of a long series of preparations for the great revelation. In the classical period, no one could be admitted to the greater mysteries at Eleusis in the autumn without first having been initiated in the lesser mysteries at Agrai in the spring. Unfortunately, very little is known about the ceremonies at Agrai. The claim which is found in late sources that they were 'as it were a preliminary purification for the greater mysteries'[14] does not indicate anything about the content of the rites, as it is merely a way of saying that the one is a preparation for the other; other writers of the Christian period use different metaphors to make the same point.[15] Nor can we infer anything from a mention of 'purification in the Ilissus at the lesser mysteries', as this is very likely to have been a mere preliminary.[16] It is more important that in one tradition these rites are said to have been founded in order to cleanse Heracles from the killing of the Centaurs.[17] Interpreted literally, this would suggest that a specific ritual of purification from blood-guilt was performed at Agrai, but, despite a Samothracian analogy,[18] this seems implausible in a cult that excluded those 'with impure hands', and it has generally been felt that the Heracles story is an explanation for a more

[12] Washing at Rheitoi: Heysch. s.v. 'Ρειτοί. Stone maidens with lustral water outside *telestērion*: Mylonas, 202. Water-carriers built into propylaea: H. Hörmann, *Die Inneren Propyläen von Eleusis*, Berlin and Leipzig, 1932, 43 f. For lustral stoups in the Eleusinion at Athens see (Lys.) 6.52.

[13] Hesych. s.v. ὑδρανός (not attested epigraphically), cf. Mylonas, 236 n. 61. E. Simon, *Ath. Mitt.* 69/70 (1954–5), 45 ff. and, independently, N. Himmelmann-Wildschütz, *Theopleptos*, Marburg, 1957, 21–2 with n. 69, have shown that the so-called 'Kore as Hydranos' (e.g. Mylonas, Fig.70), basis of so much discussion of Eleusinian 'baptism', has nothing to do with lustration: cf. C. Picard, *RHR* 154 (1958), 129–45.

[14] Schol. Ar. *Plut.* 845, cf. Clem. Al. *Strom.* 4.3.1, p. 249.8 St.

[15] e.g. Clem. Al. *Strom.* 5.70.7, p. 373.23 St. (cited Deubner, 70 n. 10), where purification precedes the lesser mysteries, which impart 'teaching' in preparation for the pure experience of the greater (the distinction from Aristotle, fr.15). For further metaphorical references see Lobeck, 188 note h. Radical doubts about the neo-Platonists' knowledge of Eleusis in K. Dowden, *RHR* 197 (1980), 409–27.

[16] Polyaenus, *Strat.* 5.17.1.

[17] Diod. 4.14.3; for the purification cf. Plut. *Thes.* 30.5, Apollod. 2.5.12. On Heracles at Eleusis see most recently N. Robertson, *Hermes* 108 (1980), 274–99.

[18] Hesych. s.v. Κοίης. (For use of the 'fleece of Zeus' by the daduch see Sud. s.v. Διὸς κώδιον.) For the connection of the Cabiri with purification see schol. Theocr. 2.11/12; might the Samothracian 'confession' (Burkert, *GR* 423 n. 34) have led up to it?

general purification which all initiates had to undergo. Such a
rite seems to be illustrated by the well-known reliefs[19] which
show a veiled and seated Heracles, behind whom stands a
priestess, holding a winnowing-fan over his head or a torch at
his side. A scene to the left portrays Demeter enthroned in
splendour. Heracles seems to be undergoing a ritual of submissive 'sitting' of a kind that is common in initiations and for
which certain acts of the grieving Demeter in the *Homeric Hymn*
provide a prototype.[20] Formally this is a purification – the
'mystic torch' cleanses the sitting man, and the purificatory
'fleece of Zeus' is also to be seen on the reliefs – but its expressive
force clearly derives largely from the symbolism of admitting a
candidate to a new status by raising him up from his humble
posture. (The symbolism of the murder purification ceremony
was similar, and so the two could be assimilated in aitiology.)

We find therefore at Agrai (if the association of this rite with
Agrai is indeed correct[21]) an important rite of purification and
induction, the beginning for the initiate of the cycle that in the
fully developed form of the mysteries was only completed some
eighteen months later. But the ceremonies at Agrai, in addition
to this prospective purification, doubtless had substantial content of their own. They were, one source reports, 'an imitation of
the events concerning Dionysus'.[22]

It has seemed worth while to illustrate fairly fully, in this
celebrated case, the fastings, abstinences, and cleansings that
preceded a major sacral act. Such preparations are recorded
wherever a rite required the worshipper's deep psychological
involvement.[23] But it is important to stress that they were not
more than preparations. They were not directed against any

[19] Reproduced e.g. Mylonas, Figs. 83, 84; Deubner, Fig. 7; cf. *Antike Kunst* 13 (1970),
64–6. Bibliography in Richardson, 211–13, Burkert, *HN* 294 f., *Antike Kunst*, loc. cit.
[20] Cf. Burkert, *HN* 294 n. 10, 296 n. 16, also Dem. 18. 259 (note 'raising up'); *Hymn
Hom. Cer.* 192–6. On the analogy with murder purification see Appendix 6.
[21] Burkert, *HN* 296 denies the connection with Agrai because in *Hymn. Hom. Cer.* the
ceremony belongs to Eleusis. But the specific reference of the Heracles *aition* to Agrai
demands explanation; and for the possibility that the scenes on the Agrai frieze
depicted Heracles' initiation see Möbius, cited by Nilsson, *GGR* 668 n. 10. Possibly,
when Agrai and Eleusis mysteries were connected as lesser and greater, the preliminary
rite was transferred to Agrai to emphasize the link. If dissociated from Agrai, the rite
would have to be assigned to 'l'initiation préalable', cf. P. Roussel, *BCH* 54 (1930),
51–74.
[22] Steph. Byz. s.v. Ἄγρα, cf. Graf, 66–78
[23] Cf. p. 20 n. 9.

doctrinally specified pollution; they could be revealed – even the solemn sitting ceremony – to outsiders through sculpture or poetry. The initiate could not proceed to the revelation without them, but they did not in themselves contribute anything to his salvation.[24] They did, it is true, perhaps acquire a special symbolic importance in the eschatology of the cult. Those not initiated were condemned to lie in the underworld in mud; this might have been because they were 'unpurified'.[25] Another punishment that threatened them was eternal water-carrying; perhaps they were conceived as trying, in vain, to fetch the water for the purificatory bath that they never took.[26] But the punishments need not be interpreted in this way, and even if they are, this means only that the omitted purification, for the sake of a vivid image, became the symbol of the omitted initiation as a whole. (The punishments seem anyway to have entered the Eleusinian eschatology from outside.[27]) All the sources insist that the salvation of the initiate depended not on purity, a mere preliminary, but on what he saw and heard on the night of Boedromion 20 in the great hall of initiation.

When Plutarch wished to assure his wife that life did not finish with physical death, he reminded her of the 'tokens' not of Eleusis, but of the mysteries of Dionysus.[28] Definite proof that eschatological hopes could already attach to cults of Dionysus in the classical period was finally provided in 1974 by the publication of a gold leaf from Hipponium, dating from the end of the fifth century, which declares that the path to felicity in the

[24] So rightly Foucart, 289.
[25] Pl. *Resp.* 363c–d ('Musaeus and his son'), *Phd.* 69c, D.L. 6.39, Graf, 103–7 (who considers a specific connection with the rite of 'wiping off with mud').
[26] Pl. *Resp.* 363c–d, *Grg.* 493a–b, Paus. 10.31.9, Graf, 107–120; on the artistic evidence most recently E. Keuls, *The Water-Carriers in Hades*, Amsterdam, 1974, 34–41, 83–103 (with a novel interpretation). At most it was by secondary adaptation that the water-carrying was related to an omitted purification. In origin, it is just a form of frustrated activity, of a kind characteristic of underworld punishments (L. Radermacher, *Rh. Mus.* 63 (1908), 535 ff., Graf, 118 n. 118); the water-carriers are not filling a bath, but 'pouring into a pierced pithos' (proverbially futile), and for the main Eleusinian purification the initiate did not fetch water but went down to the sea to bathe.
[27] Cf. Pl. *Grg.* 493a ('some Sicilian or Italian'), and, on the mud, Graf, 107.
[28] *Cons. ad Uxor.* 611d.

afterlife is one trodden by 'initiates and bacchants'.[29] Dionysus
therefore demands a place in this discussion, particularly as he
is a god who in modern, though not ancient, descriptions is
often dubbed a 'purifier'.[30] In considering him, it will be necessary to take account of the diversity of forms in which he was
worshipped.[31] His place in the official religious and even civic
life of the city was as great as that of any other god; it is a
revealing detail that in Athens, in the sacred marriage at the
Anthesteria, he received as a bride the wife of the *archon basileus*
himself. But he was also the god who in myth came from
abroad, in defiance of the local king, and led away the women to
reckless revelry in the mountains. And while even maenadism,
for all its subversive character, by the fifth century belonged to
established religion, there also existed unofficial bands of initiates of Dionysus Bacchius who roamed the streets of Greek
towns in ecstasy. Such initiations were open to men (in public
worship, by contrast, there was no place for ecstatic males) and
the cult of this unofficial Dionysus was already important by the
fifth century throughout the Greek world.[32] The god honoured
in such diverse ways was of course the same Dionysus, differentiation being introduced at most by the addition of an
epithet, and the underlying unity is expressed in Euripides'
Bacchae, a play which constantly cuts across the divisions. It is
clear, none the less, that the southern Italian initiate's hopes
and fears for the afterlife were not necessarily shared by the
Athenian farmer, drunk and happy at the Anthesteria.

Of purification or abstinence in the ordinary civic cult, virtually nothing is known. The fourteen matrons who attended the
archon basileus' wife before her sacred marriage with Dionysus
had to swear that they were pure from intercourse and other

---

[29] *SEG* xxvi 1139, cf. most recently S.G. Cole, *GRBS* 21 (1980), 223–38. On
Dionysiac scenes in funerary contexts cf. Cole, op. cit., 237, Burkert, *GR* 438 f.
Dionysus' early connection with Orphism has been confirmed by the new evidence
from Olbia, on which see F. Tinnefeld, *ZPE* 38 (1980), 67–71; W. Burkert, 'Neue
Funde zur Orphik', *Informationen zum altsprachlichen Unterricht* 2 (1980), 36–8; M.L.
West, *ZPE* 45 (1982), 17–29.

[30] e.g. Farnell, iv, 300, P. Boyancé, *REA* 40 (1938), 171.

[31] Cf. e.g. M. Detienne, in *Orfismo*, 56, 228.

[32] Hdt. 4.79 (Scythia), Ar. *Lys.* 1, *Ran.* 357, Pl. *Phd.* 69c, *LSS* 120 (Cumae); and on the
thiasos of Anacreon see W. Slater, *Phoenix* 32 (1978), 185–94. On hellenistic maenadism
see now A. Henrichs, *HSCP* 82 (1978), 121–60.

polluting contacts, but it is the nature of the ritual rather than of the god that imposes this requirement.[33] On the purity of the Maenad, a passage in the *Bacchae* offers some information, but it is hard to interpret. It comes in the *parodos*, which in this play seems to reflect the form of a cult hymn.[34] 'Blessed is he who – happy man – understanding the rites of the gods is pure in life and enters into the spirit of the revel band, dancing in the mountains with holy purifications.' The first uncertainty concerns the 'holy purifications'; it arises partly because, in Euripides' lyric manner, their syntactical relation to the rest of the sentence is very loose. A stray item of evidence attests the unsurprising fact that women might wash in preparation for Dionysiac rites,[35] but, if the reference here is to preliminary physical purification, the conjunction 'dancing in the mountains with holy purifications' is puzzling. Another possibility is that mountain dancing is itself the 'holy purification'. In myth, the maenads are freed by celebrating the rites of Dionysus from the madness that has been caused by rejecting him.[36] On an everyday level, too, Dionysiac revelry 'breaks the rope of heavy cares'.[37] It is likely that the Corybantic rites, which similarly cured mental disturbance by homoeopathic means, could be spoken of as a 'purification';[38] and observation of phenomena of this kind formed the basis of Aristotle's famous cathartic theory

[33] Above, p. 85.

[34] 72–7. In addition to the commentaries see A. J. Festugière, *Eranos* 54 (1956), 72 ff. (= *Études de religion grecque et hellenistique*, Paris, 1972, 66 ff.).

[35] Paus. 9.20.4.

[36] Cf. Boyancé, 64–73, Moulinier, 116–18. But in the historical period there is, *pace* Boyancé, little evidence for a healing Dionysus (Dodds, 95 n. 87). His title 'doctor' (Ath. 1. 22e, 36a–b) he owes to the therapeutic value of wine.

[37] Pind. fr. 248.

[38] E. Howald, *Hermes* 54 (1919), 200 disputed it; but I assume with I. M. Linforth (*Univ. Cal. Publ. in Class. Phil.* 13 (1944–50), 163–72) that the homoeopathic *katharmoi* and *teletai* that release from madness of Pl. *Phdr.* 244e are Bacchic/Corybantic. Cf. Croissant, 66. It is, however, possible that the expression 'purifications and initiations' really does refer to two stages, so that the ecstatic dancing is distinct from the *katharmos*. Pl. *Euthyd.* 277d attests for the Corybantes the often cathartic rite of *thronōsis*; LSA 23.8 speaks of 'washing' the candidate. Schol. Pind. *Pyth.* 3.139b refers to 'the mother' as καθάρτρια τῆς μανίας; in Diod 3.58.2 more generally Cybele invented purifications for sick animals and children. To appeal to authors who were themselves directly or indirectly influenced by the famous Aristotelian theory of *katharsis* is simply misleading (as e.g. Serv. ad *Georg.* 1.166, 2.389 *Liberi patris sacra ad purgationem animae pertinebant*, on which see R. Turcan, *RHR* 158 (1960), 129–44; or the passage of Aristid. Quint. cited by Dodds, 95 n. 87).

of tragedy, although it was in terms of medical purification that he interpreted them.[39] If this view of the holy purifications is correct, they are a release from anxiety or madness rather than from guilt, and immediate psychological well-being is more likely to be their aim than a better lot in the afterlife. On the more literal view, of course, they are reduced to mere preliminaries.

The expression 'is pure in life' is less ambiguous, but more surprising. Temporary rules of purity in preparation for specific rituals are common in Greek religion, and it would not be strange to find some imposed upon the maenad. A special 'life', by contrast, is the distinctive mark of the esoteric Orphic and Pythagorean movements. A famous fragment of Euripides' *Cretans* has sometimes been compared, in which the chorus of initiates explain how they have 'led a pure life' from the time they were 'consecrated and called bacchants'. 'I wear clothes all of white, and shun the birth (?and death) of mortals; tombs I do not approach, and I guard against eating food that comes from living creatures.'[40] That indeed is 'purity in life', but it is hard to believe that the ordinary maenad – Alexander's mother, as it might be – observed such restrictions. Even a less rigorous regime can scarcely be reconciled with the general outlook of the chorus of the *Bacchae*, for whom true religion and true wisdom are to avoid excessive aspirations and the exaggerated subtleties of intellect, and, accepting the values of the simple man, to relish the innocent pleasures of this life.[41] Distinctive rules of life, by contrast, separate the worshipper from the simple man, and do not seem to be observed in Greek culture except as a means to an eschatological end, in which Euripides' maenads show elsewhere no interest. The ideal of 'purity in life' can be reduced to the familiar, if it is interpreted as a general avoidance of offence against the gods rather than the observance of specific ritual prohibitions,[42] but the verb that is used, *hagisteuō*, normally has a precise application.[43] It looks as if Euripides has here derived a tint in his portrait of the Bacchae

---

[39] Arist. *Pol.* 1342a 7–11, cf. Croissant, 74 ff.
[40] Fr. 79 Austin.
[41] 370–432.
[42] Cf. Soph. *OT* 864 f.
[43] In a Dionysiac context again (Dem.) 59.78.

from initiatory cults, which did, perhaps, foster eschatological hopes, rather than from traditional maenadism.[44] If this is so, the possibility arises that the purifications too had a significance beyond that of mental release.[45]

With private initiatory cults of Dionysus we have reached or at least come near to the world of the gold tablets. (These are leaves of gold, inscribed with verses about the afterlife, that have been found in what are obviously the graves of initiates of a cult.) But since the tablets also show in crucial respects the influence of Orphic or Pythagorean teaching, these two movements will have to be considered before reverting to the Orphic–Bacchic rites. Well-known problems of method at once present themselves. No sure criterion exists for distinguishing early and late elements within Pythagorean and Orphic beliefs, nor for drawing a clear line of demarcation between the two schools. On the second question, the traditional tug-of-war between pan-Orphism and pan-Pythagoreanism has given way of late to a recognition that coincidences between the two doctrines are probably more important than divergences. Ion of Chios could ascribe an Orphic poem to Pythagoras, and Herodotus probably said that Orphic rites were really Pythagorean.[46] But similarity does not mean identity, and a further complication

[44] Cf. Boyancé, 83 n. 1, J. P. Guepin, *The Tragic Paradox*, Amsterdam, 1968, 234–6; A. Henrichs, *ZPE* 4 (1969), 238 n. 54.

[45] For completeness' sake, a few more scraps of evidence for *katharmoi* in the cult of Dionysus should be mentioned here. (1) There was a proverb Λέρνη κακῶν, which was variously explained (what seems to be the true origin, 'a bottomless pit of evils', was missed). These explanations show either that purifications were performed in the Lernaean Lake (Strabo 8.6.8, p. 371), or that offscourings were thrown into it (Apostolius 10.57, Zenobius 4.86 etc.). As the Lernaean lake was stagnant, full of water-snakes, and treacherous to the swimmer (Frazer on Paus. 2.37.5) it is more likely to have been a receptacle for *katharmata* than place of *katharmoi*. If this is right, there is no reason to connect these *katharmata* with the mystery of Dionysus' *anodos* which seems to have been celebrated there (Plut. *De Is. et Os.* 364f, Nilsson, *GF* 288–90). (2) The chorus in the *Antigone* call on Dionysus to come καθαρσίῳ ποδί to rescue the city (1144). This reveals nothing about the cult of Dionysus. The chorus, needing purification, turn to their city's greatest god (cf. Soph. *OT* 210) to supply it: a Pylian would have invoked Poseidon. (3) Even if Dionysus' leap into the sea at Hom. *Il.* 6.135–6 does reflect an initiatory rite of immersion (H. Jeanmaire, *Couroi et Courètes*, Lille, 1939, 336), its character is not one of purification. (On leaps into the sea cf. Ginouvès, 417 ff.) (4) The great purifier Melampus had Dionysiac connections (Hdt. 2.49.2, Paus. 1.43.5). (5) For a later period note *SEG* xxviii 841.3.

[46] D.L. 8.8, Hdt. 2.81 (long text); cf. Guthrie, *OGR* 216–21, Dodds 171, n. 95, Nilsson, *Gnomon* 28 (1956), 21, Burkert, *LS* 125–32, Graf, 92–4. A fine formulation in Burkert, *GR* 445.

arises from the fact that Empedocles, most tangible proponent
of a doctrine of salvation, was a man of independent thought
and imagination. We do not know whether he invented a crucial notion like that of the crime of the *daimōn*, or where he
derived it from. He will here be associated with Orphism, since
that expiation of guilt on which he insists is better attested as an
Orphic than as a Pythagorean preoccupation; but it would be
little less plausible to cite Empedocles as proof of the importance of guilt in early Pythagorean sensibility.[47]

Pythagoras subjected his followers to a code of restrictions
unique in Greek life. This it was that made such a profound
impression on all outsiders, and proved irresistible to comic
poets. He also taught a doctrine of metempsychosis; its exact
form is irrecoverable, but it must have allowed some scope for
the individual's conduct in this life to influence the form of his
next incarnation, or the 'Pythagorean life' would lose most of its
point.[48] Indeed, when Ion of Chios says of Pherecydes, 'Thus,
for his manliness and decency, he is enjoying a pleasant life even
after his death – if Pythagoras is truly a sage', the distinctive
doctrine of metempsychosis has disappeared from view, and
Pythagoreanism seems to be seen merely as a way of securing a
happier portion in a conventional afterlife, much like initiation
in the mysteries.[49] On the other hand, we cannot be sure to what
extent the thought of last things really was a daily concern of the
Pythagoreans; and it is clear that many of the rules that made
up the Pythagorean life had already existed in some form in
Greek culture, and were at most reapplied by Pythagoras for
eschatological ends.

The collection of rules near the end of the *Works and Days* is a
particularly relevant parallel.[50] Apart from their implications
for Pythagoras, it is worth pausing over them because of their
intrinsic interest for our theme. The Hesiodic, like the Pythagorean, rules provide guidance on trivial and undignified areas of
daily existence: nail-cutting, washing, excretion. Both are often

[47] Dodds, 169 n. 81, Burkert, *LS* 133 n. 72 and Zuntz, 265, however, associate him
with Pythagoras: cf. M. L. West, *Early Greek Philosophy and the Orient*, Oxford, 1971,
233–5.
[48] Burkert, *LS* 133–5.
[49] Fr. 30 West, *ap.* D.L. 1.120. Cf. the fragment of Aristophon in D.L. 8.38 (= 58
Diels/Kranz E 3).
[50] 724–59.

cast in a distinctive form, a rule followed by a curt explanation which is usually a warning of danger: 'Don't eat or wash from unconsecrated pots: a penalty follows on that' (Hesiod), 'Don't turn round at a boundary: the Erinyes are behind you' (Pythagoras).[51] The same form appears later in other magical warnings: 'Don't wear a black robe: for black belongs to death' (epilepsy purifiers), 'Gather the fruit of the wild rose from windward; otherwise there is danger to the eyes' (herbalists).[52] Another important similarity is that the Hesiodic rules are not isolated superstitions but are grouped together as a unified guide to conduct; thus there exists a 'Hesiodic life', rudimentary precursor (on the traditional chronology) of the Pythagorean and Orphic lives. There even appears in Hesiod the figure of the 'godlike man' – not, it is true, in a very godlike posture.[53] The ordinary individual can, it is implied, approach the condition of the godlike man by obedience to the rules. A kind of goal is therefore presented, even though there is no indication of the advantages enjoyed by the godlike man, and no hint that they relate to any world but this.

If the verses are Hesiod's, Pythagoras was perpetuating and developing a very ancient tradition. The very features, however, that make the comparison most interesting – the presence in Hesiod of a 'life', and a 'divine man' – do perhaps bring the ascription into doubt. There is no difficulty in supposing that the prophet of work, piety, and justice should also have felt scruples about urinating while facing the sun,[54] but it would be surprising for him to see the avoidance of this kind of thing as the distinctive mark of a 'divine man'. These rules find parallels in sacred books of the East, the *Laws of Manu*,[55] for instance, and the areas of concern that they reveal – sexuality, washing, bodily functions, purity of kitchen utensils – are commonplace in many anthropological discussions of pollution. Closely comparable evidence from the classical period is hard to find. It

[51] Iambl. *Protr.* 21.
[52] Hippoc. *Morb. Sacr.* 142.23 J., 1.17 G. (the explanations in this section of *Morb. Sacr.* seem to represent a curious blend of the original magical sanctions and rationalizing glosses by the Hippocratic); Theophr. *Hist. Pl.* 9.8.5. The form is parodied in Plato Comicus, fr. 173.
[53] 731. West interprets θεῖος here as = θεουδής, but admits this to be unique.
[54] West's introductory note to *Op.* 724–59.
[55] Cf. esp. 4.45–50, referred to by West on 727–32, 757.

would be most important to know whether a lively interest in such rules was endemic in archaic Greek peasant life, as seems to follow if the ascription to Hesiod is accepted, or something cultivated in restricted circles as a form of differentiation from the ungodlike herd. Unfortunately, authorship, date, and social context of the verses remain most uncertain.[56] Several of the Hesiodic rules have already been mentioned in other contexts. They begin with a warning against pouring libations with unwashed hands; there are also regulations to protect the hearthfire from contamination by sexuality, the male from contamination by the female, and to prevent dangerous contact between death and procreation.[57] Nine lines are given up to rules about urination and excretion. These were, of course, impure activities, and it is plausible that most of the Hesiodic principles were observed by properly trained Greeks, but no other texts show the same emphatic and explicit preoccupation. Caution is required with other bodily offscourings too: 'Do not cut the dry from the green (i.e. finger nails) at a festival.'[58] Here it is the sacred occasion that demands respect, but the sun, hearthfire, rivers and springs also require particular protection from the bodily processes. This concern for the purity of the elements perhaps suggests Persian religious sensibility, for instance, rather than Greek, and external influence is not to be excluded; but once again it is the tone and emphasis that cause surprise rather than the fundamental value, since fire is, for all Greeks, an especially pure element, rivers are divine, and springs must be guarded against various forms of contamination.[59] The claim that 'The gods are angry with the man who crosses a river "unwashed in badness and in hands", and give him sufferings afterwards', is particularly striking.[60] Washing before crossing a river is otherwise unattested in Greece, but

[56] The main linguistic difficulty is in 726, cf. West ad loc.

[57] Cf. pp. 76, 103, 53 above.

[58] 742 f., also Pythagorean, cf. West ad loc. For later antiquity see Petron. *Sat.* 104–5: hair and nails should never be cut at sea, except during a storm (when, clearly, pollution acquires healing power).

[59] Cf. *LSS* 4,50; *LSCG* 152; *IG* XII 5. 569; *SEG* xiii 521. 180–202; Pl. *Leg.* 845d–e; above, p. 230 n. 131; Paus. 3.25.8. Chrysippus praised Hesiod's rule, Plut. *de Stoic. Rep.* 1045a. Persian respect for rivers, Hdt. 1.138.2; the rule of Hes. *Op.* 739 contravenes it, as West notes.

[60] 740 f. A subjective sense for κακότης (= κακὸς εἶναι) seems inescapable here (but see Zuntz 229–232).

is a logical enough requirement granted the two premisses that rivers are divine, and that gods should be approached in purity. The idea of being 'unwashed in badness and in hands', by contrast, is singular, and not in expression alone. On the one hand, it includes moral badness of some kind within the concept of pollution; on the other, it seems to treat such badness as effaceable by washing. This is a purification from guilt like that preached by Empedocles, though without eschatological implications. Here too the ascription to Hesiod, if accepted, has surprising implications.

Other rules in the little collection relate not to avoidance of dirt but to the ordering of experience in a more general sense. There is a warning, for instance, against eating from unconsecrated pots. Between these rules and those that more specifically concern purity no distinction is drawn; 'God is indignant at' all such offences alike, or they are 'not good'. It has accordingly been claimed, since the characteristic vocabulary of pollution is absent, that the concept itself is alien to 'Hesiod'.[62] But, though he speaks of a broad set of inauspicious acts rather than a sharply defined category of *miasmata*, several of these inauspicious acts closely resemble the *miasmata* of classical times, while the idea of metaphysical taint is present in the threat posed by bodily emissions to fire and the sun. Complicated purifications are not prescribed, but, as we saw, water is credited with the power of removing badness as well as dirt. By many criteria the Hesiodic rules show more sensitivity to the threat of pollution than do classical authors. 'Do not expose yourself when you are stained with seed before your hearth', he warns. For this incompatibility between sexuality and the pure fire there is a possible parallel in Hipponax, but none later;[63] by the fifth century, Greeks had probably ceased to be troubled about contamination of this kind.

The Pythagorean *symbola* or *acousmata*[64] resemble the

[62] Rohde, 317 n. 70.

[63] p. 77 above.

[64] F. Boehm, *De symbolis Pythagoreis*, diss. Berlin, 1905. (I quote some of the symbols in what follows by their number in Boehm's collection.) Comprehensive bibliography and masterly discussion in Burkert, *LS* 166–92. On the authenticity of individual symbols note Burkert's formula, 188: 'It is like a gravel pile; there is no pebble of which we can say that it must be primitive rock, but any single one may be.'

Hesiodic code of life in containing a number of rules of purity, without recognizing a distinctive category of pollutions among the various dangers against which they warn. The range of their concerns is very wide. Some warn against magical dangers: 'Do not wear a ring'; 'Do not stir the fire with a knife'; 'Do not step over a broom'; 'When you get up in the morning, erase the marks of your body on the bed.'[65] Some protect from those spirits and demons who were ubiquitous in the Pythagorean world. 'Do not pick up scraps that fall from the table; they belong to the heroes.'[66] To approach the gods in the right condition and the right way was important; temples should be entered in clean clothing, barefoot, and from the right.[67] Above all there was a concern with partition, with not confounding man and god, dead and living, sacred and profane. 'Pour libations from the edge of the cup'; the explanation given, 'so that men and gods may not drink from the same part', is no doubt correct.[68] 'Do not cut your hair or your nails at a festival'; nails and hair are dead matter, and their cutting suits a funeral more than a feast.[69] Functions are not to be confused: 'Do not eat from a chair' (but from a table), 'Do not wipe a chair with a torch' (an ancient torch was rather like a broom), 'Don't use cedar, laurel, myrtle, cypress or oak to cleanse your body or clean your teeth: they are for honouring the gods.'[70]

Anthropological evidence shows that apparently trivial rules of conduct may assume startling importance because they derive from principles that are essential to a particular society's ordering of the world. Hawaiians are disgusted by the European habit of lying now on and now under the same blanket, because it transgresses the fundamental opposition of the above and the below.[71] The case of an Eskimo girl, who was banished for persistently eating summer foods in winter, has become

---

[65] Nn. 22, 33, 31, 34 Boehm.

[66] N. 19. On Pythagorean demonology cf. Burkert, *Gnomon* 36 (1964), 563–7.

[67] Nn. 1–3.

[68] N. 8, Iambl. *VP* 84, cf. Hom. *Il.* 16. 225–7. Cf. D.L. 8.34, sacred fish not to be eaten, 'for men and gods should not have the same privileges any more than masters and slaves.'

[69] N. 49.

[70] Nn. 38, 36, 28.

[71] Lévi-Strauss, 144 f. (with further examples), who speaks of 'meticulous rigour in the practical application of a logical system'.

notorious.[72] Parallels like these may help us to see the Pythagorean rules, too, as deriving from principles of order. The *symbola*, however, are not the norms of a whole society, but the refinements adopted by a restricted group; as their name, 'tokens, passwords', indicates, they mark off members of the group from outsiders. Some of the rules of purity seem to have this differentiating function. 'Don't dip your fingers in a lustral water stoup or wash in a bath house; it's not certain if the other people who use them are pure.'[73] Thus traditional conceptions of ritual and physical purity are rejected, in purity's own name. Images of the gods were not to be worn by Pythagoreans, because they might be brought into contact with polluting objects;[74] but to wear a ring with a god's portrait was probably in conventional terms an act of piety. The rule 'Do not kill (even) a flea in a temple'[75] is an oblique reproach to the traditions that prescribed the sacrifice of far nobler animals on sacred ground. One source states, not implausibly, that Pythagoreans avoided all contact with birth and death. If so, they regarded themselves, like priests, as too godlike to endure even those contacts with natural processes that the fact of being human, with mortal friends and kin, would normally impose.[76] About sexuality the *symbola* are surprisingly silent, but a strong tradition credits Pythagoras with insisting, amid the loose-living Greeks of Italy, on the value of reciprocal marital fidelity.[77]

This reaction against traditional religion could have two forms which, though apparently opposite in intention, served the same end. One was that of outright rejection.[78] By their refusal to eat animal flesh, the Pythagoreans (whatever the attitude of the master himself) isolated themselves from central institutions of social and even political life. The other was the reapplication of traditional elements in a way that transformed their meaning.[79] We find this in particular in connection with

[72] M. Douglas, *Implicit Meanings*, London, 1975, 244.
[73] Nn. 44–5 Boehm, Iambl. *VP* 83.
[74] N. 9.
[75] N. 6.
[76] Alexander Polyhistor in D.L. 8.33. Cf. p. 52 above, and Eur. *Cretans* fr. 79 Austin.
[77] See Burkert, 178 n. 94, also D.L. 8.21.
[78] Cf. D. Sabbatucci, *Saggio sul misticismo greco*, Rome, 1965, 69–83; M. Detienne, 'Les chemins de le déviance: Orphisme, Dionysisme et Pythagorisme', in *Orfismo*, 49–79.
[79] Burkert, *LS* 190 f., comparing Calvinism. Cf. Turner, 92–5.

the dietetic regulations. Though details are in doubt, it is almost certain that Pythagoras must have known restrictions attached to particular existing cults,[80] and he seems to have followed not only their form but also their content: 'Pythagoras told his followers to abstain from . . . and everything else that people conducting sacred rites tell the worshippers to avoid.'[81] I would be difficult to find any single food that was definitely first forbidden by Pythagoras. What was apparently his innovation, and a drastic one, was to change temporary abstinence, confined to the period preceding a ritual act, into permanent rules of life on which salvation depended. The same is true to some extent even of the rejection of animal sacrifice, since bloodless cults and altars had always existed, and the traditional ritual itself insisted that sacrifice was a crime, although a necessary one. Avoidance of natural pollutions, too, was merely the extension to a whole community of behaviour that was probably traditionally prescribed for priests.

Abstinence of various kinds was obviously integral to the Pythagorean way of life. Whether its goal would have been conceived and spoken of as precisely a 'purification' is less clear. Porphyry and Iamblichus in their biographies do indeed present purification as the key to salvation, the hub around which all Pythagoras' religious and philosophical interests revolved,[82] but these neo-Pythagoreans were also neo-Platonists, and the *Phaedo* has decisively affected their whole conception of the master. Similar doubts, except that the corrupting influence is here Aristotle rather than Plato, attach to the report that 'He believed music . . . could make a great contribution to health. He made a very serious use of this form of purification (that was his expression for musical medicine).'[83] It is likely enough that

[80] See Appendix 4.
[81] D.L. 8.33.
[82] Porph. *VP* 12,45, and passages cited in Boyancé, 86 n. 3; Iambl. *VP* 31, 68, 70, 74, 228, 'Hipparchus' in Iambl. *VP* 75–8. Also unacceptable as evidence are the purified and unpurified souls of Alexander Polyhistor in D.L. 8.31 – the next sentence betrays Platonic influence (p. 217 n. 54). Pythagoras demands purity 'both of body and soul' in Diod. 10.9.6.
[83] Iambl. *VP* 110, 68; cf. Aristoxenus, fr. 26 Wehrli. Porphyry speaks of musical therapy, but without the term *katharsis*, *VP* 30, 32–3. For Aristotle's influence on Aristoxenus see M. Pohlenz, *Die Griechische Tragödie*[2], Göttingen, 1954, ii, 195 f. As for the biographers, neo-Platonism from the time of Plutarch knew, though it could not entirely accept, the Aristotelian theory of *katharsis*: I. Bywater, *Aristotle on the Art of Poetry*, Oxford, 1909, 157–9, Croissant, 113–34.

Pythagoras used the mystical power of harmony to cure both body and mind,[84] but if he really anticipated Aristotle in seeing this process as a purification, it is surprising that Plato said nothing of a theory that would have been relevant to his rejection of the arts.[85] Such a purification would anyway, as described, have no eschatological significance. More tempting, because it helps to reconcile Pythagoras' religious and scientific concerns, is the theory that he saw intellectual activity as a form of purification from the ties of body, a mental catharsis directly beneficial to the destiny of the soul.[86] The idea of philosophy as death to this world, memorably expounded by Plato in the *Phaedo*, would then be Pythagorean. If this is correct, Pythagorean purification was a high metaphysical thing. That is not impossible; but it is not clear that Empedocles, for instance, another scientist who was also a mystic, looked on his scientific activities in this light.[87]

Secure evidence that Pythagoras saw purification as the way of salvation is of course provided if Empedocles is enlisted in the school. This, as we noted, is a very uncertain issue. It is, certainly, plausible that freedom from the pollution of animal sacrifice was much talked of by Pythagoreans, as by Empedocles, as a necessary condition of prosperous reincarnation. One tradition even claimed that the master shunned butchers and hunters.[88] The doctrines that man is bad, pleasure an evil, and 'We are here to be punished' are attested as Pythagorean, though not in early sources, but there is no evidence that a specific original pollution was identified from which man re-

[84] Cf. L. Deubner, *Neue Jahrb.* 43 (1919), 388–90 on the medical paean, Boyancé 35–8 on epodes; on the 'scientific' adoption of such methods Edelstein, *AM* 235 f., Dodds, 80.

[85] M. Pohlenz, *Gött. Nachr.* 1920, 172 f. = *Kleine Schriften* ii, Hildesheim, 1965, 466 f.; *contra*, E. Howald, *Hermes* 54 (1919), 187–207; F. Wehrli, *MH* 8 (1951), 36–62 esp. 56 ff. = *Theoria und Humanitas*, Zürich, 1972, 177–206.

[86] A. Döring, *Archiv f. Geschichte der Philosophie* 5 (1892), 505; cf. recently Guthrie, *HGP* i, 199, 204 f. Criticism in Burkert, *LS* 211–13; and cf. H. B. Gottschalk, *Heraclides of Pontus*, Oxford, 1980, 23–33. This, naturally, is the neo-Platonist interpretation: see e.g. Porph. *VP* 46. For a modern parallel cf. Edmund Gosse, *Father and Son*, ed. J. Hepburn, Oxford, 1974, 7: Philip Gosse, FRS and Plymouth Brother, valued scientific study partly because it 'kept the student "out of the world" '.

[87] E. Hussey, however, *The Presocratics* London, 1972, 71 points to B 110.

[88] But on the problem of Pythagoras' own attitude to meat-eating see Burkert, *LS* 180–2, Guthrie, *HGP* i, 187–95; against original full vegetarianism Nilsson, *HTR* 28 (1935), 206 = *Op. Sel.* ii, 657. Butchers: Eudoxus in Porph. *VP* 7.

quired purification.[89] One point that seems clear amid the general uncertainty is that Pythagoras offered his followers no short cuts through rites of lustration. Special kinds of physical purification are nowhere mentioned, and all the sources agree that it was adherence to a whole way of life that made a Pythagorean. The watchword of that way of life is perhaps as likely to have been 'piety' or 'harmony' as 'purity'.[90]

With Empedocles, Orphism, and the gold tablets the idea of deliverance through purification becomes inescapable. Empedocles' great religious poem was entitled *Katharmoi*; purifications were the main concern of the Orpheus-initiator mentioned by Plato, and the soul assures Persephone through the gold plates that it has entered the underworld in purity.[91] In each case specific pollutions are envisaged that require cleansing. Empedocles himself is a *daimōn*, banished from Olympus for 'staining his dear limbs with bloodshed'; the human race as a whole has fallen from a vegetarian golden age, when 'this was the greatest pollution among men, to wrench out (an animal's life) and eat its strong limbs', and now defiles itself daily with animal sacrifices that are, because of metempsychosis, acts of murder and cannibalism.[92] Orphic poetry too perhaps made vegetarianism the distinctive mark of the mythical golden age.[93] It broke further with Hesiodic tradition in offering an explicit account of how the human race came into being – if we accept, as we surely now must, that the myth of the Titans' crime and the birth of man from these 'unrighteous ancestors' is no hellenistic in-

---

[89] Iambl. *VP* 82,85 (among the *symbola*).

[90] Rites: only D.L. 8.33. Ion makes a better lot in the Pythagorean afterlife a consequence of 'manliness and *aidōs*' (fr. 30 West), Aristophon of 'piety' (D.L. 8.38). Plato does, it is true, use the concept of *katharsis* very widely in a context that reeks of southern Italy, *Soph.* 226b–231e, cf. Wehrli, op. cit. But in the Pythagorean table of opposed qualities, Arist. *Metaph.* 986a24 ff. (58 Diels/Kranz B 5), pure/impure does not appear.

[91] Pl. *Resp.* 364e; gold tablets A 1–3 in Zuntz's edition (*Persephone*, Oxford, 1971, 277 ff.). For gold tablets published after Zuntz see *SEG* xxvi 1139, xxvii 226 *bis*.

[92] B 115, 128, 136–7.

[93] Pl. *Leg.* 782c (not a strict proof; Guthrie, *OGR* 198 is too confident). The progressive account (*OF* 292) of native man's cannibalism gradually mitigated presumably belongs to a quite separate tradition with no place for a golden age (*pace* B. Gatz, *Weltalter, goldene Zeit und sinnverwandte Vorstellungen*, Spudasmata 16, Hildesheim, 1967, 167). Dicaearchus and Theophrastus told of a vegetarian golden age, cf. Gatz, op. cit., 156 f.

vention.[94] The character of the primal crime, which was an act of cannibalism, suggested the cure: rejection of that further cannibalism which every animal sacrifice entailed.[95] The existence of mankind had hitherto been a prime fact of experience that could not be imagined otherwise, and so required no serious explanation; the Orphic anthropogony, by presenting man as an immortal lapsed through crime, offered at the same time the possibility of redemption.[96] The gold tablets, which should probably be classed as Orphic texts,[97] also testify to the initiate's hopes of achieving divinity through expiation of guilt. 'I have paid the penalty for unjust deeds', the initiate declares in hope and confidence to the queen of the underworld.[98]

In these contexts, therefore, purification has a new significance. Where Eleusinian purification was simply the normal preparation for a solemn ritual, Dionysiac perhaps a liberation from mental strain or disturbance, Pythagorean possibly part of a more general concern for harmony, the purifications of Empedocles and Orpheus had a specific eschatological meaning, because they released the soul from a burden of personal or inherited guilt.[99] Legal notions were a natural vehicle for conceptions of this kind. Empedocles is in exile for murder, while Persephone 'accepts compensation' from mortals for her ancient grief.[100]

Encasement in flesh was in itself a punishment, but during this imprisonment further purifications were necessary in order

---

[94] Cf. Dodds, 155 f., Graf, 66–78, Burkert, *GR* 442 f. On the recent transformation of our knowledge of Orphism see Burkert, 'Neue Funde zur Orphik', *Informationen zum altsprachlichen Unterricht* 2 (1980), 27–42.

[95] Cf. M. Detienne, *Dionysos mis à mort*, Paris, 1977, Ch. 4, who ingeniously interprets the Titans' crime as a deliberately negative 'origin of sacrifice' myth, a model of cultural regression.

[96] Cf. D. Sabbatucci, *Saggio sul misticismo greco*, Rome, 1965, 116–26; Nilsson, *HTR* 28 (1935), 224 f. = *Op. Sel.* ii, 677.

[97] W. Burkert, 'Le laminette auree: da Orfeo a Lampone', in *Orfismo*, 81–104, esp. 87 f., 95; cf. S. G. Cole, *GRBS* 21 (1980), 223–38. Note too M. Schmidt, in *Orfismo*, 112–17, on a south Italian amphora of 330/20 showing Orpheus facing a dead man who holds a scroll (comparable to a gold tablet?); also the argument of Boyancé, 78, that epic verses like those of the gold tablets can scarcely have been attributed to any other poet than Orpheus.

[98] Tablet A 3, p. 305 Zuntz.

[99] For crime and expiation in Orphism cf. Pl. *Cra.* 400c, *Resp.* 364b–e, Arist. fr. 60, *OF* 232, Orph. *Hymn* 37.7–8; in Pythagoreanism?, p. 298 above. A similar atmosphere in Eur. fr. 912.

[100] Pind. fr. 133.

to escape from 'the dire cycle of deep grief' (incarnation).[101] The most important method for Empedocles was vegetarianism, since, as we have seen, to eat animal flesh was cannibalism. Very little else, unfortunately, is known of his way of salvation. He urged his followers to shun beans, and the laurel, possibly because they were staging points for human souls.[102] He may have advocated and practised a rule of life as strict as the Pythagorean, and administered or undergone rituals of purification, but of all this no evidence survives. One fragment speaks of drawing water from five springs, obviously for cathartic purposes,[103] but, though this may have been a recipe, it is equally possible that the context was rather 'this is a pollution that even the most elaborate purification cannot cure.' One Christian source states, a little ambiguously, that he urged his followers to show 'self-mastery over intercourse with women', on the grounds that it was a division rather than a union and furthered the deadly work of strife.[104] It is, of course, plausible that the ascetic movements should have enjoined sexual restraint of some kind, particularly as periodic abstinence was a part of priestly life. There are hints, suggestive though not conclusive, that Orphism in particular was hostile to sexuality, or at least to the influence of the female upon the male; Orpheus was torn to pieces by the women of Thrace, and it is probably because of his professions of chastity that Euripides' Hippolytus is accused by his father of a hypocritical entanglement in Orphic rites.[105] Nothing is said, however, of abstinence in the portrait of the initiate in the *Cretans*, and it is hard to believe that a call to full sexual renunciation, if Empedocles had made one, should have provoked so little comment in antiquity. Moderation and self-control were probably all that he preached.[106]

[101] Tablet A 1.5 Zuntz.

[102] B 140–1. Souls and laurel: fr. 127. Souls and beans: hexameters in schol. T. Hom. *Il.* 13.589 = Thesleff, 159 fr. 6.

[103] B 143.

[104] Hippol. *Haer.* 7.29–30, quoting B 110, 115; cf. Dodds, 155. Sexual differentiation is a product of the more general differentiation worked by strife: the god of B 29, 134 is sexless. This doctrine, incidentally, seems to form a bridge between Empedocles' two poems.

[105] 952–4. Cf. M. Detienne, in *Orfismo*, 70–9.

[106] *Cretans*, fr. 79 Austin. Restraint, not abstinence, is all that ἐγκράτεια (Hippolytus' word) in sexual matters entails, cf. LSJ s.v. ἐγκρατής, III.

302   *Miasma*

The prime mode of Orphic salvation was the Orphic life. Its attested components are vegetarianism, abstinence from beans and eggs, and burial in linen;[108] we should perhaps add avoidance of natural pollutions[109] and, for the reasons just noted, some degree of sexual renunciation. Orphism, however, involved ritual as well as a way of life. Ecstatic Dionysiac initiation, in particular, seems to have been adopted and given an eschatological meaning that was originally alien to it.[110] It was chosen partly, perhaps , because it had always been a 'purification', though in a different sense, but more importantly because it was a socially and psychologically abnormal form of religious action, well suited to serve as the vehicle of a new message, and the introduction to an exotic way of life.

Two problems are posed by the descriptions that we have of these Orphic 'purifications'. One is whether they are purifications merely in the broad sense – a rite of whatever form the aim of which was release from evil – or involve an actual ritual cleansing. The other, much more important, is whether there existed a popular Orphism in which the rite was not merely an introduction to the Orphic life or an element in it, but a substitute for it as a means of salvation.

In the *Cretans*, the initiate's pure and vegetarian life is paradoxically inaugurated by the characteristic Dionysiac rite of 'eating raw (flesh)'. The rite is here an introduction to the life. By reducing the initiate to bestiality as a preparation for purity, it emphasizes the transformation that he is to undergo. It is unfortunately uncertain what reality, if any, lies behind this imaginative portrayal set in the fabulous land of Crete.[111] Less exotic and less demanding ideals are suggested by Demos-

[108] Eur. *Hipp.* 952 f., Pl. *Leg.* 782c; *OF* T.219, F.291, Plut. *Quaest. Conv.* 635e; Hdt. 2.81.2. It is of course plausible that further Pythagorean dietetic rules were also Orphic (see e.g. the late *LSA* 84). Burkert, *GR* 448 refers to a ban on wine but cites no source.

[109] An inference from Eur. *Cretans*, fr. 79 Austin, and D.L. 8.33 (Pythagoras).

[110] Cf. Burkert, in *Orfismo*, 92. Main texts: Hdt. 2.81, Eur. *Hipp.* 953 f., *LSS* 120, and the new evidence from Hipponium and Olbia, cf. p. 287 n. 29.

[111] Fr. 79 Austin. Exhaustive discussion and bibliography in W. Fauth, *RE* s.v. *Zagreus*, 2226–31, 2243–57. The tradition of vegetarianism in association with the Cretan Kouretes is found elsewhere too (Porph. *Abst.* 2.21); if authentic, it doubtless relates to their role as gods of initiation, since alimentary rules in connection with initiation are commonplace.

thenes' account of the rites celebrated by Aeschines and his mother:

When you became a man you read out the books for your mother, as she performed the initiations, and helped her in other ways, by night . . . purifying the initiates, wiping them off with mud and bran, and as you raised them from the purification telling them to say 'I've escaped the bad, I've found the better' . . . and by day leading those fine revel bands through the streets.[112]

These rites seem to have been addressed to Sabazius rather than Dionysus, but he was a similar god of ecstasy. Whereas in other texts it is sometimes arguable that dancing, or some comparable activity, is itself seen as a purification,[113] the two things are here clearly distinguished. They are probably stages in the same initiation, and it is perhaps more natural to see the purification as a preparation for the dance rather than vice versa. Even so, it clearly had independent significance and efficacy. After receiving it, the candidate was at once urged to proclaim that he had 'escaped the bad'. The formula is vague, perhaps deliberately so, and need not imply eschatological hopes; but the books that Aeschines read out were probably Orphic (what else could they have been?), and are likely to have contained promises of this kind. Here, therefore, we have, unusually, clear evidence for a rite of deliverance that can reasonably be seen as Orphic, and that took the form of a physical purification.

Few other texts are so precise. An obscure sentence in the *Laws* refers to Bacchic dances, in which the participants imitate drunken Nymphs, Pan, Silens, and Satyrs, as forming part of certain purifications and initiations. It is not clear whether an actual purification preceded the dances, nor whether the whole rite was intended to benefit the candidate in this life, the next life, or in both.[114] According to Adeimantus in the *Republic*, wandering priests went to the doors of the rich, and persuaded them to expiate their own crimes or those of their ancestors by

[112] 18.259–60, cf. 19.199, 249, 281. See for details the commentary on Dem. 18 of H. Wankel, Heidelberg, 1976, ii, 1132 ff. (with his addendum *ZPE* 34 (1979), 79 f. on *LSA* 23.11). Iambl. *Myst.* 3.10 locates Sabazius' efficacy in 'Bacchic dances, spiritual purifications and release from ancient guilt'.
[113] See p. 288 n. 38; same doubt in Pl. *Leg.* 815c.
[114] 815c.

an inexpensive, playful ritual, conducted in accordance with books of Musaeus and Orpheus, and so assure themselves of a blessed lot in the life to come.[115] Of the contents of the playful ritual no details are given; purifications and Bacchic dancing probably played a part, and perhaps too an imitation of the soul's posthumous journey.[116] Plato gives no hint, any more than Demosthenes in the passage cited earlier, that such rites were the beginning, for the initiate, of a new way of life. These *en passant* remarks by contemptuous witnesses are, of course, unreliable evidence. An allusion in the *Hippolytus* shows that the link of Bacchic dances, Orphic books, and vegetarianism was familiar in fifth-century Athens.[117] It is none the less plausible that purifiers did exist who would offer their clients salvation for the cost of a ritual, without insisting on the uncomfortable requirements of an Orphic life.[118] It is interesting that Plato speaks of release, not from metempsychotic or Titanic guilt, but from the crimes of an individual or his ancestors. Thus were exotic metaphysical speculations tailored to suit the conceptions of conventional Greek morality. If Orphic and Pythagorean ideas were indeed 'a drop of alien blood in the veins of the Greeks', we see here one way in which that drop could be assimilated into the bloodstream of Greek culture without changing its fundamental character.

None the less, in its prime, the Orphic/Pythagorean movement was the only unquestionable novelty in the history of archaic Greek religion. For most of its elements parallels can be found elsewhere in Greek culture. The Eleusinian and other mysteries taught the need to take thought for the afterlife; most of the rules of life can be illustrated from cult or superstition; the idea of punishment for ancestral guilt, and of a tainted race whose members were lured into new crime, was deeply embedded in mythology; even though it is unclear whether vegetarianism was ever systematically practised before

---

[115] 364b–e. 'Play' also of Corybantic ritual, Pl. *Euthyd.* 277d. In *OF* T 208 an Orpheotelest holds a tympanon; cf. too the Gurob papyrus, *OF* 31.

[116] Pl. *Phd.* 108a, cf. Guthrie, *OGR* 176; on the ritual behind the gold plates see further Guthrie, 207–15, Burkert, *Gnomon* 46 (1974), 326 f., idem, in *Orfismo*, 95–100.

[117] 953 f.

[118] But for rejection of the dichotomy between 'authentic' and 'degenerate' Orphism see Boyancé, 9–31, idem, *REG* 55 (1942), 217–35.

Pythagoras,[119] there were certainly altars where no living beings might be offered. But it is right to emphasize that the synthesis of these elements into a life of perpetual religious concern is something almost wholly new. Despite its partial precedents, the Orphic and Empedoclean revaluation of sacrifice is particularly startling. Cannibalism was, for Greeks, one of those extreme pollutions, often imagined, though never experienced – like parricide, or incest with the mother – which served to define by contrast the proper human condition.[120] Empedocles and Orpheus now declared it to be inherent in traditional cult's most sacred act. Psychological factors have been invoked in explanation, the archaic Greek's growing burden of anxiety and guilt.[121] But it is hard to know how important were such feelings in the temperament of, for instance, Empedocles, the divine man who controlled the weather and walked among his fellows as 'a deathless god, no longer a mortal'. Perhaps emphasis should rather be placed on the ways in which these movements rejected or reversed many of Greek society's most cherished values. The motivation for such rejection, however, is obscure; it could scarcely become plain without a detailed knowledge, that will probably never be achieved, of the social environment in which the movements had their origin.[122]

Two claims that are most relevant to our theme have been made about Greek asceticism, and the age in which it emerged. One is that Greek religion was now on the road to becoming, like Hinduism or Zoroastrianism, a religion of lustrations and ceremonial purity. The other, closely connected, is that purity rather than justice was the means to salvation.[123] It should be remembered, however, that Greek religion had always been a religion of lustrations; the author in whom the act of washing is most charged with meaning is Homer. New applications the idea of purity certainly received, but it is not clear that physical lustration gained greatly in importance in these movements,

[119] Cf. p. 302 n. 111. Altars: D.L. 8.13, Paus. 1.26.5, cf. Thuc. 1.126.6.
[120] M. Detienne, *Dionysos mis à mort*, Paris, 1977, 140–5.
[121] Dodds, 151 f., cf. Boyancé, *REA* 40 (1938), 169.
[122] Speculation by F. M. Cornford, *CQ* 16 (1922), 140. Burkert, *GR* 416 emphasizes individualism. For one factor see p. 143 above.
[123] Rohde, 302; Dodds, 154.

except in the cults that substituted instantaneous purification for a way of life; and there is certainly no sign that purity was becoming a dominant idiom to which all other forms of evaluation were subordinated. As for justice, it was, as Plato knew, always possible to interpret even orthodox Greek religion as if the gods were swayed by ritual more than righteousness. A fourth-century orator could turn to Orpheus, rather than Hesiod, for the idea that justice, seated by the throne of Zeus, keeps watch over the offences of mankind; and it was Orpheus, according to Aristophanes, who 'taught us rites and to refrain from murder'.[124] Orphic poems are likely to have contained the same blend of moral and ceremonial precepts as did the teaching of Pythagoras.

The preoccupation of these movements with eschatology was, of course, uncharacteristic of Greek culture. Purification could perhaps be annexed as a means of improving one's condition in more immediate terms. Many cults seem to have offered it. The supposed baptism in the rites of Cotyto may be based on a misunderstanding,[125] but a sacred law from the Peiraeus, for instance, restricts the right of women to 'perform purifications'

---

[124] (Dem.) 25.11, Ar. *Ran.* 1032, on which see Graf, 34 ff. Cf. (with Boyancé, 24) the dire warnings of 'those who have taken an interest in such things in connection with initiations', 'priests of old', about the fate of the kin-killer, in Pl. *Leg.* 870d–e, 872d–873a. The progressive account of civilization too (*OF* 292, cf. Graf, 161 f.) upholds justice against force. Nilsson even wrote, *HTR* 28 (1935), 228 = *Op. Sel.* ii, 680, 'His (Hesiod's) craving for justice became the leading principle of Orphism.' On the relation of ritual and morality cf. Dover, 264 f., Boyancé, *REG* 55 (1942), 222.

[125] See on Cotyto the important study of S. Srebrny in *Mélanges Franz Cumont*, Brussels, 1936, 423–47, summarized by Nilsson, *GGR* 835 f. The view that ritual bathing had an important place in these rites depends on linking the title of Eupolis' *Baptai* (fr. 68–89) with his victim Alcibiades' supposed revenge; Eupolis had shown Alc. ritually baptized in the sea, the infuriated Alc. 'baptized' the poet by drowning. If this is right, are we to regard *baptai* as (*a*) a name commonly applied to adherents of Kotyto; or (*b*) one invented opprobriously by Eupolis? (*a*) would be strange. Ritual bathing was a preliminary to many cult ceremonies, and it is hard to see why it should have received this special prominence in the rites of Kotyto, whose main content was ecstatic dancing by transvestite choirs (see Srebrny, loc. cit.). As for (*b*), what is contemptible about ritual bathing? It was part of the Eleusinian cult. One should note further that *baptai* means 'dippers', not 'people initiated by dipping'. A quite different interpretation was proposed by A. Meineke, *Historia Critica Comicorum Graecorum*, Berlin, 1839, 123 (following earlier critics). Eupolis' play was an attack on effeminacy, and he noted that dyeing the hair (*baptesthai*: Men. fr. 303.4, Nicolaus Comicus 1.33) was a characteristic of luxurious, effeminate youth. Even on this view, the story of Alcibiades' revenge, with a pun on *baptō*, is not incomprehensible.

in the Thesmophoreion.[126] The Hesiodic 'divine man', who seems to observe rules of purity without thought for any future life, has a fourth-century successor in the *deisidaimōn* or Superstitious Man of Theophrastus.[127] The danger of pollution is never far from his thought. First thing in the morning he washes his hands (perhaps from three springs),[128] and sprinkles his body with lustral water; for the rest of the day he protects himself by chewing laurel. He constantly has his home purified, supposing that Hecate has been conjured against it. Like a priest, but unlike a good citizen, he declines all contact with birth, death, and tombs. He seeks out the *Orpheotelestai* every month, and repeatedly undergoes ablution in the sea. The mere sight of some poor wretch eating the meals of Hecate (?)[129] requires an elaborate ritual washing; nor is this enough, but a priestess must be summoned to perform a blood purification too. Nothing suggests that all this activity has any more distant or higher aim than the immediate appeasement of his persistent unease. Even the rites of Orpheus have become just one of many devices for this purpose. It is a piquant coincidence that we should owe this disdainful description of a life that in certain respects closely resembles the Pythagorean to that Theophrastus who, in his great lost work *On Piety*, transmitted the Orphic/Pythagorean ideal of vegetarianism to neo-Platonism, where the figures of the *deisidaimōn* and the godlike man were once again to converge.[130]

---

[126] *LSCG* 36.5.
[127] There is abundant commentary; see, besides the editions of H. Steinmetz and R. G. Ussher, H. Bolkestein, *Theophrasts Charakter der Deisidaimonia*, RGVV 21.2, Giessen, 1929; Nilsson, *GGR* 796 f. (with the important observation that this *deisidaimōn* belongs not to the lower classes, but to the bourgeois world familiar from New Comedy); convincing treatment of some textual problems, K. Borthwick, *Eranos* 64 (1966), 106–19.
[128] See Borthwick, op. cit.
[129] See Borthwick, op. cit.
[130] Marinus' life of Proclus 18, p. 160.33 Boisson. (= *OF* T.239) νύκτωρ τε καὶ μεθ' ἡμέραν ἀποτροπαῖς καὶ περιρραντηρίοις καὶ τοῖς ἄλλοις καθαρμοῖς χρώμενος, ὀτὲ μὲν Ὀρφικοῖς, ὀτὲ δὲ Χαλδαϊκοῖς.

11

SOME SCENES FROM TRAGEDY[1]

For the historian of religious beliefs tragedy provides, as was noted in the introduction, elusive evidence. In one sense, its value is unique, since, read aright, it offers insight into the minds and feelings, at a level of intense seriousness, of actual Athenians, the tragic poets themselves. The mind of Aeschylus is a much solider historical reality than any synthetic hypothesis about the Athenian mind; and fundamental beliefs that, for various reasons, lie well below the surface of everyday life may find expression through literature. The concerns of the tragedians are sometimes consigned to the melancholy category of religious philosophy,[2] but that is justified only in so far as every believer is also a philosopher of religion; there is no reason to think that the ordinary Athenian's relations with the gods were merely magical, and that the justice of Zeus was a problem left to theologians. On the other hand, when tragedy is asked to provide historical information on lower levels than this, its answers become ambiguous and hard to interpret, largely because of its setting in the mythical past. Several instances of this lack of realism have already been encountered. The situation of Oedipus, the incestuous parricide, belongs to the world of nightmare, not everyday experience. Though Orestes' dilemma had once been a real one, the emergence of homicide courts had removed it from the level of literal plausibility long before the first tragedy about him was written. Even an Oedipus left destitute by his sons could, in fifth-century Athens, have sought redress from a magistrate. The plague at the start of the *Oedipus*

---

[1] Cf. Vickers, 145–56. G. Richard, 'L'impureté contagieuse et la magie dans la tragédie grecque', *REA* 37 (1935), 301–21, is unhelpful.

[2] No mention e.g. in E. R. Dodds, 'The Religion of the Ordinary Man in Classical Greece', in *Progress*, 140–55. But is it 'religious philosophy' when an Eskimo asks: 'Why must there be snow and storms and bad weather for hunting? Why must the children of my neighbour sit shivering . . . hungry? Why must my old sister suffer pain at the end of her days? She has done no wrong that we can see' (cited in P. Radin, *Primitive Religion*, London, 1938, 54)?

Tyrannus leads to a hunt for the polluter of the city, but historical parallels for such a man-hunt are hard to find. Even the family curse of the tragedians is a metaphor as much as a dogma with fixed practical implications.

This chapter will try to make use of tragedy in a rather restricted way. On the tragic stage we see the action, and interaction, of persons who are themselves polluted or are confronted by pollution in others. No other source offers evidence of the same immediacy. Some scenes of this kind will be surveyed here, rather unsystematically, and without subordination to any general argument. But the assumption that pollution belief is one of the bizarre and impenetrable attitudes that render tragedy 'desperately alien' will perhaps be brought into doubt. At least in the tragedians' presentation, it is the flexibility of the thing and not its dogmatic rigidity that causes surprise. This must be partly a matter of art, of the successful adaptation of response to character and situation; but this adaptation would not be possible if some flexibility were not inherent in the belief itself.

We may begin with those situations where the infectiousness of pollution is either explicitly denied or nobly disregarded in favour of a higher ideal. Orestes warns Pylades of the dangers in acting as his guide.

Or.: It's disgusting to touch a sick man.
Pyl.: Not for me to touch you.
Or.: But you might be infected by my madness.
Pyl.: So be it.
Or.: You won't be afraid?
Pyl.: No. Fear ruins friendship.[3]

Pylades does not deny but disregards the dangers in the act of friendship; we might compare the action of 'those who laid some claim to virtue' in nursing their friends during the Athenian plague.[4] Theseus reassures the smitten Heracles in similar terms: 'I'm happy to share suffering with you, just as I once shared prosperity.' But he goes on to make a bolder claim. Heracles asks 'Why have you uncovered my head before the sun?' 'You are a mortal, and cannot pollute the gods', Theseus replies, and adds that from friend to friend no pollution can

[3] Eur. *Or.* 792–4.
[4] Thuc. 2.51.5.

pass. It is often and plausibly supposed that such formulations are of sophistic origin.[5] A similar scene in Sophocles does not end in a similar affirmation: Oedipus is about to embrace Theseus, then draws back. 'But what am I saying? How could I, wretch that I am, touch a man in whom no stain of evil dwells?'[6] This was an opportunity for Sophocles' Theseus magnanimously to defy or deny the reality of pollution, but he did not take it. Though treating Oedipus with all possible generosity, he kept his distance. As we saw earlier, Sophocles put the assertion 'No mortal can pollute the gods' into the mouth of Creon at a particularly unhappy moment, when Creon had just uttered the fearful blasphemy: 'Not even if eagles carry scraps of the corpse to Zeus' throne will I consent to bury it for fear of *miasma*.' The sophistic claim appears here as the last shred of self-defence of a desperate man, and stands condemned.[7] In the *Oedipus Tyrannus*, Oedipus' friends remind him of the danger that with his uncovered head he poses to the sun.[8]

It may seem that we are confronted here with a simple contrast between the conventional piety of Sophocles and Euripidean enlightenment. There does seem to be a sense in which, in Euripides, pollution has lost its sting. His famous internalization of the Erinyes, by which they are reduced to Orestes' bad conscience,[9] would, if carried through consistently, remove the need for outsiders to guard against the threat of external pollution from him. But we cannot simply detach beliefs about pollution from the whole moral fabric of the plays. For the Euripidean Theseus, it is morally inconceivable that the universe should, through pollution, set obstacles in the way of friendship, but he is not concerned to deny the need for purification;[10] Creon is defending a wanton violation of divine laws, and at its logical extreme his argument would mean that even murderers could enter the temples at will. Everywhere in Greek tragedy, propositions that in themselves might deserve serious consideration are liable to grotesque and unscrupulous

[5] Eur. *HF* 1214–34. Cf. p. 145 above.
[6] Soph. *OC* 1132–4.
[7] Soph. *Ant.* 1043 f., cf. above, p. 33.
[8] 1424–8.
[9] Eur. *Or.* 396. In his treatment of the Alcmaeon legend, however, he seems to have exploited real pollution, cf. Appendix 7 s.v. Alcmaeon.
[10] *HF* 1324.

distortion: good arguments are not reserved for good men.[11] And, though Sophocles' Theseus may not go to the length of embracing Oedipus, his behaviour throughout the play proclaims that, in the magnanimous man, human sympathy dissolves the fear of pollution. As it turns out, his nobility is also prudential, since the polluted Oedipus proves 'a benefit to those who received him, and a bane to those who drove him out'.[12] In practice, therefore, 'there is no pollution from friend to friend.'

Even in Euripides, by contrast, a superficially humanitarian disregard for pollution may assume a dim moral colour. In the *Orestes*, Helen from the height of her own good fortune commiserates with her sister's murderers, explaining: 'I'm not polluted by speaking to you; I lay all the blame on Phoebus.'[13] At first sight that might seem a humane and rational insistence that pollution attaches to the true guilty party, and not his involuntary agent. But is this the Helen we know? Electra has bitter cause to say of her in the same scene: 'She's still the same woman.'[14] Every other participant in the play is clear that laying the blame on Apollo does not vindicate Orestes. Tyndareus will not even address the 'mother-slaying snake', and is amazed that Menelaus should do so.[15] To understand Helen's attitude here it is perhaps legitimate to refer to a famous passage in the *Troades* where she justifies her own crime by the power of Aphrodite.[16] For no serious Greek thinker did divine involvement ever exclude human responsibility, and only Helen could pretend that it did. How delightful life would be for that lady if tedious people made less fuss about guilt and crime! Helen's 'I'm not polluted by speaking to you' is simply an expression of her glib moral laxity.[17]

[11] C. M. Bowra, *Sophoclean Tragedy*, Oxford, 1944, 108, though speaking of Creon's 'infatuate delusion' notes, 'In other circumstances his argument might carry weight.' Similarly K. Reinhardt, *Sophokles*[3], Frankfurt, 1947, 98; 'Was wäre der Wahn, wenn er nicht mit dem Schein der Wahreit sich umgäbe?' (He brings out the superficial plausibility in his translation, 'Der Mensch ist zu gering, Gott zu entweihen.') On Demosthenes' exploitation of a similar argument see p. 268 n. 54.

[12] *OC* 92 f.

[13] 75 f.

[14] 129.

[15] 479–81.

[16] 948–50.

[17] The Dioscuri use a similar argument at the end of the *Electra* (1293–7), without, it seems, similar moral implications; but the tone of this part of the play is hard to catch, cf. Vickers, 564–6.

It is interesting that Helen here identifies pollution with guilt; having transferred blame to Apollo, she regards Orestes as free too from pollution. The scope for debate about the relation of the two things was large;[18] and in the kind of case envisaged by the tragedians there was no authority by appeal to which the issue could be settled. In the case of Helen, it is her loose attitude to guilt rather than her willingness to equate it with pollution that appears reprehensible. The tragedians do not look on the legalistic interpretation with sympathy. Creon's claim that, by placing food in the cavern in which he incarcerates Antigone, he has made himself 'pure in respect of this girl',[19] is not commended; and, in the *Iphigeneia in Tauris*, Thoas' horror at Orestes' pollution, and his attempts to evade it by lustrations and mechanical protective devices, have an ironic effect in a king who upholds the institution of human sacrifice.[20]

Accordingly, the threat of pollution does not, in tragedy, normally impose imperatives that override the demands of ordinary human feeling. In the *Supplices*, for instance, though it is to avoid pollution that Pelasgus accepts the supplication of the Danaids, Aeschylus' presentation of the plight of the helpless girls has been such that the decision seems necessary in any terms. In the *Oresteia*, too, the Erinyes that seek to avenge Clytaemnestra are upholders of rights that, anyone would admit, are genuine, even if not absolutely valid. Pollution plays, indeed, an important part in that imaginative re-creation of the moral foundation of existing institutions that seems to be characteristic of Aeschylus. Metics are, in origin, helpless foreigners such as the Danaids who have been accepted into the state through a supplication that is backed by the threat of pollution.[21] When legal trial replaces self-help, as in the *Eumenides*, it is the same threat that forces the jurors to reach their verdicts 'with reverence for their oaths'.[22]

Because pollution and guilt can be closely associated, the imagery of pollution may be used to express moral revulsion. This is something that is commonplace even in societies that do

---

[18] Above, p. 111.
[19] 889.
[20] 1174 ff.; for the irony cf. esp. 1194.
[21] E. Schlesinger, *Die griechische Asylie*, diss. Giessen, 1933, 38–52.(on Aesch. *Supp.*).
[22] Above, p. 126.

not much fear infectious religious dangers, or practise rituals of lustration. Taints and contaminations are ubiquitous, for instance, in Elizabethan and Jacobean tragedy. The 'damned spot' of the sleep-walking scene in *Macbeth* is an obvious case; Middleton and Rowley's *Changeling* has a particularly striking example in the figure of De Flores, a man whose physical appearance is as repulsive as his soul corrupt. Of him it is said:

> he's so foul
> One would scarce touch him with a sword he loved
> And made account of; so most deadly venemous,
> He would go near to poison any weapon
> That should draw blood on him; one must resolve
> Never to use that sword again in fight,
> In way of honest manhood, that strikes him;
> Some river must devour't, 'twere not fit
> That any man should find it.

The woman he has corrupted says in penitence to her father:

> Oh, come not near me, sir; I shall defile you.[23]

The sense of contamination has here obviously passed a long way behind the metaphorical. Its source, however, is moral horror.

Pollution as guilt, the avoidance of pollution as moral revulsion are best seen in the *Hippolytus*, where purity in all its senses is of such importance. In Euripides' first play on the subject, Hippolytus responded to Phaedra's shameful proposals by covering his head to avoid pollution. In the surviving treatment, he rushes out into the pure air to escape it, furiously forbids the pandar/nurse to touch his robes, and swears that he will wash his ears free of the contaminating words in a flowing stream.[24] This reaction is not confined to the sensitive Hippolytus. Theseus, believing the accusation against his son, refuses at first even to address his reproaches to him directly, and when his passion drives him to neglect the precaution declares 'I have involved myself in pollution.'[25] With the mild ritual impurity of licit sexual contact, this *miasma* evidently has little to do. Hippolytus and Theseus vent their repugnance at the worst offence

[23] 5.2.15–23, 5.3.149, in the text of N. W. Bawcutt (*The Revels Plays*), London, 1958.
[24] 601–2, 606, 653–4.
[25] 946. Cf. Tyndareus' lapse, Eur. *Or.* 526, contrast 481.

a son could commit against his father by treating it, in word and
even in deed (Hippolytus will wash out his ears),[26] as a pollution. But Theseus in shunning Hippolytus is not protecting
himself from danger but expressing moral disgust by a form of
ostracism familiar to us all. (Tyndareus for the same reason
declares that he would not speak to the adulterous Helen.)[27]
The treatment of sexual offences in the nineteenth-century
novel will provide closer parallels than do sacred laws regulating ritual purity. This is Chekhov, for instance, describing an
encounter while bathing between a respectable matron with her
daughter and a woman living in sin: 'She (the matron) stood
between Nadezhda and Katya, as if protecting her daughter
from the water which lapped Nadezhda.'[28] Or here from Trollope is a mother advising her son, whose fiancée has unwittingly
formed a friendship with an adulterous woman: 'But it does
seem to me to be so very important! If she hasn't got your letter,
you know, it would be so necessary that you should write again,
so that the – the – the contamination should be stopped as soon
as possible.'[29] There is, therefore, a reality behind Samuel
Butler's satirical picture of a mistress expelling an unchaste
servant on the instant: 'When she thought of the fearful contamination which Ellen's continued presence even for a week
would occasion, she could not hesitate.'[29a] These pollutions are
no mere figures of speech, but demand the most drastic protective measures from those who come into contact with them.
Friendships must be broken off, servants dismissed, whole
households (where the taint occurs after marriage) dissolved; in
Tess of the D'Urbervilles, Angel Clare puts half the world between
himself and his wife's contamination. Theseus' response to
Hippolytus is no less extreme. But in none of these cases, of
course, is there any hope of banishing the pollution with lustral
water.[29b]

Naturally, the threat of pollution can have an important

[26] 653–4, cf. Alexander Aetolus, fr. 3.16 Powell, Ach. Tat. 6.12.3. The girl in
(Theoc.) 27.5 'washes off' and 'spits out' unwelcome kisses. That does not mean that
kisses pollute (cf. Catull. 99. 7 ff.).
[27] Eur. *Or.* 520–1.
[28] *The Duel*, in *The Oxford Chekhov*, vol. v, trans. R. Hingley, Oxford, 1970, 157.
[29] *The Belton Estate*, Ch. 17.
[29a] *The Way of All Flesh*, Ch. 38.
[29b] Cf. Oliver Goldsmith's song 'When lovely woman stoops to folly'.

place in the language of moral exhortation. As we noted, Pelasgus in Aeschylus is constantly warned of the danger involved in refusing the Danaids' supplication,[30] and this is the consideration that finally sways him and his people. Andromache finds Menelaus and Helen much less sensitive to such pleas.[31] In moral denunciation, too, the charge of having caused pollution is common. It tends to be hotly denied, or turned back upon the accuser; the alternative strategy, of acknowledging pollution but denying guilt, seems not to occur. The encounter between Medea and Jason after the infanticide is a striking instance. Jason exclaims against his wife: 'And do you dare to look at the sun and earth, when you've committed such a crime?' and infers: 'The gods have sent your avenging demon (*alastōr*) against me.' (Punishment for Medea's fratricide has come round upon Jason. The danger is only perceived, characteristically, once disaster has already occurred.)[32] The chorus, despite their partiality for Medea, had earlier called on the same sun and earth to prevent so foul a pollution.[33] But for Medea herself, to admit pollution would be to admit guilt. In a remarkable dialogue she turns back all Jason's accusations upon himself:

J.:   Children, what an evil mother you had
M.:   Children, your father's infatuation destroyed you.
J.:   But it wasn't my hand that killed them.
M.:   No; it was your violence against me and your new marriage . . .
J.:   They will pollute you as avenging spirits (*miastores*).
M.:   The gods know who started all these troubles.[34]

Jason may invoke the '*Erinys* of children and justice of blood' against Medea and call her 'polluted, child-killing lioness', but he can extract no admission of guilt, remorse, or pollution. 'What god listens to a cheat and perjurer like you?', she asks in defiance.[35]

---

[30] *Supp.* 366, 375, 385, 415, 473, 479, 619, 654 f.
[31] Eur. *Andr.* 258–60, 335 ff.
[32] 1327 f., 1333.
[33] 1251–60, cf. 1268.
[34] 1363–6, 1371–2.
[35] 1389 f.; 1406 f., cf. 1393; 1391 f. For a similar interchange see Eur. *Or.* 1600 ff. For reciprocal accusations of pollution cf. Trag. Adesp. fr. 358 Nauck = Soph. fr. 187 Radt; Thuc. 1.126.2–128.2.

Recognition by a hero of his own pollution does, of course, also occur. Creon at the end of the *Antigone*, who had earlier insisted on his ritual innocence towards Antigone, emphasizes his total responsibility for the suicide of his wife. From 'In respect of this maiden, I am pure', unconvincing as it was, he is reduced to 'I killed you, no-one else, it was I', and calls on his attendants to lead him away as a polluted being.[36] The killer who admits his guilt and renounces his throne or goes into voluntary exile 'according to the law' is a common figure in myth and mythical history,[37] and tragedy has several harrowing scenes where the hero confronts and feels with boundless anguish his own pollution. After the murder of his children, Heracles needs no outside admonition to hide his head from the sun; Oedipus with his own hands strikes out the eyes that had seen what they ought not to have seen, and even in his old age, convinced though he is that his crimes are no fault of his own, cannot bring himself to touch the spotless Theseus.[38] But, as always, the line between internal guilt and shame before the world cannot be sharply drawn.[39] Inseparable from the hero's perception of his own pollution is his knowledge that he will be henceforth a polluted being in the eyes of the world. Heracles explains his first suicidal impulse as a way of escaping the 'disgrace that awaits me'; his dominating emotion is one of shame, shame above all that his 'child-killing pollution' should be seen by Theseus, his dearest friend.[40] Oedipus begs the attendants to hide him away, or kill him, or hurl him into the sea 'where you will never see me again'.[41] Heracles, Orestes, and Oedipus all imagine the contumely and rejection they will suffer as polluted exiles;[42] from Neoptolemus and Creon we see the way in which ruthless enemies could exploit their misfortunes against them.[43] When heroes or their attendants say that they pollute the sun, or that earth itself will not receive them, it is tempting to see this rejection by the very elements as

---

[36] 889; 1317–46.
[37] See p. 123 n. 77.
[38] Eur. *HF* 1157 ff., cf. 1214 f.; Soph. *OT* 1270–4, *OC* 1132–5.
[39] Cf. p. 251 n. 90.
[40] Eur. *HF* 1152; 1160; 1156, 1199–1201.
[41] Soph. *OT* 1411 f., cf. 1436 f. 'Where I may be seen and addressed by nobody'.
[42] Eur. *HF* 1281–90, *El.* 1195–7, Soph. *OT* 1380–3.
[43] Eur. *Andr.* 977–8; Soph. *OC* 941–9.

an extreme extension of their exclusion from the society of men.[44]

Here as elsewhere we see a convergence between the consequences of pollution and of disgrace.[45] The Sophoclean Ajax in his shame does not react very differently from Oedipus and Heracles in their pollution. He spurns food and drink, feels hated by both gods and men, could not look his father in the eye, and devotes himself to night because he is 'unworthy to look with profit on any god or man'.[46] Helen, a disgraced woman, is reproached because 'You showed your face under the same sky as your husband, you foul creature.'[47] Demosthenes' political opponents, though they had betrayed the Greek world to Philip for bribes, 'felt no shame before the sun nor their native land, on which they stood . . .'.[48] Both pollution and disgrace should lead to the same 'shame before the sun'.

For the victim, therefore, the consequence of his pollution lies not so much in immediate danger as in social stigma. Theseus gives Heracles courage to live on by showing him that he is not, after all, wholly cut off from his fellow men. With infinite delicacy he persuades Heracles to confront the outside world, first passively by sight, then by speech, and finally by actual physical contact with one who is not polluted.[49] What disturbs and distances the modern reader in the case both of Heracles and Oedipus is the intensity of the pollution that emanates from an unintentional act. Certainly, it expresses an immediate horror that is wholly comprehensible, but it goes deeper than that because it leaves a permanent stain. Oedipus and Heracles are not, however, reduced to the level of rabid dogs which no sane man would think of approaching. Their presence inspires unease and revulsion at the thought of the fearful acts which, though unwittingly, they have perpetrated; but truly magnanimous figures are not debarred from helping them in their distress. It is perhaps not frivolous to point out that similar revulsion, with similar consequences, is far from unknown in

[44] Empedocles B 115.9–12; Soph. *OT* 1424–8; Eur. *HF* 1295–8, *Or.* 822, *Med.* 1327 f. (cf. 1251 f.), *El.* 1177–9; the Alcmaeon legend.
[45] Cf. p. 94 and p. 205.
[46] 324, 457–8, 462–5, 397–400.
[47] Eur. *Tro.* 1023–4.
[48] Dem. 19.267.
[49] Eur. *HF* 1214–34, 1398–1400.

modern western society. Unease before phenomena that threaten the order and normal assumptions of a given culture can still overrule purely moral forms of assessment. Physical illness is no longer shameful or dangerous and can be talked about freely, but mental disease remains in many circles disgraceful, unmentionable, and threatening to the highest degree. Ex-mental patients are expected to find new homes, and expend extraordinary energies in seeking to disguise their past. Such pollution is moreover eminently contagious. 'The loyal spouse of the mental patient, the daughter of the ex-con, the parent of the cripple, the friend of the blind, the family of the hangman, are all obliged to share some of the discredit of the stigmatized person to whom they are related.'[50] Immediate connections are automatically affected; friends have the choice whether to expose themselves to contamination by maintaining the association. Theseus and Pylades magnanimously risk pollution of their own free choice, but no such decision is open to the children of Oedipus. It would be useless for them to shun their father's presence, because the very blood that runs in their veins is polluted; by handling them,[51] Oedipus works no further harm. The polluted man's world is thus divided between an inside circle that shares his stigma and society at large that fears and rejects it. 'Religion demands that only relatives should see and hear a man's affliction', says Creon.[52] Orestes well knows that no outsider would offer him his daughter in marriage, although a relative might.[53] Before his father, Heracles simply laments his fate; his intense feeling of exposure and shame begins when Theseus arrives.[54]

It is appropriate to end with a few remarks on the *Oedipus at Colonus*, a play that illustrates most of the points about reactions to pollution that have been discussed in this chapter.[55] (Even in this very restricted field, Sophocles' primacy among the tragedians in the portrayal of plausible human attitudes is unmis-

[50] E. Goffman. *Stigma*, New Jersey, 1963 (London, 1968), 43, cf. 64. In both cultures, we are dealing with attitudes, not legal disabilities.

[51] Soph. *OT* 1480 f. This pollution too is social, not legal (p. 205).

[52] Soph. *OT* 1430 f. Conversely, love makes the disgusting tolerable: Aesch. fr. 137, καὶ μὴν, φιλῶ γάρ, ἀβδέλυκτ' ἐμοὶ τάδε.

[53] Eur. *Andr.* 975.

[54] Note the dramatic ὀφθησόμεσθα of 1155.

[55] I am grateful for several points about *OC* to Chris Megone.

takable.) Only under compulsion, and only by an oblique approach, does Oedipus reveal to the chorus of men of Colonus his terrible identity.[56] Their immediate reaction is one of terror, horror, and, in consequence, irrational aggression: they have been 'deceived' by Oedipus into tolerating his presence, and to break their promise will be an act of justified 'revenge'.[57] As the very voice of Oedipus would at this point be terrible to them, Antigone tactfully intervenes. The chorus are softened but not moved. 'Know, daughter of Oedipus, that we pity you and him alike for his affliction. But we fear the consequences from the gods, and can give no answer beyond what we have already said.'[58] The fear of 'consequences from the gods' is an element not normally present in modern responses to stigmatized persons; but about the concern that finds expression through this idiom there is nothing unfamiliar. Oedipus, however, persuades them at least to await the verdict of Theseus. A little later, they turn to Oedipus: 'It is terrible to stir up an evil that has long lain quiet, stranger: but none the less I long to know' the story of his affliction.[59] Many have felt that there is something heartless in the chorus's inquisition of Oedipus, but it does not lack psychological plausibility. If there is to be any semblance of normal intercourse between the tainted person and the world, the taint must be brought out into the open and publicly acknowledged. Otherwise both parties are constrained by an impossible unease.[60]

Oedipus' explanation concludes with a firm self-vindication: 'Pure by the law, unknowing, did I come to this.'[61] Before Theseus, on his arrival, no word of justification is required; Theseus' own sufferings have taught him humanity. Creon, however, reveals the sense in which Oedipus' pollution is a 'reproach' that can be exploited against him by an enemy at any time. There is no suggestion that Creon is himself frightened of

[56] 203–23; cf. E. Goffman, op. cit., 143 on 'disclosure etiquette'.
[57] 229–36.
[58] 254–7.
[59] 509 f.
[60] Cf. E. Goffman, op. cit., 143. The source of a very apposite remark unfortunately escapes me: 'Ein seltsam unglücklicher Mensch, und wenn er auch schuldlos wäre, ist auf eine fürchterliche Weise gezeichnet. Seine Gegenwart erregt in allen, die ihn gewahr werden, eine Art von Entsetzen. Jeder will das Ungeheure ihm ansehen, was ihm auferlegt ward; jeder ist neugierig und ängstlich zugleich.'
[61] 548.

Oedipus' taint, but he is happy to declare that he 'well knew that Athens would not receive an impure father-killer like this'.[62] To this charge of pollution Oedipus responds with a furiously worded assertion of his innocence.[63] The contrast with the *Oedipus Tyrannus* has often been noted, where a defence of this kind was far from Oedipus' mind; it has sometimes been supposed that the doctrine of pollution had undergone a modification in the intervening years, to take account of motive. This would be a surprising development, since in respect of guilt, at least, the relevance of intention had been well understood in Athens since at least the time of Draco. In *Oedipus Tyrannus*, we see the first reaction of passionate disgust to a crime whose very objective enormity leaves no place for rational calculation of guilt. Long years have passed in *Oedipus at Colonus*, and Oedipus has come to terms with his deeds by clearly formulating his own innocence. His self-abhorrence, though not destroyed, has been greatly reduced, and so naturally also his sense of personal pollution. It still persists, however; by a contrast of beautiful plausibility, to Creon, who taunts him with it, he makes no admission of pollution, but before Theseus, his saviour, he feels himself impure.[64]

Near the end of the play, when a thunderclap summons Oedipus to his miraculous death, the chorus suppose for a moment that they are about to be punished for associating with a polluted man.[65] They are wrong; Theseus' humanity to the wanderer, true to the Athenian tradition, did indeed bring 'benefit to those who received him'.[66] About Oedipus himself it is less easy to be confident. There is a danger of describing in too mellow and harmonious terms the ending of a play whose hero declares that his 'polluting demon will live on for ever' in Thebes,[67] and who shortly before his death has condemned his sons to mutual destruction. The idea that heroization can be a 'compensation' for suffering is attested in Pindar,[68] but no more

---

[62] 944 f.

[63] 960–1102.

[64] 1133–5. Cf. P. Easterling, *Greece and Rome* 24 (1977), 127.

[65] 1462–85.

[66] An oracle in schol. Soph. *OC* 57 perhaps implies an actual Theban defeat near Colonus, cf. Jacoby on Androtion, 324 *FGrH* fr. 62.   [67] 788.

[68] *Ol.*7.77. I. M. Linforth, *Univ. Cal. Publ. in Class. Phil.* 14 (1950–2), 102, refers also to Pind. *Nem.* 1.69–72, Eur. *Hipp.* 1423.

is envisaged for Oedipus than the power to continue helping his friends and harming his enemies from the grave. The suggestion is, however, made in the play, and is not to be entirely dismissed, that in granting him this power even the gods have in the end 'had some care' for the man they involved in the direst of all pollutions.[69]

EPILOGUE

This book has not been a history; the evidence for significant change in attitudes to pollution is too sparse. If we look forward briefly beyond the fourth century, we still find more evidence for continuity than transformation. One familiar figure does, it is true, seem to disappear, that of the polluted murderer. Little is known at all about the legal and social responses to homicide in this period, but it is probable that, if pollution had been much spoken of, it would in some way have intruded upon the sources. The function of 'purification', or the restoration of normality by a positive and public act, had been taken over by legal process, and it gradually ceased to be necessary to think of the killer as significantly different from any other malefactor whose offences were dealt with by the courts.[1] Something similar can perhaps be observed in respect of certain forms of sacrilege. In historical times, cutting sacred wood no longer evokes a savage punishment from the gods, as it does in myth, but a comparatively modest fine.[1a] The gods could afford to be more lenient because they now had precinct governors who provided effective practical protection for their groves.

In other areas, however, change is harder to find. Chrysippus, as we have seen, criticized the 'irrationality' of rules forbidding birth, copulation, and death on sacred ground, and similar feeling can already be found in Euripides;[2] but this had no influence on cult practice. More significant perhaps was the famous couplet inscribed in the fourth century above the portal of the temple of Asclepius at Epidaurus: 'He who goes inside the sweet smelling temple must be pure (*hagnos*). Purity is to have

---

[1] But for residual ritual concern see *LSS* 112, certain forms of accidental killing specifically declared pure; *BCH* (1978), 325, line 9; *LSCG* 55, earlier text (Sokolowski, p. 108); and the persistence of the Eleusinian proclamation (p. 283).

[1a] Above, p. 165. Precinct governors: Jordan, 23–8.

[2] Above, p. 34.

an honest mind (*literally*, to think *hosia*).'[3] The ideal of *hosiā* had long had a moral dimension that *hagneia* normally lacked. There was something comic about using *hagneuō* in the sense of 'be just';[4] though Sophocles' Creon said that he was *hagnos* in respect of his niece Antigone, whom he was burying alive, he could scarcely have claimed to be *hosios*;[5] and Xenophon brings out the contrast when he says that the gods 'take pleasure in good acts (*hosia*) no less than in pure offerings'.[6] A broader interpretation of *hagneia* was also possible (it appears in Sophocles),[7] but it is fair to say that the Epidaurian couplet unites two concepts that in traditional usage were always liable to be drawn apart. This moralization of ritual purity has obvious affinities with the insistence by writers of the fifth and fourth centuries that the modest offerings of a pious disposition are more welcome to the gods than hecatombs slain by the lawless rich.[8] *Katharos* had begun to be used in the same kind of way rather earlier. It had probably long been possible to say that an open and straightforward man had 'a clean mind',[9] and it was standard colloquial Greek to dub a villain *miaros*, 'dirty'.[10] Slightly more specific applications appear at the end of the fifth century. Aristophanes' mystic choir, in a parody of ritual, bans from its company all those who are 'impure in thoughts'; we begin to hear of people 'purified in soul' and of minds that 'have a pollution'.[11] The idea of a polluted mind follows naturally from the specification in homicide law that 'the planner be treated in the same way as the man who did it with his hand'.[12] This tendency culminated in such formulations as Plato's claim that the wicked have no access to the gods, because 'the bad man is impure in soul . . . and neither a good man nor a god may

[3] *Ap.* Porph. *Abst.* 2.19. Nock suggests (ii, 851 = *HSCP* 63 (1958), 418) that it was the rising Asclepius cult's imitation of the well-known Delphic temple precepts.

[4] Alexis, fr. 15.6, cf. (less clear) Eupolis, *Demes*, 62 Page (*GLP*, p. 212), 79 Austin (p. 89).

[5] Soph. *Ant.* 889.

[6] Xen. *Ages.* 11.2.

[7] *OT* 864.

[8] Cf. sources cited in Porph. *Abst.* 2.13–20; also Hdt. 1.50.1, Eur. fr. 327, 946, Pl. *Leg.* 955e, Men. fr. 683 (if genuine), Theophr. fr. 152 Wimmer.

[9] Theog. 89, Eur. *Med.* 660; καθαρῶς = honestly, Theog. 198; pure mind of modest woman, *PMG* 901.

[10] Above, p. 4. Already in Alc. 347.4 ?

[11] Ar. *Ran.* 355; Eur. *Hipp.* 317, *Or.* 1604 (in fact *hagnos*); above, p. 281 n. 3.

[12] Andoc. 1.94.

rightly receive gifts from the polluted', or in the Epicharman verse (of uncertain date): 'If you have a pure mind, you're pure in all your body.'[13]

The Epidaurian couplet enjoyed enormous popularity in the following centuries. Christian writers quoted it with appreciation, variations on the same theme entered gnomic literature,[14] and many a sacred law contained the instruction not to enter unless 'pure not only in body but also in soul'.[15] But its significance is easily overestimated. It did not make morality an object of religious concern for the first time; it merely assimilated the two entirely traditional requirements of *hagneia* and 'thinking *hosia*'. Pious Greeks may normally have seen the two things as distinct, but they had always believed both to be necessary. 'How could I pray to Zeus', asked Eumaeus, 'if I murdered my guest?'[16] More importantly, it is quite mistaken to see in the couplet a breaching of barriers, comparable to the Christian declaration that all foods are pure. Morality might be included within the category of purity, but it did not replace that category's more traditional content, any more than Philo's allegorical interpretation of the Mosaic dietetic laws exempted the worshipper from observing them literally. It is clear that, despite the doctrine of the *Phaedo*, citizens of Plato's Magnesia would be subjected to the familiar purifications and abstinences; birth and death were no more permissible within the temple at Epidaurus than in any other consecrated area;[17] the moral injunctions in sacred laws occur amid a welter of requirements for purity from birth, death, intercourse, and the eating of meat. Contact with Egyptian and oriental cults meant that the Hellenistic period saw not a decline but an increase in ritual abstinences, which were not confined to marginal superstition but were treated by a cultured Greek such as Plutarch with interest and respect. (Despite its initial impulsion towards a wholly moral view of pollution, even Christianity could not permanently stand out against what was seen as the inherent

[13] Pl. *Leg.* 716d–e; (Epicharmus), fr. 269.
[14] J. Bernays, *Theophrastos' Schrift über Frömmigkeit*, Berlin, 1866, 77; Ps.-Phocylides *Sent.* 228, *Anth. Pal.* 14.71, 74 (cf. *Philol.* 17 (1861), 551).
[15] *LSS* 91.5, cf. 59.13; 82; 86.3; 108.6–7; *LSCG* 139.3–7; Clem. Al. *Strom.* 4.22, p. 311 St.; *BCH* 51 (1927), 120. The ideal is ascribed to Pythagoras in Diod. 10.9.6.
[16] Hom. *Od.* 14.406.
[17] Cf. *SIG*³ 1168.5; Paus. 2.27.1.

impurity of, particularly, the female body.[18]) It is true that
certain specifically moral requirements were sometimes introduced, but by assimilation to the format of the ritual *hagneia*
they lost much of their force; fornication was deemed to pollute
more than legitimate intercourse, but this only meant exclusion
from the shrine for a few extra days;[19] abortion became a serious
pollution, but still one that the passage of time could cure.[20]
Only the remarkable prescriptions of a basically un-Greek
private cult centre at Philadelphia declared that those who
transgressed fundamental moral laws were permanently unfit
to worship the mighty gods of the shrine.[21] Within the main-
stream of Greek culture the Epidaurian couplet altered
nothing.

Continuity has been one theme of this book; diversity is
another. A constant, perhaps an obsessive attempt has been
made to trace divergences and mark out lines of differentiation.
The justification is that there has been a tendency in the past to
see pollution as a single homogeneous category about which
unqualified generalizations can be made: 'Pollution was unknown to Homer', or 'Ritual impurity has no relation to moral
values.' To such claims one might well respond with the tiresome 'But what do you mean by . . .?' of the philosophers. A
general theory of pollution may prove, as a goal, an *ignis fatuus*,
as 'dirtiness' is a natural source of metaphorical and symbolic
expression that is liable to be exploited in an almost unlimited
number of ways; and in the Greek case it has come to overlap
with ideas of collective responsibility and divine anger whose
logical origin is perhaps quite distinct. But it may be interesting
in conclusion to relax this vigilance in discrimination and re-
unite some of the scattered pollutions (or near pollutions) by
relating them very generally to the norms of an ordered
existence.[21a] By doing so we are once again rejecting the idea

[18] E. J. Jonkers, *Mnemos.* 11³ (1943), 156–60; G.E.M. de Ste Croix, *The Class Struggle in the Ancient Greek World*, London, 1981, 109; cf. the churching of women.
[19] See p. 75.
[20] See Appendix 3.
[21] *LSA* 20.
[21a] Cf. the very interesting attempt, which anticipates Mary Douglas, of H. Jeanmaire, *RHR* 145 (1954), 103. It begins: 'L'impureté est ressentie lorsque des contacts ou des rapports jugés anormaux s'établissent entre des ordres de choses qui doivent rester distincts.'

that a culture's beliefs about pollution derive from anxiety or a
sense of guilt. They are rather by-products of an ideal of order.
A first requirement is, it seems, the veiling or repudiation of
what is disruptively or disgracefully physical. Civilized life has
no place for those dying or being born, excreting, or engaged in
sexuality. The philosophers who made it their ideal to 'live in
agreement with nature' attacked culture's precepts in just these
areas. Rules against dying, copulating, or being born in sacred
precincts, Chrysippus pointed out, divide us, irrationally, from
the animals.[22] Herodotus, though evaluating it differently, had
seen the rule about copulation in the same way, as a mark of the
civilized or unnatural life; it distinguished the nations he most
esteemed, Greeks and Egyptians, from the brute creation and
the rest of mankind.[23] Another prerequisite for dignified,
ordered existence, again connected with control of the body, is
health. Particularly alarming are the disruptions caused by
madness, which can lead to a complete loss of control, and by
skin disease, a corruption of the body's visible form. But if the
individual is subjected to external intrusion of any kind,
through the arts of the sorcerer, purification is required. An
ordered existence is obviously impossible if nature breaks its
own rules. Unnatural occurrences such as monstrous births
may, therefore, require purification – although it is also possible
that they have been caused by the gods merely to presage
exceptional events. Diet demands no strict control; but it was
the abandonment of cannibalism that marked a decisive step
forward from the primeval savagery, and man differs from the
animals in not eating dung.[24] To sleep with a blood-relation is a
monstrous act; it is like murdering one's father, or eating the
flesh of a kinsman.[25] Here too opposition from the advocates of
nature helps to define the civilized norms. Zeno and Chrysippus taught that one should be prepared to sleep with one's
mother or daughter, should circumstances demand it, as also to
eat the limbs of one's dead parents.[26]

Further rules relate more specifically to social life. Both sexes

[22] *Ap.* Plut. *de Stoic. Rep.* 1044f–1045a.
[23] 2.64.
[24] See Appendix 4.
[25] See p. 98.
[26] *SVF*, i, nn. 253–6, iii, nn. 743–52.

must uphold the virtues that are distinctive for them. The man who accepts a passive sexual role becomes thereby a woman, while the woman who abandons her shame is a man, or a dog; both lose their right to a place in communal life. Life in society is based on the premiss that each individual must be accorded a certain minimum of respect, and the concrete vehicle of honour is the body. To deny a corpse burial is, therefore, in normal circumstances a dangerous act, because it carries contempt to a point at which shared existence becomes impossible. (Cynics, of course, care nothing for the fate of the corpse.[26a]) The most violent assault upon social order is that by murder. Before the institutions of the classical city had developed, killing disturbed the equilibrium between the two families involved; by the fifth century it had become another offence against a basic rule of life in society. 'Mutual slaughter' was now a characteristic of the primitive past, from which Orpheus by his gentle harmony had drawn civilized man away. Plato believed that man's dangerous animal nature was revealed in dreams not just of incest and cannibalism but also of murder.[27] Other obligations fell to the individual as a member of the smallest social group, the family, and almost the largest, the city. The basic needs of both were the same, nurture and protection from attack. Anyone who deprived his parent or his city of either was liable to a curse, comparable in its effects to pollution, invested with the full power of right.

Finally, in addition to obligations towards kinsmen, unrelated families, and one's native land, there were the claims of the masters and arbiters of civilized life, the gods. The most crucial institutions through which men deal with one another – hospitality, supplication, and the oath – were under their protection. The savage Cyclopes, who lived in no cities, ploughed no fields, drank no wine, and ate human flesh, also cared nothing for the gods. Respect for their images, precincts, and ceremonies was the mark of a man fit to live in society,[28] free from the disgusting and bestial quality of bold shamelessness. This was the true source of 'reverent purity in every word and deed'.

[26a] For Moschion (fr. 6. 30–33 Snell) the laws of burial are another cultural product, a consequence of progress.

[27] *Resp.* 571c–d.

[28] But not of a Cynic, *SVF*, i, nn. 264–7, 'Anacharsis', *Epistle* 9 Hercher.

Appendix 1: The Greek for Taboo

The distinctive feature of 'taboo' is that it unites the sacred and the unclean within the single category of the forbidden. It is not surprising, therefore, that taboo has often been mentioned in connection with the *ag-/hag-* word group, which seems to contain words denoting both sacred and polluted.[1] Byzantine scholars even believed that the same word could in different contexts bear both meanings; thus Cratinus is said to have used *hagios* in the sense of *miaros*.[2] The explanation that they offer for the phenomenon, 'euphemism', is unpersuasive, and some of the evidence quoted by them simply irrelevant; but the theory itself of the double value of *ag-* and *hag-* words is not a Byzantine invention,[3] and the scholars who formulated it will have been acquainted with a far wider range of evidence for classical usage than we are today. Even in the surviving texts, *agos* once means something like 'expiatory offering',[4] and *exagistos* is certainly used for both 'untouchably sacred' and 'accursed';[5] an adjective *panagēs* too is found in post-classical texts with both positive and negative senses.[6] But, as we have seen, the explanation of the ambiguity lies not in a failure to differentiate the sacred and the unclean, but in the possibility of a perilous punitive consecration. Untouchability, and hence 'pollution', is a consequence of such perilous consecration, but the merely polluted is not consecrated.

One aspect of taboo, however, that of untouchable sanctity, is certainly expressed through some words in the group. We noted earlier that this idea is not conveyed at all through *hieros*, and only partially in *hagnos/hagios*;[7] but it is inseparable from the verbs *hagizō*, *enagizō*, and *kathagizō*, which are used of a consecration that always involves complete removal from the human sphere. They commonly

---

[1] Cf. p. 6, and for documentation on what follows the important article of Chantraine/Masson cited there.

[2] Cratinus, fr. 373. Cf. e.g. Pearson on Soph. fr. 689, Moulinier, 250–2.

[3] First attested in Helladius *ap.* Phot. *Bibl.* 535a8. 'Euphemism' or *antiphrasis* is a standard topic of rhetorical handbooks.

[4] Soph. *Ant.* 775 (puzzling), cf. fr. 689.

[5] Soph. *OC* 1526; Dem. 25.93, Aeschin. 3.113 etc.; on the important but obscure epigraphic evidence see A. M. Woodward, *Hesperia* 25 (1956), 100 f. (cf. *Hesperia* 43 (1974), 177 n. 77).

[6] LSJ s.v.; Chantraine/Masson, op. cit.   [7] p. 151.

refer to the burning of offerings in the cult of the dead or heroes, but can also be applied to incense or thighs burnt in Olympian sacrifice, or to libations; the essential point is the entire destruction of the offering.[8] The verb *hagnizō* has a surprising special sense in tragedy which is closely comparable.[9] Normally it means 'purify', and is a mainly poetic variant of *kathairō*, used in similar contexts although never, of course, of simple non-religious cleansing. But there are a number of passages in which *hagnizō* or its compounds govern as objects such things as sacrificial cakes, funerary offerings, or corpses.[10] Thus we find expressions like τὸν θανόντα θ᾽ἁγνίσαι and

τάφῳ τε κρύψαι καὶ τὰ πάντ᾽ ἐφαγνίσαι
ἃ τοῖς ἀρίστοις ἔρχεται κάτω νεκροῖς.[11]

Where the reference is to burning a corpse, the rendering 'purify' is possible, because of the cathartic force of fire;[12] but it is more plausible to see even these cases as part of the same group, and regard *hagnizō* as meaning 'consecrate' (by destruction).[13] Other verbs too – *kathosiō* and *hagisteuō*[14] – are occasionally used in the same sense as *enagizō*. None of them, it is interesting to note, normally expresses the more moderate dedication of a thing or person to the service of the Olympian gods.[15] Indeed, almost without exception the object of consecration is not merely declared untouchable but actually destroyed. The act of *enagizein* does not, therefore, leave in the world a series of tabooed objects.[16]

Though a satisfactory classical Greek word for 'taboo' cannot be found, a very plausible equivalent for the negative state of *noa*, not-

---

[8] Cf. Chantraine/Masson, op. cit.; the sense 'consecrate (without destruction)' that they and LSJ admit for *kathagizō* is unnecessary – all the passages cited may, or must, refer to burning. *Hagizō* is a partial exception, being used of the consecration of altars (LSJ); but only in high poetry, and only, it seems, of the kind of altars liable to receive holocausts.

[9] Cf. Moulinier, 279 f., Williger, 48. LSJ is very inaccurate.

[10] Soph. *Ant.* 196, 545, 1081; Eur. *Ion* 707, *Supp.* 1211; cf. Ap. Rhod. 2.926. Of human sacrifice, Eur. *IT* 705, Hesych s.v. ἁγνίσαι (= Eur. fr. 314, Soph. fr. 116); and for destructive consecration cf. Eur. *Alc.* 76. ἀφαγνίζω = deconsecrate in Eur. *Alc.* 1146.

[11] Soph. *Ant.* 545, 196–7.

[12] Rohde, 334 n. 127, with parallels; but note that in Soph. *Ant.* 545 burning is not in question.

[13] By assimilation of *hagnizō* to *hagizō*?

[14] Ar. *Plut.* 661 (paratragic), Eur. *IT* 1320, Theophr. ap. Porph. *Abst.* 2.27; Soph. *Ant.* 247.

[15] On *hagizō*, a very partial exception, see above. *kathosiō* = 'consecrate' is post-classical.

[16] But there are ἐξάγιστα (see above) and of course ἐναγή.

330 *Miasma*

taboo, is available in the concept of *hosiā*.[17] *Hosios* has a basic sense of 'permitted or enjoined by the gods', 'inoffensive or pleasing to the gods'. In different contexts it is contrasted to both the sacred and the polluted. Ground, or money, which is *hosion* is that which is not sacred, since wholly free use of sacred property is not 'permitted by the gods'; on the other hand, *hosios* is often a virtual synonym of *katharos* or *hagnos*, 'pure',[18] since pollution is 'offensive to the gods'. Thus there seems to exist an enclave of *hosiā*, safe normality, between the dangerous extremes of sacredness and pollution. Threats to this normality can come from either side; *hosiō* and its compounds are used, in a more general sense than *kathairō*,[19] for the restoration of *hosiā* by the removal of that obstacle to it which is pollution, while *aphosiousthai* has a special application for the fulfilment of a religious obligation (a constraint, that is, imposed by the gods) neglect of which would be an offence against *hosiā*.[20] (Because unwelcome obligations were sometimes carried out with narrow legalism, it acquired a further sense of 'do a thing formally or perfunctorily'.[21]) In both cases it is a question of putting oneself in the clear.

In post-classical Greek this verb *aphosiousthai* underwent a remarkable development.[22] The word does not seem to be attested between the fourth century and the *Roman Antiquities* of Dionysius Halicarnassus. It reasserts itself particularly in Plutarch, with a wide variety of meanings, most of which continue classical usage or can readily be derived from it: to fulfil a religious obligation (often perfunctorily), to

[17] See esp. M. H. van der Valk, *Mnemos.* 10³ (1942), 113–40; H. Jeanmaire, *REG* 58 (1945), 66–89 (with the response of van der Valk, ibid., 64 (1951), 417–22); Benveniste, ii, 198–202. Note that Jeanmaire's concept of desacralization is inapplicable to the *hosiā* of humans; for them the relevant contrast is not ὅσιος/ἱερός but ὅσιος/ἀνόσιος (or ἐναγής).

[18] e.g. Aesch. *Ag.* 778, *Cho.* 378, Soph. *OC* 470, Eur. *Ion* 150, Andoc. 1.96. Of course the relation of 'purity' to *hosiā* is one of part to whole. On the breach of *hosiā* by death and mourning see p. 65 n. 110.

[19] Rudhardt, 169, cf. e.g. Pl. *Euthphr.* 4c, *Leg.* 873b. Dem. 23.73, 47.70. If one 'sins against the gods' by an impious speech, one should ἀφοσιοῦσθαι by recanting it, Pl. *Phdr.* 242c. When, as often, the verbs are used of responses to murder (p. 121), the senses 'purify' and 'discharge an obligation' (to the dead man) become inseparable, since the victim's rights are the source of pollution.

[20] Hdt. 1.199.4, 4.154.4, 4.203.1 (here not 'fulfil an obligation', but 'escape the threat contained in an oracle'); Pl. *Phd.* 60e, 61b, *Phlb.* 12b. For an active use, 'I put in the clear (by fulfilment of an obligation)' cf. Aeschin. 3.120 τὴν πόλιν τὰ πρὸς τοὺς θεοὺς ἀφοσιῶ, Clearchus, fr. 43a Wehrli, *ap.* Ath. 516a (for the force here, mistaken by LSJ, cf. Hdt. 1.199.4); similarly, but 'by removal of a pollution', Pl. *Euthphr.* 4c, *Leg.* 873b.

[21] See LSJ s.v. ἀφοσιόω, II.2.c, W. Wyse on Isae. 7.38, and for an instance Hdt. 4.154.4.

[22] See W. J. Terstegen, *Eusebes en Hosios,* diss. Utrecht, 1941, esp. 167 f. I discussed this word more fully in my Oxford doctoral dissertation (1977), same title as this book, 388–92.

fulfil any obligation (often again perfunctorily), to restore *hosiā* after a pollution (it now has an accusative of the pollution expiated), or to avoid a pollution. There also emerges a specialized use, rendered by LSJ 'to eschew on religious grounds, hold in abomination'. Two features of this usage are particularly noteworthy. One of course is the strong emphasis on the religious value of avoidance, which is treated as a means of preserving *hosiā*. The other is that the verb expresses the fact of religious avoidance without implying anything about its motive (thus 'eschew on religious grounds' is a better interpretation than 'hold in abomination'). The man who abstains from a food, whatever his grounds, ἀφοσιοῦται the food;[23] to abandon action on a given day because of bad omens is ἀφοσιώσασθαι τὴν ἡμέραν, but Philip, after a snake had been seen lying beside Olympias, shunned intercourse with her τὴν ὁμιλίαν ὡς κρείττονι συνούσης ἀφοσιούμενος.[24] Here then we have good Greek for 'to treat as taboo' – but, most interestingly, it is not a primitive survival but a Hellenistic development.

---

[23] Contrast e.g. Plut. *Quaest. Conv.* 635e (respect), 670f (distaste).
[24] Plut. *Caes.* 64.5, *Alex.* 2.6.

Appendix 2: The Cyrene Cathartic Law

The law is *SEG* ix 72 (cf. xx 717), *LSS* 115, Solmsen/Fraenkel⁴ 39,
Buck 115. It was discovered in 1922 in the Roman baths at Cyrene,
where it had been incorporated as a seat for bathers in the *frigidarium*,
and published with an extensive commentary by S. Ferri, *Notiziario
Archaeologico del Ministero delle Colonie* 4 (1927), 93–145. Detailed
reconsiderations of the whole were quickly offered by Wilamowitz,
Sitz. Preuss. Ak. Berl. 19 (1927), 155–76 (not in *Kl. Schr.*), G. de
Sanctis, *Riv. Fil.* n.s. 5 (1927), 185–212, A. Vogliano (helped by
P. Maas), *Riv. Fil.* n.s. 6 (1928), 255–320, K. Latte, *ARW* 26 (1928),
41–51 = *Kl. Schr.* 112–21. These contributions, together with notes
on individual passages by Schulze, Radermacher, and Maas (cited in
LSS and *SEG*), solved most of the problems in the document that
appear soluble. G. Oliverio, *La stele dei nuovi comandamenti e dei cereali*
(Documenti Antichi dell' Africa Italiana 2), Bergamo, 1933, 7–28,
35–84, republished the text, most unreliably even though he was
working from the stone, with an elaborate, eccentric, and often irrelevant commentary, but excellent plates. (The plates suggest that his
readings must be treated with caution.) G. Luzzatto, *La Lex Cathartica
di Cirene*, Milan, 1936, did not re-examine the stone, and wrote mostly
from the perspective of the legal historian. These works will be cited
by author's name in what follows. Full bibliographies are available in
LSS and *SEG*; add O. Masson, *Annuaire de l'École pratique des Hautes
Études, IVe section*, 102 (1969–70), 232 f. (linguistic notes).

The law occupies one face and about two-thirds of another of a
quadrangular stele; the third face bears *SEG* ix 2, a list of the cities
that received grain subventions during the famine of 331 to 326, while
the fourth was unworked and blank. Debate about the chronological
relation of the cathartic law and the corn subvention list has proved
inconclusive. Ferri put the corn list about 320 and the cathartic law,
on the basis of letter forms, some twenty years later; similarly
Wilamowitz. De Sanctis acknowledged that the letter forms of the
cathartic law appear younger, but explained this by the respective
ages of the stonecutters and argued for the cathartic law's priority. Cf.
too Oliverio, 10. Of the reason for the stone's publication nothing is
known. Some have supposed that it was originally topped by another
stele which explained the circumstances, as does the preamble to the

famous Founders' Oath of Cyrene (M/L 5). We do not know, therefore, whether the Cyrenaeans had only recently sought Apollo's approval for their cathartic traditions, or whether line A 1 alludes to the more distant past.

I offer here a translation of this document, with discussion of the more important uncertainties that relate to the theme of this book. No wholly satisfactory text is available (*LSS* and *SEG* are dependent on Oliverio); the most prudent is that of Fraenkel (Solmsen/Fraenkel[4] 39), and I have adopted this as the basis of my translation. A republication from the stone would be welcome, but would probably not largely affect our understanding. Some control is available through Oliverio's photographs. Sokolowski provides an extensive apparatus criticus in *LSS*. My treatment is selective, and on the interpretation of individual words I assume knowledge of Fraenkel's helpful notes.

A

1–3 'Apollo decreed that (the Cyrenaeans) should live in Libya [? for ever] observing purifications and abstinences and [   ].'

In view of Cyrene's well-known contacts with Delphi, Apollo here is surely the Delphian and not a Cyrenaean oracular Apollo; cf. M/L 5; Hdt. 4.150–8; idem, 4.161.1: Cyrenaeans ask Apollo ὄντινα τρόπον καταστησάμενοι κάλλιστα ἂν οἰκέοιεν; Diod. 8.30: Arcesilaus 3 told by Delphi that Cyrene was suffering through divine anger because of 'disrespect for piety to the gods'. On Cyrenaean respect for 'Apollo the Founder' see P. M. Fraser, *Ptolemaic Alexandria*, Oxford, 1972, i, 788.

No other sacred law containing a code of purity presents itself as an oracular response. Plato, however, envisages the possibility: see p. 140 n. 147. For citation of what 'the god decreed' in other sacred matters see *IG* I[3] 7, *SIG*[3] 735.19 f., ibid., 1158, cf. Dem. 21.51–3. It has been universally recognized that Delphi cannot have prescribed the contents of the following code. The dialect is Cyrenaean, and allusions to Cyrenaean institutions and customs are numerous. (Wilamowitz thought that at least the form χρειμένος in A 3, the proem, was Delphic, but even this is not certain, cf. Buck, §158.) Perhaps the Cyrenaeans submitted to Delphi for approval a code that they had already drafted (Wilamowitz); or it may be that Apollo's oracle was confined to the general instruction to 'live in Libya observing purifications', and that the content of the code does not even profess to be part of the response.

The code itself is somewhat disorganized, and not comprehensive; thus in B 25 there is an allusion to death-pollution, as to something familiar, but its operations are nowhere regulated. The rules it contains are doubtless very various in date; but no part of it reads like a verbatim transcript of a truly archaic code of rules.* (Note for instance the virtual absence of wholly incomprehensible words.) It perhaps manifests the same kind of retouched archaism as M/L 5, the Founders' Oath. The possibility that a more orderly code has been abbreviated and unintelligently reorganized is occasionally raised in what follows. There are inconsistencies both of phrasing (cf. below on δησεῖ/δησεῖται) and dialect (ἔκασσα/ἑκοῖσα, B 5, 7, cf. Wilamowitz).

4–7 'If disease [or   ] or death should come against the country or the city, sacrifice in front of the gates [in front of] the shrine of aversion (?) to Apollo the Averter a red he-goat.'

The interpretation of the genitive τῶ ἀποτροπαίω in 6 is very uncertain. Ferri, followed by Luzzatto, took τὸ ἀποτρόπαιον as 'the evil to be averted', whence supplements like καθαρμόν, 'a purification from the evil'. ἀποτρόπαιος as an adjective bears this sense in post-classical prose, as does ἀπότροπος in tragedy (cf. LSJ), but the substantival use seems implausible. Most scholars have followed Vogliano in taking τὸ ἀποτρόπαιον as a physical object outside the gates, a statue, unworked stone, or altar dedicated to the god (so e.g. Wilamowitz, *Glaube*, i, 173 n. 1), and in supplementing a preposition, 'in front of the *apotropaion*'. This is more attractive, even though parallels for the noun ἀποτρόπαιον are lacking.

Red victims are not often specified in sacred laws, and do not seem to have had any fixed significance (cf. P. Stengel, *Opferbräuche der Griechen*, Leipzig, 1910, 187–90, idem, *Kultusaltertümer*, 151 f.). Latte suggested, comparing Roman festivals, that in this case the red goat was a symbolic embodiment of the evil to be averted, the fiery plague; cf. p. 275, and the black bull burnt 'for' Boubrostis in Smyrna, Plut. *Quaest. Symp.* 694a–b. It certainly seems that, in a red goat, a rather disreputable animal is deliberately chosen, like the dogs sacrificed to Hecate; goats are shameless, and red hair too is a mark of shamelessness and evil generally (E. Wunderlich, *Die Bedeutung der roten Farbe im Kultus der Griechen und Römer*, *RGVV* 20.1, Giessen, 1925, 66–72). In

---

* I owe this point to Bryan Hainsworth. On the other hand, *IG* I³ 104, if a verbatim transcript of Draco's code, attests considerable lucidity for a late 7th-century law; on its style see Gagarin, *Drakon*, Ch. 8.

LSS 116 A 3, also from Cyrene, *LSCG* 18 A 33, C 33, ibid., 20 A 26, Apollo Apotropaios again receives a goat, but in Dem. 21.53 an ox.

The sacrifice to Apollo 'in front of the gates' obviously relates to the god's function as one who stands outside city gates (Propylaios) or house doors (Aguieus) and averts evil from them, and more generally 'stands in front' of threatened humans (Prostaterios); cf. Preller/Robert, i, 276 n. 1, *RE* 2.64, Farnell, iv, 148–52. For statues of Apollo outside the walls, firing his arrows to avert plague, see O. Weinreich, cited p. 276 n. 91; Weinreich's evidence is late, but cf. already Soph. *OT* 202–6. For a 'Hecate before the gates' see *SIG*³ 57 (*LSA* 50) 26, 29 f.; also Aesch. *Sept.* 164.

8–10 'Wood growing in a sacred area. If you pay the god the price, you can use the wood for sacred, profane and unclean purposes.'

Sacred purposes: statues, sacrificial fires. Unclean purposes: the burning of unclean objects, especially corpses, perhaps too use in chthonic sacrifices. Further possibilities are suggested by the Pythagorean rule, Iambl. *VP* 154, against using cedar, laurel, myrtle, or cypress for cleansing the body or the teeth, since they should be kept for honouring the gods.

On the protection of sacred wood see p. 165 above. The entirely commercial approach is unusual, but without knowing the character of the 'wood growing in a sacred area' it is rash to draw conclusions about Cyrenaean liberalism (Luzzatto). Unless 'the god' is the relevant god in each case, it looks as if this rule relates specifically to the sanctuary of Apollo.

11–15 'Coming from a woman a man, if he has slept with her by night, can sacrifice [wherever? whenever?] he wishes. If he has slept with her by day, he can, after washing [   ] go wherever he wishes, except to [*two lines missing*]

See pp. 74 ff. on such rules. Here intercourse by night requires no purification. It should be emphasized that the sacrifice here mentioned is not intended to efface the pollution of intercourse, as Ferri, Luzzatto, and Sokolowski assume. This is not attested as a function of sacrifice; the case envisaged is that of a man who wants to sacrifice but has recently had intercourse. Restoration of the limiting clause 'except to

'. . .' is quite uncertain. A specific sanctuary was probably named. Maas thought of shrines in general, but such severity would be unparalleled.

16–20 'The woman in childbed shall pollute the house. [*gap*] she shall not pollute [the person who is outside the house(?)], unless he comes in. Any person who is inside shall be polluted for three days, but shall not pollute anyone else, not wherever this person goes.'

In 16 I diverge from Fraenkel's text, reading λεχώι (nominative); for the form see Buck, §111.5. The clue to the section's articulation, as Vogliano saw, is the δ' in 17, which is unmistakable in the photograph. The previous section becomes lucid if we accept Oliverio's ἐξόροφον, as in the translation above. (For -ό- after ἐξ- cf. E. Risch, *Wortbildung der homerischen Sprache*[2], Berlin, 1974, 225, 188.) But the word is not attested, and the ξ read by Oliverio not visible on the photograph. Otherwise the stone must have said something like 'she shall not pollute a roof, unless she comes under it.' But it seems preferable to make the mobile party, liable to come under a roof, someone other than the mother.

21–5 'There is *hosiā* in respect of the Akamantia for everybody, both pure and profane. Except from the man Battus the leader and the Tritopateres and from Onymastos the Delphian, from anywhere else, where a man died, there isn't *hosiā* for one who is pure; in respect of shrines there is *hosiā* for everybody.'

A vexed section; any translation is tendentious. The different possibilities are best expressed by, respectively, Latte and Vogliano/Maas. Two main difficulties are the reading in 21, and the articulation of 22–3. In 21, *KAMANTIΩN* is certain, and a preceding trace is visible which probably belongs to an A. Wilamowitz interpreted α⟨ἴ⟩κα μαντίων, supposing accidental omission of the ι; Latte ἅ κα μαντίων; Maas Ἀκαμαντίων (from Ἀκαμαντίον, shrine of the Akamantes: a neat parallel in construction to 25).Wilamowitz translated: 'If there is *hosiā* of seers, there is it for everybody . . .'. Similarly Latte: 'Whatever *hosiā* of seers there is, there is for everybody', the point being that consultation of oracles was only permitted at certain times. (Latte suggested that μαντίων might stand for μαντείων, oracular shrines, but Vogliano

pointed out that μαντήιων would be expected.) But the postulated
omission of the verb in both conditional (or relative) and main clause
seems impossibly abbreviated, and the expression 'hosiā of seers' is
unconvincing. If seers are rejected here, the interpretation of the
following lines with reference to tomb-oracles (de Sanctis and others)
collapses. The Akamantes, introduced by Maas's interpretation, are
known as recipients of offerings in a sacred calendar from Marathon,
LSCG 20 B 32; there as here they appear close to the Tritopateres, but
as Latte points out the order of offerings in the Marathon text is by
calendar, and so the juxtaposition need not be significant. Of their
nature nothing certain is known; as 'the untiring ones' they might be
winds (cf. LSJ s.v. ἀκάμας, ἀκάματος), but in the Cyrene law, if they
are correctly introduced into it, there is perhaps a contrast with the
unusual use of κάμνω = 'die' in 24, which would make them 'undying
ones' (cf. Wilamowitz, *Glaube*, i, 309, n. 2). One of the Antenorids,
who received cult at Cyrene, was called Akamas, and some have
identified Akamantes and Antenorids (J. Defradas, *REG* 65 (1952),
299, G. Capovilla, *Aegyptus* 42 (1962), 85); but, as Vogliano noted, it is
hard to see why Antenor's second son should have given his name to
the *gens*. Two substantial difficulties in Maas's reading were indicated
by Latte. (1) The plural; did the Cyrenaeans really have a series of
shrines of the Akamantes? A possible solution would be to suppose a
mason's error for Ἀκαμάντων; or perhaps Ἀκαμαντίον was a generic
word in Cyrene meaning something like 'hero shrine'. (2) Some
contrast between the Akamantia and the ἱερά of 25 will have to be
found, or the former provision could have been left to be covered by
the latter. Vogliano suggests that the Akamantia are ἡρῷα as opposed
to ἱερά, but that in turn leaves the contrast between them and lines
22–3, which also seem to treat ἡρῷα, obscure.

The articulation of 22–4 depends on the reading at the end of 23. If
a conjunction can be introduced there, they become a subordinate
clause qualifying 21, 'there is hosiā for all . . . except that, from Battos
. . . or anywhere else, where a man died, there is not hosiā for a pure
man.' Without a conjunction, 22–4 becomes an independent sentence,
with πλάν modifying ἀπαλλῶ, as in the translation offered at the start
of this section. For καί at the end of 23 there is no space; ἤ might seem
possible, but according to Vogliano and Oliverio, the only letter
compatible with the traces is ι (a mistaken adscript ι of a common
kind: see e.g., at Cyrene, six instances in *SEG* ix 4). If this is correct,
the translation offered above becomes inescapable. On any view, the
relation between ἀπ' ἀνθρώπω Βάττω and ἀπαλλῶ presents a further
difficulty. It is generally agreed that 'from the man Battos' means
'from the (tomb of) the man Battos'. We know from Pindar of his
tomb in the market-place at Cyrene (*Pyth.* 5.93). Excavation has

revealed two round tombs in the agora, the larger of which contained two distinct altars; Wilamowitz accordingly assigned the larger tomb to a joint cult of 'Battos and the Tritopateres', the smaller to the mysterious 'Delphic Onymastos' (*Kyrene*, Berlin, 1928, 9 n. 1; cf. Oliverio, Fig. 12, F. Chamoux, *Cyrène sous la monarchie des Battiades*, Paris, 1953, 132, 285–7, with Plate 7.1, and further references in P. M. Fraser, *Ptolemaic Alexandria*, Oxford, ii, 1097 n. 508). But the conjunction of tombs and 'any other place where a man died' is illogical, as men do not die in their tombs (unless heroic tombs are envisaged as being sited at the place of death). A reference to actual places of death (though accepted by Latte) seems out of place in this context. We are perhaps dealing with a brachylogy for 'from any other place, where is buried a man who has died'.

On the Tritopateres Sokolowski gives bibliography.

'There is *hosiā* of the shrines for everybody' is normally taken to mean (cf. Wilamowitz): 'It is *hosion*, religiously inoffensive, for everybody to approach the shrines', everyone has free access to them. It is initially tempting to interpret 22–4 as indicating places where it is not *hosion* for a pure person to go. The lines would exclude 'the pure' from tombs, and thus from hero cult, with the exception of those tombs situated in the agora itself, which must have been generally recognized as an exception to the normal principle that tombs pollute; cf. p. 42, and on the similar restrictions imposed on Coan priests against approaching graves, or a house of death, p. 52. The difficulty is that these lines, in contrast to 21 and 25, speak not of '*hosiā* of' but '*hosiā* from': 'From a place where a man died there is not *hosiā* for a pure man.' Most editors have simply glossed over this ἀπό (Vogliano even translates 'al luogo dove uno è morto . . . non è data facoltà di accostarsi'), and if it is taken seriously ὁσία becomes vague: there is not *hosiā* for a pure person (coming) from a tomb – to do what? (Only those who read μαντίων in 21 can provide an answer, cf. Latte and Buck).

A possible solution would be to interpret ὁσία not in terms of freedom of access, but of freedom of consumption of sacrificial offerings. Ἀκαμαντία and ἱερά would be changed from places to offerings: 'Everyone may share in offerings made to the Akamantes . . . there is not the right of eating from the tomb of Battus for a pure man . . . everyone may share in offerings made to the gods.' This would find a parallel in the further Coan restriction for priests on παρ' ἥρωνα ἔσθεν (*LSCG* 154 A 22, 156 A 8); and on the puzzling phrase ὁσίη κρεάων in *Hymn Hom. Merc.* 130 see H. Jeanmaire, *REG* 58 (1945), 66–89, with Benveniste, ii, 198–202. But the lack of any explicit reference to eating is surprising.

The reference to a class of 'the pure' is unique (as is the earlier division of pure-profane-unclean). The pure must be priests and others who are, for whatever reason, subject to temporary *hagneiai*.

26–31 'If he sacrifices upon the altar a victim which it is not customary to sacrifice, let him remove the remaining fat (?) from the altar and wash it off and remove the other filth from the shrine and take away the ashes (?) from the altar and the fire to a pure spot, and then let him wash himself, purify the shrine, sacrifice a full grown animal as penalty, and then let him sacrifice as is customary.'

On breach of religious rules as a pollution see p. 144. Note that in this case the illicit sacrifice pollutes the sacrificer as well as the shrine.

32 'A man is bound as far as his brothers' children.'

This stands in isolation, separated by *paragraphi* from what precedes and what follows. (The first *paragraphos* is unmistakable on the photograph, and refutes attempts to make 32 run on from 31.) ὁ]κώχιμος is the only supplement that fits the space. The group of relatives extending to the sons of brothers is a familiar one (cf. Latte), but the reason for its introduction here is very obscure. A law in Dem. 43.58 (cf. Harrison, i, 128 n. 2) apparently specifies that all the heirs, and not just the direct descendants, of a man who dies owing money to a god should be *atimoi* until they pay the debt. That suggests a plausible kind of context for our regulation, especially in view of what follows; but the vagueness and brevity of the Cyrenaean law make it seem almost like a fragment of a fuller code.

33–72 'If a grown man is subject to a tithe, having purified himself with blood, he shall purify the shrine; after being sold in the market-place for the most that he is worth, he shall first sacrifice as a penalty before the tithe a fully grown victim, not from the tithe, and then he shall sacrifice the tithe and carry it away to a pure spot; otherwise, the same measures will be necessary. Everyone who sacrifices shall bring a vessel. If a [boy] is polluted unwillingly, it's sufficient for him to purify himself and a penalty isn't necessary. If he is polluted willingly, he shall purify the shrine and sacrifice first as a penalty a fully grown victim.

(43) If property is subject to a tithe, he (the owner) shall assess the

value of the property, purify the shrine and the property separately, and then sacrifice first as a penalty a fully grown victim, not from the tithe, and then sacrifice the tithe and carry it away to a pure spot. Otherwise, the same measures will be necessary. From the property, as long as it is subject to a tithe, no one shall make funerary offerings nor shall he bring libations until he pays the tithe to the god. If he brings libations or makes funerary offerings, after cleansing the temple of Apollo he shall first sacrifice as a penalty, according to his offence, a fully grown victim.

(53) If a man subject to a tithe dies, after they bury the man he (the heir?) shall place whatever he likes on the tomb on the first day, but nothing subsequent to that, until he pays the tithe to the god, and he shall not sacrifice nor go to the tomb. They shall assess him (the dead man) for the most that he was worth, being a partner to the god. After purifying the temple of Apollo and the property separately, he (the heir) having first sacrificed as a penalty a fully grown victim not from the tithe, in front of the altar, shall sacrifice the tithe in front of the altar and carry it away to a pure spot. Otherwise, the same measures will be necessary.

(63) If a man subject to a tithe dies and of the children who are left some live and some die, having assessed the [dead children?] for the most that they are worth he (the heir) shall purify the temple of Apollo and the property separately, sacrifice first the penalty of the grown man before the altar, and then sacrifice the tithe before the altar. As for the living descendant, having purified himself he shall purify the shrine separately; after being sold in the market place, he shall sacrifice the penalty of the grown man, a fully grown animal, and then he shall sacrifice the tithe and carry it away to a pure spot. Otherwise, the same measures will be necessary.'

Notes on the translation. 'The same measures will be required' is expressed by either τῶν αὐτῶν δησεῖ or δησεῖται. For the latter, other renderings have sometimes been offered, but for impersonal δεῖται with a genitive see Pl. *Men.* 79c, Dem. 18.145, LSJ s.v. δεῖ, III. In 40 and 41 μᾶι is probably middle or passive, 'incurs pollution', in view of the absence of an object and the apparently passive use of the related future μιασεῖ in B 3 (contrast active μιανεῖ in A 16), but an active sense is perhaps not inconceivable, 'pollutes (the shrine)'. The regulation, 'Everyone who sacrifices shall bring (take away?) a vessel' (39), seems misplaced here. The force of 'carrying away to the pure' in 38, 46, 62, 71 is obscure. It can scarcely mean '(thereby) restore (things) to purity', as Vogliano suggests. The sacrifice 'before the altar' has sometimes been thought to be especially appropriate to the case of a tithed man who has died, but προβώμιος has no intrinsic funerary application (for the word cf. Eur. *Ion* 376 and at Cyrene *SEG* ix 345), and the failure to specify this form of offering in earlier sections is perhaps mere carelessness (Wilamowitz).

Various forms of tithing were familiar in Greece, several of them especially associated with Apollo, who was δεκατηφόρος (*RE* s.v. *Apollo*, 47). Apart from the purely secular use of the tithe as a form of tax or rent, there was the common practice of dedicating to a god a tenth of first-fruits, plunder, or the product of any enterprise; aitiological stories told of humans sent to Delphi as tithes by their conquerors or even, in time of plague or famine, by their own people, and a penal tithing, of disputed character, was threatened against the medizers in 479 (cf. How/Wells on Hdt. 7.137. 2, Parke/Wormell i, 51–5, H. W. Parke, 'Consecration to Apollo', *Hermathena* 72 (1948), 82–114; also Diod. 11.65.5). Epigraphic evidence for the payment of tithes to Apollo is quite exceptionally abundant at Cyrene: see *SEG* ix 68, 78, 80, 84, 87 f., 94, 100, 302–17, and (partly reproducing material from *SEG*) nn. 35–42, 49, 133–42, 151 f., 248–52 of the *Supplemento Epigrafico Cirenaico* (*Annuario della Scuola Archeologica di Atene*, n.s. 23–4 (1961–2), 219–375). Beyond the fact that these are payments by individuals, the character of the tithe is impossible to determine, but apparently, in contrast to our text, it is not merely sacrificed, but in part at least goes to pay for the inscription, 'X dedicates his tithe to Apollo.' For tithes paid from spoils at Cyrene see *SEG* ix 76 f., *Suppl. Epig. Cir.* 132a. It does not seem that the institution of our inscription corresponds exactly with any of the familiar forms. It is for us bafflingly obscure, because the law assumes knowledge of the institution's general intent, and confines itself to procedural formalities and special cases (although even in these respects, for all its verbosity, it is annoyingly unexplicit and incomplete). The form of tithe that is assumed is individual, and not, as in the case of the Medizing cities, collective; on the other hand, the reference to 'penalties' seems to show that we are not dealing with the ordinary individual tithe voluntarily offered, but with an obligation that is imposed as a punishment. If the tithe is itself a punishment, the requirement of a penal sacrifice in addition to it is perhaps surprising; but the possibility of being subject to a tithe without being subject to a penal sacrifice is not envisaged, which is hard to explain on the view that voluntary thank-offerings are in question. It is perhaps conceivable that the opening provision of 30 is a brachylogy for 'If a grown man is under a tithe (and incurs pollution while under it)' (cf. 40–2); but if the stone really omits such vital specifications, it is beyond interpretation.

No direct indication is available about the offences through which such tithing was incurred. The recurrent references to purification, both of the offender and of the shrine, suggest that they were pollutions of some nature; sacrilegious pollutions, which could include almost any breach of religious rules, are the most likely kind (cf. pp. 144 ff. above). The rules for the youth who 'incurs pollution' perhaps support this view (but see below for Maas's view). It is sometimes suggested (e.g. by Wilamowitz) that the tithed man requires purification because the position of sacred debtor (κοινὸς ἐὼν τῶι θεῶι 58) is, through the contagiousness of the sacred, intrinsically polluting. But on this view one might rather expect the purification after the tithe has been sacrificed; and it offers no convincing explanation for the purification of the shrine (Wilamowitz suggests, implausibly, that the mere presence of the sacred debtor pollutes it). It is not very likely, though perhaps conceivable, that these purifications are not the response to a specific pollution, but mere preparations for the solemn act of sacrificing the tithe (for 'sacrificing off' a tithe cf. Xen. *Ages.* 1.34, idem., *Hell.* 3.3.1, 4.3.21).

The section on the youth, 40–2, perhaps, as was noted, provides a clue. In 40, the choice of reading is between ἄ]νηβος and ἔ]νηβος (the ν is certain; cf. schol. Theocr. 8.3, you are ἄνηβος till 15, ἔνηβος henceforth). ἄνηβος gives a contrast with ἡβατάς, 34; with ἔνηβος we are left to wonder about the consequences of the pollution of an ἄνηβος. According to Maas, the section has nothing to do with tithing, but refers, with its contrast between involuntary and voluntary pollution, to wet dreams and masturbation. (He sees this reference, and the severity of the penalty, as an argument in favour of ἔνηβος.) It has perhaps been misplaced here because of a desire, observable from 32–82, to divide the inscription into ten-line sections. The point about the ten-line sections is correct (cf. Vogliano 289), and, in a context that treats of 'tenths', startling; is this conscious number-symbolism, and if it is, what parallels are available at this religious level? The sexual interpretation of μιᾶι is linguistically plausible (cf. p. 76 n. 9), but its implications here are too extraordinary to be accepted without modification. Can we really imagine a Greek sacred law imposing such penalties – indeed any penalties – on young men for such offences in ordinary circumstances? If the sexual interpretation is correct, we would have to assume some specific and restricted application (temple servants, boys preparing for a specific ritual, or the like). Of this, however, the text offers no hint.

Vogliano thinks these boys are δεκατοί like the ἡβαταί. The difference in their situation lies only in the concession made for involuntary pollution. Although it is not stated, we understand that the youth voluntarily polluted must also sacrifice a tithe (note the prefix in προθύσει, 42). In favour of this it may be said that 33 seems to envisage the possibility of δεκατοί who are not full grown. But it is perhaps more plausible that the ἄνηβος has committed an offence which would have rendered him δεκατός but for his age (cf. V. Arangio-Ruiz, *Persone e famiglia nel diritto dei papiri*, Milan, 1930, 12 n. 2); as it is, he gets off more lightly. This would confirm that 'tithing' is a consequence of pollution; but the character of the pollution would remain unclear.

The assessment of a tithed man's value by 'selling him in the market' is an extraordinary and unparalleled procedure. The commentators without exception assume the sale to have been a fictional one; and if it is not, to whom do the remaining nine-tenths of the tithed man's value fall? But it is hard to see how interested participation and fair bidding at a fictional sale could be ensured. (It has been suggested that *P. Oxy.* 716.18 ff provides a parallel for the assessment of a man's value by mock-sale, but there seems no difficulty about seeing the sale there as genuine.)

The restrictions of 48–53 cause surprise by their position. Latte cited Aeschin. 3.21, a law forbidding officials who were ὑπεύθυνοι to dedicate goods, and Gaius, *Dig.* 44.6.3, 'rem de qua controversia est prohibemur in sacrum dedicare'. Our text, however, is more limited, referring only, it seems, to mortuary offerings. Ferri and Wilamowitz took this as an extreme case, 'not even for a pious duty, much less for anything else'. But the rule, which names a penalty, is oddly specific if so. It is tempting to suppose that it belongs somewhere in the following section, on the obligations of the dead *dekatos*' heir. If it is correctly placed, the point is perhaps to protect Apollo's goods from even indirect contact with funerary pollution.

Other serious difficulties, less relevant to this book's theme, can only be mentioned here without full discussion. In 33 ff. we hear of a man who is tithed, in 43 ff. of property that is tithed; the procedure in the two cases is distinct. In 58–9, however, the heir of a man tithed in his person is required to purify the inherited property, presumably in preparation for sacrificing a tenth of it to the god. Thus here the personal tithe seems to extend to the property too. Probably, therefore, the true distinction is not, as 33–48 initially imply, between a tithe on person and one on property, but between a tithe on person plus property and on property alone (Vogliano; Luzzatto, however, believes that the tithe always covers both person and property.)

The possibility 'if a man who is *dekatos* dies' is envisaged twice (53, 63). In the second case he is imagined as having produced several children, some still living and some now dead. What of the first? Vogliano, alone among scholars who have explicitly considered the problem, argued that the *dekatos* left a single child as heir. Commoner

has been the view that 53 ff. treat the case of the *dekatos* who dies
without direct heirs. Its proponents (de Sanctis, Luzzatto, Koschaker,
Abh. Sächs. Ak. 42 (1934), 53–5, and particularly V. Arangio-Ruiz,
loc. cit.) point out that in 60–3, in contrast to 69–72, there is no talk of
the heir assessing his own value and sacrificing a tithe of it, or
undergoing personal purification. The difference, they argue, implies
a qualitative distinction: the *heres externus* must pay the dead man's
tithe, but only direct descendants become polluted in their own
person. Thus the two sections treat extreme cases (no direct heirs/
various direct heirs, living and dead), on the basis of which proper
responses to intermediate situations can be worked out, if they are not
obvious anyway. The argument is ingenious; but it is impossible to be
certain that the omission of a provision in a particular part of this law
proves it to have been inapplicable there.

Amid all this uncertainty, the positive information that emerges is
disappointingly slight. The most conspicuous feature is, perhaps, the
rigorous protection of the god's rights. The condition of being *dekatos*
is, unless effaced, hereditary, and seems to extend to all the tithed
man's offspring, since the surviving son is required to pay tithes also
for his dead siblings. With the tithe, pollution too is inherited; the son
requires purification from his father's taint. Here we have one substantial gain; this is virtually the only instance that can be quoted of
an inherited pollution that has recognized legal effects (cf. pp. 204 ff.,
and p. 185 on the 'Gottesurteil von Mantinea').

73–82   (*Fragmentary beyond restoration*)

Wilamowitz remarked that the only certain fact about the content of
these lines is that it had nothing to do with either what preceded or
what followed; but even that negative conclusion is perhaps too
positive.

B

2–8   '. . . but she herself shall not be under the same roof as her
husband nor shall she incur pollution until she comes to Artemis. Any
woman who, without doing this, voluntarily incurs pollution, after
purifying the temple of Artemis shall sacrifice in addition as penalty a
full grown animal, and then shall go to the sleeping chamber. But if
she incurs pollution involuntarily, she shall purify the shrine.'

9–14 'A bride must go down to the bride-room to Artemis, whenever she wishes at the Artemisia, but the sooner the better. Any woman who does not go down [shall sacrifice in addition, *or* (Calhoun) shall not sacrifice] to Artemis [what is customary at the Artemisia]; not having gone down, [she shall purify the shrine] and sacrifice in addition [a full grown animal as penalty.]

The detailed logic of 9–14 is quite uncertain. The repetition ἃ δέ κα μὴ κατένθηι . . . μὴ κατεληλευθυῖα looks almost like a product of conflation in drafting. Calhoun suggested his οὐ θυσεῖ in *CP* 29 (1934), 345 f.

15–23 '[A pregnant woman] shall go down to the bride-room to Artemis . . . shall give to the bear (*a priestess*) the feet and head and skin. If she does not go down before giving birth she shall go down with a full grown animal. She who goes down shall observe purity on the seventh and eighth and ninth, and she who has not gone down shall observe purity on those days. But if she incurs pollution, she shall purify herself, purify the shrine and sacrifice in addition as penalty a full grown animal.'

Ferri and Wilamowitz could make little of this section. De Sanctis and Maas independently suggested that we are dealing with successive stages in a woman's career, and the ritual obligations attendant on them: 1–8 pre-marital, 9–14 the new bride, 15–23 the expectant or new mother. The interpretation is almost certainly correct; indeed, obscure though it is, this section illustrates as effectively as any text the way in which it is through ritual performances that social change is articulated and expressed. The performances are here required not merely by custom but by an actual religious law. Before marriage the girls must go to the 'sleeping-room' for the προνύμφιος ὕπνος (cf. Callim. fr. 75.2 with Pfeiffer), after it to a Nympheion in the precinct of Artemis (on its probable identity see F. Chamoux, op. cit., 315–19; its position gives special relevance to the verb 'go down'). Various passages illustrating such obligations have been collected by commentators (see too L. Deubner, 'Hochzeit und Opferkorb', *JDAI* (1925), 210–23): Suda s.v. ἄρκτος ἢ Βραυρωνίοις: ἐψηφίσαντο οἱ Ἀθηναῖοι μὴ πρότερον συνοικίζεσθαι ἀνδρὶ παρθένον εἰ μὴ ἀρκτεύσειε τῇ θεῷ; Plut. *Amat. Narr.* 772b, Suda s.v. προτέλεια, pre-marriage sacrifice to nymphs; schol. Theocr. 2.66, appeasement of Artemis by those about to marry, or pregnant for the first time; Apostolius 10.96,

Suda s.v. *Λυσίζωνος γυνή*, maidens before first intercourse dedicate girdles to Artemis.

The penalties and purifications in this section strongly recall those of the tithed man. It becomes tempting to turn back to the *dekatos* and try to interpret his condition in similar terms, as an obligation incurred by young men at a particular stage in life rather than the consequence of an offence. The temptation is strengthened by the fact that *δεκατεύω* could be used in Attic as an equivalent to *ἀρκτεύω* (Didymus *ap.* Harpocration s.v. *δεκατεύειν*); the world of the Cyrenaean girls recalls that of the Attic 'bears of Artemis', and we even find in Cyrene a bear priestess (B 16, cf. *SEG* ix 13.12, Chamoux, op. cit., 319). But it proves impossible to carry this interpretation through. The *dekatos* can be of any age (he might die, leaving children); and, in contrast to the girls of face B, no form of behaviour seems to be available to him by which he will avoid the need for penal sacrifice.

Several details in the section are elusive. What, for instance, is the pollution of 3–8, that may be incurred either voluntarily or involuntarily? Menstruation is involuntary only; intercourse may be either, but one would expect *μὴ ἑκοῖσα* to mean 'accidentally' rather than 'against her will'. If the pollution is indeed sexual, it is remarkable that the act performed in private should make necessary a purification of the temple of Artemis. In 21, *μιᾶι* probably does refer to sexual pollution, in view of the contrast with *ἁγνευσεῖ* in 19, and this supports the sexual interpretation earlier. (*ἁγνεύω* is not confined to sexual purity, but without further specification this is the most natural reference.) Unfortunately the point of this *hagneia* 'on the seventh, eighth and ninth' is uncertain. Some commentators feel that it should precede the 'going down' of 15, 18, and 19; accordingly Maas, by his supplement in 15, located the 'going down' on the tenth. But 20 f. imply rather strongly that the occasion for going down (whether performed or not) preceded the *hagneia*. Are the seventh, eighth, and ninth perhaps the days leading up to the tenth-day ceremony after birth? (cf. p. 51).

24–7 'If a woman throws out (*i.e.* miscarries), if it is distinguishable (*i.e.* if the foetus has recognizable form), they are polluted as from one who has died, but if it isn't distinguishable, the house itself is polluted as from a woman in childbed.'

On the pollution of miscarriage see p. 50 n. 67. There is doubt about the sense of 'the house itself' here: cf. p. 50, and G. M. Calhoun, *CP* 29 (1934), 345 f., whose reading *αὐτά* in 26 I adopt.

28 'Of Suppliants'
(*a new heading in large letters*)

The suppliants are helpfully discussed by J. Servais, *BCH* 84 (1960), 112–47.

29–39 'Suppliant from abroad (*or*, Visitant sent by spells). If a ('suppliant') is sent to (*or*, against) the house, if (the householder) knows, from whom he came to him, he shall name him by proclamation for three days. If (the sender of the suppliant) has died in the land or perished anywhere else, if (the householder) knows his name, he shall make proclamation by name, but if he doesn't know his name (in the form) "o man (*anthrōpos*), whether you are a man or a woman". Having made male and female figurines either of wood or of earth he shall entertain them and offer them a portion of everything. When you have done what is customary (*the change to second person appears random*), take the figurines and the portions to an unworked wood and deposit them there.'

We have here a triangular relationship between a 'suppliant', the man to whose house the 'suppliant' was sent, and the sender of the 'suppliant'. Little beyond this was clear when the text was first published, but subsequently the second half at least has been convincingly interpreted. Radermacher (*Anz. Akad. Wien*, 1927, 182 ff.) and de Sanctis independently explained that the recipient of the suppliant was required to propitiate the sender, and, since he could not do so literally, acted symbolically instead, by forming figurines to represent the sender, entertaining them to dinner with portions of food and drink, and so establishing a magically effective bond of guest-friendship. (On *kolossoi*, figurines, cf. M/L 5.44 (Cyrene), E. Benveniste, *Rev. Phil.* 58 (1932), 118–35, G. Roux, *REA* 62 (1960), 5–40, Vernant, *Pensée*, ii, 65–78). After the dinner the figurines and the food offered to them were to be carried out to an unworked wood, beyond the sphere of human activity, where their presence could do harm to none. As parallels for such symbolic entertainment, *lectisternia* and *théoxenia* (not unknown at Cyrene, cf. J. Defradas, *REG* 65 (1952), 282–301 on Pind. *Pyth.* 5. 83–6) can be quoted; Radermacher pointed out that Byzantine sailors used to seek good passage by entertaining an effigy of Saint Phokas to dinner, and Servais quoted magical parallels (*Papyri Graecae Magicae*, ed. K. Preisendanz, Leipzig, 1928, 1.40, 86, 4.54–70). Even more closely relevant, because it combines the two aspects of propitiation and expulsion, is the familiar Greek practice of sending out 'meals for Hecate' (p. 30 above).

Several different situations are envisaged in the law – the sender may be known or unknown, dead or alive – but the necessary ritual is not spelt out in each case. It is unclear whether the symbolic entertainment is always required, or only in the case specifically described where the sender is dead and unknown. The real difficulty, however, concerns the nature of the 'suppliant' and his sender. The common assumption is that he is a foreigner seeking incorporation in the community of Cyrene, and that the regulation reflects a time when this could only be achieved by admission, as a suppliant, in a private household. The ceremony described is the formal transfer of *potestas* over the suppliant from the foreign sender to the Cyrenaean recipient. To this interpretation there are serious objections. Rituals of this kind relating to *potestas* are unattested in Greece; it is very hard to see why the recipient should be ignorant of the name and sex of the sender, when the suppliant himself could readily enlighten him, or why the sender should remain so dangerous that his expulsion to an unworked wood was required. A female sender of suppliants is also surprising. A different approach was offered by H. J. Stukey, 'The Cyrenaean Hikesioi', *CP* 32 (1937), 32–43. He pointed out that the ἐπι – compounds, of which there are three in our passage, are typical of the language of magical attack. For ἐπακτός see p. 222 n. 79; for ἐπαγωγή see LSJ s.v. ἐπαγωγή, 4b; for ἐπιπέμπω (Lys.) 6.20, Xen. *Cyr.* 8.7.18, Pl. *Cri.* 46c, Dem. 24.121, LSJ s.v. ἐπιπέμπω, 2, and for later evidence Fr. Pfister, *Wochenschrift f. klassische Philologie* 29 (1912), 753–8; for ἐπηλυσία see *Hymn Hom. Cer.* 227 f., *Merc.* 37; and for the 'house' as target of magical attack see Theophr. *Char.* 16.7, Orph. *Hymn* 37.7 f., on a higher level Aesch. *Ag.* 1188–90, and probably a Sophron mime (see p. 223 above). Each of the ἐπι- compounds used in the inscription may, certainly, bear a non-magical sense, but the collocation is striking, and the further ἐπί in ἐπὶ τὰν οἰκίαν strongly suggests that the action is an aggressive one. Indeed, it is not clear that a non-aggressive sense of ἐπιπέμπω exists, except for that of 'send in addition' (which is perhaps the force of *SIG*³ 93.7, 273.24, cited by Servais). The ἱκέσιος ἐπακτός, therefore, is not a human suppliant but a demon sent against the house, as Hecate sometimes was, by an enemy. The suggestion has not been taken seriously, chiefly, no doubt, because its author rashly tried to transform the second and third suppliants, who are palpably human, into further spirits. But the same idea had occurred to Maas (*Epidaurische Hymnen*, Halle, 1933, 139, cf. *Hesperia* 13 (1944), 37 n. 4 = *Kl. Schr.* 202 n. 4), and is very likely to be correct.* It explains the characteristic language, the need for pro-

---

* On first reading the inscription, Hugh Lloyd-Jones independently thought of the same interpretation. I am grateful to him for persuading me that it is right.

pitiation and expulsion, and the possibility of a dead or unknown sender. The householder may suspect a particular enemy of working magic against him; or he may infer the fact of an attack from a series of misfortunes, but not know whom to ascribe it to specifically. Victims of murder, at least, could send out demons from the grave against their killers (Xen. *Cyr.* 8.7.18, ἐπιπέμπω), and the possibility doubtless extended to other cases; Pherecrates, fr. 174 ὁ λαγώς με βασκαίνει τεθνηκώς, may play with such ideas.

Maas saw a difficulty in the application of the term ἱκέσιος to a spirit; but this could be euphemism, and etymologically a suppliant is anyway merely a 'comer' (for the connection of the suppliant and the stranger see p. 181 above). A *prostropaios* may be an innocent human, or he may be an avenging demon (p. 108 n. 13 above). Stranger perhaps would be the intermingling of human and demonic suppliants in the same law, but even this is not inconceivable; in each case, an alien intrusion into the familiar world must be countered with due ritual procedures. (The demonic interpretation could be maintained, but the suppliant restored to humanity, by translating ἱκέσιος ἐπακτός as 'bewitched suppliant'; but this extension in the application of ἐπακτός is unattested.)

40–49 'Second suppliant, initiated or not initiated, having taken his seat at the public shrine. If an injunction is made, let him be initiated at whatever price is enjoined. If an injunction is not made, let him sacrifice fruits of the earth and a libation annually for ever. But if he omits it (*?: cf.* Buck), twice as much next year. If a child forgets and omits it, and an injunction is made to him, he shall pay to the god whatever is told him when he consults the oracle, and sacrifice, if he knows (where it is) on the ancestral tomb, and if not, consult the oracle.'

The 'injunctions' are presumably oracular, in view of the juxtaposition in 46 f.

Another regulation that is almost wholly obscure. Doubt centres on the meaning of τελέω, τελίσκω. A *telesphoria* had an important place in the cult of several gods at Cyrene (cf. Servais, op. cit., 137 n. 1; add *SEG* ix 65, 68 f., and *Supplemento Epigrafico Cirenaico*, 144–6, 252). It seems normally to be a procession, but the word could also be used with reference to initiation, Callim. *Cer.* 129. As in the case of the tithes, it is hard not to suspect a connection between the cathartic law and the institution revealed by the other epigraphic evidence; but once again it is impossible to advance beyond suspicion. If the reference here is to initiation, it is of a kind otherwise unknown, since it may entail permanent, and even hereditary, sacral obligations (perhaps it does so in all cases; or Latte may be right that, 'if an injunction is made', the initiate fulfilled his obligations by a once and for all payment). The connection between supplication and initiation is also unfamiliar. It has been thought that 'initiation' here confers admission not merely to a sacral but also a social grouping, and that the suppliant is a refugee seeking reception in Cyrene (Latte). But the uncertainties are too many for speculation to be profitable. The most useful discussion is that by Servais, op. cit.

50–55 'Third suppliant, a killer. He shall present the suppliant to the [　　] cities(?) and three tribes. When he announces that (the killer) has arrived as a suppliant, he (someone else?) shall seat him on the threshold on a white fleece, [wash] and anoint him; and (they?) shall go out into the public road, and all shall keep silent while they (the killer and his sponsor?) are outside, obeying the announcer . . . (*fragmentary: there is a reference to* 'sacrifices').'

The suppliant appears to have a sponsor, who 'presents him as a suppliant' (ἀφικετεύω, a new word, but cf. Ζεὺς ἀφίκτωρ, Aesch. *Supp.* 1) to the [　　] πολίαν καὶ τριφυλίαν. These bodies are otherwise unknown (but for the Zeus Triphylios of Euhemerus see *RE* 10 A 347); the mention of a threshold in 52 suggests that the precise reference here is to a building, or buildings, in which they met. The significant point is that the *triphylia* must in some sense represent the whole state; the purification of the murderer is thus a matter of public concern. On the further ritual details the commentary of Latte was definitive. He noted the significance of the threshold (the murderer may not yet enter), the fleece (cf. p. 373), and the 'announcer' (cf. Eur. *IT* 1208–10, 1226, ἐκποδὼν δ'αὐδῶ πολίταις τοῦδ' ἔχειν μιάσματος, and the heralds who preceded Roman flamens to stop artisans from working in their presence). 'Silence' in this context normally belongs to the killer himself (p. 371), but it can scarcely be applied to him here, and the extension is very natural. In 52–3 I read νί]ζεν rather than λευκ[μονί]ζεν (Oliverio); a rule about dress is quite out of place at this point, and the verb is ill-formed (Masson, op. cit.)

This suppliant is probably a refugee from abroad, since he requires presentation to the *triphylia*. He is designated αὐτοφόνος, but the exact force of this is uncertain (for discussion of the αὐτο- compounds used of killing cf. Fraenkel on Aesch. *Ag.* 1091, F. Zucker, *Sitz. Leipz.* 107 (1962), n. 4, 22–4, and references in p. 122 n. 69 above on *authentēs*).

The words αὐτοφόνος, αὐτοφόντης, αὐτοκτόνος, αὐτοσφαγής are used in tragedy of kin-murder, and occasionally of suicide. But that does not settle the question of αὐτοφόνος in the inscription. Tragedy is much occupied with kin-murder, and these words are used to indicate it adjectivally, not independently, in a context that clearly determines the meaning. Even in tragedy, αὐτοκτόνος once means 'killing with one's own hand' (Aesch. *Ag.* 1635), and that is perhaps the natural origin to ascribe to the proper name Autophonos of Hom. *Il.* 4.395. Of the two αὐτο- compounds used of killing that have some non-poetic existence, αὐθέντης can mean 'murderer' (Soph. *OT* 107), and αὐτόχειρ often has that sense, sometimes (Pl. *Leg.* 872a, Xen. *Hell.* 6.4.35) but not always with special emphasis on the actual physical performance of the killing. (The weakening of sense from 'killer with one's own hand' to 'killer' is very natural.) With the possible exception of Pl. *Resp.* 615c, which is anyway of elevated style, it seems nowhere to have the sense of 'kin-killer' in prose. Three renderings of αὐτοφόνος are therefore possible: kin-killer, actual killer, killer. The most plausible, because the most general, is probably the third.

Masson, op. cit., questions whether -πολίαν in 51 can derive from πόλις; but cf. ἀστυπολία, ἀλλοπολία.

Appendix 3:
Problems concerning 'Enter pure from . . .'
Requirements in Sacred Laws

(1) *Purity ἀπὸ λεχους.*

In four sacred laws purity is required ἀπὸ λεχους. (In *LSA* 51. 6 read [τ]ε[κούση]ς with Fraser rather than λ[εχοῦ]ς.) In three there is formal ambiguity between the accentuation ἀπὸ λεχοῦς (λεχώ, woman in childbed) and λέχους (λέχος, bed). In the fourth, *LSS* 115 B 27, λεχοῦς is certain, as λέχος would give λέχεος in Cyrenaean. This unambiguous Cyrenaean case is a strong argument in favour of reading λεχοῦς throughout; so too is the analogy with the commoner way of expressing the same regulation, ἀπὸ τεκούσης *vel. sim.* (cf. references in p. 50 n. 67 above).

If λέχους were read, it would still refer to childbirth, as intercourse is spoken of differently in sacred laws (P. M. Fraser, 'An Inscription from Cos', *Bulletin de la Société Archaeologique d'Alexandrie* 40 (1953), 35–62, at p. 45). There remains, however, a possibility of real difference in meaning between the two readings. With λεχοῦς, the rule refers to those who come into contact with a new mother, but says nothing explicit about the mother herself. With λέχους, interpreted as 'after (contact with) childbirth', the laws might be taken as regulating the access of:

(1) the mother herself
(2) both the mother and those in contact with her
(3) those in contact with the mother.

Option (3), of course, makes λέχους effectively synonymous with λεχοῦς; and it can practically be discounted, as it is clear from the parallels cited earlier that the way to express the outsider's ritual status is ἀπὸ τεκούσης or λεχοῦς, just as 'to approach a woman in childbed' is ἐπὶ λεχὼ ἴεναι (Theophr. *Char.* 16.9).

In *LSS* 91.15, ἀπὸ λεχους γ´, λεχώ κα´, λεχοῦς is clearly right: 'After contact with a woman lying in, 3 days; the woman herself, 21 days'. For this way of expressing the contrast between the mother and others cf. *LSCG* 124.5–6,7–8. Only in the implausible sense (3) could λέχους be admitted here. For *LSCG* 171.16–17, ἀπὸ λεχους καὶ ἐγ δια(φθ)ορᾶς (?)ἀμέρας δέκα, ἀπὸ γυναικὸς τρεῖ[ς], the arguments were well presented by Fraser in the first publication (op. cit.). The period of ten days would better suit the mother herself (cf. p. 52 n. 74), but is not inconceivable for those who have contact with her; cf. *LSS* 54.3, seven days, and perhaps the Arcadian text about to be discussed. The shrine is intended for men, line 16, and it is to them that the purity rules are addressed (ἁγνόν 15, ἀπὸ γυναικός 17). We are thus left again with the possibility of λέχους only in sense (3).

The new sacred law from an Arcadian cult of Isis is the one where λέχους has most plausibility (*BCH* 102 (1978), 325). Masculine and feminine endings alternate in this text surprisingly, and the adjective in the relevant rule is feminine, lines 5–6: ἀπὸ μὲν λεχ[ο]υς ἐναταίαν. In 8–9 we have ἀπὸ δὲ τῶν φυσικῶν (menstruation) ἑβδομαίαν. If the latter, as seems almost inevitable, refers to the menstruating woman herself, ought not the former to refer to the mother? (The intervening regulation, 6–8, on miscarriage, is itself too ambiguous to help in either direction.) This would impose the reading λέχους, interpreted in sense (1) or (2). Against this we may observe: (*a*) λέχους would be quite isolated among sacred laws (but the possibility that the formula was reapplied mistakenly here should be considered); (*b*) where the ritual status of the mother is undeniably specified, it is not done in this form; (*c*) the genitive after ἀπὸ is normally a specifically polluting object or substance; (*d*) the feminine is explicable if we assume that the law envisages the feminine birth-helpers. (This would mean that birth-pollution is here conceived as a matter of 'touching' rather than 'entering the same roof', as the possibility of male pollution is not considered.) It is, however, certainly more natural to refer the word to the mother, if we accept that the following provision about menstruation concerns the woman herself only. Here, therefore, the internal logic of the text on the whole supports λέχους; but analogy still strongly urges the claims of λεχοῦς.

(2) *What constitutes contact in 'Enter pure from . . .' laws?*
Where purity from certain foods is required, or from intercourse, there is obviously no difficulty. For death-pollution there are differential scales (above, p. 37 n. 17), but entering a house of death or attending a funeral creates some pollution even without physical contact with the corpse. For birth-pollution in the post-classical period there are no conclusive arguments; men can incur it, but they might touch the woman as well as enter the house. In the Cyrene cathartic law, 'entering the same roof' had been the determinant (Appendix 2). In Arcadia in the first century BC physical contact may have been (above).

Special problems are presented by rules requiring purity from abortion, menstruation, defloration, and the like. (We have considered in the previous section the same problem in relation to birth-pollution.) They could concern:

(a) the woman only

(b) the woman and those who touch her, during the period of active contamination

(c) the woman and those who come into social contact with her, during the same period.

In the case of menstruation, there are strong arguments for (a). In *LSCG* 55.5, *BCH* 102 (1978), p. 325, line 9, feminine endings show that the person contaminated is a woman, and in *LSS* 119.13 a menstruation rule appears in the female but not the male section of a law that appears to legislate for the two sexes successively (G. Plaumann, *Ptolemais in Oberägypten*, Leipzig, 1910, 54–8). In *LSS* 91.16 a reference to menstruation should perhaps be restored; the rule, whatever it was, was for women only. *LSS* 54, however, appears to be addressed to men (it requires purity ἀπὸ γυναικός but not ἀπ' ἀνδρός) but concludes ἀπὸ γυναικείων ἐναταίους. Interpretation (c) is hard to credit here, given the length of the exclusion, and even (b) surprising. If the rule is indeed for men, we should perhaps adopt a moderated form of (b) and understand 'after intercourse during menstruation'. But it is not inconceivable that women are envisaged; the masculine would be by attraction, and the absence of a purity rule ἀπ' ἀνδρός an omission due to the fact that the worshippers were primarily male.

In the classical period, abortion (spontaneous or contrived) certainly polluted according to principle (c) (p. 50 n. 67). There are several later sacred laws for which (a) is impossible. *LSS* 119.5 is a rule for men; unfortunately the period is lost, and we cannot see whether it was forty days as for the mother in the same law (10). Where a genitive of specification occurs, as in *LSS* 91.11 ἀπὸ φθορᾶς γυναικὸς ἢ κυνὸς ἢ ὄνου, and *LSA* 84.5, the rule is certainly not addressed to the woman (or dog, or ass), or it would be phrased γυναῖκα ἀπὸ φθορᾶς. In *LSS* 91.11 (c) is preferable to (b) – in other cases we cannot choose – as there would be little occasion for manhandling the dog or donkey in these circumstances. *LSCG* 171.17 seems to be addressed to men (above), *BCH* 102 (1978), p. 325 lines 6–8 to women, but not necessarily the mother alone (above), while *LSS* 54 is, as we have seen, ambiguous. *LSCG* 55.7 and 139.12 are quite indefinite. *LSS* 119.10 is apparently addressed to women, but has been preceded by a rule for men. Thus interpretation (a) is nowhere certain, while it is excluded in several cases. This need not necessarily mean, however, that it is to be excluded everywhere. It is quite plausible that at different times and in different places the way in which pollution was diffused should have varied.

It is often thought that *LSCG* 124.5–6 (2nd c. BC?) referred to abortion, and specified 40 days impurity for the mother and 10 for those in contact with her. If this were correct, we would see how the

40-day term was extended in later laws from the mother herself to all those involved. But, as E. Nardi notes (*Eranion Maridakis*, cf. below, 63), the mother who has aborted would not normally be called ἁ τετόκοισα (contrast *LSS* 119.11). He suggests a reference to exposure of the child, but the most polluted person should then be 'he/she who puts it out' and not the mother. Stillbirth would be a possibility, but it is not elsewhere envisaged separately in sacred laws. Perhaps the argument from τετόκοισα is too nicely drawn.

About pollution 'from a maidenhead' (*LSCG* 139.18, *LSS* 91.12) there is no evidence; both parties were probably affected.

(3) *Pollution ἀπὸ φθορᾶς vel sim.*

(The relevant laws are printed and discussed by E. Nardi, 'Antiche prescrizioni greche di purità cultuale in tema d'aborto', *Eranion in honorem G. S. Maridakis*, Athens, 1963, i, 43–85, with an addendum in *Studi in Onore di E. Volterra*, Milan, 1971, i, 141–8.)

The period of pollution for miscarriage in classical sacred laws corresponds either to that for birth or death (p. 50 n. 67 above). In later sacred laws the period leaps up to a typical 40 days (so *LSS* 54.6, probably 91.11, 119.10, *LSA* 84.5, *LSCG* 55.7, *LSCG* 139.12 (from 'abortive drugs'); *BCH* 102 (1978), p. 325 lines 6–8 has 44 days, *LSCG* 171.17 probably 10; the relevance of *LSCG* 124.5–6 is unclear, cf. above). Thus in most cases it far exceeds the periods specified after a birth or death. Scholars have often thought that these regulations concern 'procured abortion', and that the extended period of impurity reflects a new ethical condemnation of the practice (cf. *LSA* 20.20; there is disagreement whether this condemnation is indigenous or imported). The objection sometimes advanced (e.g. *Ant. u. Chr.* 4 (1933–4), 18 f.) that these laws concern ritual impurity, which has no connection with guilt, is not serious, as in just this kind of sacred law the duration of sexual pollution is influenced by moral considerations. The real difficulty is that all the Greek words in question (φθορά, διαφθορά, ἐκτρωσμός, and others) indicate merely the fact of the expulsion of the foetus but not the cause (J. Ilberg, *ARW* 13 (1910), 3). Thus it is hard to see the justification for saying that in a particular law the reference is to miscarriage and not procured abortion, or vice versa. We cannot say that φθορά in sacred laws had acquired a restricted sense of 'procured abortion', as *LSS* 91.11 is a clear counter-case: ἀπὸ φθορᾶς γυναικὸς ἢ κυνὸς ἢ ὄνου ἥμε. μ᾽ Dogs and donkeys do not have procured abortions, and the suggestion that φθορά here means something quite different, sexual assault (Nock *apud* Sokolowski ad loc., cf. Nardi, *Studi Volterra*, loc. cit.), is a desperate one, as it goes against the regular use of the word in sacred laws – and, in the case of the latter two victims, opens the door to a world of quite unsuspected pollutions. The only one of the laws, therefore, that specifically concerns procured abortion is *LSCG* 139.12, where there is explicit reference to abortive drugs; in all the other cases, any woman who entered within 40 days of an involuntary miscarriage would be violating the rule. It is however plausible that it was moral revulsion against procured abortion that rendered abortion of any kind so impure and threatening, and that the legislators had procured abortion chiefly in mind. In two laws, significantly, abortion rules are associated with rules that make exposure of the child a pollution (*LSS* 119.7, 14 days; *LSA* 84.3–4, 40 days).

Appendix 4: Animals and Food

There was no category of impure animals in Greece. Aristotle acknowledges that there are some which 'we dislike looking at', but designates them 'most lacking in honour' rather than unclean. The distinction of animals in terms of honour appears in two further places in Aristotle, and Isocrates says that Egyptians reverence 'animals despised among us'.[1] (The classification by honour extends to plants, as Callimachus' fourth *iambus* shows.) Nor was there a category of impure food.[2] A culture can, without recognizing such a category explicitly, be strictly selective about what it regards as edible (dogs are inedible for the Englishman, without being unclean); but the Greeks were ready to eat more kinds of flesh than many peoples, to judge from the Hippocratic writer *On Regimen*, who lists, as the 'animals that are eaten', cattle, goats, pigs, sheep, donkeys, horses, dogs, wild boar, deer, hares, foxes, and hedgehogs. For most of the more surprising items in this list independent evidence is available, although some of them turn out to be despised food that all but the poor would avoid.[3]

Despite this, exclusion of a particular animal, or abstinence from a food, might sometimes be required by religious rule.[4] The obvious example of the former concerns the dog. It was denied entry to the Athenian acropolis, to Delos and other sacred islands, and, no doubt, to many sacred places besides.[5] In other respects, too, the dog's status was degraded. It was a symbol of shameless behaviour, and occupied the most ignominious place in the sacrificial system, being exploited in purifications and as an offering to the marginal Eileithyia, the

---

[1] Arist. *Poet.* 1448b 12, *De An.* 404b 4, *Part. An.* 645a 15; Isoc. *Bus.* 26.

[2] This is not confuted by the fact that there are special 'pure loaves' (Hdt. 2.40.3, Alexis, fr. 220. 10, Ath. 149e; cf. Rhinthon, fr. 3 Kaibel) and 'pure piglets' (Bruneau, 286 f.); the sense of 'pure' here is anyway uncertain.

[3] Hippoc. *Vict.* 2.46 (6.544–6 L.), which refutes Porph. *Abst.* 1.14. For fox cf. Ananius, fr. 5.5 West, Mnesimachus, fr. 4.49; dog, Ar. *Eq.* 1399, Hippoc. *Morb. Sacr.* 142.18 J., 1.14 G., Alexis, fr. 220.4; ass, Ar. *Eq.* 1399, with R. A. Neil's note, Xen. *Anab.* 2.1.6 (dire need), Pollux 9.48 (sold, interestingly, in a special place).

[4] Cf. Wächter, 76–115 (much of the material irrelevant).

[5] H. Scholz, *Der Hund in der griechisch–römischen Magie und Religion*, Berlin, 1937, 7 f. (main text Plut. *Quaest. Rom.* 290a–d); add Xen. *Cyn.* 5.25, *LSS* 112 IV B.

dishonoured Ares, and the tainted Hecate.[6] On the other hand, there is no reason to think that any of these negative connotations attached to the sacred dogs of Asclepius at Epidaurus, or those kept in other temple precincts. (Even the epic tradition that knew the man-eating dogs of the *Iliad* also had place for Odysseus' faithful Argos.) As we have seen, there was no danger in eating dog flesh, and the practice seems to have been common.

Abstention from foodstuffs is attested in various forms. There are a certain number of local taboos on the consumption of particular species, usually of no great economic significance;[7] the Seriphians, for instance, threw back any lobster they caught, saying they were 'Perseus' playthings'. Of permanent abstinence from particular foods by devotees of particular cults there is no trace. We know only of a few, not very rigorous, limitations imposed on priests.[8] Temporary abstinence, however, in preparation for specific ceremonies does seem to be occasionally attested for early Greece, just as actual fasting is. Late sources tell of a proclamation that was made to Eleusinian initiates to abstain from certain foods, and something similar is recorded about another festival of Demeter, the Haloa. Combination of these sources gives as the forbidden foods: house-birds, beans, pomegranates, apples, eggs, 'egg-laying animals', the meat of animals that died naturally, and various kinds of fish.[9] The attestation is late, but the Atthidographer Melanthius, writing at some date between 350 and 270 BC, mentioned one of the forbidden fishes, the red mullet, in a work on the Eleusinian Mysteries, and it is hard to see why, unless in connection with the ban.[10] Restrictions almost certainly existed, therefore, before the Roman period, although the list may well have been extended. For a different cult, we have similar evidence, again not incontestable but very strong, for the fifth century. A fragment of Cratinus' play about the incubation oracle of Trophonius runs: 'And not to eat any more the red-skinned Aixonian *triglē*, nor the *trygōn* nor the dread *melanouros*'.[11] The lines are quoted without context, but we

---

[6] Scholz, op. cit., 14–22; cf. J. M. Redfield, *Nature and Culture in the Iliad*, Chicago, 1975, 193–202.

[7] Nilsson, *GGR* 212 f.

[8] Cheese for priestess of Athena Polias at Athens, fish for some Poseidon priests: see Arbesmann, 72 f. Eur. *Cretans* fr. 79 Austin is questionable evidence.

[9] Eleusis: Arbesmann, 76 f. Haloa: schol. Lucian 280. 22 ff. Rabe (cited Deubner, 61.5). I accept the universal view that these are merely temporary restrictions (cf. the reference to 'those being initiated', not 'those who have been initiated', in Ael. *NA* 9.51, 65), but know no conclusive evidence; devoted individuals might have extended them.

[10] 326 *FGrH* fr. 2 *ap.* Ath. 325c.

[11] Fr. 221 (? cf. Aristophanes, fr. 23, from the *Amphiaraus*). Purity at Lebadeia: Ginouvès, 344 n. 4, and generally Arbesmann, 97–102 on pre-mantic dietary restrictions.

know that the cult of Trophonius imposed several requirements of purity, and two of the three fishes mentioned are among those banned at Eleusis. There is a reference to 'refraining from' (particular foods) 'for three days' in Aristophanes' *Peace*, although it is impossible to tell what specific cult he is parodying.[12]

Even a fifth-century attestation leaves open, of course, the formal possibility of Pythagorean influence. Pythagoreanism embodied a considerable number of dietetic precepts, not for temporary observance only but as parts of a permanent way of life, and some have supposed that this was the source of all the dietary rules of cult.[13] It is perhaps not very plausible that an Eleusis to which food restrictions were alien should have adopted the eccentric regulations of a south Italian sect that was best known to Athenians as a butt of comedy; but, in view of the Orphic reinterpretation of the Eleusinian eschatology, the possibility cannot quite be excluded. Pythagorean influence on the cult of Trophonius seems at first sight even less likely, but here too we know too little of the religious climate of fifth-century Lebadeia to say absolutely, 'This cannot be.' The alternative hypothesis is that Pythagoras adopted his rules, or many of them, from cult[14] or the fund of popular magico-religious beliefs that lay behind the cult rules. As a development it seems more natural that a temporary restriction should have been taken over and extended by a sect that sought especial sanctity than that rules, the point of which lay largely in being permanently observed, should have been trimmed down for cultic use in drastically attenuated form; but the Greeks seem later to have performed just such trimming in their reception of oriental cults, reducing permanent abstention from fish, for instance, to a three-day preparation for the festival.[15] The hypothesis of borrowing from philosophy is therefore irrefutable, though implausible. The same may be said in the case of the purifiers of *On the Sacred Disease*, who told their patients to abstain from various meats, fishes, and birds.[16] They do not seem to have mentioned the bean, abhorred of Pythagoras.

---

[12] 151, cf. 162–3, noted by Latte, *Kl. Schr.* 26. For Chrysippus such rules are part of traditional religion, Plut. *de Stoic. Rep.* 1044f. The epigraphic evidence for food *hagneiai* begins only in the 2nd century BC, and initially in relation to oriental cults; the influence of popular neo-Pythagoreanism seems subsequently also to become perceptible (A. D. Nock, *HSCP* 63 (1958), 415–21 = Nock ii, 847–52). See *LSCG* 55, 95, 139; *LSS* 54, 59, 108; *LSA* 84; *CR Acad. Inscr.* 1916, 263 f.; *Altertümer von Pergamon*, viii. 3, ed. C. Habicht, Berlin, 1969, p. 168; *BCH* 102 (1978), p. 325. References to food *hagneiai* in magical papyri in Lanata, 54, n. 177.
[13] Lobeck, 190, Ziehen, 150. On the Pythagorean rules see Burkert, *LS* 180–5, M. Detienne, 'La cuisine de Pythagore', *Archives de sociologie des religions*, 29 (1970), 141–62.
[14] D. L. 8.33.
[15] See e.g. Men. fr. 754 in contrast to *LSS* 54.
[16] Hippoc. *Morb. Sacr.* 142. 16 ff. J., 1.13–16 G., well discussed by Lanata, 53–60.

Passages in comedy offer some idea of the non-gastronomic grounds on which, in a secular context, Greeks might reject particular foods. In several places large deep-sea fish are spurned because they are 'man-eating'.[17] The objection is already implicitly present in Homer, where fish are seen as uncanny creatures, hostile to man, lurking in the depths ready to devour the flesh of shipwrecked sailors.[18] This is perhaps the reason why they are excluded from the heroic diet (as also, in the main, from cult), even though it is clear from the similes that fishing was familiar to Homer's audience. Though the argument can scarcely be pressed, it is interesting to note this pre-Pythagorean evidence for an ideal diet that is very selective, particularly as it is to species of fish that the earliest evidence for abstinence at Eleusis relates. Another mark held against animals as food was the practice of 'eating excrement'.[19] It was too common to be an absolute disqualification, but it is perhaps not a coincidence that the purifiers of *On the Sacred Disease* told their patients to abstain from dog, pig, and goat (as well as deer), the three domestic animals that were commonly charged with scatophagy. By consuming such animals, one becomes a vicarious 'man-eater' and 'dung-eater' oneself. Human flesh and dung were, of course, the supremely impossible foods for a man. Cannibalism is analogous to incest,[20] while 'dung-eater' is an expression used of a man who will stop at nothing, and more loosely as one of those insults that derive, like 'temple-robber', 'murderer', and 'mother-sleeper', from the most degraded or polluting acts.[21] In their literal form these were pollutions of the imagination only, since no Greek was tempted by either diet; but, as we have seen, the taint could attach vicariously to other foods. Other objections that are brought against foodstuffs are that they are 'food for corpses' or 'for Hecate', and, sometimes in connection with this point, that they are anaphrodisiac.[22]

Such explicit interpretations of the religious rules as are available, none of them certainly early, are based on no consistent principle. It is characteristic that Aelian, referring to two of the Eleusinian rules, states that the initiate shuns the dogfish as unclean, because it gives birth through its mouth, but spares the red mullet as a mark of honour

---

[17] Antiphanes, fr. 68.12, 129.6, cf. Alexis, fr. 76. 1–4; most explicitly the didactic Archestratus *ap.* Ath. 163d, 310e (pointing out that all fishes are 'man-eating' and not some only); cf. too Pindar, fr. 306.

[18] See H. Fränkel, *Die homerischen Gleichnisse*, Göttingen, 1921, 86–8, esp. 87 n. 2.

[19] Epicharmus, fr. 63, cf. (mud) Philemon, fr. 79.19. The writers on fish often allude to 'mud-eating'. For scatophagous animals (and men) see J. Henderson, *The Maculate Muse*, Yale, 1975, 192–4.

[20] See p. 98.

[21] See Sandbach on Men. *Sam.* 550.

[22] Plato Comicus, fr. 173.19, Antiphanes, fr. 68.14, Amphis, fr. 20, Eubulus, fr. 14.

for its exceptional fertility, or its services to man.[23] The same ambiguity is found in the Pythagorean tradition. It was generally agreed, although detailed interpretations varied, that it was as an abomination that Pythagoras banned the bean from his table.[24] But the white cock was sacred (to the sun or Men) and should be spared for that reason.[25] As to fish, on the one hand sacred fish (obviously those sacred to the Olympians) were not to be eaten, 'for men and gods should not have the same privileges any more than masters and slaves.'[26] On the other, one should abstain from two particular species because they 'belong to the chthonian gods' (and were therefore impure).[27] The participants in one of Plutarch's table conversations discuss Pythagoras' rejection of fish, which they take to have been total. Three possibilities are canvassed; he held fish in honour for their silence; he regarded them, inhabitants of the deep, as wholly alien to man; or he felt that man had no right to eat inoffensive creatures that he neither tended nor fed.[28] Iamblichus sums up the ambiguities of the tradition when he states explicitly that Pythagoras banned such foods as were indigestible, or alien to the gods, or, on the contrary, sacred to the gods and so worthy of honour, or, finally, liable to interfere with the purity, moderation, or mantic powers of the soul.[29] The same ambivalence must have been already present within the oldest form of explanation, that by myth. Among the forbidden Eleusinian foods Demeter had good cause to abhor the pomegranate because of its use to trap Persephone, but she herself was the 'apple-bringer'.[30] Their sacrificial victims, too, gods either 'loved' or 'hated'. We are near once again to the 'primitive confusion of the sacred and unclean'. But, though the ancients might doubt whether a particular forbidden food was sacred or unclean, they never supposed it to be both; and nothing suggests that any of the forbidden foods were invested with a fearsome and ambiguous sanctity.

To offer an alternative explanation of most of these restrictions is,

[23] *NA* 9.51, 65. 'Honour' for mullet also in Plut. *De soll. an.* 983f. In *Anth. Pal.* 7.406 (Theodoridas 14 Gow/Page) the *mystēs* 'loves' pomegranate, apple, and myrtle (with obscene double meaning).
[24] Burkert, *LS* 183–5, with references in 183 n. 124.
[25] e.g. D. L. 8.34, Iambl. *Protr.* 21, Burkert, *LS* 172 n. 47.
[26] D. L. 8.34.
[27] Iambl. *VP* 109, *Protr.* 21.
[28] *Quaest. Conv.* 8.8 728c–730f. For other discussions of *hagneiai* see ibid., 669e–671e (ambiguity again), *De Is. et Os.* 352f–354b, Julian *Or.* 5.173d–177c (ambiguous). The Jewish exegetical tradition by contrast is clear that forbidden foods are unclean: see e.g. Philo *De Spec. Leg.* 4.100–131, *De Agr.* 130 ff.; the *Letter of Aristeas*, 144 ff.; S. Stein, *Studia Patristica* 2 (*Texte und Untersuchungen* 64), 141 ff.
[29] *VP* 106.
[30] *SIG*³ 1122.6, Paus. 1.44.3. Pomegranate: *Hymn. Hom. Cer.* 372 with Richardson.

perhaps, an impossible task. Their precise extent in the early period is uncertain; in the case of the Pythagorean rules the evidence is, at first sight, actually contradictory, and it is as though through a mist that we see the milieu in which they were observed. If the various restrictions are but a part of a more elaborate web of symbolic associations and oppositions, only this torn-off fragment remains. It is by chance only that we know that pomegranates, banned to the Eleusinian initiate, were eaten ritually at the Thesmophoria.[31] Another area of our ignorance is the archaic ethnozoology of the Greeks, their native ways of classifying plants and animals. Aristotle cannot tell us what associations a particular species or natural product may have had for the contemporaries of Homer.

But a few conclusions seem possible. The early vegetarians refused to eat animals on the grounds that this was a form of cannibalism.[32] Thus a central institution of society was subverted by appeal to that society's own values, since for all Greeks human flesh was the most impossible of foods. (The further step of repudiating bread, the staple of normal diet, as a form of dung was reserved for Herodotus' mythical Ethiopians.[33]) An Orphic poet assimilated bean-eating too to cannibalism: 'It is no better to eat beans than your father's head.'[34] As we have seen, fish-eating could be seen as a vicarious form of the same offence. Even on the more restricted interpretation of Pythagoras' teaching, by which he banned 'womb', 'heart', and 'brain', the association of these parts with vitality seems significant; to eat them is life-destroying. (The same can perhaps be said of the Orphic ban on eating eggs.[35]) The possibility of consuming a restricted set of sacrificial animals was justified by the claim that into these no human soul could pass.[36] The general purport of the cultic rules is different, since there is no question in this case of radical revaluation of accepted norms. It seems, however, that some of the same forms of assessment are at work here too. The fish that was most commonly banned was the red mullet (*triglē*), which fits neatly into the pattern. It 'delighted in polluted things,' and 'would eat the corpse of a fish or a man'. Blood-coloured itself, it was sacred to the blood-eating goddess Hecate.[37] It seems a symbolic summation of all the negative

---

[31] Deubner, 58.

[32] p. 305.

[33] Hdt. 3. 22.4; cf. J. P. Vernant, in J. P. Vernant and M. Detienne, *La Cuisine du sacrifice en pays grec*, Paris, 1979, 239–49.

[34] *OF* fr. 291, cf. Porph. *VP* 43.

[35] Womb, heart, and brain: e.g. Arist. fr. 194, Iambl. *Protr.* 21. Eggs: *OF* fr. 291.

[36] Iambl. *VP* 85, Burkert, *LS* 182.

[37] Pollution, corpses: Ael. *NA* 2.41. And Hecate: Ath. 325 a–b, cf. Antiphanes, fr. 68.14 *ap.* Ath. 358f, 313b, and Nausicrates, fr. 1–2 *ap.* Ath. 296a. Hecate and blood: *RE* s.v. *Hekate*, col. 2776. The *triglē* was banned at Eleusis and the Haloa, by the purifiers of

characteristics of the creatures of the deep. (It is therefore disconcerting that Aelian explains the Eleusinian rule as a mark of 'honour' for its good qualities.[38]) Of the other five fishes[39] certainly or probably banned at Eleusis one, the dogfish, was a 'man-eater' (as well as abnormal in its way of giving birth);[40] two were, according to Iamblichus, sacred to the chthonians,[41] and, even if that information is unreliable, alluded to the colours of blood and death in their names, *melanouros* and *erythrinos*; and one was sacred to Hecate, although not perhaps for any other reason than that it was cheap.[42] At Lebadeia, the murderous sting-ray,[43] with which Telegonus slew Odysseus, seems to have been banned. But there remains one Eleusinian fish, the *karabos* or crayfish (as also one Pythagorean), for which no such explanation is available.[44] And it does not seem that the ban on pomegranates, apples, and house-birds relates directly to their natural properties, whether actual or ascribed. The connections here are rather with Demeter's own powers and mythology – her role as 'apple-bringer', and the tricking of her daughter with a pomegranate seed.[45]

The ambiguity in the ancient interpretations, by which animals are spared for both good and bad qualities, should perhaps encourage us to look for a structural explanation, whereby two tabooed extremes mark out an area of the edible in the middle. In some societies, it has

---

Morb. Sacr., at the oracle of Trophonius, and to the priestess of Hera at Argos (Ael. *NA* 9.65). Cf. F. J. Dölger, *Ichthys*, Münster, 1922, ii, 316–330.

[38] Above, p. 361 n. 23.

[39] Exhaustive discussion in F. J. Dölger, op. cit., ii, 330–58.

[40] Archestratus *ap.* Ath. 163d, 310e (on κύων; but the point must apply to all the sharks, cf. R. Strömberg, *Studien zur Etymologie und Bildung der griechischen Fischnamen*, Göteborg, 1943, 104); Ael. *NA* 9.65. Cf. D'Arcy W. Thompson, *A Glossary of Greek Fishes*, Oxford, 1947, s.v. γαλεός.

[41] Iambl. *VP* 109, *Protr.* 21.

[42] The *mainis*: Melanthius, 326 *FGrH* fr. 2 *ap.* Ath. 325c (from which the ban is inferred). Cheapness of *mainis*: e.g. Pherecrates, fr. 56.

[43] *Trygōn*, Cratinus, fr. 221: cf. D'Arcy W. Thompson, op. cit., s.v.

[44] *Karabos*: even F. J. Dölger, op. cit., was baffled. Pythagorean fish: *akalēphē* (sea anemone), Arist. fr. 194. It was an ambiguous creature, half-plant and half-animal (see D'Arcy W. Thompson, op. cit., s.v.), but we do not know that such things mattered to Pythagoras. The apparent association with 'womb' in Ar. *Lys.* 549 may be more relevant. The ban on grey mullet and eel in *Morb. Sacr.* can be explained in either digestive (cf. Hippoc. *Int.* 12, 7.198.16 L., *Vict.* 2.48, 6.548.18 L.) or religious terms: for eels and Hecate see Ar. *Lys.* 700–2; for both fish together in a sacred pool, Ath. 331e, and for the special status of grey mullet as the 'fasting fish', the polar opposite of *triglē* (but no source makes the connection), Ath. 307 ff., D'Arcy W. Thompson, op. cit., s.v. *kestreus*. Their presumed spontaneous generation could also be relevant (Arist. *HA* 569a 22–6, 570a 3–24).

[45] 'Apple-bringer'; *SIG*³ 1122.6, Paus. 1.44.3.

been argued, there is a correlation between an animal's edibility and its 'social distance' in relation to man.[46] The scale of social distance might in a typical case extend from house-animals and labouring animals (inedible), via the domesticated but non-labouring animals (edible) and game animals (ambiguously edible), to the wild beasts (inedible). This scale, it is suggested, may be subconsciously perceived as analogous to that which determines permissible marriage-partners, who have to be sought in the middle area between close kin and strangers. (For Greece, we have already noted the connection between sexual crime and monstrous food.) Although the problems involved are complex,[47] such an approach might help to interpret the Greek sacrificial system. The sacrificial animals come from the middle range, and the less domesticated victims, in particular the goat, are to some extent favoured by the less domesticated gods.[48] There is nothing alien to Greek thought in explaining sacrificial practice in terms of an animal's moral relation to man. A Bouzygean curse is supposed to have threatened those who sacrificed the ploughing ox (by his services to man, he is brought too close for edibility); but the pig must be eaten, because he pays back his nurture in no other way than with his meat.[49] Particularly within Pythagoreanism such considerations have importance; goat and pig, on one view, are fit for sacrifice because they interfere with agriculture, but ox and sheep should be spared.[50] If these animals are too close to man to be eaten, fish by contrast are too distant. Domesticated animals 'live with men' (*synanthrōpeuō*), and in neo-Pythagoreanism this proximity becomes explicitly a reason for sparing them.[51] But, promising though the structural approach may appear for the sacrificial system in general, it can scarcely interpret the specific Eleusinian and Pythagorean restrictions that we have been considering, unless numerous subsidiary structures are to be introduced. It cannot deal with the spasmodic but precise character of the Eleusinian restrictions.

The same is true of the notorious bean taboo. Ancient explanations certainly present the bean as a bizarre, polluted, and structurally

---

[46] See the articles of Leach, Tambiah (*Ethnography*), and Halveson cited above, p. 61 n. 101.

[47] Two are pragmatic (cost and palatability). Three relate to the ideology of the sacrificial act, which demands willing submission by a live animal, bloodshed, and division of meat between men and gods. Wild animals, fish, and birds are thereby excluded.

[48] Cf. S. Dow, *BCH* (1965), 199 f.

[49] Bouzyges: Ael. *VH* 5.14. Pig: Plato Comicus, fr. 28.

[50] Aristoxenus, fr. 25, 29a Wehrli, interpreted Ov. *Met.* 15. 110–15; M. Detienne, *Archives de sociologie des religions*, 29 (1970), 141–62.

[51] Porph. *Abst.* 1.14. On fish cf. p. 361.

ambiguous product, associated with sex, the cycle of birth and death, and Hades.[52] But it is not clear what principles of classification could have caused the bean and it alone to be left in this invidious position. A new possibility has emerged with the recent discovery that, for individuals suffering from a particular hereditary enzyme deficiency, *faba vicia* is indeed a poison.[53] The phenomenon, known as favism, has been reported from Sicily, southern Italy, and Sardinia. Pragmatic interpretations of religious rules are often misguided; but the individual instance needs to be judged on its own merits. A medical explanation of the bean taboo appeals to no sage legislator with a mysterious insight into hygienic rules unknown in his own day, but to an easily observable causal connection that has lead to the avoidance of beans by peasants today in the areas where favism is prevalent. The real uncertainty concerns the occurrence of favism in antiquity. If it did occur, in an environment where magical dangers were rife, the natural classification for it would surely have been as a magical danger. The significant conclusion, however, if the favism hypothesis were correct, would be not so much that the taboo had a sound prudential origin, but that it persisted so long and insistently after this was forgotten. The bean came to symbolize polluting and threatening elements in the Pythagorean world-view, all the more strikingly, perhaps, because of its apparent innocuousness. The world-view, however, cannot explain the original choice of the bean.

An important recent study of religious symbols, and food taboos, in New Guinea explicitly rejects structural models, and emphasizes the variety of their origins (where these can be discerned at all) and complexity of their connotations. Unlike the elements in a computer language, it is pointed out, which only have meaning as part of a system, a religious symbol can derive significance directly from the reality to which it relates.[54] This is surely the kind of approach which, in its details, the Greek evidence demands. We need only add that 'abstaining from' a food is, in itself, an important mode of differentiation from everyday life, whatever the food may be. The content of the restriction, though unlikely to be wholly arbitrary, is in a sense less important than its context. The rules are found where the individual is required to shed his profane self (actual fasting is found in the same contexts): as a preparation for initiation or incubation, and as part of the permanent abnormality of the Pythagorean life.

---

[52] Cf. M. Detienne, op. cit., 153 f.
[53] R. S. Brumbaugh and J. Schwartz, 'Pythagoras and Beans: A Medical Explanation', *Classical World* 73 (1980), 421 f.
[54] Barth, *passim*, esp. 12,161, Chs. 20, 23; cf. Burkert, *SH* 48.

Appendix 5: The Ritual Status of the Justified Killer at Athens

This is an issue that has been discussed several times,[1] but it is worth reconsidering briefly, as there has been a tendency to confuse actual laws, some perhaps dating back to Draco, and the interpretations that are offered by the orators who quote them. Taken by themselves, the laws reveal a historical development that is reasonably clear, even if its significance is uncertain.

There was no formal category of 'justified homicide' at Athens. We find instead a variety of situations in which it is stated that killing should not be liable to sanctions.[2] In certain circumstances 'it is permissible to kill', or 'he shall not go into exile, having killed', or the victim shall 'die without compensation'.[3] In none of these early laws is anything said about the ritual status of the killer. Either the lawgivers thought the position on purification self-evident, or they knew nothing of pollution, or they felt that it lay outside the province of the law. The surviving portions of Draco's law are equally unrevealing.

The religious issue first emerges in the more expansive style of a decree of the late fifth century. The psephism of Demophantus, passed after the rule of the Four Hundred, prescribes that any subverter of the democracy should be 'an enemy of the Athenians and should die without compensation'.[4] That is the secular aspect; no prosecution can be brought for such a killing. There follows the specification that the killer is ὅσιος καὶ εὐαγής. The Athenians as a whole are required to ratify the decree by oath, swearing to kill all subverters of democracy and to consider those who did so ὅσιον . . . καὶ πρὸς θεῶν καὶ δαιμόνων, ὡς πολέμιον κτείναντα τῶν Ἀθηναίων. Here as elsewhere a killing is rendered non-polluting by classifying the victim as an enemy.[5] Parts of the decree seem to be taken over from earlier legislation against tyranny,[6] but even if the prescriptions about

---

[1] See MacDowell, *Homicide*, 128 f.

[2] See Calhoun, 66–71.

[3] Laws *ap.* Dem. 23.28, 53, 60; Arist. *Ath. Pol.* 16.10; Dem. 9. 44. On the sense of *atimos* in the two latter see p. 204. Similar formula in *SIG*[3] 194.

[4] *Ap.* Andoc. 1.96–8.

[5] See p. 113 n. 37.

[6] See M. Ostwald, *TAPA* 86 (1955), 103–28.

purity date back to, say, around 500, they still seem to mark a development from the earliest-attested law against tyranny, which says nothing about the ritual issue.[7]

Demosthenes' comments on the laws of justified homicide provide evidence for fourth-century views. The law quoted in 23.53 refers to three different categories of killing, and Demosthenes glosses the prescription *τούτων ἕνεκα μὴ φεύγειν κτείναντα* in three different ways: *τοῦτον ὥρισεν* (ὁ νομοθέτης) *οὐκ ἀδικεῖν*; *καὶ τοῦτον εἶναι καθαρόν*; (*τοῦτον*) *ἀθῷον ποιεῖ*. This is stylistic variation; the three expressions all gloss the same phrase of 'Draco' and all mean the same thing. In 20.158, which still refers to justified homicide, we find *καθαρὸν εἶναι*, in 23.60 *ἀθῷον εἶναι*; in 37.59[8] Demosthenes uses *ἐπιδείξας μὴ καθαρόν* for 'prove guilty' of involuntary homicide. The existence of the Delphinion court shows, argues Demosthenes, that the ancients believed certain kinds of killing to be *ὅσιον*; he glosses the old law *καὶ ἄτιμος τεθνάτω* as a case where killing is *εὐαγές* and the killer is *καθαρός*.[9] It is clear that for him 'not liable to punishment' and 'pure' are synonymous.

It has, however, been suggested that, when applied in the specific sense of 'not liable to punishment', *katharos* no longer conveys any information about ritual status.[10] 'Pure' might, therefore, mean 'not punishable (but impure)'. This is too paradoxical to be readily accepted. It is true that, as early as the *Tetralogies*, *katharos* often needs to be translated 'innocent';[11] but the legal sense is dependent on the ritual one, since in a context of murder 'pure' entails 'innocent', and there is no evidence that the meaning 'innocent' could survive dissociated from 'pure'. For Plato, certain forms of killing do require purification even though not liable to legal sanctions; but in these cases it is only after purification that the killer becomes *katharos*.[12] Porphyry's claim that all killings of whatever kind required purification should not cause us to distort the natural meaning of Demosthenes' text.[13] Individuals may have chosen to undergo purification on their own account,[14] particularly, perhaps, in the kind of cases for which Plato made it obligatory; but there can have been no legal requirement. It is interesting that Plato's Euthyphro considers it self-evident that a killing is only polluting if it is unjustified.[15]

[7] Arist. *Ath. Pol.* 16.10.
[8] = 38.22.
[9] 23.74; 9.44.
[10] Doxography and criticism in J. W. Hewitt, *TAPA* 41 (1910), 99–113.
[11] Ant. *Tetr.* 3 α 1, 4; δ 10,11. Cf. Soph. *OC* 548.
[12] *Leg.* 865b, 869a.
[13] *Abst.* 1.9.
[14] MacDowell, *Homicide*, 128 f.
[15] Pl. *Euthphr.* 4b–c.

By the late fourth century, even a law could subsume the legal aspect of justified homicide under the religious. Eucrates' law of 336 against subverters of the democracy, based largely on earlier legislation, says only that anyone who kills such a subverter should be *hosios*. It is no longer necessary to state that his victim dies 'without compensation'. Outside Athens, the same is true of a third century decree from Teos, which states simply that anyone who kills a rebellious garrison-commander shall be 'not polluted (*miaros*)'.[16]

The situation in the early period remains uncertain. One cannot prove that purification was not required, but there is no firm evidence to suggest that it was, and the laws were clearly not so interpreted in the fourth century. One may wonder too in what sense purification could have been obligatory, if there was no explicit requirement in the law.[17]

A scholion on Demosthenes makes a claim that, if correct, would invalidate the whole preceding argument.[18] It tells how the Athenians granted 'citizenship and a gift' to certain individuals who had killed 'Myrrhine the daughter of Peisistratus', but forced them to live in Salamis, because 'anyone who had killed in any circumstances was not permitted to set foot in Attica.' The incident seems to be unattested elsewhere, and the scholion contains one evident mistake: Myrrhine was wife of Hippias, and thus not daughter but daughter-in-law of Peisistratus.[19] The circumstantial details, however, suggest that the ultimate source for the story might even have been an inscription. The scholiast's interpretation is based on a very strong claim about the pollution created by justified killing. But it cannot be correct; to say nothing of the evidence already discussed, Phrynichus' assassins were invited to live in Athens, and Xenophon contrasts the impurity of the normal murderer with the honours paid to the tyrannicide.[20] This evidence is not decisive for attitudes early in the fifth century, but from the time of Draco it had been quite normal for the involuntary killer to 'set foot in Attica' after a period of exile. The details fit into place, however, if we assume that Myrrhine's assassins were not 'ordered to reside in Salamis' but received a plot of land there as their 'gift',[21] one of the shares in the Salaminian cleruchy that the

---

[16] *SEG* xii 87.11; *SEG* xxvi 1306.23–6.

[17] For a year's purificatory exile in early Sicyon in consequence of (justified) fratricide see Nic. Dam. 90 *FGrH* fr. 61 – scarcely trustworthy evidence.

[18] Schol. Patm. Dem. 23.71 (*BCH* 1 (1877), 138).

[19] Thuc. 6.55.1; Davies, 450.

[20] *IG* I³ 102. 30–2 (M/L 85), cf. Lys. 7.4, 13.70; Xen. *Hiero* 4.4–5. Rewards for killers: M/L 43, Ar. *Av.* 1072–5, Dem. 23. 119. No pollution in killing a rogue, Dem. 19.66 (cf. *Anth. Pal.* 7.230,433, 531 on the Spartan mother).

[21] Cf. Hdt. 8.11.3.

Athenians seem recently to have established.[22] This was no banishment but, for a foreigner, a remarkable privilege (cleruchs were all
Athenian citizens); the scholion is thus virtually the earliest evidence
for the extraordinary honour enjoyed by tyrannicides in the Greek
world.[23]

---

[22] See Meiggs and Lewis on M/L 14.
[23] H. Friedel, *Der Tyrannenmord in Gesetzgebung und Volksmeinung der Griechen*, Stuttgart,
1937. 'No *nemesis*' from gods for tyrannicide, Theog. 1181.

Appendix 6: The Ritual of Purification from Homicide[1]

The fullest account comes in the fourth book of Apollonius' *Argonautica* – a valuable source, given its author's antiquarian learning. Jason had murdered Medea's brother by treachery in a temple, with Medea's connivance, and the Erinys had seen the deed (452–76). Jason mutilated the corpse, and thrice sucked out its blood and spat it back 'in the way that murderers expiate treacherous killings' (476–81),[2] but Zeus was outraged at the crime and resolved that after purification by Circe they should suffer endless troubles before reaching home (557–61). As the Argo sailed on, the mast itself, made of oak from Dodona, announced the need for purification (580–8). On reaching Circe's island, the Argonauts found her on the shore cleansing herself from a terrifying dream of blood (662–71); Jason and Medea alone followed her back to her palace. Circe offered them seats, but they rushed without a word to the hearth and sat down there; Medea covered her face with her hands, Jason planted in the ground the great sword with which he had slain Apsyrtus; neither raised their eyes from the ground. Circe understood, and in respect for Zeus of Suppliants 'performed the sacrifice by which innocent suppliants are cleansed, when they come to a person's hearth'. Holding up a sucking pig she cut its throat and sprinkled their hands with its blood; then she poured offerings to Zeus of Purification, with invocations. This completed the purification itself, and Circe's attendants carried outside the polluted remnants (*lumata*). She herself remained at the hearth and made burnt offerings and libations to appease the Erinyes and Zeus, 'whether they were stained by a stranger's or related blood' (685–717). Only then did she raise Medea and Jason from the hearth, give them seats, and ask their names and story.

The priestess at the opening of the *Eumenides* discovers Orestes in the same position of silent submission at the *omphalos* as Jason and Medea at Circe's hearth. His hands are still dripping with blood; in one hand he holds the sword he killed with, in the other the suppliant's olive branch with a woollen fleece around it.[3] Little that is

[1] See recently Ginouvès, 319–25, R. R. Dyer, *JHS* 89 (1969), 38–56, Burkert, *GR* 137–9.
[2] Cf. p. 133 n. 111.
[3] 40–5.

clear emerges from the surviving fragments of the Athenian exegetic rules for the 'purification of suppliants',[4] but the Cyrene cathartic law offers suggestive hints. Details are obscure, but we read of a threshold which the polluted suppliant probably may not cross; he must be seated there on a fleece, washed and anointed; when he is led out into the public street, all those present must be silent, and apparently a special herald goes ahead to warn passers-by of the coming pollution.[5]

That law is a mere fragment, but it is sufficient to show again, outside poetry, the constrictions placed on the polluted man, the danger that he is for normal people, and his helplessness. A purification is a ritual drama, more effective even than simple supplication. The polluted man is excluded from society, and in his appeal for purification he expresses that isolation by silence and, perhaps, veiled head.[6] Other participants and bystanders confirm his abnormal condition. They too are silent, and may cover their heads.[7] Not words but symbolic actions tell the murderer's story and make his appeal. He sits at the hearth or threshold; sitting itself, in ritual, expresses submission, and no normal person chooses such a place.[8] His part is one of complete passivity, since he cannot purify himself. The 'doer' of the killing has been reduced to mere 'suffering'.

Washing with water sometimes formed part of the rites themselves. It is mentioned in the Cyrene law, and an obscure fragment of the cathartic regulations of the Athenian Eupatridai,[9] but it seems only to have been a subsidiary. The central act, already criticized by Heraclitus in a famous passage, was the cleansing of blood by blood. 'Vainly they cleanse themselves with blood when they are polluted by blood, as if a man who had stepped into mud were to wash himself in

---

[4] Jacoby, 16.

[5] See p. 350.

[6] Silence: Aesch. *Eum.* 448, Eur. *HF* 1219, idem, fr. 1008 *ap.* schol. Aesch. *Eum.* 276, Appendix 7 s.v. Telephus. Veiled head: Eur. *IT* 1207, *HF* 1214 ff. (not demonstrable for the ceremony itself). The silence in theory covers the entire period before purification (Aesch. *Eum.* 448, Telephus legend): an ideal that, taken seriously, proves ridiculous (Arist. *Poet.* 1460a 32).

[7] Bystanders are silent in the Cyrene inscription; so is Circe when she understands the situation. Note too Eur. *IT* 951. Thoas, Eur. *IT* 1218 (slightly different context), covers his head.

[8] On-sitting and the hearth in supplication see J. Gould, *JHS* 93 (1973), 95–7.

[9] 356 *FGrH* fr. 1 *ap.* Ath. 410b (associated with blood). Ovid, *Fast.* 2.45 f., chides the ancients for supposing water could efface bloodshed. It was sufficient after battle or justified killing (Hom. *Il.* 6.266–8, *Od.* 22.478 f.), but Heraclitus, Aeschylus, and Apollonius imply that blood was necessary in cases of murder. Ovid was perhaps misled by traditions associating particular springs or areas of sea with the purification of famous killers: e.g. Paus. 2.31.9, Ovid, loc. cit., Amm. Marc. 22.16.3, Ginouvès, 323, Appendix 7 s.v. Achilles, Cadmus, Heracles. On the Apolline purification by water and laurel postulated by P. Amandry, *Rev. Arch.* 11[6] (1938), 19–27, see the criticisms of Ginouvès and Dyer, locc. citt.

mud.'[10] Heraclitus was only emphasizing a paradox of which all who
thought about the rite were aware, and which seems to have been
essential to its meaning. The strangeness of washing blood with
blood, of purifying by defilement, is constantly underlined in other
references: 'to wash away foul blood by blood'; 'he washed the trace of
killing from my hand by slaughtering fresh blood upon it'; (you will
not be clean) 'until the slaughter of a young animal, by a man who
purifies from the stain of blood, bloodies your hands'; 'until Zeus
himself stains you with drops of pig's blood'.[11]

The language of 'wiping out blood with blood' is sometimes found
not in relation to the purification ceremony, but to actual vengeance
killing.[12] The ritual has accordingly been seen as a substitution, the
pig dying in place of the murderer himself.[13] The verbal parallel
suggests that this idea did hover in the background, but the details of
the ceremony cannot be explained in these terms: a sucking pig, the
cheapest of offerings, or a lamb[14] is a poor replacement for the life of a
man, and the substitution theory ignores what is central to the rite,
the sprinkling of the animal's blood on the killer's hands. It is more
plausible to see here merely one of several special applications of
Greek religion's most powerful form of action, the killing of an
animal;[15] a comparable case, also involving the manipulation of
bloody remnants, is the ritual that accompanied oaths. Purification
'by blood' often occurs where there is no question of purification 'from
blood'. Temples, assemblies, and armies were regularly cleansed in
this way; so were priests who had contracted a pollution, the
mysterious tithed men of the Cyrene law, the 'sixteen women' and
Hellanodikai at Elis before any ceremony, and persons mad,
epileptic, or bewitched.[16] The exact procedure is not clear in all these
cases, but vases that show the cleansing of the daughters of Proetus
suggest that actual sprinkling with the victim's blood was not

[10] B 5 (86 Marcovich).
[11] Eur. *IT* 1223 f., *Stheneboea*, prologue 25 v. Arnim, Aesch. *Eum.* 449 f., fr. 327. But
despite the 'defiling' the process is a washing, Aesch. *Eum.* 281, Eur. *IT* 1224, 1338,
Sthen., loc. cit.; cf. Ginouvès, 321.
[12] e.g. Pl. *Leg.* 872e–873a, Soph. *OT* 100; cf. R. Hirzel, 'Die Talion', *Philol. Suppl.* 11
(1907–10), 405–82.
[13] Rohde, 296, Diels, 69 n. 2, 122, Stengel, 159 f., J. P. Guépin, *The Tragic Paradox*,
Amsterdam, 1968, 160–7. *Contra*, Schwenn 81–4, Nilsson, *GGR* 104, Rudhardt, 166.
Language like that of *LSCG* 156 A 14 περιταμέσθω χοίρῳ is irreconcilable with the
substitution theory.
[14] Eur. *IT* 1223. Still less explicable is the dog (p. 230 n. 136). There is no explicit
Greek testimony for the idea that the evil passes into the animal: for Rome see Val.
Flacc. *Arg.* 3.439–43 (clearly implicit), Appian, *BC* 5.96.401, Serv. Auct. ad Virg. *Aen.*
2.140 (explicit).
[15] Nilsson, *GGR* 106.
[16] See p. 21 f., p. 30 n. 66, pp. 230 and 339 ff.; *LSCG* 156 A 14, 157 A 2; Paus. 5.16.8.

restricted to the purification of murderers.[17] Unless, therefore, we suppose this specific form to have been transferred to other contexts from that of murder purification, the homoeopathic idea of 'washing blood with blood' is a secondary development. The original source of power is the contact with blood, a repugnant, polluting substance, in a controlled ritual context that renders the threat tolerable.[18] For a murderer, this sanctification of pollution is particularly apposite. Blood falls on his hands again, but this time it is not he who has struck the blow. The original blood, profanely shed, clung to his hands; the animal blood, shed in ritual, may be wiped off or washed away, and the bloody remains are readily disposed of.

It is clear from Apollonius and other evidence that the actual purification was followed by rites of appeasement addressed to underworld powers.[19] The two aspects seem to be united in the symbolism of the so-called 'fleece of Zeus',[20] on which the candidate for purification sometimes stood. He placed on it his left or inferior foot, which suggests that it was a receptacle for his impurity;[21] indeed, ancient scholars were perhaps correct in deriving the verb *apodiopompeisthai*, 'send away (pollution)', from the fleece of Zeus. But since it came from a ram sacrificed to Zeus Meilichios or Ktesios, it also brought the candidate into symbolic contact with the god he sought to appease.

As we have seen, a rite that recalls that of murder purification seems to have formed part of initiation at Eleusis or Agrai. The sitting posture, veiled head, silence, and passive submission of the candidate are all the same; even the fleece of Zeus appears in the Eleusinian context.[22] It is generally agreed that the explanation lies in the

[17] References in p. 230 n. 134. Burkert has accordingly suggested (Gaisford lecture held in Oxford, 9 Mar. 1982) derivation from a Babylonian healing ritual which uses a pig (R. C. Thompson, *The Devils and Evil Spirits of Babylonia*, London 1903–4, ii, 16–21). But for the Babylonian rite goats seem to have been used as commonly as pigs (Thompson, op. cit., 21–37), and the essential symbolism is quite distinct in the two cases ('washing' with blood in Greece, laying parts of the animal on corresponding parts of the sick human being in the Babylonian text).   [18] Cf. Vickers, 142 f.

[19] e.g. Arctinus, OCT Homer v, p. 105.29, *LSS* 115 B 58, Dem. 23.72, Plut. *Thes.* 12.1, Val. Flacc. *Arg.* 3.444–58 (cf. P. Boyancé, *REL* 13 (1935), 107–36).

[20] Cf. J. Harrison, *Prolegomena to the Study of Greek Religion*², Cambridge, 1908, 23ƀ–7; Cook, i, 422–8; Burkert, *GR* 87 (Mycenaean fleece of Zeus?). A comparison has sometimes been made with the ancient Roman practice in cases of involuntary homicide. The killer gave the victim's relatives a ram *qui pro se agatur, caedatur* (Festus, p. 476.20 L.). This is a clear case of substitution. Cincius *ap.* Festus p. 470.21 L. says this was done *exemplo at . . .* (*Atheniensium* Scaliger); Greek sources offer no support for Scaliger's restoration.   [21] Hesych. s.v. Διὸς κώδιον.

[22] p. 285 above. Note however that there is no hint that the piglet on the Lovatelli urn is to be used for purification. Thus the claim that the rites of murder purification are in origin simply those used in any induction would outrun the evidence – though it would not be absurd.

common character of the two ceremonies as rites of passage. The candidate at Eleusis is inducted into the society of the initiated; homicide purification means the reacceptance of the killer into social and religious life. The killer in the Cyrene inscription supplicates a body that represents the whole of Cyrene.[23] In Athenian law, the involuntary homicide on return from exile was purified as a token of reintegration into his old community.[24] When Plato in the *Laws* prescribed that the killer should be purified before going into exile, he seems to have severed an organic link that he no longer understood between purification and admission to a social group.[25] A killer may in theory be purified in one place and go to settle in another, but in the predominant mythical pattern he starts life anew at the place of purification. Conversely, the man guilty of a particularly repugnant crime may be refused purification, because the person supplicated is not prepared to tolerate his continuing presence.[26] (The alternative response, of purifying and then expelling, seems to be found only in Apollonius.[27] Of course if, as in Apollonius and a passage in Herodotus,[28] the purifier was really expected to postpone inquiry about the candidate's identity until after the ceremony, it is hard to see how he could avoid applying 'the rites by which innocent suppliants are cleansed', as did Apollonius' Circe, to the very guilty. There are obscurities here that we cannot resolve; but the point remains that purification without reception is quite untypical.) It is important to hold fast to this social context. Purification for murder was not performed by chance persons, amateurs, peripheral seers, disreputable magicians; if it was, public opinion could have denied its efficacy. In myth, the purifier is the man of wealth, position, and responsibility; in history, a priest or official of the community, perhaps representative of an ancient aristocratic family.[29] Only when these rites are considered outside their social context do they seem wholly mechanical and amoral; in context, they have a logic which, though not exactly that of morality, suits well enough their patron, Zeus the arbiter of social life.

[23] See p. 350 above.

[24] Dem. 23.72.

[25] 865d, 866a.

[26] Myth of Ixion; Eur. *Or.* 429 f.; cf. p. 118 n. 58.

[27] Expulsion: 4.745.

[28] 1.35.

[29] On Cyrene see text. In Samothrace, a special priest purified murders: Hesych. s.v. κοιῆς. The Eleusinian daduch used the 'fleece of Zeus', but it is not clear what for (Suda s.v. Διὸς κώδιον, cf. above, p. 285). At Athens the Eupatrid exegetes (Jacoby 16) supervised the ritual, and the *exēgētai pythochrēstoi* offered advice. The Phytalid *gens* controlled an altar at which purifications seem to have been performed, Plut. *Thes.* 12.1, Paus. 1.37.4, cf. Töpffer, 249 f. The role of the ἐγχυτρίστριαι (p. 36 n. 15) will have been subordinate.

Appendix 7:
Exile and Purification of the Killer in Greek Myth

This appendix collects evidence for acts of homicide in Greek myth that lead to the exile, purification, or, occasionally, trial of the killer. This means that certain classes of homicide are omitted:

(1) Killings that lead to simple human revenge: the Hippocoontids kill Licymnius and are killed in turn by Heracles (Apollod. 2.7.3), Aegisthus kills Agamemnon and is killed by Orestes, and so on.

(2) Semi-justified homicide: a bad character is killed and no conse- quences are reported – Neleus and Peleus kill (at the very altars) their wicked stepmother (Apollod. 1.9.8), Oeneus kills his son or brother- in-law Toxeus for jumping over his wall (Apollod. 1.8.1, cf. *Heldensage*, 86), Cycnus kills his wife who had slandered her stepson (Apollod. *Epit.* 3.25, cf. *RE* 11. 2440 f., *Heldensage*, 387), Aepytus/ Cresphontes kills the Aegisthus figure Polyphontes (Apollod. 2.8.5), the sons of Antiope kill their wicked stepmother and found Thebes (Apollod. 3.5.5), Cercyon kills his unchaste daughter Alope (Hyg. *Fab.* 187).

(3) Only slightly distinct from the former, cases where no conse- quences of killing are reported although these might have been ex- pected: Aetolus slays his hosts (Apollod. 1.7.6), Apollo accidentally kills Hyacinthus (Apollod. 1.3.3 with Frazer), the daughters of Cocalus kill Minos (Apollod. *Epit.* 1.15, *Heldensage*, 367 f.).

(4) Aitiological myths of the killing of individuals particularly dear to the gods (like Linus): cf. p. 274 n. 80.

(5) Killings where the perpetrator commits suicide (Themisto, Deianeira) or suffers transformation (Procne, Harpalyce, etc.).

The fact that categories two and three can be omitted has, of course, some negative significance; purification is not indispensable to every myth about killing. But there is no consistency in this area (again an interesting fact); in terms of moral justification, several instances in the following list might well find a place in category two.

Even with these exclusions the following list makes no pretence to comprehensiveness (though I have included all the cases known to me). Especial emphasis has been placed on the function that these killings have within a particular hero's career. Vickers has recently protested against the tendency to dismiss as insignificant the 'standard elements' in Greek myths and concentrate on the search for distinctive features; these standard elements − murder, sacrilege, offences against the gods or family − are, he insists, the very key to understanding the mythology as a whole (Vickers, Appendix 2). That protest needed to be made. None the less, as most scholars since Lobeck (*Aglaophamus*, 969) have recognized, and the following analysis confirms, killing is constantly used as a purely structural device in myths whose main concern is genealogical. The number of myths in which the moral implications of murder are of central importance is by contrast small (although a poet was, of course, free at any time to transform a structural device into a main theme).

Achilles: (1) on Achilles and Thersites see p. 131 n. 102.

(2) in a raid from Troy, on Lesbos or in Miletus, Achilles killed the local hero Trambelus, and, on learning him to be a son of Telamon, lamented him deeply (Istrus, 334 *FGrH* fr. 57, Parth. *Amat. Narr.* 26). A miraculous well was shown in Miletus where Achilles had purified himself from this killing (139 *FGrH* fr. 6 *ap.* Ath. 43d).

Local legend of indeterminate date (*RE* 6 A 2129, Jacoby on Istrus, loc. cit.).

Aeolus: in exile for a year for 'a killing' (hypothesis to Eur. *Melanippe ἡ σοφή, ap.* H. v. Arnim, *Supplementum Euripideum*, Bonn, 1913, 25 f.)

Probably an invention by Euripides to allow Melanippe's seduction in her father's absence.

Aetolus: An Elean by birth, he killed Apis accidentally and fled to the Couretan country (65 *FGrH* fr.1, Apollod. 1.7.6, schol. Pind. *Ol.* 3.22c), which subsequently took his name, Aetolia.

The Eleans were of Aetolian stock, through Oxylus (Pind. *Ol.* 3.12, Ephorus, 70 *FGrH* fr. 115, 122, *RE* 5.2380 f.). Aetolus, who in Hecataeus was born and bred in Aetolia (1 *FGrH* fr. 15), was transformed into an Elean to show that Oxylus in invading Elis was reclaiming an ancient heritage, perhaps to make Aetolia derive from Elis and not vice versa (cf. *RE* 1.1129, *Heldensage*, 281).

Agave: exiled for Pentheus' death, Eur. *Bacch.* 1330−92.

Alcathous: (1) cf. s.v. *Pelopids*.

(2) when king of Megara, killed his own son Callipolis in a comprehensible fit of anger; was purified, without exile, by the Melampodid Polyidus (Paus. 1.42.6, 43.5).

Local legend of uncertain but probably not early origin (cf. Jacoby on 485 *FGrH* fr. 10 n. 45) uniting (1) Megara's chief hero Alcathous (2) the Megarian connection of Polyidus (3) an existing monument, the 'monument of Callipolis'.

Alcmaeon: The early tradition about the consequences of the matricide cannot be recovered with certainty (cf. M. Delcourt, *Oreste et Alcméon*, Paris, 1959; *Heldensage*, 956 ff.). Asclepiades of Tragilus, a writer on tragic plots, offers two unusual features (12 *FGrH* fr. 29): the matricide precedes the expedition of the *Epigoni* against Thebes (if we accept, as we surely must on Proppian principles, that Alcmaeon on this point obeyed his father's behest), and when Alcmaeon goes mad in consequence of the murder the gods themselves intervene to cure him. Some have supposed this to be an earlier version (*Heldensage*, 956 f., following Bethe) than the more familiar one by which the matricide followed the expedition, and Alcmaeon fled to Acarnania in consequence, in search of a land invisible to the sun when the matricidal blow was struck (Thuc. 2.102.5–6). An alternative explanation for the migration is available: he had marched up in that direction to help Diomedes recover his Aetolian heritage. Several scholars have ascribed this motivation to the epic *Alcmaeonis*, because the source for it, Ephorus (70 *FGrH* fr. 123), went on to cite the poem (fr. 5 Kinkel = Ephorus, fr. 124): so e.g. *RE* 1.1563, P. Friedlaender, *Rh. Mus.* 69 (1914), 330 f. = *Studien zur Antiken Literatur und Kunst*, Berlin, 1969, 44. There is nothing compelling about this reconstruction; Asclepiades' version could well derive from tragedy, and the Ephoran account of the Acarnania expedition looks like a rationalization, which had the further advantage of explaining a mythographical problem, the Acarnanians' absence from the Trojan expedition (Ephorus, loc. cit.). A polluted, wandering Alcmaeon could therefore have appeared in early epic (even Friedlaender, loc. cit. postulated him for *Epigoni*). A Tyrrhenian amphora (570–60) shows a serpent rising from Eriphyle's corpse to pursue Alcmaeon (K. Schefold, *Myth and Legend in Early Greek Art*, London, 1966, 80, Fig. 30).

For the elaborated Alcmaeon romance with various purifications, relapses, and marriages see Apollod. 3.7.5–7. Much of this we owe to Euripides, cf. *Heldensage*, 959 ff.

Miasma

Althaemenes: a Cretan who, on learning that his father Catreus was destined to die at the hand of one of his children, emigrated to Rhodes. There he killed his sister for her supposed unchastity, and unwittingly killed his father too when he landed secretly on the island. On realizing what he had done, he prayed and was swallowed into the earth (Apollod. 3.2.2) or went out into the wilderness and there died (Diod. 5.59.4).

Althaemenes was a Rhodian hero, credited with introducing the worship of Zeus Atabyrios (Diod. 5.59.2). The tradition that made him a Heraclid was probably secondary (*Heldensage*, 373). His two murder myths have no obvious aitiological meaning, but their date is uncertain; Rohde thought them Hellenistic (cf. *Heldensage*, 371 n. 6).

Amphitryon: killed his father-in-law Electryon, accidentally (3 *FGrH* fr. 13b, Apollod. 2.4.6) or in anger (Hes. *Asp.* 11,82; 3 *FGrH* fr. 13c), and fled from Argos to Thebes, where he was received (Hes. *Asp.* 13, 3 *FGrH* fr. 13c) or purified (Apollod. 2.4.6, Hes. *Asp.* hypoth. D, E Rzach) by Creon.

There is some reason to think that Amphitryon was originally a Theban (cf. Hes. *Asp.* 1 f.); when he was adopted into the Perseid genealogy at Argos, the killing of Electryon was necessary to take him back to Thebes: Robert, *Oidipus*, ii, 40–2; P. Friedlaender, *Herakles* (*Philol. Untersuch.* 19), Berlin, 1907, 47 f.; *Heldensage*, 605 ff.

Apollo: (1) forced to serve Admetus for a year as penance for the killing of the Cyclopes (or the Delphic dragon, 404 *FGrH* fr. 5). This service was already known to the Hesiodic catalogue (fr. 54b–c, cf. Eur. *Alc.* 1–7, 3 *FGrH* fr. 35a; P/R 270).

(2) after the slaying of the dragon at Delphi, Apollo fled to Tempe or Crete (via Aegialeia, Paus. 2.7.7) for purification. The Homeric hymn knows nothing of purification; the Tempe tradition derives from an aitiological connection of uncertain date with the Septerion (? first attested in the fourth century, Theopompus, 115 *FGrH* fr. 80, cf. Parke/Wormell, i, 14 n. 12); the Cretan tradition might be older (cf. p. 142) though one could argue that the very idea that the dragon's death required purification was created by the Septerion aition.

Archias: of Corinth killed his lover Actaeon (Plut. *Amat. Narr.* 772e–773b, Diod. 8.10); Actaeon's father committed suicide, plague followed, Archias went into voluntary exile and founded Syracuse, where another lover killed him. According to another tradition, the

Bacchiads in general were responsible for the crime and were expelled because of it (Alex. Aetolus, fr. 3.7–10, *Coll. Al.* p. 122; schol. Ap. Rhod. 4.1212; cf. A. Andrewes, *CQ* 32 (1949), 70 f.).

A rationalized version of the Actaeon myth has been adopted to explain political change or colonization.

Archelaus: a Temenid, who kills the Thracian king Cisseus, with every justification, but on Apollo's advice flees to Macedonia (Hyg. *Fab.* 219).

The very hero seems to be a courtly invention, perhaps entirely Euripides', to please king Archelaus of Macedon (*Heldensage*, 669 f.).

Ares: killed Halirrhothius, Poseidon's son, who was trying to rape Ares' daughter Alcippe. Prosecuted by Poseidon, tried before the twelve gods, and adjudged to have committed justified homicide (Eur. *El.* 1258–63, implied by counter-etymology in Aesch. *Eum.* 685–90; cf. Apollod. 3.14.2 with Frazer).

A simple charter for the Areopagus and for the category of justified homicide (killing of rapist as justified homicide, Dem. 23. 53), confusing only in that such cases were in fact tried at the Delphinion. Halirrhothius' only other legend seems secondary (*RE* 7. 2270).

Athamas: killed his son Learchus in madness, was expelled from Boeotia, and after wanderings settled at Halos or Athamantia in Thessaly (Apollod. 1.9.2, cf. Jacoby on 4 *FGrH* fr. 126).

Infanticide is an element proper to the Athamas myth, but these wanderings link the Boeotian and Thessalian Athamas legends and provide an etymology for Halos (ἄλη; cf. *Heldensage*, 43 f., Jacoby, loc. cit.).

Atreus: cf. s.v. *Pelopids*.

Bellerophon: killed his brother accidentally and went to Proetus to be purified (Apollod. 2.3.1 with Frazer). In Homer his presence at Proetus' palace was unexplained; the killing and purification first appear in Euripides' *Stheneboea* (prologue 23–5 v. Arnim) and might be his invention (cf. *Heldensage*, 181–3, esp. 183 n. 1).

Cadmus: served Ares for a great year (8 years) in appeasement for the killing of the dragon (Apollod. 3.4.2, containing 3 *FGrH* fr. 89; Ares' anger against the Cadmaeans, Eur. *Phoen.* 931–5).

Jacoby on 3 *FGrH* fr. 89 and Latte, *RE* 10. 1464, regard the service as ancient, a necessary preliminary to marriage with Ares' daughter Harmonia.

For Nonnus (5.4) Cadmus purified himself from the dragon's blood in Dirce.

Carnabas: son of Triopas, the savage Perrhaebian prince, killed his father and was honoured by the people for this liberation, but fled none the less through his blood-guilt; he sailed to the Troas, was purified by king Tros, and given land where he founded Zeleia (schol. T and Eustath. ad Hom. *Il.* 4.88).

'One of the many mythical reflections of Thessalian colonization in this region', *RE* 10. 1950; for various myths linking Triopas and Triopids with east Greek colonization cf. *RE* 7 A 171.

Cephalus: killed his wife Procris accidentally (383 *FGrH* fr. 2, Apollod. 3.15.1) or in passion (3 *FGrH* fr. 34), was arraigned by her father Erechtheus before the Areopagus (4 *FGrH* fr. 169a, Apollod. 3.15.1, cf. 334 *FGrH* fr. 14), and condemned to permanent exile. Pausanias and Aristodemus (Paus. 1.37.6, 383 *FGrH* fr. 2) tell how he went in his exile to Thebes; according to Aristodemus, supposedly deriving from the epic cycle (*Epigoni*, fr. 2, OCT Homer v, p. 115 Allen; cf. *Heldensage*, 162 n. 5), he was purified by the Cadmaeans and then aided them with his miraculous dog against the Teumessian fox; his involvement with the fox was elsewhere narrated independently of his exile in Thebes (Apollod. 2.4.7).

It looks as if two substantive elements in Cephalus' myth – the Procris romance (already Hom. *Od.* 11.321), the fox episode – were conveniently linked, perhaps already in the *Epigoni*, by the Theban exile.

Copreus: a son of Pelops, killed Iphitus, fled to Mycenae, and was purified by Eurystheus (Apollod. 2.5.1).

In Hom. *Il.* 15.639 Copreus was Eurystheus' herald, and properly named for that office. Impossible to say when and how he became a Pelopid (*RE* 11.2.1364).

Daedalus: murdered his nephew Talos/Perdix in jealousy of his skills, was condemned to death by the Areopagus, and fled to Crete (Apollod. 3.15.8 with Frazer; the murder already implicit, Soph. fr. 323).

M. Ventris and J. Chadwick, *Documents in Mycenaean Greek²*, Cambridge, 1973, n. 200 (Cnossus) shows that Daedalus is a Cretan, appropriated by Athens for his intellectual sharpness and sent back to his homeland through the murder myth.

Danaids: after the murder of their husbands they were purified by Athena and Hermes at the command of Zeus (Apollod. 2.1.5, and no other source). A. F. Garvie, *Aeschylus' Supplices: Play and Trilogy*, Cambridge, 1969, 211–33, discusses whether this detail is Aeschylean, inconclusively.

Epeigeus, Lycophron, Medon (Hom. *Il.* 16.571; 15.430; 13.695): all Homeric warriors said to have fled their homes through murder. They have no existence outside Homer; Homer makes them killers to give them a touch of individuality at the point of death.

Heracles: (1) after the murder of his children, Heracles condemned himself to exile, and was purified by Thespius; he consulted Delphi, and was told to serve Eurystheus (Apollod. 2.4.12). For Menecrates (schol. Pind. *Isthm.* 4.104g) he was purified by Sicalus, for Ap. Rhod. 4.539–41 by Nausithous the Phaeacian; several sources make the murder prelude to the service with Eurystheus (Moschus 4.13–16, 36–45; 90 *FGrH* fr. 13; Diod. 4.11.1–2).

Considered by Wilamowitz (ed. Eur. *HF*, Berlin, 1895, i, 87) followed by P. Friedlaender (*Herakles, Philol. Untersuch.* 19, Berlin, 1907, 51) 'ein Hilfsmotiv ohne innerliche Bedeutung', whereby the Thebans explained the activity of 'their' Heracles in Argos and his lack of Theban progeny. If so, this is a clear case of a structural device that grew into a central theme; but it is hard to accept so banal an origin for the motif (cf. *Heldensage*, 628).

(2) while feasting with his father-in-law Oeneus, accidentally killed the cupbearer, a relative of his host, and though Oeneus was prepared to forgive the involuntary crime chose 'to undergo exile according to the law' and went to Trachis (Apollod. 2.7.6, cf. Frazer ad. loc., *Heldensage*, 576 f.; first reference 4 *FGrH* fr. 2).

The story set Heracles on the road for his encounter with Nessus, illustrated his uncontrollable strength, and provided an aition for cult of the variously named cupbearer (*Heldensage*, 576 f.).

(3) after the treacherous murder of Iphitus, Heracles was purified at Amyclae by one Deiphobus (Diod. 4.31.5, Apollod. 2.6.2), after Neleus in Pylos had refused this service because of his friendship with Iphitus' father Eurytus (Diod., Apollod., loc. cit.; *Heldensage*, 537 n. 3; cf. schol. Pind. *Ol.* 9.43, 44c). Despite purification, Heracles' illness continued; he sought a cure at Delphi, where Apollo enjoined his sale to Omphale and the payment of the proceeds of the sale to Eurytus or Iphitus' sons (Diod., Apollod., loc. cit.; in the probably older version of 3 *FGrH* fr. 82b, Soph. *Tr.* 274–6, Zeus himself saw to Heracles' sale).

The murder of Iphitus, known to Homer and older perhaps than the sack of Oechalia, probably served originally to motivate the servitude under Omphale (P. Friedlaender, op. cit., 73–8). The sack of Pylos by Heracles is mentioned in Homer, but not its motive (*Il.* 11.690). According to one prominent later tradition, it was due to Neleus' refusal to purify him from the murder of Iphitus (cf. above), but it is not safe to attribute this motive to Hesiod on the strength of schol. AD Hom. *Il.* 2. 333–5 (1.102.17 Dindorf), which concludes a narrative along these lines with 'Hesiod tells the story in the *Catalogues*'. Lobeck long ago warned that there might be conflation here (*Aglaophamus*, 309), as there commonly is in the Homeric mythographic scholia (E. Schwartz, *Jahrb. f. Klass. Phil. Suppl.* 12 (1881), 405 ff.); we now have a Hesiodic fragment describing the sack of Pylos (fr. 33), and it seems clear that the scholion referred to Hesiod merely for the picturesque detail of Periclymenus' transformations. Other explanations for the sack of Pylos were known (cf. the controversy in the scholia to Hom. *Il.* 11.690, *Heldensage*, 537).

(4) the Lesser Mysteries at Agrai were founded to purify Heracles from the blood of the Centaurs: cf. p. 284.

(5) in his youth Heracles killed Linus, his lyre-teacher, in anger because Linus had struck him. Heracles cited a law of Rhadamanthys to show that this was justified homicide, and went free (Apollod. 2.4.9 with Frazer).

(6) Heracles cleansed himself from Cacus in a neighbouring stream: Dion. Hal. *Ant. Rom.* 1.39.4.

(7) after killing the wicked sons of Proteus, he was purified by their own father: Conon 26 *FGrH* para. 32.

(8) while returning from Troy Heracles was blown to Cos, fought with the Meropes and defeated them, was purified, and married ? Chalciope (Plut. *Quaest. Graec.* 58, 304c–e; for Heracles on Cos cf. Hom. *Il.* 14.255, Apollod. 2.7.1).

A Coan aition.

For other killings by Heracles, even that of the sons of Boreas (2 *FGrH* fr. 31, Ap. Rhod. 1.1300–6 with schol.), purifications seem not to be recorded. He was, of course, the 'justest of homicides' (Peisander of Rhodes fr. 10, p. 252 Kinkel).

Hippotes: the Heraclid, killed the seer Carnus, mistaking him for a malevolent magician; plague afflicted the Heraclids, and Hippotes was banished for ten years (Apollod. 2.8.3, Paus. 3.13.4). The killing of Carnus followed by plague was an aition of common type for a festival, the Carneia. The exile and wandering of the killer, not typical of such aitia, explained the name of Hippotes' son Aletes, the conqueror of Corinth (*RE* 8.1923).

Hyettus: killed Molurus son of Arisbas *flagrante delicto* and fled from Argos to king Orchomenus, who received him and gave him great wealth, including the village now called Hyettus (Paus. 9.36.6–7, citing Hes. fr. 257).

Hyettus, Molurus, and Arisbas are otherwise unknown (Arisbe is a place name, *RE* 2.847); the name Hyettus itself belongs originally to a place, not a person (*RE* 9.91, citing Kretschmer). A simple but early aitiological invention.

Ixion: treacherously murdered his bride's father, and as first shedder of 'kindred blood' went mad. No one would purify him until Zeus was moved to pity; he now attempted to seduce his benefactor's wife, and was condemned in punishment to spin endlessly on his wheel (for the sources see *RML* s.v. *Ixion, Nephele*; first in Pind. *Pyth.* 2.32; Aesch. *Eum.* 441, 718, idem, the Ixion trilogy; cf. *Heldensage*, 12–15).

A tightly knit myth of social crime, whose solar origins (*Heldensage*, 15), if genuine, were quickly forgotten.

Jason: in flight from Colchis murdered the brother of Medea (*Heldensage*, 800–2, *RE* 2.285). It is very uncertain whether the purification from this crime described Ap. Rhod. 4.662–717 belongs to the old legend (contrast *Heldensage*, 827, *RE* 15.37 *pro*; *RE* 11.504, *RML*

2.1202 f. *contra*). It is true that Circe, sister of Aietes (Hom. *Od.* 10.37), belongs rather to the *Argonautica* than the *Odyssey*, but her role will surely have been to give advice about the voyage on the journey out, not to perform purification on the return (K. Meuli, *Odyssee und Argonautika*, Berlin, 1921, 95 ff., esp. 112–14, = *Ges. Schr.*, ii, 661 ff. esp. 672 f.).

Jason's participation in the funeral games for Pelias was recorded (Paus. 5.17.10), which suggests, although it does not prove (cf. the Homeric Orestes' funeral feast for Aegisthus), that his revenge against Pelias was unknown to the earliest tradition (*Heldensage*, 37). When the murder was added, Jason and Medea were expelled from Iolcus or left it voluntarily, and travelled to Corcyra or Corinth (*Heldensage*, 869, *RE* 9. 767; cf. Eumelus, fr. 2, p. 188 Kinkel, for Medea's ancient Corinthian connection).

Leucippus: the Lycian accidentally slew his father and so was forced to leave home; according to the Magnesian legend the god of Delphi appointed him leader of a group of displaced Thessalians who were seeking new homes, and he established the colony of Magnesia (*Inscr. Magn.* 17.36 ff. = Parke/Wormell, nn. 381–2; Parth. *Amat. Narr.* 5: cf. *RE* 12.2264).

A typical oecist romance.

Lycus and Nycteus: fled from Hyria (?) to Thebes after killing Phlegyas (Apollod. 3.5.5; on the text cf. Robert, *Oedipus*, i, 398).

Brings Nycteus' daughter Antiope, a Hyrian in Hesiod (fr. 181), to Thebes (*RE* 17.1511 f.).

Medea: her flight to Athens after the murder of Creon's children and her own is familiar from Eur. *Med.* Pre-tragic tradition on the consequences of the infanticide, and Medea's presence at Athens, is hard to recover (*RE* 15.46, ibid., *Suppl.* 13.1081). The history of the latter is complicated by problems surrounding the interpretation of several sets of vases; but C. Sourvinou-Inwood, *Theseus as Son and Stepson*, London, 1979, has argued strongly for detecting an Athenian Medea from early in the fifth century. If so, it will have been after accidental infanticide (the version of Eumelus, cf. *RE* 15.42 f.) that she was originally received in Athens. Purification only in Ov. *Fast.* 2.42.

Odysseus: (1) some told how the kinsmen of the slain suitors submitted the issue between themselves and Odysseus to Neoptolemus as arbitrator, who sent him into banishment (Apollod. *Epit.* 7.40, cf. Plut. *Quaest. Graec.* 14. 294c–d).

The banishment explained those Aetolian connections of Odysseus that existed in other versions too; Neoptolemus' arbitration seems also to have served as aition in an Ithacan cult of Telemachus (cf. W. R. Halliday on Plut., loc. cit.).

(2) killed Euryalus, his son by a Thesprotian princess; this may have been brought into connection with his own death at Telegonus' hands (cf. Pearson and Radt, introductions to Soph. *Euryalus*).

Oedipus: the problems of the literary treatment are complex; see after Robert, *Oidipus*, Nilsson's review of Robert, *Gött. Anz.* 184 (1922), 36–46 = *Op. Sel.* i. 335–48; idem, *The Mycenaean Origin of Greek Mythology*, California, 1932, 102–12; L. Deubner, *Oedipusprobleme*, *Berl. Abh.* 1942, n. 4; F. Wehrli, *MH* 14 (1957), 108–17 = *Theoria und Humanitas*, Zürich, 1972, 60–71; Jacoby on 3 *FGrH* fr. 95, 16 *FGrH* fr. 10; M. Delcourt, *Oedipe, ou la légende du conquerant*, Liège, 1944, introduction; L. W. Daly, *RE Suppl.* 7. 769–86; W. Burkert, 'Seven against Thebes', in *I poemi epici rapsodici non omerici e la tradizione orale*, Padova, 1981, esp. 29–35.

For the *Iliad*, Oedipus perhaps died in battle and certainly received funerary games (*Il.* 23.679, Robert, *Oidipus*, i, 115; but note the reservation of Burkert, op. cit.). The Odyssean *Nekyia* knows the parricide and incest, but leaves Oedipus on the throne, suffering, and says nothing of blindness (*Od.* 11. 271–80; blindness unknown?, Robert, *Oidipus*, i, 112). According to Pherecydes, Oedipus contracted two further marriages after the incestuous one (3 *FGrH* fr. 95; cf. 16 *FGrH* fr. 10.8, Paus. 9.5.11), and it is almost certain, although Robert disputed it, that the remarriage of the polluted Oedipus already occurred in early epic (Jacoby on Pherecydes, loc. cit., Nilsson, *Op. Sel.*, i. 345, Deubner, op. cit., 27 ff., Wehrli, op. cit., 112 (65). Even the third wife may have been in the *Catalogue*, cf. Hes. fr. 190. 13 ff., 193. 1–8 with M/W's notes). If ἄφαρ in Hom. *Od.* 11.274 is taken in its normal sense, the *Nekyia* poet too must have known though not mentioned a further marriage (Paus. 9.5.11), unless we suppose, implausibly, that he did not know of the great expedition against Thebes, or did not connect it with a quarrel between the sons of Oedipus (so Nilsson).

On the character of these early traditions see above, p. 136. Later poets rendered Oedipus coherent by gradual elimination of incongruous elements. He seems already to be blind and in his sons' power in the *Thebais*, fr. 2,3, pp. 11 f. Kinkel, with the parody in schol. Soph. *OC* 1375 (Robert, *Oidipus*, i, 171). In Pherecydes, a purificatory year apparently preceded the second marriage (this might, of course, be traditional). The tradition by which 'Jocasta' is mother of Eteocles and Polyneices, and lives on after the incest is discovered, is now attested in the Lille Stesichorus, cf. *ZPE* 26 (1977), 7–36; it excludes subsequent marriages. Exile first appears in Sophocles, hinted at in *OT* (e.g. 1518), worked out in *OC*; but it does not obliterate the older tradition whereby Oedipus stayed in Thebes (Eur. *Phoen.*, cf. Soph. *OC* 765–7). Oedipus is never chased by Erinyes (although he suffers from those of a mother in Homer), or purified.

Orestes: on the Homeric treatment see p. 136. Other pre-tragic traditions are little known. Orestes' act was perhaps sometimes mitigated by being seen as self-defence against the axe-carrying Clytaemnestra (M. Delcourt, *Oreste et Alcméon*, Paris, 1959, 26; on the axe see Lesky, *RE* 18. 973 f.). The Erinyes first appear in Stesichorus, as does Apollo, who gives Orestes a bow to ward them off (*PMG* 217). Apollo's support for Orestes need not exclude moral conflict or the need for purification (*RE* 18. 977) any more than it does in Aeschylus. Some of the local traditions about Orestes' healing may date back to the sixth century (Paus. 2.31.4 – purification –, ibid., 3.22.1, 8.34.2; later traditions *RE* 18. 990 f.); so too that of his Arcadian residence (Eur. *El.* 1273–5, *Or.* 1643–5), which it is natural to connect with his frenzied wanderings. Jacoby believed that the trial before the Areopagus was Aeschylus' invention (commentary on 323a *FGrH* fr. 1), but more probably the poet's innovation was only to make Orestes' trial the one for which the Areopagus was founded (*RE* 18.980 f.). His aitiological association with the Choes (Eur. *IT* 947–60) is likely to be ancient, but does not have to be. For a possible representation of Orestes struggling with a snake (Erinys?) see P. Zancani Montuoro and U. Zanotti-Bianco, *Heraion alla Foce del Sele*, ii, Rome, 1954, 289–300 with Plates 46,89.

Aeschylus' treatment is helpfully discussed by O. P. Taplin, *The Stagecraft of Aeschylus*, Oxford, 1977, 381–4. The purification occurs in three stages. The first is the physical rite performed at Delphi by Apollo (*Cho.* 1059 f., *Eum.* 282 f.), who in this assumes the role that normally belongs to a human purifier (therefore ἀνδρός, *Eum.* 449, is not a problem). Aeschylus insinuates into our minds the fact that this purification occurs, even though we do not see it on stage and cannot identify a point during the action at which it could have been performed. There follows a period of exile, during which Orestes' pollution is 'rubbed off' by social intercourse and 'purified' by time, because the blood on his hands 'falls asleep' (*Eum.* 238, 280, 286). Aeschylus may be hinting at the Peloponnesian traditions concerning Orestes (above), but the basic conception is the well-attested one by which the killer's exile is itself a form of purification (p. 114). The cleansing at Delphi was not redundant because it permitted him to be received by hosts abroad during this exile. He points out (*Eum.* 285, cf. 238 f.) that he brought no harm to them – a reasonable point, as purification did not always take (Apollod. 2.6.2,3.7.5; for the 'proof by safe contact' cf. Ant. 5.82 f.). The final stage, which permitted him finally to return to Argos, free from the Erinyes, was the trial before the Areopagus.

There is nothing unusual in the combination of purification and 'purificatory' exile; it was the fate of any killer who was not to be banned in perpetuity (MacDowell, *Homicide*, 120–5). The trial is, of course, an intrusive element among mythological responses to homicide, and even from a fifth-century perspective misplaced, since it would normally precede exile and not follow it. Given the trial's actual position, however, the Erinyes in a sense correspond to the victim's relatives, whose pardon was necessary before an involuntary killer could return from exile. There may also have been a reversal in the order of physical purification and purificatory exile, but it is not clear at what stage a killer going into temporary exile would normally have received purification. There is no reliable historical evidence, and the mythological or semi-mythological instances of temporary exile do not normally mention physical purification (Eur. *Hipp.* 34–7, *Or.* 1643–5, 90 *FGrH* fr. 45, 61; Aeolus above; but note Poemander below, purified abroad). Common sense suggests that he underwent it on arrival abroad, as did the permanent exile; would he not otherwise be too dangerous to associate with? It also seems to be necessary, except in the abnormal conception of Plato (p. 374), that purification should occur away from the scene of the crime; Achilles sailed to Lesbos to be cleansed from the killing of Thersites, and then at once returned. If this is correct, Orestes conforms to the normal pattern. Demosthenes, however, seems to attest for Athens purification on return (23.72). It is perhaps not impossible that a killer could be purified more than once, but such a repetition is unattested; if we reject this possibility, it will be necessary, in order to keep *Eumenides* consistent with Athenian practice, either to postulate a change between the time of the play and of Demosthenes, or to suppose that the killer already cleansed abroad was exempt from purification on return (cf. perhaps *Eum.* 235–43). There are irresoluble uncertainties here; but on any view of them, it does not emerge that Aeschylus is concerned, as is often supposed, to dispute the importance of ritual purification or deny its efficacy. Though he presents it as merely one stage in the process by which the killer was prepared for return to his home territory, it was, as we have seen, never anything else.

In Soph. *El.*, notoriously, the question of pollution is not raised explicitly. In Eur. *El.* 1250–75, Orestes is required to leave Argos, undergo trial at Athens, and settle in Arcadia. In Eur. *Or.* 1643–60 the trial is to be preceded by a year of (purificatory) exile in Arcadia, but he may then return to Argos.

Oxylus: who by capturing Elis recovered the ancient heritage of his ancestor Aetolus (above), was in some versions in exile in Elis for accidental homicide when he met the returning Heraclids and in obedience to an oracle was chosen by them as leader (Apollod. 2.8.3 with Frazer; Paus. 5.3.7).

The exile is a simple mechanism to put him in the Heraclids' path.

Patroclus: born in Opus, he killed a youth in anger over a game of knuckle-bones and fled to Peleus with his father (Hom. *Il.* 23. 84–90; 4 *FGrH* fr. 145; Apollod. 3.13.8).

Perhaps an attempt to reconcile two traditional homes of Patroclus, Phthia and Opus (*RE* 18.4.2275 f.).

Peleus: (1) Peleus and/or Telamon murdered their brother Phocus (first in *Alcmaeonis*, fr. 1, p. 76 Kinkel; the accidental tradition of Ap. Rhod. 1.92 f., Diod. 4.72.6 is certainly secondary), and were expelled by Aeacus from Aegina. Peleus went to Phthia, was purified by king Eurytion, and married his daughter (3 *FGrH* fr. 1b, Apollod. 3.13.1). (In Ov. *Met.* 11. 409 he is purified from Phocus by Acastus.)

(2) in a boar-hunt (sometimes the Calydonian boar-hunt) he accidentally killed Eurytion (Pind. fr. 48), fled to Acastus at Iolcus, and was purified by him (Apollod. 3.13.2). Then followed the attempt to seduce him by Acastus' wife, on whom he subsequently achieved revenge (Apollod. 3.13.3,7: ? from Pherecydes, *RE* 19.278).

The killings served to move Peleus, who though Thessalian had acquired an Aeginetan father and other local connections, up and down the Greek world (*RE* 19.274,277).

Peliades: the consequences of their involuntary parricide in the earliest versions are uncertain; perhaps the question was not raised. The Chest of Cypselus showed them as spectators at the funerary games of Pelias, but this detail is commonly taken (e.g. *RE* 19. 309 f.) to reflect an earlier legend in which Pelias did not die at their hands (cf. above s.v. *Jason*). Hyg. *Fab.* 24 and Paus. 8.11.1 make them flee; Palaephatus 40 (*Mythographi Graeci*, 3.2, ed. N. Festa, Leipzig, 1902) has them expelled by Acastus (cf. *RE* 19.310). Eur. *Med.* 504 f. (perhaps not decisive evidence) envisages them still in Iolcus; nothing in Apollod. 1.9.27. Subsequently we hear that the Iolcians forgave them their involuntary act, and young noblemen took them in marriage 'as being pure of bloodshed' (90 *FGrH* fr. 54). Another version even made Jason himself act as matchmaker for them (Diod. 4.53.2 = Dionysius Skytobrachion, 32 *FGrH* fr. 14). The happy ending is, no doubt, 'sentimental invention' (*Heldensage*, 869), even though its exact source is hard to define; Dionys. Skyt., loc. cit., is believed to be dependent on post-Euripidean tragedy (Jacoby ad loc.), but 90 *FGrH* fr. 54 cannot come from quite the same source.

Pelopids: some or all, were expelled (along with Hippodameia, Paus. 6.20.7) by Pelops for murdering their half-brother Chrysippus (4 *FGrH* fr. 157, Thuc. 1.9.2, *RE* 3.2498 f., *Heldensage*, 217–19). The names commonly mentioned are Atreus and Thyestes; 485 *FGrH* fr. 10 adds Alcathous, and schol. Eur. *Or.* 4 envisages a general *diaspora* of the Pelopids.

Whatever its origin, the story had useful consequences in interpreting or creating Pelopid links throughout the Peloponnese (*Heldensage*, 218). It explained, for instance, how the Pelopid Alcathous was at Megara to build its walls (already Theog. 773).

Pelops: (1) the plague that followed his murder of Stymphalus (Apollod. 3.12.6; *Heldensage*, 74 n. 5) was aitiological.

(2) According to Apollod. *Epit.* 2.8–9 Pelops was cleansed from the blood of Myrtilus by Hephaestus (the choice of god is unexplained) at Ocean. The detail seems ancient; it might have stood in Pherecydes, for whom the killing of Myrtilus was justified response to a gross offence (3 *FGrH* fr. 37b) and so perhaps fit to be cleansed by a god (*Heldensage*, 214; *RE* 16.1154; Jacoby on Pherecyd., loc. cit.). Jacoby suggests that this was originally a purification from the blood of Oenomaus, not Myrtilus; but it was Myrtilus whom Pelops killed with his own hands. Concurrent versions of the saga ignored Myrtilus (*RE* 16.1152).

Penthesilea: came to Troy and was purified by Priam after accidentally killing her sister while hunting (Apollod. *Epit.* 5.1, cf. Quint.
Smyrn. 1.24 f.).

The *Aethiopis* may, but need not, have used this mechanical device
to explain her presence at Troy; 4 *FGrH* fr. 149 has a quite different
explanation (cf. *Heldensage*, 1176 f., *RE Suppl.* 7.870).

Perseus: when he finally fulfils the prophecy and kills his grandfather,
Acrisius of Argos, by an accidental discus cast, he is 'ashamed' to
accept his inheritance and exchanges it with Megapenthes king of
Tiryns; he settles in Tiryns and founds Mycenae (3 *FGrH* fr. 12; Paus.
2.15.4, 2.16.2–3; Apollod. 2.4.4).

Acrisius' death is of course essential to the folk-tale motif; but
Perseus' reaction to it is used to bring him into the proper aitiological
connection with Mycenae (*Heldensage*, 237).

Phalces: a Temenid, kills his sister Hyrnetho unintentionally at
Epidaurus, and flees to Sicyon (Paus. 2.6.7, 2.28.3–7; *Heldensage*,
667).

Explains cult of Hyrnetho at Epidaurus, and continues dispersion
of Temenids (q.v.).

Poemander: king of Tanagra, accidentally killed his own son, fled to
Chalcis, where he was purified by Elpenor, and apparently then
returned to Tanagra (Plut. *Quaest. Graec.* 37, 299c–e; a new variant of
the killing in *P. Oxy.* 2463.6–20).

Telamon: see s.v. *Peleus*. The murder of Phocus took him back from
Aegina to Salamis, mythologically his original or at least early
adopted home (*Heldensage*, 1043–5, Jacoby on 3 *FGrH* fr. 60).

Telegonus: son of Odysseus and Circe, slays his father in ignorance
(first in the *Telegonia*). Nowhere do we hear of exile or purification; on
the contrary, in the *Telegonia* and perhaps Sophocles, the story ended
with a double marriage and a heroization (*RE* 6 A 315; Pearson's
introduction to Soph. Ὀδυσσεὺς Ἀκανθοπλήξ).

Telephus: killed his uncles the Aleads and on Delphi's instructions fled to Mysia (Hyg. *Fab.* 244.2, *Corp. Paroem. Graec.* ed. Leutsch/Schneidewin, 1.412) – the famous journey which he conducted in strict observance of the killer's silence (Arist. *Poet.* 1460 a 32, Amphis, fr. 30.7, Alexis, fr. 178.3; that the same homicide is in question is not demonstrable, *Heldensage*, 1146, but very plausible). Telephus ultimately achieved kingship in Mysia; there is no record of a purification.

The traditions about Telephus and Auge are, chiefly through imaginative elaboration by all the tragedians, remarkably involved; the killing is only one of the ways in which the anomaly of the Mysian king's Tegean birth was resolved (*Heldensage*, 1138–60).

Temenids: murdered their father Temenus, jealous of the honour he paid to his son-in-law Deiphontes; the army expelled the Temenids in consequence and made Deiphontes king (90 *FGrH* fr. 30, Diod. 7.13.1, Paus. 2.19.1, Apollod. 2.8.5; probably from Ephorus, cf. 70 *FGrH* fr. 18).

The legend as we find it seems to derive from Euripides' Τημενίδαι. It explains the dispersion of Temenids through the Peloponnese (*Heldensage*, 665 f.; cf. s.v. *Pelopids*).

Theoclymenus: was probably invented for his role in the *Odyssey*. To bring a Melampodid to Ithaca a murder was necessary.

Theseus: (1) on reaching the Cephisus, he was purified by the Phytalids at the altar of Zeus Meilichios from the blood of 'various robbers, and Sinis his relative through Pittheus' (Plut. *Thes.* 12.1, Paus. 1.37.4; cf. *RE Suppl.* 13.1080, citing the vase *JHS* 56 (1936), 77 with Plate 5).

Aition for the Zeus Meilichios cult, and the role of the Phytalids in cults of Theseus (cf. Töpffer, 249 f.).

(2) for the killing of his relatives the Pallantids (*RE Suppl.* 13.1091 f.) he was either tried at the newly instituted Delphinium (e.g. Pollux 8.119), which recognized his plea of justification, or went into a year's exile at Troizen (Eur. *Hipp.* 33–7; Paus. 1.22.2). The trial is an aition of uncertain age, while the exile was probably Euripides' invention to take Theseus to Troizen (Eur. *Hipp.*, ed. W. S. Barrett, Oxford, 1964, p. 33; Jacoby on 328 *FGrH* fr. 108).

Thyestes: see s.v. *Pelopids*.

Tlepolemus: killed Licymnius accidentally or in anger (*RE* 6 A 1615), and fled to Rhodes with a large band of followers (Hom. *Il.* 2.653–70).
  A simple aition for the foundation of Rhodes by a Heraclid.

Tydeus: expelled from Calydon for shedding 'kindred blood' (Soph. fr. 799.3, Eur. *Supp.* 148, fr. 558.2; details vary, cf. Apollod. 1.8.5, *RE* 7 A 1705, Robert *Oidipus*, i, 140 f.); fled to Argos, was purified by Adrastus, and married his daughter (3 *FGrH* fr. 122).
  Tydeus' migration was already known to Homer (*Il.* 14.113 ff.), though not there explained. The obvious motive was subsequently supplied (Robert, loc. cit.; speculations on Tydeus' original home, *Heldensage*, 924 f.).

The theme of servitude as a form of expiation for blood-guilt appears in several of those stories: Apollo (1), Cadmus, Heracles (1) and (3). Cadmus was actually enslaved to the father of his victim, while the price of Heracles' sale was paid to his victim's relatives. It is known in some cultures for the killer to be taken into his victim's family to work in his place; Glotz, p. 173, suggested that we have in these myths the faint reflection of such a custom in Greece. But specific explanations can be thought of for this form of penalty in each case.
  The list of those who, but for the need to transfer them from one mythological homeland to another (or other aitiological reasons), need never have killed is a long one. One may dispute individual cases, but it seems to include Aetolus, Amphitryon, Bellerophon, Daedalus, Hyettus, Lycus and Nycteus, Oxylus, Patroclus, Peleus and Telamon, Penthesilea, Theoclymenus, Tydeus, the Pelopids and Temenids. The motif of the killer who, perhaps after consulting Delphi, founded a foreign colony, was a natural development of this: cf. Archias, Carnabas, Leucippus, Tlepolemus, Triopas. In some cases, murders that had an independent place in a hero's story were also exploited aitiologically: cf. Athamas, Cephalus, Perseus, and Oedipus.
  A final point that deserves emphasis is the lack of uniformity in the consequences of particular forms of killing. This is clearest, perhaps, from the contrast between two involuntary parricides, Oedipus and Telegonus, but numerous smaller instances emerge from the preceding catalogue. The task of exploiting these stories as historical evidence is thereby much complicated.

Appendix 8:
Gods Particularly Concerned with Purity

It is commonly assumed that the status of Apollo and Artemis in this respect was unique. As we have seen, not all the arguments are very strong. Being born or dying was forbidden in all temple precincts, and contact with birth or death seems to have made the affected person 'impure', not 'impure in respect of Apollo' (see pp. 33 and 37 above). The god who presided over purification from killing was Zeus (p. 139 above), and if Apollo assumed the role of the human purifier for Orestes, Hephaestus did the same for Pelops, and 'all the gods' for Alcmaeon (see Appendix 7). On the other hand, several items of evidence, though individually inconclusive, suggest in combination that certain forms of purity were particularly although not exclusively required by the Delian gods. The dramatic motif of the god who departs to avoid contact with death, used more widely in the fourth century, was initially applied by Euripides to Apollo and Artemis (see p. 33 n. 3). It was the purity of Delos that caused particular concern to the Athenians. Above all, Apollo and Artemis are the gods who dominate the cathartic law of Cyrene (see Appendix 2). They probably owe this special position to their role as senders and healers of disease. This is the function of Apollo that appears at the start of the Cyrene cathartic law, and disease could be viewed as a form of pollution (see Chapter 7). The connection of thought becomes almost explicit when the Athenians purify Delos in response to plague.

Other gods were perhaps distinguished in terms of their concern for purity. On a general level this was a difference between gods of the upper and lower worlds, since Hecate and the heroes were impure. (Presumably, therefore, it was not necessary to approach them in a state of purity.) About more detailed discriminations we can only guess. On Cos we find the priests of, at least, Demeter and Zeus subject to stringent rules (see p. 52). Dionysus was involved with purifications, although of a special kind (see Chapter 10). But the attitude of country deities to sexual purity was relaxed (see p. 76).

INDEXES

PRINCIPAL PASSAGES

Where several passages are covered by a heading in the General Index (e.g. 'Plato on homicide') they are not listed separately here. Nor are the sources for Appendix 7.
References to this book are printed in italics. An Asterisk indicates discussion of a textual problem.

Achilles Tatius (4.7.7) *102 n. 115*; (6.12.3) *314 n. 26*

Aelian:
  NA (9.51, 65) *360 f., 363*
  VH (5.14) *364 n. 49*; (8.5) *129 n. 97, 279 n. 108*; (12.50) *142 n. 162*
  Fr. (11) *33 n. 3*; (39) *23 n. 24*; (44) *81 n. 32, 179*

Aelius Aristides (48.31) *30 n. 66*

Aeneas Tacticus (22.17) *159*

Aeschines:
  1 (19) *153 nn. 46–7*; (28) *197*; (183) *94 n. 82, 96 n. 88*
  2 (87–8) *126 n. 86*; (133–4) *155 n. 58*
  3 (77) *64 n. 109*; (107–112) *164 n. 114*; (111) *191 n. 3*; (118–9) *166 n. 127*; (132–4) *173 n. 166*
  (Aeschines) *Epistles* (1.2) *33 n. 46, 43 n. 43, 218*; (2.5) *197 n. 40*

Aeschylus:
  Ag. (1505–8) *201*; (1644–5) *111*; (1645) *145 n. 8*
  Cho. (98) *230 n. 132*; (269–96) *110*; (278–82) *218*; (472–4) *201*; (635) *8 n. 35*; (909) *123 n. 71*; (923) *117 n. 55*; (967–8) *223 n. 87*; (1055–6) *129 n. 94*
  Eum. (40–5) *370*; (62–3) *139 n. 140*; (236) *224 n. 92*; (238) *118*; (278–96) *129*; (280) *118*; (285) *129 n. 97*; (286) *118*; (304) *6*; (448) *371 n. 6*; (449 f.) *372*; (902–87) *257 f., 279 f.*
  Sept. (4–6) *267*; (679–82) *113 n. 37*; (681–2) *137 n. 135*; (764–5) *266*; (859) *33 n. 3*
  Supp. (225–6) *98*; (262–7) *211 n. 24*; (375) *146 n. 12*; (459–79) *185*; (646–50) *217 n. 56*; (656–709) *257 f., 279 f.*
  Theori/Isthmiastae (29–31) *84 n. 42*
  Fr. (137) *318 n. 52*; (327) *372*; (354) *133 n. 111*

Alcaeus (Fr.346.4) *101 n. 111*

Alcmaeonis 377

Alexander Aetolus (Fr.3.16) *314 n. 26*

Alexis Fr. (15.6) *323 n. 4*; (76.1–4) *360 n. 17*; (178.3) *391*

Amphis Fr. (20) *360 n. 22*; (30.7) *391*

'Anacharsis' (*Epistle* 9) *327 n. 28*

Anaxandrides (Fr.39.10) *175 n. 177*

Andocides (1.29) *179 n. 193*; (1.94) *114 n. 41, 323*; (1.96–8) *366*; (4.33) *98 n. 98*

Androtion, *FGrH* 324 (Fr.30) *161 n. 99, 166 n. 130*

Anthologia Palatina (7.406) *361 n. 23*; (14.71, 74) *324 n. 14*

Antiphanes Fr. (68.12–14) *360 nn. 17, 22*; (129.6) *360 n. 17*

Antiphon:
  5 (11) *122*; (11–12) *187 n. 241*; (82–4) *9 n. 39, 109, 129, 191 n. 4, 387*; (87) *119 n. 62*; (93) *254*
  6 (1) *254*; (4) *119, 254*; (37) *38 n. 20*; (45–6) *268 n. 52*
  Tetr. (1 β 9) *204 n. 84*; (2 α 2, γ 7–8) *117*

Apollodorus, *FGrH* 244 (Fr.89) *83 n. 37*

Apollodorus (3.5.1) *260*; (3.12.6) *274*

Apollonius Rhodius, *Argon.* 4 (452–745) *370–4, 383 f.*; (477–9) *108*; (479) *133 n. 111*; (699–717) *108*; (710) *283 n. 11*; (1669 ff.) *251 n. 89*

Archedikos (Fr.4) *97, 99*

Archestratus (*ap.* Ath. 163d, 310e) *360 n. 17*

Aristophanes:
  Ach. (44) *21*
  Av. (463–4) *20*; (524–5) *219 n. 67*; (1490–3) *244 n. 50*
  Eccl. (128) *21 n. 12*; (647) *99 n. 101*; (1033) *35 n. 10*

Aristophanes: (*cont.*)
  Eq. (445–8) *206*; (1280–9) *99 n. 101, 101
    n. 111*
  Lys. (181–237) *85 n. 46*; (549) *363 n. 44*;
    (641–7) *79 f.*; (700–2) *363 n. 44*;
    (742–3) *33 n. 5*; (911–3) *75, 76 n. 8*;
    (914–5) *186 n. 235*; (1129 f.) *22 n. 18*
  Nub. (243) *248 n. 68*; (1321–1450) *196*
  Pax (151, 162–3) *283 n. 9, 359*; (1250)
    224 n. 92
  Plut. (21) *153 n. 46*; (656–8) *213 n. 31*;
    (845) *180 n. 201*
  Ran. (338) *283 n. 11*; (355) *323 n. 11*;
    (366) *162 n. 101*; (630) *253 n. 105*;
    (1032) *143 n. 164, 306*
  Thesm. (330) *82 n. 35*; (332–67) *193 f.*
  Vesp. (118–24) *208, 246*; (394) *162 n. 101*;
    (1037 ff.) *248 n. 69*; (1043) *211 n. 24*
  Fr. (58 Austin) *243 f.*; (320–1) *83 n. 36*;
    (692a) *244*
Aristotle:
  Ath. Pol. (13.5) *262 n. 31, 263 n. 33*;
    (16.10) *194, 366 f.*; (56.4) *283 n. 9*;
    (57.4) *159 n. 85*; (60.2) *165 n. 120*
  Pol. (1329a 27–34) *87 n. 53, 97 n. 92, 175
    n. 177*; (1335b 12–16) *49 n. 63*; (1335b
    24–6) *50 n. 67*
  (*De somniis* 459b 23–460a 23) *102*; (*Rhet.*
    1418a 23–6) *210 n. 17*; (*Poet.* 1448b
    12) *357*; (*Poet.* 1460a 32) *391*
  Fr. (60) *300 n. 99*; (101) *35 n. 12, 64
    n. 107*; (194) *362 n. 35, 363 n. 44*; (496)
    232 n. 153; (611.10) *65 n. 110*
Aristoxenus (ed. Wehrli) Fr. (25) *364
    n. 50*; (26) *297 n. 83*; (29a) *364 n. 50*
Arrian:
  Anabasis (1.9.7) *277 n. 103*; (1.9.9) *168
    n. 134, 176 n. 179*; (4.9.5) *252*
  (*Cyn.* 33) *113 n. 37*; (*diss. Epict.* 3.21.16)
    88 n. 55
Athenaeus (46e–f) *37 n. 17*; (150a) *85
    n. 43*; (171e) *157 n. 69*; (461c) *244 n. 50*

Babrius (63) *244 n. 50*
Bacchylides (11.95–110) *209 n. 14, 213
    n. 30*

Callimachus:
  (*Dem.* 130–2) *49 n. 64*; (*Jov.* 11–13) *49
    n. 64*; (*Pall.*) *27 f.*; (*Epigr.* 9 Pf.) *43*
  Fr. (63.9–12) *82 n. 35*; (194.28–31) *208
    n. 7, 228*; (194.37–44) *35 n. 11, 53 n. 80,
    228*; (194.40–56) *229 n. 124*;
    (194.101 ff.) *229 n. 124*

Carmen Priapeum (14) *78 n. 18*
Censorinus (*De die natali* 11.7) *48 n. 58,
    52 n. 74*
Chairemon (*Achilles Thersitoktonos*) *260
    n. 22*
Chariton (1.5.5) *47 n. 54*
Chrysippus (ap. Plut. *de Stoic. Rep.* 1044f–
    1045a) *34, 293 n. 59, 326, 359 n. 12*
Cleidemus, *FGrH* 323 (Fr.14) *36 n. 15*
Clemens Alexandrinus, *Strom.* (4.19
    p. 302.1–3) *82 n. 33*; (4.22. p. 311) *324
    n. 15*; (7.4.26.2–3, vol. iii, p. 19)
    225–32
Com. Adesp. (239 Austin Fr.1) *183 n. 213*
Com. Nov. Adesp. (Fr.214) *263 n. 38*
Cratinus (Fr.221) *358*
Curtius Rufus (10.9.11) *23 n. 21*

Damophilus, *FGrH* 70 (Fr.96) *172
    nn. 164–5.*
Democritus (B 262) *253 n. 99*
Demosthenes (9.44) *366, 367 n. 9*; (12.2–4)
    188 n. 249; (18.159) *268 n. 53*; (18.259)
    231; (18.259–60) *303*; (18.296) *268
    n. 53*; (19.267) *317 n. 48*; (20.158) *125
    n. 82, 367*; (21.16) *151 n. 39*; (21.53)
    155; (21.126) *176 n. 180*; (21.180) *158
    n. 74*; (22.2) *123 n. 72*; (22.78) *88 n. 55,
    97*; (23.28) *366–7*; (23.53) *366–7*;
    (23.60) *366–7*; (23.72) *114, 116 n. 49,
    373 n. 19, 374 n. 24, 387*; (23.73) *121
    n. 66*; (23. 74) *141 n. 156, 366–7*;
    (24.29, 31) *157*; (24.55) *175 n. 175*;
    (25.11) *306*; (25.30) *204 n. 80*; (25.61)
    194 n. 17; (37.59) *108 n. 10, 367*;
    (43.57–8) *38 n. 21*; (43.62) *36 n. 14, 70
    n. 123*; (47.70) *38 n. 20, 41 n. 36, 121
    n. 66*; (49.66) *6 n. 23*; (54.39) *21 n. 12*;
    (57.55) *263 n. 33*; (59.72–117) *97, 178
    n. 190*; (59.78) *85 n. 45*; (59.85–7) *94
    n. 82, 95 nn. 84, 87*; (59.92) *97 n. 92*;
    (59.116–7) *178 n. 189*; (60.30) *64
    n. 108*
Dinarchus (2.5) *263 n. 38*
Diodorus Siculus (3.58.2–3) *224 n. 93, 232
    n. 153, 288 n. 38*; (4.14.3) *284*; (10.9.6)
    297 n. 82, 324 n. 15; (10.30) *46 n. 48*;
    (12.58.6–7) *276*; (13.86.1–3) *39 n. 24*;
    (15.48–9) *176 n. 181*; (15.49.6) *10
    n. 44*; (16.23–39, 56–64) *172–5*;
    (16.58.6) *168 n. 133*; (16.61.3) *240
    n. 25*; (17.64.3) *58 n. 94*; (32.12.2) *221
    n. 75*

Indexes

397

Diogenes Laertius (1.110) *210 n. 17, 211 n. 23*; (8.31) *297 n. 82*; (8.32) *217 n. 54*; (8.33) *296 n. 76, 297, 299 n. 90*; (8.34) *295 n. 68, 361*; (8.38) *299 n. 90*; (8.43) *82 n. 33*; (9.43) *37 n. 17*

Diphilus Fr. (32.17) *263 n. 38*; (126) *207, 225–32*

Donatus (on Ter. *Andr.* 483.3) *51 n. 69*

'Ekphantos' (p. 80. 15 ff. Thesleff) *266 n. 47*

Empedocles (B 110) *298 n. 87*; (B 115.9–12) *317 n. 44*

Ephippus, *FGrH* 126 (Fr.3) *163 n. 109, 278 n. 104*

Epicharmus Fr. (63) *360 n. 19*; (269) *324*

Epigoni (Fr.ii Allen) *131 n. 102, 380*

Erinna (v. 19 Page, *GLP* 488) *53 n. 80*

Eubulus (Fr.14) *360 n. 22*

Eupolis (*Demes* 31–2 Page) *191 n. 3*; (Fr.120) *221 n. 75*

Euripides:

 Alc. (22–3) *33 n. 3*; (98 ff.) *35 n. 10*; (1143–6) *37 n. 17*; (1146) *329 n. 10*

 Andr. (155–60) *251 n. 89*; (258–60) *315*; (293–4) *221 n. 75, 230 n. 133; (335 ff.) 315*; (614–5) *111 n. 25*; (654–9) *122*; (975) *318 n. 53*; (974–6) *205 n. 86*; (977–8) *316 n. 43*

 Bacch. (72–7) *288–90*

 El. (256) *86 n. 51*; (654) *52 n. 74*; (1124–33) *52 n. 74*; (1177–9) *317 n. 44*; (1195–7) *316 n. 42*; (1198–1200) *205 n. 86*; (1293–7) *311 n. 17*; (1350–5) *9 n. 39*

 Hec. (345) *6 n. 25*; (1276) *219 nn. 64–5*

 Hel. (985–7) *185 n. 228*; (1430) *38 n. 20*

 Heracl. (71) *145 n. 9, 146 n. 12*; (255–6) *185 n. 226*; (259 f.) *183 n. 215*; (264) *145 n. 8, 146 n. 12*; (558–9) *108 n. 10*

 HF (225) *211 n. 24*; (722) *253 n. 101*; (757) *145 n. 8, 146*; (922 ff.) *10 n. 42, 114*; (928–9) *20 n. 7*; (966–7) *129 n. 94*; (1214 ff.) *371 n. 6*; (1219) *371 n. 6*; (1232) *145 n. 7*; (1258–62) *200 n. 60*; (1361) *123 n. 71*

 Hipp. (73–81) *164, 190*; (141 ff.) *245, 252*; (316) *129 n. 94*; (316–9) *245*; (317) *323 n. 11*; (317–8) *222*; (831–3) *201 n. 67*; (952–4) *301, 302 n. 108, 304*; (1379–81) *199 n. 52, 201 n. 67*; (1415) *192*; (1437 ff.) *33, 67*; (1447–51) *108 n. 10*

 IA (938–47) *111*; (1191–2) *123 n. 71*

 Ion (80) *228 n. 121*; (434–5) *228 n. 118*; (936–9) *76 n. 8;* (1118) *145 n. 8*; (1334) *113 n. 37*

 IT (380–4) *34, 37*; (468–9) *157 n. 72*; (693) *205 n. 89*; (798–9) *175 n. 178*; (949–57) *195 n. 25*; (1040–1) *53 n. 79*; (1174 ff.) *312*; (1176–7) *53 n. 79*; (1193) *227 n. 108*; (1199–1201) *27 n. 50, 53 n. 79*; (1207) *371 n. 6*; (1208–10) *350*; (1216) **228 n. 118*; (1218) **108 n. 14, 110, 371 n. 7*; (1223–4) *372 nn. 11, 14*; (1226) *350*; (1226–9) *49*; (1462–3) *90 n. 66*

 Med. (607–8) *197 f.*; (665–81) *86 n. 49*; (1055) *253 n. 105*; (1251–68) *315*; (1327–1407) *315*; (1327–8) *317 n. 44*; (1333) *108 n. 14*

 Or. (75–6) *311*; (339) *129 n. 94*; (396) *254, 310*; (429 f.) *374 n. 26*; (479–81) *311*; (500–4) *137 n. 133*; (515) *121 n. 66*; (526) *313 n. 25*; (580–4) *110 n. 20*; (792–4) *309*; (793) *129 n. 98*; (822) *317 n. 44*; (1600–4) *111*; (1604) *323 n. 11*

 Phoen. (944–5) *81 n. 29*; (1050) *98 n. 96*

 Supp. (220–8) *205 n. 89, 219 n. 66*

 Tro. (41–2) *93 n. 79*; (251–8) *93 n. 77*; (501) *86 n. 51*; (1023–4) *317 n. 47*

 (*Aeolus*) *98*; (*Antiope* 80, Page) *65 n. 110*; (*Auge*) *34 n. 7*; (*Cretans*, Fr.79, Austin) *33 n. 2, 39 n. 23, 142 n. 162, 289, 301–2*; (*Melanippe*) *221 n. 75*; (*Oedipus*, Fr.98, Austin) *183 n. 215*; (*Stheneboea*, prologue 22–5, v. Arnim) *134 n. 120, 372, 379*

 Fr. (82) *107 n. 6, 110 n. 19*; (292) *243*; (368) *145 n. 8*; (645.4) *123 n. 76*; (662) *101 n. 109*; (912) *300 n. 99*; (1008) *371 n. 6*

Festus (p. 470.21, p. 476.20 L.) *373 n. 20*

FGrH (356 Fr.1) *134 n. 119, 141 n. 151, 283 n. 11, 371 n. 9*; (532 D 2) *27 n. 50, 53 n. 79, 122 n. 67, 185 n. 228*

Heliodorus *Aeth.* (1.2.7) *33 n. 3*; (10.4.5) *102 n. 112*

Herodotus:

 1 (19–22) *250*; (35) *123 n. 77, 134 n. 121, 374*; (44) *134 n. 120*; (64.2) *73*; (91) *202 n. 69*; (157–60) *185*; (182) *93 n. 77*; (198) *77*

Herodotus: (*cont.*)
2 (64) *74, 326*; (81) *290*; (81.2) *302 n. 108*;
(86.2) *64 n. 108*; (175) *253 n. 104*
3 (22.4) *362 n. 33*; (47.3) *185 n. 226*;
(50–53) *123 nn. 71, 77, 194 n. 17*
4 (154.4) *155 n. 55*; (161.1) *266 n. 47*
6 (56) *7, 192–3*; (58.1) *41 n. 33*; (58.3)
65 n. 110; (86) *187*; (91) *10 n. 42, 184,
191 n. 1*; (106.3) *154 n. 53, 159 n. 82*;
(121.1) *206 n. 95*; (134–6) *179*;
(134.2) *81 n. 32*
7 (39.3) *22 n. 20*; (133–7) *188*; (134.2)
191 n. 4, 264; (137.1) *17*; (137.2) *200
n. 59*; (141.2) *185 n. 228*; (169) *272
n. 73* (171) *272 n. 70*; (197) *203 n. 73,
259*; (206.1) *154 n. 53*; (220.3–4) *264
n. 40*; (231) *194 n. 17*
8. (54) *253*
9 (93.1–3) *176*; (116–20) *75 n. 3*
Hesiod:
Op. (90–104) *241*; (102–4) *236*; (121–6)
244; (225–47) *257 f., 266*; (336–7) *149
n. 26, 150 n. 34*; (704–5) *103 n. 118*;
(706–64) *241*; (724–59) *291–4*;
(733–4) *76*; (735–6) *70*; (753–5) *103*
Fr. (30.16–19) *273 n. 76*; (37.14) *209
n. 14*; (133) *218 n. 58*
Scut. (11) *122 n. 68*; (13) *135 n. 125*
Hesychius s.v. ('Αλμυρίδες) *47 n. 52*; (ἐν
Πυθίῳ χέσαι) *162 n. 101*; (Κοίης) *284
n. 18, 374 n. 29*; (παναγεῖς, παναγία) *90
n. 68*; (περίστιον) *21 n. 15, 38 n. 20*
Hippocrates (*Flat.* 5, 6 (6.96, 98 L.))
3 n. 10, 218; (*Morb. Sacr.* 148.38 J.,
1.40 G.) *224 n. 92*; (*Morb. Sacr.* 148.55
J., 1.46 G.) *19*; (*Vict.* 2.46 (6.544–6
L.)) *357: see also General Index*
Hippolytus (*Haer.* 7.29–30) *301 n. 104*
Hipponax Fr. (6) *231 n. 145*; (78) *258 n. 8*;
(92) *208, 258 n. 8*; (104.20) *77*
Homer:
Il. (1.65) *273*; (1.314–7) *210 n. 18, 217,
229 n. 130*; (3.56–7) *195*; (4.160–2)
201; (4.234–9) *187 n. 243*; (6.135–6)
290 n. 45; (6.266–8) *19*; (16.228–30)
67 f.; (16.666–83) *67*; (16.795–9) *68*;
(18.23–5) *68*; (21.75) *182 n. 207*;
(21.83) *201*; (21.218–21) *66 f.*;
(22.213) *67 n. 116*; (22.358) *70*;
(22.402 f.) *68*; (23.39–41) *68 n. 120*;
(23.44–6) *68*; (23.49–53) *59 f.*;
(23.579 ff.) *187 n. 242*; (24.33–76) *70*;
(24.480) *135 n. 124*; (24.505–6) *122
n. 68*; (24.592–5) *134 n. 116*

Od. (3.215) *265*; (4.377–8) *201*; (5.394–
7) *240*; (9.197–201) *176*; (9.411–2)
240; (11.73) *70*; (12.340–51) *254*;
(12.374–419) *176*; (19.109–14) *265*;
(19.395–6) *186*; (21.258–9) *158*;
(22.310–29) *182 n. 210*; (22.481–94)
114 n. 39; (22.481) *227 n. 114*
Horace (*Ars P.* 471) *218 n. 60*
Hymn Hom. Cer. (192–6) *285*
Hyperides (*Euxen.* 14–17) *160*

Iamblichus, *VP* (68) *297 n. 83*; (82) *299
n. 89*; (83) *296*; (84) *295*; (85) *299 n. 89,
362 n. 36*; (106) *361 n. 29*; (109) *361
n. 27, 363 n. 41*; (110) *297 n. 83*; (*Myst.*
3.10) *303 n. 112*; (*Protr.* 21) *361–3,
nn. 27, 35, 41*
Ion of Chios (Fr.30 W.) *291, 299 n. 90*
Isaeus (6.49 f.) *178 n. 191*
Istros, *FGrH* 334 (Fr.50) *259*

Livy (40.6.1–5) *22 n. 19*
Lucian (*Tim.* 17) *89 n. 65*
Lycurgus, *Leocr.* (79) *186*; (112–115)
45 n. 47; (117) *206*; (133) *118*
Lysias (1.14) *65 n. 110*; (2.7) *145 n. 7*; (6.4)
268 n. 52; (6.53) *259*; (12.5) *263*;
(13.79) *194 n. 17*; (13. 79–87) *114*;
(24.13) *153 n. 47, 268 n. 52*; (26.8) *268
n. 52*; (31.31) *194 n. 16*; (32.13) *187*;
(Fr.53 Thalheim) *159 n. 84,
170 n. 146, 239 f.*

Melanthius, *FGrH* 326 (Fr.2) *358*
Menander (*Asp.* 97–8) *33 n. 3*; (*Asp.* 216
ff.) *33 n. 2*; (*Asp.* 466–7) *35 n. 10*; (*Epit.*
440) *80, 85 n. 46*; (*Epit.* 749 f.) *82 n. 35*;
(*Epit.* 880–1) *248 n. 67*; (*Phasma* 50–
6) *207, 225–32*; (Fr.394) *244 n. 50*;
(Fr.754) *359 n. 15*

Neanthes of Cyzicus, *FGrH* 84 (Fr.16) *259*
Nicolaus of Damascus, *FGrH* 90 Fr.(45)
114 n. 42, 123 n. 77, 204 n. 85, 275 n. 81;
(47.10) *202 n. 69*; (52) *159 n. 87*; (61)
123 n. 77, 368 n. 17

Orphicorum Fragmenta (ed. O. Kern) (156)
142 n. 162; (232) *300 n. 99*; (291) *302
n. 108, 362*; (292) *143 n. 164, 299 n. 93,
306 n. 124*; (T. 219) *302 n. 108*; (T.239)
307 n. 130
'Orphic' *Lithica* (208–18) *224 n. 93*; (210)
225 n. 97; (214 f.) *229 n. 124*; (591
(585)) *223 n. 85*

Ovid (*Fast.* 2.45–6) *131 n. 103, 371 n. 9*;
  (*Fast.* 5.681–2) *10 n. 46*; (*Met.* 10.
  434–5) *82 n. 33*; (*Met.* 15.110–5) *364
  n. 50*; (*Met.* 15.322–8) *230 n. 131*

Parthenius, *Amat. Narr.* (9.5) *261 n. 24*;
  (14.5) *123 n. 77*
Pausanias:
  1 (3.4) *275 n. 88*; (37.4) *374 n. 29*; (43.3)
    71 n. 126
  2 (10.4) *88 n. 58, 90 n. 67, 92 n. 73*; (14.1)
    88 n. 55; (20.2) *124 n. 78*; (22.6–7) *85
    n. 44*; (24.1) *93 n. 77*; (27) *33 n. 5, 324
    n. 17*; (29.10) *119 n. 61*; (32.6) *275 n. 86*
  4 (12.6) *52 n. 75*
  5 (5.10) *230 n. 131*; (5.11) *212, 217 n. 53*;
    (13.3) *39 n. 25*; (14.5) *27 n. 46*; (16.8)
    372 n. 16; (27.10) *117 n. 54*
  6 (11.6) *117 n. 54*; (20.9) *85 n. 43*
  7 (2.1) *266 n. 47*; (25.13) *88 n. 58*
  8 (41.7–9) *275 n. 86*
  9 (27.6) *93 n. 76*; (20.4) *288 n. 35*; (39.7)
    213 n. 31; (39.5) *215 n. 43*
  10 (11.5) *275 n. 88*; (31.9) *286 n. 26*
Peisander, *FGrH* 16 (Fr.10) *199 n. 55*
Petronius, *Sat.* (104–5) *293 n. 58*; (134)
  218 n. 60
Pherecrates (Fr.174) *349*
Philemon (Fr.79.19) *360 n. 19*
Philetas (*Epigr.* 1.5 G/P) *102 n. 114*
Philippides (Fr.25.2–7) *269*
Philochorus, *FGrH* 328 Fr. (86) *31 n. 68*;
  (155) *161 n. 99, 166 n. 130*; (190) *30
  n. 63*
Phylarchus, *FGrH* 81 (Fr.45) *47 n. 53*
Pindar (*Ol.* 7.77) *320 n. 68*; (*Pyth.* 3.43–4)
  67; (*Pyth.* 3.76–9) *247 n. 65*; (Fr. 133)
  300 n. 100
Plato comicus Fr. (28) *364 n. 49*; (173) *292
  n. 52*; (173.19) *360 n. 22*
Plato:
  Cra. (396c–e) *221*; (400c) *300 n. 99*;
    (405a–b) *215 n. 45*; (405b) *139 n. 140*
  Ep. (329b) *6*; (356d–357a) *159 n. 85, 175
    n. 177*
  Euthphr. (2d) *263 n. 38*; (3e–4d) *119
    n. 63, 121 n. 66*; (4b–c) *367*; (4c) *111
    n. 21*
  Euthyd. (277d) *247 n. 64, 288 n. 38*
  Grg. (493a–b) *286 nn. 26–7*
  Leg. (716d–e) *323 f.*; (729e–730a) *182*;
    (735a–736c) *264*; (759c) *97 n. 92, 175
    n. 177, 205*; (759d) *87 n. 53, 92 n. 75*;
    (782c) *299 n. 93, 302 n. 108*; (800d–e)

  159 n. 84; (815c) *303*; (838a–39a) *95
    n. 86*; (838a–b) *100 n. 104*;
    (839e–840a) *84 n. 42*; (845d–e) *293
    n. 59*; (845e) *222 n. 80*; (854b) *221*;
    (869d) *113 n. 37*; (870d–e,
    872d–873a) *143 n. 164, 306 n. 124*;
    (881d–e) *194 n. 17*; (917b) *145 n. 8*;
    (926e–927a) *244 n. 48*; (932e–933e)
    222 n. 80; (933a–b) *251*; (937d) *217
    n. 56*; (947b–d) *43 n. 40*; (947d) *53
    n. 80, 70 n. 123*; (949e–950a) *263 n. 35*;
    (956a) *52 n. 78*
  Menex. (238b) *64 n. 108*
  Phd. (58a–c) *153 n. 46*; (67c, 69c) *282
    n. 6*; (108a) *304 n. 116*
  Phdr. (244e) *288 n. 38*; (265a) *243 n. 44*
  Resp. (363c–d) *286*; (364b–e) *303 f.*;
    (364c) *202*; (364e) *299, 300 n. 99*;
    (399e) *263 n. 38*; (567c) *263 n. 38*;
    (501a) *264 n. 39*; (571c–d) *98 n. 99,
    327*
  Soph. (226b–231e) *299 n. 90*; (226d) *18*
Plutarch:
  Ages. (3.9) *86 n. 50*; (29.7) *43 n. 42*;
    (30.1) *277 n. 102*
  Alc. (18–21) *168–70*; (23.9) *86 n. 50*;
    (29.5) *176 n. 179*; (34.1–2) *26*
  Alex. (11.12) *176 n. 179*; (13.4) *163
    n. 109, 278 n. 104*; (16.2) *155 n. 55*;
    (57.3) *220 n. 72*; (75) *220 n. 72*
  Arat. (53.2–4) *43 n. 40*
  Arist. (20.4) *23*; (20.6) *71 n. 125*; (25.1)
    186 n. 235
  Cim. (4.5–7) *98 n. 98*; (6.4–7) *107, 129
    n. 94, 277 n. 101*
  Dem. (21.3) *268 n. 54*
  Demetr. (30.2) *171 n. 155*
  Dion (56.2) *254 n. 108*
  Lyc. (27.1) *71*; (27.4) *36 n. 16*
  Lys. (8.4–5) *187*; (30.1) *183 n. 214*
  Nic. (16.7) *171 n. 155*
  Num. (9.11) *88 n. 58, 92 nn. 73, 75*
  Pel. (33.5) *43 n. 40*; (33.8) *39 n. 27*
  Per. (30.3) *188 n. 249*; (33.1–2) *206*
  Phoc. (28.2–3) *158 n. 75*; (37.2) *158*;
    (37.3–4) *47 n. 52*
  Sol. (12) *211 n. 23*
  Sull. (35.2) *40 n. 29*
  Thes. (12.1) *139 n. 143, 373 n. 19, 374 n. 29*
  Timol. (22.2) *39 n. 24*; (30.7–9) *10 n. 44*;
    (39.3) *43 n. 40*
  De Superst. (166a) *220 n. 71*; (170b) *222 f.*
  Apophth. Lac. (223e 11) *208 n. 5*; (238d)
    41 n. 33

Plutarch: (*cont.*)
  De mul. vir. (252e) *261 n. 24*
  Quaest. Rom. (5.264f–265a) *60 n. 100*;
    (51. 276f–277a) *217 n. 55*;
    (68.280b–c) *230 n. 136*; (68.280c) *30
    n. 65*; (85.284f) *80 n. 25*; (111.290d) *22
    n. 19*; (111.290a–d) *357 n. 5*
  Quaest. Graec. (2.291e–f) *95 n. 87*;
    (24.297a) *35 n. 10*; (26.297c) *265*;
    (40.300f) *85 n. 44, 279*; (46.302b) *231
    n. 142*; (54.303c) *208 n. 10*
  De Pyth. or. (397a) *228 n. 121*; (403f)
    84 n. 40, 87 n. 54, 92 n. 75; (404a) *253
    n. 105*
  Cons. ad Uxor. (611d) *286*
  Quaest. Conv. (635e) *302 n. 108*; (655d)
    78 n. 15; (694a–b) *334*; (700e) *103
    n. 116*; (728c–730f) *361 n. 28*
  Praec. Reip. Ger. (814b) *21 n. 16*
  Quaest. Nat. (36) *95 n. 87*
(Plutarch) (*Cons. ad Apoll.* 118c–119d) *40
  n. 29*; (*Par. Min.* 19a.310b) *98 n. 96,
  280 n. 111*; (*Am. Narr.* 773c–774d) *198
  n. 48, 277 n. 101*; (*X Orat.* 833a–4a) *45
  n. 47*
P.MG (895) *160*
Pollux (1.35) **90 n. 68*
Polyaenus (*Strat.* 5.17.1) *284*
Polybius (4.21.8–9) *22 n. 17, 225*;
  (23.10.17) *22 n. 19*
Porphyry:
  Abst. (1.9) *367*; (1.14) *356 n. 3, 364 n. 51*;
    (2.13–20) *323 n. 8*; (2.19) *323 n. 3*;
    (2.44) *180 n. 199*; (2.50) *102 n. 112*;
    (4.16 p. 255.6) *283 n. 9*
  VP (7) *298 n. 88*; (12) *297 n. 82*; (45) *297
    n. 82*
Posidippus Fr. (1.5–6) *99*; (26.21) *89 n. 65*
Propertius (4.8.83–6) *95 n. 87*

Scholia (Ar. *Ach.* 747) *283 n. 10*; (Ar. *Plut.*
  845) *284*; (Schol. Patm. Dem. 23.71)
  368; (AD Hom. *Il.*2. 333–5) *382*;
  (T Hom. *Il.* 13.589) *301 n. 102*;
  (Lucian p. 112.5 Rabe) *89 n. 65*;
  (Lucian p. 276.5) *82 n. 33*; (Lucian
  p. 279.21) *89 n. 65*; (Lucian
  p. 280.16–17) *83 n. 39*; (Lucian
  p. 280.22 ff.) *358 n. 9*; (Soph. *OC* 477)
  225 n. 97; (Soph. *OC* 680) *83 n. 36*;
  (Theocr. 2.11/12) *223 n. 86*
Seneca (*Ag.* 163) *259 n. 15*; (*Tro.* 634–5)
  259 n. 15

Servius (on Virg. *Georg.* 1.166, 2.389) *288
  n. 38*
Simonides (*PMG* 531.3–4) *43 n. 41*
Solon Fr. (9.3) *270*; (13.23–32) *199*
Sophocles:
  Aj. (172–86) *246, 252*; (184–5) *243 n. 45*;
    (655 f.) *217 n. 54*; (756–77) *246, 252*
  Ant. (196–7) *329*; (256) *8 n. 34, 192*;
    (545) *329*; (775) *6 n. 22, 328 n. 4*;
    (775–6) *111*; (889) *312, 316, 323*;
    (999–1047) *33, 44, 65 f.*; (1043–4) *145
    n. 7, 310*; (1070–1) *62*; (1144) *290
    n. 45*; (1317–46) *316*
  El. (84) *35 n. 11*; (434) *35 n. 11*
  OC (292) *253 n. 101*; (367 ff.) *204*; (407)
    123 n. 73; (466–92) *10 n. 42*; (466) *4,
    146*; (490–2) *146, 195 n. 25*; (548) *111,
    124*; (941–9) *118 n. 58, 316 n. 43*; (964–
    5) *201, 252 n. 96*; (1132–5) *310, 316 n.
    38*; (1482–4) *17*
  OT (181) *219 n. 68*; (194–7) *230 n. 132*;
    (202–6) *335*; (236–75) *193 f.*;
    (236–41) *83*; (269–72) *191 n. 3*; (313)
    107; (656) *6*; (833) *219 n. 66*; (864) *150
    n. 34, 323 n. 7*; (1424–8) *310*; (1426) *8
    n. 35*; (1486 ff.) *205*; (1492–1502) *205
    n. 86*
  (*Phil.* 758 f.) *248 n. 68*; (*Tr.* 1012) *211
    n. 24*; (*Tr.* 1201 f.) *192 n. 11* (Fr. 34)
    208; (Fr.734) *231 n. 141*
Sophron (Fr.68, 70) *248 n. 69*
Stesichorus (Fr.223) *202 n. 70*
Strabo (7.7.12) *93 n. 77*; (8.3.19, p. 346)
  213 n. 29; (8.6.8, p. 371) *290 n. 45*
SVF:
  i (253–6) *326*; (256) *100 n. 104*; (264–7)
    327 n. 28
  iii (743–52) *326*; (743–6) *100 n. 104*

Tacitus (*Ann.* 3.60) *183 n. 216*
Theocritus (2.12–16) *223 n. 85*; (5.121)
  223 n. 85; (7.107–8) *231 n. 145*;
  (24.88–100) *225–32*; (24.89–92) *221
  n. 75*; (27.5) *314 n. 26*
Theodorus Priscianus (*Physica*
  p. 251.2–5) *233*
Theognis (731–42) *200 n. 59*
Theophrastus:
  Char. (16) *225–32, 307*; (16.7) *222*;
    (16.9) *39 n. 23, 51 n. 73*; (16.14) *220 n.
    72*; (16.15) *219 n. 67*
  Hist. Pl. (7.12.1) *231–2*; (7.13.4) *231–2*;
    (9.8.5) *292*; (9.8.7) *152–3*; (9.10.4)
    216, 224 n. 93

Thucydides:
1 (126.2–35.1) *183 f.*; (139.2) *166 n. 128*
2 (13.4–5) *173*; (17.1–2) *164 n. 115*;
(51.4–6) *219 n. 68, 220*; (52.3) *33 n. 5*;
(64.2) *280*
3 (56.2) *156*; (58) *122 n. 68*; (65.1) *156*;
(70.4–5) *165 n. 123*; (81.3) *185 n. 227*;
(104.1–2) *163 n. 107*
4 (97.2–99) *44, 190 n. 255*; (97.3)
162 n. 102
5 (1) *203*; (16.1) *253 n. 102*; (32.1) *253
n. 102*; (49.5) *175 n. 176*; (54.3) *155
n. 55*
7 (18.2) *188, 253 n. 102*; (50.4) *253 n. 104*
Timaeus, *FGrH* 566 Fr. (29) *268 n. 55*;
(56) *213 n. 31*; (101) *47 n. 53*; (146) *221
n. 75*
Trag. Adesp. (Fr.358) *315 n. 35*

Valerius Flaccus, *Arg.*3 (439–43) *226*;
(444–458) *373 n. 19*

Xenophon:
Ages. (5.7) *75 n. 3*; (11.2) *323*

An. (4.5.35) *52 n. 78, 176*; (5.3.13) *253
n. 105*; (5.4.33–4) *76 n. 7*; (5.7.13–35)
22 f.; (5.7.35) *124 n. 78*; (6.4.9–13) *42
n. 38*; (7.8.1–6) *250 n. 85*
Hell.
1 (2.15) *219 n. 66*; (4.12) *26.158*; (7.20)
47 n. 52; (7.22) *45 n. 47*; (7.35) *194
n. 17*
2 (3.21) *262 n. 30*; (3.23, 26, 51) *195 n. 24*
3 (1.9) *196 n. 27*; (3.1) *65 n. 110*; (3.3) *266
n. 47*; (4.11) *187 n. 243*; (5.24) *44 n. 46*
4 (4.2–4) *159 n. 89*; (5.1–2) *155 n. 58*;
(7.2–3) *155 f.*
5 (4.1) *188*
7 (4.34) *199*
Lac. (9.4–6) *194 n. 17*; (14.4) *219 n. 62,
263*
Mem. (3.8.10) *162 n. 103*; (3.12.6) *243
n. 44*; (3.13.3) *213 n. 31*; (4.4.19–23)
100 n. 104
(*Cyn.* 5.25) *163 n. 108, 357 n. 5*; (*Cyr.*
8.7.18) *107, 129 n. 94*; (*Hiero* 4.4–5)
129, 368; (*Symp.* 1.4) *281 n. 3*
(Xenophon) *Ath.* (2.6) *257 n. 3*; (3.2–8)
157 n. 68

Zeno: *see SVF*

INSCRIPTIONS

Altertümer von Pergamon viii 3 (p. 168.11–
14) *74 n. 4, 359 n. 12*

BCH (51, 1927, 120) *324 n. 15*; (60, 1936,
182 f.) *161 n. 97*; (102, 1978, 326) *37
n. 17, 50 n. 67, 74 n. 4, 102 n. 112, 322
n. 1, 353–5, 359 n. 12*
Buck (17) *185*; (64) = Ziehen 61
Bull. Épig. (69, 1956, n. 110) *230 n. 131*

Chiron (11, 1981, 7) *195*
CR Acad. Inscr. (1916, 263 f.) *359 n. 12*

Der Eid von Plataiai, ed. P. Siewert (50–1)
7, 191
Die Inscriften von Ilion (25.86) *3 n. 10*

Epigraphica, ed. H. W. Pleket (i n. 43)
162 n. 104

Hesperia (11, 1942, p. 265 n. 51) *89 n. 65*

Inscr. Cos (319) *253 n. 105*
Inscr. Cret. (4.76) *38 n. 21*; (4.146) = *LSS*
114
IG
I³ (1 A 14) *27 n. 46*; (6 C 48) *89 n. 62*; (7)
26 nn. 40, 42; (35) *89 n. 60*; (45) *183
n. 216*; (52 A 18–22) *171*; (78.54–7)
164 n. 115, 165 n. 121; (84) *161, 162
n. 105*; (102.30–2) *368*; (104.20) *125*;
(257) *229 n. 130, 293 n. 59*
II² (1035.10) *33 n. 5, 162 n. 106*; (1316)
89 n. 65; (1635.134–40) *176 n. 181*;
(1672.126–7) *30 n. 66*; (2342.31) *89
n. 59*; (2501) *161 n. 97, 162 n. 104*;
(2874) *90 n. 66*; (3462) *89 n. 64*; (3512)
88 n. 55; (3606.15) *90 n. 68*; (3607) *89
n. 65*; (3629) *89 n. 62*; (3725) *89 n. 65*;
(4076) *89 n. 62*; (4851) *89 n. 62*
IV² (123) *249 n. 73*
XII (5.569) *293 n. 59*; (5.593) = *LSCG*
97

IG (*cont.*)
  XIV (645.137) *162 n. 106*; (865)
    198 n. 46

LSA (12) *37 n. 17, 50 n. 67, 74 n. 4*; (16) *41
    n. 34, 65 n. 110, 191 n. 4*; (18) *37 n. 17,
    74 n. 4*; (20) *74 n. 4, 325, 355*; (23.8) *288
    n. 38*; (29) *37 n. 17, 74 n. 4*; (36.36) *30
    n. 66*; (42 A) *84 n. 40*; (51) *37 n. 17, 50
    n. 67, 74 n. 4, 352*; (52 B 10) *52 n. 74*;
    (56.11) *139 n. 143*; (61.8–9) *81 n. 32*;
    (73) *97 n. 92, 175 n. 177*; (74) *170
    n. 149*; (79) *27 n. 50, 88 n. 56, 283 n. 11*;
    (83) *33 n. 5*; (84) *37 n. 17, 302 n. 108,
    354–6, 359 n. 12*
LSCG (5) = *IG* I³ 78; (14) = *IG*³ 84;
    (15) = *IG* I³ 7; (32.23 ff.) **161 n. 99,
    163 n. 111*; (32.58) *145 n. 6*; (36.5)
    306 f.; (39.23–4, 26) *27 n. 47, 30 n. 66*;
    (47) *161 n. 97, 162 n. 104*; (55) *37 n. 17,
    74 n. 4, 102 n. 112, 322 n. 1, 354 f., 359
    n. 12*; (56) *3 n. 10, 37 n. 17, 112, 223
    n. 87*; (58.12 f.) *27 n. 47*; (60) *171
    n. 155*; (63.10) *81 n. 32*; (65.12–13) *49
    n. 62*; (65.16–23) *83 n. 36*; (65.23) *52
    n. 78*; (65.37) *20 n. 9*; (65.50, 66, 67 f.)
    30 n. 66; (65.66–8) *30 n. 66*; (65.107–
    12) *20 n. 9*; (68) *83 n. 36, 144 n. 5*; (76)
    145 n. 6; (77 D 13) *52 n. 74*; (78.15–
    21) *166 n. 127*; (79) *176 n. 182*; (82) *85
    n. 44*; (83.40) *88 n. 56*; (95.5) *74 n. 4,
    359 n. 12*; (96.9) *85*; (97) *34–41, 53, 54
    n. 81, 58, 69*; (97 A 28–9) **40 n. 30*; (97
    B 5) **38 n. 22*; (108) *229 n. 130*; (109)
    85 n. 44; (116.22–5) *170 n. 149*; (124)
    *36 n. 15, 37 n. 17, 50 n. 67, 52 n. 74, n. 78,
    74 n. 4, 85 n. 44, 354 f.*; (130) *253 n. 105*;
    (136) *145 n. 6, 165 n. 121*; (139) *37
    n. 17, 74 n. 4, 324 n. 15, 354–6, 359 n. 12*;
    (149) *145 n. 6*; (150 A 5) *165 n. 121*;
    (151 A 42–4) *75 n. 6, 86 n. 48, 94 n. 81*;
    (151 B 23) *180 n. 198, 227 n. 108*; (152)
    145 n. 6, 293 n. 59; (154) *see below*;
    (156) *see below*; (157 A 2) *372 n. 16*;
    (166.9) *175 n. 177*; (171.16–17) *50
    n. 67, 74 n. 4, 352–5*
  154 A (14) *253 n. 105*; (16–18) *52 n. 76*;
    (21–45) *52*; (22, 37) *39 n. 25*; (24, 39)
    50 n. 67, 51 n. 73; (24–6) *37 n. 17* (27)
    52 n. 78; (29, 30, 44) *228 n. 118, 231
    n. 141*; (39–41) *37 n. 17*
  154 B (1–16) *145 n. 6*; (2, 6, 15, 26) *228
    n. 118, 231 n. 141*; (17–32) *38 n. 21, 39

    n. 23*; (17) **39 n. 23*; (24–32) *53*; (24–
    5) *27 n. 50*; (33–6) *42 n. 37, 52 n. 77,
    185 n. 228*
  156 (A 7–16) *52*; (A 8–10) *39 n. 25*: (A
    11) *37 n. 17*; (A 12–3) *51 n. 73*; (A 13)
    50 n. 67; (A 14) *372 nn. 13, 16*; (A 15)
    228 n. 118, 231 n. 141; (B 29–35) *88
    n. 56*
LSS (1) = *IG* I³ 1; (4) = *IG* I³ 257; (24)
    170 n. 149; (27) *170 n. 149*; (28) *83 n.
    36, 145 n. 6*; (31) *37 n. 17, 145 n. 6*; (32)
    83 n. 36, 144 n. 5; (33) *83 n. 36, 144 n. 5*;
    (38 A 32) *283 n. 11*; (50) *293 n. 59*; (54)
    *50 n. 67, 74 n. 4, 102 n. 112, 354–5, 359
    n. 12*; (59) *74 n. 4, 324 n. 15, 359 n. 12*;
    (63) *84 n. 40*; (64) *43 n. 41, 253 n. 105*;
    (65) *83 n. 37, 139 n. 143*; (69) *158 n. 77*;
    (72 A 5) *253 n. 105*; (82) *324 n. 15*;
    (86.3) *324 n. 15*; (88) *85 n. 44*; (91) *37
    n. 17, 50 n. 67, 52 n. 74, 74 n. 4, 102 n.
    112, 324 n. 15, 354 f.*; (106) *37
    n. 17*; (108) *74 n. 4, 324 n. 15, 359 n. 12*;
    (112) *112, 322 n. 1, 357 n. 5*; (114) *21
    n. 14, 22 n. 19*; (115) *see below*; (117)
    170 n. 149 (119) *37 n. 17, 50 n. 67, 74 n.
    4, 102 n. 112, 354–6*; (120) *302
    n. 110*; (133) *177*
  115 *Appendix 2*; *also* (A 1–3) *140, 393*;
    (A 4–7) *275*; (A 16–20) *37 n. 17, 49 f.,
    54*; (A 21–5) *39 n. 25*; (B 24–7) *40*,
    49 f., (B 50 ff.) *134, 371, 373 n. 19*

MAMA (iv 279–90) *254 f.*
Michel (524 C 1) *3 n. 10*
M/L (13.12–14) *132 n. 107, 180 n. 202, 196
    n. 29*; (30) *193–5, 222 n. 80*

Schwyzer (272) *198 n. 46*; (412) = Ziehen
    61; (661) *185*
SEG (iv 64) *116 n. 46*; (ix 72) = *LSS* 115;
    (xii 80) *89 n. 60*; (xii 87) *204, 368*; (xiii
    521.180–202) *293 n. 59*; (xix 427) *139
    n. 144, 141, 279*; (xxiv 116) *89 n. 59*;
    (xxv 447.6) *3 n. 10*; (xxvi 121) = *IG*
    II² 1035; (xxvi 136.52–4) *26 n. 42*;
    (xxvi 1306.23–6) *3 n. 10, 195 n. 23a,
    368*; (xxvi 1139) *287*; (xxviii 421) =
    BCH 102, 1978, 326; (xxviii 841.3)
    290 n. 45
SGDI (1153) *7*; (1561–1587) *250*; (5398)
    = *LSCG* 97
*SIG*³ (360) *193, 194 n. 16*; (711) *26 n. 37*;
    (943.7–10) *219 n. 68*; (963) *161 n. 97*;

(965.15–17) *161 n. 100*; (1161) *250*;
(1168.1) *33 n. 5*; (1168.47–55) *213 n.
31*; (1168. vii and xxxvi) *249 n. 73*;
(1184.7) *253 n. 105*; (1218) =
LSCG 97; (1236) *253 n. 105*
Solmsen/Fraenkel⁴ (5) *185*; (3ℓ) = *LSS*
115

P. Steinleitner, *Die Beicht im Zusammenhange
mit der sakralen Rechtspflege in der Antike*,
Leipzig 1913 (*passim*) *254 f.*

Ziehen (61) *74 n. 3, 144 n. 3*

GREEK

ἀγίζω 328 f.
ἅγιος 147 n. 16, 329
ἁγιστεύω 289, 329
ἀγνίζω 329
ἁγνίτης 135 n. 124
ἁγνός 12, 147–51, 323
ἄγος 5–12, 328
αἰσχύνω 3 n. 8, 95 n. 84
αἰτιῶμαι ἐμαυτόν 253 n. 105
ἀκαθαρσία 214
ἀλάστωρ 15, 109, 224 n. 92
ἀλιτήριος 109, 268, 270
ἀναπίμπλημι 219 f.
ἀποδιοπομποῦμαι 29, 373
ἀπόνιμμα 36 n. 15
ἀποτρόπαιος 220 n. 71, 334
ἀραῖος 192 n. 11
ἀρεστήριον 145 n. 6
αὐθέντης 122
αὐτοφόνος 350 f.
ἀφαγνίζω 329 n. 10
ἀφοσιῶ, -οῦμαι 121, 330 f.
βάπτω 306 n. 125
βοηθῶ τῷ θεῷ 165 n. 119
δαιμονῶ 246, 248
ἐγχυτρίστρια 36 n. 15, 374 n. 29
ἔκθυμα, ἐκθύομαι 10 n. 42
ἐκκαθαίρω 263
ἐκμιαίνομαι 76 n. 9
ἐλατήριος 214 n. 34
ἐλαύνω, ἐξελαύνω 223 n. 87
ἐναγής see ἄγος
ἐναγίζω 328 f.
ἐνθύμιος, ἐνθυμοῦμαι 252 f.
ἐξάγιστος 328
ἐπακτός 222 n. 79, 348
ἐπι- compounds, of magic 348
θνησείδια 52 n. 78, 358
θρόνωσις 285, 373 f.
ἱερομηνία 154–8
ἱερός 151 f.

καθαγίζω 328 f.
καθαίρω 4, 227 n. 114
κάθαρμα 229 n. 130, 259
καθαρμός 4, 18
καθαρός 323, 367
κάθαρσις (medical) 55 n. 87, 213 f.
καθοσιῶ 329
κακότης 293 n. 60
λαικάζω 99 n. 101
λοῖμος 257
λουτρόν 35 n. 11
λυμαίνομαι 195 n. 24
μελαγχολῶ 246 n. 61, 248 n. 67
μιαίνω 3
μιαρός 3–5
μίασμα 3 f., 12 f.
νόσος 220
ὀξυθύμια 30
ὀργάς 164 n. 113
ὁσία 338
ὅσιος 323, 330
ὁσιῶ 121, 330
παλαμναῖος 108
παναγής 328
περικαθαίρω 222 n. 80, 225 f.
περιρραντήριον 19
περιστίαρχος 21
προσπερμεία 231 n. 141
προστρόπαιος 108
ῥάκος 102 n. 113
σκατοφάγος 360
συνανθρωπεύω 364
συνείδησις 253 n. 105
τραγῳδῶ 15
ὑδρανός 284
φαρμακεύω, φάρμακον 214, 222 n. 80
φαρμακός 24–6, 258 f.
φθορά 354–6
φοιβ- 139 n. 140
χέρνιψ 35 n. 11

GENERAL

Names from Appendix 7, which is arranged alphabetically, are not included.

Abaris 209
Abaton 167
Abortion 325, 354–6
Achilles, kills Thersites 130 f.
Achilles Tatius, virgin sacrifice in 259 n. 15
Acousmata, Pythagorean 294–6, 298
Adultery 75 n. 4, 94–7, 325
Aelian, on divine vengeance 179 n. 193
Aeschines, on Demosthenes as pollution 268 f.; religious attitudes in 14 n. 60, 16 n. 73, 128 n. 90, 187 n. 241
   Speeches 1 and 2, on sexual pollution 94–7
Aeschylus, and institutions 312; communal moral responsibility in 279 f.; on family curses 199 n. 53; on the prosperous city 257 f.
   Choephori, pollution threatening Orestes in 110, 129
   Eumenides, Erinyes in 107 f., 126, 196, 279, 312; purification of Orestes in 139 f., 386–8
   Septem, fratricide in 137
   Supplices, expressions for pollution in 5 n. 21, 8, 9; incest in? 98 n. 99; threat of pollution in 185, 279, 312, 315
Aesop, as scapegoat 260; death of 274
Aethiopis, purification in 131 n. 102, 138–40, 373 n. 19
Agesilaus, lameness of 277
Agis, king 86
Agora, burial in 42, 337 f.; purity of 19, 125
Agrai, mysteries of 284 f., 373 f.
Agriculture, and sexual purity 77
Aidōs 189
Aigeus 86
Akamantia 336–8
Alcmaeon 124, 136, 377
Alcmaeonidai 16 f., 131, 204, 206, 211 n. 23, 270
Alcman, *Partheneion* 1 80
Alētrides 80
Alexander, murders Cleitus 252
Altars, murder at 184 n. 223
Alyattes, disease of 250
Amphiaraus, death of 43 n. 42; purifications in cult of 213 n. 31, 359 n. 11; sacred land of 160

Amphidromia 51
Anairesis, denial of 44 n. 46
Anathema 7 n. 30
Anchisteia 40
Andocides, on events of 415 168–70; religious attitudes in 16 n. 73
'*Angelos*' (= Hecate) 223 n. 86
Anigrus, marsh 212 f.
Animals, in Greek religion 357–64; 'dung-eating' 360; sacred 176; sacrificial, range of 364
'Announcer', of pollution 350
Anthesteria 39, 85, 287 f.
Anthropogony, Orphic 299 f.
Antiphon, *Speeches* 1, 5, 6, religious arguments in 119, 126 f., 254
   Tetralogies, enthumēmata in 253; on 'accidents' 117; pollution in 104–10, 127, 129 f., 278
Aphrodisia, of magistrates 85 n. 43
Apollo, and archaic healers 209; and plague 275 f.; and purity 393; and Sarpedon 67; and Thargelia 25
   Apotropaios 334 f.; Delphinios 141 f.; inassociable with grief 33 n. 3, 67 nn. 114, 116; Nomios 244 f.; of Delphi 138–43; purified 378
Apples, and Demeter 361–3
Aratus of Sicyon, burial of 42
Areopagus, mythical origin of 379, 386; sessions on impure days 159; supervision of religion 118, 178
Ares 85, 244 f., 358
Argives, devious 13, 155
Aristophanes, contagious qualities in 219; expressions for madness in 246 n. 61, 248 n. 67; on disease 243; religious outlook of 14
   Lysistrata, Lysistrata and Myrrhine in 89
   Nubes, values in 189, 196
Aristotle, on parricide 124; on tragic *katharsis* 288 f., 297 n. 83
Armies, purification of 22 f., 226
Arrēphoroi 80
Artemis, and brides 345 f.; and purity 393; 'bears' of 80, 345 f.; Hemera, at Lousoi 213
Asclepieia, bathing at 213 n. 31

Asclepius, and irrationality 249; and morality 248 f.; brought to Athens 275; *see also* Epidaurus
Atē 16 n. 73
Athamas, as scapegoat 259
Athletes, sexual abstinence of 84 n. 42
Atimia 19, 46, 94–6, 197; as outlawry 194 f., 204; hereditary 204, 339

Babylonian purification 373 n. 20
Bacis 209
Baptimism, in rites of Cotyto? 306 n. 125; not at Eleusis 284 n. 13
Barbarians, purified off 23
Barley-groats 227
Barth F. 363
Bath, after birth 50; after funeral 36; before ritual 36
Baths, abstention from 215; healing 212 f.
Battle, purification after? 113 n. 37
Battus 179, 336–8
Beans 301, 302, 358–65
'Bears': *see* Artemis
Beckett S. 50 n. 68
Bees, hostility to sexuality 77, 83, 95
Bestiality 355
Bewitchment 222–4, 251, 348 f.; purification from 222, 372
Birth, pollution of Ch. 2, esp. 48–52; 336, 353
Birth and death, avoidance of contact with 33 f., 52 f., 289, 296, 302, 307
Birthdays, during Thargelia 25
Black bile, and madness 246, 248 n. 67
Blood, purification by 230, 371–3
Blood-feud 125
Blood-money 116, 131
Boulē, purification of 21
Boys, in ritual 81 n. 28
'Boy from the hearth' 81 n. 28
Bran-mash 231
Brides, ritual duties of 345 f.
Bronze 228 n. 118
Buckthorn 231
Burial, in *agora* 42; intramural 70–73; of purificatory relics 229 f.; pollution of 37 n. 17; refusal of 45, 70, 170, 190, 195; right to 44, 327
Burning, of polluting objects 221
Butchers 298
Butler S. 314

Cabiri 223 n. 86, 284 n. 18
Cambyses, madness of 243

Camus A. 60
Cannibalism 305, 326, 360; metaphorical 362
Cassandra, and Apollo 93; rape of 185, 202 f., 273
Categories, violation of 62, 189
Chekhov, A. 314
Children, burial of 41, 72; ritual roles of 79–81
Christianity, and purifications 234, 324 f.
Chrysippus, on rules of purity 34, 322, 326
Cimon, his incest with Elpinice 98, 270
Cinesias 239 f.
Cirrhaean plain 164, 166
Citizenship, exclusivity of 262 f.
Cleisthenes 16
Cleomenes, madness of 242
Clothing, purity of 52, 68
Codrus 260
Collective responsibility, two forms 278
Colonization, 'purifies' city 264 n. 39
Confession 236 f., 249 n. 73, 254 f.
Confession-inscriptions, Lydo-Phrygian 254 f.
Conscience 252–4
'Consecration', by destruction 328 f.; punitive 6–12
Contagion, Greek views of 218–20
Corpses, deprived of burial 45–47; futility of punishing 45 n. 47; polluting Ch. 2
Corybantic rites 245–7; as purification 288 n. 38
Cos, rules of purity on 52 f., 393
Cotyto, baptism in rites of? 306 n. 125
Crete, and purification 142
Crop-failure 130, 257, 271–5; *see also Loimos*
Crossroads, purificatory remains sent to 30 n. 65, 229
Crown 35 n. 12, 36, 145, 153, 176
Cunnilinctus 99
Curses 7, 186 n. 234, Ch. 6; Bouzygean 44, 192, 364; hereditary 199–206; hereditary, tragedians' interpretation of 200 f.; parental 196 f.; power of cursing effectively 192 f.; public 193–6; spoken by inanimate objects 198 n. 46
Cybele, and purification 245 f., 288 n. 38
Cynicism 325–7
Cypress 35 n. 10
Cyrene, cathartic law Appendix 2; relations with Delphi 333

Daduch, and sexuality 89
Daidala, in Plataea 27 n. 51
Dancing, as purification 212, 283, 303
Days, impure 102 n. 113, 158 f.
Death, and pollution Ch. 2; 353; false
    report of 61; in battle, not polluting
    42; of good men, not polluting 43
Debts to gods 175; hereditary 339, 344,
    349 f.
Defixiones 191 n. 2, 198, 251, 269 n. 58
Defloration 75 n. 4, 355
Delos, Athenian attitudes to its purity 17,
    73, 276–7; no dogs on 357;
    purifications of 33 n. 6, 73, 163, 203,
    218, 276–7, 393; regular purification
    of temples on 30
Delphi, and Cyrene 333; and sacred laws
    140, 333; and the great plague 275;
    and the Eleusinian *orgas* 161; its
    explanations of disease 250; and
    of public disaster 271–6, 280;
    influences doctrine of pollution?
    138–43
Deme, purified 38
Demeter, and purity 393; festivals of
    81–3, 82 n. 33; Thesmophoros, and
    sexual propriety 83 n. 36, 144 f.
Demons, and pollution 55, 107, 217; in
    Pythagoreanism 295
Demosthenes, attacked as a pollution 97
    n. 93, 268 f.; on his own luck 268
    n. 54; on judicial oaths 187; on
    Megarians 166 n. 130; religious
    attitudes in 14 n. 60, 16 n. 73, 128
    n. 90, 168 n. 133, 219 n. 64
Speech 22, on sexual pollution 94–7
Desacralization 179 f.
Descent, 'purity' of 262
Diagoras of Melos 178 n. 192
Dickens C. 18
Diet, Greek 357, 360
Dinarchus, on Demosthenes as a
    pollution 268 f.
Diodorus, on purification of Delos 276;
    his source for Third Sacred War 172
    n. 165
Dionysius of Syracuse 268
Dionysus, and eschatology 286 f.; and
    Orphism 287 n. 29; and purification
    218, 286–90; Dionysiac/Orphic
    ritual 302–4; diverse forms of his cult
    287; unmentionable in funerary
    context 64
Disaster, public, explanations of 271–80

Disease, caused by pollution 217 f.;
    chronic 240; contagious 58, 219; in
    mythology 239; not formally a
    pollution 219; purification from
    Ch. 7; rationale of purification from
    216–8; religious explanations of
    Ch. 8;
    see also Epilepsy, Impotence,
    Madness, Skin-disease
Diseases, animal names for 248
Dodds E.R. 2, 9, 110
Dodona, responses 141, 250, 279
Dogs 357 f.
Douglas M. 56, 61, 63, 179
Draco, homicide law of 115, 125
Dreams, ritual responses to 219 n. 71;
    significance of, determined by
    dreamer's status 266 n. 48; wet 342
Dumont L. 63
Durkheim E. 150 f., 225

Earthquakes 86, 276
Eggs, in purifications 230; not eaten 302,
    358, 362
Egg-laying animals 358
Eiresiōnē 25
Eisangelia 195
Ekklēsia, purification of 21
Eleusinian Mysteries, and Orphism 282;
    dietetic restrictions before 358–63;
    eschatology of 286; Heracles and
    284 f., 373 f.; initiates dedicate
    clothing 180; precinct purified
    30 n. 66; purification as aim of? 285 f.;
    purifications before 283–5; *see also*
    Agrai, Daduch, *Hiereus Panagēs*,
    Hierophant, Hierophantids,
    Mysteries, Priestess of Demeter and
    Kore.
Eliade M. 11
Empedocles, *Katharmoi* 208 f., 242, 291,
    299–301, 305
Encirclement, in purifications 225 f.
Enodia 244
Enthumion, survival of the concept 253
    n. 105
Ephialtes, demon 248
Epic, early, purifications in 131 n. 102,
    377, 380, 382–4
Epicureans, purified off 23
Epidaurus, inscription over temple
    322–5; temple record 248; *see also*
    Asclepius

Epilepsy, impurity used to cure 234; purifiers of, *see* Hippocrates, *Morb. Sacr.*

Epimenides 142, 209 f., 211 n. 23, 259, 276

Erinyes 107, 109 n. 15, 196 n. 34; as conscience 310; unreal in 4th century 14; *see also* Aeschylus, Homer

Eunostos 85 n. 44

Eupolis, *Baptai* 306 n. 125

Euripides, attitude to pollution 310 f.; criticism of rules of purity in 34, 322; Erinyes in 254, 310; family curses in 199 n. 53; interest in religious phenomena 91, 93, 164, 288–90; mythological innovations in 376, 377, 378, 391

    Bacchae, Dionysus in 14; maenadism in 288–90

    HF, Heracles' pollution in 109, 309 f., 316–8

    Helen, character of Theonoe 93 f.

    Hippolytus, character of Hippolytus 75, 84 n. 42, 301; sexual pollution in 95 n. 84, 313 f.

    IA, metaphorical pollution in 111

    Ion, character of Ion in 91

    Medea, debate about pollution in 315

    Orestes, ascription of pollution in 111, 309–11

    Supplices, debate about burial in 44

    Cretans, purity of initiate in 289

Evenius of Apollonia 274

Excommunication, informal 194

Excretion 162, 293

Execution, forbidden during festivals 157

Exegetes, Athenian 112, 131, 141; Athenian, their cathartic rules 371, 374 n. 29

Exile, as purification 114, 118, 386 f.; in myth Appendix 7; voluntary, because of pollution 123

Exposure of child 356

Family, in oaths and curses 186; punishment of 186, 198–206

Fast, Eleusinian 283; in mourning 36 n. 16

Favism 365

Fellatio 99

Festivals, confined to men 83–5; to women 81–3; restrictions on profane activities during 154–8; revolutions during 159; surprise attacks during 156

Fig-trees 42 n. 37, 221

Figurines 347

Fines, payable to god 180

Fire, and sexuality 77; cathartic 227; new 23, 25, 35

Fish, abstention from certain species 360–3; 'man-eating' 360

Fleece of Zeus 28 f., 230, 284 n. 18, 285, 350, 373

Food, purity required to prepare 77 f., 80, 99

Foods, abstention from 52 n. 78, 283, 297, 357–65; ancient explanations for abstention from 360 f.; abstention from in magic 359 n. 12

Foreigners, contamination by 263

'Forty days', and Greek gynaecology 48, 52

Fratricide 137

Frazer J. G. 11

Fumigation 215 n. 41, 227

Functionalism 59

Funerals, pollution of Ch. 2

Gates, gods outside 335

Generals, trials of 267

Ginouvès R. 19 n. 4

'Godlike man' 292

Gods, accept humble offerings 323; cannot suffer pollution 309; debts to 175; forgive 14; particularly concerned with purity 393; shun pollution 33, 37, 65; suffer pollution 145

Goffman E. 318

Gold, as purifier 228

Gold Leaves 286, 290 f., 299–301

Goldsmith O. 314

Gorgias, *Palamedes* 127

Gosse P. 298 n. 86

Grave-cult, impure 38

Groves, sacred 164 f., 322, 335; penalties for offences against sacred 165 n. 121

Guilt, and shame 251

    hereditary 199–206; of states 202 f.; post-Homeric? 201

    purification from 294, 300; sense of 254, 305

Hair-cutting 293, 295

Haloa 83, 358–63

Hardy T. 314

Harvest, purity required for 78
'Healer-seer' 209–11
Hearth, purity/purification of 21, 38
    n. 20, 51, 77, 293
Hearth-temple 167
Hecate, and dogs 358; exorcism of 222–4;
    'food for' 360; impurity of 222, 223
    n. 86; meals of 30, 224, 307, 347;
    sacred fish of 362 f.
Helike and Boura, destruction of 176, 277
Hellebore 215 f.
Helots 261
Hemerology 29
Hephaestus, and purification 389, 393
Hera, bath of 27
Heracles, as 'purifier' 211; at
    Agrai/Eleusis 284 f., 373 f.; 'woman-
    hater', priest of 87; women excluded
    from cults of 84
Heraclitus, on purification by blood 371 f.
Herald 188
Herbalists 153, 292
Hermaphrodites, burnt 221 n. 75
Herms, mutilation of 168–70
Hero-cult, impure 39, 180
Herodotus, divine vengeance in 164
    n. 117, 168 n. 133; on communal
    afflictions 272–8; on disease 242 f.
Heroes, send disease 243 f.
Heroization, as compensation 320
Hesiod, hemerology in 29; on disease 236,
    241; on just and unjust city 257 f.,
    265 f., 278–9
    Op. 724–59 291–4
Hiereus panagēs 89 n. 62, 90 n. 68
Hiereia panagia 90 n. 68
Hierophant, and sexuality 87, 89
Hinduism 32, 46 n. 51, 65, 225
'Hippocrates', *Morb. Sacr.*, attitude of
    author 207 f., 215 f., 233; methods of
    the purifiers attacked in 207 f., 210,
    215 n. 43, 217, 222, 230, 232–4, 244,
    292, 359 f., 363 n. 44, 372
Hippocratic Corpus, bathing in 215; no
    infection in 220; 'purification' in
    213 f.
Hippocratic medicine, and temple-
    medicine 249; its origins in popular
    medicine 213; success of 238 f.
Hittite purifications 22, 231 n. 146
Homer, disease in 240; divine anger in
    241, 273; Erinyes and curses in 133,
    196 f.; homicide in 130–7;

no pollution in? 9, 66–70, 130–43,
    176, 189; plague in *Iliad* 1 176, 209 f.,
    217, 266 f., 273, 275; purifications in
    19 f., 67 f., 114 n. 39, 210, 227, 305;
    religious scruples in 253 f.;
    supplication in 181 f.
Homicide Ch. 4; 322, 327; disasters
    caused by pollution of 128–30, 273 f.;
    in hellenistic period 322 n. 1; in
    Homer 130–7; in mythology
    Appendix 7; purification from 114,
    135, 350, Appendix 7; rite of
    purification from Appendix 6;
    ritual status of justified homicide
    Appendix 5
Homosexuality 94
'Hopes', good and bad 175
House, destroyed 194; object of magical
    attack 348
Humiliations, public 95 n. 87, 195 f.
Hunters, impure 298; sexual abstinence
    by? 84 n. 42
Hunting, purification after 113 n. 37
Hyperbolus 270

Iamblichus, on dietary rules 361; on
    Pythagoras and purification 297
Iguvium, purifications at 225 n. 98
Images, sacred 168
Impiety, trials for 189
Impotence, purification from 208
Incantations 232, 298
Incest 97 f., 100, 326
Incubation, bathing before 213 n. 31;
    dietary restrictions before 358 f.
Insult, forms of 97–100, 132, 171, 206,
    258 f., 262, 268, 360
Islands, sacred 163
Iulis, funerary laws of 34–41, 69

James W. 57
Jurors, imperilled 126–8; their oath 187
    n. 241

Kallynteria 26–8
Kanēphoroi 80
Keos: *see* Iulis
King, as scapegoat 259, 265; dreams of
    266; public welfare dependent on
    265, 274; without blemish 266
Kings of Sparta, polluted 276 f.; trials of
    267

Kinsman, killing of 122 f., 129, 133, 137, 351; possibility of prosecuting 137 n. 133
Kisses, impure 99; washed off 314 n. 26

Lamb, in purifications 372
Land, sacred 160–6
Laurel 228, 301
Leather 52 n. 78
Legalistic devices, to avoid religious guilt 133, 154 f., 184, 186 f., 312
Leges sacratae 7, 12
Lemnos, fire-festival on 82
Lentils 227
Lerna, lake of 290 n. 45
Leuctra 198, 202, 277
Leviticus 61 f.
Lochial bleeding 55
Locrian tribute 202 f.
Loimos, meaning of 257; mythological explanations of 271–5; ritual responses to 275
Love, purification from 221
Luck, contagious 219; of leader 268
Lustral water, distributed before sacrifice 20; sharing of 22; sources of 226; stoups for 19
Lycurgus of Sparta, funerary laws 71
Lycurgus, orator, religious attitudes in 16 n. 73, 128 n. 90, 183 n. 215
Lydian purifications 134
Lysander, and oaths 187
Lysias, 'hatred of people' in 206; on Cinesias 239
  Speeches 1 and 12 128
  Speech 6, religious attitudes in 16 n. 73, 179 n. 193
  Speech 22 262
  Speeches 28 and 29 267 n. 51
Lysimache 88

Madness, caused by murder 129, 218; causes of 243–8; cure of, as a purification 288; purification from 208, 215 f., 372; treatments of 246
Magic, pollution in 223 nn. 84 f.
Magical rules, form of 292
Magistracies, purity required for 153 n. 47, 268
Maiden-choirs 80
Maimakterion 28
Maimonides M. 57

Manu, Laws of 292
Marriage, ritual obligations attached to 345 f.
Marriage-bed, pollution of 95 n. 84
Masturbation 342
Medical materialism 57
Megacles 17
Megara, and Athens: *see Orgas*
Melampodids 210 f.
Melampus 207–9, 212 f., 215, 230, 290 n. 45
Menstrual blood, properties of 102
Menstruation 100–3, 354
Metics 261 f.
Middleton and Rowley, *Changeling* 313
Miltiades, impiety of 179
Mind, pure 323
Miscarriage 50 n. 67, 346, 354–6
Modi J. J. 57
Monsters, burnt 221
Moon, and menstruation 102 n. 113
Moschion, on burial 45 n. 47, 48 n. 56, 327 n. 26a
Mother, impurity after birth 52 n. 74
Mother of gods 244 f., 288 n. 38
Moulinier L. 4 n. 13
Mourners, purification of 36
Mourning, and pollution 64, 65 n. 110; forbidden 43
Mouth, purity of 99
Mud, purification by 231; lying in, as underworld punishment 286
Mullet, red 362 f.
Murder: *see Homicide*
Musaeus 242, 304
Music, as purification 212, 297 f.
Myrrhine, wife of Hippias, assassinated 368
Mysteries, profanation of in 415 168–70, 191; secrecy of 177 f.

Nail-cutting 293, 295
Nuer, murder-pollution among 120 f.

Oaths 186–8; in homicide trials 126; of sexual purity 85
Oedipus 199, 308, 385 f.; as scapegoat 259; in Homer 136, 385
Olive-wood 229
Olympia, women excluded from stadium 85
Omens, responses to 219–221

Oracle, consulted on religious change 161 n. 100; enjoins death of king 265; enjoins sexual abstinence 86

Orestes 124, 308; in Homer 136; purification of 139 n. 142, 386–8

Orgas, sacred 161, 163 f., 166

Orphism, and Eleusis 282 f.; and inherited guilt 201 f.; and justice 305; and killing 143, 306; and purification 299–307; and Pythagoreanism 290 f.; its dietary rules 302, 362; its ritual 302–4, 307

Ostracism 269 f.

Outlawry: *see Atimia*

Pan, and madness 245; copulation in precincts of 76

Pardon, removes killer's pollution 108

Parricide 124

Pausanias, regent 107, 183

Pausanias, periegete, magic in 275 n. 90

Peisistratids 206

Peisistratus, and Delos 73

Pelargikon 164

Pentheus, as scapegoat 259 n. 18

Pericles, and Alcmaeonid pollution 16, 206; his citizenship law 262 f.

Perjury 10, 186 f., 199

Pheretima 242

Philippides, on Stratocles 269

Phocians, in Third Sacred War 172–5

Phreatto, court at 119

Phrynichus, assassins of 368

Phytalids 374 n. 29

Pig, mystic 283; purification by 30 n. 66, 283 n. 11, 371–3

Pindar, and pollution 16, 67

Pitch 228

Plague, Athenian 218, 275 f.

Plagues, caused by polluted air 218; god-sent 257; semi-magical cures of 275; *see also Loimos*

Plants, purifying 231

Plato, mental and spiritual purification in 281 f., 323

Leges, on inherited guilt 205; on offences against parents 196 f.; on purification from homicide 374; on the pollution of killing 107, 108 n. 10, 110–29, 137, 367; right of burial denied in 45 f., 47 n. 52; role of Delphi in 140 f.

Phaedo, on purification 281 f., 324

Pleistoanax 277

Plutarch, defender of religious traditions 29 f., 57, 324; on dietary rules 361 n. 28; on 'tragic' history 15 n. 71; 'taboo' in 330 f.

Timoleon, luck in 268 n. 54

Plynteria 26–8

Pollution, and dirt 56; and disgrace 94, 205, 316 f.; and divine anger 9–11, 110, 146; and law 37 n. 17, 114–25; and morality 34, 75, 94, 111–4, 117, 312, 325, 355, 367; and order 325–7; anthropological definitions of 3, 61–4; its consequences social, not legal 98, 205, 317 f.; conveys moral revulsion 111, 312–4; definition of 2–11, 96; emotional implications of 53; Greek interpretations of 44, 55, 107; healing properties of 233, 373; hereditary 185, 204–6, 344; how diffused 39 f., 49 f., 54, 110, 318, 353–5; how intensely feared 128, 211; in hellenistic period 322–5; in magic 222 f.; intermittent concern with 16, 315; invoked in curses 191; not mentioned or present 42–4, 128, 159 f.; object of dispute 111, Ch. 11; of abstract values 3, 146; of mind 323; possibility of, denied 309; practical effects of 53, 205, 318; 'sleeps' 17; spoils marriage prospects 205, 318; spread by relationship 40, 318; without physical basis 8, 144 f.

Pomegranate 358, 362 f.

Pompaia 28

Poseidon 85, 244

Praxiergidai 26

Pregnancy 48 f., 344–6

Priest of Heracles at Thespiai 93 n. 76

Priests/priestesses, age and marital status of 87–94; descent of 97; diet of 52, 238; exceptional attendance at funerals 43, 53 n. 80; excluded from hero-cult 39; inviolable 175; no contact with birth and death 52 f.; purity of 175, 205; sexual abstinence by 87–94

Priestess of Demeter and Kore, at Eleusis 89

Priestesses, Athenian, marital status of 88–90

Proclamation, against killer 125; Eleusinian 283

Proclus 307 n. 130
Procreation, imperilled by contact with death 53, 70
Prodigies, burnt 221
Proetus, daughters of: *see* Melampus
Prophecy, purification before 20
Prophetesses, sexual status of 93
Prostitute, impurity of intercourse with 75 n. 4
Prostitutes, male 94, 95 n. 84
Prytaneum, court of 117
Pulvillus, Horatius 40 n. 29
Puppy, in purifications 30 n. 65, 230
Purges, medical 213–5
Purification, animal victims used in inedible 283 n. 11; as broad term for elimination of evils 211 f.; performed facing east 225; techniques of 224–34, Appendix 6; *see also* Armies, Bath, Battle, Bewitchment, *Boulē*, Corybantic rites, Dancing, Disease, *Ekklēsia*, Exile, Guilt, Hearth, Homicide, Hunting, Impotence, Love, Mourners, Music, Perjury, Prophecy, Sacrifice, Sacrilege, Sex, Shipyards, Temples
Purificatory materials, disposal of 229 f.
Purifiers, standing of 207–9, 374
Purity, of mind and soul 281 f., 323
Pythagoreanism, and Orphism 290 f.; and purification 290–9; dietary rules in 296 f., 359, 361 f.; guilt in? 291, 298 f.
Pythagoreans, pogroms of 267 n. 50
Pythia 93

Rape 185
Red sacrificial victims 334
Relatives, polluted 40, 58, 318
Ritual omissions, bring disaster 272 f.; not shaming 252
Ritual rules, kinds of 176–8; violation of 144–6, 176–8
Rivers, respect for 293
Roman purifications/rules of purity 23 n. 24, 24, 65, 77, 225 n. 98
Roof, sharing of 122, 336
Rowley: *see* Middleton

Sabazius 303
Sacred:*see* Animals, Groves, Images, Islands, Land, Triremes
'Sacred laws' 176 f.

Sacred marriage 85, 287 f.
Sacred War, third 166, 172–5; fourth 166
Sacredness, and *agos* 6; confused with pollution? 11, 159, 180, 233, 361; meaning of 150–4; of the city 153, 193 f.
Sacrifice, as purification 10, 209 f.; murder at 159; omitted, causes disease 252; penal 339–46; purificatory, inedible 283 n. 11
Sacrifice, human, as purification 259; of king's daughter 264 f.; requires virgin victim 81, 259
Sacrilege Ch. 5; causes public disaster 272–4, 276–8; mob responses to 196; purification after 144–6
Sacrum anniversarium Cereris 82 n. 33, 89 n. 65
Salamis, cleruchy on 368
Salt 227
Samothrace, Mysteries of 284 n. 18, 374 n. 29
Sanctuary: *see* Supplication
Scapegoats, non-ritual 260–71; ritual and mythological 24–6, 258–60; whipped 226
Sea, pollution thrown into 230; purification in 226
Seers, mockery of 15
Self-defilement, in mourning 41, 68
Septerion 25 n. 30
Servitude, for killing 392
Sex, Empedocles' attitude to 301; impurity of Ch. 3, 335 f.; Orphic attitude to 301; purification from 74; Pythagorean attitude to 296; 'unnatural' forms of 98
Sexual abstinence, before hunting? 84; before magic 91 n. 71; before warfare? 84; enjoined by oracle 86; of athletes 84; of hierophant 87; of laymen involved in ritual 85 f.; of priests and priestesses 86–8; provoked by portent 86
Shakespeare, *Macbeth* 313
Shame, and guilt 251
Shipwreck 9, 17, 129
Shipyards, purification of 21 n. 14
Silence, of homicide 350, 371, 391
Sin, and disease 236 f.
Sitting, rituals of 285, 371, 373 f.
Skin-disease, caused by pollution 218; purification from 208, 212 f.

Skira 82 n. 34

Slaughter, impure techniques? 52 n. 78

Solon, funerary legislation of 34, 40; his religious optimism 14 n. 60

Sophocles, on family curses 199 n. 53
Ajax, Ajax's shame in 317; debate on burial in 44
Antigone, Creon's attitude to pollution 33, 310, 316; exposure of corpse in 46–8; pollution by corpse in 33, 44
OC, death of Oedipus 43 n. 42; Oedipus' pollution in 137, 318–21
OT, Oedipus' pollution in 316–20; plague in 130, 141, 257, 278

Sophron, invocation of Hecate in 222 f.
The Women who claim . . . 223 f.

Sorcery: *see* Bewitchment

Soul, purity of 281 f., 323

Sparta, expulsion of foreigners 263; intramural burial in 71

Spartan religious attitudes 12 f., 43 n. 42, 155 f., 184, 188, 264, 276 f., 279

Spartans and rape 277

'Spitting-out' pollution 108, 133 n. 11, 219

Springs, healing 212 f.; pollution thrown into 230; rules protecting purity of 293 n. 59; special, used for ritual purposes 51, 150, 227 n. 108

Squill 231 f.

Statues, washing and bathing of 27; after pollution 27 n. 50, 53

Steiner F. 235

Stigma 317 f.

Stoicism, critical of rules of purity 34, 326 f.

Stoning 194

Storm, due to pollution 257

Stratocles 269

Study, as purification 298

Substitution, in sacrifice 372, 373 n. 20

Suicide 42, 52, 198 n. 48; of suppliants 185

Sulla 40 n. 29

Sulphur 57 f., 227 f.

Sun, pollution of 293, 310, 316 f.

'Suppliants', Cyrenaean 347–51

Supplication 146, 181–6; at tomb 152; rejection of, as pollution 146

Sycophants 263

Symbola, Pythagorean 294–6

Taboo 11; Greek for Appendix 1

Talthybius, wrath of 17, 188, 191, 264

Tarantism 247

Temenē, leasing of 160–3; purity of 161–3

Temples, closed on impure days 26; defilement of 162; exclusion from, after impure contacts 37 n. 17, 50 n. 67, 52 n. 74, 64–6, 74 n. 4, 102 n. 112, 352–6, 359 n. 12; exclusion from, of killer 119, 125, 185; exclusion from, of sexual offenders 94; founded in response to plague 275; loans by 173; murder in 185; no birth, death or copulation in 33, 74; purified 30, 53, 144 f., 339–46; rape in 185; siting of 162

Temple-robbery 170–5

Teos, public curses in 193–5

Thaletas 209, 212

Thargelia 25 f.

Thebes, sack of 163, 168, 175, 277

Themistocles, accursed 270

Theophrastus, *On Piety* 307
The Superstitious Man 307

Thersites 130 f., 260

Thesmophoria 81–3, 179; and menstruation 102 n. 113

Thirty Tyrants, butcher metics 262; 'purify city' 263

Thomas K. 13

Threshold 350

Thucydides, festival truces in 154–6; on events of 415 168–70; on the plague 220, 271; pollution in 1, 8, 13, 183 f., 203; religious explanations of public disaster in 276 f.

Time, purifies 386 f.

Titans, crime of 299 f.

Tithing 341; in Cyrene 339–44

Tombs, impure 38; re-used 39

Torches 227

Tragedy, as evidence for religious attitudes 13–15, 308

Treachery 5 n. 18, 45 n. 47, 193–6, 206, 270

Triremes, sacred 153

Tritopateres 336–8

Trollope A. 314

Trophonius, purifications in cult of 213 n. 31, 358 f.

Truces, of festivals 155 f.

Tylor E. B. 55

Tyrannicides, honoured 368 f.

Tyranny, legislation against 366–8

Urination 162, 293

Van Gennep A. 59
Vegetarianism, importance of 304 f.; in
    Empedocles and Orphism 299 f.,
    302; in Euripides, *Cretans* 289, 302;
    Pythagorean 296, 298, 362
Vengeance, divine: against cities 271–80;
    and disease Ch. 8; delayed 175;
    delayed until descendants 199;
    forms of 257; instantaneous 179; *post
    mortem* 186; through human agency
    165, 194
Vico G. B. 63
Virgin priestesses 90–3
Virgins, in ritual 79–81, 81 n. 28

Warfare, obstructed by festivals 154–6;
    religious explanations for failure in
    276–8

Water, in purifications 226 f., 371; new 35
Water-carrying, in underworld 286
Water-vessel, outside house of death 35
Weasel, in purifications? 21 n. 12
'Wiping off' 215 n. 41, 231
Witchcraft: *see* Bewitchment
Women, dangerous and debilitating 84,
    101, 261; impure? 101
Wood, Mrs. H. 46 n. 48
Wool 229; shunned by Orphics 302

Xanthippus, ostracon against 270
Xenophon, his sacred horse 176; on
    pollution of killer 129; purifies army
    23; religious attitudes in 16 n. 73, 168
    n. 133

Zeus Alastoros 224 n. 92; Hikesios 181 f.;
    Katharsios 139
Zoroastrianism 32, 46 n. 51, 57, 65, 229